THE BARBOUR COLLECTION OF CONNECTICUT TOWN VITAL RECORDS

THE BARBOUR COLLECTION OF CONNECTICUT TOWN VITAL RECORDS

TORRINGTON 1740–1850
UNION 1734–1850
VOLUNTOWN 1708–1850

Compiled by
Marsha Wilson Carbaugh

General Editor
Lorraine Cook White

Copyright © 2002
Genealogical Publishing Co., Inc.
Baltimore, Maryland
All Rights Reserved
Library of Congress Catalogue Card Number 94-76197
International Standard Book Number 0-8063-1695-0
Made in the United States of America

INTRODUCTION

As early as 1640 the Connecticut Court of Election ordered all magistrates to keep a record of the marriages they performed. In 1644 the registration of births and marriages became the official responsibility of town clerks and registrars, with deaths added to their duties in 1650. From 1660 until the close of the Revolutionary War these vital records of birth, marriage, and death were generally well kept, but then for a period of about two generations until the mid-nineteenth century, the faithful recording of vital records declined in some towns.

General Lucius Barnes Barbour was the Connecticut Examiner of Public Records from 1911 to 1934 and in that capacity directed a project in which the vital records kept by the towns up to about 1850 were copied and abstracted. Barbour previously had directed the publication of the Bolton and Vernon vital records for the Connecticut Historical Society. For this new project he hired several individuals who were experienced in copying old records and familiar with the old script.

Barbour presented the completed transcriptions of town vital records to the Connecticut State Library where the information was typed onto printed forms. The form sheets were then cut, producing twelve small slips from each sheet. The slips for most towns were then alphabetized and the information was then typed a second time on large sheets of rag paper, which were subsequently bound into separate volumes for each town. The slips for all towns were then interfiled, forming a statewide alphabetized slip index for most surviving town vital records.

The dates of coverage vary from town to town, and of course the records of some towns are more complete than others. There are many cases in which an entry may appear two or three times, apparently because that entry was entered by one or more persons. Altogether the entire Barbour Collection--one of the great genealogical manuscript collections and one of the last to be published--covers 137 towns and comprises 14,333 typed pages.

TABLE OF CONTENTS

TORRINGTON 1

UNION 67

VOLUNTOWN 129

ABBREVIATIONS

ae	age
b.	born, both
bd.	buried
B.G.	burying ground
bp.	baptized
d.	died, day, or daughter
decd.	deceased
f.	father
h.	hour or husband
J.P.	Justice of Peace
Inten. Pub.	Intention Published (an announcement of marriage)
m.	married or month
res.	resident
s.	son
st. b.	stillborn
w.	wife
wid.	widow
wk.	week
y.	year

THE BARBOUR COLLECTION OF CONNECTICUT TOWN VITAL RECORDS

TORRINGTON VITAL RECORDS
1740 – 1850

	Page
ABBEY, Henry S., of Buffalo, N.Y., m. Elizabeth **SMITH**, of Torrington, Oct. 30, 1831, by Rev. William R. Gould	114
ABERNETHY, Charlotte L., m. George P. **COWLES**, b. of Wolcottville, Sept. 18, 1844, by Rev. Samuel Day, of Wolcottville	128
Charlotte Leaming, d. Russell C. & Orrel, b. Oct. 2, 1820	59
Elisha Smith, s. Russell & Orrel, b. Oct. 24, 1805	59
Lucy S., d. Russell & Orrel, b. Sept. 7, 1807	59
Lucy S., m. George D. Wadhams, b. of Torrington, Dec. 25, 1828, by Rev. William R. Gould	85
Mary L., of Torrington, m. William B. **DeFOREST**, (Rev.), of Watertown, May 3, 1836, by Rev. H. P. Armes	122
Mary Lucretia, d. Russell C. & Orrel, b. Mar. 27, 1812	59
Orrel S., w. Russell C., d. May 26, 1835	59
Russell C., of Washington, m. Orrel **SMITH**, of Torrington, Sept. 17, 1803	59
Russell C., d. Sept. 16, 1861, ae 81	59
ADAMS, Augustus, of Breakesville, O., m. Anna **BAEBEE**, of Torrington, Apr. 5, 1847, by Rev. S. T. Seelye	131
ADDIS, George S., m. Sarah O. **GROSS**, b. of Torrington, Aug. 22, 1841, by Rev. B. Emerson	126
AGARD, Alvin, s. Benjamin & Rhoda, b. Jan. 14, 1797	10
Aurelia, [d. Benjamin & Rhoda], b. Mar. 6, 1799	10
Benjamin, m. Rhoda **LOOMIS**, b. of Torrington, Apr. 7, 1796	10
Bradley R., m. Mary Ann **CHURCH**, b. of Wolcottville, Nov. 3, 1841, by Rev. Samuel Day, of Wolcottville	126
Chloe, m. Aaron **MARSHALL**, b. of Torrington, Dec. 4, 1777	68
Hannah, of Litchfield, m. Benjamin **EGLESTONE**, of Torrington, Jan. 5, 1769	28
Mary, m. Oliver **COE**, b. of Torrington, Oct. 7, 1762	16
Rhoda, [d. Benjamin & Rhoda], b. July 23, 1802	10
Roman, [s. Benjamin & Rhoda], b. Dec. 3, 1804	10
ALLEN, ALLINE, [see also **ALLYN**], Abigail, b. Oct. 5, 1756; of Windsor, m. Guy **WOLCOTT**, of Torrington, Oct. 5, 1781	13
Anniss M., of Wolcottville, m. George P. Roberts, of St. Louis, Mo., May 15, 1843, by Rev. Samuel Day, of Wolcottville	127
Henry, m. Rebecca **WHITING**, b. of Torrington, Feb. 17, 1824, by Rev. Epaphras Goodman	56
Thankfull, of Middletown, m. Ebenezer **MILLER**, of Torrington, Feb. 16, 1761	76
ALLINE, [see under **ALLEN**]	
ALLYN, [see also **ALLEN**], Amelia, d. Oliver & Lucy, b. July 1, 1803	60
Amelia, m. James **WHITING**, b. of Torrington, Apr. 16, 1828, by Rev. William R. Gould	85
Chauncey, s. Joseph & Elizabeth, b. Dec. 2, 1767	1b
Chauncey, s. Joseph & Elizabeth, d. May 20, 1784	1b
Chancey, s. Henery & Betsey, b. July 7, 1802	79

	Page
ALLYN, (cont.)	
Elizabeth, d. Joseph & Elizabeth, b. June 23, 1762	1b
Elizabeth, w. Joseph, Sr., d. July 15, 1810	1b
Gilbert, s. Joseph & Elizabeth, b. Oct. 11, 1780	1b
Hannah, s. Joseph & Elizabeth, b. Sept. 26, 1778	1b
Henry, s. Joseph & Elizabeth, b. May 20, 1773	1b
Henery, of Torrington, m. Betsey **PALMER**, of Windsor, July 26, 1798	79
Henery, s. Henery & Betsey, b. July 17, 1799, at Windsor	79
Horatio Nelson, [s. Oliver & Lucy], b. Mar. 11, 1805	60
Jonah, s. Joseph & Elizabeth, b. May 27, 1770	1b
Joseph, s. Joseph & Elizabeth, b. May 14, 1765	1b
Joseph, Jr., m. Phebe **SMITH**, Mar. 28, 1793	2
Joseph, Jr., m. Sabra **LOOMIS**, Mar. 18, 1801	2
Joseph, s. Oliver & Lury, b. May 29, 1809	60
Joseph, s. Thomas & Elizabeth, d. Apr. 14, 1831	1b
Joseph, of Torrington, m. Esther M. **WESTLAKE**, of Wolcottville, Apr. 21, 1845, by Rev. Samuel Day	129
Julia, d. Henery & Betsey, b. July 4, 1801	79
Julia, of Torrington, m. Lyman **BEACH**, of Litchfield, Apr. 7, 1823, by Rev. Epaphras Goodman	55
Nelson, m. Speedy **BIRGE**, June 7, 1832, by Rev. William R. Gould	115
Oliver, s. Joseph & Elizabeth, b. Dec. 15, 1775	1b
Oliver, m. Lury **LOOMIS**, b. of Torrington, May 7, 1801	60
Phebe, w. Joseph, Jr., d. Sept. 2, 1798	2
ALVORD Nilson, of Torrington, m. Adelia **SKIFF**, of New York, July 4, 1848, by Rev. S. T. Seelye	133
ANDREWS, Harriet, of Harwinton, m. Abram M. Humphreyville, of Litchfield, Oct. 26, 1834, by Rev. David Miller	121
APLEY, Elizabeth, of Torrington, m. Hiram **JOHNSON**, of Canaan, Oct. 10, 1833, by Rev. Charles Sherman	119
ASHBORN, James, of Litchfield, m. Lucinda **SMITH**, of Wolcottville, Dec. 26, 1847, by Rev. Henry Zell, of Wolcottville	133
ATWATER, Asaph, of Farmington, m. Lucy Ann **DIBBLE**, of Torrington, May 27, 1772	2
Asaph, s. Asaph & Lucia Ann, b. Jan. 28, 1778	2
Asaph & Lucy, had d. [ ], b. Aug. 4, 1785	2
Benaroy, d. Asaph & Lucy Anne, b. Apr. 16, 1781	2
Charles, of Waterbury, m. Amanda **MERRELLS**, of Naugatuck, Sept. 20, 1849, by Rev. S. T. Seelye	135
Enos, s. Asaph & Lucy Anne, b. Feb. 14, 1783	2
Lucy, d. Asaph & Lucy Anne, b. Mar. 20, 1779	2
Mehitibell, d. Asaph & Lucy, b. Mar. 9, 1773	2
Mehitibel, d. Asaph & Lucy Ann, d. Mar. 7, 1775	2
Mehitibel, d. Asaph & Lucy Ann, b. Aug. 15, 1776	2
Thomas, s. Asaph & Lucy, b. Sept. 11, 1777	2
AUSTIN, Abigail, d. Nathaniell & Anne, b. Jan. 26, 1790	3
Anna, m. Hiram **RIDER**, July 20, 1837, in Torringford by Rev. Thomas Bainbridge	123
Anne, d. Nathaniell & Anne, b. Nov. 24, 1787	3
Anne, w. Nathaniell, d. May 7, 1793	3
Charlotte, m. John **HUNGERFORD**, Jr., b. of Torrington, June 5, 1820, by Samuel J. Mills	24

	Page
AUSTIN, (cont.)	
Charlotte, m. John **HUNGERFORD**, Jr., June 5, 1820	48
Clarecy, d. Nathaniell & Anne, b. Mar. 26, 1793	3
Clymena, d. Samuell & Ruth, b. Mar. 15, 1772	3
Cyrenius, s. Samuel & Mary, b. Mar. 5, 1779	4
Eliphalet, s. Aaron, b. June 8, 1760	2
Eliphalet, m. Sibel **DUDLEY**, b. of Torrington, [ ]	3
Elizabeth, d. Eliphalet & Sibel, b. May 25, 1780	3
Esther, m. Giles A. **GAYLORD**, b. of Torrington, Dec. 4, 1823, by Rev. Epaphras Goodman	56
Euseba, s. Aaron, b. Apr. 7, 1758	2
Fanny, m. Larrin **WETMORE**, Sept. 12, 1828, by Rev. William R. Gould	85
Joab, s. Nathaniell & Anne, b. Mar. 15, 1785	3
Mindwell, d. Samuell & Ruth, b. Aug. 25, 1766	3
Nathaniell, of Torrington, m. Anne **BIDWELL**, of Windsor, Sept. 28, 1775	3
Nathaniell, s. Nathaniell & Anne, b. Aug. 20, 1783	3
Norman, of Goshen, m. Ann B. **CADY**, of Torrington, Jan. 1, 1823, by Rev. Joseph Harvey, of Goshen	54
Polly, d. Samuel & Mary, b. Apr. 8, 1776	4
Priscilla, m. Asa **LOOMIS**, June 11, 1778	69
Rachel, d. Samuel & Mary, b. July 29, 1781	4
Rozwell, s. Aaron, b. Mar. 23, 1765	2
Rozel, s. Eliphalet & Sibel, b. July 21, 1781	3
Ruth, d. Samuell & Ruth, b. Feb. 12, 1769	3
Samuel, m. Ruth **GILLET**, b. of Torrington, Nov. 19, 1765	3
Samuel, m. Mary **BISSELL**, b. of Torrington, Oct. 28, 1774	4
Samuel, s. Samuel & Mary, b. Sept. 15, 1783	4
Sarah, d. Samuel & Ruth, b. Mar. 6, 1768	3
AVERED, Eunice, d. Israel & Abigail, b. Apr. 16, 1755	1a
Hannah, d. Israel & Abigail, b. May 7, 1747	1a
Israel, s. Israel & Abigail, b. June 16, 1752	1a
BACON, Ann, d. James & Hannah, b. Jan. 5, 1766; d. Jan. 6, 1766	8
Eldad, s. James & Hannah, b. Dec. 17, 1768	8
Esther, d. James & Hannah, b. Apr. 2, 1764	8
Hannah, d. James & Hannah, b. June 6, 1762	8
James, s. James & Hannah, b. Sept. 23, 1775	8
Phebe*, m. Epaphras **LOOMIS**, Jr., b. of Torrington, Dec. 1, 1777 *("Phebe **BROWN**" in Orcutt's Hist.)	66
Rachel, d. James & Hannah, b. Aug. 1, 1772	8
BAEBEE, [see under **BEEBE**]	
[**BAILEY**], **BALEY**, Damaries, m. Capt. Amos **WILLSON**, b. of Torrington, Aug. 19, 1777	104
BALCOM, Anson, m. Margarette **McKENZIE**, June 2, 1831, by Rev. David Miller	87
BALL, Almira, m. Jabez **GIBBS**, Mar. 17, 1828, by Rev. William R. Gould	84
Hannah, m. Jeremiah **BOWNS**, b. of Torrington, Oct. 23, 1820, by Samuel J. Mills	24
Mercy, m. Harmon **DALY**, Nov. 27, 1836, by Rev. Joseph Eldredge, of Norfolk	123
BANCROFT, Charles F., m. Eunice **EAVES**, Oct. 2, 1847, by Rev. John K. Still	131
Charlotte, m. Miles **BEACH**, Apr. 26, 1824, by Rev. Joseph Harvey, of Goshen	56
Ephraim, Jr., m. Jemima **LOOMIS**, b. of Torrington, Nov. 2, 1775	19

4 BARBOUR COLLECTION

Page

BANCROFT, (cont.)
Erastus, s. Noadiah & Jerusha, b. Oct. 27, 1782; d. [   ], 17[   ]   19
Erastus, s. Noadiah & Jerusha, b. Oct. 31, 1790   19
Esther, m. Rozel **COE**, s. Ebenezer & Jane, b. of Torrington, Apr. 22, 1766   12
Harris, s. Ephraim & Jemima, b. Sept. 30, 1791   19
Hellen, twin with Hellois, d. Horace & Damaras, b. Jan. 15, 1822   43
Hellois, twin with Hellen, d. Horace & Damaras, b. Jan. 15, 1822   43
Heloise, m. George H. **BOWNE**, Oct. 23, 1844, by J. A. McKinstry   128
Horace, s. Horace & Damaras, b. Dec. 9, 1830   43
Huldah, d. Ephraim & Jemima, b. Aug. 12, 1784   19
Huldah, d. Ephraim & Jemima, d. July 2, 1788   19
Jemima, d. Ephraim & Jemima, b. May 30, 1781   19
Jerusha, d. Noadiah & Jerusha, b. May 19, 1788   19
Jerusha, m. Miles **WILLCOX**, b. of Torrington, Oct. 22, 1807   17
John S., of East Windsor, m. Duliete **HUDSON**, of Torrington, June 12,
    1843, by Rev. B. Emerson   127
Luman, s. Noadiah & Jerusha, b. Mar. 23, 1784   19
Mahlon Wing, s. Horace & Damaras, b. Sept. 4, 1827   43
Miles, s. Ephraim & Jemima, b. July 27, 1776   19
Miles, s. Ephraim & Jemima, d. Apr. 5, 1795   19
Moses, s. Ephraim & Jemima, b. Aug. 27, 1789   19
Noadiah, m. Jerusha **LOOMIS**, b. of Torrington, Sept. 7, 1780   19
Noadiah, s. Noadiah & Jerusha, b. Apr. 12, 1786   19
Oliver, s. Ephraim & Jemima, b. June 9, 1787   19
Reuben, s. Ephraim & Jemima, b. Aug. 3, 1794   19
Ruth, m. Reuben **THRALL**, b. of Torrington, Aug. 11, 1765   95
Tryphena, d. Ephraim & Jemima, b. Feb. 5, 1779   19
Warren, m. Laura **PIERPOINT**, Feb. 17, 1828, by Rev. Walter Smith, of
    Cornwall   84
BARBER, Abijah, of Torrington, m. Mary **LOOMIS**, of Torrington, Feb. 19, 1795   22
Benham, of Harwinton, m. Mary **WILLSON**, of Torrington, Dec. 27, 1822,
    by Rev. H. P. Armes   117
Chester, of Harwinton, m. Marilla **BIRGE**, of Torringford, Feb. 6, 1821, by
    Samuel J. Mills   24
Chloe, d. Nathaniel & Hipzibah, b. Mar. 21, 1751   5
Chloe, m. Abner **LOOMIS**, b. of Torrington, June 9, 1785   65
Eli, s. Nathaniel & Hipzibah, b. Feb. 9, 1761   5
Eli, s. Nathaniel & Mercy, b. Apr. 22, 1775   5
Elihu, m. Jemima **NORTH**, b. of Torrington, Apr. 19, 1787   58
Elihu, s. Elihu & Jemima, b. Feb. 24, 1798   58
Elijah, m. Mary **HILLS**, b. of Torrington, July 10, 1766   9
Elizabeth, of Windsor, m. Joseph **DRAKE**, of Torrington, Mar. 7, 1750/1   22
Elkanah, s. Elihu & Jemima, b. June 25, 1803   58
Hipzibah, d. Nathaniel & Hipzibah, b. [   ]; d. Jan. 2, 1760   5
Hipzibah, twin with Jemimah, d. Nathaniel & Hipzibah, b. July 20, 1763   5
Hipzibah, wid. Nathaniell, d. Mar. 26, 1793   5
Hiram, m. Roxyana **BURDICK**, b. of Torrington, Dec. 6, 1830, by Rev.
    William R. Gould   87
Jane, m. Edward **ROOT**, May 17, 1848, by Rev. S. T. Seelye   134
Jemimah, twin with Hipzibah, d. Nathaniel & Hipzibah, b. July 20, 1763   5
Jemima, m. Benony **LOOMIS**, b. of Torrington, Mar. 9, 1786   66
Jemima, d. Elihu & Jemima, b. Apr. 16, 1800   58
Jockebod (?), of Torrington, m. Elijah **HUBBARD**, of Winchester, Oct. 26,

TORRINGTON VITAL RECORDS 5

	Page
BARBER, (cont.)	
1791	43
John C., m. Sarah **MILLER**, b. of Torrington, Oct. 1, 1841, by Rev. Brown Emerson	126
Kezia, d. Nathaniel & Hepzibah, b. Oct. 11, 1755	5
Kezia, d. Nathaniel & Hipzibah, d. May 22, 1779	5
Levi, s. Nathaniell & Mercy, b. June 11, 1771	5
Loana P., m. William **DURAND**, Feb. 3, 1843, by Rev. B. Emerson	127
Lois, d. Nathaniel & Hipzibah, b. June 2, 1753	5
Lois, m. Friend **THRALL**, b. of Torrington, May 27, 1773	95
Lucy, d. Nathaniel & Hipzibah, b. Dec. 18, 1757	5
Luman, s. Elijah & Mary, b. Nov. 12, 1766	9
Marain, m. Eliza **WHITNEY**, Feb. 16, 1832, by Rev. William R. Gould	115
Marvin, s. Abijah & Mary, b. Aug. 6, 1796	22
Mary, d. Elihu & Jemima, b. Jan. 22, 1793	58
Mary Ann, m. Anson **COLT**, Jr., b. of Torrington, Sept. 12, 1824, by Rev. George E. Pierce	57
Nathaniel, s. Nathaniel & Hipzibah, b. July 11, 1742	5
Nathaniel, s. Nathaniell & Hipzibah, d. Mar. 9, 1743	5
Nathaniel, s. Nathaniel & Hipzibah, b. Feb. 5, 1745	5
Nathaniel, s. Nathaniel, m. Mercy **SPAFFORD**, of Salisbury, Mar. 17, 1769	5
Nathaniell, Jr., d. Mar. 31, 1782	5
Nathaniell, Lieut., d. Mar. 8, 1788	5
Olive, m. Harvey **WHITEING**, b. of Torrington, Sept. 5, 1790	105
Orson, s. Elihu & Jemima, b. Nov. 6, 1806	58
Orson, m. Roxa A. **EGGLESTON**, b. of Torrington, Dec. 8, 1829, by Frederick Marsh	86
Orson, m. Martha **STARK**, Dec. 4, 1842, by Thomas Benedict	126
Roselandey, of Simsbury, m. Joseph **PRESTON**, Jr., of Torrington, Oct. 17, 1793	89
Sheldon, m. Sally E. **HODGES**, b. of Torrington, Apr. 10, 1833, by Rev. Milton Huxley	117
Timothy, s. Nathaniel & Hipzibah, b. Oct. 23, 1748	5
Uri, s. Nathaniel & Mercy, b. June 1, 1769	5
Zimri, s. Nathaniel & Mercy, b. May 29, 1773	5
BARNES, Sextus, of New Hartford, m. Abigail **OMSTEAD**, of Torrington, Sept. 14, 1836, by Rev. Seth Higbey	123
BASOM, Eliza, m. Horace **GIBBS**, b. of Torrington, Oct. 26, 1824, by Rev. Epaphras Goodman	57
BEACH, BEECH, Aaron Loomis, s. Wait & Huldah, b. Dec. 9, 1767	10
Abel, m. Margaret **PICKETT**, Apr. 5, 1738	5
Abel, s. Abel & Margaret, b. Dec. 18, 1740	5
Abel, s. John & Marcy, b. Jan. 3, 1775	9
Abel, Capt., d. Oct. 3, 1796	5
Abiah, w. Joel, d. Aug. 7, 1766	8
Adah, d. John & Marcy, b. Mar. 12, 1787	9
Ahira, s. Joseph & Jerusha, b. Oct. 20, 1784	6
Almeda, d. Miles & Huldah, b. Oct. 24, 1795	61-2
Anan, s. Noah & Sarah, b. Jan. 22, 1787	11
Benjamin, s. Joseph & Experience, b. Mar. 25, 1740	6
Benjamin, m. Abiah **LOOMIS**, b. of Torrington, Aug. 31, 1763	8
Dinah, d. Joseph & Experience, b. May 6, 1750; d. May 31, 1750	6
Dinah, d. Joseph & Experience, b. Nov. 2, 1751	6

	Page
BEACH, BEECH, (cont.)	
Ebenezer W., m. Lucy **WALLING**, b. of Torrington, Oct. 5, 1833, by Rev. Epaphras Goodman	119
Edee, w. Joseph, d. Apr. 29, 1776	6
Elah, s. Joseph & Jerusha, b. Oct. 14, 1780	6
Eliza, d. Julius & Jerusha, b. Apr. 30, 1807	59
Eliza, of Otis, Mass., m. Orson **MOSS**, of Litchfield, July 8, 1849, by Rev. J. A. McKinstry	134
Easther, d. Abel & Esther, b. Aug. 20, 1780	5
Experience, d. Joseph & Experiece, b. Sept. 10, 1744	6
Ezra, s. Benjamin & Abiah, b. Oct. 26, 1766	8
George, m. Mary **DELLINER**, Nov. 28, 1822, by Rev. Joseph Hargey, of Goshen	54
Hannah, d. Joseph & Experience, b. May 17, 1736	6
Hannah, of Torrington, m. Henry **JUDD**, of Litchfield, Nov. 10, 1830, by William R. Gould	86
Hannah B. L., m. David **COOK**, b. of Torrington, Dec. 21, 1806	23
Harris, s. Joseph & Jerusha, b. Mar. 3, 1786	6
James, s. Abel & Margaret, b. Nov. 24, 1752	5
James, s. John & Marcy, b. June 10, 1780, in Winchester	9
Joel, of Winchester, m. Abiah **FILLEY**, of Torrington, Oct. 18, 1757	8
John, s. Abel & Margaret, b. May 2, 1750	5
John, s. John & Marcy, b. Feb. 26, 1783	9
Joseph, s. Joseph & Experience, b. July 26, 1753	6
Joseph, Jr., s. Joseph, m. Edee **COOK**, b. of Torrington, Jan. [ ], 1776	6
Joseph, Jr., m. Jerusha **PHELPS**, b. of Torrington, Aug. 19, 1779	6
Julus, s. Noah & Sarah, b. Oct. 27, 1783	11
Julius, of Torrington, m. Jerusha **WEEKS**, of Litchfield, Apr. 30, 1806	59
Keziah, d. Samuel & Keziah, b. Oct. 10, 1768	5
Keziah, d. Samuel & Keziah, d. Feb. 8, 1776	5
Keziah, d. Samuel & Keziah, b. Aug. 16, 1779	5
Keziah, of Torrington, m. Reuben **HALL**, of Wallingford, May 19, 1829, by Rev. William R. Gould	85
Levi, s. Benjamin & Abiah, b. Oct. 24, 1764	8
Levi, s. Benjamin & Abiah, d. Oct. 19, 1768	8
Levi, s. Benjamin & Abiah, b. Feb. 6, 1772	8
Lewis, s. Miles & Huldah, b. Mar. 14, 1797	61-2
Lewis, of Goshen, m. Almira **WHITE**, of Torrington, Feb. 27, 1831, by Isaac Jones, at Wolcottville	87
Luandrus, of Dover, N.H., m. Harriet **BURR**, of Torrington, July 11, 1831, by Rev. Epaphras Goodman	87
Lyman, of Litchfield, m. Julia **ALLYN**, of Torrington, Apr. 7, 1823, by Rev. Epaphras Goodman	55
Malinda, of Torrington, m. Zenas **WRIGHT**, of Plainfield, N.Y., Nov. 21, 1811, by Rev. Mr. Gilbert	6
Margaret, d. Abel & Margaret, b. Sept. 3, 1747	5
Margaret, m. Abijah **WILLSON**, b. of Torrington, Oct. 5, 1767	103
Martha, d. Abel & Margaret, b. Jan. 13, 1759	5
Martha, m. William **WILSON**, b. of Torrington, Aug. 6, 1783	109
Mary, d. John & Marcy, b. Aug. 19, 1778, in Winchester	9
Mary, d. Noah & Sarah, b. July 7, 1779	11
Mary, d. Noah [& Sarah], d. Apr. 4, 1798	11
Mary, m. Caleb **JOHNSON**, b. of Torrington, Dec. 20, 1798	29

TORRINGTON VITAL RECORDS 7

	Page
BEACH, BEECH, (cont.)	
Miles, s. Wait & Huldah, b. Aug. 20, 1779; d. [Aug.] 25, [1769]	10
Miles, s. Wait & Huldah, b. Mar. 17, 1773	10
Miles, of Torrington, m. Huldah **GRANT**, of Litchfield, Aug. 11, 1793	61-2
Miles, m. Charlotte **BANCROFT**, Apr. 26, 1824, by Rev. Joseph Harvey, of Goshen	56
Miles G., s. Miles & Huldah, b. Mar. 16, 1800	61-2
Mindwell, d. Samuell & Kezia, b. Dec. 16, 1770	5
Miriam, d. Joseph & Experience, b. Dec. 5, 1734	6
Miriam, d. Benjamin & Abiah, b. Sept. 9, 1768; d. Nov. 12, 1768	8
Miriam, d. Benjamin & Abiah, b. Nov. 19, 1769	8
Nancy, d. Wait & Huldah, b. Aug. 23, 1770	10
Nancy, m. Dr. Penfield **GOODSELL**, b. of Torrington, Oct. 26, 1791	39
Noah, s. Abel & Margaret, b. Sept. 13, 1755	5
Noah, of Torrington, m. Sarah **BRADLEY**, of Winchester, Feb. 19, 1778	11
Phebe, d. Joseph & Experience, b. Apr. 4, 1738	6
Rebeckah, d. Abel & Margaret, b. May 23, 1745	5
Rhoda, d. Samuel & Keziah, b. May 8, 1776	5
Samuel, s. Abel & Margaret, b. Dec. 2, 1742	5
Samuel, s. Samuel & Keziah, b. Aug. 21, 1781	5
Sarah, d. Abel & Esther, b. July 4, 1776	5
Sarah, d. Noah & Sarah, b. Mar. 7, 1781	11
Sarah, m. Pomeroy **LEACH**, b. of Torrington, Sept. 24, 1797	70
Selden, of Lexington, N.Y., m. Mary A. **DUNBAR**, of Torrington, Dec. 31, 1848, by Rev. S. T. Seelye	134
Silvah, m. Jonathan **PHELPS**, b. of Torrington, Jan. 20, 1785	88
Susanna, d. Noah & Sarah, b. Feb. 21, 1786; d. Mar. 6, 1786	11
Wait, of Goshen, m. Huldah **LOOMIS**, of Torrington, July 9, 1767	10
BEARDSLEY, Adaline M., of Wolcottville, m. Lucius Fowler **LEACH**, of Torrington, Sept. 13, 1842, by Rev. Samuel Day, of Wolcottville	127
BECKLEY, Daniel, m. Lucy Anna **MERRILL**, b. of Winchester, July 13, 1837, by Thomas Benedict, at his house	123
Norris, m. Maryan **HART**, Dec. 27, 1841, by Thomas Benedict	126
[BEEBE], BAEBEE, BEBEE, Anna, of Torrington, m. Augustus **ADAMS**, of Breakesville, O., Apr. 5, 1847, by Rev. S. T. Seelye	131
Rhoda, of East Haddam, m. David **WILLIAMS**, of Colchester, Jan. 31, 1790	113
BEERS, Charles C., of Goshen, m. Emma Rosetta **PALMER**, of Torrington, Sept. 28, 1831, by Rev. William R. Gould	114
BELLAMIE, Lorenzo, m. Elenor **FREEMAN**, b. of Torrington, June 28, 1830, by Rev. David Miller	86
BENEDICT, Noah, m. Harriet A. **CURTIS**, b. of Winchester, Mar. 5, 1835, by Rev. H. P. Armes	122
BENHAM, Charles, m. Lois F. **BRUN**(?), Mar. 4, 1838, by Rev. Stephen Hubbell, of Wolcottville	124
Jay, of Waterbury, m. Salina **BRACE**, of Torrington, Nov. 28, 1830, by Rev. David Miller	86
BENNETT, Benoni, of Amesville, N.Y., m. Ursula Ann **COOK**, of Whitestown, N.Y., Aug. 18, 1840, by Samuel Day	125
BENTON, Sina, of Harwinton, m. David **EGGLESTON**, of Torrington, Dec. 25, 1796	28
BERNARD, Henry, of Winchester, m. Joan C. **STONE**, of Litchfield, Jan. 30, 1848, by Rev. George A. Hubbell. Witnesses Alfred Brown & Hiram Lyman	132

	Page
BIDWELL, Anne, of Windsor, m. Nathaniell **AUSTIN**, of Torrington, Sept. 28, 1775	3
Hannah, of Windsor, m. Samuel **FOOT**, of Simsbury, Mar. 27, 1766	35
BIRD, James S., of Bethlem, m. Fanny M. **NORTHROP**, of Torrington, May 24, 1846, by Rev. Henry Zell, of Wolcottville, at his house	132
BIRGE, Aranda, s. John & Lydia, b. Sept. 1, 1782	8
Caroline G., m. Wait B. **WILLCOX**, b. of Torrington, Oct. 3, 1832, by Rev. Milton Huxley	117
Chester, s. John & Lydia, b. July 23, 1788	8
David, s. David & Elizabeth, b. Aug. 9, 1763	7
David, m. Rhodah **HUDSON**, b. of Torrington, Dec. 16, 1784	7
David, s. David & Rhodah, b. Oct. 31, 1790	7
Elizabeth, d. David & Elizabeth, b. Mar. 21, 1759	7
Elizabeth, d. David & Rhodah, b. Mar. 8, 1788	7
Elizabeth, m. Amos **WILLSON**, b. of Torrington, Dec. 13, 1820, by Samuel J. Mills	25
Eunice, d. David & Rhodah, b. Jan. 7, 1786	7
John, s. John & Mary, b. Mar. 15, 1753	7
John, of Torrington, m. Lydia **HOPKINS**, of Canaan, Mar. 23, 1779	8
John, s. John & Lydia, b. May 4, 1785	8
Laura, Mrs., m. Norman **GRISWOLD**, b. of Torrington, Nov. 6, 1821, by Rev. Epaphras Goodman	26
Marilla, of Torringford, m. Chester **BARBER**, of Harwinton, Feb. 6, 1821, by Samuel J. Mills	24
Mary, d. John & Mary, b. Oct. 31, 1752	7
Nathaniel, m. Olive **PECK**, b. of Torrington, May 8, 1831, by Rev. Epaphras Goodman	87
Polly, d. John & Lydia, b. Feb. 22, 1781	8
Speedy, m. Nelson **ALLYN**, June 7, 1832, by Rev. William R. Gould	115
Willard, m. Julia Ann **MERRILL**, Nov. 9, 1833, by Rev. H. P. Armes	120
BISHOP, Mary, Mrs., m. Eli **PHELPS**, Jan. 3, 1841, by Rev. Samuel Day, of Wolcottville	125
BISSELL, **BYSSEL**, Ann M., m. Thomas **MOSES**, b. of Torrington, Nov. 15, 1826, by Rev. Epaphras Goodman	81
Augustus E., of Georgia, m. Melissent W. **WATSON**, of Torrington, Feb. 29, 1836, by Rev. Epaphras Goodman	123
Catharine, m. Burritt **TUTTLE**, Oct. 1, 1848, by Rev. S. T. Seelye	134
Elijah, m. Rachel **SOPER**, b. of Torrington, Jan. 22, 1789	29
Elijah, s. Elijah & Rachel, b. Feb. 28, 1791	29
George, m. Sarah **WOODRUFF**, Oct. 26, 1823, by Rev. Joseph Harvey, of Goshen	56
Hannibal, s. Elijah & Rachel, b. Apr. 10, 1793	29
Lucy, of Wolcottville, m. George H. **MASON**, Jan. 1, 1846, in Wolcottville, by Rev. Henry Zell, of Wolcottville	132
Martha, m. Daniel **WINCHEL**, b. of Torrington, June 15, 1779	113
Mary, m. Samuel **AUSTIN**, b. of Torrington, Oct. 28, 1774	4
Mary E., m. Henry P. **COE**, b. of Wolcottville, Aug. 23, 1841, by Samuel Day	126
Nancy, m. John **WADKINS**, Aug. 28, 1822, by Rev. Epaphras Goodman	54
Rachel M., of Torrington, m. Henry A. Perkins, of New Hartford, June 14, 1831, by Rev. Epaphras Goodman	87
Roderick, m. Fanny **GAYLORD**, b. of Torrington, May 11, 1824, by Rev. Epaphras Goodman	56

	Page
BISSELL, BYSSEL, (cont.)	
Rosetta, m. Charles S. **MASON**, b. of Wolcottville, Nov. 28, 1841, by Rev. Samuel Day, of Wolcottville	126
BLAKE, Allen, s. Elijah & Sarah, b. May 19, 1792	43
Barzillai, s. Joseph & Marana, b. Nov. 5, 1772	9
Barzilla, m. Ruth **MURRAY**, b. of Torrington, Sept. 27, 1798	20
Elijah, m. Sarah **HAMLIN**, b. of Middletown, Sept. 27, 1779, at Middletown	43
Elijah, s. Elijah & Sarah, b. June 26, 1784	43
Harry, s. Elijah & Sarah, b. June 29, 1788	43
Ithiel, s. Elijah & Sarah, b. Aug. 1, 1790	43
Jesse, s. Joseph & Marana, b. July 2, 1769	9
Jesse, s. Joseph & Marana, d. May 22, 1773	9
Jesse, s. Joseph & Marana, b. Dec. 14, 1776	9
Jonathan, s. Elijah & Sarah, b. Aug. 13, 1786	43
Joseph, m. Marana **GRANT**, b. of Torrington, Aug. 27, 1767	9
Lowrain, d. Joseph & Marana, b. Dec. 27, 1778	9
Maria, d. Elijah & Sarah, b. Oct. 18, 1797	43
Polly, d. Elijah & Sarah, b. Sept. 15, 1782	43
Rheube, d. Barzillia & Ruth, b. Dec. 20, 1800	20
Sally, d. Elijah & Sarah, b. Dec. 12, 1780	43
Sally, d. Elijah & Sarah, d. June 17, 1793	43
Sally, s. Elijah & Sarah, b. Dec. 16, 1794	43
Sarah, d. Joseph & Marana, b. Nov. 22, 1770	9
Seth, s. Joseph & Marana, b. Dec. 7, 1767	9
William, s. Barzilla & Ruth, b. Sept. 25, 1799	20
BLAKESLEE, George, of Torrington, m. Marion **DAVIS**, of Newtown, July 2, 1848, by Rev. S. T. Seelye	133
BOOGUE, Henry O., m. Julia M. **WEED**, of Harwinton, Sept. 8, 1845, in Wolcottville, by Rev. Henry Zell, of Wolcottville	132
BOOTH, David, of Naugatuck, m. Emeline **SCOTT**, of Litchfield, Jan. 1, 1845, by Rev. Samuel Day	129
BOSTWICK, Eliza Potter, d. William & Philomela, b. Feb. 6, 1800	91
Harmon B., s. William & Philomela, b. Mar. 29, 1805	91
William Frederick, s. William & Phelomela, b. June 8, 1798	91
BOWLER, Adelia, m. William **SMITH**, b. of Waterbury, Oct. 2, 1831, by Daniel Coe	114
BOWNE, BOWNS, Caroline, of Torrington, m. Caleb C. **TRACY**, of Washington, Jan. 9, 1845, by J. A. McKinstry	128
George H., m. Heloise **BANCROFT**, Oct. 23, 1844, by J. A. McKinstry	128
Jeremiah, m. Hannah **BALL**, b. of Torrington, Oct. 23, 1820, by Samuel J. Mills	24
Laura L., of Torrington, m. Robert O. **MARTIN**, of Goshen, Oct. 15, 1849, by Rev. J. A. McKinstry	135
BOWNELLY, John, m. Candace **HAYDEN**, b. of Torrington, Jan. 12, 1823, by Cirus Yale	54
BOWNS, [see under **BOWNE**]	
BRACE, Deborah, m. Watrous **PERKINS**, b. of Torrington, Aug. 21, 1823, by Rev. Epaphras Goodman	55
Harlan, s. Rial & Deborah, b. Aug. 11, 1787	10
Jared, s. Ariel & Deborah, b. Dec. 7, 1773	10
Lucy, d. Rial & Deborah, b. Mar. 12, 1793	10
Rial, s. Rial & Deborah, b. July 8, 1781	10
Rodney, s. Rial & Deborah, b. May 1, 1790	10

BRACE, (cont.)
Salina, of Torrington, m. Jay **BENHAM**, of Waterbury, Nov. 28, 1830, by
   Rev. David Miller — 86
Samantha, d. Rial & Deborah, b. Dec. 10, 1784 — 10
Truman, s. Rial & Deborah, b. Aug. 11, 1783 — 10
Willys, s. Ariel & Deborah, b. Aug. 31, 1779 — 10
BRADFORD, A. G., m. Maria **SCOTT**, May 4, 1848, by Rev. S. T. Seelye — 133
BRADLEY, Almeda, d. Seymour & Tryphena G., b. May 13, 1793 — 4
   Clarissa, of Torrington, m. Salmon **HUNT**, of Canaan, Jan. 8, 1823, by Rev.
      Rodney Rossiter, of Plymouth — 54
   Elvira, d. Seymour & Tryphena, b. Dec. 10, 1794 — 4
   Emeline, m. William C. **RUSSELL**, b. of Torrington, May 24, 1827, by Rev.
      John L. Stone, of Litchfield — 83
   Laura, d. Seymour & Tryphena, b. July 24, 1796 — 4
   Minerva S., of Cornwall, m. Sterling **WOODRUFF**, of Torrington, Sept. 1,
      1834, by Rev. Milton Huxley — 120
   Ralph, s. Seymour & Tryphena G., b. June 17, 1791 — 4
   Sarah, of Winchester, m. Noah **BEACH**, of Torrington, Feb. 19, 1778 — 11
   Seymour, m. Tryphena Grant **NORTH**, b. of Torrington, May 30, 1791 — 4
   Seymour, s. Seymore & Tryphena, b. Mar. 15, 1798 — 4
BRAW, Hezekiah H., of Hartford, m. Mary Ann **LOOMIS**, of Torrington, Mar.
   27, 1833, by Rev. Epaphras Goodman — 118
BRISTOL, Chester, of Elizabethtown, N.J., m. Mindwell **PHELPS**, of Torrington,
   May 1, 1825, by Rev. Epaphras Goodman — 83
   Lewis, of Brookfield, m. Mary Anne **LONG**, of Wolcottville, Oct. 12, 1846,
      in Wolcottville, by Rev. Henry Zell,of Wolcottville — 132
BROCKET, Mary, of Waterbury, m. Silas **PARDEE**, of Bristol, Mar. 31, 1844, by
   Rev. Samuel Day, of Wolcottville — 128
BRONSON, BRUNSON, Lois, of Winchester, m. Seth **WETMORE**, of
   Torrington, Dec. 9, 1779 — 107
   Luther, of Winchester, m. Flora M. **GRANT**, of Torrington, Nov. 3, 1842, by
      Thomas Benedict — 126
   Thereon, m. Maria R. **MUNSILL**, July 7, 1841, by Thomas Benedict — 126
BROOKER, BROKER, Chester, m. Phebe Anne **SMITH**, b. of Litchfield, June
   21, 1846, by Rev. Samuel Day — 130
   Ede, d. John & Jerusha, b. Mar. 19, 1783 — 7
   John, m. Jerusha **WILSON**, b. of Torrington, Feb. 18, 1783 — 7
   Lucy, d. John & Jerusha, b. Sept. 25, 1789 — 7
   Martin, m. Maria **SEYMOUR**, May 1, 1838, by Rev. Stephen Hubbell, of
      Wolcottville — 124
   Riley, s. John & Jerusha, b. Mar. 28, 1791 — 7
   Russel, m. Jennett **McKINZIE**, b. of Torrington, Nov. 12, 1826, by Rev.
      Epaphras Goodman — 81
   Warren, s. John & Jerusha, b. Sept. 29, 1786 — 7
   Warren, s. John & Jerusha, d. Sept. 1, 1787 — 7
BROOKS, Keziah, of Springfield, m. Daniel **THRALL**, Jr., of Torrington, June 2,
   1785 — 96
   Lydia, m. David R. **KIMBERLEY**, Oct. 7, 1824, by Rev. Rodney Rossiter,
      of Plymouth — 57
   Maria Ann, of Wolcottville, m. Edmund **WOODING**, of Bristol, Sept. 11,
      1842, by Rev. Samuel Day, of Wolcottville — 127
   Orson, of Waterbury, m. Louisa **JOHNSON**, of Torrington, Nov. 22, [1843?],
      by John A. McKinstry — 127

	Page
BROOKS, (cont.)	
Samuel, Jr., m. Julia A. **SEYMOUR**, May 18, 1834, by Rev. H. P. Armes	120
BROWN, Anna Bertha*, d. Owen & Berthe*, b. July 5, 1798, at Norfolk *("Ruth")	17
Caroline, of Canton, m. Sylvester **COE**, of Torrington, Jan. 20, 1825, by Rev. Epaphras Goodman	57
Elizabeth, of Windsor, m. Joel **LO[O]MIS**, of Torrington, June 4, 1752	68
Elizabeth, m. James H. **HURLBUT**, Sept. 9, 1832, by Rev. David L. Parmelee	116
John, s. Owen & Berthe*, b. May 9, 1800, at Torrington *("Ruth")	17
Oliver Owen, s. Owen & Berthe*, b. Oct. 20, 1804 *("Ruth")	17
Owen, late of Symsbury, now of Torrington, m. Berthe ***MILLS**, of Symsbury, Feb. 11, 1793, at Symsbury *("Ruth")	17
Phebe, m. Epaphras **LOOMIS**, Jr., b. of Torrington, Dec. 1, 1777	66
Salmon, s. Owen & Berthe*, b. Apr. 30, 1802 *("Ruth")	17
William, m. Polly **HUBBARD**, Feb. 4, 1821, by Datus Ensign	25
BRUN(?), Lois F., m. Charles **BENHAM**, Mar. 4, 1838, by Rev. Stephen Hubbell, of Wolcottville	124
BUCKLAND, Almansor A., of East Windsor, m. Sarah **NORTHROP**, of Torrington, Feb. 4, 1835, by Rev. Daniel Smith	121
BUNCE, Horace H., m. Anna **CURTISS**, b. of Torrington, May [ ], 1849, by Rev. J. A. McKinstry	135
BUNNELL, Mansfield, of Plymouth, m. Sophronia A. **MILLER**, of Torrington, Apr. 24, 1833, by Rev. Epaphras Goodman	118
BURBANK, Aaron, m. Mrs. Abigail **TREADWAY**, b. of Winsted, Dec. 18, 1842, by Rev. B. Emerson	126
BURDICK, Roxyana, m. Hiram **BARBER**, b. of Torrington, Dec. 6, 1830, by Rev. William R. Gould	87
BURGESS, Lewis G., of New Haven, m. Eliza T. **HURLBUT**, of Winchester, July 12, 1848, by Rev. James H. Dill, of Winchester	134
BURR, Allin, s. Reuben & Mehetable, b. Feb. 15, 1780	6
Almira, of Torrington, m. Converse **CLARK**, of Saybrook, Mar. 17, 1825, by Cyrus Yale	57
Arnold, s. John & Jael, b. Dec. 10, 1778	6
Chloe, d. John & Tabitha, b. Sept. 27, 1764	6
Chloe, d. Reuben & Mehetable, b. May 15, 1786	6
Eliza, d. Reuben & Martha, b. Jan. 16, 1801	6
Eliza, m. Daniel G. **HUMPHREY**, Jr., b. of Torrington, Oct. 31, 1820, by Samuel J. Mills	25
Esther G., m. James B. **TALLMADGE**, Apr. 22, 1845, by D. W. Clark	129
Fanny, d. Reuben & Martha, b. Dec. 4, 1798	6
Harriet, d. Reuben & Martha, b. Jan. 13, 1803	6
Harriet, of Torrington, m. Luandrus **BEACH**, of Dover, N.H., July 11, 1831, by Rev. Epaphras Goodman	87
Horatio, s. John & Jael, b. Aug. 30, 1781	6
Jael, d. John & Jael, b. Aug. 7, 1775	6
Jael, d. John & Jael, d. Oct. 17, 1775	6
Jehiel, s. John & Tabitha, b. Apr. 11, 1757	6
John, Jr., Lieut., m. Jael **MARKHAM**, b. of Torrington, Dec. 13, 1770	6
John, s. John & Jael, b. May 2, 1773	6
John, s. John & Jael, d. Aug. 26, 1775	6
John, s. John & Jael, b. Sept. 13, 1776	6
Mehetable, d. Reuben & Mehetable, b. Nov. 22, 1777	6

	Page
BURR, (cont.)	
Mehetable, w. Reuben, d. Sept. 29, 1793	6
Milo, s. Reuben & Martha, b. Jan. 1, 1797	6
Reuben, s. John & Tabitha, b. Jan. 13, 1752	6
Reuben, m. Mehitabel **STARK***, b. of Torrington, July 2, 1772 *("Stanley" in Orcutt's Hist. of Torrington)	6
Reuben, s. Reuben & Mehetable, b. Aug. 15, 1773	6
Reuben, m. Martha **WILLSON**, Aug. 20, 1794	6
Rufus, of Winchester, m. Anna S. **HUDSON**, of Torrington, May 10, 1827, by Rev. Epaphras Goodman	84
Russell, s. John & Tabitha, b. Oct. 19, 17[ ]	6
Sally, d. Reuben & Mehetable, b. Aug. 4, 1789	6
Salmon, s. Reuben & Mehetable, b. May 26, 1775	6
Sarah J., of Torrington, m. Andrew E. Hull, of Burlington, May 9, 1849, by Rev. S. T. Seelye	135
Tabitha, d. John & Tabitha, b. June 23, 1754	6
Theodore, s. John & Jael, b. Aug. 16, 1771	6
Uriel, s. Reuben & Martha, b. May 19, 1795	6
Uriel, m. Esther **CURTIS**, b. of Torrington, Dec. 13, 1820, by Samuel J. Mills	25
BURRETT, Joseph H., m. Mercia **STOCKING**, b. of Torrington, May 4, 1836, by Rev. H. P. Armes	122
CALDWELL, Samantha, b. Sept. 30, 1780; m. Joshua **CADY**, Oct. 19, 1799	64
Urania, m. Ralph **JUDD**, b. of Torrington, May 10, 1825, by Rev. George E. Pierce	83
CADY, Alonzo, s. Joshua & Samantha, b. Sept. 8, 1804	64
Ann B., of Torrington, m. Norman **AUSTIN**, of Goshen, Jan. 1, 1823, by Rev. Joseph Harvey, of Goshen	54
Anna Brace, d. Joshua & Samantha, b. Apr. 3, 1802	64
Horatio Nelson, s. Joshua & Samantha, b. Mar. 10, 1800	64
Joshua, b. July 2, 1771; m. Samantha **CADWELL**, Oct. 19, 1799	64
[**CAMPBELL**], **CAMBELL**, Jean, of Canaan, m. Ephraim **LOOMIS**, of Torrington, Oct. 18, 1764	65
CANFIELD, Abial, of Torrington, m. Bede **KENNA**, of Wolcott, Mar. 31, 1831, by Rev. Epaphras Goodman	87
Samantha, m. Spencer **TURREL**, b. of Torrington, Mar. 10, 1831, by Rev. Epaphras Goodman	87
CARR, Clement, of Torrington, m. Jedidiah* **PELTON**, of Chatham, May 18, 1785 *("Jedidiah")	20
Florilley, d. Clement & Jedidiah, b. July 25, 1792	20
Lemuel, s. Clement & Jedidiah, b. Sept. 29, 1785	20
Loas, d. Robert & Mary, b. Nov. 4, 1790	17
Poley, d. Robert & Mary, b. Dec. 10, 1786	17
Robert, m. Mary **PRESTON**, b. of Torrington, Dec. 29, 1785	17
Ruth, d. Robert & Mary, b. Mar. 1, 1788	17
Stillman, s. Clement & Jedidiah, b. Jan. 15, 1788; d. Jan. [ ], 1790	20
CARRINGTON, Polly, m. Eliada **PIERPOINT**, Aug. 25, 1848, by Rev. William H. Moore	134
CARTER, Ezra, s. Ithiel & Lois, b. Apr. 19, 1789	13
George H., of Sharon, m. Julia **HARRISON**, of Milton, Dec. 26, 1843, by Rev. Samuel Day, of Wolcottville	128
Julius, s. Ithiel, b. July 5, 1786	13
Lois, Jr., d. Ithiel & Lois, b. Feb. 28, 1792	13

TORRINGTON VITAL RECORDS

	Page
CARTER, (cont.)	
Lucas, s. Ithiel, b. Sept. 12, 1787	13
Marcia*, d. Ithiel & Lois, b. Aug. 15, 1790 *("Martha"?)	13
Marsha*, d. Ithiel & Lois, b. Aug. 17, 1790 *("Martha"?)	13
Sarah, d. Ithiel & Lois, b. Aug. 18, 1793	13
[**CARTWRIGHT**], **CARTWRITE**, Emily, m. Seth B. **ST. JOHN**, Mar. 10, 1839, by Thomas Benedict	124
CASE, Hosea, m. Angeline **ROBERTS**, b. of Torrington, Jan. 18, 1846, by Rev. H. D. Kitchel	130
CASTLE, Annis A., of Harwinton, m. Harvey **DAYTON**, of Torrington, Feb. 25, 1849, by Rev. J. A. McKinstry	135
Eliza, d. Ransom & Nancy, b. Oct. 21, 1827	59
CASWELL, Francis, of Plymouth, m. Mary Ann **DUNBAR**, of Torrington, Sept. 5, 1842, by Frederick Marsh	126
CATLIN, Charles, m. Anna B. **CHURCHILL**, b. of Wolcottville, Jan. 14, 1849, by Frederick Marsh	135
CHAMBERLAIN, Mercy, of Middletown, m. Franklin **HEDGE**, of Torrington, Sept. 3, 1826, by Rev. E. W. Goodman	81
CHAMPION, Henry S., of Winsted, m. Mary A. **GILLETT**, of Torrington, Oct. 17, 1842, by John A. McKinstry	127
CHASE, Adaline, of Winchester, m. Matthew R. **HART**, of Goshen, Oct. 23, 1845, by Rev. Miles N. Olmstead	130
Reuben, m. Lucy **CURTIS**, Oct. 18, 1823, by Rev. Julius Field	55
CHATFIELD, Dennis, of Waterbury, m. Mary Jane **MATTHEWS**, of Torrington, Dec. 18, 1835, by Rev. H. P. Armes	122
CHURCH, Charles S., m. Charlotte A. **TAYLOR**, b. of Torrington, Nov. 28, 1833, by H. P. Armes	119
George W., of Torrington, m. Evaline B. **LATHROP**, of Sheffield, Nov. 19, 1848, by Rev. S. T. Seelye	134
John H., of Bethlem, m. Mary Ann **WILCOX**, of Torrington, Dec. 4, 1823, by Rev. Epaphras Goodman	56
Mary Ann, m. Bradley R. **AGARD**, b. of Wolcottville, Nov. 3, 1841, by Rev. Samuel Day, of Wolcottville	126
Susanna, of Wolcottville, m. A. P. **KLINE**, of Wilmington, N.C., Aug. 20, 1843, by Rev. B. Emerson	127
CHURCHILL, Anna B., m. Charles **CATLIN**, b. of Wolcottville, Jan. 14, 1849, by Frederick Marsh	135
CLARK, Converse, of Saybrook, m. Almira **BURR**, of Torrington, Mar. 17, 1825, by Cyrus Yale	57
Francis, of Winsted, m. Mary J. **PERKINS**, of Wolcottville, Feb. 28, 1847, by Rev. S. T. Seelye	131
George R., m. Susan R. **GRANT**, Apr. 10, 1849, by Rev. Thomas Benedict	135
Hannah, m. Daniel **MURRAY**, [ ]	78
Marilla, of Winchester, m. John C. **WOODRUFF**, of New Hartford, Jan. 12, 1847, by Rev. S. T. Seelye	131
CLEMMINS, Sophia, m. Frederick **FORBES**, b. of Torrington, Sept. 28, 1826, by Rev. Janes Beach, of Winsted	81
CLEVELAND, Ellen, of Torrington, m. William L. **MERREL**, of Waterbury, May 14, 1849, by Rev. John A. McKinstry	135
COBB, Nathan, of Torrington, m. Eliza **COLYER**, of Burlington, Sept. 25, 1826, by Rev. E. W. Goodman	81
COE, Abner, s. Oliver & Mary, b. Apr. 12, 1763	16
Ann Eliza, of Torrington, m. Norris **NORTH**, of Torrington, June 28, 1843,	

	Page
COE, (cont.)	
by Rev. B. Emerson	127
Artemecia, d. Oliver & Sarah, b. Dec. 5, 1799	16
Asahel, of Waterbury, m. Maria **WETMORE**, of Torrington, June 2, 1830, by Rev. William R. Gould	86
Dorcas, s. Oliver & Sarah, b. Jan. 11, 1794	16
Ebenezer, s. Jonathan & Elizabeth, b. Dec. 2, 1750	12
Ebenezer, Jr., s. Jonathan & Elizabeth, d. Oct. 18, 1784	12
Elizabeth, d. Jonathan & Elizabeth, b. Feb. 15, 1743	12
Eunice, d. Ebenezer & Jane, b. Apr. 29, 1742	12
Henry P., m. Mary E. **BISSELL**, b. of Wolcottville, Aug. 23, 1841, by Samuel Day	126
Jerusha, d. Jonathan & Elizabeth, b. Mar. 27, 1746	12
Jonathan, of Torrington, m. Elizabeth **ELMER**, of Windsor, Sept. 23, 1737	12
Jonathan, s. Jonathan & Elizabeth, b. Aug. 20, 1742	12
Jonathan, Jr., m. Eunice **COOK**, b. of Torrington, Apr. 15, 1767	16
Jonathan, s. Jonathan & Eunice, b. Mar. 23, 1770	16
Jonathan, of Winsted, m. Betsey **WETMORE**, of Torrington, Nov. 30, 1848, by Rev. S. T. Seelye	134
Lovina, d. Jonathan & Eunice, b. Feb. 11, 1768	16
Lovine, of Winchester, m. Asahel **MILLER**, of Torrington, Oct. 26, 1788	76
Lucretia, d. Jonathan & Elizabeth, b. June 9, 1755	12
Lucretia, m. Daniel **MURREY**, b. of Torrington, Mar. 18, 1776	78
Lyman W., m. Eliza **SEYMOUR**, Nov. 3, 1841, by Rev. Samuel Day, of Wolcottville	126
Martha, d. Jonathan & Elizabeth, b. Jan. 5, 1748/9	12
Mary, d. Ebenezer & Jane, b. Sept. 7, 1744	12
Norman, m. Nancy **WHITING**, Aug. 26, 1827, by Rev. William R. Gould. Int. Pub.	84
Norris, s. Oliver & Sarah, b. May 1, 1792	16
Oliver, s. Jonathan & Elizabeth, b. Sept. 3, 1738	12
Oliver, m. Mary **AGARD**, b. of Torrington, Oct. 7, 1762	16
Oliver, m. Sarah **MARSHALL**, Dec. 1, 1791	16
Orrel, of Torrington, m. Samuel J. **STOCKING**, of Waterbury, Mar. 22, 1835, by Rev. H. P. Arrnes	122
Rhoda P., of Wolcottville, m. Joseph **GOULD**, of Winchester, Oct. 2, 1842, by Rev. Samuel Day, of Wolcottville	127
Robert, s. Jonathan & Elizabeth, b. Mar. 28, 1740	12
Robert, m. Chloe **THRALL**, b. of Torrington, Dec. 26, 1761	16
Rozel, s. Ebenezer & Jane, b. Sept. 20, 1746	12
Rozel, s. Ebenezer & Jane, m. Esther **BANCROFT**, b. of Torrington, Apr. 22, 1766	12
Seth, s. William, b. Dec. 21, 1757	16
Seth, of Torrington, m. Dorcas **KIES**, of Middletown, Nov. 15, 1829, by Rev. David Miller	86
Sylvester, of Torrington, m. Caroline **BROWN**, of Canton, Jan. 20, 1825, by Rev. Epaphras Goodman	57
William, s. William, b. Mar. 23, 1764	16
COLE, [see also **COWLES**], Ira, of Kent, m. Lavina **THRALL**, of Torrington, Nov. 23, 1820, by Joseph Harvey	25
COLEBY, Eliza J., m. John **OSTRAM**, b. of Goshen, Aug. 10, 1829, at Wolcottville, by Rev. David Miller	85
COLLINS, Abigail, m. John **GILLETT**, b. of Torrington, Aug. 30, 1770	43

TORRINGTON VITAL RECORDS 15

	Page
COLT, Anson, Jr., m. Mary Ann BARBER, b. of Torrington, Sept. 12, 1824, by Rev. George E. Pierce	57
Charlotte, of Torrington, m. Burton POND, of Bristol, Oct. 6, 1829, by Rev. Epaphras Goodman	85
Chloe, m. Leverett TUTTLE, b. of Torrington, Feb. 10, 1830, by Rev. Epaphras Goodman	86
COLYER, Eliza, of Burlington, m. Nathan COBB, of Torrington, Sept. 25, 1826, by Rev. E. W. Goodman	81
Polly, m. Stephen FYLER, b. of Windsor, July [ ], 1778	36
COMBS, Eliza, of Torrington, m. Edward HILL, of Charlton, Mass., Nov. 17, 1839, by Rev. W. A. Stickney	125
Letitia, of Wolcottville, m. Stephen C. WARNER, of Nagatuc, Sept. 2, 1841, by Samuel Day	126
CONE, Marilla W., of Torrington, m. William Henry JUDD, of Norfolk, Aug. 14, 1845, by Rev. Niles N. Olmstead	129
COOK, Ansel, m. Sophronia EGLESTON, b. of Torrington, May 7, 1834, by Rev. Milton Huxley	120
Anson, s. Urijah & Submit, b. Oct. 4, 1779	18
David, s. John & Bethyah, b. Jan. 31, 1781	14
David, m. Hannah B. L. BEACH, b. of Torrington, Dec. 21, 1806	23
Deborah, d. John & Deborah, b. Nov. 25, 1769	14
Deborah, d. John & Deborah, d. Oct. 14, 1774	14
Deborah, w. John, d. Aug. 25, 1775	14
Edee, d. John & Rachel, b. Nov. 28, 1752	11
Edee, m. Joseph BEACH, Jr., s. Joseph, b. of Torrington, Jan. [ ], 1776; d. Apr. 29, 1776	6
Edee, w. Dea. Jonathan, of Winsted, d. Oct. 29, 1781	102
Elihu, s. John & Rachel, b. Feb. 18, 1760; d. Feb. 20, 1760	11
Elihu, s. John & Rachel, b. Mar. 29, 1761	11
Elihu, m. Huldah YALE, b. of Torrington, June 6, 1787	18
Esther, d. Joseph & Joehebed, b. Aug. 19, 1756	15
Eunice, d. John & Rachel, b. Mar. 5, 1746	11
Eunice, m. Jonathan COE, Jr., b. of Torrington, Apr. 15, 1767	16
Florilla, of Harwinton, m. Albro GRISWOLD, of Weathersfield, Jan. 4, 1835, by Rev. H. P. Armes	121
Francis, s. John & Rachel, b. Sept. 18, 1747	11
Francis, s. John & Rachel, d. Dec. 23, 1750	11
Hannah, d. John & Rachel, b. Mar. 13, 1758	11
Hannah, m. Simeon MOOR, Jr., b. of Torrington, June 21, 1784	77
Harmon*, s. John & Lydia, b. Feb. 2, 1807 *("Herman")	23
Herman, m. Angeline DARE, b. of Torrington, May 22, 1836, by Rev. H. P. Armes	122
Horace L., of Wolcottville, m. Ruth E. HOYT, of Newfield, Nov. 9, 1845, by Rev. J. B. Beach, of M. E. Ch.	130
Huldah, d. Elihu & Huldah, b. Feb. 14, 1788	18
John, m. Rachel WILLSON, b. of Windsor, June 22, 1741	11
John, s. John & Rachel, b. Aug. 29, 1743	11
John, Jr., of Torrington, m. Deborah PALMER, 2nd, of Windsor, May 25, 1769	14
John, s. John & Deborah, b. Dec. 2, 1771; d. Feb. 29, 1772	14
John, m. Dethyah WINCHEL, b. of Torrington, Feb. 2, 1779	14
John, s. John & Bethyah, b. May 27, 1779	14
John, Dea., d. Sept. 8, 1779	11

BARBOUR COLLECTION

	Page
COOK, (cont.)	
John, Jr., of Torrington, m. Lydia **LOOMIS**, of Harwington, Mar. 19, 1806	23
John Winthrop, s. Luther, b. Mar. 12, 1818	60
Lewis, s. John & Lydia, b. Sept. 23, 1817	23
Lois, d. Urijah & Submit, b. Mar. 25, 1781	18
Leucy, d. John & Rachel, b. Oct. 2, 1756	11
Lucy, m. Moses **LOOMIS**, Jr., b. of Torrington, Aug. 8, 1782	64
Luther, s. John & Bethyah, b. Sept. 21, 1783	14
Maria Louisa, d. Luther, b. Sept. 26, 1833	60
Mary, d. John & Rachel, b. Nov. 10, 1764	11
Mary, d. John, decd. & Rachel, d. Nov. 14, 1784	11
Ophela, d. Elihu & Huldah, b. Jan. 3, 1794	18
Rachel, d. John & Rachel, b. May 2, 1742	11
Rachel, m. David **SOPER**, b. of Torrington, Jan. 26, 1764	94
Rachel, wid. John, d. Apr. 8, 1789	11
Rhoda, m. Joseph **FERAN**, b. of Harwinton, Nov. 14, 1838, at the house of Hiram Burr, by Rev. Herman L. Vaill	124
Riley, s. Elihu & Huldah, b. June 14, 1797	18
Rowzanda, d. Shubael & Sarah Basset, b. Mar. 17, 1774	14
Roxey, d. Elihu & Huldah, b. Oct. 28, 1790	18
Sally, d. Urijah & Submit, b. Mar. 28, 1782	18
Sarah, d. John & Rachel, b. Oct. 31, 1750	11
Sarah, m. Levi **HURLBUT**, July 28, 1777	49
Shubael, s. John & Rachel, b. Apr. 21, 1749	11
Shubael, m. Sarah Basset **GILLET**, b. of Torrington, Sept. 17, 1773	14
Urijah, s. John & Rachel, b. Sept. 1, 1754	11
Urijah, m. Submit **TUTTLE**, b. of Torrington, Feb. 8, 1779	18
Ursula Ann, of Whitestown, N.Y., m. Benoni **BENNETT**, of Amesville, N.Y., Aug. 18, 1840, by Samuel Day	125
CORNISH, Deidamia, of Simsbury, m. James **SMITH**, of Lexington, N.Y., Oct. 16, 1825, by Rev. Alexander Gillett	81
COTTON, Justus, of Longmeadow, Mass., m. Emeline **PHELPS**, of Torrington, Nov. 1, 1830, by Rev. William R. Gould	86
Polley, m. William **MILLER**, [ ], 1783	73
COWLES, [see also **COLE**], Abigail, m. John **WILLIAMS**, a regular, b. of Torrington, June 20, 1780	108
Albro W., m. Eliza **TALLMADGE**, Mar. 5, 1828, by Rev. William R. Gould	84
George P., m. Charlotte L. **ABERNETHY**, b. of Wolcottville, Sept. 18, 1844, by Rev. Samuel Day, of Wolcottville	128
Jerusha, m. Ebenezer **NORTH**, s. Ebenezer, b. of Torrington, Feb. 16, 1769	84
Lois, d. Samuel & Sibella, b. Apr. 25, 1757	15
Noah, s. Samuel & Sibella, b. Oct. 17, 1759	15
Samuel, Jr., m. Sibella **NORTH**, Apr. 14, 1756	15
Zilpah, d. Samuel & Sibella, b. June 7, 1762	15
CRAMPTON, Levi, of Goshen, m. Elizabeth **MUNN**, of Torrington, Aug. 31, 1824, by Rev. Arnold Scholfield. Int. Pub.	57
Willis, of Farmington, m. Pluma **LOOMIS**, of Torrington, Feb. 2, 1836, by Milton Huxley	122
CRANE, Milo R., of Sandisfield, Mass., m. Cordelia S. **WAUGH**, of Torrington, Oct. 8, 1839, by Frederick Marsh	125
CROOK, Benjamin N., of Torrington, m. Adeline **THOMPSON**, of Waterbury, Jan. 11, 1846, by J. A. McKinstry	130
CUMMINGS, COMMINS, CUMMINS, Cordelia, of Goshen, m. Joseph B.	

TORRINGTON VITAL RECORDS 17

	Page
CUMMINGS, COMMINS, CUMMINS, (cont.)	
LEWIS, of Winsted, Feb. 6, 1833, by Rev. H. P. Armes	117
Esther Roberts, d. Samuel & Margaret, b. Nov. 20, 1782	17
Lovell, s. Samuel & Margaret, b. Apr. 17, 1791	17
Nathaniel Roberts, s. Samuel & Margaret, b. July 6, 1780	17
Reuben, s. Samuel & Margaret, b. Sept. 4, 1786	17
Roma, d. Samuel & Margaret, b. Sept. 6, 1778	17
Samuel, m. Margaret **ROBERTS**, b. of Torrington, Sept. 28, 1778	17
Zilpha, d. Samuel & Margaret, b. Oct. 17, 1788	17
CURTIS, CURTICE, CURTISS, Anna, m. Horace H. **BUNCE**, b. of Torrington, May [ ], 1849, by Rev. J. A. McKinstry	135
Elizabeth, m. Edward **EGGLESTON**, b. of Torrington, Dec. 4, 1760	27
Esther, m. Uriel **BURR**, b. of Torrington, Dec. 13, 1820, by Samuel J. Mills	25
Frances W., m. John P. **GULLIVER**, Sept. 8, 1845, at the house of Dea. Elizur Curtiss, by Lavalette Perrin	129
Harriet A., m. Noah **BENEDICT**, b. of Winchester, Mar. 5, 1835, by Rev. H. P. Armes	122
Huldah, d. John & Mary, b. Feb. 17, 1772	13
Jeremiah, s. John & Mary, b. Apr. 8, 1770	13
Job, s. Zebulon & Lydia, b. July 5, 1745	13
John, s. Zebulon & Lydia, b. Mar. 10, 1746	13
John, m. Mary **FILLEY**, b. of Torrington, June 4, 1769	13
Jonny, s. John & Mary, b. Feb. 16, 1774	13
Lois, m. James **SOUTHWICK**, Apr. 28, 1830, by Rev. William R. Gould	86
Lorrain, s. John & Mary, b. Sept. 16, 1775	13
Lucy, m. Reuben **CHASE**, Oct. 18, 1823, by Rev. Julius Field	55
Lydia, d. Zebulon & Lydia, b. Dec. 29, 1751	13
Lydia, w. Capt. Zebulon, d. June 22, 1776	13
Lyd[i]a, m. Joseph **HOMES**, b. of Torrington, Sept. 9, 1778	51
Mary, d. John & Mary, b. Dec. 26, 1779	13
Rufus, m. Ursula **FOWLER**, b. of Torrington, Oct. 21, 1820, by Samuel J. Mills	24
Sedelia, of Goshen, m. George **PLATT**, of Sharon, Apr. 4, 1843, by Rev. Samuel Day, of Wolcottville	127
Thomas, Capt., d. Jan. 20, 1751/2	13
Thomas, s. John & Mary, b. Apr. 3, 1778	13
Truman A., of New Hartford, m. Laura **WOODWARD**, of Torrington, Mar. 18, 1840, by Rev. Herman L. Vaill	125
DAILY, DALY, Harmon, m. Mercy **BALL**, Nov. 27, 1836, by Rev. Joseph Eldredge, of Norfolk	123
Julius, m. Lois **WILLSON**, Aug. 9, 1832, by Rev. William R. Gould	116
DANIELS, Caleb F., of Norwich, m. Sarah R. **TALLMADGE**, of Torrinford, Apr. 28, 1839, by Rev. Herman L. Vaill	124
David F., of Preston, m. Laura **SPERRY**, of Torrington, Sept. 25, 1831, by Rev. Herman Ellis, of Norfolk	114
Martha, d. George & Elizabeth, b. May 4, 1783	96
DARE, Angeline, m. Herman **COOK**, b. of Torrington, May 22, 1836, by Rev. H. P. Armes	122
DAVIS, Marion, of Newtown, m. George **BLAKESLEE**, of Torrington, July 2, 1848, by Rev. S. T. Seelye	133
DAYTON, Caroline, m. Newton **POTTER**, Nov. 17, 1837, by Rev. Stephen Hubbell, of Wolcottville	124
Emily, of Wolcottville, m. Julius **SCOVILLE**, of Litchfield, Sept. 22, 1842,	

	Page
DAYTON, (cont.)	
in Wolcottville, by Rev. John H. Still	126
Harvey, of Torrington, m. Annis A. **CASTLE**, of Harwinton, Feb. 25, 1849, by Rev. J. A. McKinstry	135
Martha M., of Wolcottville, m. Squire **SCOVILLE**, of Litchfield, July 14, 1844, by Rev. Samuel Day, of Wolcottville	128
Mary Ann, of Torrington, m. Gilbert **MASON**, of New London, Sept. 13, 1835, by Rev. John B. Beach	122
DeFOREST, William B., Rev. of Watertown, m. Mary L. **ABERNETHY**, of Torrington, May 3, 1836, by Rev. H. P. Armes	122
[DELEBER], DELLEBUR, Daniel G., [s. Samuel & Minerva], b. June 24, 1812	109
Lucius T., [s. Samuel & Minerva], b. Apr. 12, 1815	109
Mary K., [d. Samuel & Minerva], b. Oct. 17, 1808	109
Raphael M., [s. Samuel & Minerva], b. Feb. 1, 1810	109
Samuel, b. May 31, 1785; m. Minerva **MARSHALL**, June 19, 1806	109
Samuel, [s. Samuel & Minerva], b. July 18, 1819	109
DELLEBUR, [see under **DELEBER**]	
DELLINER, Mary, m. George **BEACH**, Nov. 28, 1822, by Rev. Joseph Harvey, of Goshen	54
DEMING, Jannah, of Barkhamsted, m. Lydia **THORP**, of Torrington, Dec. 22, 1824, by Rev. Epaphras Goodman	57
DIBBLE, DIBELL, Anna, w. Daniel, b. Mar. [ ], 1744; m. Daniel, Nov. 17, 1768	23
Anna, w. Daniel, d. Feb. 14, 1786	23
Aurelia*, d. Daniel & Anna, b. Mar. 5, 1772 *(Arnold Copy has "Orealea")	23
Aurelia, of Torrington, m. Chauncey **HAYDEN**, of Randolph, Vt., Oct. 28, 1834, by Rev. H. P. Armes	121
Daniel, s. Thomas & Hannah, b. Oct. 20, 1744; m. Anna [ ], Nov. 17, 1768	23
Daniel & Anna, had d. [ ], b. Jan. 28, 1770	23
Daniel, of Torrington, m. Ruth **PHELPS**, of Windsor, Jan. 8, 1788	23
Ebenezer, s. Thomas & Hannah, b. June 21, 1750	22
Hannah, d. Thomas & Hannah, b. Jan. 11, 1753	22
Isaac Haydon, s. Daniel & Anna, b. Oct. 31, 1781	23
Lucretia, d. Daniel & Anna, b. Jan. 17, 1784	23
Lucretia, m. Jannah B. **PHELPS**, Nov. 26, 1812	45
Lucy Ann, of Torrington, m. Asaph **ATWATER**, of Farmington, May 27, 1772	2
Mehetibel, twin with Meriam, d. Daniel & Anna, b. Mar. 22, 1776	23
Mehitable, b. Mar. 22, 1776, at Torrington; m. Harvey **PALMER**, Nov. 25, 1795	69
Meriam, twin with Mehetibel, d. Daniel & Anna, b. Mar. 22, 1776	23
Marriam, m. John P. **WETMORE**, Nov. 25, 1795	44
Orealea*, d. Daniel & Anna, b. Mar. 5, 1772 *("Aurelia")	23
Thomas, s. Thomas & Hannah, b. May 25, 1757; d. Dec. 2, 1759	22
Thomas, d. Aug. 20, 1758	22
DIX, Osmus Alvin, s. Orren & Nancy, b. Aug. 7, 1805	93
DOOLITTLE, David, s. David & Taphath, b. Oct. 31, 1777	23
Eli, s. David & Taphath, b. July 15, 1773	23
Lydia, d. David & Taphath, b. July 23, 1775	23
DOWD, Mary, of Goshen, m. Aaron **THRALL**, of Torrington, Feb. 20, 1766	96
DRAKE, Annis, of Windsor, m. Aaron **LOOMIS**, of Torrington, Feb. 12, 1789	68
Elizabeth, d. Joseph & Elizabeth, b. Feb. 1, 1754	22
Flora P., m. Thomas A. **STARKS**, May 20, 1840, by Thomas Benedict	125

TORRINGTON VITAL RECORDS 19

	Page
DRAKE, (cont.)	
Hannah, d. Joseph & Elizabeth, b. Mar. 12, 1761	22
John Eson, s. Joseph & Olive, b. Sept. 10, 1777	22
Joseph, of Torrington, m. Elizabeth **BARBER**, of Windsor, Mar. 7, 1750/1	22
Jul[i]aana, d. Joseph & Elizabeth, b. Mar. 28, 1769	22
Lorinda, d. Joseph & Elizabeth, b. Nov. 18, 1765	22
Martin V., m. Sally A. **DRAKE**, Oct. 27, 1847, by Thomas Benedict	131
Mary Ann, of Torrington, m. Harvey **FORD**, of Winchester, June 26, 1825, by Rev. F. Marsh, of Winchester	83
Moses, m. Reuby **LOOMIS**, Oct. 29, 1839, by Thomas Benedict	125
Sally A., m. Martin V. **DRAKE**, Oct. 27, 1847, by Thomas Benedict	131
Sarah, d. Joseph & Elizabeth, b. May 13, 1756	22
Ursula, d. Joseph & Elizabeth, b. Jan. 23, 1751/2	22
DUDLEY, Morgan, of Winchester, m. Almira **WILLSON**, of Torrington, May 3, 1834, by Rev. Epaphras Goodman	120
Sibel, m. Eliphalet **AUSTIN**, b. of Torrington, [ ]	3
DUNBAR, Harriet, of Torrington, m. Leroy **MILLIMAN**, of Winsted, Sept. 13, 1843, by Rev. B. Emerson	127
Mary A., of Torrington, m. Selden **BEACH**, of Lexington, N.Y., Dec. 31, 1848, by Rev. S. T. Seelye	134
Mary Ann, of Torrington, m. Francis **CASWELL**, of Plymouth, Sept. 5, 1842, by Frederick Marsh	126
Riley, m. Rhoda **HUNTINGTON**, b. of Torrington, Jan. 29, 1835, by Rev. H. P. Armes	121
DURAND, William, m. Loana P. **BARBER**, Feb. 3, 1843, by Rev. B. Emerson	127
EAVES, Eunice, m. Charles F. **BANCROFT**, Oct. 2, 1847, by Rev. John K. Still	131
EDMONDS, EDMOND, Anna, d. Sarah **PRESTON**, b. Feb. 16, 1794; f. Stephen **EDMOND**	89
Ebenezer, m. Sarah C. **NORTH**, b. of Torrington, Oct. 6, 1833, by Rev. H. P. Armes	118
Isaac H., m. Sally **FAIRBANKS**, b. of Torrington, May 3, 1835, by Rev. H. P. Armes	122
EGGLESTON, EGLESTON, EGLESTONE, Alexa, d. David & Sina, b. Nov. 2, 1808	28
Alma, d. David & Sina, b. Oct. 3, 1806	28
Alma, m. Robert **PELTON**, Apr. 8, 1829, by Frederick Marsh	85
Amarilla*, d. Curtis & Amarilla, b. Feb. 11, 1805 *(Arnold Copy has "Annarilla")	27
Ann, d. Benjamin & Hannah, b. Sept. 30, 1773	28
Anna, d. David & Sina, b. Aug. 28, 1804	28
Annarilla*, d. Curtis & Annarilla*, b. Feb. 11, 1805 *("Amarilla")	27
Anramia, of Torrington, m. Cyrus **HUBBARD**, of Harwinton, Oct. 18, 1820, by Frederick Marsh	24
Anson, s. Joseph & Lusanna, b. July 15, 1794	28
Aurinda, d. David & Sina, b. Oct. 28, 1802	28
Barbarina, s. David & Sina, b. Dec. 2, 1800	28
Barnabus, s. David & Sina, b. May 7, 1797	28
Benjamin, of Torrington, m. Hannah **AGARD**, of Litchfield, Jan. 5, 1769	28
Benjamin, s. Benjamin & Hannah, b. Apr. 16, 1788	28
Curtis, s. Edward & Elizabeth, b. Apr. 4, 1774	27
Curtis, m. Annarilla* **FOWLER**, June 27, 1799 *("Amarilla" in Boyd's Annals)	27
David, s. Joseph & Lusanna, b. Apr. 29, 1776	28

	Page
EGGLESTON, EGLESTON, EGLESTONE, (cont.)	
David, of Torrington, m. Sina **BENTON**, of Harwinton, Dec. 25, 1796	28
David Mason, s. David & Sina, b. Dec. 13, 1813	28
Edward, m. Elizabeth **CURTIS**, b. of Torrington, Dec. 4, 1760	27
Edward, d. Sept. 28, 1807	27
Elizabeth, w. Edward, d. Nov. 27, 1801	27
Elizabeth, d. Curtis & Annarilla, b. July 7, 1803	27
Elmina, of Litchfield, m. Daniel A. **GRANT**, of Torrington, Nov. 6, 1845, by Rev. Miles N. Olmstead	130
Esther, d. Edward & Elizabeth, b. Mar. 5, 1762	27
Ethan, s. Benjamin & Hannah, b. Jan. 7, 1785	28
Eunice, d. Edward & Elizabeth, b. Oct. 30, 1766	27
Eunice, d. Joseph & Lusanna, b. Aug. 31, 1791	28
Eunice, d. Edward & Elizabeth, d. Nov. 11, 1801	27
Ezekiel, s. Edward & Elizabeth, b. Mar. 13, 1769	27
Frederick Benton, s. David & Sina, b. Mar. 13, 1811	28
James, s. Edward & Elizabeth, b. May 17, 1764	27
James, m. Jemiah **PHELPS**, b. of Torrington, Dec. 24, 1789	27
Jedediah, s. Benjamin & Hannah, b. Dec. 30, 1777	28
Jerusha, d. James & Jemiah, b. June 25, 1791	27
John, s. Benjamin & Hannah, b. May 9, 1770	28
John, s. Benjamin & Hannah, d. Mar. 6, 1791	28
John, s. David & Sina, b. Feb. 28, 1799	28
Jonathan, s. Benjamin & Hannah, b. Sept. 12, 1780	28
Joseph, of Torrington, m. Lusanna **MASON**, of Litchfield, Mar. 23, 1775	28
Joseph, s. Joseph & Lusanna, b. Dec. 2, 1777	28
Judah, d. Benjamin & Hannah, b. Oct. 8, 1775	28
Linda, d. Benjamin & Hannah, b. Dec. 17, 1772	28
Mollie, d. Benjamin & Hannah, b. Nov. 21, 1782	28
Morilla, m. Bennet **PALMER**, b. of Torrington, Mar. 30, 1830, by Frederick Marsh	86
Nabby, d. Joseph & Lusanna, b. June 15, 1789	28
Norman Fowler, s. Curtis & Annarilla, b. July 17, 1800	27
Phylo, s. Edward & Elizabeth, b. Apr. 7, 1771	27
Roxa A., m. Orson **BARBER**, b. of Torrington, Dec. 8, 1829, by Frederick Marsh	86
Sophronia, m. Ansel **COOK**, b. of Torrington, May 7, 1834, by Rev. Milton Huxley	120
Timothy, s. Joseph & Lusanna, b. Oct. 21, 1779	28
William, s. Joseph & Lusanna, b. June 21, 1787	28
ELLSWORTH, Polly, of Torrington, m. Justin P. **LEWIS**, of Ohio, Aug. 7, 1831, by Rev. Epaphras Goodman	87
ELMER, Elizabeth, of Windsor, m. Jonathan **COE**, of Torrington, Sept. 23, 1737	12
EMMONS, Ethiel, m. Almira **LEACH**, Oct. 14, 1827, by Rev. Isaac Dwinel	84
Lucius, of Litchfield, m. Almeda S. **LEACH**, of Torrington, Sept. 23, 1849, by Rev. John A. McKinstry	135
Luther, of Cornwall, m. Mary **WILLEY**, of Torringford, Oct. 19, 1829, by William R. Gould	86
ENO, Abigail, m. Martin **NORTH**, b. of Torrington, Apr. 2, 1760	83
Eunice, d. Eliphalet & Sarah, b. Nov. 23, 1794	48
EVANS, Susan, m. Artemas **ROWLEY**, b. of Torrington, Sept. 20, 1826, by Rev. E. W. Goodman	81
EVERITT, EVERIT, Abi, d. Israel & Abi, b. Dec. 28, 1792	1a

	Page
EVERITT, EVERIT, (cont.)	
Fyler, s. Israel & Abi, b. Apr. 7, 1787	1a
Israel, m. Abi **FYLER**, b. of Torrington, Sept. 26, 1782	1a
Israel, s. Israel & Abi, b. June 18, 1783	1a
Josiah, s. Israel & Abi, b. Nov. [ ], 1785	1a
[ ]aler*, s. Israel & Abi, b. Apr. 7, 1787 *("Fyler" in Orcutt's Hist. of Torrington)	1a
FAIRBANKS, Sally, m. Isaac H. **EDMONDS**, b. of Torrington, May 3, 1835, by Rev. H. P. Armes	122
FARLEY, Francis D., of Lenox, Mass., m. Rhoda **ROOD**, of Torrington, May 22, 1849, by Rev. John A. McKinstry	135
FELLOWS, Ephraim, of Cornwall, m. Sabra **ROBERTS**, of Torrington, Nov. 2, 1825, by Rev. Epaphras Goodman	81
FERAN, Joseph, m. Rhoda **COOK**, b. of Harwinton, Nov. 14, 1838, at the house of Hiram Burr, by Rev. Herman L. Vaill	124
FERGUSON, FIRGUSON, FURGUSON, Anna, of Haddam, m. Abner **IVES**, of Wallingford, May 11, 1768	53
James, m. Martha **SQUIRES**, b. of Durham, Jan. 9, 1767	35
James, s. James & Martha, b. Mar. 1, 1769	35
Joseph, s. James & Martha, b. Feb. 1, 1771	35
Lettes, m. Ebenezer **LEACH**, b. of Torrington, [ ]	70
Samuel, s. James & Martha, b. May 20, 1767	35
FIELD, Gustavus G., Dr. of Guilford, m. Lura A. **MORSE**, of Canaan, Oct. 14, 1838, by Rev. James Beach, of Winsted. Settled in Torrington	125
FILLEY, Isaac, s. Abraham & Marey, b. Dec. 8, 1761	33-4
Mary, m. John **CURTICE**, b. of Torrington, June 4, 1769	13
FITCH, John Mills, s. Luther & Clarissa, b. May 20, 1803	32
Julia Bethiah, d. Luther & Clarissa, b. Feb. 5, 1805	32
William Beecher, s. Luther & Lydia, b. Feb. 11, 1801	32
FOOT, Cornelia, of Torrington, m. Elias **HATCH**, of Winchester, Oct. 8, 1833, by Rev. H. P. Armes	118
Julia, m. William **LEACH**, b. of Torrington, Aug. 19, 1828, by Rev. Epaphras Goodman	85
Roger, s. Samuel & Hannah, b. Dec. 27, 1766	35
Samuel, of Simsbury, m. Hannah **BIDWELL**, of Windsor, Mar. 27, 1766	35
Samuel, s. Samuell & Hannah, b. Mar. 27, 1771	35
FORBES, Frederick, m. Sophia **CLEMMINS**, b. of Torrington, Sept. 28, 1826, by Rev. Janes Beach, of Winsted	81
FORD, Harriet, m. Lorrain **NORTH**, b. of Torrington, May 4, 1834, by Frederick Marsh	120
Harvey, of Wincheester, m. Mary Ann **DRAKE**, of Torrington, June 26, 1825, by Rev. F. Marsh, of Winchester	83
FOREST, FORREST, Emma, m. James **GAUNT**, Feb. 3, 1837, by Rev. Stephen Hubbell	123
Jemima J., of Wolcottville, m. Burr **MANVILLE**, of Watertown, Dec. 24, 1847, by Rev. Henry Zell, of Wolcottville	133
Samuel, m. Ann **PICKERING**, b. of Torrington, Dec. 25, 1835, by Rev. H. P. Armes	122
FOSTER, FORSTER, Anna, m. Jotham **IVES**, b. of Wallingford, May 10, 1769	53
Lois, of Wallingford, m. William **GRANT**, of Torrington, Nov. 18, 1762	41
Phebe, of Wallingford, m. Matthew **GRANT**, of Torrington, Nov. 18, 1762	40
Sarah, of Wallingford, m. John **WHITING**, of Torrington, Jan. 18, 1749/50	105
FOWLER, Ammarilla, d. Noah & Rhoda, b. Feb. 6, 1776	33-4

	Page
FOWLER, (cont.)	
Annarilla*, m. Curtis **EGLESTON**, June 27, 1799 *("Amarilla")	27
Desier, d. Noah & Rhoda, b. June 3, 1783	33-4
Desire B., m. Daniel S. **ROGERS**, b. of Torrington, Apr. 17, 1832, by Rev. Epaphras Goodman	115
George, s. Noah & Rhoda, b. Dec. 5, 1778	33-4
Mary, m. Issachey **LOOMIS**, b. of Torrington, Dec. 10, 1765	67
Noah, s. Joseph & Ruth, b. Sept. 24, 1750; m. Rhoda **TUTTLE**, b. of Torrington, Feb. 10, 1774	33-4
Norman, s. Noah & Rhoda, b. Apr. 9, 1777	33-4
Parleman, s. Noah & Rhoda, b. Aug. 14, 1780	33-4
Raphael, s. Noah & Rhoda, b. July 22, 1785	33-4
Ramus, twin with Romulus, s. Noah & Rhoda, b. Aug. 3, 1791	33-4
Rhoda, d. Noah & Rhoda, b. Oct. 9, 1781	33-4
Rhoda, m. Daniel Coe **HUDSON**, Jan. 24, 1805	37
Romulus, twin with Remus, s. Noah & Rhoda, b. Aug. 3, 1791	33-4
Sibel, d. Noah & Rhoda, b. Aug. 7, 1787	33-4
Ursula, d. Noah & Rhoda, b. [ ], 1794; d. June [ ], 1873, at Florence, Mass.	33-4
Ursula, m. Rufus **CURTIS**, b. of Torrington, Oct. 21, 1820, by Samuel J. Mills	24
Warren, s. Noah & Rhoda, b. Mar. 2, 1775	33-4
FOX, Charity, of Hebron, (wid.), m. Oliver **SKINNER**, of Torrington, July 3, 1823, by Alexander Gillett	55
FREEMAN, Almyra, m. William **HARRISON**, b. of Torrington, Oct. 3, 1847, by Rev. S. T. Seelye	131
Amos, of Torrington, m. Sarah Emeline **ROMANS**, of Enfield, Jan. 9, 1831, by Rev. Epaphras Goodman	87
Charles S., m. Lucy A. **FREEMAN**, b. of Torrington, Aug. 1, 1843, by Rev. B. Emerson	127
Charlotta, m. Pinus **WATERMAN**, b. of Torrington, Aug. 19, 1830, by Rev. Epaphras Goodman	87
Drusilla, of Harwinton, m. Horace **PRINCE**, of Torrington, June 1, 1845, by Rev. Samuel Day, of Wolcottville	129
Elenor, m. Lorenzo **BELLAMIE**, of Torrington, June 28, 1830, by Rev. David Miller	86
Emeline, of Torringford, m. James **JONES**, Dec. 9, 1840, by W. B. Ransom	125
Henry, m. Julia Ann **PHELPS**, b. of Torringford (colored), Apr. 28, 1839, by Rev. Herman L. Vaill	124
John, m. Susanna **PRINCE**, Jan. 6, 1833, by Rev. Epaphras Goodman	117
Laura Ann, m. Benjamin **PETERSON**, b. of Wolcottville, Sept. 27, 1843, by Rev. Samuel Day, of Wolcottville	127
Lucinda, of Torrington, m. Chauncey B. **MIX**, of Northfield, Nov. 30, 1820, by Samuel J. Mills	25
Lucy A., m. Charles S. **FREEMAN**, b. of Torrington, Aug. 1, 1843, by Rev. B. Emerson	127
Nancy, m. James **JONES**, b. of Torrington, May 21, 1821, by Rev. David Miller	25
FRENCH, Esther, of Torrington, m. John **SMITH**, of Winchester, Aug. 27, 1823, by David Miller	55
FROST, Mary M., d. Selah & Ursula, b. Jan. 8, 1824	31
Warren, s. Selah & Ursula, b. Jan. 18, 1827	31
FULLER, David S., of Torrington, m. Maria **PORTER**, of Waterbury, Oct. 3,	

FULLER, (cont.)	
1824, by Rev. Epaphras Goodman	57
FYLER, [see also **TYLER**], Abi, m. Israel **EVERIT**, b. of Torrington, Sept. 26, 1782	1a
Cata, d. Stephen & Polly, b. July 30, 1786	36
George, s. Stephen & Polly, b. Feb. 13, 1782	36
Harlow, d. Stephen & Polly, b. Dec. 21, 1795	36
Harlow, m. Sybel **TOLLES**, b. of Torrington, July 6, 1823, by Rev. Epaphras Goodman	55
Jane, m. Ephraim **LOOMIS**, Jr., b. of Torrington, Oct. 30, 1784	65
Jerusha, of Torrington, m. Pitts **GOODWIN**, of New Hartford, Dec. 25, 1822, by Rev. Epaphras Goodman	54
Juba, d. Stephen & Polly, b. Aug. 5, 1793	36
Lucy, d. Silas & Lucy, b. Feb. 26, 1780	35
Mason W., of Winsted, m. Martha W. **MUNSON**, of Wolcottville, Apr. 17, 1843, by Rev. Samuel Day, of Wolcottville	127
Polly, d. Stephen & Polly, b. Mar. 10, 1784	36
Reuben, s. Stephen & Polly, b. July 9, 1791	36
Roxcey, d. Stephen & Polly, b. Oct. 12, 1788	36
Sabra, m. Junia **NORTH**, b. of Torrington, Jan. 25, 1785	80
Silas, s. Silas & Lucy, b. May 31, 1782	35
Stephen, m. Polly **COLYER**, b. of Windsor, July [ ], 1778	36
Stephen, s. Stephen & Polly, b. Mar. 6, 1780	36
GATES, Maria, of Torrington, m. Chester **JOHNSON**, of Harwinton, Apr. 27, 1821, by Alexander Gillett	25
GAUNT, James, m. Emma **FORREST**, Feb. 3, 1837, by Rev. Stephen Hubbell	123
GAYLORD, Ann E., of Torrington, m. Peter A. **GIBBS**, of Harwinton, Apr. 22, 1835, by Rev. Epaphras Goodman	122
Betsey, of Torrington, m. John S. **PRESTON**, of Harwinton, Oct. 1, 1837, by Rev. Herman L. Vaill	123
Dorety, of Middletown, m. Ebenezer **MILLER**, Jr., of Torrington, Feb. 7, 1787	77
Elijah, of Torrington, m. Margaret **TAYLOR**, of Windsor, Nov. 11, 1749	42
Elijah, Capt., m. Margaret **HENMAN**, b. of Torrington, Feb. 18, 1790	42
Elijah Milo, s. Elijah & Margaret, b. Dec. 5, 1795	42
Esther W., of Torrington, m. John H. **NORTH**, of Cornwall, May 3, 1826, by Rev. Epaphras Goodman	81
Fanny, m. Roderick **BYSSEL**, b. of Torrington, May 11, 1824, by Rev. Epaphras Goodman	56
Giles, s. Elijah & Margaret, b. Aug. 1, 1793	42
Giles A., m. Esther **AUSTIN**, b. of Torrington, Dec. 4, 1823, by Rev. Epaphras Goodman	56
Joseph, s. Nehemiah & Lucy, b. Feb. 15, 1751/2	41
Lucy, d. Nehemiah & Lucy, b. Apr. 14, 1750	41
Lucey, m. Zachariah **MATHER**, b. of Torrington, Apr. 20, 1769	77
Margaret, w. Capt. Elijah, d. Nov. 25, 1789	42
Margaret T., m. Thaddeus **GRISWOLD**, b. of Torrington, June 11, 1822, by Rev. Epaphras Goodman	26
Margaret Taylor, d. Elijah & Margaret, b. May 23, 1791	42
Nehemiah, s. Nehemiah & Lucy, b. Oct. 14, 1754	41
GIBBS, Eber N., m. Abigail W. **HUDSON**, b. of Torrington, Apr. 19, 1837, by Rev. Herman L. Vaill	123
Harriet E., m. David **SAMMIS**, b. of Goshen, Oct. 21, 1827, by Rev. William	

	Page
GIBBS, (cont.)	
R. Gould. Int. Pub.	84
Horace, m. Eliza **BASCOM**, b. of Torrington, Oct. 26, 1824, by Rev. Epaphras Goodman	57
Jabez, m. Almira **BALL**, Mar. 17, 1828, by Rev. William R. Gould	84
Peter A., of Harwinton, m. Ann E. **GAYLORD**, of Torrington, Apr. 22, 1835, by Rev. Epaphras Goodman	122
GILBERT, Amos, m. Sarah **HOLLIS**, b. of Wolcottville, Nov. 12, 1844, by Rev. Henry Zell, of Wolcottville	129
James, of Waterbury, m. Lucy M. **ROYS**, of Norfolk, Oct. 17, 1847, by Rev. Henry Zell, of Wolcottville, at his house	133
GILLETT, GILLET, Abigail, d. John & Abigail, b. May 6, 1771	43
Abigail, wid. John, d. May 13, 1835, ae 84	43
Ann, d. Jabez & Ann, b. Dec. 11, 1762	42
Ann, w. Capt. Jabez, d. May 13, 1795	42
Aurelia, d. Jabez & Ann, b. Apr. 24, 1776	42
Benjamin Catlin, s. John & Abigail, b. Aug. 20, 1782; d. July 27, 1837, in Wilmington, N.C.	43
Benjamin Catlin, d. July 27, 1837, in Wilmington, N.C.	43
Caroline, of Windsor, m. Abel S. **LEACH**, of Torrington, June 5, 1822, by Rev. Isaac Merriam	26
Caroline M., of Torringford, m. Charles N. **HENDERSON**, of New Hartford, July 31, 1839, by Rev. Herman L. Vaill	124
Chloe, d. Jabez & Ann, b. Jan. 23, 1765	42
Eliza, of Torrington, m. Jesse **PRITCHARD**, of Lee, Mass., Jan. 20, 1830, by Rev. William R. Gould	86
Elizabeth, d. Jabez & Ann, b. Aug. 10, 1773	42
Esther, d. Jabez & Ann, b. Mar. 1, 1771	42
Horrace, s. Jabez & Ann, b. Oct. 6, 1779	42
Jabez, m. Ann **LOOMIS**, b. of Windsor, June 15, 1762	42
Jabez, of Torrington, m. Laurana **ROBERTS**, of Windsor, Jan. 11, 1798	42
John, m. Abigail **COLLINS**, b. of Torrington, Aug. 30, 1770	43
John, s. John & Abigail, b. Mar. 30, 1776	43
John, Jr., m. Mary **WOODWARD**, Feb. 2, 1824	43
John, Jr., m. Mary **WOODWARD**, b. of Torrington, Feb. 2, 1824, by Rev. Epaphras Goodman	56
John, d. Jan. 15, 1826, ae 87 y.	43
John Catlin, s. John & Mary, b. June 5, 1827	43
Mary A., of Torrington, m. Henry S. Champion, of Winsted, Oct. 17, 1842, by John A. McKinstry	127
Roxana, d. Jabez & Ann, b. [ ]	42
Rufus W., m. Charlotte M. **SMITH**, b. of Torrington, May 26, 1847, by Rev. William H. Moore	131
Rufus Woodward, s. John & Mary, b. Apr. 22, 1825	43
Ruth, m. Samuel **AUSTIN**, b. of Torrington, Nov. 19, 1765	3
Sarah Basset, m. Shubael **COOK**, b. of Torrington, Sept. 17, 1773	14
GILMAN, Elias E., m. Charlotte S. **JUDSON**, July 1, 1838, by Rev. Stephen Hubbell, of Wolcottville	124
GOODSELL, Aurelia, d. Penfield & Nancy, b. Mar. 21, 1792	39
Penfield, Dr., m. Nancy **BEACH**, b. of Torrington, Oct. 26, 1791	39
Penfield, s. Penfield & Nancy, b. Sept. 16, 1796	39
GOODWIN, Ebenezer, of New Hartford, m. Hannah **POND**, of Torrington, July 3, 1832, by Rev. Epaphras Goodman	115

	Page
GOODWIN, (cont.)	
George, m. Sally **WEEKS**, Apr. 10, 1832, by Rev. William R. Gould	115
Olive, m. Hiram **WINCHEL**, b. of Torrington, Oct. 5, 1825, by Rev. Epaphras Goodman	81
Pitts, of New Hartford, m. Jerusha **FYLER**, of Torrington, Dec. 25, 1822, by Rev. Epaphras Goodman	54
GORE, Lorenzo E., m. Clarinda **WILCOX**, of Litchfield, Oct. 12, 1846, by Rev. Henry Zell, of Wolcottville	132
GOULD, Joseph, of Winchester, m. Rhoda P. **COE**, of Wolcottville, Oct. 2, 1842, by Rev. Samuel Day, of Wolcottville	127
GRANGER, Betsey, m. Thomas **SPARKS**, Feb. 14, 1821, by Rev. Ebenezer Washburn	24
GRANT, Albert, s. Matthew & Roseannah, b. June 20, 1802; d. Feb. 18, 1804	45
Albert, s. Matthew & Roseannah, b. June 20, 1804	45
Augustus, d. Matthew & Phebe, b. Aug. 1, 1773	40
Augustus, s. Matthew & Phebe, d. Nov. 15, 1777	40
Augustus, s. Ira & Susanna, b. Jan. 29, 1797	58
Daniel, s. William & Sarah, b. Dec. 28, 1743	40
Daniel A., of Torrington, m. Elmina **EGGLESTON**, of Litchfield, Nov. 6, 1845, by Rev. Miles N. Olmstead	130
Electa Spafford, w. Asahel, d. Aug. 4, 1831	71
Electa Spafford, see also Electa Spafford **LOOMIS**	71
Flora, d. Ira & Susanna, b. Aug. 28, 1803	58
Flora M., of Torrington, m. Luther **BRONSON**, of Winchester, Nov. 3, 1842, by Thomas Benedict	126
Gerry, s. Matthew & Roseannah, b. May 23, 1798	45
Gerry, m. Louisa **WHITING**, b. of Torrington, Nov. 2, 1825, by Rev. Alexander Gillett	81
Harriet Laphely, d. William & Candace (**HILLS**), b. July 8, 1795	14
Horatio, s. Matthew & Roseannah, b. Apr. 1, 1800	45
Huldah, of Litchfield, m. Miles **BEACH**, of Torrington, Aug. 11, 1793	61-2
Ira, s. William & Lois, b. June 30, 1765	41
Ira, s. William & Lois, d. Oct. 16, 1772	41
Ira, s. William & Lois, b. Oct. 2, 1773	41
Ira, m. Susanna **MUNSELL**, Mar. 10, 1796	58
John, of Torrington, m. Cynthia **PAINE**, of Southhold, L.I., June 4, 1823, by Rev. Epaphras Goodman	55
Lewis Cicero, s. William & Candace, b. May 26, 1797	14
Lois, w. William, d. Oct. 25, 1777	41
Lovisa Foster, d. William & Candace, b. July 6, 1793	14
Lydia Ann, d. John, b. Aug. 24, 1824	60
Lydia Anne, of Wolcottville, m. Francis M. **HALE**, Jan. 1, 1846, in Wolcottville, by Rev. Henry Zell, of Wolcottville	132
Marana, d. William & Sarah, b. June 1, 1746	40
Marana, m. Joseph **BLAKE**, b. of Torrington, Aug. 27, 1767	9
Matthew, of Torrington, m. Phebe **FORSTER**, of Wallingford, Nov. 18, 1762	40
Matthew, s. Matthew & Phebe, b. Sept. 4, 1763	40
Matthew, Capt., d. Jan. 14, 1794	40
Matthew, m. Roseannah **LEE**, Sept. 29, 1795	45
Phebe, d. Matthew & Phebe, b. Nov. 22, 1765	40
Phebe, d. Daniel, b. Apr. 17, 1769	38
Phebe, w. Lieut. Matthew, d. Nov. 7, 1777	40
Phebe, m. Seth **HOMES**, b. of Torrington, Mar. 31, 1785	44

	Page
GRANT, (cont.)	
Philee, m. Raphael **MARSHALL**, b. of Torrington, Nov. 1, 1787	75
Sarah, m. Abner **LOOMIS**, b. of Torrington, July 28, 1757	65
Sarah, w. William, d. Mar. 19, 1791	40
Susan R., m. George R. **CLARK**, Apr. 10, 1849, by Rev. Thomas Benedict	135
Thomas, s. Matthew & Roseannah, b. Feb. 18, 1806	45
William, s. William & Sarah, b. Nov. 23, 1741	40
William, of Torrington, m. Lois **FORSTER**, of Wallingford, Nov. 18, 1762	41
William, s. William & Lois, b. Feb. 26, 1771	41
William, d. Nov. 10, 1786	40
William, Jr., of Torrington, m. Candace **HILLS**, of Winchester, Jan. 8, 1793	14
Zerviah, m. Amos **WILLSON**, b. of Torrington, Oct. 26, 1752	104
GREY, Joseph, of Haddam, m. Emeline H. **MORGAN**, of Torrington, Nov. 15, 1831, by Rev. William R. Gould	115
GRISWOLD, Albro, of Weathersfield, m. Florilla **COOK**, of Harwinton, Jan. 4, 1835, by Rev. H. P. Armes	121
Frederick, of Litchfield, m. Elizabeth **LOOMIS**, of Torrington, Sept. 30, 1845, by Thomas Benedict	130
Harriet S., of Torringford, m. Addison N. **WILLSON**, of Harwinton, June 30, 1841, by Samuel Day	126
Hiram, of Goshen, m. Harriet **WHITING**, of Torrington, Nov. 29, 1820, by Joseph Harvey	25
Mary, b. July 17, 1757, at Torrington; m. Samuel **WOODWARD**, Feb. 10, 1782	9
Midian, of Litchfield, m. Lury **NORTH**, of Torrington, Mar. 19, 1822, by Frederick Marsh	26
Norman, m. Mrs. Laura **BIRGE**, b. of Torrington, Nov. 6, 1821, by Rev. Epaphras Goodman	26
Sabra, of Winchester, m. Amos **WILLSON**, Jr., of Torrington, Mar. 25, 1801	15
Thaddeus, m. Margaret T. **GAYLORD**, b. of Torrington, June 11, 1822, by Rev. Epaphras Goodman	26
GROSS, Ann P., of Torringford, m. Henry R. **SEYMOUR**, of Colebrook, Oct. 12, 1840, by Samuel Day	125
Oliver E., m. Amanda Rood **HAZEN**, b. of Torrington, Nov. 12, 1827, by Rev. Epaphras Goodman	84
Sarah O., m. George S. **ADDIS**, b. of Torrington, Aug. 22, 1841, by Rev. B. Emerson	126
GUIGALL, Richard, of Norfolk, m. Lucia W. **WHITING**, of Torrington, Apr. 3, 1848, by Rev. John A. McKinstry	133
GULLEY, Marshall J., m. Amanda W. **LEACH**, Jan. 8, 1845, by Thomas Benedict	128
GULLIVER, John P., m. Frances W. **CURTISS**, Sept. 8, 1845, at the house of Dea. Elizur Curtiss, by Lavalette Perrin	129
HALE, [see also **HALL**], Francis M., m. Lydia Anne **GRANT**, of Wolcottville, Jan. 1, 1846, in Wolcottville, by Rev. Henry Zell, of Wolcottville	132
HALL, [see also **HALE & HULL**], Joseph Catlin, m. Almira Ann **WILLEY**, Oct. 24, 1830, at Wolcottville, by Rev. Isaac Jones, of Litchfield	87
Reuben, of Wallingford, m. Keziah **BEACH**, of Torrington, May 19, 1829, by Rev. William R. Gould	85
HAMLIN, Sarah, m. Elijah **BLAKE**, b. of Middletown, Sept. 27, 1779, at Middletown	43
HARMON, Nathan W., m. Harriet **MERREL**, b. of Torrington, Sept. 12, 1824, by Rev. George E. Pierce	57

TORRINGTON VITAL RECORDS 27

	Page
HARRIS, Hannah, m. Thomas **MATTHEWS**, b. of Torrington, Apr. 16, 1775	78
Sarah, m. John **STANCLIFT**, b. of Torrington, Oct. 21, 1778	111
Smith, of Winchester, m. Huldah **LOOMIS**, of Torrington, May 13, 1838, by Thomas Benedict	123
HARRISON, Julia, of Milton, m. George H. **CARTER**, of Sharon, Dec. 26, 1843, by Rev. Samuel Day, of Wolcottville	128
William, m. Almyra **FREEMAN**, b. of Torrington, Oct. 3, 1847, by Rev. S. T. Seelye	131
HART, Jeremiah, s. Stephen & Eunice, b. May 28, 1791	8
Martin, s. Stephen & Eunice, b. Oct. 30, 1792	8
Maryan, m. Norris **BECKLEY**, Dec. 27, 1841, by Thomas Benedict	126
Matthew R., of Goshen, m. Adaline **CHASE**, of Winchester, Oct. 23, 1845, by Rev. Miles N. Olmstead	130
Seymour, s. Stephen & Eunice, b. Aug. 5, 1794	8
Stephen, m. Eunice **SEYMOUR**, Sept. 9, 1790	8
Stephen & Eunice, had twin sons b. June 28, 1796; d. same day	8
HARWINTON, Archobel, of Goshen, m. Huldah **WILCOX**, late of Torrington, now of Goshen, Jan. 28, 1792	43
HATCH, Elias, of Winchester, m. Cornelia **FOOT**, of Torrington, Oct. 8, 1833, by Rev. H. P. Armes	118
HAYDEN, HEYDON, Candace, m. John **BOWNELLY**, b. of Torrington, Jan. 12, 1823, by Cirus Yale	54
Charlotte Augusta, m. Dr. J. W. **PHELPS**, Dec. 23, 1846, by W. H. Moore	130
Chauncey, of Randolph, Vt., m. Aurelia **DIBBLE**, of Torrington, Oct. 28, 1834, by Rev. H. P. Armes	121
Irena, m. Jonathan **WILLEY**, Oct. 2, 1828, by Rev. William R. Gould	85
Sidney, of Barkhamsted, m. Florella E. **MILLER**, of Torrington, Mar. 23, 1836, by Rev. Epaphras Goodman	123
HAYES, Gaylord, of Hartland, m. Mary **HUMPHREY**, of Torrington, Oct. 12, 1820, by Samuel J. Mills	24
HAZEN, Amanda Rood, m. Oliver E. **GROSS**, b. of Torrington, Nov. 12, 1827, by Rev. Epaphras Goodman	84
HEDGE, Franklin, of Torrington, m. Mercy **CHAMBERLAIN**, of Middletown, Sept. 3, 1826, by Rev. E. W. Goodman	81
HENDERSON, Charles N., of New Hartford, m. Caroline M. **GILLETT**, of Torringford, July 31, 1839, by Rev. Herman L. Vaill	124
HENISEE, Timothy, of Farmington, m. Milly **JOHNSON**, of Litchfield, Sept. 21, 1829, by Rev. Epaphras Goodman	85
HENMAN, Margaret, m. Elijah **GAYLORD**, b. of Torrington, Feb. 18, 1790	42
HICKCOX, Jane E., of Stafford, N.Y., m. Edwin **HODGES**, of Torrington, Jan. 13, 1836, by Milton Huxley	122
[HIGBEE], HIGGBEE, Rachel, m. Richard **LOOMIS**, b. of Torrington, May 30, 1780	71
HIGLEY, Isaac, of Torrington, m. Sarah **LOOMIS**, of Harwinton, Feb. 24, 1757	48
Sarah, w. Isaac, d. July 19, 1753	48
Susanna, d. Isaac & Sarah, b. Dec. 8, 1741	48
Susannah, m. Timothy **OSBORN**, b. of Torrington, Feb. 28, 1764	87
HILL, HILLS, Albert, of Bristol, m. Angeline E. **TIFFANY**, of Torrington, Nov. 28, 1833, by Rev. Epaphras Goodman	119
Amanda, d. Benony, Jr. & Elizabeth, b. June 18, 1780	50
Candace, of Winchester, m. William **GRANT**, Jr., of Torrington, Jan. 8, 1793	14
Edward, of Charlton, Mass., m. Eliza **COMBS**, of Torrington, Nov. 17, 1839, by Rev. W. A. Stickney	125

BARBOUR COLLECTION

	Page
HILL, HILLS, (cont.)	
Hannah, m. Aaron **LOOMIS**, June 6, 1745	64
Huldah, w. Levi, d. Apr. 15, 1820	71
Lucy, of Torrington, m. Abel S. **WETMORE**, of Winchester, Nov. 24, 1829, by Rev. William R. Gould	85
Mary, of Goshen, m. Epaphras **LOOMIS**, of Torrington, Sept. 9, 1755	66
Mary, m. Epaphras **LOOMIS**, Sept. 9, 1755	68
Mary, m. Elijah **BARBER**, of Torrington, July 10, 1766	9
Mary, m. Sylvester **HURLBUT**, Nov. 14, 1831, by Rev. William R. Gould	114
Zerviah, of Simsbury, m. Ephraim **LOOMIS**, Jr., of Torrington, July 20, 1789	65
HINSDALE, Gilman, m. Amanda **WARD**, Mar. 27, 1827	31
Gilman, m. Amanda **WARD**, b. of Torrington, Mar. 27, 1827, by Rev. W. R. Gould. Int. Pub.	83
Mary Loiza, d. Gilman & Amanda, b. Jan. 30, 1830	31
HODGES, Alpha, s. Elkanah & Rebeckah, b. May 4, 1792	48
Edwin, s. Erastus & Laura, b. June 26, 1810	46-7
Edwin, of Torrington, m. Jane E. **HICKCOX**, of Stafford, N.Y., Jan. 13, 1836, by Milton Huxley	122
Elkanah, m. Rockselany **NORTH**, b. of Torrington, Jan. 14, 1777	48
Elkanah, m. Rebeckah **WHITING**, b. of Torrington, Mar 26, 1778	48
Elkanah, d. May 21, 1797	48
Elkanah Higby, s. Erastus & Laura, b. Jan. 11, 1812	46-7
Erastus, s. Elkanah & Rebeckah, b. Mar. 8, 1781	48
Erastus, m. Laura **LOOMIS**, b. of Torrington, Jan. 5, 1809	46-7
Harry*, s. Elkanah & Rebeckah, b. Oct. 3, 1794 *("Henry Elkanah **HODGES**" in Orcutt's Hist.)	48
Rockselany, w. Dr. Elkanah, d. Feb. 13, 1777	48
Rowelana*, d. Elkanah & Rebeckah, b. Apr. 27, 1784 *("Roxalany" in Orcutt's)	48
Sally, d. Elkanah & Rebeckah, b. Mar. 29, 1787	48
Sally E., m. Sheldon **BARBER**, b. of Torrington, Apr. 10, 1833, by Rev. Milton Huxley	117
Willard, s. Elkanah & Rebeckah, b. Dec. 16, 1778	48
William, s. Elkanah & Rebeckah, b. Aug. 24, 1789	48
HOLBROOK, Huldah, d. Sylvanus & Betsey, b. June 27, 1804	38
Uri, s. Sylvanus & Betsey, b. Mar. 11, 1806	38
HOLLIS, Elizabeth, of Wolcottville, m. Christopher **SENIOR**, of New Britain, Dec. 6, 1846, in Wolcottville, by Rev. Henry Zell, of Wolcottville	132
Sarah, m. Amos **GILBERT**, b. of Wolcottville, Nov. 12, 1844, by Rev. Henry Zell, of Wolcottville	129
HOLLISTER, Betty, of Glassonbury, m. Samuel **KELSEY**, of Torrington, Oct. 25, 1774	59
HOLMES, HOMES, David, s. Joseph & Lydia, b. Apr. 27, 1779	51
Delight, m. Elisha **HOSKINS**, Dec. 24, 1766	50
Jerusha, d. Joseph & Lydia, b. Apr. 25, 1783	51
Joseph, m. Lyda **CURTIS**, b. of Torrington, Sept. 9, 1778	51
Lavinia, m. Cyrus **NORTH**, b. of Torrington, Dec. 14, 1820, by Frederick Marsh	24
Marens, s. Seth & Phebe, b. May 5, 1786	44
Nancy, m. Frederick **TIBBALS**, Mar. 11, 1841, by Thomas Benedict	126
Rufus, s. Joseph & Lydia, b. Apr. 29, 1781	51
Seth, m. Phebe **GRANT**, b. of Torrington, Mar. 31, 1785	44

TORRINGTON VITAL RECORDS

	Page
HOPKINS, Lydia, of Canaan, m. John **BIRGE**, of Torrington, Mar. 23, 1779	8
HOSFORD, Ruth, of Litchfield, m. Ephraim **LOOMIS**, of Torrington, Oct. 31, 1756	65
HOSKINS, Benjamin, s. Elisha & Delight, b. Nov. 27, 1767	50
Calvin, s. Elisha & Delight, b. Sept. 24, 1778	50
Delight, d. Elisha & Delight, b. Jan. 8, 1782	50
Elisha, m. Delight **HOLMES**, Dec. 24, 1766	50
Elisha, s. Elisha & Delight, b. June 18, 1769	50
Elisha, s. Elisha & Delight, d. July 26, 1771	50
Elisha, s. Elisha & Delight, b. Jan. 16, 1773	50
Lodema, d. Elisha & Delight, b. May 17, 1771	50
Luther, s. Elisha & Delight, b. Jan. 5, 1777	50
Tamma, d. Elisha & Delight, b. Jan. 5, 1775	50
HOYT, Ann, of Torrington, m. Isaac W. **RIGGS**, of Middlebury, Nov. 24, 1833, by Rufus Babcock, of Colebrook	119
Harriet, m. Frederick **NORTH**, June 14, 1830, by Rufus Babcock	86
Ira, of Torrington, m. Helen **ROBERTS**, of Torrington, Nov. 4, 1842, by Rev. Brown Emerson	126
Ruth E., of Newfield, m. Horace L. **COOK**, of Wolcottville, Nov. 9, 1845, by Rev. J. B. Beach, of M.E.Ch.	130
William, of Waterbury, m. Lucy **LEACH**, of Torrington, Oct. 2, 1831, by Daniel Coe	114
HUBBARD, Cyrus, of Harwinton, m. Anramia **EGGLESTON**, of Torrington, Oct. 18, 1820, by Frederick Marsh	24
Cyrus, m. Harriet **TAYLOR**, of Torrington, July 8, 1849, by Rev. William H. Moore	134
Dorothy, of Glastonbury, m. Daniel **HUDSON**, of Torrington, Dec. 10, 1788	37
Edward R., of Winsted, m. Tryphena S. **PALMER**, of Litchfield, Sept. 19, 1847, at the house of Mrs. Palmer, by Rev. Henry Zell, of Wolcottville	133
Elijah, of Winchester, m. Jockebod **BARBER**, of Torrington, Oct. 26, 1791	43
Hiram W., of Wolcottville, m. Betsey **WHEELER**, of Litchfield, Mar. 30, 1845, by Rev. Samuel Day, of Wolcottville	129
Polly, m. William **BROWN**, Feb. 4, 1821, by Datus Ensign	25
Samuel C., m. Merilla **WELLS**, Apr. 6, 1846, by Thomas Benedict	130
HUDSON, Abigail W., m. Eber N. **GIBBS**, b. of Torrington, Apr. 19, 1837, by Rev. Herman L. Vaill	123
Adah, d. Daniel & Mary, b. Feb. 8, 1778	37
Anna S., of Torrington, m. Rufus **BURR**, of Winchester, May 10, 1827, by Rev. Epaphras Goodman	84
Anna Squires, d. Barzillia & [Content], b. Oct. 21, 1803	38
Barzillai, s. Daniel & Mary, b. Aug. 13, 1780	37
Barzillia, m. Content **PICKET**, Jan. 26, 1803	38
Claresy, d. Daniel & Mary, b. June 7, 1782; d. Dec. 5, 1782	37
Claresy, d. Daniel & Mary, b. Dec. 29, 1785	37
Daniel, of Torrington, m. Dorothy **HUBBARD**, of Glastonbury, Dec. 10, 1788	37
Daniel, s. Daniel C. & Mary, b. Mar. 9, 1798	37
Daniel, s. Daniel C. & Mary, d. Mar. 16, 1805	37
Daniel C., s. Daniel C. & Mary Hary, b. Jan. 15, 1809; d. [ ], at Freeborn, O	37
Daniel Coe, s. Daniel & Mary, b. Apr. 24, 1774	37
Daniel Coe, m. Mary **LOOMIS**, Feb. 16, 1797	37
Daniel Coe, m. Rhoda **FOWLER**, Jan. 24, 1805	37

BARBOUR COLLECTION

	Page
HUDSON, (cont.)	
Dorothy, w. Daniel, d. May 4, 1807	37
Duliete, of Torrington, m. John **BANCROFT**, of East Windsor, June 12, 1843, by Rev. B. Emerson	127
Erasmus Darwin, s. Daniel C. & Rhoda, b. Dec. 15, 1806; d. [ ], 1874, at New York (profession), physician	37
Eunice, d. Daniel & Mary, b. Feb. 5, 1776	37
Florella H., m. James H. **SEYMOUR**, b. of Torrington, Nov. 2, 1835, by Rev. Epaphras Goodman	123
Grace, d. Daniel & Mary, b. Apr. 17, 1772	37
Mary, w. Daniel, d. Dec. 8, 1787	37
Mary, w. Daniel C., d. July 22, 1804	37
Mary C., m. Thomas A. **MILLER**, b. of Torrington, Apr. 1, 1829, by Rev. Epaphras Goodman	85
Mary Coe, d. Barzillia & Content, b. Apr. 12, 1806	38
Molly, d. Daniel & Mary, b. May 1, 1770	37
Rhodah, m. David **BIRGE**, b. of Torrington, Dec. 16, 1784	7
Sarah, d. Daniel & Mary, b. Nov. 18, 1783; d. Jan. 17, 1784	37
HULL, [see also **HALL**], Andrew E., of Burlington, m. Sarah J. **BURR**, of Torrington, May 9, 1849, by Rev. S. T. Seelye	135
HUMPHREY, Daniel G., Jr., m. Eliza **BURR**, b. of Torrington, Oct. 31, 1820, by Samuel J. Mills	25
Mary, of Torrington, m. Gaylord **HAYES**, of Hartland, Oct. 12, 1820, by Samuel J. Mills	24
Susan M., of Guilford, N.Y., m. Harvey L. **ROOD**, of Torrington, Oct. 15, 1848, by Rev. William H. Moore	134
HUMPHREYVILLE, Abram M., of Litchfield, m. Harriet **ANDREWS**, of Harwinton, Oct. 26, 1834, by Rev. David Miller	121
HUNGERFORD, Charlotte, d. John & Charlotte, b. Apr. 3, 1825	48
Charlotte A., of Torrington, m. Dr. R. S. **OLMSTEAD**, of Brooklyn, N.Y., Nov. 8, 1849, by Rev. S. T. Seelye	135
Elizabeth, w. John, Jr., d. June 12, 1819	48
Elizabeth W., of Wolcottville, m. Roderick A. **WHITE**, of Simsbury, Nov. 6, 1844, by Rev. Samuel Day	129
Elizabeth Webster, d. John & Elizabeth, b. Apr. 19, 1817	48
John, Jr., m. Elizabeth **WEBSTER**, Mar. 3, 1814	48
John, Jr., m. Charlotte **AUSTIN**, b. of Torrington, June 5, 1820, by Samuel J. Mills	24
John, Jr., m. Charlotte **AUSTIN**, June 5, 1820	48
John Thompson, s. John & Elizabeth, b. June 4, 1815	48
Nathaniel Austin, s. John & Charlotte, b. Oct. 20, 1823	48
Walter Mills, s. John & Charlotte, b. Feb. 6, 1822	48
HUNT, Salmon, of Canaan, m. Clarissa **BRADLEY**, of Torrington, Jan. 8, 1823, by Rev. Rodney Rossiter, of Plymouth	54
HUNTINGTON, Rhoda, m. Riley **DUNBAR**, b. of Torrington, Jan. 29, 1835, by Rev. H. P. Armes	121
HURLBUT, Clarissa, of Winchester, m. Theodore **ROBBINS**, of Norfolk, Feb. 9, 1845, in Newfield, by Rev. J. B. Beach, of the M.E.Ch.	128
Eliza A., m. Lewis S. **SMITH**, July 15, 1845, by Thomas Benedict	129
Eliza T., of Winchester, m. Lewis G. **BURGESS**, of New Haven, July 12, 1848, by Rev. James H. Dill, of Winchester	134
James H., m. Elizabeth **BROWN**, Sept. 9, 1832, by Rev. David L. Parmelee	116
Levi, m. Sarah **COOK**, July 28, 1777	49

	Page
HURLBUT, (cont.)	
Levi, d. June 5, 1798	49
Naomy, d. Levi & Sarah, b. Feb. 12, 1778	49
Phebee, m. George **MILLER**, b. of Torrington, [ ]	75
Robert, s. Levi & Sarah, b. June 18, 1784	49
Roxelana, d. Levi & Sarah, b. Apr. 9, 1795	49
Sally, of Torrington, m. James B. **WHITE**, of Winchester, Sept. 20, 1831, by Daniel Coe	87
Sarah, d. Levi & Sarah, b. Apr. 4, 1780	49
Sylvester, m. Mary **HILLS**, Nov. 14, 1831, by Rev. William R. Gould	114
INGRAHAM, Elkanah, of Norfolk, m. Highla **TURRELL**, of Torrington, Sept. 5, [1820], by Samuel J. Mills	24
Elkanah, Jr., of Colchester, m. Loisa **TURRELL**, of Torrington, Jan. 1, 1825, by Rev. Epaphras Goodman	57
IVES, Abner, of Wallingford, m. Anna **FIRGUSON**, of Haddam, May 11, 1768	53
Abner, s. Abner & Anna, b. Sept. 29, 1772	53
Amasa, s. Abner & Anna, b. Oct. 18, 1776	53
Anna, d. Jotham & Anna, b. Sept. 26, 1771	53
Anna, d. Abner & Anna, b. July 11, 1774	53
Catharine, d. Abner & Anna, b. Aug. 11, 1778	53
Charlotte, d. Abner & Anna, b. Feb. 25, 1781	53
Dimedice*, d. Abner & Anna, b. Aug. 6, 1787 *("Diamedia" in Orcutt's)	53
Eunice, d. Abner & Anna, b. Mar. 19, 1769	53
Jesse, s. Abner & Anna, b. Oct. 30, 1770	53
Joel, s. Jotham & Anna, b. May 13, 1770	53
Jotham, m. Anna **FORSTER**, b. of Wallingford, May 10, 1769	53
Nanncy, d. Abner & Anna, b. July 8, 1785	53
Shebourne, s. Abner & Anna, b. Feb. 2, 1783	53
Trumbull, s. Abner & Anna, b. Oct. 24, 1789	53
JACKINS, Abigail, of Wolcottville, m. Chauncey B. **MIX**, Oct. 2, 1843, by Rev. Samuel Day, of Wolcottville	127
JOHNSON, Abner Adolphus, s. Jacob, b. Jan. 11, 1788	54
Adolphus, s. Jacob, b. Apr. 25, 1784	54
Adolphus, s. Jacob, d. Dec. 16, 1787	54
Caleb, s. Jacob, b. May 1, 1774	54
Caleb, m. Mary **BEACH**, b. of Torrington, Dec. 20, 1798	29
Caleb, s. Caleb & Mary, b. Apr. 10, 1804, at Johnstown, Cty. of Montgomery, N.Y.	29
Charity, d. Jacob, b. Dec. 25, 1779	54
Chester, of Harwinton, m. Maria **GATES**, of Torrington, Apr. 27, 1821, by Alexander Gillett	25
Clarissa, m. James **WALLIN**, Sept. 20, 1832, by Rev. Epaphras Goodman	116
Enoch, m. Adaline **PALMER**, Jan. 7, 1847, by Rev. S. T. Seelye	131
Frederick, s. Caleb & Mary, b. Dec. 15, 1799	29
Hezekiah, of Harwinton, m. Flora **MOTT**, of Wolcottville, [July 4, 1841(?)], by Samuel Day	126
Hiram, of Canaan, m. Elizabeth **APLEY**, of Torrington, Oct. 10, 1833, by Rev. Charles Sherman	119
Jacob, s. Jacob, b. Feb. 8, 1782	54
James Willard, s. Caleb & Mary, b. Dec. 27, 1801, at Johnstown, Cty. of Montgomery, N.Y.	29
Jerusha, d. Jacob, b. Nov. 24, 1789	54
John Beach, s. Caleb & Mary, b. Sept. 26, 1806	29

JOHNSON, (cont.)

	Page
Laura, m. John **SNYDER**, Apr. 13, 1835, by Rev. David Miller	122
Louisa, of Torrington, m. Orson **BROOKS**, of Waterbury, Nov. 22, [1843?], by John A. McKinstry	127
Mealley, of Torrington, m. Daniel **POTTER**, of Farmington, Jan. 24, 1792	87
Milly, of Litchfield, m. Timothy **HENISEE**, of Farmington, Sept. 21, 1829, by Rev. Epaphras Goodman	85
Rial, of Harwinton, m. Flora **WILLEY**, of Torrington, Oct. 25, 1821, by Alexander Gillett	26
Stephen, s. Jacob, b. May 9, 1778	54
Susannah, d. Jacob, b. Apr. 23, 1786	54
Thankful, d. Jacob, b. Oct. 16, 1776	54

JONES, James, m. Nancy **FREEMAN**, b. of Torrington, May 21, 1821, by Rev. David Miller — 25

James, m. Emeline **FREEMAN**, of Torringford, Dec. 9, 1840, by W. B. Ransom — 125

JUDD, Henry, of Litchfield, m. Hannah **BEACH**, of Torrington, Nov. 10, 1830, by William R. Gould — 86

Ralph, m. Urania **CADWELL**, b. of Torrington, May 10, 1825, by George E. Pierce — 83

Sarah, of Farmington, m. Nathan **KELSEY**, of Torrington, Dec. 10, 1760 — 58

William Henry, of Norfolk, m. Marilla W. **CONE**, of Torrington, Aug. 14, 1845, by Rev. Niles N. Olmstead — 129

JUDSON, Charlotte S., m. Elias E. **GILMAN**, July 1, 1838, by Rev. Stephen Hubbell, of Wolcottville — 124

KELSEY, Amos, s. Nathan & Sarah, b. Mar. 8, 1767 — 58

Esaies, s. Jonathan & Ruth, d. Sept. 21, 1759 — 58

Jonathan, s. Jonathan, of Torrington, m. Rachel **LEWIS**, of Windsor, Nov. 12, 1767 — 58

Jonathan, s. Jonathan, d. Sept. 15, 1776, ae 37 y. — 58

Jonathan, Dea., d. Apr. 13, 1792, ae 89 y. 6 m. — 58

Lois, d. Nathan & Sarah, b. Sept. 8, 1763 — 58

Mary, w. Samuel, d. May 10, 1770 — 59

Nathan, of Torrington, m. Sarah **JUDD**, of Farmington, Dec. 10, 1760 — 58

Nathan, s. Nathan & Sarah, b. Feb. 19, 1762 — 58

Noah, s. Nathan & Sarah, b. June 13, 1765 — 58

Rozel, s. Nathan & Sarah, b. June 7, 1768 — 58

Samuel, of Torrington, m. Betty **HOLLISTER**, of Glassonbury, Oct. 25, 1774 — 59

[**KENDALL**], **KEENDALL**, Emeline, of Suffield, m. Merriel Burwell **RIGGS**, of Torrington, Apr. 9, 1848, by Rev. George A. Hubbell — 133

KENNA, Bede, of Wolcott, m. Abial **CANFIELD**, of Torrington, Mar. 31, 1831, by Rev. Epaphras Goodmn — 87

KIES, Dorcas, of Middletown, m. Seth **COE**, of Torrington, Nov. 15, 1829, by Rev. David Miller — 86

KIMBERLEY, David R., m. Lydia **BROOKS**, Oct. 7, 1824, by Rev. Rodney Rossiter, of Plymouth — 57

Helen A., of Wolcottville, m. Cornelius A. **WINSHIP**, of Litchfield, Sept. 19, 1847, by Rev. S. T. Seelye — 131

Jane E., m. Hiram **PALMER**, b. of Torrington, Mar. 11, 1849, by Rev. S. T. Seelye — 135

KLINE, A. P., of Wilmington, N.C., m. Susanna **CHURCH**, of Wolcottville, Aug. 20, 1843, by Rev. B. Emerson — 127

TORRINGTON VITAL RECORDS 33

	Page
KNAPP, Amelia, of Canaan, m. Joshua B. **TROWBRIDGE**, of Danbury, May 20, 1839, by Thomas Benedict	124
LATHROP, Evaline B., of Sheffield, m. George W. **CHURCH**, of Torrington, Nov. 19, 1848, by Rev. S. T. Seelye	134
LEACH, Abel S., of Torrington, m. Caroline **GILLETT**, of Windsor, June 5, 1822, by Rev. Isaac Merriam	26
Abel Strong, s. Pomeroy & Sarah, b. May 22, 1800	70
Aleymena, d. Pomeroy & Sarah, b. Sept. 16, 1798	70
Almira, d. Pomeroy & Sarah, b. May 13, 1804	70
Almira, m. Ethiel **EMMONS**, Oct. 14, 1827, by Rev. Isaac Dwinel	84
Almeda S., of Torrington, m. Lucius **EMMONS**, of Litchfield, Sept. 23, 1849, by Rev. John A. McKinstry	135
Amanda W., m. Marshall J. **GULLEY**, Jan. 8, 1845, by Thomas Benedict	128
Benoni, s. Caleb & Experience, b. Apr. 12, 1770	70
Betsey, d. Richard & Mary, b. Mar. 3, 1789	70
Candace, m. Charles **PIERPOINT**, b. of Torrington, Sept. 29, 1824, by Rev. Epaphras Goodman	57
Destemony, d. Ebenezer & Lettis, b. Dec. 20, 1788	70
Ebenezer, m. Lettes **FERGUSON**, b. of Torrington, [ ]	70
Eunice, d. Nathaniell & Eunice, b. Nov. 29, 1780	73
Experience, w. Caleb, d. Apr. 21, 1770	70
Experience, of Torrington, m. Daniel **RICHARDS**, of Litchfield, Sept. 20, 1823, by Rev. Epaphras Goodman	55
George, of Torrington, m. Mary J. **MORSE**, of Litchfield, Jan. 22, 1843, by John A. McKinstry	126
Hannah, d. Nathaniell & Eunice, b. Aug. 5, 1785	73
Jacob, s. Richard & Mary, b. Dec. 8, 1777	70
Joshua, m. Anna **STODDARD**, Dec. 13, 1826, by Rev. William R. Gould	81
Lorenda, d. Ebenezer & Lettis, b. July 6, 1785	70
Lucinda C., of Torrington, m. Elmore D. **SQUIRES**, of Utica, N.Y., Dec. 20, 1842, by John A. McKinstry	126
Lucius Fowler, of Torrington, m. Adaline M. **BEARDSLEY**, of Wolcottville, Sept. 13, 1842, by Rev. Samuel Day, of Wolcottville	127
Lucy, of Torrington, m. William **HOYT**, of Waterbury, Oct. 2, 1831, by Daniel Coe	114
Lyman, s. Richard & Mary, b. Dec. 14, 1786	70
Mary, w. Richard, Jr., d. Apr. 19, 1791	70
Mary, m. Lewis **MURRAY**, May 10, 1826, by Rev. Epaphras Goodman	81
Miles, s. Richard & Mary, b. Apr. 7, 1791	70
Nathaniell, m. Eunice **MARSHALL**, b. of Torrington, Nov. 19, 1779	73
Nathaniell, s. Nathaniell & Eunice, b. Feb. 12, 1788	73
Olive, d. Nathaniell & Eunice, b. Nov. 10, 1782	73
Orphelia, d. Pomeroy & Sarah, b. May 12, 1806	70
Orphelia, m. Elisha **LOOMIS**, b. of Torrington, Apr. 3, 1833, by Rev. Milton Huxley	117
Percy, d. Richard & Mary, b. Sept. 3, 1782	70
Polly, d. Richard & Mary, b. May 28, 1780	70
Pomeroy, s. Richard & Mary, b. Dec. 10, 1775	70
Pomeroy, m. Sarah **BEACH**, b. of Torrington, Sept. 24, 1797	70
Rhoda, m. Ephraim W. **WOLCOTT**, b. of Torrington, May 10, 1824, by Rev. Epaphras Goodman	56
Richard, Jr., m. Mary **STRONG**, b. of Torrington, Mar. 23, 1775	70
Richard, 3rd, s. Richard & Mary, b. May 10, 1784	70

	Page
LEACH, (cont.)	
Richard, Jr., of Torrington, m. Elizabeth **LYMAN**, of New Hartford, Jan. 12, 1792	70
Roxy M., m. Merrell **WHITE**, Sept. 23, 1834, by H. P. Armes	120
Sarah, of Torrington, m. Jeremiah H. **PHILLIPS**, of Ovid, N.Y., Nov. 11, 1828, by Rev. William R. Gould	85
Sarah, m. Julius **ROGERS**, Oct. 29, 1844, by Thomas Benedict	128
Sophia, m. Charles **WELTON**, b. of Torrington, Apr. 9, 1848, by Rev. George A. Hubbell	133
Washington, s. Ebenezer & Lettis, b. Nov. 1, 1783	70
William, m. Julia **FOOT**, b. of Torrington, Aug. 19, 1828, by Rev. Epaphras Goodman	85
LEAMING, Elizabeth, of Middletown, m. John **WETMORE**, of Torrington, May 19, 1757	107
Jean, of Middletown, m. Amasa **MARSHALL**, of Torrington, Feb. 27, 1759	75
LEAVENWORTH, Rebecca, m. Joseph **PHELPS**, Oct. 27, 1804	21
LEE, Elizabeth, m. Remembrance **NORTH**, Sept. 21, 1795	11
Roseannah, m. Matthew **GRANT**, Sept. 29, 1795	45
LEFFINGWELL, Levi, of Goshen, m. Maria **MILLER**, of Torrington (colored), Jan. 1, 1827, by Rev. Epaphras Goodman	83
Lura, m. Joseph **SHIRW**, Sept. 25, 1831, by Rev. William R. Gould	115
LeGUETT, Joseph Charles, of Winchester, m. Elizabeth **WILLSON**, of Torringford, May 1, 1842, by Rev. B. Emerson	126
LEWIS, Jemima, m. Noah **NORTH**, b. of Torrington, Mar. 25, 1756	83
Joseph B., of Winsted, m. Cordelia **CUMMINS**, of Goshen, Feb. 6, 1833, by Rev. H. P. Armes	117
Justin P., of Ohio, m. Polly **ELLSWORTH**, of Torrington, Aug. 7, 1831, by Rev. Epaphras Goodman	87
Mindwell, m. Ichabod **LOMIS**, s. Ichabod, b, of Torrington, Jan. 29, 1766	70
Rachel, of Windsor, m. Jonathan **KELSEY**, s. Jonathan, of Torrington, Nov. 12, 1767	58
LONG, Jane Elizabeth, m. William **MANN**, b. of Torrington, Jan. 17, 1836, by Rev. H. P. Armes	122
Mary Anne, of Wolcottville, m. Lewis **BRISTOL**, of Brookfield, Oct. 12, 1846, in Wolcottville, by Rev. Henry Zell, of Wolcottville	132
LOOMIS, LOMIS, Aaron, m. Hannah **HILLS**, June 6, 1745	64
Aaron, s. Aaron & Hannah, b. Jan. 9, 1745/6	64
Aaron, s. Aaron & Hannah, d. Feb. 23, 1745/6	64
Aaron, s. Ephraim & Jean, b. May 25, 1766	65
Aaron, of Torrington, m. Annis **DRAKE**, of Windsor, Feb. 12, 1789	68
Aaron, s. Aaron & Annis, b. May 16, 1790	68
Abiah, m. Benjamin **BEACH**, b. of Torrington, Aug. 31, 1763	8
Abigail, d. Asa & Priscilla, b. July 16, 1779	69
Abigail, d. Lemuel & Abigail, b. Apr. 28, 1805	92
Abner, m. Sarah **GRANT**, b. of Torrington, July 28, 1757	65
Abner, s. Abner & Sarah, b. Nov. 22, 1757	65
Abner, s. Abner & Sarah, d. Sept. 11, 1776	65
Abner, m. Chloe **BARBER**, b. of Torrington, June 9, 1785	65
Abner, s. Richard & Rachel, b. June 1, 1799	71
Abner, d. Jan. 18, 1809	65
Abraham, s. Abraham, of Torrington, m. Mary **TAYLOR**, of Litchfield, Feb. 10, 1757	66
Abraham, s. Abraham & Mary, b. July 25, 1764	66

TORRINGTON VITAL RECORDS 35

	Page
LOOMIS, LOMIS, (cont.)	
Abraham, of Torrington, m. Mary **WETMORE**, of Winchester, Nov. 12, 1775	66
Abraham, s. Alexander & Submit, b. Oct. 9, 1795	61-2
Alanson, of Winchester, m. Sally **RICHARDS**, of Torrington, Mar. 20, 1827, by Rev. Epaphras Goodman	83
Alexander, s. Abraham & Mary, b. June 11, 1770	66
Alexander, m. Submit **SPENCER**, b. of Torrington, June 3, 1792, by [ ]	61-2
Allin, s. Timothy & Anna, b. Sept. 2, 1781	69
Almeda, d. Lemuel & Abigail, b. Aug. 1, 1797	92
Alvin, s. Aaron & Annis, b. Dec. 22, 1800	68
Amey, d. Ephraim & Ruth, b. Apr. 25, 1764	65
Amaret, d. Richard & Rachel, b. Dec. 15, 1802	71
Amaret, d. Richard & Rachel, d. Aug. 4, 1809	71
Ann, d. Joel & Elizabeth, b. Sept. 17, 1756	68
Ann, m. Jabez **GILLETT**, b. of Windsor, June 15, 1762	42
Anna, d. Timothy & Anna, b. Nov. 2, 1774	69
Annis, d. Aaron & Annis, b. June 23, 1797	68
Ansel, s. Joel & Prudence, b. July 3, 1795	79
Asa, s. Epaphras & Mary, b. July 7, 1767	68
Asa, m. Priscilla **AUSTIN**, June 11, 1778	69
Asahel, s. Ephraim & Zeruiah, b. Apr. 8, 1790	65
Belinda, see under Lynda	
Benoni, s. Abraham & Mary, b. Feb. 27, 1758	66
Benony, m. Jemima **BARBER**, b. of Torrington, Mar. 9, 1786	66
Betsey, d. Joel & Prudence, b. Apr. 15, 1793	79
Betsey, d. Elisha & Marcy, late of Winchester, now of Torrington, b. Mar. 26, 1806	103
Bildad, s. Ephraim & Jean, b. Feb. 12, 1773	65
Calven, s. Alexander & Submit, b. Apr. 19, 1793	61-2
Candace, d. Solomon & Elizabeth, b. Nov. 6, 1807	67
Caroline, d. Ephraim, Jr. & Zeruiah, b. Oct. 9, 1807	65
Caroline, of Torrington, m. Zebulon **MERRILL**, of New Hartford, Nov. 13, 1842, by Thomas Benedict	126
Chester, s. Michael & Huldah, b. July 1, 1778	72
Chester, s. Michael & Huldah, d. Mar. 26, 1779	72
Chester, s. Michael & Huldah, b. June 25, 1780	72
Chester, s. Richard & Rachel, b. Apr. 20, 1785	71
Chloe, d. Abner & Chloe, b. May 14, 1788	65
Chloe, d. Abner & Chloe, d. Sept. 9, 1816	65
Clarissa, d. Richard & Rachel, b. Oct. 29, 1780	71
Cyrus, s. Eli & Dorothy, b. June 30, 1775	67
Deborah, d. Aaron & Hannah, b. Jan. 4, 1751/2	64
Dorothy, m. Eli **LOOMIS**, b. of Torrington, Nov. 18, 1762	67
Dorothy, d. Eli & Dorothy, b. Nov. 10, 1766	67
Earl, s. Alexander & Submit, b. May 16, 1798	61-2
Edgar, of Windsor, m. Harriet J. **SMITH**, of Torrington, Aug. 26, 1835, by Rev. Epaphras Goodman	122
Electa Spafford, d. Richard & Rachel, b. Apr. 9, 1807	71
Eli, m. Dorothy **LOOMIS**, b. of Torrington, Nov. 18, 1762	67
Eli, s. Eli & Dorothy, b. Jan. 11, 1770	67
Elias, s. Ephraim & Jean, b. Nov. 13, 1776	65

LOOMIS, LOMIS, (cont.)

	Page
Elisha, s. Benoni & Jemimah, b. July 27, 1798	66
Elisha, of Torrington, m. Anna **WADSWORTH**, of Hartford, Nov. 14, 1804	21
Elisha, m.. Orphelia **LEACH**, b. of Torrington, Apr. 3, 1833, by Rev. Milton Huxley	117
Elizabeth, d. Joel & Elizabeth, b. Sept. 25, 1753	68
Elizabeth, d. Hiram & Abigail, b. July 22, 1822	52
Elizabeth, of Torrington, m. Frederick **GRISWOLD**, of Litchfield, Sept. 30, 1845, by Thomas Benedict	130
Emily, d. Grandison & Fanny, b. Jan. 29, 1830	31
Emory, of Torrington, m. Laura **LYMAN**, of Torrington, Sept. 12, 1841, by Rev. Brown Emerson	126
Epaphras, of Torrington, m. Mary **HILLS**, of Goshen, Sept. 9, 1755	66
Epaphras, m. Mary **HILLS**, Sept. 9, 1755	68
Epaphras, s. Epaphras & Mary, b. Mar. 31, 1756	66
Epaphras, Jr., s. Epaphras & Mary, b. Mar. 31, 1756	68
Epaphras, Jr., m. Phebe **BACON***, b. of Torrington, Dec. 1, 1777 *("Phebe" **BROWN**" in Orcutt's Hist.)	66
Ephraim, of Torrington, m. Ruth **HOSFORD**, of Litchfield, Oct. 31, 1756	65
Ephraim, s. Ephraim & Ruth, b. July 12, 1758	65
Ephraim, of Torrington, m. Jean **CAMBELL**, of Canaan, Oct. 18, 1764	65
Ephraim, Jr., m. Jane **FYLER**, b. of Torrington, Oct. 30, 1784	65
Ephraim, Jr., of Torrington, m. Zerviah **HILL**, of Simsbury, July 20, 1789	65
Ephraim, 3rd, s. Ephraim, Jr. & Zeruiah, b. July 16, 1796	65
Ephraim, d. Apr. 4, 1812	65
Esther, m. Rev. Nathaniel **ROBEARTS**, b. of Torrington, Nov. 7, 1748	90
Flora, d. Ira & Mary, b. Jan. 2, 1794	114
George Ward, s. Hiram & Abigail, b. Jan. 27, 1827	52
Grandison, s. Ephraim, Jr. & Zeruiah, b. Mar. 28, 1798	65
Guy, s. Timothy & Anny, b. Feb. 7, 1784	69
Hannah, d. Aaron & Hannah, b. Dec. 6, 1746	64
Hannah, m. Caleb **LYMAN**, b. of Torrington, Sept. 28, 1768	63
Harlow, s. Joel & Prudence, b. May 30, 1798	79
Harriet, d. Richard & Rachel, b. Oct. 7, 1794	71
Harris Allyn, s. Benony & Jemimah, b. Aug. 3, 1793	66
Hepzibah, m. Issacher **LOOMIS**, b. of Torrington, May 6, 1802	67
Hiram, s. Solomon & Elizabeth, b. Nov. 28, 1794	67
Hiram, m. Abigail **WARD**, b. of Torrington, Mar. 29, 1821, by Frederick Marsh	25
Hiram, m. Abigail **WARD**, Mar. 29, 1821	52
Horrace, s. Solomon & Elizabeth, b. Nov. 19, 1796	67
Horace, m. Permelia **LOOMIS**, b. of Torrington, Apr. 21, 1824, by Alexander Gillett	56
Horace, m. Roxalana **LOOMIS**, Jan. 29, 1828, by Rev. William R. Gould. Int. Pub.	84
Huldah, d. Aaron & Hannah, b. Mar. 2, 1748	64
Huldah, of Torrington, m. Wait **BEACH**, of Goshen, July 9, 1767	10
Huldah, m. Michael **LOOMIS**, b. of Torrington, Oct. 9, 1777	72
Huldah, d. Richard & Rachel, b. May 18, 1797	71
Huldah, d. Lemuel & Abigail, b. Dec. 20, 1806	92
Huldah, of Torrington, m. Smith **HARRIS**, of Winchester, May 13, 1838, by Thomas Benedict	123
Ichabod, s. Ichabod, m. Mindwell **LEWIS**, b. of Torrington, Jan. 29, 1766	70

TORRINGTON VITAL RECORDS 37

	Page
LOOMIS, LOMIS, (cont.)	
Ira, s. Epaphras & Mary, b. July 7, 1766	66
Ira, s. Epaphras & Mary, b. Sept. 14, 1770	66
Ira, s. Epaphras & Mary, b. Sept. 15, 1770	68
Ira, m. Mary **THRALL**, July 25, 1793	114
Isabel, m. Benjamin **PHELPS**, Oct. 16, 1755	88
Issachey, m. Mary **FOWLER**, b. of Torrington, Dec. 10, 1765	67
Issacher, m. Hepzibah **LOOMIS**, b. of Torrington, May 6, 1802	67
Jane, w. Ephraim, Jr., d. [ ]	65
Jean, d. Ephraim & Jean, b. Dec. 10, 1769	65
Jean, d. Aaron & Annis, b. Mar. 11, 1792	68
Jemimah, d. Moses & Sarah, b. July 9, 1758	64
Jemima, m. Ephraim **BANCROFT**, Jr., b. of Torrington, Nov. 2, 1775	19
Jerusha, d. Epaphras & Mary, b. Feb. 6, 1761	66
Jerusha, d. Epaphras & Mary, b. Feb. 6, 1761	68
Jerusha, d. Abraham & Mary, b. Sept. 4, 1780	66
Jerusha, m. Noadiah **BANCROFT**, b. of Torrington, Sept. 7, 1780	19
Joel, of Torrington, m. Elizabeth **BROWN**, of Windsor, June 4, 1752	68
Joel, s. Joel & Elizabeth, b. May 22, 1760	68
Joel, m. Prudence **WEST**, May 23, 1792	79
Joseph, s. Isaac & Sarah, b. June 26, 1758	69
Joseph, s. Issacher & Mary, b. Jan. 14, 1767	67
Julia, d. Abner & Chloe, b. Dec. 20, 1790	65
Julia, d. Abner & Chloe, d. July 6, 1817	65
Laphela, d. Ira & Mary, b. Nov. 12, 1795	114
Larry, d. Richard & Rachel, b. May 20, 1787	71
Laura, d. Aaron & Annis, b. Feb. 17, 1794	68
Laura, m. Erastus **HODGES**, b. of Torrington, Jan. 5, 1809	46-7
Lemuel, s. Aaron & Deborah, b. May 8, 1744	64
Lemuel, s. Aaron & Deborah, d. June 6, 1761	64
Lemuel, s. Eli & Dorothy, b. Oct. 17, 1769	67
Lemuel, of Torrington, m. Abigail **PARSON**, of Farmington, Oct. 17, 1793	92
Lemuel, s. Lemuel & Abigail, b. Apr. 3, 1800	92
Levi, s. Richard & Rachel, b. June 23, 1783	71
Levi, s. Solomon & Elizabeth, b. May 8, 1806	67
Lorrain, s. Epaphras & Mary, b. Jan. 9, 1764	68
Lorine, s. Epaphras & Mary, b. June 9, 1764	66
Lovicey, d. Abner & Sarah, b. Aug. 28, 1772	65
Lovice, d. Abner & Sarah, b. Sept. 27, 1779	65
Lovicy, m. Artemus **PHILLOW**, Dec. 11, 1800	80
Lovice, d. Abner & Sarah, d. [ ]	65
Lucinda, d. Lemuel & Abigail, b. Dec. 6, 1809	92
Lucy, d. Aaron & Hannah, b. Apr. 20, 1756	64
Lucy, m. Elisha **SMITH**, Nov. 25, 1773	111
Luman, s. Moses, Jr. & Lucy, b. July 13, 1783	64
Luman, m. Amanda **THRALL**, b. of Torrington, June 7, 1807	12
Lury, m. Oliver **ALLYN**, b. of Torrington, May 7, 1801	60
Lydia, d. Lemuel & Abigail, b. Aug. 4, 1802	92
Lydia, of Harwington, m. John **COOK**, Jr., of Torrington, Mar. 19, 1806	23
Lynda*, d. Asa & Priscilla, b. May 30, 1781 *("Belinda" in Orcutt's)	69
Mabel, d. Abraham & Mary, b. June 26, 1767	66
Margaret, d. Eli & Dorothy, b. Sept. 7, 1772	67
Margaret King, d. Elisha & Anna, b. July 4, 1809	21

LOOMIS, LOMIS, (cont.)

	Page
Mary, d. Abraham & Mary, b. Dec. 15, 1760	66
Mary, d. Issacher & Mary, b. Nov. 14, 1769	67
Mary, w. Abraham, d. May 20, 1773	66
Mary, d. Epaphras & Mary, b. Mar. 15, 1775	68
Mary, m. Abijah **BARBER**, b. of Torrington, Feb. 19, 1795	22
Mary, m. Daniel Coe **HUDSON**, Feb. 16, 1797	37
Mary Ann, of Torrington, m. Hezekiah H. **BRAW**, of Hartford, Mar. 27, 1833, by Rev. Epaphras Goodman	118
Michael, m. Huldah **LOOMIS**, b. of Torrington, Oct. 9, 1777	72
Moses, of Torrington, m. Sarah **ROBERTS**, of Simsbury, Nov. 3, 1752	64
Moses, s. Moses & Sarah, b. June 18, 1760	64
Moses, Jr., m. Lucy **COOK**, b. of Torrington, Aug. 8, 1782	64
Naomi, d. Abner & Sarah, b. Aug. 26, 1769	65
Naomi, had s. Riley Lyman, b. Dec. 13, 1789	1b
Nathan Wadsworth, s. Elisha & Anna, b. Sept. 22, 1805	21
Oliver, s. Ephraim & Jane, b. May 29, 1787	65
Orlen, s. Solomon & Elizabeth, b. Mar. 1, 1792; d. July 26, 1827	67
Orlean, m. Ruba **NORTH**, Nov. 27, 1820, by James Beebe, J.P.	25
Orril, d. Timothy & Anna, b. June 18, 1792	69
Parmelia, d. Benoni & Jemima, b. Jan. 18, 1804	66
Permelia, m. Horace **LOOMIS**, b. of Torrington, Apr. 21, 1824, by Alexander Gillett	56
Plume, d. Lemuel & Abigail, b. Aug. 10, 1794	92
Pluma, of Torrington, m. Willis **CRAMPTON**, of Farmington, Feb. 2, 1836, by Milton Huxley	122
Rachel, d. Epaphras & Mary, b. May 29, 1772	68
Rachel, d. Epaphras & Mary, d. Mar. 6, 1774	68
Rachel, d. Richard & Rachel, b. Feb. 29, 1792	71
Rachel, Mrs. of Torrington, m. John **WHITING**, of Colebrook, Jan. 3, 1827, by Rev. William R. Judd	83
Rebecca, d. Ephraim & Jean, b. Sept. 26, 1774	65
Remembrance, s. Epaphras & Mary, b. Feb. 27, 1759	66
Remembrance, s. Epaphras & Mary, b. Feb. 27, 1759	68
Remembrance, s. Epaphras & Mary, d. Jan. 6, 1777	68
Remembrance, s. Epaphras, Jr. & Phebe, b. June 24, 1780	66
Reuben, s. Ephraim & Jane, b. Oct. 9, 1785	65
Reuben, s. Lemuel & Abigail, b. Feb. 11, 1796	92
Reuby, m. Moses **DRAKE**, Oct. 29, 1839, by Thomas Benedict	125
Rhoda, m. Ebenezer **ROOD**, b. of Torrington, Sept. 6, 1770	91
Rhoad, d. Issacher & Mary, b. Feb. 27, 1777	67
Rhoda, m. Benjamin **AGARD**, b. of Torrington, Apr. 7, 1796	10
Richard, s. Aaron & Deborah, d. May 15, 1753	64
Richard, s. Abner & Sarah, b. Dec. 25, 1758	65
Richard, m. Rachel **HIGGBEE**, b. of Torrington, May 30, 1780	71
Richard, Jr., s. Richard & Rachel, b. Aug 2, 1789	71
Richard, d. Aug. 9, 1826, ae 67	71
Riley, s. Joel & Prudence, b. Aug. 18, 1800	79
Roman, s. Ephraim, Jr. & Zeruiah, b. Sept. 6, 1800	65
Rockalaney, d. Benony & Jemimah, b. Mar. 27, 1791	66
Roxalana, m. Horace **LOOMIS**, Jan. 29, 1828, by Rev. William R. Gould. Int. Pub.	84
Roxsa, d. Timothy & Anna, b. Apr. 14, 1778	69

	Page
LOOMIS, LOMIS, (cont.)	
Ruhamer, d. Timothy & Anna, b. May 9, 1790	69
Ruth, d. Ephraim & Ruth, b. Mar. 11, 1762	65
Ruth, w. Ephraim, d. May 1, 1764	65
Ruth, d. Ephraim, Jr. & Zeruiah, b. Aug. 9, 1793	65
Sabra, m. Joseph **ALLYN**, Jr., Mar. 18, 1801	2
Sally Wells, d. Elisha & Anna, b. Dec. 25, 1806	21
Salmon, s. Ephraim & Jean, b. Jan. 23, 1768	65
Sarah, d. Moses & Sarah, b. Nov. 28, 1755	64
Sarah, of Harwinton, m. Isaac **HIGLEY**, of Torrington, Feb. 24, 1757	48
Sarah, m. Moses **ROOD**, b. of Torrington, Jan. 5, 1768	91
Sarah, w. Abner, d. May 19, 1784	65
Sarah, d. Moses & Lucy, b. Aug. 30, 1789	64
Sarah Talcot, d. Timothy & Anna, b. July 27, 1776	69
Silas, s. Ephraim & Jean, b. Apr. 12, 1771	65
Simeon, s. Elisha & Mercy, b. June 9, 1808	103
Solomon, of Torrington, m. Elizabeth **OLCOTT**, of New Hartford, Aug. 31, 1791	67
Sophronia, d. Wait & Sally, b. Dec. 28, 1800	69
Sibbel*, d. Ichabod & Mindwell, b. June 25, 1770 *("Sybil")	70
Sylvey, d. Abner & Sarah, b. Jan. 6, 1759	65
Silvey, m. John **WHITEING**, Jr., b. of Torrington, Mar. 23, 1779	105
Sylvia, d. Alexander & Submit, b. Mar. 12, 1801	61-2
Theadas, s. Ichabod & Mindwell, b. Nov. 27, 1766	70
Timothy, Jr., s. Timothy & Anna, b. Nov. 14, 1779	69
Trypheney, d. Abner & Sarah, b. Nov. 10, 1763	65
Tryphena, m. Seth **WHITEING**, b. of Torrington, Apr. 16, 1789	105
Wait, s. Epaphras & Mary, b. Nov. 22, 1765	68
Waite, s. Epaphras & Mary, b. Nov. 23, 1765	66
Wait, m. Sally **STONE**, [ ] 27, 1796	69
Warrin, s. Benony & Jemimah, b. Nov. 9, 1787	66
Wells, s. Timothy & Anna, b. Jan. 17, 1786	69
Zeruiah, d. Ephraim & Zeruiah, b. May 16, 1791	65
LYMAN, Amanda, d. Ebenezer & Ann, b. Sept. 22, 1790	63
Amanda, d. Lyman & Elizabeth, b. Jan. 25, 1808	44
Caleb, s. Ebenezer & Sarah, b. May 1, 1748	63
Caleb, m. Hannah **LOOMIS**, b. of Torrington, Sept. 28, 1768	63
Ebenezer, d. Apr. 1, 1753	63
Ebenezer, d. Feb. 15, 1762	63
Ebenezer, s. Ebenezer & Ann, b. July 16, 1779	63
Ebenezer, m. Ann **YOUNGS**, b. of Torrington, [ ]	63
Eleanor, d. Caleb & Hannah, b. Mar. 21, 1784	63
Elijah Smith, s. Elijah & Lucinda, b. Apr. 26, 1812	18
Elizabeth, of New Hartford, m. Richard **LEACH**, Jr., of Torrington, Jan. 12, 1792	70
Esther, d. Ebenezer & Sarah, b. Aug. 5, 1745	63
Experience, wid. Ebenezer, d. Nov. 14, 1769	63
George, s. Caleb & Hannah, b. Aug. 1, 1790	63
Hannah, m. Asahel **STRONG**, b. of Torrington, Mar. 20, 1749	92
Hannah, of Goshen, m. Epaphras **SHELDON**, Jr., of Torrington, Nov. 17, 1774	93
Hiram, m. Julia M. **OSTURN**, b. of Torrington, May 7, 1848, by Rev. George A. **HUBBELL**	133

BARBOUR COLLECTION

LYMAN, (cont.)

	Page
Larre, d. Ebenezer & Ann, b. Oct. 17, 1788	63
Laura, of Torrington, m. Emory **LOOMIS**, of Torrington, Sept. 12, 1841, by Rev. Brown Emerson	126
Lydia, d. Ebenezer & Sarah, b. June 16, 1738	63
Medad, s. Caleb & Hannah, b. Nov. 24, 1769	63
Mindwell, m. Jacob **STRONG**, b. of Torrington, Oct. 29, 1741	92
Phinehas, s. Ebenezer & Ann, b. June 14, 1776	63
Rhoda, d. Ebenezer & Sarah, b. July 12, 1753	63
Rhoda, d. Caleb & Hannah, b. Nov. 7, 1782	63
Riley, s. Naomi Loomis, b. Dec. 13, 1789	1b
Roxselany, d. Ebenezer & Ann, b. Oct. 15, 1777	63
Ruth, d. Ebenezer & Sarah, b. Nov. 25, 1735	63
Ruth, m. Asahel **NORTH**, b. of Torrington, Jan. 26, 1757	82
Sarah, d. Ebenezer & Sarah, b. July 1, 1740	63
Sibel, d. Ebenezer & Sarah, b. May 25, 1742	63
Sibbel, d. Ebenezer & Sarah, d. May 1, 1766	63
Sibel, d. Caleb & Hannah, b. June 8, 1778	63
McKENZIE, McKINZIE, Jennett, m. Russel **BROOKER**, b. of Torrington, Nov. 12, 1826, by Rev. Epaphras Goodman	81
Margarette, m. Anson **BALCOM**, June 2, 1831, by Rev. David Miller	87
Nancy, of Torrington, m. Samuel **WELLMAN**, of Bethleham, Apr. 25, 1836, by Rev. H. P. Armes	122
McKINLEY, Clarissa, of Torrington, m. Rufus **PATCHEN**, of Derby, Mar. 11, 1821, by Nathan Emery, Elder	24
MAGRANNIS, Francis, of Hartford, m. Beulah **PHELPS**, of Harwinton, Mar. 1, 1835, by Rev. H. P. Armes	122
MAINE, Harriet, m. James **SMITH**, b. of Torrington, Nov. 5, 1848, by Rev. John A. McKinstry	134
MALTBY, Deborah S., of Torrington, m. Moses M. **WEED**, of Barkhamstead, Jan. 11, 1848, by Rev. William H. Moore	131
MANN, William, m. Jane Elizabeth **LONG**, b. of Torrington, Jan. 17, 1836, by Rev. H. P. Armes	122
MANVILLE, Burr, of Watertown, m. Jemima J. **FOREST**, of Wolcottville, Dec. 24, 1847, by Rev. Henry Zell, of Wolcottville	133
MARKHAM, Jael, m. Lieut. John **BURR**, Jr., b. of Torrington, Dec. 13, 1770	6
MARSH, Margaret, Mrs. of Windsor, m. Rev. Nathaniel **ROBEARTS**, of Torrington, Nov. 22, 1743; d. Oct. 1, 1747	90
MARSHALL, MARSHAL, Aaron, m. Chloe **AGARD**, b. of Torrington, Dec. 4, 1777	68
Abigail, d. Abner & Hannah, b. July 13, 1769	74
Abner, s. Abner & Hannah, b. Nov. 17, 1761	74
Amasa, of Torrington, m. Jean **LEAMING**, of Middletown, Feb. 27, 1759	75
Ambrose, s. Noah & Sarah, b. Apr. 12, 1756	74
Asenath, d. Aaron & Cloe, b. Aug. 5, 1786	68
Chloe, d. Aaron & Chloe, b. Oct. 6*, 1779 *("Oct. 4"?)	68
Chloe, w. Aaron, d. Dec. 24, 1795	68
Eunice, d. Amasa & Jane, b. June 1, 1761	75
Eunice, m. Nathaniell **LEACH**, b. of Torrington, Nov. 19, 1779	73
Hannah, m. Roger **WILLSON**, b. of Torrington, Jan. 23, 1780	109
Hannah, w. Abner, d. June 24, 1800	74
Harvey, s. Thomas & Desire, b. June 29, 1768	75
John, s. Noah & Sarah, b. Apr. 30, 1759	74

MARSHALL, MARSHAL, (cont.)
Julius, s. Abner & Hannah, b. Jan. 7, 1767; d. Jan. 23, 1767	74
Minerva, d. Raphael & Phebee, b. May 30, 1789; m. Samuel **DELLEBUR**, June 19, 1806	109
Nancy, d. Abner & Hannah, b. Jan. 19, 1765	74
Noah, of Torrington, m. Sarah **TAYLOR**, of Litchfield, Nov. 15, 1753	74
Noah, s. Noah & Sarah, b. Sept. 8, 1754	74
Noah, d. Feb. 3, 1777	74
Oliver, s. Noah & Sarah, b. Nov. 23, 1757	74
Oliver, s. Noah & Sarah, d. Jan. 10, 1777	74
Raphael, s. Thomas & Desire, b. May 14, 1765	75
Raphael, m. Philee **GRANT**, b. of Torrington, Nov. 1, 1787	75
Reuben, s. Thomas & Desire, b. Nov. 29, 1766	75
Roger, s. Abner & Hannah, b. Aug. 2, 1763	74
Rozel, s. Noah & Sarah, b. June 10, 1761	74
Sarah, d. Noah & Sarah, b. May 12, 1767	74
Sarah, d. Thomas & Desire, b. June 10, 1771	75
Sarah, m. Giles **WHITEING**, b. of Torrington, May 30, 1791	106
Sarah, m. Oliver **COE**, Dec. 1, 1791	16

MARTIN, Robert O., of Goshen, m. Laura L. **BOWNS**, of Torrington, Oct. 15, 1849, by Rev. J. A. McKinstry — 135

MASON, Charles S., m. Rosetta **BISSELL**, b. of Wolcottville, Nov. 28, 1841, by Rev. Samuel Day, of Wolcottville — 126

George H., m. Lucy **BISSELL**, of Wolcottville, Jan. 1, 1846, by Rev. Henry Zell, of Wolcottville — 132

Gilbert, of New London, m. Mary Ann **DAYTON**, of Torrington, Sept. 13, 1835, by Rev. John B. Beach — 122

Lusanna, of Litchfield, m. Joseph **EGLESTONE**, of Torrington, Mar. 23, 1775 — 28

MASTERS, Eliza A., of Torringford, m. Merret S. **WHITE**, of Canaan, July 18, 1839, by Rev. Herman L. Vaill — 124

MATHER, Ann, m. Emery **TAYLOR**, b. of Torrington, Mar. 27, 1831, by Rev. Epaphras Goodman — 87

Elizabeth, d. Zachariah & Lucey, b. Dec. 1, 1783	77
Harriet, of Torrington, m. Emory Taylor, of Bristol, Mar. 11, 1824, by Rev. Epaphras Goodman	56
Lucinda, d. Zachariah & Lucey, b. May 6, 1775	77
Lucinda, d. Zachariah & Lucia, b. May 6, 1775	77
Lucey, d. Zachariah & Lucy, b. June 2, 1776	77
Naomi, d. Zachariah & Lucy, b. Nov. 27, 1777	77
Polly, d. Zachariah & Lucia, b. Sept. 11, 1772	77
Sarah, Ann, of Torrington, m. William **OLCOTT**, of Harwinton, Jan. 1, 1834, by Rev. Epaphras Goodman	119
Sibel, d. Zachariah & Lucy, b. July 24, 1781	77
Zachariah, m. Lucey **GAYLORD**, b. of Torrington, Apr. 20, 1769	77

MATTHEWS, Mary Jane, of Torrington, m. Dennis **CHATFIELD**, of Waterbury, Dec. 18, 1835, by Rev. H. P. Armes — 122

Sarah, d. Thomas & Hannah, b. Dec. 17, 1776 — 78

Thomas, m. Hannah **HARRIS**, b. of Torrington, Apr. 16, 1775 — 78

MERCUM, Esther, of Wallingford, m. Benjamin **WHITING**, of Torrington, Oct. 14, 1755 *("Merriman" in Orcutt's book) — 106

MERRILL, MERREL, MERRELLS, Amanda, of Naugatuck, m. Charles **ATWATER**, of Waterbury, Sept. 20, 1849, by Rev. S. T. Seelye — 135

BARBOUR COLLECTION

	Page
MERRILL, MERREL, MERRELLS, (cont.)	
Augustus, of New Hartford, m. Adaline **WOODING**, of Torrington, Nov. 3, 1846, by J. A. McKinstry	130
Harriet, m. Nathan W. **HARMON**, b. of Torrington, Sept. 12, 1824, by Rev. George E. Pierce	57
Julia Ann, m. Willard **BIRGE**, Nov. 9, 1833, by Rev. H. P. Armes	120
Lucy Anna, m. Daniel **BECKLEY**, b. of Winchester, July 13, 1837, by Thomas Benedict, at his house	123
William L., of Waterbury, m. Ellen **CLEVELAND**, of Torrington, May 14, 1849, by Rev. John A. McKinstry	135
Zebulon, of New Hartford, m. Caroline **LOOMIS**, of Torrington, Nov. 13, 1842, by Thomas Benedict	126
MERRIMAN, Charles, s. Ichabod & Rebecca, b. Mar. 7, 1782	78
Esther*, of Wallingford, m. Benjamin **WHITING**, of Torrington, Oct. 14, 1755 *(Arnold Copy has "Esther **MERCUM**")	106
Lucy E., of Torrington, m. Malvin **PACKARD**, of Bridgewater, Mass., Dec. 8, 1833, by H. P. Armes	119
MILLARD, McKensie, m. Ellen E. **MUNN**, Aug. 29, 1848, by Rev. S. T. Seelye	134
MILLER, Abigail, d. Ebenezer & Thankfull, b. May 24, 1767	76
Asahel, s. George & Sarah, b. Oct. 24, 1760	76
Asahel, of Torrington, m. Lovine **COE**, of Winchester, Oct. 26, 1788	76
Beulah, s. Ebenezer & Thankfull, b. Mar. 21, 1782	76
Daniel, s. William & Polly, b. Jan. 5, 1785	73
David, s. George & Sarah, b. Feb. 23, 1765	76
David, m. Hannah **SMITH**, Jan. 1, 1795	75
David Smith, s. David & Hannah, b. Apr. 2, 1808	75
Ebenezer, of Torrington, m. Thankfull **ALLINE***, of Middletown, Feb. 16, 1761 *("Allins" in Orcutt's book)	76
Ebenezer, s. Ebenezer & Thankfull, b. Jan. 7, 1764	76
Ebenezer, Jr., of Torrington, m. Dorety **GAYLORD**, of Middletown, Feb. 7, 1787	77
Elihu Rockwell, s. David & Hannah, b. Sept. 28, 1801	75
Elizabeth, d. Ebenezer & Thankfull, b. Aug. 11, 1765	76
Elizabeth, d. Ebenezer & Thankfull, d. Oct. 11, 1767	76
Elizabeth, d. Ebenezer & Thankfull, b. Nov. 8, 1770	76
Elizabeth, m. E. Lyman **WETMORE**, b. of Torrington, Sept. 3, 1795	44
Experience, d. Ebenezer & Thankfull, b. May 5, 1778	76
Experience, d. Ebenezer & Thankfull, d. June 3, 1778	76
Fanna Sophronia, d. David & Hannah, b. Nov. 3, 1797	75
Florella E., of Torrington, m. Sidney **HAYDEN**, of Barkhamsted, Mar. 23, 1836, by Rev. Epaphras Goodman	123
George, s. George & Sarah, b. Mar. 7, 1755	76
George, d. Feb. 13, 1775	76
George, s. George & Phebee, b. July 2, 1777	75
George, m. Phebee **HURLBUT**, b. of Torrington, [ ]	75
George, d. [ ]	75
Hannah, d. George & Sarah, b. Sept. 14, 1772	76
Hannah Eliza, d. David & Hannah, b. Oct. 8, 1805	75
Henry, s. Ebenezer & Thankfull, b. Oct. 11, 1776	76
Huldah, d. David & Hannah, b. Sept. 15, 1795	75
Joel, s. George & Sarah, b. Jan. 10, 1758	76
Joel, s. Asahel & Lovine, b. June 26, 1790	76
Jonathan, s. Ebenezer & Thankfull, b. Nov. 26, 1761	76

TORRINGTON VITAL RECORDS 43

	Page
MILLER, (cont.)	
Joseph, s. Ebenezer & Thankfull, b. Oct. 29, 1779	76
Joseph, s. William & Polly, b. Mar. 1, 1790	73
Joshua, s. Ebenezer & Thankfull, b. Mar. 8, 1775	76
Josiah, s. George & Sarah, b. Apr. 12, 1767	76
Josiah, m. Harriet **MOORE**, b. of Torringtford, Nov. 18, 1821, by Epaphras Goodman	26
Maria, of Torrington, m. Levi **LEFFINGWELL**, of Goshen, (colored), Jan. 1, 1827, by Rev. Epaphras Goodman	83
Nancy, d. William & Polly, b. Feb. 5, 1787	73
Phebe, d. George & Sarah, b. Jan. 23, 1757	76
Phebe, d. George & Phebee, b. Apr. 13, 1776	75
Phebe, m. William Anson **STONE**, Apr. 24, 1796	15
Polly, d. William & Polly, b. Apr. [ ], 1791	73
Ruth, d. George & Sarah, b. Nov. 19, 1762	76
Samuel, s. Ebenezer & Thankfull, b. Sept. 2, 1773	76
Sarah, d. George & Sarah, b. July 12, 1769	76
Sarah, m. John C. **BARBER**, b. of Torrington, Oct. 1, 1841, by Rev. Brown Emerson	126
Sophronia A., of Torrington, m. Mansfield **BUNNELL**, of Plymouth, Apr. 24, 1833, by Rev. Epaphras Goodman	118
Thankfull, d. Ebenezer & Thankfull, b. June 9, 1772	76
Thomas A., m. Mary C. **HUDSON**, b. of Torrington, Apr. 1, 1829, by Rev. Epaphras Goodman	85
Thomas Alline, s. Ebenezer & Thankfull, b. Sept. 13, 1769	76
Willard, s. Ebenezer & Dorety, b. Dec. 31, 1787	77
William, m. Polley **COTTON**, [ ], 1783	73
MILLIMAN, Leroy, of Winsted, m. Harriet **DUNBAR**, of Torrington, Sept. 13, 1843, by Rev. B. Emerson	127
MILLS, Berthe*, of Symsbury, m. Owen **BROWN**, late of Symsbury now of Torrington, Feb. 11, 1793, at Symsbury *("Ruth")	17
MINER, John, m. Hannah **STRONG**, b. of Torrington, Apr. 5, 1775	75
John, s. John & Hannah, b. Aug. 15, 1775	75
MITCHELL, Amanda, m. Henry L. **SMITH**, b. of Torrington, June 23, 1850, by Rev. Ira Pettebone	135
MIX, Chauncey B., of Northfield, m. Lucinda **FREEMAN**, of Torrington, Nov. 30, 1820, by Samuel J. Mills	25
Chauncey B., m. Abigail **JACKINS**, of Wolcottville, Oct. 2, 1843, by Rev. Samuel Day, of Wolcottville	127
Jane L., of Torringford, m. George B. **MORSE**, Sept. 29, 1846, by Rev. S. T. Seelye	130
MOORE, MOOR, Benjamin, s. Simeon & Hannah, b. Mar. 1, 1756	77
Chloe, d. Simeon & Hannah, b. Aug. 17, 1758	77
Eldad, s. Simeon & Hannah, b. Oct. 10, 1762	77
Harriet, m. Josiah **MILLER**, b. of Torringford, Nov. 18, 1821, by Rev. Epaphras Goodman	26
Maria, of Torrington, m. Jonathan **WHITNEY**, of Granville, Mass., Sept. 19, 1827, by Rev. Epaphras Goodman	84
Philander, s. Simeon & Hannah, b. Feb. 18, 1759	77
Polly, d. Simeon & Hannah, b. Nov. 1, 1784	77
Polly, of Winchester, m. Rowland **WILLSON**, of Torrington, Oct. 24, 1806	60
Simeon, s. Simeon & Hannah, b. Mar. 25, 1760	77
Simeon, Jr., m. Hannah **COOK**, b. of Torrington, June 21, 1784	77

	Page
MOREHOUSE, Elizabeth, d. Huldah **WILCOX**, b. Jan. 25, 1788	78
MORGAN, Emeline H., of Torrington, m. Joseph **GREY**, of Haddam, Nov. 15, 1831, by Rev. William R. Gould	115
MORSE, George B., m. Jane L. **MIX**, of Torringford, Sept. 29, 1846, by Rev. S. T. Seelye	130
Lura A., of Canaan, m. Dr. Gustavus G. **FIELD**, of Guildford, Oct. 14, 1838, by Rev. James Beach, of Winsted. Settled in Torrington	125
Mary J., of Litchfield, m. George **LEACH**, of Torrington, Jan. 22, 1843, by John A. McKinstry	126
MOSES, Charlotte, m. Stephen **SMITH**, b. of Torrington, Oct. 14, 1829, by William R. Gould	86
Thomas, m. Ann M. **BISSELL**, b. of Torrington, Nov. 15, 1826, by Rev. Epaphras Goodman	81
MOSS, Orson, of Litchfield, m. Eliza **BEACH**, of Otis, Mass., July 8, 1849, by Rev. J. A. McKinstry	134
MOTT, Flora, of Wolcottville, m. Hezekiah **JOHNSON**, of Harwinton, [July 4, 1841(?)], by Samuel Day	126
MUNN, Abijah, s. Jedidiah & Molly, b. Feb. 14, 1790, at Southbury	30
Betsey, d. Jedidiah & Molly, b. Apr. 6, 1797	30
Clarry, d. Jedidiah & Molly, b. Feb. 26, 1787, at Southbury	30
Elizabeth, of Torrington, m. Levi **CRAMPTON**, of Goshen, Aug. 31, 1824, by Rev. Arnold Scholfield. Int. Pub.	57
Ellen E., m. McKensie **MILLARD**, Aug. 29, 1848, by Rev. S. T. Seelye	134
Jedidiah, s. Jedidiah & Molly, b. Jan. 23, 1799	30
Jedediah, Sr., d. May 28, 1805	30
Ranson, s. Jedidiah & Molly, b. Jan. 8, 1793	30
MUNSELL, MUNSILL, Maria R., m. Theron **BRONSON**, July 7, 1841, by Thomas Benedict	126
Susanna, m. Ira **GRANT**, Mar. 10, 1796	58
MUNSON, Martha W., of Wolcottville, m. Mason W. **FYLER**, of Winsted, Apr. 17, 1843, by Rev. Samuel Day, of Wolcottville	127
Mary, of Torrington, m. Albert B. **WILCOX**, of Bristol, May 31, 1832, by Rev. William R. Gould	115
William, of Bristol, m. Lucretia **PALMER**, of Torrington, Nov. 21, 1832, by Rev. H. P. Arms	116
MURRAY, MURREY, Ammi, s. Daniel & Lucrecia, b. July 29, 1787	78
Daniel, m. Lucretia **COE**, b. of Torrington, Mar. 18, 1776	78
Daniel, s. Daniel & Lucrecia, b. Apr. 4, 1785	78
Daniel, m. Hannah **CLARK**, [ ]	78
Lewis, twin with Lucrecia, s. Daniel & Hannah, b. Mar. 19, 1795	78
Lewis, m. Mary **LEACH**, May 10, 1826, by Rev. Epaphras Goodman	81
Lucrecia, w. Daniel d. June 5, 1792	78
Lucrecia, twin with Lewis, d. Daniel & Hannah, b. Mar. 19, 1795	78
Riely, s. Daniel & Lucrecia, b. Jan. 9, 1792	78
Ruth, d. Daniel & Lucrecia, b. Sept. 7, 1776	78
Ruth, m. Barzilla **BLAKE**, b. of Torrington, Sept. 27, 1798	20
Truman, s. Daniel & Lucrecia, b. Oct. 25, 1781	78
Warren, s. Daniel & Lucrecia, b. July 8, 1779	78
NASH, John, m. Esther **WHITING**, b. of Torrington, Jan. 17, 1783	79
Lucy, d. John & Esther, b. May 8, 1783	79
NEW, Henry, m. Almira **PALMER**, b. of Torrington, Feb. 8, 1835, by Milton Huxley	121
NORTH, Abigail, d. Martin & Abigail, b. Apr. 3, 1764	83

	Page
NORTH, (cont.)	
Abigail Mariann, m. Seth Sidney **TREADWAY**, b. of Torrington, May 22, 1831, by Rev. Epaphras Goodman	87
Achsah, s. Ebenezer & Sibella, b. Aug. 19, 1748	82
Ared, s. Willard & Lucina, b. Mar. 19, 1824	30
Arial, s. Junia* & Sabra, b. Aug. 13, 1788 *("Junius" in Orcutt's)	80
Asahel, s. Ebenezer & Sibella, b. May 15, 1743	82
Asahel, m. Ruth **LYMAN**, b. of Torrington, Jan. 26, 1757	82
Betsey, d. Remembrance & Elizabeth, b. Apr. 20, 1795	11
Cyrus, s. Remembrance & Elizabeth, b. May 6, 1797	11
Cyrus, m. Lavinia **HOLMES**, b. of Torrington, Dec. 14, 1820, by Frederick Marsh	24
Ebenezer, s. Ebenezer & Sibella, b. June 27, 1746	82
Ebenezer, s. Ebenezer, m. Jerusha **COWLES**, b. of Torrington, Feb. 16, 1769	84
Ebenezer, Sr., d. Aug. 5, 1789	82
Enos, s. Ebenezer & Jerusha, b. Nov. 17, 1773	84
Frederick, m. Harriet **HOYT**, June 14, 1830, by Rufus Babcock	86
Jemima, d. Noah & Jemima, b. Apr. 17, 1766	83
Jemima, m. Elihu **BARBER**, b. of Torrington, Apr. 19, 1787	58
John H., of Cornwall, m. Esther W. **GAYLORD**, of Torrington, May 3, 1826, by Rev. Epaphras Goodman	81
Junia, s. Noah & Jemima, b. Sept. 24, 1760	83
Junia, m. Sabra **FYLER**, b. of Torrington, Jan. 25, 1785	80
Lemuel, s. Asahel & Ruth, b. Dec. 14, 1767; d. Mar. 3, 1787	82
Lemuel, s. Phinehas & Cloe, b. Sept. 23, 1790	82
Lorrain, m. Harriet **FORD**, b. of Torrington, May 4, 1834, by Frederick Marsh	120
Lucina, d. Martin & Abigail, b. June 6, 1767	83
Lucy, d. Remembrance & Elizabeth, b. May 21, 1789	11
Lury, of Torrington, m. Midian **GRISWOLD**, of Litchfield, Mar. 19, 1822, by Frederick Marsh	26
Maria, d. Noah & Jemima, b. Dec. 29, 1767	83
Martin, m. Abigail **ENO**, b. of Torrington, Apr. 2, 1760	83
Martin, s. Martin & Abigail, b. June 10, 1761	83
Mary, d. Remembrance & Elizabeth, b. June 14, 1793	11
Noah, m. Jemima **LEWIS**, b. of Torrington, Mar. 25, 1756	83
Noah, s. Noah & Jemima, b. May 12, 1757	83
Noah, s. Remembrance & Elizabeth, b. Sept. 4, 1787	11
Norris, of Torrington, m. Ann Eliza **COE**, of Torrington, June 28, 1843, by Rev. B. Emerson	127
Pamela, m. Martin **WEBSTER**, Sept. 28, 1820, by Lyman Beecher	24
Phinehas, m. Cloe **SKINNER**, b. of Torrington, [ ], 17[ ]*	
*(Date of m. obtained from A. C. Hitchcock, of Waterbury, "Dec. 3, 1787")	82
Phinehas, s. Asahel & Ruth, b. July 19, 1762	82
Phinehas, s. Phinehas & Cloe, b. Feb. 9, 1803	82
Phinehas, m. Louisa **WETMORE**, Oct. 10, 1832, by Rev. William R. Gould	116
Prudence, d. Ebenezer & Jerusha, b. Nov. 16, 1769	84
Prudence, d. Remembrance & Elizabeth, b. Mar. 28, 1791	11
Remembrance, s. Noah & Jemima, b. Oct. 13, 1762	83
Remembrance, m. Elizabeth **LEE**, Sept. 21, 1786	11
Remembrance, d. Aug. 10, 1802	11
Rocksilany, d. Asahel & Ruth, b. Nov. 23, 1759	82

BARBOUR COLLECTION

	Page
NORTH, (cont.)	
Rockselany, m. Elkanah **HODGES**, b. of Torrington, Jan. 14, 1777	48
Roxalaney, d. Junia & Sabra, b. Nov. 2, 1785	80
Rocselana, d. Phinehas & Cloe, b. Dec. 27, 1796	82
Ruby, d. Junia & Sabra, b. July 28, 1790	80
Ruba, m. Orlean **LOOMIS**, Nov. 27, 1820, by James Beebe, J.P.	25
Rufus, s. Martin & Abigail, b. Dec. 29, 1769	83
Sarah, d. Ebenezer & Sibella, b. Dec. 1, 1752	82
Sarah C., m. Ebenezer **EDMONDS**, b. of Torrington, Oct. 6, 1833, by Rev. H. P. Armes	118
Sibella, m. Samuel **COWLES**, Jr., Apr. 14, 1756	15
Tryphena, d. Junia & Sabra, b. Mar. 14, 1787	80
Tryphena Grant, m. Seymour **BRADLEY**, b. of Torrington, May 30, 1791	4
Willard, s. Junia & Sabra, b. June 5, 1783* *(Arnold Copy note says "1793"?)	80
Willard, m. Lucina **PELTON**, Nov. 20, 1820, by James Beebe, J.P.	25
William, s. Remembrance & Elizabeth, b. Oct. 1, 1799	11
NORTHROP, Fanny M., of Torrington, m. James S. **BIRD**, of Bethlem, May 24, 1846, by Rev. Henry Zell, of Wolcottville, at his house	132
Herman, of Winsted, m. Fanny **WHITE**, of Torrington, Sept. 24, 1827, by Rev. William R. Gould. Int. Pub.	84
Sarah, of Torrington, m. Almansor A. **BUCKLAND**, of East Windsor, Feb. 4, 1835, by Rev. Daniel Smith	121
NORTON, David, s. David & Lois, b. Feb. 9, 1773	84
OLCOTT, Elizabeth, of New Hartford, m. Solomon **LOOMIS**, of Torrington, Aug. 31, 1791	67
William, of Harwinton, m. Sarah Ann **MATHER**, of Torrington, Jan. 1, 1834, by Rev. Epaphras Goodman	119
OLMSTEAD, OMSTEAD, Abigail, of Torrington, m. Sextus **BARNES**, of New Hartford, Sept. 14, 1836, by Rev. Seth Higby	123
R. S., Dr. of Brooklyn, N.Y., m. Charlotte A. **HUNGERFORD**, of Torrington, Nov. 8, 1849, by Rev. S. T. Seelye	135
OSBORN, [see also **OSTURN**], Isaac Higley, s. Timothy & Susannah, b. Apr. 12, 1772	87
Justin, s. Timothy & Susannah, b. Dec. 5, 1765	87
Susannah, d. Timothy & Susannah, b. Mar. 10, 1770	87
Susanna, m. Henry **WATTLES**, Feb. 10, 1818	67
Timothy, m. Susannah **HIGLEY**, b. of Torrington, Feb. 28, 1764	87
OSTRAM, John, m. Eliza J. **COLEBY**, b. of Goshen, Aug. 10, 1829, at Wolcottville, by Rev. David Miller	85
OSTURN, [see also **OSBORN**], Julia M., m. Hiram **LYMAN**, b. of Torrington, May 7, 1848, by Rev. George A. Hubbell	133
PACKARD, Malvin, of Bridgewater, Mass., m. Lucy E. **MERRIMAN**, of Torrington, Dec. 8, 1833, by H. P. Armes	119
PAINE, Cynthia, of Southhold, L.I., m. John **GRANT**, of Torrington, June 4, 1823, by Rev. Epaphras Goodman	55
PALMER, Adaline, m. Enoch **JOHNSON**, Jan. 7, 1847, by Rev. S. T. Seelye	131
Addison, s. Harvey & Mehitable, b. Sept. 17, 1802	69
Almira, m. Henry **NEW**, b. of Torrington, Feb. 8, 1835, by Milton Huxley	121
Anna, d. Harvey & Mehitable, b. Nov. 8, 1796	69
Aurelia, d. Harvey & Mehitable, b. Oct. 11, 1800	69
Bennet, m. Morilla **EGLESTON**, b. of Torrington, Mar. 30, 1830, by Frederick Marsh	86

TORRINGTON VITAL RECORDS

	Page
PALMER, (cont.)	
Betsey, of Windsor, m. Henery **ALLYN**, of Torrington, July 26, 1798	79
Deborah, 2nd, of Windsor, m. John **COOK**, Jr., of Torrington, May 25, 1769	14
Eliza, d. Harvey & Mehitable, b. July 5, 1798	69
Emma Rosetta, of Torrington, m. Charles C. **BEERS**, of Goshen, Sept. 28, 1831, by Rev. William R. Gould	114
Harvey, b. Nov. 30, 1770, at Windsor; m. Mehitable **DIBBLE**, Nov. 25, 1795	69
Hiram, m. Jane E. **KIMBERLEY**, b. of Torrington, Mar. 11, 1849, by Rev. S. T. Seelye	135
Lucretia, d. Harvey & Mehitable, b. June 16, 1806	69
Lucretia, of Torrington, m. William **MUNSON**, of Bristol, Nov. 21, 1832, by Rev. H. P. Arms	116
Tryphena S., of Litchfield, m. Edward R. **HUBBARD**, of Winsted, Sept. 19, 1847, at the house of Mrs. Palmer, by Rev. Henry Zell, of Wolcottville	133
PARDEE, Eugene, of Wadsworth, O., m. Eleanor A. **TAYLOR**, of Torrington, June 5, 1836, by R. W. Chipman, V.D.M.	122
Silas, of Bristol, m. Mary **BROCKET**, of Waterbury, Mar. 31, 1844, by Rev. Samuel Day, of Wolcottville	128
PARKER, Rebeckah, d. Peter & Esther, b. July 28, 1777	89
PARMELE[E], William, of Goshen, m. Ann Eliza **WHITE**, of Torrington, Mar. 22, 1824, by Rev. Joseph Harvey, of Goshen	56
PARSON, Abigail, of Farmington, m. Lemuel **LOOMIS**, of Torrington, Oct. 17, 1793	92
PATCHEN, Rufus, of Derby, m. Clarissa **McKINLEY**, of Torrington, Mar. 11, 1821, by Nathan Emery, Elder	24
PEASE, Sylvanus H., of Somers, m. Emeline **ROBERTS**, of Torrington, July 7, 1833, by Rev. Epaphras Goodman	118
PECK, Harriet Ann, Mrs., m. Eli **TERRY**, Oct. 28, 1840, by Rev. Merrell Richardson	125
Olive, m. Nathaniel **BIRGE**, b. of Torrington, May 8, 1831, by Rev. Epaphras Goodman	87
PELTON, Jedidiah, of Chatham, m. Clement **CARR**, of Torrington, May 18, 1785	20
Lucina, m. Willard **NORTH**, Nov. 20, 1820, by James Beebe, J.P.	25
Robert, m. Alma **EGGLESTON**, Apr. 8, 1829, by Frederick Marsh	85
PERKINS, Henry A., of New Hartford, m. Rachel M. **BISSELL**, of Torrington, June 14, 1831, by Rev. Epaphras Goodman	87
Mary J., of Wolcottville, m. Francis **CLARK**, of Winsted, Feb. 28, 1847, by Rev. S. T. Seelye	131
Watrous, m. Deborah **BRACE**, b. of Torrington, Aug. 21, 1823, by Rev. Epaphras Goodman	55
PERRY, Orville, of New Haven, m. Elizabeth A. **WEBSTER**, of Torringford, June 14, 1837, by Rev. Herman L. Vail	123
PETERSON, Benjamin, m. Laura Ann **FREEMAN**, b. of Wolcottville, Sept. 27, 1843, by Rev. Samuel Day, of Wolcottville	127
PHELPS, Adin, m. Maria **PHELPS**, b. of Torrington, Oct. 26, 1834, by Rev. David Miller	121
Almira, d. Jonathan & Silvah, b. Sept. 22, 1789	88
Anna, d. Jonathan & Silvah, b. Oct. 8, 1785	88
Benjamin, m. Isabel **LOMIS**, Oct. 16, 1755	88
Benjamin, s. Benjamin & Isabil, b. June 15, 1769	88
Beulah, of Harwinton, m. Francis **MAGRANNIS**, of Hartford, Mar. 1, 1835, by Rev. H. P. Armes	122
Cornelia, m. Frederick B. **WADHAMS**, b. of Torrington, Sept. 9, 1829, by	

48   BARBOUR COLLECTION

	Page
PHELPS, (cont.)	
Rev. William R. Gould	85
Daniel, s. Benjamin & Isabil, b. Nov. 9, 1766	88
Eli, m. Mrs. Mary **BISHOP**, Jan. 3, 1841, by Rev. Samuel Day, of Wolcottville	125
Emeline, of Torrington, m. Justus **COTTON**, of Longmeadow, Mass., Nov. 1, 1830, by Rev. William R. Gould	86
Frederick, s. Jannah B. & Lucretia, b. Dec. 15, 1814	45
Isabil, d. Benjamin & Isabil, b. June 15, 1761	88
Isabel, w. Benjamin, d. Dec. 15, 1784	88
J. W., Dr., m. Charlotte Augusta **HAYDEN**, Dec. 23, 1846, by W. H. Moore	130
Jannah B., m. Lucretia **DIBBLE**, Nov. 26, 1812	45
Jemima, d. Benjamin & Isabil, b. Feb. 16, 1765	88
Jemiah, m. James **EGLESTONE**, b. of Torrington, Dec. 24, 1789	27
Jerusha, d. Benjamin & Isabil, b. May 2, 1757	88
Jerusha, m. Joseph **BEACH**, Jr., b. of Torrington, Aug. 19, 1779	6
Jerusha, d. Jonathan & Silvah, b. Sept. 13, 1791	88
Jonathan, s. Benjamin & Isabil, b. May 17, 1763	88
Jonathan, m. Silvah **BEACH**, b. of Torrington, Jan. 20, 1785	88
Jonathan, d. Sept. 27, 1791	88
Joseph, s. Benjamin & Isabil, b. Mar. 16, 1759	88
Joseph, m. Rebecca **LEAVENWORTH**, Oct. 27, 1804	21
Joseph Nelson, s. Joseph & Rebecca, b. Nov. 29, 1806	21
Julia Ann, m. Henry **FREEMAN**, b. of Torringford (colored), Apr. 28, 1839, by Rev. Herman L. Vaill	124
Lucinda, of Torrington, m. Sylvester **SPENCER**, of Litchfield, Dec. 6, 1821, by Rev. Joseph Harvey, of Goshen	26
Luman, s. Jonathan & Silvah, b. June 26, 1787	88
Maria, m. Adin **PHELPS**, b. of Torrington, Oct. 26, 1834, by Rev. David Miller	121
Mindwell, of Torrinton, m. Chester **BRISTOL**, of Elizabethtown, N.J., May 1, 1825, by Rev. Epaphras Goodman	83
Ruth, of Windsor, m. Daniel **DIBBLE**, of Torrington, Jan. 8, 1788	23
Sally, d. Joseph & Rebecca, b. Sept. 6, 1805	21
Sylvia, wid. m. Nathan **THRALL**, Feb. [ ], 1800	95
PHILLIPS, Jeremiah H., of Ovid, N.Y., m. Sarah **LEACH**, of Torrington, Nov. 11, 1828, by Rev. William R. Gould	85
PHILLOW, Addison, s. Artemas & Lovicy, b. Nov. 27, 1804	80
Ad[e]line, d. Artemas & Lovicy, b. Apr. 30, 1807	80
Artemus, m. Lovicy **LOOMIS**, Dec. 11, 1800	80
Dennis, s. Artemas & Lovicy, b. Dec. 5, 1803	80
Edmund Augustus, s. Artemas & Lovicy, b. Oct. 6, 1802	80
Emily, d. Artemas & Lovicy, b. Dec. 16, 1805	80
Lury Loomis, d. Artemas & Lovicy, b. Oct. 9, 1801	80
Orphelia, d. Artemas & Lovicy, b. Nov. 9, 1808	80
PICKERING, Ann, m. Samuel **FORREST**, b. of Torrington, Dec. 25, 1835, by Rev. H. P. Armes	122
PICKETT, PICKET, Content, m. Barzillia **HUDSON**, Jan. 26, 1803	38
Margaret, m. Abel **BEACH**, Apr. 5, 1738	5
PIERPOINT, Charles, m. Candace **LEACH**, b. of Torrington, Sept. 29, 1824, by Rev. Epaphras Goodman	57
Eliada, m. Polly **CARRINGTON**, Aug. 25, 1848, by Rev. William H. Moore	134
Laura, m. Warren **BANCROFT**, Feb. 17, 1828, by Rev. Walter Smith, of	

TORRINGTON VITAL RECORDS 49

	Page
PIERPOINT, (cont.)	
Cornwall	84
PILGRIM, Charles, m. Elizabeth M. **SMITH**, of Wolcottville, Aug. 22, 1847, at the house of Mr. Horton, by Rev. Henry Zell, of Wolcottville	133
PITKIN, John R., of Winchester, m. Sophia **THRALL**, of Torrington, Oct. 1, 1823, by Rev. Frederick Marsh, of Winchester	55
PLATT, George, of Sharon, m. Sedelia **CURTISS**, of Goshen, Apr. 4, 1843, by Rev. Samuel Day, of Wolcottville	127
POND, Burton, of Bristol, m. Charlotte **COLT**, of Torrington, Oct. 6, 1829, by Rev. Epaphras Goodman	85
Hannah, of Torrington, m. Ebenezer **GOODWIN**, of New Hartford, July 3, 1832, by Rev. Epaphras Goodman	115
Hannah D., m. Jeremiah D. **ROOT**, June 16, 1833, in Wolcottville, by Rev. J. Boyden, Jr.	118
Lucia, d. Preston & Esther, b. Mar. 5, 1815	31
Lyman, of Litchfield, m. Lucy **SPENCER**, of Torrington, June 5, 1823, by Rev. Epaphras Goodman	55
Preston, m. Esther **WHEADON**, Apr. 27, 1814	31
Russel L., m. Frances L. **ROUS**, b. of Torrington, Oct. 17, 1849, by Rev. J. A. McKinstry	135
POPE, Augustus F., m. Abba J. **SPENCER**, Dec. 27, 1846, by Rev. S. T. Seelye	131
PORTER, Maria, of Waterbury, m. David S. **FULLER**, of Torrington, Oct. 3, 1824, by Rev. Epaphras Goodman	57
POTTER, Adelia, d. Ambrose & Abigail, b. June 14, 1805	22
Ambrose, m. Abigail **SEWARD**, b. of Torrington, Apr. 18, 1805	22
Daniel, of Farmington, m. Mealley **JOHNSON**, of Torrington, Jan. 24, 1792	87
Lucius Foot, s. Ambrose & Abigail, b. Aug. 27, 1808	22
Newton, m. Caroline **DAYTON**, Nov. 12, 1837, by Rev. Stephen Hubbell, of Wolcottville	124
PRATT, Ezra D., of Cornwall, m. Aurilla Anne **ROOD**, of Torringford, July 1, 1846, by Rev. S. t. Seelye	130
PRESTON, Argabas Drake, s. Joseph & Roselandey, b. Mar. 6, 1795	89
John S., of Harwinton, m. Betsey **GAYLORD**, of Torrington, Oct. 1, 1837, by Rev. Herman L. Vaill	123
Joseph, Jr., of Torrington, m. Roselandey **BARBER**, of Simsbury, Oct. 17, 1793	89
Mary, m. Robert **CARR**, b. of Torrington, Dec. 29, 1785	17
Mary Polly, d. Joseph & Roselandey, b. July 16, 1798	89
Roseperphena, d. Joseph & Roselandey, b. July 26, 1796	89
Sarah, had d. Anna **EDMOND**, b. Feb. 16, 1794; f. Stephen **EDMOND**	89
Zerepta, d. Junia & Artemessy, b. Apr. 23, 1779	89
PRINCE, Horace, of Torrington, m. Drusilla **FREEMAN**, of Harwinton, June 1, 1845, by Rev. Samuel Day, of Wolcottville	129
Susanna, m. John **FREEMAN**, Jan. 6, 1833, by Rev. Epaphras Goodman	117
PRITCHARD, Jesse, of Lee, Mass., m. Eliza **GILLETT**, of Torrington, Jan. 20, 1830, by Rev. William R. Gould	86
RAY, Abigail, d. Timothy & Lovicy, b. Nov. 23, 1786	90
Abner, s. Timothy & Lovicey, b. Apr. 9, 1791	90
Lovicey, d. Timothy & Lovicey, b. June 20, 1788	90
Rachel, d. Timothy & Lovicy, b. Dec. 26, 1784	90
Rachel, had d. Clarinda **WHITING**, b. Sept. 23, 1806	7
Rachel, m. Richard **SPERRY**, Mar. 10, 1807	7
Timothy, m. Lovicy **RICHARDS**, b. of Torrington, Sept. 15, 1784	90

	Page
RICE, William, s. Daniel & Anna, b. Oct. 26, 1798	73
RICHARDS, Alpheas, s. John & Rachel, b. Aug. 26, 1778	90
Daniel, of Litchfield, m. Experience **LEACH**, of Torrington, Sept. 20, 1823, by Rev. Epaphras Goodman	55
Elizabeth, d. Capt. Eli & Elizabeth, b. Apr. 16, 1785	79
Lovicy, m. Timothy **RAY**, b. of Torrington, Sept. 15, 1784	90
Sally, of Torrington, m. Alanson **LOOMIS**, of Winchester, Mar. 20, 1827, by Rev. Epaphras Goodman	83
Samuel Sackit, s. John & Rachel, b. Aug. 5, 1776	90
RICHARDSON, David, of Prospect, m.. Anne **TYLER**, of Harwinton, Nov. 26, 1844, in Wolcottville, by Rev. John Morrison Reid, of M. E. Ch.	128
RIDER, Hiram, m. Anna **AUSTIN**, July 20, 1837, in Torringford, by Rev. Thomas Bainbridge	123
RIGGS, Isaac W., of Middlebury, m. Ann **HOYT**, of Torrington, Nov. 24, 1833, by Rufus Babcock, of Colebrook	119
Merriel Burwell, of Torrington, m. Emeline **KEENDALL**, of Suffield, Apr. 9, 1848, by Rev. George A. Hubbell	133
ROBBINS, Theodore, of Norfolk, m. Clarissa **HURLBUT**, of Winchester, Feb. 9, 1845, in Newfield, by Rev. J. B. Beach, of the M. E. Ch.	128
ROBERTS, ROBEARTS, Adah, of Torrington, m. Joseph **WOOSTER**, of Goshen, Oct. 20, 1841, by Rev. Brown Emerson	126
Augeline, m. Hosea **CASE**, b. of Torrington, Jan. 18, 1846, by Rev. H. D. Kitchel	130
Chloe, d. Joel, b. Apr. 15, 1765	90
Emeline, of Torrington, m. Sylvanus H. **PEASE**, of Somers, July 7, 1833, by Rev. Epaphras Goodman	118
Esther, w. Rev. Nathaniell, d. Feb. 6, 1783	90
George P., of St. Louis, Mo., m. Anniss M. **ALLEN**, of Wolcottville, May 15, 1843, by Rev. Samuel Day, of Wolcottville	127
Helen, of Torrington, m. Ira **HOYT**, of Torrington, Nov. 4, 1842, by Rev. Brown Emerson	126
Henry, of Torrington, m. Betsey **TIFFANY**, of Barkhamsted, Dec. 11, 1826, by Rev. Epaphras Goodman	81
Joel, s. Joel & Esther, b. June 16, 1772	90
Judah, s. Joel, b. Sept. 13, 1763	90
Laurana, of Windsor, m. Jabez **GILLETT**, of Torrington, Jan. 11, 1798	42
Margaret, w. Rev. Nathaniel, d. Oct. 1, 1747	90
Margaret, d. Rev. Nathaniell & Esther, b. June 5, 1750	90
Margaret, m. Samuel **CUMMINGS**, b. of Torrington, Sept. 28, 1778	17
Nama, d. Joel, b. Sept. 26, 1760	90
Nathaniel, Rev. of Torrington, m. Mrs. Margaret **MARSH**, of Windsor, Nov. 22, 1743	90
Nathaniel, Rev., m. Esther **LOMIS**, b. of Torrington, Nov. 7, 1748	90
Nathaniel, Rev., d. Mar. 4, 1776	90
Sabra, of Torrington, m. Ephraim **FELLOWS**, of Cornwall, Nov. 2, 1825, by Rev. Epaphras Goodman	81
Samuel, s. Joel, b. Jan. 26, 1762	90
Sarah, of Simsbury, m. Moses **LOOMIS**, of Torrington, Nov. 3, 1752	64
ROBERTSON, Daniel, m. Mary Jane **SEYMOUR**, Aug. 22, 1838, by Rev. Stephen Hubbell, of Wolcottville	130
ROCKWELL, Chester, of East Windsor, m. Jerusha **TAYLOR**, of Torrington, Feb. 28, 1805	15
ROGERS, Daniel S., m. Desire B. **FOWLER**, b. of Torrington, Apr. 17, 1832, by	

TORRINGTON VITAL RECORDS 51

	Page
ROGERS, (cont.)	
Rev. Epaphras Goodman	115
Julius, m. Sarah **LEACH**, Oct. 29, 1844, by Thomas Benedict	128
ROMANS, Sarah Emeline, of Enfield, m. Amos **FREEMAN**, of Torrington, Jan. 9, 1831, by Rev. Epaphras Goodman	87
ROOD, Aaron, s. Moses & Sarah, b. Nov. 17, 1784	91
Amos, s. Moses & Sarah, b. Jan. 3, 1772	91
Anne, d. Ebenezer & Rhoda, b. May 28, 1780	91
Aurilla Anne, of Torringford, m. Ezra D. **PRATT**, of Cornwall, July 1, 1846, by Rev. S. T. Seelye	130
Clarissa W., b. Mar. 3, 1818	91
Ebenezer, m. Rhoda **LOMIS**, b. of Torrington, Sept. 6, 1770	91
Ebenezer, s. Ebenezer & Rhoda, b. Mar. 27, 1776	91
Eunice, d. Ebenezer & Rhoda, b. July 24, 1783	91
Hannah, d. Moses & Sarah, b. Feb. 16, 1779	91
Harvey L., of Torrington, m. Susan M. **HUMPHREY**, of Guilford, N.Y., Oct. 15, 1848, by Rev. William H. Moore	134
Isaac, s. Ebenezer & Rhoda, b. Sept. 13, 1771	91
John, s. Ebenezer & Rhoda, b. May 10, 1778	91
Loran, s. Moses & Sarah, b. May 29, 1787	91
Lydia, d. Moses & Sarah, b. June 12, 1774	91
Mary, d. Moses & Sarah, b. Oct. 17, 1776	91
Moses, m. Sarah **LOMIS**, b. of Torrington, Jan. 5, 1768	91
Moses, s. Moses & Sarah, b. June 12, 1781	91
Norman W., b. Nov. 14, 1819	91
Rhoda, d. Ebenezer & Rhoda, b. Apr. 6, 1774	91
Rhoda, of Torrington, m. Francis D. **FARLEY**, of Lenox, Mass., May 22, 1849, by Rev. John A. McKinstry	135
Sarah, d. Moses & Sarah, b. Oct. 26, 1768	91
ROOT, Caroline, of Bristol, m. Harlihigh **SKINNER**, of Winchester, Sept. 2, 1833, by Rev. Epaphras Goodman	118
Edward, m. Jane **BARBOUR**, May 17, 1848, by Rev. S. T. Seelye	134
Jeremiah D., m. Hannah D. **POND**, June 16, 1833, in Wolcottville, by Rev. J. Boyden, Jr.	118
ROSSITER, ROSSETER, Adaline, d. Newton & Maria, b. Feb. 11, 1821	72
Amos H., s. Newton & Maria, b. Mar. 20, 1815	72
Charlotte, d. Newton & Maria, b. Mar. 23, 1819	72
Gilbert, s. Newton & Maria, b. Feb. 9, 1823	72
Harriet Newell, d. Newton & Maria, b. Mar. 10, 1817	72
Jonathan A., of Harwinton, m. Huldah A. **WETMORE**, of Torrington, Apr. 18, 1844, by Rev. B. Emerson	128
Luther, s. Newton & Maria, b. Feb. 19, 1813	72
ROUS, Frances L., m. Russel L. **POND**, b. of Torrington, Oct. 17, 1849, by Rev. J. A. McKinstry	135
ROWLEY, Artemas, m. Susan **EVANS**, b. of Torrington, Sept. 20, 1826, by Rev. E. W. Goodman	81
ROYS, Lucy M., of Norfolk, m. James **GILBERT**, of Waterbury, Oct. 17, 1847, by Rev. Henry Zell, of Wolcottville, at his house	133
RUSSELL, William C., m. Emeline **BRADLEY**, b. of Torrington, May 24, 1827, by Rev. John L. Stone, of Litchfield	83
ST. JOHN, Seth B., m. Emily **CARTWRITE**, Mar. 10, 1839, by Thomas Benedict	124
SAMMIS, David, m. Harriet E. **GIBBS**, b. of Goshen, Oct. 21, 1827, by Rev. William R. Gould. Int. Pub.	84

	Page
SANFORD, Melicent, m. Asa **SPENCER**, b. of Torrington, Nov. 6, 1783	111
SCOTT, Emeline, of Litchfield, m. David **BOOTH**, of Naugatuck, Jan. 1, 1845, by Rev. Samuel Day	129
Maria, m. A. G. **BRADFORD**, May 4, 1848, by Rev. S. T. Seelye	133
SCOVILLE, Charles F., of Wolcottville, m. Clarissa **SPENCER**, of Litchfield, Jan. 1, 1846, in Wolcottville, by Rev. Henry Zell, of Wolcottville	132
John W., m. Martha **WILLSON**, Oct. 17, 1832, by Rev. William R. Gould	116
Julius, of Litchfield, m. Emily **DAYTON**, of Wolcottville, Sept. 22, 1842, in Wolcottville, by Rev. John H. Still	126
Mary Lord, of Wolcottville, m. Abner Marshall **WILSON**, of Vernon, N.Y., Apr. 4, 1847, at the house of Col. Foot, by [Rev. Henry Zell, of Wolcottville]	132
Squire, of Litchfield, m. Martha M. **DAYTON**, of Wolcottville, July 14, 1844, by Rev. Samuel Day, of Wolcottville	128
SENIOR, Christopher, of New Britain, m. Elizabeth **HOLLIS**, of Wolcottville, Dec. 6, 1846, in Wolcottville, by Rev. Henry Zell, of Wolcottville	132
SEWARD, Abigail, m. Ambrose **POTTER**, b. of Torrington, Apr. 18, 1805	22
SEYMOUR, Eliza, m. Lyman W. **COE**, Nov. 3, 1841, by Rev. Samuel Day, of Wolcottville	126
Eunice, m. Stephen **HART**, Sept. 9, 1790	8
Henry R., of Colebrook, m. Ann P. **GROSS**, of Torringford, Oct. 12, 1840, by Samuel Day	125
James H., m. Florella H. **HUDSON**, b. of Torrington, Nov. 2, 1835, by Rev. Epaphras Goodman	123
Julia A., m. Samuel **BROOKES**, Jr., May 18, 1834, by Rev. H. P. Armes	120
Maria, m. Martin **BROOKER**, May 1, 1838, by Rev. Stephen Hubbell, of Wolcottville	124
Mary Jane, m. Daniel **ROBERTSON**, Aug. 22, 1838, by Rev. Stephen Hubbell, of Wolcottville	130
Wager W., of Sanfordville, N.Y., m. Adah **SHATTUCK**, of Torrington, Dec. 10, 1832, by Rev. James Beach, of Winstead	117
SHATTUCK, Adah, of Torrington, m. Wager W. **SEYMOUR**, of Sanfordville, N.Y., Dec. 10, 1832, by Rev. James Beach, of Winsted	117
SHAWS, Joseph, of South Lester, m. Artemesia **WERRELL**, of Torrington, Aug. 15, 1832, by Rev. Daniel Miller	116
SHELDON, Allyn, s. Epaphras & Eunice, d. Feb. 9, 1762	93
Allyn, s. Epaphras & Hannah, b. July 20, 1786	93
Daniel, s. Epaphras & Hannah, b. Aug. 13, 1781	93
Epaphras, Jr., of Torrington, m. Hannah **LYMAN**, of Goshen, Nov. 17, 1774	93
Esther, d. Epaphras & Hannah, b. Mar. 1, 1784	93
Henry, s. Epaphras & Hannah, b. Oct. 27, 1791	93
Samuel Lyman, s. Epaphras & Hannah, b. Nov. 16, 1782	93
William, s. Epaphras & Hannah, b. Dec. 12, 1788	93
SHIRW(?), Joseph, m. Lura **LEFFINGWELL**, Sept. 25, 1831, by Rev. William R. Gould	115
SIMONS, Erastus, of Colebrook, m. Rosetta M. **SIMONS**, of Torrington, [ ], [1847], by Rev. Thomas Benedict, of Bap. Ch.	131
Rosetta M., of Torrington, m. Erastus **SIMONS**, of Colebrook, [ ], [1847], by Rev. Thomas Benedict, of Bap. Ch.	131
SKIFF, Adelia, of New York, m. Nilson **ALVORD**, of Torrington, July 4, 1848, by Rev. S. T. Seelye	133
SKINNER, Cloe, m. Phinehas **NORTH**, b. of Torrington, [ ] 17, [ ]* *(Date of m. obtained from A. C. Hitchcock of Waterbury, "Dec. 3,	

TORRINGTON VITAL RECORDS 53

	Page
SKINNER, (cont.)	
1787")	82
Harlihigh, of Winchester, m. Caroline **ROOT**, of Bristol, Sept. 2, 1833, by Rev. Epaphras Goodman	118
Oliver, of Torrington, m. wid. Charity **FOX**, of Hebron, July 3, 1823, by Alexander Gillett	55
SMITH, Almira, d. Elisha & Lucy, b. Jan. 12, 1780; d. Apr. 21, 1781	111
Charlotte M., m. Rufus W. **GILLETT**, b. of Torrington, May 26, 1847, by Rev. William H. Moore	131
Ebenezer, s. Ebenezer & Hannah, b. Apr. 18, 1763	93
Elisha, b. Aug. 14, 1751, in Farmington; m. Lucy **LOOMIS**, Nov. 25, 1773	111
Elisha, s. Elisha & Lucy, b. July 19, 1775, in Winchester	111
Elisha, s. Elisha & Lucy, d. Aug. 9, 1776, in Torrington	111
Elisha, d. Jan. 9, 1813	111
Elizabeth, of Torrington, m. Henry S. **ABBEY**, of Buffalo, N.Y., Oct. 30, 1831, by Rev. William R. Gould	114
Elizabeth M., of Wolcottville, m. Charles **PILGRIM**, Aug. 22, 1847, at the house of Mr. Horton, by Rev. Henry Zell, of Wolcottville	133
Hannah, d. Ebenezer & Hannah, b. July 21, 1765	93
Hannah, m. Jesse **WHITEING**, b. of Torrington, Sept. 30, 1784	105
Hannah, m. David **MILLER**, Jan. 1, 1795	75
Harriet J., of Torrington, m. Edgar **LOOMIS**, of Windsor, Aug. 26, 1835, by Rev. Epaphras Goodman	122
Henry L., m. Amanda **MITCHELL**, b. of Torrington, June 23, 1850, by Rev. Ira Pettebone	135
Ira, s. Ebenezer & Hannah, b. Jan. 14, 1769	93
James, of Lexington, N.Y., m. Deidamia **CORNISH**, of Simsbury, Oct. 16, 1825, by Rev. Alexander Gillett	81
James, m. Harriet **MAINE**, b. of Torrington, Nov. 5, 1848, by Rev. John A. McKinstry	134
Jesse, s. Ebenezer & Hannah, b. Oct. 28, 1766	93
John, of Winchester, m. Esther **FRENCH**, of Torrington, Aug. 27, 1823, by David Miller	55
Joseph, s. Ebenezer & Hannah, b. Oct. 29, 1773	93
Lewis S., m. Eliza A. **HURLBUT**, July 15, 1845, by Thomas Benedict	129
Lucinda, of Wolcottville, m. James **ASHBORN**, of Litchfield, Dec. 26, 1847, by Rev. Henry Zell, of Wolcottville	133
Miles, s. Ebenezer & Hannah, b. Sept. 11, 1775	93
Norman, s. Ebenezer & Hannah, b. Aug. 7, 1782	93
Orrel, d. Elisha & Lucy, b. Jan. 30, 1778	111
Orrel, of Torrington, m. Russell C. **ABERNETHY**, of Washington, Sept. 17, 1803	59
Orvell*, d. Elisha & Lucey, b. Jan. 30, 1778 *("Orrell"?)	111
Phebe, m. Joseph **ALLYN**, Jr., Mar. 28, 1793; d. Sept. 2, 1798	2
Phebe Anne, m. Chester **BROOKER**, b. of Litchfield, June 21, 1846, by Rev. Samuel Day	130
Polly, d. Ebenezer & Hannah, b. Nov. 20, 1787	93
Polly A., m. Myron **STONE**, b. of Litchfield, Dec. 25, 1843, by Rev. Samuel Day, of Wolcottville	128
Sarah, d. Ebenezer & Hannah, b. Nov. 8, 1777	93
Stephen, m. Charlotte **MOSES**, b. of Torrington, Oct. 14, 1829, by William R. Gould	86
William, m. Adelia **BOWLER**, b. of Waterbury, Oct. 2, 1831, by Daniel Coe	114

BARBOUR COLLECTION

	Page
SNYDER, John, m. Laura **JOHNSON**, Apr. 13, 1835, by Rev. David Miller	122
SOPER, David, m. Rachel **COOK**, b. of Torrington, Jan. 26, 1764	94
Lucinda, of New Hartford, m. William **WHITING**, of Torrington, Mar. 9, 1784	110
Naomi, d. David & Rachel, b. May 9, 1774; d. July 2, 1774	94
Olive, d. David & Rachel, b. July 23, 1768	94
Rachel, d. David & Rachel, b. Apr. 12, 1772	94
Rachel, m. Elijah **BISSELL**, b. of Torrington, Jan. 22, 1789	29
SOUTHWICK, James, m. Lois **CURTIS**, Apr. 28, 1830, by Rev. William R. Gould	86
SPAFFORD, Mercy, of Salisbury, m. Nathaniel **BARBER**, s. Nathaniel, Mar. 17, 1769	5
SPARKS, Thomas, m. Betsey **GRANGER**, Feb. 14, 1821, by Rev. Ebenezer Washburn	24
SPENCER, Abba J., m. Augustus F. **POPE**, Dec. 27, 1846, by Rev. S. T. Seelye	131
Asa, m. Melicent **SANFORD**, b. of Torrington, Nov. 6, 1783	111
Clarissa, of Litchfield, m. Charles F. **SCOVILLE**, of Wolcottville, Jan. 1, 1846, in Wolcottville, by Rev. Henry Zell, of Wolcottville	132
Lucy, d. Asa & Melicent, b. Jan. 23, 1794	111
Lucy, of Torrington, m. Lyman **POND**, of Litchfield, June 5, 1823, by Rev. Epaphras Goodman	55
Mary, d. Asa & Melicent, b. May 29, 1786	111
Miles, s. Asa & Melicent, b. Mar. 30, 1785	111
Roxey, d. Asa & Melicent, b. June 21, 1788	111
Submit, m. Alexander **LOOMIS**, b. of Torrington, June 3, 1792	61-2
Sylvester, of Litchfield, m. Lucinda **PHELPS**, of Torrington, Dec. 6, 1821, by Rev. Joseph Havey, of Goshen	26
Theodosia, d. Asa & Mellicent, b. Sept. 26, 1791	111
SPERRY, Albert, s. Richard & Rhodah, b. May 4, 1811	7
Homer, s. Richard & Rhodah, b. May 31, 1815	7
Lorra*, d. Richard & Rachel, b. Feb. 20, 1808 *("Laura")	7
Laura, of Torrington, m. David F. **DANIELS**, of Preston, Sept. 25, 1831, by Rev. Herman Ellis, of Norfolk	114
Lewis, s. Richard & Rhodah, b. Mar. 24, 1809	7
Louice, d. Richard & Rhodah, b. May 27, 1820	7
Lucy, d. Richard & Rhodah, b. Mar. 31, 1818	7
Richard, m. Rachel **RAY**, Mar. 10, 1807	7
Samuel, s. Richard & Rhodah, b. Dec. 20, 1822	7
SPICER, Harvey, m. Mary A. **TAYLOR**, Apr. 30, 1827, by Rev. William R. Gould. Int. Pub.	84
SQUIRES, Elmore D., of Utica, N.Y., m. Lucinda C. **LEACH**, of Torrington, Dec. 20, 1842, by John A. McKinstry	126
Martha, m. James **FURGUSON**, b. of Durham, Jan. 9, 1767	35
STANCLIFT, John, m. Sarah **HARRIS**, b. of Torrington, Oct. 21, 1778	111
STARK, STARKS, Martha, m. Orson **BARBER**, Dec. 4, 1842, by Thomas Benedict	126
Mehitabel, m. Reuben **BURR**, b. of Torrington, July 2, 1772	6
Thomas A., m. Flora P. **DRAKE**, May 20, 1840, by Thomas Benedict	125
STOCKING, Mercia, m. Joseph H. **BURRETT**, b. of Torrington, May 4, 1836, by Rev. H. P. Armes	122
Samuel J., of Waterbury, m. Orrel **COE**, of Torrington, Mar. 22, 1835, by Rev. H. P. Armes	122
STODDARD, STODARD Anna, m. Joshua **LEACH**, Dec. 13, 1826, by Rev.	

TORRINGTON VITAL RECORDS 55

	Page
STODDARD, STODARD, (cont.)	
William R. Gould	81
Anne, d. Ebenezer & Abigail, b. May 8, 1787	112
Ebenezer, m. Abigail **STRONG**, b. of Torrington, May 6, 1785	112
Pheney, d. Ebenezer & Abigail, b. Mar. 18, 1786	112
STONE, Joan C., of Litchfield, m. Henry **BERNARD**, of Winchester, Jan. 30, 1848, by Rev. George A. Hubbell. Witnesses Alfred Brown & Hiram Lyman	132
Myron, m. Polly A. **SMITH**, b. of Litchfield, Dec. 25, 1843, by Rev. Samuel Day, of Wolcottville	128
Ransley, s. William Anson & Phebe, b. June 3, 1798	15
Sally, m. Wait **LOOMIS**, [ ] 27, 1796	69
William Anson, m. Phebe **MILLER**, Apr. 24, 1796 *(Perhaps "**STOWE**")	15
William Anson & Phebe, had child b. Feb. 19, 1797; d. [ ]	15
STOW, Daniel Belding, s. Daniel, b. Aug. 10, 1771	112
Polle, d. Daniel, b. Sept. 7, 1775	112
Prudence, d. Daniel, b. Sept. 11, 1769	112
William, s. Daniel, b. June 2, 1773	112
William Anson*, m. Phebe **MILLER**, Apr. 24, 1796 *(Perhaps "William Anson **STONE**"?)	15
STRICKLAND, Chloe S., of Warren, m. John S. **WILCOX**, of Torrington, [ ] 27, 1849, by Rev. S. T. Seelye	135
STRONG, Abigail, d. Jacob & Mindwell, b. Jan. 27, 1751	92
Abigail, m. Ebenezer **STODARD**, b. of Torrington, May 6, 1785	112
Asahel, m. Hannah **LYMAN**, b. of Torrington, Mar. 20, 1749	92
Asahel, s. Asahel & Hannah, b. Apr. 17, 1750	92
David, s. Asahel & Hannah, b. May 31, 1768	92
Dorcas, d. Asahel & Hannah, b. Feb. 28, 1758	92
Elizabeth, d. Jacob & Mindwell, b. Sept. 10, 1755	92
Elizabeth, d. Jacob & Mindwell, d. Jan. 2, 1756	92
Experience, d. Jacob & Mindwell, b. Aug. 13, 1743	92
Experience, d. Jacob & Mindwell, d. Aug. 13, 1743	92
Experience, d. Jacob & Mindwell, b. Mar. 28, 1749/50	92
Fanny, m. John **TAYLOR**, b. of Torrington, Apr. 27, 1823, by Rev. Epaphras Goodman	55
Hannah, d. Asahel & Hannah, b. Nov. 30, 1753	92
Hannah, w. Asahel, d. Feb. 19, 1771	92
Hannah, m. John **MINER**, b. of Torrington, Apr. 5, 1775	75
Jacob, m. Mindwell **LYMAN**, b. of Torrington, Oct. 29, 1741	92
Jacob, d. Sept. 1, 1776	92
Mary, d. Jacob & Mindwell, b. July 2, 1757	92
Mary, m. Richard **LEACH**, Jr., b. of Torrington, Mar. 23, 1775	70
Mindwell, d. Jacob & Mindwell, b. July 28, 1742	92
Return, s. John, b. Mar. 11, 1764	94
[**TAINTOR**], [see under **TANTER**]	
TALMADGE, TALLMADGE, Anstin, m. William B. **WILLSON**, b. of Torrington, [Aug. 18, 1833], by Rev. Epaphras Goodman	118
Eliza, m. Albro W. **COWLES**, Mar. 5, 1828, by Rev. William R. Gould	84
James B., m. Esther G. **BURR**, Apr. 22, 1845, by D. W. Clark	129
Sarah R., of Torringford, m. Caleb F. **DANIELS**, of Norwich, Apr. 28, 1839, by Rev. Herman L. Vaill	124
TANTER, Joseph, of Torrington, m. Mary **WILLSON**, of Windsor, Sept. 19, 1771. Was on Sept. 20, 1771, 26 y. old	97

	Page
TANTER, (cont.)	
Joseph, s. Joseph & Mary, b. Mar. 2, 1772	97
TAYLOR, Abial, s. Joseph & Ann, b. July 4, 1788	98
Charlotte A., m. Charles S. **CHURCH**, b. of Torrington, Nov. 28, 1833, by H. P. Armes	119
Eleanor A., of Torrington, m. Eugene **PARDEE**, of Wadsworth, O., June 5, 1836, by R. W. Chipman, V.D.M.	122
Emory, of Bristol, m. Harriet **MATHER**, of Torrington, Mar. 11, 1824, by Rev. Epaphras Goodman	56
Emery, m. Ann **MATHER**, b. of Torrington, Mar. 27, 1831, by Rev. Epaphras Goodman	87
Harriet, m. Cyrus **HUBBARD**, July 8, 1849, by Rev. William H. Moore	134
Henrietta M., m. Merril **TREAT**, b. of Torrington, Apr. 19, 1849, by Rev. S. T. Seelye	135
Jerusha, d. Joseph & Ann, b. Aug. 22, 1782	98
Jerusha, of Torrington, m. Chester **ROCKWELL**, of East Windsor, Feb. 28, 1805	15
John, m. Fanny **STRONG**, b. of Torrington, Apr. 27, 1823, by Rev. Epaphras Goodman	55
Joseph, m. Ann **WILLSON**, b. of Torrington, Aug. 31, 1775	98
Joseph, s. Chester & Jerusha, b. Apr. 29, 1806	15
Margaret, of Windsor, m. Elijah **GAYLORD**, of Torrington, Nov. 11, 1749	42
Mary, of Litchfield, m. Abraham **LOOMIS**, s. Abraham, of Torrington, Feb. 10, 1757	66
Mary A., m. Harvey **SPICER**, Apr. 30, 1827, by Rev. William R. Gould. Int. Pub.	84
Rockey, d. Joseph & Ann, b. Nov. 11, 1779	98
Sarah, of Litchfield, m. Noah **MARSHALL**, of Torrington, Nov. 15, 1753	74
Silva, d. Joseph & Ann, b. Feb. 5, 1777	98
Uri, s. Joseph & Ann, b. July 22, 1786	98
TERRY, Eli, m. Mrs. Harriet Ann **PECK**, Oct. 28, 1840, by Rev. Merrell Richardson	125
THOMPSON, Adeline, of Waterbury, m. Benjamin N. **CROOK**, of Torrington, Jan. 11, 1846, by J. A. McKinstry	130
THORP, Lydia, of Torrington, m. Jannah **DEMING**, of Barkhamsted, Dec. 22, 1824, by Rev. Epaphras Goodman	57
THRALL, Aaron, s. Joel & Margaret, b. May 29, 1742	95
Aaron, of Torrington, m. Mary **DOWD**, of Goshen, Feb. 20, 1766	96
Alexander, s. Reuben & Ruth, b. Mar. 19, 1768	95
Amanda, d. Levi & Mary, b. Mar. 17, 1785	96
Amanda, m. Luman **LOOMIS**, b. of Torrington, June 7, 1807	12
Amy, d. Joseph & Elizabeth, b. Mar. 7, 1772	95
Anna, d. Nathan & Sylvia, b. Jan. 31, 1805	95
Augustus, s. Levi & Mary, b. Oct. 9, 1773	96
Car[o]line, d. Daniel & Elizabeth, b. May 31, 1755	95
Chloe, d. Joel & Margaret, b. Mar 5, 1745	95
Chloe, m. Robert **COE**, b. of Torrington, Dec. 26, 1761	16
Daniel, Jr., of Torrington, m. Keziah **BROOKS**, of Springfield, June 2, 1785	96
Elizabeth, d. Daniel & Elizabeth, b. Dec. 11, 1739	95
Elizabeth, wid. Joseph, d. May 3, 1803	95
Friend, s. Joel & Margaret, b. June 9, 1752	95
Friend, m. Lois **BARBER**, b. of Torrington, May 27, 1773	95
Ira, s. Nathan & Sylvia, b. Sept. 12, 1802	95

TORRINGTON VITAL RECORDS

	Page
THRALL, (cont.)	
Jerusha, d. Charles & Margaret, b. Jan. 2, 1777	98
Joel, s. Joel & Margaret, b. Apr. 15, 1739	95
Joel, d. Oct. 15, 1777	95
Joseph, s. Joseph & Elizabeth, b. Apr. 20, 1770	95
Joseph, d. Aug. 5, 1776	95
Joshua, s. Daniel & Keziah, b. July 21, 1799	96
Keziah, d. Daniel & Keziah, b. Feb. 12, 1791	96
Lavine, d. Daniel & Keziah, b. Jan. 13, 1793	96
Lavina, of Torrington, m. Ira **COLE**, of Kent, Nov. 23, 1820, by Joseph Harvey	25
Levi, s. Joel & Margaret, b. June 11, 1749	95
Lois, d. Friend & Lois, b. June 26, 1773	95
Lois, w. Friend, d. July 5, 1773	95
Lois, d. Friend & Lois, d. Oct. 17, 1773	95
Luke, s. Nathan & Sylvia, b. May 22, 1800	95
Margaret, d. Joel & Margaret, b. Jan. 9, 1756	95
Martha, d. Daniel & Elizabeth, b. June 19, 1757	95
Mary, d. Levi & Mary, b. Feb. 1, 1776	96
Mary, m. Ira **LOOMIS**, July 25, 1793	114
Nancy, d. Daniel & Keziah, b. July 25, 1787	96
Nathan, s. Joseph & Elizabeth, b. Apr. 4, 1769	95
Nathan, m. wid. Sylvia **PHELPS**, Feb. [ ], 1800	95
Noah, s. Joel & Margaret, b. Apr. 3, 1754	95
Pardon, s. Joel & Margaret, b. Feb. 10, 1759	95
Reuben, s. Joel & Margaret, b. Feb. 20, 1746/7	95
Reuben, m. Ruth **BANCROFT**, b. of Torrington, Aug. 11, 1765	95
Rhoda, d. Charles & Margaret, b. Apr. 22, 1776	98
Roger, s. Aaron & Mary, b. Mar. 21, 1767	96
Sabra, d. Aaron & Mary, b. Apr. 3, 1769	96
Samuel, s. Daniel & Keziah, b. Feb. 6, 1797	96
Samuel, m. Harriet **WILLSON**, b. of Torrington, May 9, 1822, by Alexander Gillett	26
Sarah, d. Daniel & Keziah, b. July 28, 1789	96
Silas, s. Charles & Margaret, b. June 22, 1774	98
Sophia, of Torrington, m. John R. **PITKIN**, of Winchester, Oct. 1, 1823, by Rev. Frederick Marsh, of Winchester	55
TIBBALS, Frederick, m. Nancy **HOLMES**, Mar. 11, 1841, by Thomas Benedict	126
TIFFANY, Angeline E., of Torrington, m. Albert **HILL**, of Bristol, Nov. 28, 1833, by Rev. Epaphras Goodman	119
Betsey, of Barkhamsted, m. Henry **ROBERTS**, of Torrington, Dec. 11, 1826, by Rev. Epaphras Goodman	81
TOLLES, Sybel, m. Harlow **FYLER**, b. of Torrington, July 6, 1823, by Rev. Epaphras Goodman	55
TRACY, Caleb C., of Washington, m. Caroline **BOWNE**, of Torrington, Jan. 9, 1845, by J. A. McKinstry	128
TREADWAY, Abigail, Mrs., m. Aaron **BURBANK**, b. of Winsted, Dec. 18, 1842, by Rev. B. Emerson	126
Clarissa, m. Darius **WILLSON**, b. of Torrington, Oct. 2, 1821, by Frederick Marsh	26
Seth Sidney, m. Abigail Mariann **NORTH**, b. of Torrington, May 22, 1831, by Rev. Epaphras Goodman	87
TREAT, Merril, m. Henrietta M. **TAYLOR**, b. of Torrington, Apr. 19, 1849, by	

	Page
TREAT, (cont.)	
Rev. S. T. Seelye	135
TROWBRIDGE, Joshua B., of Danbury, m. Amelia **KNAPP**, of Canaan, May 20, 1839, by Thomas Benedict	124
TURRELL, TURREL, Highla, of Torrington, m. Elkanah **INGRAHAM**, of Norfolk, Sept. 5, [1820], by Samuel J. Mills	24
Loisa, of Torrington, m. Elkanah **INGRAHAM**, Jr., of Colchester, Jan. 1, 1825, by Rev. Epaphras Goodman	57
Spencer, m. Samantha **CANFIELD**, b. of Torrington, Mar. 10, 1831, by Rev. Epaphras Goodman	87
TUTTLE, Bedee, s. Isaiah & Ruth, b. May 31, 1777	97
Burritt, m. Catharine **BISSELL**, Oct. 1, 1848, by Rev. S. T. Seelye	134
Hilpah, of Barkhamsted, m. Minard **VAN De BOGERT**, of Torrington, Oct. 14, 1821, by Daniel Coe	26
Isaiah, m. Ruth **WILLSON**, b. of Torrington, Mar. 22, 1774	97
Leverett, m. Chloe **COLT**, b. of Torrington, Feb. 10, 1830, by Rev. Epaphras Goodman	86
Lovicey, d. Isaiah & Ruth, b. Oct. 25, 1775	97
Rhoda, m. Noah **FOWLER**, b. of Torrington, Feb. 10, 1774	33-4
Submit, m. Urijah **COOK**, b. of Torrington, Feb. 8, 1779	18
Uriel, s. Isaiah & Ruth, b. June 8, 1774	97
Uriel, s. Isaiah & Ruth, d. Feb. 7, 1778	97
Uriel, s. Isaiah & Ruth, b. Oct. 13, 1779	97
Zurviah, d. Isaiah & Ruth, b. May 22, 1782	97
TYLER, [see also **FYLER**], Anne, of Harwinton, m. David **RICHARDSON**, of Prospect, Nov. 26, 1844, in Wolcottville, by Rev. John Morrison Reid, of M. E. Ch.	128
VAN, DeBOGERT, Minard, of Torrington, m. Hilpah **TUTTLE**, of Barkhamsted, Oct. 14, 1821, by Daniel Coe	26
WADHAMS, Frederick B., m. Cornelia **PHELPS**, b. of Torrington, Sept. 9, 1829, by Rev. William R. Gould	85
George D., m. Lucy S. **ABERNETHY**, b. of Torrington, Dec. 25, 1828, by Rev. William R. Gould	85
WADKINS, John, m. Nancy **BISSELL**, Aug. 28, 1822, by Rev. Epaphras Goodman	54
WADSWORTH, Anna, of Hartford, m. Elisha **LOOMIS**, of Torrington, Nov. 14, 1804	21
[WALLEN], WALLIN, WALLING, James, m. Clarissa **JOHNSON**, Sept. 20, 1832, by Rev. Epaphras Goodman	116
Lucy, m. Ebenezer W. **BEACH**, b. of Torrington, Oct. 5, 1833, by Rev. Epaphras Goodman	119
WARD, Abigail, m. Hiram **LOOMIS**, b. of Torrington, Mar. 29, 1821, by Frederick Marsh	25
Abigail, m. Hiram **LOOMIS**, Mar. 29, 1821	52
Amanda, m. Gilman **HINSDALE**, Mar. 27, 1827	31
Amanda, m. Gilman **HINSDALE**, b. of Torrington, Mar. 27, 1827, by Rev. W. R. Gould. Int. Pub.	83
WARNER, Stephen C., of Nagatuc, m. Letitia **COMBS**, of Wolcottville, Sept. 2, 1841, by Samuel Day	126
WATERMAN, Pinus, m. Charlotta **FREEMAN**, b. of Torrington, Aug. 19, 1830, by Rev. Epaphras Goodman	87
WATSON, Melissent W., of Torrington, m. Augustus E. **BISSELL**, of Georgia, Feb. 29, 1836, by Rev. Epaphras Goodman	123

TORRINGTON VITAL RECORDS 59

	Page
WATTLES, Charles, s. Henry & Susanna, b. Jan. 6, 1825	67
Henry, m. Susanna **OSBORN**, Feb. 10, 1818	67
Mary J., d. Henry & Susanna, b. Feb. 14, 1819	67
Sarah, d. Henry & Susanna, b. May 10, 1831	67
William H., s. Henry & Susanna, b. Dec. 14, 1820	67
WAUGH, Cordelia S., of Torrington, m. Milo R. **CRANE**, of Sandisfield, Mass., Oct. 8, 1839, by Frederick Marsh	125
George R., of Torrington, m. Anne **WILLIAMS**, of New Britain, Apr. 6, 1845, by Frederick Marsh	129
WEBSTER, Elizabeth, m. John **HUNGERFORD**, Jr., Mar. 3, 1814	48
Elizabeth A., of Torringford, m. Orville **PERRY**, of New Haven, June 14, 1837, by Rev. Herman L. Vail	123
Martin, m. Pamela **NORTH**, Sept. 28, 1820, by Lyman Beecher	24
WEED, Julia M., of Harwinton, m. Henry O. **BOOGUE**, Sept. 8, 1845, in Wolcottville, by Rev. Henry Zell, of Wolcottville	132
Moses M., of Barkhamstead, m. Deborah S. **MALTBY**, of Torrington, Jan. 11, 1848, by Rev. William H. Moore	131
WEEKS, Jerusha, of Litchfield, m. Julius **BEACH**, of Torrington, Apr. 30, 1806	59
Sally, m. George **GOODWIN**, Apr. 10, 1832, by Rev. William R. Gould	115
WELLMAN, Samuel, of Bethleham, m. Nancy **McKENZIE**, of Torrington, Apr. 25, 1836, by Rev. H. P. Armes	122
WELLS, Merilla, m. Samuel C. **HUBBARD**, Apr. 6, 1846, by Thomas Benedict	130
WELTON, Charles, m. Sophia **LEACH**, b. of Torrington, Apr. 9, 1848, by Rev. George A. Hubbell	133
WERRELL, Artemesia, of Torrington, m. Joseph **SHAWS**, of South Lester, Aug. 15, 1832, by Rev. Daniel Miller	116
WEST, Prudence, m. Joel **LOOMIS**, May 23, 1792	79
WESTLAKE, Esther M., of Wolcottville, m. Joseph **ALLYN**, of Torrington, Apr. 21, 1845, by Rev. Samuel Day	129
WETMORE, Abel S., of Winchester, m. Lucy **HILL**, of Torrington, Nov. 24, 1829, by Rev. William R. Gould	85
Abigail, d. Seth & Lois, b. Mar. 27, 1787	107
Alphonso, s. Seth & Lois, b. Feb. 5, 1793	107
Artemisia, d. Seth & Lois, b. Nov. 7, 1789	107
Betsey, of Torrington, m. Jonathan **COE**, of Winsted, Nov. 30, 1848, by Rev. S. T. Seelye	134
Delia, d. John P. & Mariam, b. July 29, 1797	44
E. Lyman, m. Elizabeth **MILLER**, b. of Torrington, Sept. 3, 1795	44
Huldah A., of Torrington, m. Jonathan A. **ROSSETER**, of Harwinton, Apr. 18, 1844, by Rev. B. Emerson	128
John, of Torrington, m. Elizabeth **LEAMING**, of Middletown, May 29, 1757	107
John, s. Seth & Lois, b. Oct. 7, 1780	107
John, d. Aug. 27, 1795	107
John P., m. Marriam **DIBBLE**, Nov. 25, 1795	44
Larrin, m. Fanny **AUSTIN**, Sept. 12, 1828, by Rev. William R. Gould	85
Louisa, m. Phinehas **NORTH**, Oct. 10, 1832, by Rev. William R. Gould	116
Lyman, s. Lyman & Elizabeth, b. July 29, 1801	44
Lyman & Elizabeth, had child b. Apr. 3, 1803; d. Apr. 10, 1803	44
Maria, d. Lyman & Elizabeth, b. May 14, 1805	44
Maria, of Torrington, m. Asahel **COE**, of Waterbury, June 2, 1830, by Rev. William R. Gould	86
Mary, of Winchester, m. Abraham **LOOMIS**, of Torrington, Nov. 12, 1775	66
Nancy, d. Lyman & Elizabeth, b. July 17, 1796	44

60   BARBOUR COLLECTION

	Page
WETMORE, (cont.)	
Sally, m. Giles **WHITING**, Dec. 26, 1804	106
Salmon Brownson, s. Seth & Lois, b. Sept. 2, 1795	107
Seth, s. John & Elizabeth, b. Mar. 20, 1761	107
Seth, of Torrington, m. Lois **BRUNSON**, of Winchester, Dec. 9, 1779	107
Seth, s. Seth & Lois, b. Oct. 3, 1784	107
WHEADON, Esther, m. Preston **POND**, Apr. 27, 1814	31
WHEELER, Betsey, of Litchfield, m. Hiram W. **HUBBARD**, of Wolcottville, Mar. 30, 1845, by Rev. Samuel Day, of Wolcottville	129
Betsey A., m. Gilbert G. **WHEELER**, b. of Stonington, Sept. 26, 1839, by Rev. Gad N. Smith	124
Gilbert G., m. Betsey A. **WHEELER**, b. of Stonington, Sept. 26, 1839, by Rev. Gad N. Smith	124
Mary G., of Litchfield, m. Virgil **WILSON**, of Harwinton, Mar. 19, 1843, by Rev. Samuel Day, of Wolcottville	127
WHITE, Almira, of Torrington, m. Lewis **BEACH**, of Goshen, Feb. 27, 1831, by Isaac Jones, at Wolcottville	87
Ann Eliza, of Torrington, m. William **PARMELE**, of Goshen, Mar. 22, 1824, by Rev. Joseph Harvey, of Goshen	56
Anna Eliza, d. Thomas & Jedidah, b. Oct. 30, 1803	61-2
Calvin, s. Dan & Ravene*, b. July 6, 1786 *("Roena")	108
Dan, m. Roena **WILSON**, b. of Torrington, Apr. 6, 1786	102
Dan, m. Ravene **WILSON**, b. of Torrington, Apr. 6, 1786	108
Fanny, of Torrington, m. Herman **NORTHROP**, of Winsted, Sept. 24, 1827, by Rev. William R. Gould. Int. Pub.	84
Hiram Jacob, s. Thomas & Jedidah, b. July 26, 1802	61-2
James B., of Winchester, m. Sally **HURLBUT**, of Torrington, Sept. 20, 1831, by Daniel Coe	87
Merrell, m. Roxy M. **LEACH**, Sept. 23, 1834, by H. P. Armes	120
Merret S., of Canaan, m. Eliza A. **MASTERS**, of Torringford, July 18, 1839, by Rev. Herman L. Vaill	124
Roderick A., of Simsbury, m. Elizabeth W. **HUNGERFORD**, of Wolcottville, Nov. 6, 1844, by Rev. Samuel Day	129
WHITING, WHITEING, Abner, s. John & Silvey, b. May 24, 1779	105
Aurilla*, d. Harvey & Olive, b. July 28, 1795 *("Amelia" in Orcutt's book)	105
Benjamin, of Torrington, m. Esther **MERCUM***, of Wallingford, Oct. 14, 1755 *("Merriman" in Orcutt's book)	106
Benjamin, s. Benjamin & Esther, b. Dec. 11, 1765	106
Billy, s. William & Lucinda, b. Jan. 9, 1794	110
Candace, d. Harvey & Olive, b. Dec. 4, 1792	105
Christopher, s. Benjamin & Esther, b. Aug. 3, 1757	106
Cicero Lewis, s. Giles & Sally, b. Apr. 23, 1807	106
Clarinda, d. Rachel Ray, b. Sept. 23, 1806	7
Esther, d. Benjamin & Esther, b. Sept. 13, 1763	106
Esther, m. John **NASH**, b. of Torrington, Jan. 17, 1783	79
Florilla, d. Giles & Sarah, b. May 31, 1796	106
Frederick Parmelee, s. William & Lucinda, b. Feb. 18, 1800	110
Giles, s. John & Sarah, b. Jan. 8, 1771	105
Giles, m. Sarah **MARSHAL**, b. of Torrington, May 30, 1791	106
Giles, m. Sally **WETMORE**, Dec. 26, 1804	106
Harriet, d. Giles & Sarah, b. May 29, 1800	106
Harriet, of Torrington, m. Hiram **GRISWOLD**, of Goshen, Nov. 29, 1820, by Joseph Harvey	25

	Page
WHITING, WHITEING, (cont.)	
Harvey, s. John & Sarah, b. Oct. 27, 1760	105
Harvey, m. Olive **BARBER**, b. of Torrington, Sept. 5, 1790	105
Ira, s. John & Silvey, b. Nov. 28, 1780	105
James, m. Amelia **ALLYN**, b. of Torrington, Apr. 16, 1828, by Rev. William R. Gould	85
James Foster, twin with Nancy, s. Giles & Sarah, b. Aug. 10, 1798	106
Jesse, s. John & Sarah, b. Feb. 4, 1763	105
Jesse, m. Hannah **SMITH**, b. of Torrington, Sept. 30, 1784	105
John, of Torrington, m. Sarah **FOSTER**, of Wallingford, Jan. 18, 1749/50	105
John, s. John & Sarah, b. July 24, 1758	105
John, Jr., m. Silvey **LOOMIS**, b. of Torrington, Mar. 23, 1779	105
John, of Colebrook, m. Mrs. Rachel **LOOMIS**, of Torrington, Jan. 3, 1827, by Rev. William R. Judd	83
John Newton, s. Frederick P. & Mary Ann, b. July 28, 1827	110
Josiah, s. John & Sarah, b. Aug. 15, 1752	105
Julius, s. Jesse & Hannah, b. Dec. 31, 1784	105
Louisa, m. Gerry **GRANT**, b. of Torrington, Nov. 2, 1825, by Rev. Alexander Gillett	81
Louisa, [d. Frederick P. & Mary Ann], b. Feb. 23, 1836	110
Lucia, d. Giles & Sarah, b. Oct. 21, 1792	106
Lucia W., of Torrington, m. Richard **GUIGALL**, of Norfolk, Apr. 3, 1848, by Rev. John A. McKinstry	133
Lucian N., [s. Frederick P. & Mary Ann], b. Nov. 15, 1840	110
Lucresia, d. William & Lucinda, b. Dec. 18, 1801	110
Marcia, d. Harvey & Olive, b. Dec. 15, 1790	105
Marcus, s. Giles & Sarah, b. Feb. 9, 1794	106
Mary, d. John & Sarah, b. July 10, 1754	105
Melinda B., of Torrington, m. Jerome B. Woodruff, of Litchfield, Sept. 5, 1836, by Milton Huxley	123
Nancy, twin with James Foster, d. Giles & Sarah, b. Aug. 10, 1798	106
Nancy, m. Norman **COE**, Aug. 26, 1827, by Rev. William R. Gould. Int. Pub.	84
Orphela, d. Giles & Sarah, b. July 8, 1791	106
Rebeckah, d. John & Sarah, b. Dec. 6, 1756	105
Rebeckah, m. Elkanah **HODGES**, b. of Torrington, Mar. 26, 1778	48
Rebecca, m. Henry **ALLEN**, b. of Torrington, Feb. 17, 1824, by Rev. Epaphras Goodman	56
Reuby, d. Giles & Sarah, b. Mar. 28, 1802	106
Roxy, d. Frederick P. [& Mary Ann], b. Apr. 3, 1830	110
Sarah, d. John & Sarah, b. Dec. 1, 1750	105
Sarah, d. Seth & Tryphena, b. July 18, 1790	105
Sarah, w. Giles, d. Aug. 5, 1803, in the 35th y. of her age	106
Selah, s. William & Lucinda, b. Feb. 13, 1786	110
Seth, s. John & Sarah, b. Sept. 25, 1765	105
Seth, m. Tryphena **LOOMIS**, b. of Torrington, Apr. 16, 1789	105
Uri, s. William & Lucinda, b. Aug. 6, 1788	110
William, s. Benjamin & Esther, b. Sept. 4, 1759	106
William, of Torrington, m. Lucinda **SOPER**, of New Hartford, Mar. 9, 1784	110
WHITNEY, Eliza, m. Marain **BARBER**, Feb. 16, 1832, by Rev. William R. Gould	115
Jonathan, of Granville, Mass., m. Maria **MOORE**, of Torrington, Sept. 19, 1827, by Rev. Epaphras Goodman	84
WILCOX, WILLCOX, Abiather, s. Asahel & Mary, b. Mar. 31, 1771	107

	Page
WILCOX, WILLCOX, (cont.)	
Abiather, s. Asahel & Mary, d. Apr. 18, 1774	107
Abiather, s. Asahel & Mary, b. Aug. 24, 1777	107
Albert B., of Bristol, m. Mary **MUNSON**, of Torrington, May 31, 1832, by Rev. William R. Gould	115
Asahel, s. Asahel & Mary, b. Mar. [ ], 1773	107
Asenath, d. Asahel & Mary, b. Sept. 3, 1775	107
Clarinda, of Litchfield, m. Lorenzo E. **GORE**, Oct. 12, 1846, by Rev. Henry Zell, of Wolcottville	132
Ebenezer, s. Asahel & Mary, b. Dec. 6, 1779	107
Edmond, s. Asahel & Mary, b. Aug. 4, 1789	107
Emeline, d. Miles & Jerusha, b. Nov. 17, 1808	17
Huldah, d. Asahel & Mary, b. Dec. 23, 1766	107
Huldah, had d. Elizabeth **MOREHOUSE**, b. Jan. 25, 1788	78
Huldah, late of Torrington, now of Goshen, m. Archobel **HARWINTON**, of Goshen, Jan. 28, 1792	43
John S., of Torrington, m. Chloe S. **STRICKLAND**, of Warren, [ ] 27, 1849, by Rev. S. T. Seelye	135
Luther, s. Asahel & Mary, b. Dec. 15, 1764	107
Mary, d. Asahel & Mary, b. May 7, 1769	107
Mary Ann, of Torrington, m. John H. **CHURCH**, of Bethlem, Dec. 4, 1823, by Rev. Epaphras Goodman	56
Miles, s. Asahel & Mary, b. Mar. 8, 1787	107
Miles, m. Jerusha **BANCROFT**, b. of Torrington, Oct. 22, 1807	17
Obediah, s. Asahel & Mary, b. Dec. 23, 1781	107
Sarah, d. Asahel & Mary, b. Dec. 8, 1762	107
Wait B., m. Caroline G. **BIRGE**, b. of Torrington, Oct. 3, 1832, by Rev. Milton Huxley	117
William, s. Asahel & Mary, b. July 21, 1784	107
William, s. Asahel & Mary, d. Apr. 8, 1797	107
WILLEY, Almira Ann, m. Joseph Catlin **HALL**, Oct. 24, 1830, at Wolcottville, by Rev. Isaac Jones, of Litchfield	87
Flora, of Torrington, m. Rial **JOHNSON**, of Harwinton, Oct. 25, 1831, by Alexander Gillett	26
Jonathan, m. Irena **HEYDON**, Oct. 2, 1828, by Rev. William R. Gould	85
Mary, of Torringford, m. Luther **EMMONS**, of Cornwall, Oct. 19, 1829, by William R. Gould	86
WILLIAMS, Anne, of New Britain, m. George R. **WAUGH**, of Torrington, Apr. 6, 1845, by Frederick Marsh	129
David, of Colchester, m. Rhoda **BEBEE**, of East Haddam, Jan. 31, 1790	113
David, s. David & Rhoda, b. May 13, 1796	113
Dorrance, s. David & Rhoda, b. Sept. 22, 1798	113
Huldah, d. John & Abigail, b. Nov. 10, 1780	108
John, a regular, m. Abigail **COWLES**, b. of Torrington, June 20, 1780	108
Matilda, d. David & Rhoda, b. May 24, 1793	113
Menoris, s. David & Rhoda, b. July 1, 1791	113
WILSON, WILLSON, Abiel, s. Noah & Ann, b. Dec. 16, 1748	102
Abiel, s. Noah & Ann, d. Oct. 4, 1749	102
Abijah, s. Noah & Ann, b. Dec. 18, 1746	102
Abijah, m. Margaret **BEACH**, b. of Torrington, Oct. 5, 1767	103
Abijah, Jr., s. Abijah & Margaret, b. June 8, 1779	103
Abner Marshall, of Vernon, N.Y., m. Mary Lord **SCOVILLE**, of Wolcottville, Apr. 4, 1847, at the house of Col. Foot, by [Rev. Henry	

TORRINGTON VITAL RECORDS 63

	Page
WILSON, WILLSON, (cont.)	
Zell, of Wolcottville]	132
Addison N., of Harwinton, m. Harriet S. **GRISWOLD**, of Torringford, June 30, 1841, by Samuel Day	126
Almira, of Torrington, m. Morgan **DUDLEY**, of Winchester, May 3, 1834, by Rev. Epaphras Goodman	120
Amos, m. Zerviah **GRANT**, b. of Torrington, Oct. 26, 1752	104
Amos, Capt., m. Damaries **BALEY**, b. of Torrington, Aug. 19, 1777	104
Amos, s. Capt. Amos & Damaris, b. Aug. 14, 1778	104
Amos, Jr., of Torrington, m. Sabra **GRISWOLD**, of Winchester, Mar. 25, 1801	15
Amos, m. Elizabeth **BIRGE**, b. of Torrington, Dec. 13, 1820, by Samuel J. Mills	25
Ann, d. Noah & Ann, b. Apr. 6, 1741	102
Ann, d. Noah & Ann, d. June 14, 1741	102
Ann, d. Noah & Ann, b. Oct. 28, 1751	102
Ann, had d. Edee, b. Jan. 1, 1768; d. Feb. 13, 1768 & Clymeney, b. Oct. 17, 1770	102
Ann, m. Joseph **TAYLOR**, b. of Torrington, Aug. 31, 1775	98
Armira, d. Roger & Hannah, b. Mar. 15, 1780	109
Aurelia, d. Roger & Hannah, b. Mar. 6, 1802	109
Charlotte, d. Noah & Hannah, b. Aug. 26, 1764	102
Clymeney, d. Ann, b. Oct. 17, 1770	102
Crasscendey, d. Noah & Hannah, b. Mar. 28, 1771	102
Damaris, w. Capt. Amos, d. Jan. 22, 1792	104
Darius, m. Clarissa **TREADWAY**, b. of Torrington, Oct. 2, 1821, by Frederick Marsh	26
Edee, d. Noah & Ann, b. Jan. 4, 1744/5	102
Edee, d. Noah & Ann, d. Apr. 11, 1746	102
Edee, d. Ann, b. Jan. 1, 1768; d. Feb. 13, 1768	102
Elizabeth, of Torringford, m. Joseph Charles **LeGUETT**, of Winchester, May 1, 1842, by Rev. B. Emerson	126
Harmon, s. Amos & Sabra, b. Sept. 12, 1802	15
Harriet, d. Amos & Sabra, b. Dec. 27, 1804	15
Harriet, m. Samuel **THRALL**, b. of Torrington, May 9, 1822, by Alexander Gillett	26
Harry, s. Roger & Hannah, b. Nov. 12, 1795	109
Heman, s. Roger & Hannah, b. May 24, 1783	109
Huldah, d. William & Martha, b. Jan. 31, 1784	109
Jerusha, d. Noah & Ann, b. Aug. 16, 1758	102
Jerusha, m. John **BROKER***, b. of Torrington, Feb. 18, 1783	
*("**BROOKER**")	7
Josiah, s. Roger & Hannah, b. July 1, 1794	109
Lathrop, s. Roger & Hannah, b. May 31, 1800	109
Lenard, s. Roger & Hannah, b. Apr. 23, 1791	109
Lois, m. Julius **DAILY**, Aug. 9, 1832, by Rev. William R. Gould	116
Martha, m. Reuben **BURR**, Aug. 20, 1794	6
Martha, m. John W. **SCOVILLE**, Oct. 17, 1832, by Rev. William R. Gould	116
Mary, of Windsor, m. Joseph **TANTER**, of Torrington, Sept. 19, 1771	97
Mary, of Torrington, m. Benham **BARBER**, of Harwinton, Dec. 27, 1832, by Rev. H. P. Armes	117
Noah, s. Noah & Ann, b. Sept. 13, 1742	102
Noah, s. Noah, m. Hannah **YOUNGS**, b. of Torrington, Nov. 24, 1764	102

	Page
WILSON, WILLSON, (cont.)	
Norman, s. Roger & Hannah, b. July 19, 1785	109
Orel, d. Abijah & Margaret, b. Jan. 5, 1777	103
Parlaman, s. Roger & Hannah, b. Aug. 15, 1797	109
Rachel, m. John **COOK**, b. of Windsor, June 22, 1741	11
Ravene, m. Dan **WHITE**, b. of Torrington, Apr. 6, 1786	108
Rhoda, d. Amos & Zerviah, b. Nov. 5, 1768	104
Roena, m. Dan **WHITE**, b. of Torrington, Apr. 6, 1786	102
Roger, s. Amos & Zerviah, b. Aug. 2, 1756	104
Roger, m. Hannah **MARSHALL**, b. of Torrington, Jan. 23, 1780	109
Rowlan, s. Roger & Hannah, b. Sept. 25, 1781	109
Rowland, of Torrington, m. Polly **MOORE**, of Winchester, Oct. 24, 1806	60
Roxelany, d. Roger & Hannah, b. Sept. 29, 1792	109
Rozel, s. Amos & Zerviah, b. Oct. 1, 1758	104
Rozel, s. Amos & Zerviah, d. Nov. 2, 1758	104
Rozel, s. Amos & Zerviah, b. May 14, 1765	104
Reuby, d. Roger & Hannah, b. Jan. 17, 1790	109
Ruth, d. Amos & Zerviah, b. Dec. 17, 1754	104
Ruth, m. Isaiah **TUTTLE**, b. of Torrington, May 22, 1774	97
Rynnol, s. Abijah & Margaret, b. June 18, 1774	103
Solomon, s. Abijah & Margaret, b. Feb. 8, 1772	103
Solomon, s. Abijah & Margaret, d. Nov. 26, 1775	103
Virgil, of Harwinton, m. Mary G. **WHEELER**, of Litchfield, Mar. 19, 1843, by Rev. Samuel Day, of Wolcottville	127
William, s. Amos & Zerviah, b. Oct. 31, 1753	104
William, s. Amos & Zerviah, d. June 1, 1754	104
William, s. Noah & Ann, b. Sept. 14, 1754	102
William, m. Martha **BEACH**, b. of Torrington, Aug. 6, 1783	109
William, s. William & Martha, b. July 24, 1785	109
William, s. William & Martha, d. Sept. 19, 1786	109
William B., m. Austin **TALMADGE**, b. of Torrington, [Aug. 18, 1833], by Rev. Epaphras Goodman	118
Zenas, s. Abijah & Margaret, b. Jan. 22, 1768; d. Apr. 15, 1769	103
Zenas, s. Abijah & Margaret, b. Apr. 11, 1769	103
Zerviah, w. Amos, d. May 3, 1776	104
[WINCHELL], WINCHEL, Bethyah, m. John **COOK**, b. of Torrington, Feb. 2, 1779	14
Daniel, m. Martha **BISSELL**, b. of Torrington, June 15, 1779	113
Daniel, s. Daniel & Martha, b. May 20, 1788	113
David, s. Daniel & Martha, b. July 4, 1791	113
Ebenezer, d. Jan. 2, 1778	113
Harriet, d. Daniel & Martha, b. Nov. 30, 1783	113
Hiram, m. Olive **GOODWIN**, b. of Torrington, Oct. 5, 1825, by Rev. Epaphras Goodman	81
Oliver, s. Daniel & Martha, b. Jan. 31, 1786	113
Thankful, d. Daniel & Martha, b. Oct. 20, 1781	113
WINSHIP, Cornelius A., of Litchfield, m. Helen A. **KIMBERLEY**, of Wolcottville, Sept. 19, 1847, by Rev. S. T. Seelye	131
WOLCOTT, Abigail, twin with Guy, d. Guy & Abigail, b. July 2, 1785	13
Allyn, s. Guy & Abigail, b. Mar. 12, 1809	13
Almira, d. Guy & Abigail, b. May 26, 1799	13
Amanda, d. Guy & Abigail, b. Nov. 15, 1802	13
Anna, d. Guy & Abigail, b. May 16, 1797	13

	Page
WOLCOTT, (cont.)	
Elezur, s. Guy & Abigail, b. July 17, 1792	13
Ephraim W., m. Rhoda **LEACH**, b. of Torrington, May 10, 1824, by Rev. Epaphras Goodman	56
Frederick, s. Guy & Abigail, b. Jan. 13, 1795	13
George, s. Guy & Abigail, b. July 26, 1805	13
Guy, b. Aug. 7, 1760, at Windsor, now of Torrington; m. Abigail **ALLEN**, of Windsor, Oct. 5, 1781	13
Guy, twin with Abigail, d. Guy & Abigail, b. July 2, 1785	13
Guy, s. Guy & Abigail, b. Oct. 15, 1787	13
James, s. Guy & Abigail, b. Nov. 3, 1789	13
WOODING, Adaline, of Torrington, m. Augustus **MERRILL**, of New Hartford, Nov. 3, 1846, by J. A. McKinstry	130
Edmund, of Bristol, m. Maria Ann **BROOKS**, of Wolcottville, Sept. 11, 1842, by Rev. Samuel Day, of Wolcottville	127
WOODRUFF, Jerome B., of Litchfield, m. Melinda B. **WHITING**, of Torrington, Sept. 5, 1836, by Milton Huxley	123
John C., of New Hartford, m. Marilla **CLARK**, of Winchester, Jan. 12, 1847, by Rev. S. T. Seelye	131
Sarah, m. George **BISSELL**, Oct. 26, 1823, by Rev. Joseph Harvey, of Goshen	56
Sterling, of Torrington, m. Minerva S. **BRADLEY**, of Cornwall, Sept. 1, 1834, by Rev. Milton Huxley	120
WOODWARD, Charles, s. Samuel & Mary, b. Aug. 16, 1798	9
Elijah, s. Samuel & Mary, b. Apr. 25, 1789	9
Elijah, s. Samuel & Mary, d. Jan. 8, 1817	9
Griswold, s. Samuel & Mary, b. Feb. 3, 1791	9
Harry, s. Samuel & Mary, b. May 26, 1795	9
Laura, d. Samuel & Mary, b. June 29, 1785	9
Laura, d. Samuel & Mary, d. Dec. 5, 1801	9
Laura, of Torrington, m. Truman A. **CURTIS**, of New Hartford, Mar. 18, 1840, by Rev. Herman L. Vaill	125
Mary, d. Samuel & Mary, b. Sept. 20, 1783	9
Mary, m. John **GILLETT**, Jr., Feb. 2, 1824	43
Mary, m. John **GILLETT**, Jr., b. of Torrington, Feb. 2, 1824, by Rev. Epaphras Goodman	56
Mary, [w. Samuel], d. Mar. 28, 1834	9
Rufus, s. Samuel & Mary, b. July 16, 1793	9
Rufus, s. Samuel & Mary, d. Nov. 24, 1823	9
Samuel, b. Nov. 8, 1750, at Watertown; m. Mary **GRISWOLD**, Feb. 10, 1782	9
Samuel, Dr., d. Jan. 26, 1835	9
Samuel Bord, s. Samuel & Mary, b. June 11, 1787	9
WOOSTER, Joseph, of Goshen, m. Adah **ROBERTS**, of Torrington, Oct. 20, 1841, by Rev. Brown Emerson	126
WRIGHT, Huldah, d. Timothy, decd. of Berkamstead & Tryphena, b. Oct. 19, 1800, in Berkamstead	63
Zenas, of Plainfield, N.Y., m. Malinda **BEACH**, of Torrington, Nov. 21, 1811, by Rev. Mr. Gilbert	6
YALE, Huldah, m. Elihu **COOK**, b. of Torrington, June 6, 1787	18
YOUNGS, Ann, m. Ebenezer **LYMAN**, b. of Torrington, [ ]	63
Hannah, m. Noah **WILLSON**, s. Noah, b. of Torrington, Nov. 24, 1764	102

UNION VITAL RECORDS
1734 - 1850

	Vol.	Page
ABBE, Eleazer, of Mansfield, m. Mrs. Lydia **OSGOOD**, of Stafford, Feb. 16, 1801, by Sol[omo]n Wales, J.P.	TM	14
Elizabeth, m. Jesse **WARD**, May 22, 17[ ]	2LR	295
ABBOTT, C[h]loe, d. Samuel & Elizabeth, b. Feb. 15, 1770	2LR	269
Hannah, m. John **HENDRICK**, Mar. 24, 1761	2LR	295
Margaret, wid., d. Jan. 11, 1806	1-D	1
Samuel, m. Rachel **WARD**, b. of Union, Jan. 11, 1770	2LR	290
Sarah, m. Jonathan **BIRK**, Nov. 11, 1754	2LR	295
Sarah, of Woodstock, m. Jonas **HAUGHTON**, of Union, Nov. 24, 1768	2LR	290
ADAMS, Mary, m. Leicester **FULLER**, b. of Barre, Oct. 22, 1834, by Rev. Stephen Fairbanks	1-M	27
Morey, of Bolton, Mass., m. Calista **MOORE**, of Union, Jan. 1, 1828, by Neh[emiah] B. Beardsley	1-M	1
AGARD, Isaac, of Stafford, m. Sarah Ann **FAIRBANKS**, of Union, July 25, 1838, by Rev. Erastus Benton, of Eastford	1-M	67
Lucius, of Stafford, m. Mary M. **CORBIN**, of Union, Feb. 13, 1854, by Rev. Samuel J. Curtice	1-M	90
ALDRICH, Edward, of Thompson, m. Adelia **COMSTOCK**, of Union, Feb. 22, 1830, by Rev. Ira M. Bidwell	1-M	1
ALLEN, Betsey, of Sturbridge, m. Gideon **WALES**, of Union, Oct. 30, 1800, by Sol[omo]n Wales, J.P.	TM	12
Betty, of Sturbridge, m. Gideon **WALES**, of Union, Oct. 30, 1800	1-M	23
Elisha, s. William & Sybble, b. May 13, 1761	2LR	294
Philip, of Ashford, m. Mrs. Lucinda **BUGBEE**, of Union, Nov. 26, 1801, by Sol[omo]n Wales, J.P.	TM	14
Smith Bates, s. William French & Polly, b. Sept. 23, 1815	1-B	26
AMES, [see also **EAMES**], Jerusha, m. Hezekiah **WALKER**, Nov. 23, 1767	2LR	290
Phebe, Mrs., of Union, m. Warham **MASON**, of Sturbridge, Oct. 24, 1792, by Sol[omo]n Wales, J.P.	TM	4
AMIDOWN, AMIDON, Gardner, s. Henry & Lidia, b. Nov. 8, 1797	1-B	1
Jonathan P., of Southbridge, m. Sally **MOORE**, of Union, June 17, 1824, by Nehemiah B. Beardsley	1-M	31
Joseph, of Southbridge, m. Mary M. **HAMMOND**, of Union, Dec. 7, 1826, by Neh[emiah] B. Beardsley	1-M	1
ANDERSON, Abigail Apama, d. Lester & Polly, d. May 21, 1841, ae 19 y.	1-D	1
Abner Howard, s. Lester & Polly, b. Sept. 16, 1818	1-B	26
Ira Willard, s. Lester & Polly, b. Mar. 16, 1824	1-B	83
Juliana, of Union, m. James **BUFFINGTON**, of Ashford, Sept. 12, 1824, by Neh[emiah] B. Beardsley	1-M	33
Leicester, of Ashford, m. Polly **HOWARD**, of Union, Aug. 3, 1817	1-M	1
Roxa Alice, d. Lester & Polly, b. July 14, 1826	1-B	83
Thomas Asbury Philander, s. Lester & Polly, b. Aug. 14, 1830	1-B	43
ANDRESS, Mary L., m. Ebenezer **COLBURN**, b. of Stafford, Feb. 28,		

	Vol.	Page
ANDRESS, (cont.)		
1836, by Moses C. Sessions, J.P.	1-M	43
ANTHONY, Paul, of Sturbridge, m. Mrs. Levine **HOOD**, of Leicister, June 24, 1802, by Sol[omo]n Wales, J.P.	TM	15
ARMOUR, Almira, d. John & Sarah, b. May 14, 1801	1-B	26
Almira, d. Orinda **SESSIONS**, b. Dec. 26, 1811	1-B	72
Arnold, s. James & Eunice, b. July 17, 1791	1-B	1
Charles, s. James & Eunice, b. July 12, 1787	1-B	1
Danforth, s. John & Sarah, b. Jan. 5, 1799	1-B	26
Dolly, d. John & Sarah, b. Oct. 24, 1796	1-B	26
Eunice, b. July 12, 1755	1-B	1
Ire, s. James & Eunice, b. Mar. 28, 1789	1-B	1
James, s. James & Marg[a]ret, b. Apr. 1, 1756	2LR	289
James, Jr., b. Apr. 4, 1756	1-B	1
James, Jr., m. Eunice **ARNOLD**, b. of Union, Oct. 18, 1776	1-M	1
James, Jr., s. James & Eunice, b. Dec. 26, 1778	1-B	1
Joan, d. James & Marg[a]ret, b. Mar. 2, 1758	2LR	289
John, s. James & Eunice, b. May 12, 1783; d. Aug. 3, 1793	1-B	1
John, s. John & Sarah, b. June 5, 1807	1-B	26
Laura, d. John & Sarah, b. June 20, 1811. Recorded Aug. 16, 1843	1-B	83
Lyman, s. James & Eunice, b. Jan. 24, 1781	1-B	1
Lyman, s. John & Sarah, b. Apr. 23, 1803	1-B	26
Maria, d. James & Eunice, b. July 2, 1801	1-B	26
Martha, d. James & Marg[a]ret, b. July 16, 1760	2LR	293
Martha, of Bennington, m. Job **RANSOM**, of Colrain, Aug. [ ], 1784, by Sol[omo]n Wales, J.P.	TM	1
Mary, d. James & Marg[a]ret, b. June 1, 1754	2LR	289
Patty, d. John & Sarah, b. Nov. 22, 1794	1-B	26
Polly, m. Chauncey **PAUL**, b. of Union, Sept. 17, 1820, by Ingoldsby W. Crawford, J.P.	1-M	16
Preston, s. John & Sarah, b. Aug. 15, 1793	1-B	26
Preston, s. Alice **GLEAZIER**, b. Jan. 20, 1820	1-B	83
Preston, s. Alice **GLAZURE**, d. Feb. 20, 1827	1-D	1
Sally, d. James & Eunice, b. Mar. 19, 1777	1-B	1
Samuel, s. James & Eunice, b. Oct. 8, 1794	1-B	1
Sarah, of Union, m. Charles **MARTIN**, of Woodstock, June 24, 1804	1-M	13
Volney, s. John & Sarah, b. June 11, 1805	1-B	26
William, s. James & Eunice, b. June 24, 1784	1-B	1
ARMSTRONG, Susannah, m. Samuel **CODY**, b. of Union, June 6, 1782	1-M	3
ARNLEY, Nathan, m. Frances P. **ROBBINS**, Jan. 9, 1845, by Rev. Samuel J. Curtiss	1-M	75
ARNOLD, Eunice, m. James **ARMOUR**, Jr., b. of Union, Oct. 18, 1776	1-M	1
Rebeckah, d. Lowdon & Lucy, b. Nov. 1, 1798	1-B	1
BABCOCK, Luke, s. Rev. Caleb & Sarah, b. Apr. 29, 1752	2LR	288
BACK, Lucius, of Holland, Mass., m. Sophia **MOORE**, of Union, Jan. 27, 1835, by Rev. Abial Williams	1-M	50
Tryphenia A , of Holland, m. John W. **MOORE**, of Union, June 12, 1826, by Neh[emiah] B. Beardsley	1-M	32
BACKUS, Aaron, s. Josiah & Elizabeth, b. Jan. 11, 1798	1-B	76
Abigail, d. Josiah & Elizabeth, b. Apr. 28, 1800	1-B	76
Diana, d. Josiah & Elizabeth, b. Feb. 11, 1796	1-B	75
Elizabeth, d. Josiah & Elizabeth, b. Jan. 20, 1794	1-B	75

	Vol.	Page
BACKUS, (cont.)		
Johannah, d. Josiah & Elizabeth, b. June 16, 1803	1-B	76
Josiah, s. Josiah & Elizabeth, b. Nov. 6, 1791	1-B	2
Josiah, Jr., s. Josiah & Elizabeth, b. Nov. 6, 1791	1-B	75
BADGER, Abigail, d. Daniel, Jr. & Elizabeth, b. Mar. 10, 1747	2LR	287
Abigail, d. Daniel, Jr. & Elizabeth, b. Mar. 10, 1746/7	2LR	287
Abner, m. Mrs. Phebe **HOWARD**, b. of Union, Nov. 26, 1801, by Sol[omo]n Wales, J.P.	TM	13
Asher, of Union, m. Mrs. Polly **GOODHILL**, of Holland, Aug. 22, 1796, by Sol[omo]n Wales, J.P.	TM	7
Augusta, d. Asher & Polly, b. Jan. 28, 1798	1-B	75
Daniel, s. Daniel & Phillippi, b. Aug. 2, 1748	2LR	287
Daniel, Capt., d. Feb. 22, 1769	2LR	270
Daniel, Jr., m. Eward **WALKER**, b. of Union, Oct. 5, 1769	2LR	290
Diantha, d. Asher & Polly, b. Feb. 28, 1807	1-B	75
Dwight, s. Asher & Polly, b. Apr. 5, 1803	1-B	75
Elisha, s. Daniel, Jr. & Phillippi, b. Feb. 3, 1749/50	2LR	288
Elisha, of Union, m. Susannah **CHAPPELL**, of Norwich, July 20, 1769	2LR	290
Elizabeth, m. Archible **COY**, Dec. 25, 1760	2LR	295
Gideon, m. Mary **DODGE**, Dec. 19, 1754	2LR	295
Gideon, s. Daniel & Phillippe, b. Feb. 24, 1765	2LR	267
Giles, m. Olive **SPRAGE**, Jan. 7, 1790, by Sol[omo]n Wales, J.P.	TM	2
Hamilton, s. Asher & Polly, b. Apr. 15, 1811	1-B	75
Ichabod, d. Mar. 26, 1892, at Southbridge, Mass.	1-D	1a
Irena, d. Jeremiah & Zerviah, b. Sept. 9, 1767	2LR	268
Jeremiah, m. Zerviah **PEAK**, Jan. 15, 1767	2LR	290
Jonathan, s. Samuel & Patience, d. Jan. 25, 1757	2LR	291
Joshua, s. David & Ann, b. June 1, 1751	2LR	269
Josiah, s. Daniel, Jr. & Phillippi, b. Aug. 25, 1751	2LR	288
Lorin, s. Asher & Polly, b. Mar. 12, 1809	1-B	75
Lydia, d. Enoch & Mary, b. July 17, 1746	2LR	287
Lidia, d. Gideon & Mary, b. Sept. 15, 1755	2LR	292
Marvin, s. Willard & Tabitha, b. Feb. 10, 1795	1-B	2
Mary, d. Daniel & Phillippe, b. May 20, 1762	2LR	294
Melenda, d. Jeremiah & Zerviah, b. June [ ], 1788	1-B	27
Patience, wid., d. Sept. 28, 1793	1-D	2
Phillippe, d. Daniel, Jr. & Phillippe, b. Mar. 2, 1768	2LR	268
Ransom, s. Asher & Polly, b. Apr. 5, 1814	1-B	75
Rocksey, d. Asher & Polly, b. Dec. 13, 1796	1-B	75
Ruth, d. Daniel, Jr. & Phillippi, b. Feb. 22, 1760	2LR	293
Samantha, d. Asher & Polly, b. Mar. 1, 1805	1-B	75
Sarah, d. David & Ann, b. Oct. 10, 1746	2LR	292
Sarah, of Union, m. Royal **JEN[N]INGS**, of Ashford, Dec. 20, 1749	2LR	295
Winthrop, s. Asher & Polly, b. Sept. 28, 1801	1-B	75
BAILEY, Cyrus, m. Sarah **SPRAGE**, July 20, 1797, by Sol[omo]n Wales, J.P.	TM	9
BAKER, Davis, of Southbridge, Mass., m. Ann M. **FAULKNER**, of Conn., Sept. 3, 1851, by Rev. D. P. Livermore	1-M	81
BALLARD, Hooker, of Westmoreland, m. Mrs. Abigail **THOMPSON**, of Brimfield, Sept. 30, 1793, by Sol[omo]n Wales, J.P.	TM	5
BARNES, John, m. Mary Ann **GILBERT**, May 19, 1836, by Ebenezer Lindsey, J.P.	1-M	61

BARBOUR COLLECTION

	Vol.	Page
BARNET, Jacob, of Lime, m. Esther WALES, of Union, Nov. 8, 1791, by Sol[omo]n Wales, J.P.	TM	3
BARRY, James, of New Salem, m. Harriet B. ROBINSON, of Barre, Aug. 17, 1833, by Augustus Moore, J.P.	1-M	49
BARTLETT, Elizabeth, w. Robert, d. Jan. 19, 1781	1-D	2
John S., of Ashford, m. Louisa MOORE, of Union, Nov. 27, 1834, by Rev. Abial Williams	1-M	50
Richard, d. Apr. 20, 1791	1-D	2
BASCOM, BOSCOMB, Alles, d. John & Sarah, b. Sept. 18, 1768	2LR	266
Daniel, m. Elizabeth WARD, Oct. 9, 1760	2LR	295
Elias, s. John & Sarah, b. May 4, 1764	2LR	267
John, m. Sarah BURLEY, June 9, 1763	2LR	290
Meriam, d. John & Sarah, b. May 12, 1766	2LR	268
Olive, d. Daniel & Elizabeth, b. July 15, 1761	2LR	294
Uriah, s. Daniel & Elizabeth, b. Apr. 9, 1764	2LR	267
BATCHELLOR, BATCHELDER, Bettee, d. Elijah & Elizabeth, b. June 3, 1769	2LR	266
Elizabeth, d. Elijah & Elizabeth, b. June 22, 1769	2LR	266
James, s. Nehemiah & Experience, b. July 29, 1759	2LR	266
BATES, Anna, d. Labon & Chloe, b. Apr. 30, 1807	1-B	51
David, d. Mar. 8, 1793	1-D	2
Nathaniel Sampon, s. Labon, Jr. & Chloe, b. Jan. 19, 1811	1-B	51
Osro(?), s. Labon, Jr. & Chloe, b. Apr. 30, 1813	1-B	70
Sally, d. Labon, & Chloe, b. Apr. 11, 1809	1-B	51
Smith, s. Labon, Jr. & Chloe, b. Jan. 30, 1805, at Pelham, Mass.	1-B	70
BEAL, Levi, m. Sally MOREY, Jan. 21, 1798, by Sol[omo]n Wales, J.P.	TM	9
BEAMAN, Abigail, m. Sylvanus NELSON, of South Brimfield, Jan. 30, 1803, by Sol[omo]n Wales, J.P., at his house	TM	16
BELCHER, Sally, Mrs., of Stafford, m. John PERRY, Apr. 25, 1802, by Sol[omo]n Wales, J.P.	TM	15
BELKNAP, Anna Fuller, d. Daniel & Margaret, d. Mar. 2, 1809	1-D	2
Chloe, d. Daniel W. & Margaret, b. Mar. 5, 1816	1-B	76
Chloe, d. Daniel & Margaret, b. Mar. 5, 1816	1-B	81
Daniel, m. Margaret WALKER, Feb. 19, 1807	1-M	2
Daniel Ozina, s. Daniel W. & Marg[ar]et, b. Nov. 8, 1821	1-B	85
Frank Sherman, s. Daniel W. & Barget*, b. Feb. 3, 1826 (*Margaret)	1-B	86
Lorin, s. Daniel & Margaret, b. Sept. 19, 1811	1-B	70
Lydia Walker, d. Daniel W. & Margaret, b. Aug. 25, 1818	1-B	76
Marg[ar]et, s. Daniel W. & Marg[ar]et, b. July 2, 1823	1-B	85
Moses Chester, s. Daniel W. & Marg[a]ret, b. June 13, 1828	1-B	45
Simon Walker, s. Daniel W. & Margaret, b. July 29, 1813	1-B	59
Simons Walker, s. Daniel & Margaret, b. July 29, 1813	1-B	70
Sophia Thazar, d. Daniel & Margaret, b. Jan. 18, 1810	1-B	70
BEN[N]ET, Royal, of Killingly, m. Mrs. Persis ELLENWOOD, of Brimfield, Apr. 22, 1802, by Sol[omo]n Wales, J.P.	TM	15
BENSON, Andrew, s. Lewis & Merah, b. May 17, 1819	1-B	70
BIRK, Jonathan, m. Sarah ABBOTT, Nov. 11, 1754	2LR	295
BISHOP, Benjamin, s. Jeremiah & Martha, b. Mar. 4, 1750	2LR	294
Eleazer, s. Jeremiah & Martha, b. Sept. 8, 1745	2LR	294
James, s. Jeremiah & Martha, d. Nov. 9, 1751	2LR	270
Joel, s. Jeremiah & Martha, b. June 4, 1743	2LR	294
Rhoda, d. Jeremiah & Martha, b. Jan. 31, 1747/8	2LR	288

UNION VITAL RECORDS 71

	Vol.	Page
BISHOP, (cont.)		
Seth, s. Jeremiah & Martha, b. July 30, 1754	2LR	294
BLANCHARD, BLANCHER, Chester, s. Jonathan & Sarah, b. Dec. 6, 1765	2LR	268
Jonathan, s. Jonathan & Sarah, b. Apr. 29, 1768	2LR	266
Jonathan, of Monson, m. Mrs. Ruth **LAWSON**, of Union, Oct. 6, 1828, by Neh[emiah] B. Beardsley	1-M	34
Lydia, d. Jonathan & Sarah, b. July 9, 1763	2LR	267
BLANDING, Eliza Ann, m. John **NILES**, July 3, 1842, by Moses C. Sessions, J.P.	1-M	57
BLISS, Lucy, Mrs., of Wilbraham, m. David **MUNGER**, of Union, June 25, 1800, by Sol[omo]n Wales, J.P.	TM	12
Lucy, of Wilbraham, m. David **MUNGER**, of Union, June 25, 1800	1-M	13
BLODGETT, Alden Willard, s. Willard & Almira, b. May 18, 1817, at Stafford. Recorded Oct. 17, 1838	1-B	108
Almira, Jr., d. Willard & Almira, b. June 5, 1826	1-B	86
Austin Abbott, s. Willard & Almira, d. Oct. 26, 1821	1-D	2
Hannah, d. Willard & Almira, b. Jan. 18, 1829	1-B	45
Levina, d. Willard & Almira, b. May 16, 1831	1-B	47
Minerva F., of Union, m. Perry L. **GOODELL**, of Sturbridge, Mass., July 3, 1845, by Rev. Samuel J. Curtiss	1-M	58
Minerva Flint, d. Willard & Almira, b. Nov. 18, 1818, at Stafford. Recorded Oct. 17, 1838	1-B	108
Patty, Mrs., m. Malachi **NICHOLS**, May 8, 1792, by Sol[omo]n Wales, J.P.	TM	3
R[e]uben, s. Willard & Almira, b. Nov. 16, 1822	1-B	85
Ruth, d. Willard & Almira, b. June 18, 1824	1-B	85
Ruth, m. Aureleas O. **CORBIN**, Mar. 29, 1848, by Rev. Samuel J. Curtiss	1-M	75
Sarah, d. Willard & Almira, b. Dec. 14, 1820	1-B	76
Walter Moore, s. Alden, Jr. & Parmela, b. Apr. 5, 1822	1-B	86
BOLES, Abigail, d. Lemuel & Lucy, b. Sept. 25, 1802	1-B	27
Abigail had s. Joseph Boles **ROODE**, b. Jan. 5, 1820	1-B	76
Abigail, m. Casper L. **LAWSON**, b. of Union, Sept. 25, 1831, by Rev. Stephen Fairbanks	1-M	47
David Ho[l]mes, s. Lemuel & Lucy, b. Aug. 14, 1800	1-B	27
Jedediah Morse, s. Lemuel & Lucy, b. Jan. 23, 1799	1-B	27
Lemuel, s. Lemuel & Lucy, b. Sept. 28, 1792	1-B	2
Leonard, s. Lemuel & Lucy, b. Aug. 27, 1796	1-B	27
Lucy, w. Lemuel, d. Feb. 2, 1805	1-D	2
Nathaniel, s. Lemuel & Lucy, b. Aug. 19, 1794	1-B	2
BOND, Eleanor, Mrs., of Holland, m. Elisha **TOWN**, of Sturbridge, Aug. 18, 1796, by Sol[omo]n Wales, J.P.	TM	9
William, m. Mrs. C[h]loe **BROWN**, of Westown, Mar. 16, 1801, by Sol[omo]n Wales, J.P.	TM	13
BOOTH, BOOTHE, Benjamin, s. Isaac & Deborah, b. May 17, 1768	2LR	266
Benjamin, s. Rebeckah Eames, b. July 28, 1793	1-B	2
Betsey, d. Isaac, Jr. & Elizabeth, b. July 7, 1792	1-B	2
Betsey, d. Isaac, Jr. & Elizabeth, d. Aug. 19, 1793	1-D	2
Elam, s. Isaac & Elizabeth, b. May 25, 1801	1-B	51
Henry, s. Isaac & Elizabeth, b. Oct. 22, 1798	1-B	51
Isaac, s. Isaac & Deborah, b. Dec. 14, 1765	2LR	268
Isaac, Jr., of Union, m. Elizabeth **FOSKET**, of Stafford, Nov. 4, 1790	1-M	2

72 BARBOUR COLLECTION

	Vol.	Page
BOOTH, BOOTHE, (cont.)		
Isaac, d. Jan. 13, 1798	1-D	2
Isaac B., m. Lydia C. **PHILLIPS**, b. of Union, Apr. 4, 1833, by Augustus Moore, J.P.	1-M	49
Isaac Billings, s. Isaac & Elizabeth, b. Feb. 3, 1805	1-B	51
Juliaett, d. Sullivan & Minerva, b. Nov. 7, 1841	1-B	70
Lydia, d. Isaac & Elizabeth, b. Feb. 11, 1791	1-B	51
Mary C., m. Anson **BUCKLAND**, Apr. 6, 1848, by Rev. Samuel J.* Curtiss (*handwritten correction to "I" on original manuscript)	1-M	75
Mary Elizabeth, d. Isaac Billings & Mary, b. Aug. 18, 1830	1-B	46
Melvine, s. Sullivan & Minerva, b. Nov. 17, 1839	1-B	52
Milo Sullivan, s. Sullivan & Minerva, b. Dec. 23, 1845	1-B	70
Rosett, d. Sullivan & Minerva, b. Oct. 12, 1843	1-B	70
Rosett, d. Sullivan & Minerva, b. Oct. 12, 1843	1-B	127
Samuel Chandler, s. Isaac, Jr. & Elizabeth, b. June 4, 1795	1-B	27
Sanford, s. Sullivan & Minerva, b. Apr. 14, 1838	1-B	108
Sarah, d. Isaac & Deborah, b. Apr. 15, 1770	2LR	266
Sullivan, s. Isa[a]c & Elizabeth, b. June 5, 1808. Recorded Nov. 9, 1831	1-B	45
Sullivan, m. Minerva **COYE**, b. of Union, Nov. 14, 1831, by Rev. Andrew R. Reed	1-M	49
Sullivan, d. Aug. 7, 1845	1-D	20
BOSCOMB, [see also **BASCOM**], Uriah, s. Daniel & Elizabeth, b. Apr. 9, 1764	2LR	267
BOSS, Luther, of Ashford, m. Betsey **HAWES**, of Union, Sept. 19, 1822, by William Foster, J.P.	1-M	2
BOSWORTH, Mary, Mrs., of Ashford, m. John **HOLMAN**, of Union, Apr. 6, 1809	1-M	8
BOWERS, Esek S., of Thompson, m. Tryphenia **RUSS**, of Ashford, [June] 4, [1826], by Luther Crawford, J.P.	1-M	34
John Sanford, s. Jerahmall & Rhoda, b. Aug. 13, 1818	1-B	84
Paris H., of Thompson, m. Orrilla **RUBY**, of Union, Mar. 14, 1824, by William Foster, J.P.	1-M	33
BOYDEN, Justus, of Sturbridge, m. Mrs. Molley **COY**, of Union, Mar. 10, 1800, by Sol[omo]n Wales, J.P.	TM	11
Polly, m. Gideon **WALES**, Jr., b. of Union, Jan. 19, 1830, by Neh[emiah] B. Beardsley	1-M	45
BRAYTON, Daniel, of Sturbridge, m. Almira **CONE**, of Ashford, Aug. 17, 1829, by Neh[emiah] B. Beardsley	1-M	34
BROUGHTON, Andrew, of Eastford, m. Julia A. **COOK**, of Union, May 21, 1854, by Rev. Samuel J. Curtiss	1-M	36
BROWN, Annis Maria, d. Othniel, Jr. & Annis, b. Sept. 24, 1826	1-B	86
Charles Pinckney, s. John & Lovina, b. Jan. 29, 1798	1-B	27
C[h]loe, Mrs., of Westown, m. William **BOND**, Mar. 16, 1801, by Sol[omo]n Wales, J.P.	TM	13
David Richard, s. David & Lucy, b. Nov. 18, 1821	1-B	85
Eunice, d. Othniel & Annis, b. Apr. 26, 1817	1-B	76
Frances A., m. Emory **PEARLES**, Jan. 21, 1849, by Harvey Walker, J.P.	1-M	77
Freeman Munroe, s. David & Lucy, b. Feb. 26, 1817	1-B	85
Holstein, s. Othniel & Annis, b. Feb. 26, 1821	1-B	76
John, s. David & Lucy, b. May 16, 1819	1-B	85
Mary, m. John **LAWSON**, Sept. 12, 1751	1-B	295

	Vol.	Page
BROWN, (cont.)		
Mary, d. Othniel, Jr. & Annis, b. Feb. 13, 1823	1-B	86
Mary, m. Benjamin M. **GOLD**, Dec. 14, 1843, by Rev. Washington Munger	1-M	56
Othniel, Jr., d. Dec. 27, 1843, ae 47 y.	1-D	2
Robert Othnial, s. Othniel, Jr. & Annis, b. Jan. 22, 1837	1-B	108
BRUMBLEY, Daniel, s. Daniel, b. Dec. 7, 1747	2LR	287
BUCK, Lucius, of Holland, Mass., m. Sophia **MOORE**, of Union, Jan. 27, 1835, by Rev. Abial Williams (Lucius **BACK**?)	1-M	50
BUCKLAND, Anson, m. Mary C. **BOOTH**, Apr. 6, 1848, by Rev. Samuel J. Curtiss	1-M	75
BUFFINGTON, James, of Ashford, m. Juliana **ANDERSON**, of Union, Sept. 12, 1824, by Neh[emiah] B. Beardsley	1-M	33
BUGBEE, Amos, s. Eleazer & Suviah, b. July 20, 1802. Recorded June 26, 1833	1-B	46
Amos, of Union, m. Nancy S. **HOWARD**, of Woodstock, Dec. 11, 1850, by Bela Hicks, Adm., Woodstock	1-M	80
Annis, d. Eleazer & Suviah, b. June 12, 1811. Recorded June 26, 1833	1-B	46
Annis, d. Marcus & Sylvia, b. Sept. 13, 1816	1-B	84
Annis, of Union, m. Aaron **GAGE**, of Ashford, Oct. 12, 1835, by Rev. Leonard Gage, of Ashford	1-M	55
Anses, d. Isaiah & Huldah, b. Dec. 1, 1754	2LR	292
Armina, d. Marcus & Sylvia, b. Mar. 11, 1805	1-B	84
Betsey, of Union, m. John **DIXON**, of Holland, Mass., Oct. 4, 1842, by Rev. Samuel T. Curtiss	1-M	4
Edwin Gilman, s. Amos & Betsey, b. Oct. 24, 1830	1-B	47
Eleazer Gilbert, s. Amos & Betsey, b. Mar. 18, 1823. Recorded June 26, 1833	1-B	46
Elijah, s. Marcus & Sylvia, b. Apr. 3, 1809	1-B	84
Eunice, Mrs., m. John **FISH**, Oct. 11, 1801, by Sol[omo]n Wales, J.P.	TM	13
Horatio Nelson, s. Newman & Eliza, b. Sept. 24, 1833	1-B	61
Jason, s. Marcus & Sylvia, b. Feb. 7, 1803	1-B	84
Jasper, [twin with Justice], s. Marcus & Silva, b. June 2, 1821	1-B	45
Jedediah, m. Molly **HISCOCK**, Oct. 29, 1767	2LR	290
Jesse, s. Jedediah & Molly, b. Nov. 2, 1768	2LR	266
Joseph Snell, s. Marcus & Betsey, b. Mar. 23, 1832	1-B	47
Justice, [twin with Jasper], s. Marcus & Silva, b. June 2, 1821	1-B	45
Loring, s. Marcus & Sylvia, b. Apr. 20, 1807	1-B	84
Lucinda, Mrs., of Union, m. Philip **ALLEN**, of Ashford, Nov. 26, 1801, by Sol[omo]n Wales, J.P.	TM	14
Lucius Smith, s. Numan & Eliza, b. June 9, 1826. Recorded Jan. 6, 1834	1-B	61
Lucy, m. William **MARCY**, May 2, 1756	2LR	295
Lydia, d. Eleazer & Sarviah, b. Sept. 7, 1804. Recorded June 26, 1833	1-B	46
Lydia, m. John **HOWARD**, b. of Union, Oct. 2, 1825, by Ingoldsby W. Crawford, J.P.	1-M	39
Marcus, b. Oct. 16, 1772	1-B	84
Marcus, m. Betsey **SNELL**, b. of Union, Mar. 4, 1830, by Nehemiah B. Beardsley	1-M	34
Martha Ann Surviah, d. Amos & Betsey, b. Sept. 25, 1834	1-B	52

BUGBEE, (cont.)

	Vol.	Page
Mehetable, w. Stephen, of Woodstock, d. May 14, 1821	1-D	2
Newman, s. Marcus & Sylvia, b. Dec. 18, 1798	1-B	84
Olive, d. Amos & Betsey, b. Apr. 25, 1825. Recorded June 26, 1833	1-B	47
Olive, m. Erastus C. BURLEY, Oct. 27, 1844, by Rev. Washington Munger	1-M	61
Parmelia, see under Permelia		
Pattee, m. Joseph Morse KENT, July 11, 1799, by Sol[omo]n Wales, J.P.	TM	11
Parmetia, d. Marcus & Sylvia, b. Feb. 21, 1814	1-B	84
Permelia, m. Luther HISCOCK, b. of Union, Dec. 28, 1837, by Rev. Washington Munger, at the house of Marcus Bugbee	1-M	26
Polly, d. Marcus & Sylvia, b. Jan. 3, 1801	1-B	84
Polly, m. Porter VINTON, July 27, 1828, by Augustus Moore, J.P.	1-M	22
Stephen, of Woodstock, m. Susanna DOLPH, of Holland, Dec. 13, 1821, by William Foster, J.P.	1-M	2
Sylvia, b. Feb. 28, 1775	1-B	84
Sylvia Corbin, d. Newman & Eliza, b. Apr. 1, 1831	1-B	61
Willard, s. Marcus & Sylvia, b. June 18, 1811	1-B	84
William Harrison, s. Newman & Eliza, b. Apr. 16, 1828	1-B	61
BULLARD, Lula, of South Brimfield, m. Jesse OLDS, of Sturbridge, Sept. 7, 1795, by Sol[omo]n Wales, J.P.	TM	7
[BURKE], [see under BURK]		
BURLEY, BURLEIGH, Amelia, Mrs., of Union, m. Elijah HIGGENS, Jr., of Worthington, Mass., Aug. 15, 1849, by Ebenezer Lindsey, J.P.	1-M	58
Amy Caroline, d. Luke & Ruammey, b. May 2, 1811	1-B	70
Asa, [twin with Polly], s. Jacob & Lucy, b. May 22, 1802	1-B	51
Asa, of Union, m. Laura DORCHESTER, of Tolland, Aug. 29, 1824, by Neh[emiah] B. Beardsley	1-M	33
Austin, s. Jacob & Lucy, b. Jan. 28, 1794	1-B	2
Cyrel, s. Josiah & Hannah, b. Apr. 9, 1767	2LR	266
Ellathear, d. John & Meriam, b. Apr. 18, 1751	2LR	288
Elwell P., of Holland, Mass., m. Charlotte P. PATRIDGE, of Union, Apr. 9, 1840, by G. H. Woodward	1-M	61
Erastus C., m. Olive BUGBEE, Oct. 27, 1844, by Rev. Washington Munger	1-M	61
Esther, d. Samuel & Rachel, b. Oct. 26, 1796	1-B	27
Ferdinand Lithbridge, s. Silas & Dorothy, b. Aug. 26, 1809	1-B	70
Hiram, s. Jacob & Lucy, b. May 22, 1804	1-B	51
Huldah, d. Josiah & Hannah, b. Nov. 29, 1767	2LR	266
Ithel, s. Jacob & Lucy, b. Jan. 23, 1792	1-B	2
John, s. John & Meriam, b. Oct. 8, 1738	2LR	288
John, s. Jacob & Lucy, b. May 25, 1796	1-B	27
Josiah, s. John & Meriam, b. Nov. 8, 1742	2LR	288
Laura Symantha, d. Luke & Ruammy, b. Aug. 15, 1809	1-B	51
Lois, d. Samuel & Rachel, b. Feb. 5, 1799	1-B	27
Luke, of Union, m. Ruammey PERREY, of Stafford, Nov. 22, 1808	1-M	2
Nancy, d. Samuel & Rachel, b. Feb. 16, 1794	1-B	27
Orren, s. Jacob & Lucy, b. July 10, 1799	1-B	27
Owen, m. Joanna Merrebeth FERRY*, b. of Union, Jan. 21, 1823, by William Foster, J.P. (*Perhaps "Terry")	1-M	2
Phylenia, d. Jacob & Lucy, b. Feb. 16, 1790	1-B	2

	Vol.	Page
BURLEY, BURLEIGH, (cont.)		
Polly, [twin with Asa], d. Jacob & Lucy, b. May 22, 1802	1-B	51
Polly, m. Nathaniel **ORMSBY**, Feb. 6, 1822, by Zenas E. Leonard Sturbridge	1-M	15
Rachel, d. Samuel & Rachel, b. Oct. 11, 1789	1-B	2
Salona, d. Roxana **THOMPSON**, b. June 24, 1807	1-B	51
Samuel, s. John & Merriam, b. Sept. 22, 1745	2LR	287
Samuel, s. Samuel & Rachel, b. Nov. 25, 1791	1-B	2
Sarah, d. John & Meriam, b. Mar. 22, 1740	2LR	288
Sarah, m. John **BASCOM**, June 9, 1763	2LR	290
Sarah, d. Josiah & Hannah, b. July 28, 1768	2LR	266
Tryphenia, d. Jacob & Lucy, b. Mar. 25, 1788	1-B	2
Tryphenia, Mrs., m. Erastus **HORTON**, b. of Union, Apr. 28, 1808	1-M	8
BURLINGAME, Annis, m. Justus K. **FAY**, b. of Union, July 3, 1827, by Ingoldsby W. Crawford, J.P.	1-M	27
BURNETT, Orrin, m. R[h]oda **LILLIE**, Mar. 23, 1834, by Stephen Haskell	1-M	50
BURT, Pamela, Mrs., m. Thad[d]eus **FOWBOOK***, b. of Brimfield, May 21, 1801, by Sol[omo]n Wales, J.P. (***FARABOOK?**)	TM	13
BUTTERWORTH, Timothy D., of Holland, m. Esther **TOWN**, of Union, Jan. 9, 1851, by Ebenezer Lindsey, J.P.	1-M	79
CADY, Cyrael, of Orange, m. Mrs. Joanna **PADDOCK**, of Holland, Feb. 29, 1796, by Sol[omo]n Wales, J.P.	TM	7
Lois, m. David **MOOR**, b. of Union, Sept. 11, 1783	1-M	13
Lois, d. Lemuel & Susannah, b. July 24, 1785	1-B	3
Lucy, d. Jan. 4, 1807	1-D	3
Lyman, s. Samuel & Susannah, b. Sept. 2, 1783	1-B	3
CAMBO, Isabel, Mrs., m. Peter **DICKEY**, b. of Union, May 26, 1791	1-M	4
CAMP, Abijah, s. John & Eleanor, b. Apr. 12, 1751	2LR	267
Asa, s. John & Eleanor, b. Sept. 19, 1759, at Rehobath	2LR	267
Eleanor, d. John & Eleanor, b. Mar. [ ], 1747	2LR	287
Eleanor, d. John & Eleanor, b. Feb. 12, 1753	2LR	267
Sarah, d. John & Eleanor, b. Mar. 23, 1755, at Diton	2LR	267
Simeon, s. John & Eleanor, b. Oct. 15, 1757, at Rehobath	2LR	267
-----, s. John & Eleanor, b. Dec. 30, 1748	2LR	288
CAMPBELL, Alexander, Jr., s. Alexander & Charlotte, b. Feb. 29, 1820	1-B	94
Almedia, d. Alexander & Charlotte, b. Mar. 26, 1818	1-B	93
Charlotte, Jr., d. Alexander & Charlotte, b. Oct. 9, 1822	1-B	94
Mason, s. Alexander & Charlotte, b. Oct. 12, 1830. Recorded Apr. 26, 1830 (Probably dates should be reversed)	1-B	94
Minerva, s. Alexander & Charlotte, b. Jan. 27, 1816	1-B	93
CAREY, Hannah, m. John **LILLIE**, b. of Union, Nov. 29, 1827, by Neh[emiah] B. Beardsley	1-M	12
CARPENTER, Adaline Permelia, d. Palmer, Jr., & Lydia, b. June 5, 1843	1-B	125
Charles Palmer, s. Palmer, Jr., & Lydia, b. May 17, 1841	1-B	111
Ephraim L., of Ashford, m. Hannah **JAMES**, of Union, Feb. 15, 1827, by Ingoldsby W. Crawford, J.P.	1-M	38
Grace, m. James **CRAWFORD**, Jr., Sept. 8, 1755	2LR	295
Martha, d. Uriah & Lucy, b. Nov. 30, 1761	2LR	294
Mary, Mrs., of Sturbridge, m. Washington **WELLS**, of Great Barrington, Nov. 2, 1798, by Sol[omo]n Wales, J.P.	TM	10
Richard, m. Mrs. Annis **MALTON**, Jan. 31, 1804, by Sol[omo]n Wales, J.P.	TM	15

	Vol.	Page
CARPENTER, (cont.)		
Uriah, Jr., m. Lucy **WYMAN**, Dec. 5, 1759	2LR	295
CASE, Horatio, m. Pamela **SCARBOROUGH**, Nov. 8, 1846, by Rev. Samuel J. Curtiss	1-M	73
CASS, Libeas, d. Sept. 27, 1844, ae 28 y.	1-D	27
Sally, m. George W. **TOWN**, b. of Union, Apr. 12, 1847, by Ingoldsby W. Crawford, J.P.	1-M	72
CHAFFEE, CHAFFE, Deadamia, m. Eleazer **WALES**, June 11, 1783, by Sol[omo]n Wales, J.P.	TM	18
Hannah, of Ashford, m. Joseph **SNELL**, Jr., of Union, Nov. 25, 1813	1-M	19
Matilda, of Union, m. Thomas **SELDON**, of New Stamford, Feb. 27, 1786, by Sol[omo]n Wales, J.P.	TM	1
Patey, Mrs., of South Brimfield, m. Jeremiah **MOLTON**, of Munson, June 30, 1794, by Sol[omo]n Wales, J.P.	TM	8
CHAMBERLAIN, Dianna(?), d. Samuel & Lydia, b. July 28, 1748	2LR	287
Lydia, d. Samuel & Lydia, b. [ ], 1744	2LR	287
Mary, of Union, m. Rindalder B. **MARCY**, of Woodstock, Oct. 16, 1836, by Leonard Gage	1-M	42
Rhoda, m. John **KINNEY**, b. of Union, June 16, 1811	1-M	11
Samuel, s. Samuel & Lydia, b. Sept. 14, 1746	2LR	287
CHANDLER, Fanny, of Woodstock, m. Nathaniel **SESSIONS**, of Union, Oct. 30, 1794	1-M	19
CHAPPELL, Susannah, of Norwich, m. Elisha **BADGER**, of Union, July 20, 1769	2LR	290
CHARLES, Anne, Mrs., of Brimfield, m. James **DEMICK**, of So. Brimfield, Feb. 4, 1802, by Sol[omo]n Wales, J.P.	TM	14
CHASE, Lucy Ann, of Southbridge, m. John W. **MOORE**, of Union, Aug. 6, 1837, by Rev. Abial Williams	1-M	63
Sarah,, d. Silas & Lydia, b. Jan. 1, 1822	1-B	68
CHICKERING, Nathaniel, of Weston, m. Mrs. Ruth **RICHARDSON**, of Brookfield, Feb. 22, 1804, by Sol[omo]n Wales, J.P.	TM	17
CHILD, Elizabeth, of Woodstock, m. Abijah **SESSIONS**, Jr., of Union, May 25, 1814	1-M	29
Seth, of Woodstock, m. Delotia **CRAWFORD**, of Union, Jan. 2, 1832, by George B. Atwell	1-M	43
CLARK, Aaron, s. Aaron & Sarah, b. Apr. [ ], 1747	2LR	287
David, s. Aaron & Sarah, b. July 15, 1749	2LR	288
David, s. Aaron & Sarah, d. Jan. 27, 175[ ]	2LR	291
David, s. Aaron & Sarah, b. Aug. 20, 1756	2LR	293
Eli, m. Mrs. Polly **SMALLEDGE**, Mar. 5, 1801, by Sol[omo]n Wales, J.P.	TM	12
Elizabeth, d. Aaron & Sarah, b. July 27, 1759	2LR	293
Esther, d. Aaron & Sarah, b. Aug. 19, 1752	2LR	292
George W., of Woodstock, m. Olive **CRAWFORD**, of Union, Sept. 9, 1838, by Samuel Crawford, J.P.	1-M	44
Mary, d. Aaron & Sarah, b. Sept. 19, 1743	2LR	287
Phebe, of Union, m. Schuyler M. **WRIGHT**, of Woodstock, May 21, 1837, by Ebenezer Lindsey, J.P.	1-M	59
Sarah, d. Aaron & Sarah, b. June 15, 1745	2LR	288
CLEVELAND, CLEAVELAND, Allice, w. Pain, d. Oct. 18, 1820	1-D	3
Anna, d. Pain & Allice, b. Apr. 20, 1808	1-B	79
Anna, of Union, m. Augustus **TOURTELLOT**, of Sturbridge, May 31, 1832, by Augustus Moore, J.P.	1-M	20

UNION VITAL RECORDS 77

	Vol.	Page
CLEVELAND, CLEAVELAND, (cont.)		
Clarissa, d. Solomon & Lucy, b. Feb. 23, 1838	1-B	122
Frances, s. Solomon & Lucy, b. Mar. 23, 1843	1-B	122
Freeman, s. Pain & Allice, b. Mar. 16, 1804	1-B	79
John, s. Pain & Allice, b. May 18, 1806	1-B	79
Martin, s. Pain & Ellice, b. June 12, 1798	1-B	79
Mary Ann, d. Solomon & Lucy, b. June 12, 1833, at Vernon	1-B	122
Orange, of Union, m. Sarah **MORGAN**, of Brimfield, Sept. 1, 1819	1-M	3
Patty, d. Pain & Allice, b. Mar. 23, 1802	1-B	79
Sarah J., of Union, m. Ephraim W. **SQUIRE**, of Eastford, Mar. 26, 1853, by Rev. Samuel J. Curtiss	1-M	68
Sarah Jane, d. Solomon & Lucy, b. Jan. 24, 1835	1-B	122
Solomon, s. Pain & Allice, b. Jan. 27, 1842(?) (1812?)	1-B	79
Susanna, d. Pain & Ellice, b. Apr. 23, 1800	1-B	79
CODY, Samuel, m. Susannah **ARMSTRONG**, b. of Union, June 6, 1782	1-M	3
COGGESHALL, Cornelius, of Springfield, Mass., m. Sophronia M. **DAVIS**, of Palmer, Mass., Jan. 5, 1851, by Rev. Samuel J. Curtiss	1-M	80
COLBURN, Ebenezer, m. Mary L. **ANDRESS**, b. of Stafford, Feb. 28, 1836, by Moses C. Sessions, J.P.	1-M	43
COLLYER, Sarah J., of Union, m. Lurandus **JOHNSON**, of Tolland, Jan. 30, 1853, by Ebenezer Lindsey, J.P.	1-M	85
COLTON, Mary, Mrs., of Munson, m. Thomas **MOOR**, of Union, Mar. 16, 1793, by Sol[omo]n Wales, J.P.	TM	5
COMSTOCK, Adelia, of Union, m. Edward **ALDRICH**, of Thompson, Feb. 22, 1830, by Rev. Ira M. Bidwell	1-M	1
Eurilla, of Union, m. Gurdon **MAY**, of Holland, Sept. 9, 1827, by Neh[emiah] B. Beardsley	1-M	17
Israel Taft, s. Israel, Jr. & Deborah, b. Nov.19, 1830	1-B	97
Janett, of Union, m. Merchant **GOODELL**, of Charlton, Mass., Apr. 8, 1834, by John Crawford, J.P.	1-M	55
Martha, of Union, m. Roswell **GOODALE**, of Charlton, Mass., Mar. 14, 1838, by Moses C. Sessions, J.P.	1-M	56
CONE, Almira, of Ashford, m. Daniel **BRAYTON**, of Sturbridge, Aug. 17, 1829, by Neh[emiah] B. Beardsley	1-M	34
CONVERSE, Jared, of Ashford, m. Amanda M. **SESSIONS**, of Union, Mar. 27, 1851, by Ebenezer Lindsey, J.P.	1-M	80
John Tyler, of Ashford, m. Marcia **CRAWFORD**, of Union, Mar. 29, 1846, by Rev. Thomas Holman	1-M	38
Rebeckah, Mrs., of Union, m. George **LEONARD**, of Woodstock, Apr. 22, 1802, by Sol[omo]n Wales, J.P.	TM	15
COOK, Esther, d. Thomas & Sybble, b. May 19, 1766	2LR	268
Julia A., of Union, m. Andrew **BROUGHTON**, of Eastford, May 21, 1854, by Rev. Samuel J. Curtiss	1-M	36
COPELAND, Azel, s. Azel & Desire, b. Feb. 3, 1793	1-B	3
CORBIN, Almira, Jr., d. Lathrop & Almira, b. Mar. 21, 1826	1-B	93
Almira, m. James **PHILLIPS**, Mar. 15, 1835, by Luther Crawford, J.P.	1-M	51
Ann, m. Charles W. **MOORE**, b. of Union, [May] 30, [1830], by Leonard Gage	1-M	41
Augustus, s. Philip & Rhobe, b. Sept. 28, 1801	1-B	28
Aureleas O., m. Ruth **BLODGETT**, Mar. 29, 1848, by Rev. Samuel J. Curtiss	1-M	75

78   BARBOUR COLLECTION

	Vol.	Page
CORBIN, (cont.)		
Aurelius Orvella, s. Samuel & Charlotte, b. Apr. 17, 1821	1-B	80
Charles A., m. Louisa **LAWSON**, b. of Union, Jan. 17, 1849, by Thomas Holman, Jr.	1-M	77
Charles Augustus, [s. Samuel & Charlotte], b. Dec. 16, 1824	1-B	132
Charlotte Juliette, d. Samuel & Charlotte, b. Feb. 10, 1817	1-B	68
Charlotte Juliette, d. Samuel & Charlotte, d. May 12, 1828	1-D	27
Charlotte Juliette, [d. Samuel & Charlotte], b. Feb. 3, 1834	1-B	132
Eleazer, m. Dicea **CRAWFORD**, June 1, 1826, by George B. Atwell	1-M	37
Emeline Mariah, d. Benjamin & Mariah, b. June 11, 1831	1-B	97
Healey, s. Philip & Rhobe, b. June 8, 1799	1-B	28
Hedy, m. Nancy **COYE**, b. of Union, Oct. 13, 1825, by Neh[emiah] B. Beardsley	1-M	37
Henry Fielder, [s. Samuel & Charlotte], b. Apr. 27, 1829	1-B	132
Hermon, s. Philip & Roby, b. May 20, 1806	1-B	68
Joseph Perrin, of Woodstock, m. Louisa **CRAWFORD**, of Union, Sept. 24, 1795, by Sol[omo]n Wales, J.P.	TM	7
Lathrop, of Woodstock, m. Amira **CRAWFORD**, of Union, June 16, 1825, by Luther Crawford, J.P.	1-M	3
Levina, of Woodstock, m. Halsey **LEONARD**, of Union, Aug. 17, 1823, by Ingoldsby W. Crawford, J.P.	1-M	12
Lovica Roby, d. Samuel & Charlotte, b. Mar. 16, 1823	1-B	80
Lucy R., of Union, m. Philip F. **GAGE**, of West Woodstock, Aug. 31, 1853, by Rev. Samuel J. Curtice	1-M	87
Mary M., of Union, m. Lucius **AGARD**, of Stafford, Feb. 13, 1854, by Rev. Samuel J. Curtice	1-M	90
Nancy D., m. Edwin W. **UPHAM**, Nov. 12, 1848, by Rev. Samuel J. Curtis	1-M	78
Philip, s. Philip & Rhobe, b. Apr. 4, 1797	1-B	3
Philo Roderick, [s. Samuel & Charlotte], b. Jan. 25, 1827	1-B	132
Polly, d. Philip & Rhobe, b. May 28, 1795	1-B	3
Samuel, s. Philip & Rhobe, b. Feb. 17, 1792, at Dudley	1-B	28
Samuel Aurelius, s. Samuel & Charlotte, b. Jan. 28, 1816	1-B	68
Samuel Aurelius, s. Samuel & Charlotte, d. June 10, 1817	1-D	3
Samuel Morello, s. Samuel & Charlotte, b. Dec. 15, 1818	1-B	80
COY, COYE, Abigail, d. Nathaniel & Abigail, d. Aug. 3, 1749	2LR	291
Abigail, of Union, m. Abner **HOWARD**, of Sturbridge, Apr. 16, 1799	1-M	8
Amasa, s. Levi & Hannah, b. Apr. 30, 1798	1-B	3
Amasa, m. Orinda **SESSIONS**, b. of Union, June 30, 1825, by Rev. Alvan Underwood, of Woodstock	1-M	37
Amasa, of Union, m. Lydia **WALKER**, of Brookfield, Mass., July 2, 1848, by Rev. Samuel J. Curtis	1-M	57
Antone, s. Levi & Hannah, b. Jan. 8, 1804	1-B	28
Archible, m. Elizabeth **BADGER**, Dec. 25, 1760	2LR	295
Archibald, d. Apr. 1, 1794	1-D	3
Asa, s. David & Lucy, b. Sept. 17, 1799	1-B	60
Asa, m. Anna **GRIGGS**, b. of Union, Dec. 14, 1826, by Neh[emiah] B. Beardsley	1-M	37
Charlotte, d. Lucy* (sic) & Hannah, b. June 26, 1791 (*Levi?)	1-B	3
C[h]loe, Mrs., m. Joel **KENNEY**, b. of Union, May 10, 1792, by Sol[omo]n Wales, J.P.	TM	4
Chloe, m. Joel **KINNEY**, b. of Union, May 10, 1792	1-M	11

UNION VITAL RECORDS 79

	Vol.	Page
COY, COYE, (cont.)		
Cyrus, s. David & Lucy, b. Jan. 27, 1802	1-B	28
David, m. Mrs. Lucy **KENNEY**, Oct. 22, 1797, by Sol[omo]n Wales, J.P.	TM	9
David, m. Lucy **KINNEY**, b. of Union, Oct. 22, 1797	1-M	3
David, d. Sept. 18, 1831	1-D	4
Eli, m. Nancy **WALKER**, Feb. 19, 1827, by James D. Barnett, Woodstock	1-M	38
Eliza, d. David & Lucy, b. Dec. 28, 1805	1-B	60
Eliza, d. Hannah, b. Feb. 6, 1825	1-B	97
Elizabeth, Mrs., m. Ezra **PUTNEY**, b. of Union, Oct. 6, 1807	1-M	16
Elizabeth, wid., d. May 29, 1806	1-D	3
Hannah, d. Levi & Hannah, b. June 3, 1806	1-B	60
Hannah, w. Levi, d. Aug. 25, 1828, ae 65 y. 2 m. 22 d.	1-D	4
Irena, m. William **WALKER**, b. of Union, Feb. 2, 1823, by William Foster, J.P.	1-M	23
Levi, m. Hannah **LILLIE**, Feb. 15, 1785, by Sol[omo]n Wales, J.P.	TM	1
Levi, d. Jan. 1, 1831; ae 67 y. 10 m.	1-D	4
Lucy, d. Levi & Hannah, b. Apr. 13, 1808	1-B	60
Lucy, Jr., d. Feb. 7, 1835	1-D	4
Luke, m. Mercy **HEVILAND**, b. of Rensseloeville, Oct. 15, 1799, by Sol[omo]n Wales, J.P.	TM	11
Luranna, d. David & Lucy, b. Mar. 1, 1798	1-B	3
Lurana, m. Jason **HAWSE**, b. of Union, Mar. 16, 1815	1-M	8
Mariam(?), d. Nathaniel & Abigail, d. Aug. 29, 1749	2LR	291
Minerva, d. David & Lucy, b. Aug. 24, 1812	1-B	68
Minerva, m. Sullivan **BOOTH**, b. of Union, Nov. 14, 1831, by Rev. Andrew R. Reed	1-M	49
Molley, Mrs., of Union, m. Justus **BOYDEN**, of Sturbridge, March 10, 1800, by Sol[omo]n Wales, J.P.	TM	11
Nancy, d. David & Lucy, b. Dec. 16, 1803	1-B	60
Nancy, m. Hedy **CORBIN**, b. of Union, Oct. 13, 1825, by Neh[emiah] B. Beardsley	1-M	37
Orinda, d. Apr. 27, 1845, ae 65 y.	1-D	24
CRAM, Chloe, d. Humphrey & Hannah, b. Nov. 25, 1750	2LR	288
Jonathan, s. Humphrey & Hannah, b. Mar. 9, 1746/7	2LR	287
Mehetable, d. Humphrey & Hannah, b. Apr. 15, 1745	2LR	287
Mehetable, m. Jonas **LOOMIS**, Nov. 29, 1764	2LR	290
CRAWFORD, Albert, s. Samuel, Jr. & Lydia, b. Apr. 15, 1822	1-B	80
Albert, m. Mercy **PULNAM***, May 10, 1846, by Rev. Samuel J. Curtiss (***PUTNAM**?)	1-M	67
Almira, d. Luther & Elizabeth, b. July 18, 1802	1-B	28
A[l]mira, of Union, m. Lathrop **CORBIN**, of Woodstock, June 16, 1825, by Luther Crawford, J.P.	1-M	3
Alonzo, s. Ingoldsby W. & Rhoda, b. Mar. 3, 1834	1-B	98
Amanda, d. John & Susanna, b. Apr. 12, 1806	1-B	60
Andrew, s. Andrew & Mary, d. Dec. 17, 1769	2LR	270
Anna, d. Samuel, Jr. & Lucy, b. Mar. 6, 1811	1-B	60
Anne, d. James, Jr. & Grace, b. July 20, 1762	2LR	267
Benjamin, s. Luther & Eliza, b. Apr. 24, 1794	1-B	3
Burton, s. Samuel, Jr. & Lydia, b. Dec. 5, 1815	1-B	79
Calista, d. Ingoldsby W. & Rhoda, b. Aug. 1, 1811, at Woodstock	1-B	68
Calista, of Union, m. Sanford **LYON**, of Woodstock, Nov. 21, 1832,		

BARBOUR COLLECTION

	Vol.	Page
CRAWFORD, (cont.)		
by Rev. Alvan Underwood, of Woodstock	1-M	48
Caroline, d. Ingoldsby W. & Rhoda, b. Jan. 17, 1816	1-B	68
Caroline, m. David L. **NEWELL**, b. of Union, Nov. 29, 1835, by John H. Willis	1-M	14
Chester, s. James, Jr. & Grace, b. Jan. 26, [ ]	2LR	293
Chester, s. James, Jr. & Grace, d. Feb. 1, 1759	2LR	270
Daniel Taft, s. Ingoldsby W. & Rhoda, b. Aug. 27, 1813	1-B	68
Deborah, d. Robert & Lydia, b. Aug. 26, 1764	2LR	267
Delatia, d. Samuel, Jr. & Lydia, b. Feb. 17, 1804	1-B	28
Delotia, of Union, m. Seth **CHILD**, of Woodstock, Jan. 2, 1832, by George B. Atwell	1-M	43
Dicea, d. Samuel, Jr. & Lydia, b. Jan. 8, 1802	1-B	28
Dicea, m. Eleazer **CORBIN**, June 1, 1826, by George B. Atwell	1-M	37
Eliza, d. Luther & Elizabeth, b. Aug. 4, 1804	1-B	60
Eliza, d. Luther & Elizabeth, d. May 12, 1817	1-D	3
Elizabeth, d. Hugh & Marg[a]ret, b. Dec. 21, 1739	2LR	292
Elizabeth, d. James, Jr. & Grace, d. Apr. 30, 1760	2LR	270
Fayett, m. Mary **MARSHALL**, Apr. 1, 1846, by Rev. Samuel J. Curtiss	1-M	67
Frances, d. James, Jr. & Grace, b. Apr. 30, 1760	2LR	293
French, s. John & Susanna, b. Feb. 23, 1801	1-B	28
French, of Union, m. Zida **WEBBER**, of Holland, Jan. 1, 1829, by Ingoldsby W. Crawford, J.P.	1-M	43
George Washington, s. Daniel Taft & Martha, b. May 28, 1849	1-B	132
Harriet, d. Ingoldsby W. & Rhoda, b. Mar. 19, 1831	1-B	97
Huldah, d. Robert & Lydia, b. Sept. 2, 1766	2LR	268
James, Jr., m. Grace **CARPENDER**, Sept. 8, 1755	2LR	295
John, s. Hugh & Marg[a]ret, b. Mar. 12, 1754	2LR	292
John, s. Robert & Lydia, b. July 10, 1758	2LR	289
John, m. Mary **ROSEBROOKS**, Dec. 14, 1758	2LR	295
John, of Union, m. Susanna **HAYWARD**, of Ashford, Apr. 24, 1800	1-M	3
John Laman, s. Andrew & Mary, b. Mar. 5, 1766	2LR	268
Laurens, s. John & Susanna, b. Jan. 24, 1809	1-B	60
Levina, d. Samuel, Jr. & Lucy, b. Oct. 28, 1807	1-B	60
Liberty Webber, s. French & Zida, b. June 24, 1834	1-B	98
Logan, s. Ingoldsby W. & Rhoda, b. Jan. 13, 1822	1-B	80
Louisa, of Union, m. Joseph Perrin **CORBIN**, of Woodstock, Sept. 24, 1795, by Sol[omo]n Wales, J.P.	TM	7
Lucian, s. Luther & Elizabeth, b. Jan. 26, 1807	1-B	60
Lucian, s. Luther & Elizabeth, d. Nov. 17, 1827	1-D	4
Luther, of Union, m. Elizabeth **WILBUR**, of Woodstock, June 14, 1792	1-M	3
Luther, s. Daniel T. & Martha, b. Aug. 29, 1839	1-B	111
Marcia, d. Ingoldsby W. & Rhoda, b. Nov. 15, 1824	1-B	80
Marcia, of Union, m. John Tyler **CONVERSE**, of Ashford, Mar. 29, 1846, by Rev. Thomas Holman	1-M	38
Margaret, d. Luther & Elizabeth, d. Aug. 5, 1820	1-D	3
Mariah Louisa, d. Charles & Polly, b. Mar. 21, 1823	1-B	80
Martha Eliza, d. Daniel Taft & Martha, b. July 26, 1851	1-B	132
Mary Eddy, d. Charles & Polly, b. Mar. 30, 1826	1-B	93
Meriah, s. Samuel, Jr. & Lucy*, b. Aug. 6, 1805 (*Probably Lydia)	1-B	60
Minerva, Jr., d. Daniel T. & Minerva, b. Dec. 25, 1836	1-B	111

UNION VITAL RECORDS 81

	Vol.	Page
CRAWFORD, (cont.)		
Minerva, Sr., w. Daniel T., d. Jan. 30, 1837	1-D	24
Newton, s. Luther & Elizabeth, b. Oct. 29, 1809	1-B	68
Olive, d. Andrew & Mary, b. Sept. 18, 1767	2LR	268
Olive, d. Samuel, Jr. & Lydia, b. July 29, 1818	1-B	79
Olive, of Union, m. George W. **CLARK**, of Woodstock, Sept. 9, 1838, by Samuel Crawford, J.P.	1-M	44
Oscar, s. Daniel T. & Martha, b. Dec. 14, 1840	1-B	111
Ossian, s. Ingoldsby W. & Rhoda, b. Nov. 3, 1827	1-B	93
Ossian French, s. French & Zida, b. Dec. 25, 1829	1-B	94
Peggy, d. Luther & Elizabeth, b. May 30, 1800	1-B	28
Polly, d. John & Mary, b. Dec. 20, 1764	2LR	267
Polly, d. Samuel & Olive, b. Nov. 7, 1794	1-B	3
Randall, s. Luther & Elizabeth, b. Feb. 23, 1798	1-B	28
Rebeckah F., d. Oct. 17, 1842, ae 29 y.	1-D	24
Robert, m. Lidia **PEIRCE**, June 16, 1757	2LR	295
Rosebrook, s. John & Mary, b. Apr.1, 1761	2LR	294
Sally, d. Luther & Elizabeth, b. June 24, 1792	1-B	3
Samuel, s. Hugh & Marg[a]ret, b. July 22, 1748	2LR	292
Samuel, Dea., of Union, m. Mrs. Olive **EDDY**, of Woodstock, Dec. 26, 1793	1-M	3
Samuel, Jr., of Union, m. Lydia **HOWARD**, of Ashford, Aug. 20, 1801	1-M	3
Samuel, d. May 11, 1824	1-D	3
Samuel D., m. Rebecca **FOSTER**, Mar. 15, 1840, by Augustus Moore, J.P.	1-M	44
Samuel Dwight, s. Samuel, Jr. & Lucy, b. Aug. 19, 1813	1-B	68
Samuel Edward, s. Samuel D. & Rebeckah F., b. Mar. 30, 1841, at Ashford	1-B	120
Samuel Preston, s. Charles & Polly, b. May 16, 1820	1-B	80
Sarah, d. Hugh & Marg[a]ret, b. Oct. 18, 1745	2LR	292
Sarah, m. Daniel **LOOMIS**, Feb. 9, 1764	2LR	290
Sarah, d. James, Jr. & Grace, b. Apr. 2, 1768	2LR	266
Sarah, w. Dea. Samuel, d. May 25, 1793	1-D	3
Sarah Ann, d. Ingoldsby W. & Rhoda, b. Mar. 9, 1819	1-B	79
Sarah Ann, d. Daniel T. & Martha, b. Mar. 4, 1843	1-B	120
Sidney, s. John & Susanna, b. Feb. 13, 1804	1-B	28
Stephen, s. Robert & Lidia, b. July 25, 1761	2LR	294
Stephen Howard, s. Samuel, Jr. & Lydia, b. Aug. 1, 1820	1-B	80
Stephen Howard, s. Samuel, Jr. & Lydia, d. Oct. 27, 1820	1-D	3
Susan Emily, d. French & Zida, b. Nov. 3, 1841	1-B	120
Susan Zida, d. French & Zida, b. May 3, 1836	1-B	98
Susan Zida, d. French & Zida, d. Sept. 12, 1838, ae 2 y. 4 m. 9 d.	1-D	24
Sibyll, d. John & Mary, b. Aug. 8, 1762	2LR	269
Theophilus, s. James, Jr. & Grace, b. Apr. 25, 1764	2LR	267
Theresa, d. Luther & Elizabeth, b. July 28, 1812	1-B	68
Theresa, d. Luther & Elizabeth, d. Mar. 26, 1813	1-D	3
Willard, s. Luther & Elizabeth, b. Feb. 5, 1796	1-B	28
William Foster, s. Samuel D. & Rebeckah F., b. Oct. 4, 1842	1-B	120
W[illia]m M., of Union, m. Almeda J. **POTTER**, of Willington, Oct. 9, 1854, by Rev. Samuel J. Curtis	1-M	73
William Merrell, s. French & Zida, b. July 31, 1831	1-B	98
CROSBY, Jonathan Hopkins, s. Prince & Tamison, b. Jan. 1, 1796	1-B	3

	Vol.	Page
CROSBY, (cont.)		
Orra, s. Prince & Tamison, b. Nov. 14, 1793	1-B	3
CUMBO, Isabel, Mrs., m. Peter **DICKEY**, May 6, 1791, by Sol[omo]n Wales, J.P.	TM	3
CUMMINGS, George W., m. Mrs. Chloe **NEEDHAM**, b. of Union, [, 1827], by Neh[emiah] B. Beardsley. Recorded Oct. 29, 1827	1-M	17
CURTIS, CURTISS, Charles M., of Eastford, m. Abigail P. **WALKER** of Union, Dec. 17, 1854, by Rev. Samuel J. Curtis	1-M	73
Horace, of Woodstock, m. Lucinda **FERRY**, of Union, Jan. 3, 1837, by Rev. Washington Munger	1-M	44
Lydia, of Ashford, m. Luther **MOORE**, of Union, Mar. 27, 1839, by Rev. Stephen Fairbanks	1-M	63
Polly, Mrs., of Ashford, m. Noah **MOOR[E]**, of Union, June 15, 1794	1-M	13
Samuel Ives, Jr., s. Samuel Ives & Eliza, b. Feb. 5, 1844	1-B	125
DANDLESON, Elizabeth, wid., of Brimfield, m. Capt. William **EATON**, of Windsor, Vt., Aug. 21, 1792, by Sol[omo]n Wales, J.P.	TM	4
Pol[l]ey, m. Jonathan **PHILLIPS**, b. of Brimfield, Aug. 1, 1792, by Sol[omo]n Wales, J.P.	TM	4
DAVIS, Sophronia M., of Palmer, Mass., m. Cornelius **COGGESHALL**, of Springfield, Mass., Jan. 5, 1851, by Rev. Samuel J. Curtiss	1-M	80
DAVISSON, Lucy, m. Gurdon **HORTON**, b. of Union, May 1, 1816	1-M	30
DAY, Samuel, m. Mrs. Elizabeth **MUNGER**, Oct. 10, 1793, by Sol[omo]n Wales, J.P.	TM	5
DEMICK, [see under **DIMICK**]		
DICKERMAN, John, s. Comfort & Elizabeth, b. May 26, 1791	1-B	4
Lidia, d. Comfort & Elizabeth, b. May 21, 1794	1-B	4
DICKEY, Clara, d. Peter & Isebel, b. May 14, 1799	1-B	4
Lucinda, d. Peter & Isebel, b. Oct. 7, 1802	1-B	4
Lucy, d. Peter & Isebel, b. Nov. 25, 1804	1-B	4
Peter, m. Mrs. Isabel **CUMBO**, May 6, 1791, by Sol[omo]n Wales, J.P.	TM	3
Peter, m. Mrs. Isabel **CAMBO**, b. of Union, May 26, 1791	1-M	4
Sibble, d. Peter & Isebel, b. July 16, 1796	1-B	4
Walter, s. Peter & Isabel, b. July 16, 1793	1-B	4
William, s. Peter & Isebel, b. Nov. 25, 1791	1-B	4
DIKE, Nathan, s. Jabez & Easter, b. Nov. 26, 1751	2LR	288
DIMICK, DEMICK, James, of So. Brimfield, m. Mrs. Anne **CHARLES**, of Brimfield, Feb. 4, 1802, by Sol[omo]n Wales, J.P.	TM	14
Timothy D., m. Laura **JOHNSON**, Dec. 13, 1840, by Augustus Moore, J.P.	1-M	4
DIXON, Betsey, m. Jonathan **LARNARD**, b. of Union, Sept. 2, 1852, by Rev. Samuel J. Curtice	1-M	83
John, of Holland, Mass., m. Betsey **BUGBEE**, of Union, Oct. 4, 1842, by Rev. Samuel T. Curtiss	1-M	4
Sarah S., m. William S. **PRATT**, of Vernon, Ct., Oct. 2, 1842, by Rev. Samuel J. Curtis	1-M	52
DODGE, Hiram, of Medway, m. Mary **WALKER**, of Union, Nov. 8, 1837, by Moses C. Sessions, J.P.	1-M	4
Mary, m. Gideon **BADGER**, Dec. 19, 1754	2LR	295
DOLPH, Amasa, of Holland, m. Mrs. Susannah **WALKER**, of Union, May 18, 1800, by Sol[omo]n Wales, J.P.	TM	11

UNION VITAL RECORDS 83

	Vol.	Page
DOLPH, (cont.)		
Susanna, of Holland, m. Stephen **BUGBEE**, of Woodstock, Dec. 13, 1821, by William Foster, J.P.	1-M	2
DORCHESTER, Laura, of Tolland, m. Asa **BURLEY**, of Union, Aug. 29, 1824, by Neh[emiah] B. Beardsley	1-M	33
DORSETT, Eliza, m. Ebenezer G. **SMITH**, b. of Union, June 8, 1825, by Rev. Alvan Underwood, of Woodstock	1-M	35
DOWD, Sarah, Mrs., m. Amasa **MUNGER**, Jan. 21, 1798, by Sol[omo]n Wales, J.P.	TM	9
DUNCAN, Leander, m. Eliza J. **FAULKNER**, Nov. 25, 1847, by Rev. Samuel J. Curtiss	1-M	74
DUPE, Joshua, of Stafford, m. Mrs. Lucy **ROOP**, of Union, Sept. 24, 1793, by Sol[omo]n Wales, J.P.	TM	6
EAMES, EMES, [see also **AMES**], Rebecca, d. James & Mehetable, b. July 2, 1763	2LR	267
Rebeckah had s. James **MILLER**, b. Sept. 18, 1789	1-B	13
Rebeckah had s. Benjamin **BOOTH**, b. July 28, 1793	1-B	2
EASTMAN, Erastus S., of Ashford, m. Lucina **MORAY**, of Union, Aug. 26, 1830, by Rev. Ezekiel Skinner	1-M	5
EATON, Catharine, d. Josiah, Jr. & Lydia, b. Jan. 26, 1811	1-B	5
Dianna Perrin, d. William & Fanny, b. Dec. 21, 1824. Recorded Dec. 23, 1831	1-B	5
Edwin Ruthvin, s. William & Fanny, b. Dec. 1, 1828	1-B	5
Eliza, d. Josiah, Jr. & Lydia, b. Nov. 3, 1807	1-B	5
Erasmus, m. Mrs. Polly **McINTIER**, b. of Union, Aug. 8, 1804, by Sol[omo]n Wales, J.P.	TM	17
Fidella, d. William & Fanny, b. Apr. 7, 1827. Recorded Dec. 23, 1831	1-B	5
Josiah, Jr., m. Lydia **WEBBER**, b. of Union, Sept. 11, 1806	1-M	5
Lovisa, m. Asa F. **SNELL**, b. of Union, Dec. 6, 1821, by William Foster, J.P.	1-M	29
Lydia, of Union, m. Saunders **FERRY**, of Vernon, N.Y., Dec. 19, 1827, by Neh[emiah] B. Beardsley	1-M	27
Sabrina, d. Josiah, Jr. & Lydia, b. Apr. 17, 1813	1-B	5
Urilla, d. William & Fanny, b. Oct. 20, 1831	1-B	5
William, Capt., of Windsor, Vt., m. Wid. Elizabeth **DANDLESON**, of Brimfield, Aug. 21, 1792, by Sol[omo]n Wales, J.P.	TM	4
William, s. Josiah, Jr. & Lydia, b. June 18, 1816	1-B	5
William, m. Fanna **SESSIONS**, b. of Union, Nov. 28, 1822, by William Foster, J.P.	1-M	5
EDDY, Lucy, of Monson, m. Rufus **HOLMAN**, of Union, Sept. 1, 1803	1-M	30
Olive, Mrs., of Woodstock, m. Dea. Samuel **CRAWFORD**, of Union, Dec. 26, 1793	1-M	3
EDSON, Maria S., m. Jos[eph] Warner **TOWN**, b. of Petersham, Mass., May 9, 1848, by Rev. Samuel J. Curtis	1-M	76
ELLENWOOD, Persis, Mrs., of Brimfield, m. Royal **BEN[N]ET**, of Killingly, Apr. 22, 1802, by Sol[omo]n Wales, J.P.	TM	15
ENOS, Aaron, S. Joab & Susanna, b. Mar. 2, 1767	2LR	268
Aaron, s. Joab & Susanna, d. Mar. 15, 1767	2LR	270
Abijah, s. Benjamin & Jerusha, b. Nov. 4, 1747	2LR	287
Abner, s. James & Silence, b. Nov. 14, 1766	2LR	268
Alexander, s. Benjamin & Jerusha, b. Feb. 1, 1753	2LR	292
Benjamin, s. James & Mary, d. Dec. 7, 1760	2LR	270

	Vol.	Page
ENOS, (cont.)		
Ebenezer, s. Joab & Susanna, b. May 9, 1765	2LR	268
Elisha, s. Benjamin & Jerusha, b. May 18, 1754	2LR	292
Erasmus, s. James & Silence, b. Apr. 8, 1765	2LR	267
Hannah, w. James, d. July 15, 1760	2LR	291
James, d. May 22, 1762	2LR	270
James, m. Silence **SESSIONS**, Oct. 18, 1764	2LR	290
Joseph, m. Elizabeth **WHITE**, Mar. 7, 1750	2LR	295
Mary, d. Benjamin & Jerusha, b. Jan. 16, 1751	2LR	292
Mary, d. Joab & Susanna, b. Aug. 25, 1768	2LR	266
Rachel, d. Joseph & Rachel, b. Feb. 15, 1746/7	2LR	287
ESTABROOKS, Sarah Louisa, d. John S. & Louisa, b. Dec. 20, 1842	1-B	92
FAIRBANKS, FAREBANKS, Joseph, m. Tabitha **MARCY**, Nov. 4, 1762	2LR	290
Joseph Newton, s. Stephen & Martha, b. Nov. 2, 1826	1-B	91
Joshua, s. Joseph & Tabitha, b. Dec. 23, 1764	2LR	268
Molly, d. Joseph & Tabaly, b. Nov. 2, 1767	2LR	268
Orrin Metter, s. Stephen & Martha, b. Sept. 4, 1829	1-B	91
Peter Fletcher, s. Stephen & Martha, b. Mar. 8, 1824	1-B	91
Sarah Ann, d. Stephen & Martha, b. Dec. 31, 1816	1-B	67
Sarah Ann, of Union, m. Isaac **AGARD**, of Stafford, July 25, 1838, by Rev. Erastus Benton, of Eastford	1-M	67
Stephen, s. Joseph & Tabitha, b. Mar. 4, 1763	2LR	267
Stephen, s. Joseph & Tabitha, b. July 11, 1787	1-B	6
Stephen, of Union, m. Martha **SABIN**, of Thompson, Apr. 10, 1810	1-M	6
Stephen Sabins, s. Stephen & Martha, b. Oct. 15, 1822	1-B	91
Sibbel had d. Mary Ann **HAMMOND**, b. Apr. 9, 1807	1-B	62
Tabitha Marcy, d. Stephen & Martha, b. May 8, 1818	1-B	67
FARNHAM, Eli, s. Eliasaph & Sally, b. May 6, 1797	1-B	6
Joseph, of Eastford, m. Harmony C. **HISCOX**, of Union, Aug. 13, 1851, by Rev. Henry Forbush	1-M	82
Juliana, d. Eliasaph & Sally, b. Apr. 23, 1799	1-B	6
Zilpha, d. Eliasaph & Sally, b. Apr. 13, 1795, at Ashford	1-B	6
FAULKNER, Ann M., of Conn., m. Davis **BAKER**, of Southbridge, Mass., Sept. 3, 1851, by Rev. D. P. Livermore	1-M	81
Eliza J., m. Leander **DUNCAN**, Nov. 25, 1847, by Rev. Samuel J. Curtiss	1-M	74
Joseph H., m. Caroline V. **HOLT**, Nov. 29, 1845, by Rev. Samuel S. Curtiss	1-M	28
Mary, m. A. H. **VAN SHAACK**, Nov. 25, 1847, by Rev. Samuel J. Curtiss	1-M	22
FAY, Justus K., m. Annis **BURLINGAME**, b. of Union, July 3, 1827, by Ingoldsby W. Crawford, J.P.	1-M	27
FEARSELL, Elizabeth, Mrs., of Holland, m. John **TREAT**, of Granvil, May 14, 1793, by Sol[omo]n Wales, J.P.	TM	5
FENTON, Jason, m. Lois **WALKER**, b. of Sturbridge, June 27, 1796, by Sol[omo]n Wales, J.P.	TM	8
FERRY, Andrew, s. Jason & Betsey, b. July 30, 1829	1-B	91
Sintha, Mrs., m. Royal **FULLER**, b. of Holland, May 12, 1802, by Sol[omo]n Wales, J.P.	TM	15
Jason, of Stafford, m. Mrs. Polly **RULY**, of Union, Feb. 12, 1801, by Sol[omo]n Wales, J.P.	TM	12
Jason, m. Elizabeth **RIDER**, Apr. 1, 1829, by Augustus Moore, J.P.	1-M	27

UNION VITAL RECORDS 85

	Vol.	Page
FERRY, (cont.)		
Joanna Merrebeth, m. Owen **BURLEY**, b. of Union, Jan. 21, 1823, by William Foster, J.P. (Perhaps "**TERRY**")	1-M	2
Justin, s. Jason & Polly, b. Aug. 18, 1801	1-B	6
Lucinda, of Union, m. Horace **CURTISS**, of Woodstock, Jan. 3, 1837, by Rev. Washington Munger	1-M	44
Saunders, of Vernon, N.Y., m. Lydia **EATON**, of Union, Dec. 19, 1827, by Neh[emiah] B. Beardsley	1-M	27
FISH, John, m. Mrs. Eunice **BUGBEE**, Oct. 11, 1801, by Sol[omo]n Wales, J.P.	TM	13
FISHER, Almira, of Union, m. James R. **GUILE**, of Flushing, N.Y., Mar. 10, 1833, by Rev. Leonard Gage, of Ashford	1-M	7
FISK, Rufus, of Brandon, Vt., m. Mrs. Mary **WRIGHT**, of Union, Jan. 5, 1800, by Sol[omo]n Wales, J.P.	TM	11
FOSKET, Elizabeth, of Stafford, m. Isaac **BOOTH**, Jr., of Union, Nov. 4, 1790	1-M	2
FOSTER, Alvin, s. Edward, Jr. & Rebeckah, b. Mar. 23, 1805	1-B	67
Anna, d. Edward & Rachel, b. Sept. 11, 1793	1-B	6
Anna, of Union, m. Philip **GAGE**, of Monson, Sept. 25, 1822, by Ingoldsby W. Crawford, J.P.	1-M	7
Burk, s. William & Kaziah, b. Mar. 26, 1802	1-B	6
Burke, m. Hannah **GRIGGS**, Jan. 11, 1835, by Rev. Moses B. Church	1-M	28
Charles, m. Louisa **SESSIONS**, b. of Union, June 6, 1809	1-M	6
Charles May, s. Charles & Louisa, b. Sept. 2, 1811	1-B	66
Daniel, of Andover, m. Mrs. Sally **STRALTON***, of Brimfield, Oct. 1, 1790, by Sol[omo]n Wales, J.P. (***STRATTON**?)	TM	2
Dorothy, d. William & Kaziah, b. Jan. 27, 1800	1-B	6
Dorothy, m. John **POTTER**, Oct. 25, 1821, by Luther Crawford, J.P.	1-M	16
Dwight, s. Edward & Kaziah, b. Apr. 16, 1801	1-B	6
Ebbert, s. William & Kaziah, b. Oct. 21, 1805	1-B	6
Edward, m. Mrs. Rebeckah **STRONG**, Nov. 27, 1800, by Sol[omo]n Wales, J.P.	TM	12
Edward, Jr., m. Rebekah **STRONG**, b. of Union, Nov. 27, 1800	1-M	6
Edward Henry, s. William & Keziah, b. July 1, 1821	1-B	67
Edward Newell, s. Edward, Jr. & Rebecca, b. July 9, 1810, in Springfield, Mass.	1-B	66
Eleazer Byron, s. William & Keziah, b. May 20, 1824	1-B	67
Esther, d. Edward & Rachel, d. Mar. 20, 1790	1-D	6
Esther, d. William & Kaziah, b. Mar. 4, 1804	1-B	6
Esther, of Union, m. Ephraim H. **HYDE**, of Stafford, June 25, 1840, by Augustus Moore, J.P.	1-M	39
Hannah Newell, d. Charles & Louisa, b. June 7, 1813	1-B	66
John Newell, s. William & Keziah, b. July 26, 1816	1-B	67
Louisa, d. Charles & Louisa, b. Mar. 21, 1816	1-B	66
Louisa, d. William & Keziah, b. Feb. 7, 1819	1-B	67
Mary, d. William & Keziah, b. Oct. 7, 1807	1-B	66
Mary, m. Samuel S. **NEEDHAM**, b. of Union, Apr. 6, 1841, by Rev. Samuel S. Needham	1-M	65
Rachel, d. Edward & Rachel, d. Mar. 8, 1790	1-D	6
Rachel Ann, d. William & Keziah, b. Oct. 27, 1811	1-B	66
Rebeckah, d. Edward & Rachel, d. Mar. 20, 1790	1-D	6
Rebeccah, d. William & Keziah, b. Oct. 18, 1813	1-B	66

86 BARBOUR COLLECTION

	Vol.	Page
FOSTER, (cont.)		
Rebecca, m. Samuel D. **CRAWFORD**, Mar. 15, 1840, by Augustus Moore, J.P.	1-M	44
Rebeckah **STRONG**, d. Edward & Rebeckah, b. June 8, 1813, in Augusta, N.Y.	1-B	66
Susannah, of Stafford, m. Silas **HENRY**, of Holland, May 12, 1803, by Sol[omo]n Wales, J.P.	TM	16
William, of Union, m. Kaziah **MASON**, of Woodstock, Nov. 10, 1799	1-M	6
William, s. Edward & Rebeckah, b. Dec. 22, 1816, at Augusta, N.Y.	1-B	67
William, s. Edward & Rebeckah, d. Dec. 24, 1816, at Augusta, N.Y.	1-D	6
William Mason, s. William & Keziah, b. Oct. 21, 1809	1-B	66
FOWBOOK, Thad[d]eus, m. Mrs. Pamela **BURT**, b. of Brimfield, May 21, 1801, by Sol[omo]n Wales, J.P. (**FARABOOK**?)	TM	13
FREEMAN, Daniel, of Mansfield, m. Dinah **THOMPSON**, of Union, Oct. 24, 1842, by Rev. Samuel S. Curtiss	1-M	28
FULLER, Abigail, d. William & Mehetable, b. Aug. 30, 1763	2LR	267
Abigail, m. Samuel **PEAK**, Dec. 6, 1764	2LR	290
Abner, s. William & Mehetable, b. Feb. 24, 1769	2LR	266
Adna, s. Hezekiah & Marg[a]ret, b. Mar. 8, 1768	2LR	268
Amos, s. Hezekiah & Marg[a]ret, b. Aug. 7, 1752	2LR	288
Calvin, s. William & Mehetable, b. May 6, 1758	2LR	289
David, of Stafford, m. R[h]oda **JAMES**, of Union, Dec. 25, 1823, by William Foster, J.P.	1-M	6
Dorot[h]y, d. William & Mehetable, b. Oct. 21, 1751	2LR	292
Elizabeth, d. Hezekiah & Marg[a]ret, b. Sept. 6, 176[ ]	2LR	293
Elizabeth, Mrs., of Stafford, m. Thomas **RULY**, of Union, Feb. 11, 1801, by Sol[omo]n Wales, J.P.	TM	12
Elizabeth, of Stafford, m. Thomas **RUBY**, of Union, Feb. 11, 1801	1-M	18
Hezekiah, m. Margaret **TYLER**, Feb. 15, 1748	2LR	295
James, d. Jan. 29, 1749	2LR	291
James, s. Hezekiah & Marg[a]ret, b. Mar. 21, 1763	2LR	294
Joanna L., d. Joseph & Lucena, b. Feb. 11, 1807	1-B	6
Joseph, of Union, m. Lucena **LORING**, of Barrey, Feb. 26, 1805	1-M	6
Leicester, m. Mary **ADAMS**, b. of Barre, Oct. 22, 1834, by Rev. Stephen Fairbanks	1-M	27
Lucy, d. Hezekiah & Marg[a]ret, b. July 10, 1752 (sic)	2LR	288
Luther, s. William & Mehetable, b. May 10, 1766	2LR	266
Phineas, s. Hezekiah & Marg[a]ret, b. Aug. 28, 1865* *(1765)	2LR	268
Royal, m. Mrs. Sintha **FERRY**, b. of Holland, May 12, 1802, by Sol[omo]n Wales, J.P.	TM	15
-----, s. William & Mehitable, b. July 26, 1750; d. Sept. 6, 1750	2LR	288
GAGE, Aaron, of Ashford, m. Annis **BUGBEE**, of Union, Oct. 12, 1835, by Rev. Leonard Gage, of Ashford	1-M	55
Joel E., s. Enos & Patty, b. Dec. 31, 1809, at Casanova	1-B	32
Loran Orange, s. Enos & Patty, b. Aug. 26, 1815	1-B	32
Lucy, [twin with Lydia], d. Enos & Patty, b. July 16, 1812, at Woodstock	1-B	32
Lydia, [twin with Lucy], d. Enos & Patty, b. July 16, 1812, at Woodstock	1-B	32
Philip, of Monson, m. Anna **FOSTER**, of Union, Sept. 25, 1822, by Ingoldsby W. Crawford, J.P.	1-M	7
Philip F., of West Woodstock, m. Lucy R. **CORBIN**, of Union,		

	Vol.	Page
GAGE, (cont.)		
Aug. 31, 1853, by Rev. Samuel J. Curtice	1-M	87
GALE, Betsey, m. Ely **MOORE**, b. of Union, Dec. 19, 1822, by William Foster, J.P.	1-M	31
GALLOP, Abigail, of Montville, m. Gideon **WALES**, of Union, Jan. 25, 1798	1-M	23
GAUNDEY, Berah*, of South Brimfield, m. Mrs. Rhoda **PERRY**, of Gera, Oct. 31, 1793, by Sol[omo]n Wales, J.P. (*Perhaps "Borah")	TM	6
GAY, Amasa, m. Mary **MOORE**, b. of Union, Feb. 10, 1789	1-M	7
Persis, [twin with Polly], d. Amasa & Mary, b. Dec. 30, 1790	1-B	7
Polly, [twin with Persis], d. Amasa & Mary, b. Dec. 30, 1790	1-B	7
Sally, d. Amasa & Mary, b. Aug. 25, 1789	1-B	7
Walter Woodard, s. Amasa & Mary, b. Jan. 23, 1793	1-B	7
GIBSON, John, of Windham, m. Mary **HUTCHISSON**, of Union, Mar. 1, 1767	2LR	290
GILBERT, Mary Ann, m. John **BARNES**, May 19, 1836, by Ebenezer Lindsey, J.P.	1-M	61
GLAZURE, GLEAZIER, [see also **GLEASURE**], Alice had s. Preston **ARMOUR**, who d. Feb. 20, 1827	1-D	1
Alice had s. Preston **ARMOUR**, b. Jan. 20, 1820	1-B	83
GLEASURE, [see also **GLAZURE**], Roxalana, of Holland, m. Samuel **WEBBER**, Jr., of Union, Feb. 14, 1812	1-M	23
GOLD, Benjamin M., m. Mary **BROWN**, Dec. 14, 1843, by Rev. Washington Munger	1-M	56
GOODALE, GOODELL, [see also **GOODHILL**], Alles, of Pomfret, m. John **SESSIONS**, of Union, Nov. 5, 1766	2LR	290
Harvey, of Hartford, m. Lovina H. **HOLMAN**, of Union, May 1, 1839, by Samuel J. Curtiss	1-M	56
Merchant, of Charlton, Mass., m. Janett **COMSTOCK**, of Union, Apr. 8, 1834, by John Crawford, J.P.	1-M	55
Perry L., of Sturbridge, Mass., m. Minerva F. **BLODGETT**, of Union, July 3, 1845, by Rev. Samuel J. Curtiss	1-M	58
Roswell, of Charlton, Mass., m. Martha **COMSTOCK**, of Union, Mar. 14, 1838, by Moses C. Sessions, J.P.	1-M	56
GOODHILL, [see also **GOODALE**], Hulda, Mrs., m. Lovel **POWIN***, b. of Holland, July 24, 1793, by Sol[omo]n Wales, J.P. (***PARVIN**?)	TM	5
Polly, Mrs., of Holland, m. Asher **BADGER**, of Union, Aug. 22, 1796, by Sol[omo]n Wales, J.P.	TM	7
GOWDY, Jane, d. James & Anne, b. July 23, 1761	2LR	294
GREEN, James, s. Israel & Mary, b. Apr. 12, 1749	2LR	288
Lucy, d. Israel & Mary, d. Jan. 15, 1749	2LR	291
Lucy, d. Israel & Mary, b. Feb. 10, 1750/51	2LR	288
Mary, d. Israel & Mary, d. Feb. 3, 1750	2LR	291
GREGG, [see also **GRIGGS**], Hendrick, m. Mrs. Sarah Winchester **SESSIONS**, May 16, 1803, by Sol[omo]n Wales, J.P.	TM	17
GRIGGS, [see also **GREGG**], Anna, d. Elisha & Sarah, b. Jan. 29, 1797	1-B	7
Anna, m. Asa **COYE**, b. of Union, Dec. 14, 1826, by Neh[emiah] B. Beardsley	1-M	37
Chester, s. Elbijenks* & Lydia, b. Feb. 21, 1794 (*Albigence)	1-B	7
Elam, s. Joseph C. & Polly, b. Sept. 7, 1824	1-B	32
Elisha Ela, s. Joseph C. & Polly, b. June 6, 1818	1-B	32

	Vol.	Page
GRIGGS, (cont.)		
Esther, d. Elisha & Sarah, b. Jan. 13, 1800	1-B	7
Est[h]er, m. Norman **HORTON**, Nov. 27, 1823, by Henry Smith	1-M	30
Hannah, m. Burke **FOSTER**, Jan. 11, 1835, by Rev. Moses B. Church	1-M	28
John, s. Elisha & Sarah, b. Dec. 6, 1799	1-B	7
John, s. Elisha & Sarah, d. Dec. 8, 1799	1-D	7
John P., of Ashford, m. Emeline **HISCOX**, of Union, Jan. 20, 1845, by Rev. Samuel J. Curtiss	1-M	58
John T., of Ashford, m. Dolly Ann **HISCOCK**, of Union, Feb. 12, 1838, by Moses C. Sessions, J.P.	1-M	55
Joseph Cheney, s. Elisha & Sarah, b. Feb. 16, 1795	1-B	7
Joseph Maitland, s. Joseph C. & Polly, b. Oct. 8, 1816	1-B	32
Laura, m. Dexter **MOORE**, b. of Union, July 4, 1839, by Geo[rge] H. Woodward	1-M	63
Lucinda, d. Elisha & Sarah, b. Feb.8, 1793	1-B	7
Lucina, d. Joseph & Ele[a]nor, b. Sept. 30, 1794	1-B	7
Lucinda, m. Alexander **STRONG**, Jr., b. of Union, Nov. 28, 1816	1-M	29
Lydia, d. Joseph & Eleanor, b. Mar. 13, 1791	1-B	7
Lyman, s. Elbijencks* & Lydia, b. Mar. 30, 1797 (*Albigence)	1-B	7
Mahaleth, d. Elbijenks* & Lydia, b. Dec. 6, 1799 (*Albigence)	1-B	7
Orlando, s. Joseph C. & Lotty, b. Sept. 26, 1830	1-B	107
Philip, s. Joseph C. & Polly, b. May 7, 1820	1-B	32
Sally, of Union, m. David **JAMES**, of Ashford, June 12, 1823, by W[illia]m Foster, J.P.	1-M	10
GUILE, GUILD, Hugh Wellington, s. James R. & Almira, b. Aug. 27, 1835	1-B	107
James R., of Flushing*, N.Y., m. Almira **FISHER**, of Union, Mar. 10, 1833, by Rev. Leonard Gage, of Ashford (*Written "Slushing")	1-M	7
William Henry, s. James R. & Almira, b. Nov. 16, 1833	1-B	32
GURLEY, Aseneth D., m. Harvey **MARCY**, b. of Union, Apr. 10, 1825, by S. W. Crawford, J.P.	1-M	31
HALLADAY, HALLIDAY, Martha, w. Isaac, d. Nov. 28, 1760	2LR	270
Roseanna, d. Zuriah **WALKER**, b. Mar. 3, 1765; d. Apr. 19, 1765	2LR	267
HAMILTON, James F., of Stafford, m. Mary E. **WALES**, of Union, Mar. 6, 1844, by Rev. Samuel J. Curtiss	1-M	39
Tyler, m. Siloma **MOULTON**, b. of Union, Mar. 26, 1832, by Rev. Setephen (sic) Fairbanks	1-M	47
HAMMOND, Charles, s. Dr. Shubael & Polly, b. June 15, 1813	1-B	73
Cynthia, d. Dr. Shubael & Polly, b. Aug. 4, 1814	1-B	73
Cynthia, m. Judson **SMITH**, b. of Union, Jan. 17, 1838, by Rev. Alvan Underwood	1-M	65
Frances, s. Dr. Shubael & Polly, b. Jan. 21, 1816	1-B	73
Maria, d. Shubael & Polly, b. Feb. 26, 1820	1-B	26
Mary Ann, d. Sibbel **FAIRBANKS**, b. Apr. 9, 1807	1-B	62
Mary M., of Union, m. Joseph **AMIDOWN**, of Southbridge, Dec. 7, 1826, by Neh[emiah] B. Beardsley	1-M	1
Persis, d. Shubael & Polly, b. Aug. 9, 1827	1-B	36
Persis, of Union, m. Marcus N. **POTTER**, of Sturbridge, N.Y., Feb. 12, 1851, by Rev. Samuel J. Curtiss	1-M	81
Polly, wid. Dr. Shubael, & d. of Robert **PAUL**, d. Aug. 17, 1863, at Dexter, N.Y.; bd. at Union	1-D	9

	Vol.	Page
HAMMOND, (cont.)		
Samuel, s. Dr. Shubael & Polly, b. Apr. 18, 1818	1-B	73
Shubael, Dr., m. Polly **PAUL**, b. of Union, Oct. 4, 1812	1-M	8
HANES*, Ruth, of Union, m. Hiram **WATKINS**, of Ashford, Oct. 9, 1834, by Rev. Stephen Fairbanks (***HAWES**?)	1-M	46
HARVEY, William, of Palmer, Mass., m. Achsah **RUBY**, of Union, May 22, 1834, by Augustus Moore, J.P.	1-M	25
HASKELL, Amasa, of Woodstock, m. Amanda **PAUL**, of Union, Aug. 24, 1823, by Ingoldsby W. Crawford, J.P.	1-M	30
HATCH, Emily Almira, [d. John B. & Prescilla L.], b. May 26, 1845	1-B	134
Harriet, m. Arnold **PAINE**, b. of Union, Apr. 20, 1841, by Rev. Samuel J. Curtiss	1-M	52
Jarvis Bliss, [s. John B. & Prescilla L.], b. Sept. 30, 1838	1-B	134
Roswell Jarvis, [s. John B. & Prescilla L.], b. Oct. 28, 1841	1-B	134
Sarah Hinkson, [d. John B. & Prescilla L.], b. July 30, 1836	1-B	134
HAUGHTON, HOUGHTON, Amasa, s. Jonas & Sarah, b. Feb. 17, 1769	2LR	266
Celinda, d. Nehemiah & Esther, b. Nov. 17, 1830	1-B	96
Celinda, d. Sept. 3, 1833	1-D	8
Celinda R., d. Nehemiah & Esther, b. Dec. 27, 1838	1-B	96
Cemantha, [see under Samantha]		
Cinthia, d. Asa & Sybble, b. Sept. 25, 1768	2LR	266
Delana, d. Nehemiah & Esther, b. July 6, 1840	1-B	96
Diana, d. Nehemiah & Esther, b. June 17, 1817	1-B	73
Diana, of Union, m. Jedediah P. **WEBSTER**, of Wilbraham, [Oct.] 8, [1837], by Rev. Leonard Gage, of Ashford	1-M	60
Diantha, d. Nehemiah & Esther, b. Aug. 15, 1828	1-B	95
[E]lecta L., d. Nehemiah, b. Aug. 29, 1842	1-B	96
Jonas, of Union, m. Sarah **ABBOTT**, of Woodstock, Nov. 24, 1768	2LR	290
Lucy, d. Nehemiah & Esther, b. Dec. 31, 1818	1-B	73
Marcus Taft, s. Nehemiah & Esther, b. July 28, 1833	1-B	105
Mary, m. Daniel **HENDRICK**, May 27, 1752	2LR	295
Mary A., of Union, m. Hiram **STEBBINS**, of Wilbraham, Mass., Apr. 9, 1844, by Rev. Samuel J. Curtiss	1-M	68
Mary Ann, d. Nehemiah & Esther, b. Aug. 10, 1823	1-B	95
Myranda, d. Nehemiah & Esther, b. Mar. 8, 1821	1-B	73
Nehemiah, of Thompson, m. Esther **LAWSON**, of Union, Mar. 27, 1817	1-M	30
Sarah, d. Jonas & Hannah, b. Feb. 17, 1770	2LR	269
Semantha, d. Nehemiah & Esther, b. Apr. 5, 1826	1-B	95
Walter, s. Asa & Sybble, b. Feb. 20, 1770	2LR	266
[HAVILAND], [see under **HEVILAND**]		
HAWSE, Amos, s. Elijah & Rebeckah, b. Jan. 25, 1796	1-B	33
Asa, Jr., of Woodstock, m. Olive **SESSIONS**, of Union, May 20, 1824, by Neh[emiah] B. Beardsley	1-M	31
Betsey, d. Elijah & Rebeckah, b. Dec. 12, 1784, at Worcester	1-B	33
Betsey, of Union, m. Luther **BOSS**, of Ashford, Sept. 19, 1822, by William Foster, J.P.	1-M	2
Jason, s. Elijah & Rebeckah, b. Oct. 11, 1791	1-B	8
Jason, m. Lurana **COYE**, b. of Union, Mar. 16, 1815	1-M	8
Polly, d. Elijah & Rebeckah, b. Aug. 23, 1798	1-B	33
Polly, d. Elijah, d. Mar. 27, 1800	1-D	8
Ruth, d. Elijah & Rebeckah, b. Sept. 12, 1793	1-B	8
Ruth, of Union, m. Hiram **WATKINS**, of Ashford, Oct. 9, 1834, by		

	Vol.	Page
HAWSE, (cont.)		
Rev. Stephen Fairbanks (Written "Ruth **HANES**")	1-M	46
Sally, d. Elijah & Rebeckah, b. Oct. 23, 1786, at Worcester	1-B	33
Sally, m. Ebenezer **SESSIONS**, 3rd, b. of Union, Nov. 21, 1805	1-M	19
HAYWARD, HAYWOOD, Anna, d. Josiah & Anna, b. June 8, 1794	1-B	8
Betsey, d. Josiah & Anne, b. Oct. 26, 1792	1-B	8
Esther Work, d. Manasseth & Lucy, b. Dec. 1, 1790	1-B	8
Huldah, of Ashford, m. Ebenezer **SESSIONS**, of Union, May 18, 1769	2LR	290
Susanna, of Ashford, m. John **CRAWFORD**, of Union, Apr. 24, 1800	1-M	3
HENDRICK, HENDRICKS, HENDRICKES, Amasa, s. Daniel & Mary, b. Oct. 2, 1753	2LR	292
Benjamin, s. Jabes, d. Sept. 9, 1749	2LR	291
Benjamin, s. Sam[ue]l & Tabatha, b. Apr. 18, 1756	2LR	294
Benjamin, s. Samuel & Tabitha, d. Apr. 26, 1756	2LR	270
Daniel, m. Mary **HOUGHTON**, May 27, 1752	2LR	295
David, s. Jabes & Louis, d. Nov. 2, 1749	2LR	291
David, s. Jabes & Lois, b. Jan. 28, 1754	2LR	292
Ezra, s. John & Hannah, b. Feb. 2, 1762	2LR	294
James, s.Israel & Ann, d. Sept. 17, 1760	2LR	270
John, m. Hannah **ABBOTT**, Mar. 24, 1761	2LR	295
John, s. John & Hannah, b. Apr. 4, 1764	2LR	267
Marsilla, d. Sam[ue]l & Tabitha, b. May 23, 1757	2LR	294
Mary, d. John & Hannah, b. Dec. 5, 1765	2LR	268
Nathan, s. Jabes & Louis, d. Oct. 31, 1754	2LR	291
Samuel, m. Tabitha **SNA----**, June 19, 1755	2LR	295
Samuel, s. Sam[ue]l & Tabitha, b. July 26, 1759	2LR	294
HENRY, Silas, of Holland, m. Mrs. Susannah **FOSTER**, of Stafford, May 12, 1803, by Sol[omo]n Wales, J.P.	TM	16
HEVILAND, Mercy, m. Luke **COY**, b. of Rensseloeville, Oct. 15, 1799, by Sol[omo]n Wales, J.P.	TM	11
HIGGENS Elijah, Jr., of Worthington, Mass., m. Mrs. Amelia **BURLEY**, of Union, Aug. 15, 1849, by Ebenezer Lindsey, J.P.	1-M	58
HINES, Archilus, of Holland, m. Mary **RIMOND**, Jan. 2, 1788, by Sol[omo]n Wales, J.P.	TM	2
HISCOCK, HISCOX, Abby, d. David & Anna, b. May 5, 1808	1-B	48
Almira, of Union, m. Otis **LYON**, of Woodstock, Mar. 19, 1832, by Rev. Stephen Hiscox	1-M	47
David, Jr. of Ashford, m. Mrs. Anna **THOMPSON**, of Union, May 10, 1805	1-M	8
David Thompson, s. David & Anna, b. Sept. 8, 1809	1-B	62
Dolly Ann, d. Isaiah & Dolly, b. Oct. 22, 1818	1-B	35
Dolly Ann, of Union, m. John T. **GRIGGS**, of Ashford, Feb. 12, 1838, by Moses C. Sessions, J.P.	1-M	35
Emeline, d. Isaiah & Dolly, b. July 1, 1823	1-B	35
Emeline, of Union, m. John P. **GRIGGS**, of Ashford, Jan. 20, 1845, by Rev. Samuel J. Curtiss	1-M	58
Harmony C., of Union, m. Joseph **FARNHAM**, of Eastford, Aug. 13, 1851, by Rev. Henry Forbush	1-M	82
Isaiah, s. Isaiah & Dolly, b. Sept. 26, 1813	1-B	62
Lucius Griggs, s. Isaiah & Dolly, b. June 17, 1821	1-B	35
Luke, of Union, m. Mrs. Eliza **WAKEFIELD**, of Stafford, June 15,		

UNION VITAL RECORDS 91

	Vol.	Page
HISCOCK, HISCOX, (cont.)		
1845, by Amos Babcock, Holland, Mass.	1-M	62
Luther, m. Permelia **BUGBEE**, b. of Union, Dec. 28, 1837, by Rev. Washington Munger, at the house of Marcus Bugbee	1-M	26
Luther Rich, s. Isaiah & Dolly, b. Feb. 22, 1812	1-B	62
Lyman, s. David & Anna, b. Dec. 29, 1805	1-B	48
Mary, of Union, m. William **RICHARDS**, of Sturbridge, Jan. 11, 1838, by Rev. Stephen Fairbanks	1-M	18
Mary, of Union, m. James **WALKER**, of Woodstock, Nov. 5, 1838, by Rev. Stephen Fairbanks	1-M	60
Molly, m. Jedediah **BUGBEE**, Oct. 29, 1767	2LR	290
Phillellia, d. Isaiah & Sally, b. June 5, 1826	1-B	36
Rebeckah, Mrs., m. Rufus **ROOD**, Nov. 29, 1798, by Sol[omo]n Wales, J.P.	TM	10
Rebecca, of Union, m. Schuyler **SPENCER**, of Southbridge, Jan. 1, 1829, by Ingoldsby W. Crawford, J.P.	1-M	17
William, s. David & Anna, b. Jan. 21, 1807	1-B	48
Zelotes Palmer, s. Isaiah & Dolly, b. June 23, 1816	1-B	35
HITCHCOCK, Caleb, Rev., m. Sarah **WINCHESTER**, Nov. 30, 1750	2LR	295
Elizabeth, d. Rev. Caleb & Sarah, b. Feb. 29, 1754	2LR	293
Gad, s. Caleb & Sarah, b. July 10, 1766	2LR	268
Martha, d. Rev. Caleb & Sarah, b. Dec. 9, 1757	2LR	293
Molly, d. Caleb & Sarah, b. Aug. 27, 1761	2LR	294
Winchester, s. Caleb & Sarah, b. Sept. 5, 1763	2LR	267
HODGES, Fanny, of Monson, m. Fred[e]rick **LADD**, of Coventry, Dec. 16, 1788, by Sol[omo]n Wales, J.P.	TM	2
HOLMAN, HOLLMAN, Almira, d. Thomas, Jr. & Levina, b. May 19, 1804	1-B	48
Almira, of Union, m. Samuel **SHEPHARD**, of Sturbridge, Oct. 16, 1827, by Neh[emiah] B. Beardsley	1-M	21
Amey, d. Rufus & Lucy, b. Aug. 16, 1815	1-B	35
Annis, d. Rufus & Lucy, b. Aug. 20, 1810	1-B	35
Calista, d. Thomas, Jr. & Lovina, b. Apr. 19, 1807	1-B	62
Calista, of Union, m. Rev. Justus H. **VINTON**, of Willington, [May*] 9, [1834], by Rev. Samuel S. Mallory (*April?)	1-M	22
Chester, s. Rufus & Lucy, b. Nov. 1, 1804	1-B	34
Chester, s. Rufus & Lucy, d. Apr. 19, 1808	1-D	8
Clarissa, d. Rufus & Lucy, b. June 11, 1818	1-B	35
Clarissa, d. Rufus & Lucy, d. Feb. 11, 1819	1-D	8
Elijah, s. Thomas, Jr. & Levina, b. May 31, 1803	1-B	48
Elijah, m. Hannah **WILBUR**, b. of Union, Jan. 5, 1834, by Rev. Leonard Gage, of Ashford	1-M	25
Elijah, d. Feb. 28, 1837	1-D	8
Henrietta Almira, d. Elijah & Hannah, b. Feb. 4, 1836	1-B	105
Jeremiah, of Union, m. Polly **McINTIER**, of Charlton, Dec. 14, 1809	1-M	8
John, of Union, m. Mrs. Mary **BOSWORTH**, of Ashford, Apr. 6, 1809	1-M	8
Levina Howard, d. Thomas, Jr. & Lovina, b. Apr. 10, 1809	1-B	62
Lovina H., of Union, m. Harvey **GOODALE**, of Hartford, May 1, 1839, by Samuel J. Curtiss	1-M	56
Lucy, b. Sept. 19, 1781	1-B	34
Lucy, d. Rufus & Lucy, b. Nov. 11, 1820	1-B	35

BARBOUR COLLECTION

HOLMAN, HOLLMAN, (cont.)

	Vol.	Page
Lusina, d. Rufus & Lucy, b. Apr. 1, 1807	1-B	34
Lydia, d. Thomas, Jr. & Levina, b. June 22, 1801	1-B	33
Lydia, m. Paul **LAWSON**, b. of Union, Dec. 9, 1824, by Neh[emiah] B. Beardsley	1-M	12
Minerva, d. Thomas & Levina, b. Mar. 4, 1816	1-B	34
Minerva, of Union, m. Rev. Rhodolphus **WESTON**, of Carthage, Ill., Sept. 1, 1840, by Rev. Samuel J. Curtiss	1-M	60
Moses, s. Jeremiah & Sally, b. Feb. 11, 1811	1-B	62
Numan, s. John & Mary, b. Dec. 24, 1809	1-B	62
Palmer, s. Rufus & Lucy, b. Feb. 20, 1813	1-B	35
Rufus, b. Oct. 20, 1780	1-B	34
Rufus, of Union, m. Lucy **EDDY**, of Monson, Sept. 1, 1803	1-M	30
Rufus Milton, s. Rufus & Lucy, b. Oct. 8, 1826	1-B	36
Salam, s. Thomas, Jr. & Levina, b. July 1, 1802	1-B	48
Sarah Crawford, d. Elijah & Hannah, b. Dec. 18, 1834	1-B	105
Thomas, Jr., of Union, m. Mrs. Levina **HOWARD**, of Ashford, June 5, 1800	1-M	8
Thomas, Jr., s. Thomas & Levina, b. July 15, 1812	1-B	62
HOLMES, Harvey L., m. Fanney **SEVERY**, b. of Union, Nov. 7, 1852, by Rev. Samuel J. Curtice	1-M	84
HOLT, Caroline V., m. Joseph H. **FAULKNER**, Nov. 29, 1845, by Rev. Samuel S. Curtiss	1-M	28
HOOD, Levine, Mrs., of Leicester, m. Paul **ANTHONY**, of Sturbridge, June 24, 1802, by Sol[omo]n Wales, J.P.	TM	15
HORTON, Almira, d. Ezra & Olive, b. Apr. 27, 1801	1-B	34
Almira Minerva, d. Erastus & Tryphenia, b. June 1, 1809	1-B	62
Alonzo Erastus, s. Erastus & Tryphenia, b. Oct. 24, 1813	1-B	73
Anna, d. Rev. Ezra & Mary, b. Apr. 15, 1763	2LR	294
Carlo, s. Norman & Esther, b. Feb. 13, 1826	1-B	36
Charles, s. Ezra, Jr. & Lucy, b. July 3, 1834	1-B	105
Cha[u]nc[e]y, s. Ezra & Olive, b. May 13, 1797	1-B	8
Edward Haskall, s. Ezra, Jr. & Lucy, b. July 27, 1830	1-B	25
Eli, s. Ezra & Olive, b. May 6, 1803	1-B	34
Elvira, d. Ezra, Jr. & Lucy, b. July 30, 1828. Recorded Dec. 28, 1833	1-B	25
Erastus, m. Mrs. Tryphenia **BURLEY**, b. of Union, Apr. 28, 1808	1-M	8
Eserord (?), s. Ezra, Jr. & Lucy, b. Jan. 18, 1822	1-B	17
Ezra, s. Rev. Ezra & Mary, b. Apr. 12, 1761	2LR	294
Ezra, s. Ezra & Olive, b. June 12, 1794	1-B	8
Ezra Mason, s. Ezra, Jr. & Lucy, b. June 3, 1832	1-B	25
Fidellia, d. Ezra & Olive, b. Jan. 5, 1809	1-B	34
Gurdon, s. Ezra & Olive, b. Feb. 24, 1791	1-B	8
Gurdon, m. Lucy **DAVISSON**, b. of Union, May 1, 1816	1-M	30
Harriet, d. Norman & Esther, b. Aug. 22, 1824	1-B	35
Hellen, d. Ezra, Jr. & Lucy, b. Aug. 3, 1823. Recorded Dec. 28, 1833	1-B	17
Laurens, s. Ezra & Olive, b. Mar. 21, 1807	1-B	34
Lucinda, d. Ezra & Olive, b. Aug. 28, 1792	1-B	8
Lucinda, m. Alfred **MOORE**, b. of Union, Jan. 28, 1819	1-M	13
Mary, Jr., Mrs., of Union, m. Rev. Calvin **INGOLS**, of Pomfrett, May 28, 1795	1-M	9
Mary, d. Ezra & Olive, b. Oct. 17, 1798	1-B	8

	Vol.	Page
HORTON, (cont.)		
Mary, m. Elijah **KINNEY**, May 31, 1821, by Rev. Cyrus W. Gray, of Stafford	1-M	11
Mary Emily, d. Erastus & Tryphenia, b. July 19, 1811	1-B	62
Norman, m. Est[h]er **GRIGGS**, Nov. 27, 1823, by Henry Smith	1-M	30
Norman Sanford, s. Norman & Esther, b. Apr. 17, 1828	1-B	95
Norton, s. Ezra & Olive, b. Dec. 5, 1795	1-B	8
Olive, d. Ezra & Olive, b. Apr. 1, 1805	1-B	34
Philena, d. Ezra & Olive, b. June 12, 1789	1-B	8
Philena, m. Salmon **STRONG**, b. of Union, Jan. 9, 1812	1-M	19
Robert Bruce, s. Ezra & Lucy, b. Oct. 13, 1843	1-B	131
Thomas, s. Ezra, Jr. & Lucy, b. May 4, 1825. Recorded Dec. 28, 1833	1-B	25
Thomas, m. Delight A. **WALES**, b. of Union, Apr. 22, 1850, by Rev. Samuel J. Curtiss	1-M	79
HOUGHTON, [see under **HAUGHTON**]		
HOW, Ele[a]ner, wid., d. Nov. 6, 1806	1-D	8
HOWARD, Abner, of Sturbridge, m. Mrs. Abigail **COYE**, of Union, Apr. 16, 1799	1-M	8
Abner, d. Apr. 7, 1825	1-D	8
Anna, [twin with Sally], d. Manassah & Lucy, b. Sept. 24, 1801	1-B	48
Augustus, s. Manassah & Dorothy, b. June 19, 1806	1-B	62
Clamantine, s. Jotham & Polly, b. Apr. 31 (sic), 1804	1-B	48
Clinton, s. Manassah & Dorothy, b. Dec. 17, 1815. Recorded July 11, 1833	1-B	17
Eleazer, s. Manassah & Lucy, b. Aug. 21, 1793	1-B	48
Grosvenor, s. Jotham & Polly, b. June 10, 1799	1-B	48
Harris, s. Jotham & Polly, b. Apr. 6, 1806	1-B	48
John, s. Manassah & Dorothy, b. May 31, 1804	1-B	62
John, m. Lydia **BUGBEE**, b. of Union, Oct. 2, 1825, by Ingoldsby W. Crawford, J.P.	1-M	39
Levina, Mrs., of Ashford, m. Thomas **HOLMAN**, Jr., of Union, June 5, 1800	1-M	8
Louisa, d. Manassah & Dorothy, b. Sept. 5, 1808. Recorded July 11, 1833	1-B	17
Lucy, d. Manassah & Lucy, b. Oct. 15, 1795	1-B	48
Lydia, of Ashford, m. Samuel **CRAWFORD**, Jr., of Union, Aug. 20, 1801	1-M	3
Marvin, of Eastford, m. Betsey **WALES**, of Union, Oct. 26, 1851, by Rev. Henry B. Blake, of So. Coventry	1-M	82
Nancy S., of Woodstock, m. Amos **BUGBEE**, of Union, Dec. 11, 1850, by Bela Hicks, Adm., Woodstock	1-M	80
Phebe, Mrs., m. Abner **BADGER**, b. of Union, Nov. 26, 1801, by Sol[omo]n Wales, J.P.	TM	13
Polly, of Union, m. Leicester **ANDERSON**, of Ashford, Aug. 3, 1817	1-M	1
Sally, d. Manassah & Lucy, b. Sept. 5, 1798	1-B	48
Sally, [twin with Anna], d. Manassah & Lucy, b. Sept. 24, 1801	1-B	48
Sally, of Union, m. Pearley **WALKER**, Jr., of Ashford, June 6, 1826, by Ingoldsby W. Crawford, J.P.	1-M	24
Stillman, s. Jotham & Polly, b. Jan. 2, 1802	1-B	48
William, s. Manassah & Dorothy, b. July 25, 1812. Recorded July 11, 1833	1-B	17

	Vol.	Page
HOWARD, (cont.)		
-----, of Palmer, m. Amanda **RUBY**, of Union, Apr. 5, 1827, by Neh[emiah] B. Beardsley	1-M	25
HOWLET, Nancy, of Woodstock, m. George **THOMPSON**, Jr., of Union, Mar. 14, 1816	1-M	20
HUMPHREY, Ebenezer, of Ashford, m. Mary **SIMONS**, of Union, May 5, 1795, by Sol[omo]n Wales, J.P.	TM	7
HUNT, Daniel, s. John & Anna, b. Oct. 12, 1792	1-B	33
Ira, s. John & Anna, b. Feb. 15, 1797	1-B	33
Ira, s. John, d. Aug. 19, 1800	1-D	8
Jerrethmell, s. John & Anna, b. Jan. 3, 1794	1-B	33
John, of Union, m. Anna **WESTON**, of Willington, Sept. 8, 1791	1-M	8
Lydda, w. John, d. May 3, 1790	1-D	8
Mary, d. John & Anna, b. June 14, 1795	1-B	33
Timothy Westen, s. John & Anna, b. July 18, 1799	1-B	33
HURLBUTT, Daniel, of Trumbull Cty., O., m. Amy Louisa **NEWELL**, of Union, Aug. 14, 1837, by Rev. Alvin Underwood	1-M	26
HUTCHINSON, HUTCHISSON, Mary, of Union, m. John **GIBSON**, of Windham, Mar. 1, 1767	2LR	290
Parcy, d. Amos & Mary, b. May 16, 1767	2LR	268
HYDE, Ephraim H., of Stafford, m. Esther **FOSTER**, of Union, June 25, 1840, by Augustus Moore, J.P.	1-M	39
INGALLS, INGALS, Calvin, Rev., of Pomfrett, m. Mrs. Mary **HORTON**, Jr., of Union, May 28, 1795	1-M	9
Catharine, d. Calven & Mary, b. June 12, 1796	1-B	9
JAMES, Aaron Rathbone, s. Benjamin & Cynthia, b. Sept. 26, 1811. Recorded Oct. 3, 1831	1-B	31
Benjamin, m. Cynthia **RUSSELL**, b. of Ashford, Feb. 8, 1794	1-M	10
Benjamin Reynolds, s. Benjamin & Cynthia, b. Nov. 22, 1796	1-B	10
Benjamin Reynolds, d. Sept. 14, 1819. Recorded Oct. 3, 1831	1-D	10
Betsey, d. Benjamin & Cynthia, b. Mar. 30, 1807. Recorded Oct. 3, 1831	1-B	31
David, of Ashford, m. Sally **GRIGGS**, of Union, June 12, 1823, by W[illia]m Foster, J.P.	1-M	10
Diana, d. Benjamin & Cynthia, b. Oct. 15, 1794, at Ashford	1-B	10
Diana, d. Benjamin & Cynthia, d. Mar. 6, 1796. Recorded Oct. 3, 1831	1-D	10
Elisha Benjamin Reynolds, s. Benjamin & Cynthia, b. Jan. 22, 1814. Recorded Oct. 3, 1831	1-B	31
Hannah, of Union, m. Ephraim L. **CARPENTER**, of Ashford, Feb. 15, 1827, by Ingoldsby W. Crawford, J.P.	1-M	38
Hannah Diana, d. Benjamin & Cynthia, b. June 10, 1801, at Ashford	1-B	10
Jonathan, s. Benjamin & Lydia*, b. Apr. 13, 1799, at Ashford (*Probably Cynthia?)	1-B	10
Jonathan, m. Parmela **MOORE**, b. of Union, Nov. 24, 1825, by Neh[emiah] B. Beardsley	1-M	10
Josiah R., m. Lucretia **WATSON**, Oct. 12, 1845, by Rev. Samuel J. Curtiss	1-M	10
Josiah Russell, s. Benjamin & Cynthia, b. Sept. 12, 1809. Recorded Oct. 3, 1831	1-B	31
Nancy Diana, d. Jonathan & Parmela, b. Jan. 12, 1832	1-B	31
Rebeckah, d. Benjamin & Cynthia, b. Mar. 17, 1805	1-B	10
Rebecca, of Union, m. Joseph **WALKER**, of Ashford, June 25,		

UNION VITAL RECORDS

	Vol.	Page
JAMES, (cont.)		
1829, by Ingoldsby W. Crawford, J.P.	1-M	24
Rhoda, d. Benjamin & Cynthia, b. Mar. 27, 1803, at Ashford	1-B	10
R[h]oda, of Union, m. David **FULLER**, of Stafford, Dec. 25, 1823, by William Foster, J.P.	1-M	6
Willard Reynolds, s. Jonathan & Parmela, b. Nov. 21, 1827	1-B	10
JEN[N]INGS, Royal, of Ashford, m. Sarah **BADGER**, of Union, Dec. 20, 1749	2LR	295
JOHNSON, Dinah, of Union, m. Lyman E. **THOMPSON**, of Mansfield, Oct. 3, 1833, by Augustus Moore, J.P.	1-M	20
Huldah, d. David & Huldah, b. Sept. 28, 1820	1-B	10
Huldah, of Union, m. David G. **WHITTEMORE**, of Sturbridge, Mass., Nov. 25, 1849, by Rev. Samuel J. Curtiss	1-M	79
Laura, m. Timothy D. **DIMICK**, Dec. 13, 1840, by Augustus Moore, J.P.	1-M	4
Lurandus, of Tolland, m. Sarah J. **COLLYER**, of Union, Jan. 30, 1853, by Ebenezer Lindsey, J.P.	1-M	85
KELLEY, KILLY, Frances, s. Nathan & Olive, b. Feb. 5, 1810	1-B	11
Wing, s. Nathan & Olive, b. May 13, 1807	1-B	11
KENNEY, [see also **KINNEY**], Abigail, d. Eleazer & Mary, b. Mar. 18, 1792	1-B	11
Abigail, d. Joel & Chloe, b. Sept. 23, 1793	1-B	11
Archibal, s. Joel & Chloe, b. Oct. 24, 1794	1-B	11
Daniel, s. Joel & Chloe, b. Mar. 11, 1798	1-B	11
Eleazer, s. Nathan & Abigail, b. Mar. 28, 1771	1-B	11
Joel, s. Nathan & Abigail, b. Aug. 1, 1769	1-B	11
Joel, m. Mrs. C[h]loe **COY**, b. of Union, May 10, 1792, by Sol[omo]n Wales, J.P.	TM	4
John, s. Nathan & Abigail, b. May 30, 1776	1-B	11
Louise, d. John & Lucy (?), b. Nov. 21, 1809	1-B	11
Lucy, d. Nathan & Abigail, b. Dec. 4, 1774	1-B	11
Lucy, Mrs., m. David **COY**, Oct. 22, 1797, by Sol[omo]n Wales, J.P.	TM	9
Ruth, d. Nathan & Abigail, b. Aug. 14, 1772	1-B	11
KENT, Joseph Morse, m. Pattee **BUGGBEE**, July 11, 1799, by Sol[omo]n Wales, J.P.	TM	11
KEYES, Elnathan, s. John & Mary, b. Oct. 11, 1769	2LR	266
John Lyman, s. John **KEYES** & Polly **WALKER**, b. Nov., 16, 1810. Recorded Mar. 26, 1830	1-B	40
Sarah Ann, d. Cyrel & Margaret, b. Sept. 26, 1816	1-B	40
KINNEY, [see also **KENNEY**], Abigail, d. Eliazer & Mary, d. Apr. 5, 1792	1-D	11
Abigail, d. Joel & Chloe, d. Sept. 27, 1792	1-D	11
Abigail, of Woodstock, m. Benoni **WALKER**, of Union, Nov. 14, 1799	1-M	23
Albert, s. Nathan & Lucy, b. Aug. 15, 1839	1-B	50
Alpheas, s. Nathan & Eunice, b. July 29, 1781	1-B	39
Ami Eliza, d. Nathan & Lucy, b. Apr. 1, 1831	1-B	49
Ann E., m. Robert B. **PAUL**, b. of Union, Mar. 16, 1852, by Rev. Samuel J. Curtice	1-M	83
Daniel, s. Joel & Chloe, d. Mar. 12, 1798	1-D	11
David, s. Nathan & Eunice, b. Mar. 28, 1789	1-B	39
David, s. Alpheas & Lucy, b. Jan. 5, 1813	1-B	39
Eleazer, m. Mary **PAUL**, b. of Union, Nov. 24, 1791, by Sol[omo]n		

BARBOUR COLLECTION

	Vol.	Page
KINNEY, (cont.)		
Wales, J.P.	TM	3
Eleazer, m. Phebe **MOORE**, b. of Union, May 20, 1849, by Ebenezer Lindsey, J.P.	1-M	78
Eli Edwin, s. Elijah & Mary, b. July 20, 1827	1-B	49
Elijah, m. Mary **HORTON**, May 31, 1821, by Rev. Cyrus W. Gray, of Stafford	1-M	11
Elisha Edwin, s. Elijah & Mary, b. Sept. 25, 1822. Recorded Mar. 31, 1830	1-B	40
Elisha Edwin, s. Elijah & Mary, d. Mar. 27, 1828	1-D	11
Elizabeth, m. Moses C. **SESSIONS**, b. of Union, Jan. 2, 1821, by William Foster, J.P.	1-M	29
Esther, d. Nathan & Lucy, b. May 6, 1842	1-B	50
Friend Scot, s. Alpheas & Lucy, b. Nov. 10, 1808	1-B	39
Harrison, s. Elijah & Mary, b. July 7, 1825	1-B	40
Joel, m. Chloe **COYE**, b. of Union, May 10, 1792	1-M	11
John, m. Rhoda **CHAMBERLAIN**, b. of Union, June 16, 1811	1-M	11
John, Jr., s. John & Rhoda, b. Aug. 30, 1819	1-B	40
Lucy, m. David **COYE**, b. of Union, Oct. 22, 1797	1-M	3
Mariah Jane, d. Nathan & Lucy, b. Feb. 14, 1835	1-B	49
Mary Makiey, d. Alpheas & Lucy, b. Jan. 29, 1811	1-B	39
Mary Olive, d. Elijah & Mary, b. Dec. 1, 1823. Recorded Mar. 31, 1830	1-B	40
Meriam, s. John & Rhoda, b. Feb. 23, 1818	1-B	39
Milton Horace, s. Nathan & Lucy, b. July 9, 1837	1-B	50
Miran, s. Nathan & Lucy, b. Feb. 24, 1833	1-B	49
Nathan, Jr., s. Nathan & Eunice, b. Nov. 6, 1785	1-B	39
Nathan, m. Lucy **WALES**, b. of Union, Jan. 18, 1830, by Ingoldsby W. Crawford, J.P.	1-M	11
Orren Jefferson, s. Alpheas & Lucy, b. Feb. 12, 1806	1-B	39
Permilla, d. John & Rhoda, b. July 10, 1814	1-B	39
Permilla, d. John & Rhoda, d. Jan. 16, 1815	1-D	11
Ruth, m. Thomas **LAWSON**, Jr., b. of Union, Jan. 1, 1795	1-M	12
Sanford, s. Alpheas & Lucy, b. Mar. 13, 1815	1-B	39
Truman, s. John & Rhoda, b. July 1, 1815	1-B	39
Warren, s. Alpheas & Lucy, b. Aug. 14, 1804	1-B	39
LADD, Fred[e]rick, of Coventry, m. Fanny **HODGES**, of Monson, Dec. 16, 1788, by Sol[omo]n Wales, J.P.	TM	2
LAFLEN, Abraham, s. John & Susanna, b. Jan. 26, 1754	2LR	292
Hannah, d. John & Susanna, b. Nov. 10, 1758	2LR	294
James, s. John & Susanna, b. Apr. 8, 1747	2LR	292
Jean, d. John & Susanna, d. Sept. 8, 1748	2LR	291
John, s. John & Susanna, b. May 5, 1752	2LR	292
Mary, d. John & Susanna, b. Feb. 12, 1749	2LR	292
Mary, d. John & Susanna, d. Sept. 7, 1749	2LR	291
Mary, m. Edmund **MARIAM**, Nov. 27, 1788, by Sol[omo]n Wales, J.P.	TM	2
Nancy, d. John & Susanna, b. Apr. 5, 1760	2LR	294
Polly, Mrs., m. Stephen **MOOR**, July 4, 1799, by Sol[omo]n Wales, J.P.	TM	10
Samuel, s. John & Susanna, b. Apr. 7, 1757	2LR	294
Susanna, d. John & Susanna, b. July 24, 1753	2LR	294
LAMB, Mary of Ashford, m. James **RUBY**, of Union, Dec. 31, 1801	1-M	18

UNION VITAL RECORDS 97

	Vol.	Page
LAMB, (cont.)		
Stephen A., m. Mary A. **RIDER**, Sept. 8, 1845, by Rev. Samuel J. Curtiss	1-M	54
LARNED, LARNARD, [see also **LEONARD**], Abijah, m. Anne **WALES**, Dec. 31, 1753	2LR	295
Abijah, s. Abijah & Anne, b. Feb. 2, 1760	2LR	293
Ann, d. Abijah & Ann, b. Apr. 2, 1769	2LR	266
Anna, d. Abijah & Anna, d. Sept. 4, 1770	2LR	270
David, s. Abijah & Anne, b. July 28, 1754	2LR	292
Eunice, d. Abijah, d. Aug. 21, 1758	2LR	291
Irene, d. Abijah & Ann, b. Feb. 25, 1765	2LR	267
James, s. Abijah & Ann, b. Nov. 18, 1761	2LR	294
Jonathan, m. Betsey **DIXON**, b. of Union, Sept. 2, 1852, by Rev. Samuel J. Curtice	1-M	83
Silvanus, s. Abijah & Anne, b. May 26, 1763	2LR	267
LAWSON, Adaline, d. Ira & Amy, b. Mar. 31, 1830	1-B	114
Amy, Mrs., m. Nathaniel **NEWELL**, Jr., b. of Union, Dec. 7, 1808	1-M	14
Amy, w. Ira, d. June 29, 1836, ae 41 y.	1-D	25
Amy Heflin, d. Ira & Anna, b. Sept. 25, 1839	1-B	114
Ann, w. Ira, d. Feb. 23, 1860	1-D	25
Anna, wid. Robert, d. Dec. 14, 1841, ae 78 y.	1-D	12
Caleb, s. David & Sarah, b. Mar. 11, 1792	1-B	12
Caleb, s. David & Sarah, d. June 29, 1792	1-D	12
Caroline, d. Ira & Amy, b. May 29, 1828	1-B	114
Caroline, d. Ira & Amy, d. Aug. 6, 1831, ae 3 y.	1-D	25
Caroline Louisa, d. Ira & Ann, b. May 27, 1847	1-B	129
Casper L., m. Abigail **BOLES**, b. of Union, Sept. 25, 1831, by Rev. Stephen Fairbanks	1-M	47
Casper Monroe, s. Casper L. & Abigail, b. Dec. 8, 1835	1-B	129
Daniel, s. Thomas & Esther, b. Feb. 17, 1763	2LR	294
Daniel Webster, s. Ira & Anna, b. Jan. 12, 1838	1-B	114
David, s. Robert & Anna, b. July 8, 1800	1-B	12
David, d. Jan. 19, 1836	1-D	12
Ebenezer, s. John, Jr. & Mary, b. Jan. 26, 1760	2LR	293
Edwin Newton, s. Paul & Lydia, b. Jan. 26, 1832	1-B	30
Emoline, d. Ira & Amy, b. Mar. 28, 1832	1-B	114
Esther, d. Thomas & Esther, b. Feb. 7, 1767	2LR	268
Esther, m. Alpheas **TWIST**, b. of Union, Feb. 3, 1795	1-M	20
Esther, d. Thomas, Jr. & Ruth, b. May 6, 1799	1-B	12
Esther, [twin with Mary], d. Robert & Anna, b. Mar. 14, 1803	1-B	12
Esther, w. Thomas, d. Jan. 22, 1804	1-D	12
Esther, of Union, m. Nehemiah **HOUGHTON**, of Thompson, Mar. 27, 1817	1-M	30
Esther, of Union, m. John **MOORE**, of Ashford, Nov. 29, 1827, by Neh[emiah] B. Beardsley	1-M	41
Esther Calista, d. Paul & Lydia, b. Jan. 16, 1830	1-B	30
George Milton, s. Paul & Lydia, b. Aug. 22, 1847	1-B	121
Hannah, d. Thomas & Esther, d. June 22, 1756	2LR	291
Ira, s. Robert & Anna, b. July 4, 1796	1-B	12
Ira Remmington, s. Ira & Amy, b. Apr. 25, 1834	1-B	114
Jane Brown, d. Ebenezer & Elizabeth, b. Sept. 28, 1795	1-B	12
John, m. Mary **BROWN**, Sept. 12, 1751	2LR	295
John, s. John, Jr. & Mary, b. Nov. 12, 1752	2LR	292

LAWSON, (cont.)

	Vol.	Page
John, d. Jan. 20, 1795	1-D	12
John Fields, s. Ira & Anna, b. May 24, 1841, at Ashford	1-B	114
Julia Ann, d. Ira & Amey, b. June 3, 1824	1-B	74
Justus Vinton, s. Paul & Lydia, b. Apr. 4, 1834	1-B	30
Louisa, m. Charles A. **CORBIN**, b. of Union, Jan. 17, 1849, by Thomas Holman, Jr.	1-M	77
Lovisa, d. Paul & Lydia, b. Dec. 9, 1826	1-B	74
Lydia Ann, d. Paul & Lydia, b. Nov. 15, 1839	1-B	113
Lydia Ann, d. Paul & Lydia, d. Mar. 26, 1840	1-D	25
Margaret, d. Thomas & Est[h]er, d. Apr. 18, 1758	2LR	291
Margaret, d. David & Sarah, b. Oct. 19, 1790	1-B	12
Martha, d. Thomas & Esther, b. Mar. 19, 1765	2LR	267
Mary, m. Matthew **PAULL**, Jr., Nov. 13, 1755	2LR	295
Mary, [twin with Esther], d. Robert & Anna, b. Mar. 14, 1803	1-B	12
Matthew, m. Rebeckah **ROSS**, b. of Union, Feb. 19, 1795	1-M	12
Mehetabel, d. Thomas & Esther, b. Mar. 17, 1761	2LR	294
Minerva, d. Paul & Lydia, b. Mar. 18, 1837	1-B	113
Nancy Elizabeth, d. Casper L. & Abigail, b. Nov. 19, 1832	1-B	129
Paul, m. Lydia **HOLLMAN**, b. of Union, Dec. 9, 1824, by Neh[emiah] B. Beardsley	1-M	12
Paul Clinton, s. Paul & Lydia, b. Sept. 2, 1828	1-B	30
Phebe, d. Robert & Anna, b. Feb. 12, 1792	1-B	12
Phebe, of Union, m. Lyman **MOORE**, of Smithfield, May 31, 1827, by Nehemiah B. Beardsley	1-M	32
Robert, s. Thomas & Esther, b. Jan. 11, 1759	2LR	293
Robert, s. Ira & Amey, b. May 8, 1827	1-B	74
Robert, d. Apr. 19, 1835, ae 76	1-D	12
Ruth, Mrs., of Union, m. Jonathan **BLANCHARD**, of Monson, Oct. 6, 1828, by Neh[emiah] B. Beardsley	1-M	34
Sara[h] An[n], d. David & Sarah, b. Dec. 6, 1806	1-B	12
Susan, d. David & Sarah, d. Mar. 13, 1810	1-D	12
Susan, d. Paul & Lydia, b. July 10, 1843	1-B	121
Thomas, m. Esther **PAULL**, Dec. 31, 1754	2LR	295
Thomas, s. John, Jr. & Mary, b. Jan. 7, 1758	2LR	293
Thomas, s. Thomas & Esther, b. Mar. 22, 1769	2LR	266
Thomas, Jr., m. Ruth **KINNEY**, b. of Union, Jan. 1, 1795	1-M	12
Thomas, Jr., d. Dec. 20, 1819, in the 51st y. of his age	1-D	12
Thomas, s. Ira & Amey, b. Aug. 6, 1822, at Cranston, R.I.	1-B	74
Thomas, d. Jan. 5, 1825	1-D	12
Thomas Ansel, s. Ira & Ann, b. July 3, 1844	1-B	129
Truman* Ansel, [s.] Ira & Ann, d. Apr. 13, 1862 (*Thomas?)	1-D	25
LEDOYT, Otis, s. Jonathan & Lydia, b. Mar. 16, 1801, at Woodstock	1-B	12
Schuyler, s. Jonathan & Lydia, b. Aug. 21, 1809	1-B	12
LELAND, Sarah, m. Smith **TOURTELLOT**, Apr. 2, 1848, by Rev. Samuel J. Curtiss	1-M	16
LEONARD, [see also **LARNED**], George, of Woodstock, m. Mrs. Rebeckah **CONVERSE**, of Union, Apr. 22, 1802, by Sol[omo]n Wales, J.P.	TM	15
Halsey, of Union, m. Levina **CORBIN**, of Woodstock, Aug. 17, 1823, by Ingoldsby W. Crawford, J.P.	1-M	12
Lusina, d. George & Rebeckah, b. May 30, 1803	1-B	12
Polly, d. Daniel & Mehetobel, b. May 17, 1816	1-B	74

UNION VITAL RECORDS 99

	Vol.	Page
LEONARD, (cont.)		
Rhoda, of Union, m. Stephen **PA[I]NE**, of Woodstock, Dec. 15, 1825, by Luther Crawford, J.P.	1-M	16
LEWIS, Esther, d. John & Hannah, b. June 20, 1794	1-B	12
File, d. John & Hannah, b. Apr. 15, 1792	1-B	12
Sarah M., of Union, m. Harvey **WILSON**, of Springfield, Mass., Jan. 5, 1851, by Rev. Samuel J. Curtiss	1-M	80
LILLIE, LILLEY, Hannah, m. Levi **COY**, Feb. 15, 1785, by Sol[omo]n Wales, J.P.	TM	1
John, m. Hannah **CAREY***, (*handwritten correction to **COREY**), b. of Union, Nov. 29, 1827, by Neh[emiah] B. Beardsley	1-M	12
Johnathan, m. Betsey **WILLIAMS**, b. of Union, July 2, 1843, by Rev. Samuel J. Curtiss	1-M	48
Nancy, of Union, m. Benjamin Mills **WENTWORTH**, of Dorchester, Nov. 29, 1827, by Neh[emiah] B. Beardsley	1-M	24
Phebe, of Union, m. Benjamin **STONE**, of Sturbridge, Apr. 17, 1842, by Rev. Samuel J. Curtiss	1-M	65
Polly, m. Elijah **SAVERY**, b. of Union, Sept. 14, 1828, by Neh[emiah] B. Beardsley	1-M	21
R[h]oda, m. Orrin **BURNETT**, Mar. 23, 1834, by Stephen Haskell	1-M	50
Ruby, m. Nathan **WALKER**, Oct. 6, 1841, by Rev. Samuel J. Curtiss	1-M	69
LOOMIS, LUMMIS, Abigail, d. Abner & Charity, b. Feb. 7, 1763	2LR	267
Abner, m. Charity **SPRAGUE**, July 12, 1754	2LR	295
Anna, m. Walter **SESSIONS**, b. of Union, July 20, 1786	1-M	19
Caleb, Jr., m. Mary **WYMAN**, Jan. 7, 1758	2LR	295
Calvin, m. Eunice **MOORE**, b. of Union, Nov. 23, 1790, by Sol[omo]n Wales, J.P.	TM	3
Daniel, d. Jan. 1, 1758	2LR	291
Daniel, m. Sarah **CRAWFORD**, Feb. 9, 1764	2LR	290
Elisha, s. Daniel & Sarah, b. Aug. 7, 1747	2LR	287
Jonas, m. Mehetable **CRAM**, Nov. 29, 1764	2LR	290
Luther, s. Abner & Charity, b. July 25, 1758; bp. Sept. 17, 1758, by Rev. David. Ripley, in Abbentown, Pomfret	2LR	289
Phebe, d. Dr. Caleb & Abigail, d. Oct. 15, 1756, in the 24th y. of her age	2LR	291
Phebe, d. Abner & Charity, b. Mar. 3, 1761	2LR	294
Reuben, s. Daniel & Sarah, b. May 22, 1750; d. Aug. 29, 1750	2LR	288
Rufus, of Woodstock, m. Amey W. **MOORE**, of Union, Mar. 28, 1844, by Rev. Samuel J. Curtiss	1-M	54
Sarah, m. Timothy **WALES**, Nov. 11, 1762	2LR	290
Sarah, d. Jonah & Mehetable, b. July 9, 1767	2LR	268
Walter, of Union, m. Hannah **SESSIONS**, of Brimfield, [ ]	1-M	12
LORING, LOWRING, Lucena, of Barrey, m. Joseph **FULLER**, of Union, Feb. 26, 1805	1-M	6
Mary, m. Linus **WALES**, b. of Union, Aug. 18, 1811	1-M	23
LOVEJOY, Elizabeth, d. Phineas & Susanna, b. Nov. 21, 1765	2LR	268
LOWRING, [see under **LORING**]		
LUMBARD, Otis, of Ashford, m. Lydia **MOORE**, of Union, Oct. 8, 1844, by Rev. Samuel J. Curtiss	1-M	54
LYON, Alvin Moore, s. Lyman & Olive H. W., b. July 3, 1843	1-B	121
Emily Deliza, d. Orrin & Matilda, b. Sept. 10, 1838	1-B	113
Emily Deliza, d. Orrin & Matilda, d. Sept. 29, 1842, ae 4 y.	1-D	25

	Vol.	Page

LYON, (cont.)
Harriet Lucinda, d. Orrin & Matilda, b. Oct. 24, 1843, at Holland — 1-B — 124
Mary Ann, d. Walter & Hannah, b. Jan. 15, 1840 — 1-B — 113
Mary Ann Margaree, d. Orren & Matilda, b. Jan. 20, 1842 — 1-B — 114
Mary Jerusha, d. Lyman & Olive H. W., b. Apr. 24, 1845 — 1-B — 129
Nancy Hannah, d. Orrin & Matilda, b. Mar. 8, 1846 — 1-B — 124
Orrin, m. Matilda **SNOW**, b. of Union, Sept. 3, 1837, by Rev.
   Nathan D. Benedict — 1-M — 48
Otis, of Woodstock, m. Almira **HISCOX**, of Union, Mar. 19, 1832,
   by Rev. Stephen Hiscox — 1-M — 47
Sanford, of Woodstock, m. Calista **CRAWFORD**, of Union, Nov.
   21, 1832, by Rev. Alvan Underwood, of Woodstock — 1-M — 48
Sarah Salome Frances, d. Walter & Hannah, b. May 21, 1843 — 1-B — 121
MALTON, [see under **MOULTON**]
MARBLE, Levi, m. Mrs. Persis **SMITH**, of Sturbridge, Oct. 25, 1793, by
   Sol[omo]n Wales, J.P. — TM — 5
MARCY, Alvan, s. Samuel, Jr. & Lois, b. June 22, 1765 — 2LR — 267
Avis, d. Samuel, Jr. & Lois, b. Sept. 5, 1769 — 2LR — 266
Dwight, s. Calvin, Jr. & Elvira, b. June 8, 1840 — 1-B — 115
Esther, d. Samuel, Jr. & Lois, b. Aug. 28, 1763 — 2LR — 267
Harvey, m. Aseneth D. **GURLEY**, b. of Union, Apr. 10, 1825, by S.
   W. Crawford, J.P. — 1-M — 31
Laura Mariah, d. Calvin, Jr. & Elvira, b. Feb. 8, 1837 — 1-B — 115
Merrick, s. Calvin & Abigail, b. Oct. 11, 1812, in Holland, Mass.
   Recorded Sept. 10, 1835 — 1-B — 102
Mer[r]ick, m. Rinda **MOORE**, b. of Union, Nov. 17, 1842, by Rev.
   Samuel J. Curtiss — 1-M — 70
Merrick Augustus, s. Merrick & Rinda M., b. Aug. 29, 1843 — 1-B — 126
Prosper, d. (s ?) Samuel, Jr. & Lois, b. July 26, 1767 — 2LR — 268
Prosper, s. Samuel, Jr., d. Jan. 26, 1770 — 2LR — 270
Rindalder B., of Woodstock, m. Mary **CHAMBERLAIN**, of Union,
   Oct. 16, 1836, by Leonard Gage — 1-M — 42
Samuel, Jr., m. Louis **PEACK**, Apr. 10, 1763 — 2LR — 290
Sibbel, m. Moses **PEACK**, Feb. 29, 1763 — 2LR — 290
Tabitha, m. Joseph **FAIRBANKS**, Nov. 4, 1762 — 2LR — 290
William, m. Lucy **BUGBEE**, May 2, 1756 — 2LR — 295
MARIAM, [see under **MERRIAM**]
MARSH, Sophronia, m. Edson **SMITH**, Feb. 19, 1845, by Rev. Samuel J.
   Curtis — 1-M — 68
MARSHALL, Mary, m. Fayett **CRAWFORD**, Apr. 1, 1846, by Rev.
   Samuel J. Curtiss — 1-M — 67
MARTIN, Charles, of Woodstock, m. Sarah **ARMOUR**, of Union, June
   24, 1804 — 1-M — 13
MASON, Kaziah, of Woodstock, m. William **FOSTER**, of Union, Nov.
   10, 1799 — 1-M — 6
Warham, of Sturbridge, m. Mrs. Phebe **AMES**, of Union, Oct. 24,
   1792, by Sol[omo]n Wales, J.P. — TM — 4
MAY, Gurdon, of Holland, m. Eurilla **COMSTOCK**, of Union, Sept. 9,
   1827, by Neh[emiah] B. Beardsley — 1-M — 17
Nehemiah, of Holland, m. Mrs. Martha **STRONG**, of Union, Jan.
   16, 1794, by Sol[omo]n Wales, J.P. — TM — 8
[McCLELLAN], [see under **McLELLAN**]
McINTIRE, McINTIER, Nathaniel, m. Betsey **RANDALL**, b. of

UNION VITAL RECORDS 101

	Vol.	Page
McINTIRE, McINTIER, (cont.)		
Sturbridge, Sept. 3, 1826, by Neh[emiah] B. Beardsley	1-M	32
Polly, Mrs., m. Erasmus **EATON**, b. of Union, Aug. 8, 1804, by Sol[omo]n Wales, J.P.	TM	17
Polly, of Charlton, m. Jeremiah **HOLMAN**, of Union, Dec. 14, 1809	1-M	8
McKINSTREY, Alexander, of Sturbridge, m. Mrs. Sally **RIDER**, of Charlton, Jan. 14, 1802, by Sol[omo]n Wales, J.P.	TM	13
McLELLAN, Silas, m. Abigail T. **PARKHURST**, Mar. 25, 1836, by Ebenezer Lingsbury*, J.P. (*Kingsbury?)	1-M	42
McNALL, MACKNALL, McNELL, Alexander, m. Anne **MOOR**, Apr. 10, 1758	2LR	295
Alexander, s. James & Hannah, b. July 21, 1789	1-B	53
Charles, s. Henry & Hannah, b. Mar. 15, 1769	2LR	266
Elizca, d. James & Hannah, b. Apr. 6, 1804	1-B	53
Elizabeth, wid., d. Sept. 13, 1749	2LR	270
Hannah, d. James & Hannah, b. Nov. 24, 1799	1-B	53
Henry, s. Henry & Hannah, b. Jan. 11, 1763	2LR	294
James, s. James & Hannah, b. Oct. 8, 1794	1-B	53
Jean, w. James, d. Dec. 30, 1773, in the 65th y. of her age or thereabout	2LR	270
Lyman, s. James & Hannah, b. Dec. 14, 1791	1-B	53
Rachel, d. Alexander & Agnes, b. Feb. 12, 176[ ]	2LR	294
William, d. Sept. 22, 17[ ]	2LR	291
MERRIAM, MARIAM, MERIAM, Charles, s. Edmond & Mary, b. Jan. 31, 1794	1-B	13
Edmund, m. Mary **LAFLEN**, Nov. 27, 1788, by Sol[omo]n Wales, J.P.	TM	2
Edmond, d. July 24, 1801	1-D	13
Mary, Mrs., of Union, m. Samuel **WEBBER**, of Munson, Sept. 15, 1803, by Sol[omo]n Wales, J.P.	TM	17
Otis, s. Edmond & Mary, b. Mar. 31, 1792	1-B	13
METCALF, MEDCALF, Azubah, m. William **WILLIAMS**, Feb. 17, 1746/7	2LR	295
Fisher, s. Judson & Anna, b. July 9, 1812	1-B	38
Mary Ann, d. Judson & Anna, b. Oct. 19, 1813	1-B	38
MILLER, James, s. Rebeckah Eames, b. Sept. 18, 1789	1-B	13
Joseph, of Wales, Mass., m. Fidellia **SAVERY**, May 8, 1847, by Rev. Samuel J. Curtiss	1-M	70
MOORE, MOOR, Abigail, wid., of Union, m. Benjamin **SMITH**, of Holland, Apr. 9, 1794, by Sol[omo]n Wales, J.P.	TM	8
Alfred, s. Thomas & Azubah, b. Jan. 16, 1796	1-B	38
Alfred, m. Lucinda **HORTON**, b. of Union, Jan. 28, 1819	1-M	13
Almira, of Holland, Mass., m. George W. **WALKER**, of Hartford, Conn., Oct. 13, 1836, by Moses C. Sessions, J.P.	1-M	59
Alvin, s. Thomas & Lucy, d. May 22, 1843, ae 4 y. 7 m.	1-D	21
Amey W., of Union, m. Rufus **LUMMIS**, of Woodstock, Mar. 28, 1844, by Rev. Samuel J. Curtiss	1-M	54
Amy Whiton, d. Samuel & Amey, b. Nov. 8, 1798	1-B	37
Anne, m. Alexander **MACKNALL**, Apr. 10, 1758	2LR	295
Augustus, s. Ichabod & Phebe, b. May 23, 1791	1-B	37
Austin, s. Thomas & Azubah, b. June 7, 1802	1-B	38
Austin Noah, s. Austin & Sally, b. Mar. 24, 1832	1-B	101
Azubah, d. Thomas & Azubah, b. Jan. 25, 1804	1-B	38

102 BARBOUR COLLECTION

	Vol.	Page
MOORE, MOOR, (cont.)		
Azubah, d. Thomas & Azubah, d. Jan. 5, 1805	1-D	13
Betsey, w. Eli, d. Oct. 13, 1823	1-D	13
Calista, d. William & Bethiah, b. Mar. 26, 1805	1-B	41
Calista, of Union, m. Morey **ADAMS**, of Bolton, Mass., Jan. 1, 1828, by Neh[emiah] B. Beardsley	1-M	1
Caroline, d. Thomas & Azubah, b. Feb. 6, 1809	1-B	38
Caroline, m. James **MOORE**, b. of Union, Apr. 24, 1831, by Augustus Moore, J.P.	1-M	41
Charles W., m. Ann **CORBIN**, b. of Union, [May] 30, [1830], by Leonard Gage	1-M	41
Charles Wesley, s. Ichabod & Phebe, b. Aug. 14, 1802	1-B	42
Chauncey, s. Ichabod & Phebe, b. July 24, 1799	1-B	37
Cynthia Jane, d. Festus & Cynthia, b. Apr. 26, 1830	1-B	102
Daniel, s. David & Lois, b. Jan. 11, 1784	1-B	13
David, m. Lois **CADY**, b. of Union, Sept. 11, 1783	1-M	13
Dexter, m. Laura **GRIGGS**, b. of Union, July 4, 1839, by Geo[rge] H. Woodward	1-M	63
Ebenezer Morris, s. Augustus & Anna, b. Mar. 29, 1818	1-B	89
Eleazer, s. William & Bethiah, b. Dec. 19, 1802	1-B	41
Eli, s. Thomas & Azubah, b. Oct. 8, 1799	1-B	38
Eli Gale, s. Eli & Betsey, b. Sept. 27, 1823	1-B	42
Elizabeth Tryphenia, d. John Wesley & Tryphenia, b. May 4, 1829	1-B	90
Elmira, d. William & Bethiah, b. July 26, 1810	1-B	41
Ely, m. Betsey **GALE**, b. of Union, Dec. 19, 1822, by William Foster, J.P.	1-M	31
Erastus, s. Ichabod & Phebe, b. Mar. 5, 1793	1-B	37
Esther, d. Thomas & Lucy, d. [ ], 1848	1-D	21
Eunice, m. Calvin **LOOMIS**, b. of Union, Nov. 23, 1790, by Sol[omo]n Wales, J.P.	TM	3
Fanny, d. Ichabod & Phebe, b. Oct. 23, 1795	1-B	37
Festus, s. Ichabod & Phebe, b. Apr. 10, 1789	1-B	37
Festus, of Union, m. Cintha **UNDERWOOD**, of Holland, July 8, 1829, by Augustus Moore, J.P.	1-M	41
Festus R[e]uben, s. Festus & Cynthia, b. Apr. 15, 1833	1-B	102
George, s. Tho[ma]s & Lucy, d. June 16, 1842, ae 4 m. 5 d.	1-D	21
Hannah, d. Samuel & Ama, b. Nov. 22, 1808	1-B	42
Harriet, m. Abner **SHAW**, b. of Brimfield, Mass., Aug. 31, 1842, by French Crawford, J.P.	1-M	66
Henry Samuel, s. Samuel W. & Angeline, b. Dec. 30, 1844	1-B	126
Hiram, s. Stephen & Polly, b. Nov. 30, 1799	1-B	37
Horace Walter, s. Austin & Sally, b. Apr. 19, 1836	1-B	115
Ikebod, s. John & Sarah, b. Oct. 9, 1758	2LR	293
Ichabod, s. John & Sarah, b. Oct. 9, 1759	2LR	267
Isaac, s. David & Lois, b. Apr. 12, 1785	1-B	13
James, s. John & Sarah, b. Nov. 17, 1760	2LR	267
James, s. John & Sarah, d. Nov. 15, 1761	2LR	270
James, s. Ichabod & Phebe, b. Dec. 25, 1804	1-B	42
James, s. Samuel & Ama, b. Aug. 18, 1812	1-B	42
James, m. Caroline **MOORE**, b. of Union, Apr. 24, 1831, by Augustus Moore, J.P.	1-M	41
Jenet, d. John & Sarah, b. Dec. 20, 1763	2LR	267
John, s. John & Sarah, b. July 21, 1762	2LR	267

UNION VITAL RECORDS 103

	Vol.	Page
MOORE, MOOR, (cont.)		
John, d. Nov. 10, 1827	1-D	13
John, of Ashford, m. Esther **LAWSON**, of Union, Nov. 29, 1827, by Neh[emiah] B. Beardsley	1-M	41
John, s. John Wesley & Tryphenia A., b. Jan. 17, 1828	1-B	90
John, s. John W. & Tryphenia, d. Sept. 30, 1830	1-D	21
John, s. John W., d. [ ]	1-D	21
John W., of Union, m. Tryphenia A. **BACK**, of Holland, June 12, 1826, by Neh[emiah] B. Beardsley	1-M	32
John W., of Union, m. Lucy Ann **CHASE**, of Southbridge, Aug. 6, 1837, by Rev. Abial Williams	1-M	63
John Wesley, s. John & Martha, b. Dec. 21, 1802	1-B	38
Leonard, s. David & Lois, b. Aug. 28, 1789	1-B	13
Lois, d. David & Lois, b. Sept. 2, 1787	1-B	13
Louisa, d. Samuel & Ama, b. June 28, 1810	1-B	42
Louisa, of Union, m. John S. **BARTLETT**, of Ashford, Nov. 27, 1834, by Rev. Abial Williams	1-M	50
Lucinda, d. Samuel & Ama, b. Sept. 30, 1804	1-B	42
Lucinda, of Union, m. Chauncey **WHITON**, of Ashford, Mar. 26, 1833, by Rev. Elliott Palmer	1-M	45
Luther, s. Ichabod & Phebe, b. May 26, 1806	1-B	42
Luther, of Union, m. Lydia **CURTISS**, of Ashford, Mar. 27, 1839, by Rev. Stephen Fairbanks	1-M	63
Lydia, d. Samuel & Amey, b. June 30, 1801	1-B	37
Lydia, d. Samuel & Ama, b. Mar. 28, 1814	1-B	42
Lydia, of Union, m. Otis **LUMBARD**, of Ashford, Oct. 8, 1844, by Rev. Samuel J. Curtiss	1-M	54
Lyman, s. Thomas & Azubah, b. Jan. 3, 1798	1-B	38
Lyman, of Smithfield, m. Phebe **LAWSON**, of Union, May 31, 1827, by Nehemiah B. Beardsley	1-M	32
Margaret, of Union, m. Benjamin **SMITH**, of Holland, Apr. 9, 1794, by Sol[omo]n Wales, J.P.	TM	6
Margaret, Mrs., m. Samuel **PAUL**, b. of Union, Apr. 24, 1798	1-M	16
Marlin, s. Joseph & Ellice, b. Aug. 18, 1795	1-B	13
Martha, d. Tho[ma]s & Lucy, d. Mar. 26, 1848, ae 1 y. 2 m. 5 d.	1-D	21
Mary, m. Amasa **GAY**, b. of Union, Feb. 10, 1789	1-M	7
Mehetable, d. David & Lois, b. Oct. 26, 1792	1-B	13
Mehetable, d. John & Martha, b. Feb. 27, 1794	1-B	13
Nancy, d. William & Bethiah, b. June 15, 1800	1-B	41
Noah, of Union, m. Mrs. Polly **CURTIS**, of Ashford, June 15, 1794	1-M	13
Permela, d. William & Bethiah, b. Apr. 6, 1797	1-B	41
Parmela, m. Jonathan **JAMES**, b. of Union, Nov. 24, 1825, by Neh[emiah] B. Beardsley	1-M	10
Persis, d. William & Bethiah, b. Oct. 22, 1806	1-B	41
Persis, d. William & Bethiah, b. July 22, 1826	1-D	13
Phebe, d. Ichabod & Phebe, b. Apr. 11, 1796	1-B	37
Phebe, Jr., of Union, m. Eli **WEBBER**, of Holland, Mass., Jan. 23, 1845, by Augustus Moore, J.P.	1-M	69
Phebe, m. Eleazer **KINNEY**, b. of Union, May 20, 1849, by Ebenezer Lindsey, J.P.	1-M	78
Pliney, s. William & Bethiah, b. Apr. 25, 1814	1 D	41
Rinda, d. Augustus & Anna, b. Aug. 22, 1820	1-B	89
Rinda, m. Merick **MARCY**, b. of Union, Nov. 17, 1842, by Rev.		

	Vol.	Page
MOORE, MOOR, (cont.)		
Samuel J. Curtiss	1-M	70
Rowena, d. Samuel & Amey, b. Mar. 17, 1800	1-B	37
Sally, of Union, m. Jonathan P. **AMIDOWN**, of Southbridge, June 17, 1824, by Nehemiah B. Beardsley	1-M	31
Sally Louisa, d. Austin & Sally, b. Mar. 7, 1827	1-B	89
Samuel, of Union, m. Amy **WHITON**, of Ashford, Jan. 30, 1798	1-M	13
Samuel W., m. Angeline **RUBY**, b. of Union, Nov. 7, 1842, by Rev. Washington Munger	1-M	64
Samuel Whiton, s. Samuel & Ama, b. Aug. 28, 1817	1-B	42
Sarah, d. Ichabod & Phebe, b. July 29, 1797	1-B	37
Sarah Rosebrook, d. William & Bethiah, b. Oct. 22, 1798	1-B	41
Shubael, m. Mrs. Patience **UTLEY**, b. of Union, Feb. 20, 1794, by Sol[omo]n Wales, J.P.	TM	8
Sophia, of Union, m. Lucius **BUCK***, of Holland, Mass., Jan. 27, 1835, by Rev. Abial Williams (***BACK**?) (a handwritten note indicated that **BACK** "is right")	1-M	50
Stephen, m. Mrs. Polly **LAFLEN**, July 4, 1799, by Sol[omo]n Wales, J.P.	TM	10
Susannah, d. David & Lois, b. Jan. 3, 1797	1-B	38
Thomas, of Union, m. Mrs. Mary **COLTON**, of Munson, Mar. 16, 1793, by Sol[omo]n Wales, J.P.	TM	5
Thomas, s. John & Martha, b. Feb. 5, 1806	1-B	38
Thomas, Jr., s. Thomas & Azubah, b. Oct. 7, 1806	1-B	38
Thomas, s. Thomas & Lucy, d. June 23, 1842	1-D	21
Tryphenia A., w. John W., d. Nov. 10, 1839	1-D	21
Washington, s. William & Bethiah, b. May 1, 1813	1-B	41
Willard Wells, s. William Wells & Mary **SMITH**, b. June 24, 1834	1-B	115
William, s. Robert & Elizabeth, b. Apr. 6, 1749	2LR	292
William, of Union, m. Bethiah **WELD**, of Sturbridge, May 30, 1796	1-M	13
William W., of Holland, m. Mary S. **TRUMBULL**, of Union, Apr. 28, 1834, by John Crawford, J.P.	1-M	42
William Weld, s. William & Bethiah, b. Dec. 6, 1808	1-B	41
MOREY, MORAY, Frances Newton, s. Harvey & Asenath, b. Dec. 29, 1825	1-B	89
Lucina, of Union, m. Erastus S. **EASTMAN**, of Ashford, Aug. 26, 1830, by Rev. Ezekiel Skinner	1-M	5
Lucy Philena, d. Harvey & Asenath, b. Mar. 19, 1827	1-B	89
Sally, m. Levi **BEAL**, Jan. 21, 1798, by Sol[omo]n Wales, J.P.	TM	9
MORGAN, Sarah, of Brimfield, m. Orange **CLEVELAND**, of Union, Sept. 1, 1819	1-M	3
MORRIS, MOORIS, Chester P., m. Betsey **WALES**, Mar. 24, 1785, by Sol[omo]n Wales, J.P.	TM	1
Laura, m. W[illia]m P. **SESSIONS**, Jan. 19, 1841, by Augustus Moore, J.P.	1-M	65
MORSE, Danford, of Union, m. Huldah **SCARBOROUGH**, of Ashford, Jan. 18, 1846, by Augustus Moore, J.P.	1-M	70
Huldah, m. Freeman **PUTNAM**, b. of Union, Nov. 20, 1853, by Rev. Samuel J. Curtice	1-M	89
Ira, s. Jedediah & Persy, b. Sept. 9, 1826	1-B	102
Lucius, s. Jedediah & Persy, b. Jan. 14, 1812. Recorded June 26, 1833	1-B	101
Luke, s. Jedediah & Persy, b. Jan. 24, 1820	1-B	101

UNION VITAL RECORDS 105

	Vol.	Page
MORSE, (cont.)		
Luke, m. Huldah **SCARBOROUGH**, b. of Union, Feb. 1, 1841, by Rev. Samuel J. Curtiss	1-M	64
Maria, d. Jeremiah & Persis, b. Jan. 9, 1807; m. Ira **WALKER**	1-B	90
Maria, m. Ira **WALKER**, b. of Union, Mar. 11, 1830, by Neh[emiah] B. Beardsley	1-M	45
Nancy H., of Union, m. Horace **MOULTON**, of Wales, Mass., Nov. 23, 1839, by Rev. Gilman Noyes, Southbridge	1-M	64
Orrin, s. Jedediah & Persy, b. Jan. 27, 1822	1-B	101
Otis, s. Jedediah & Persy, b. Feb. 25, 1805	1-B	101
Stephen Hiscock, s. Lucius & Loudica, b. Aug. 28, 1831	1-B	90
MOULTON, MOLTON, MALTON, Annis, Mrs., m. Richard **CARPENTER**, Jan. 31, 1804, by Sol[omo]n Wales, J.P.	TM	15
Horace, of Wales, Mass., m. Nancy H. **MORSE**, of Union, Nov. 23, 1839, by Rev. Gilman Noyes, Southbridge	1-M	64
Jeremiah, of Munson, m. Mrs. Patey **CHAFFE**, of South Brimfield, June 30, 1794, by Sol[omo]n Wales, J.P.	TM	8
Siloma, m. Tyler **HAMILTON**, b. of Union, Mar. 26, 1832, by Rev. Stephen Fairbanks	1-M	47
MUNGER, MUNGAR, Amasa, m. Mrs. Sarah **DOWD**, Jan. 21, 1798, by Sol[omo]n Wales, J.P.	TM	9
David, of Union, m. Mrs. Lucy **BLISS**, of Wilbraham, June 25, 1800, by Sol[omo]n Wales, J.P.	TM	12
David, of Union, m. Lucy **BLISS**, of Wilbraham, June 25, 1800	1-M	13
Elizabeth, Mrs., m. Samuel **DAY**, Oct. 10, 1793, by Sol[omo]n Wales, J.P.	TM	5
Ephraim, of Union, m. Mrs. Sally **ROBBINS**, of Sturbridge, Feb. 6, 1794	1-M	13
Gaus, s. David & Lucy, b. Nov. 2, 1800	1-B	37
Horace, s. Jonathan & Elizabeth, b. Oct. 24, 1792	1-B	13
Joanna, w. Ephraim, d. Aug. 5, 1793	1-D	13
Jonathan, m. Mrs. Elizabeth **PAUL**, b. of Union, Dec. 1, 1791	1-M	13
Palace, d. Jonathan & Elizabeth, b. Dec. 23, 1794	1-B	13
Salmon, s. Ephraim & Joanna, b. Aug. 5, 1791	1-B	13
Susanna, d. Ephraim, d. Nov. 9, 1794	1-D	13
Tera, s. Jonathan, d. Jan. 5, 1794	1-D	13
MUNROW, Lemuel, of Charlton, m. Mrs. Arseneth **WALBRIDGE**, of Stafford, Aug. 27, 1789, by Sol[omo]n Wales, J.P.	TM	2
NEDSON, Diantha Christiana, of Woodstock, m. William **WATERMAN**, of Sturbridge, Mass., Sept. 24, 1853, by Rev. Samuel J. Curtice	1-M	88
Robert, m. Gene **PECANKER**, Apr. 4, 1802, by Sol[omo]n Wales, J.P.	TM	11
NEEDHAM, Anna, of South Brimfield, m. Samuel **STRONG**, of Union, Sept. 19, 1770	2LR	290
Chloe, Mrs., m. George W. **CUMMINGS**, b. of Union, [1827], by Neh[emiah] B. Beardsley. Recorded Oct. 29, 1827	1-M	17
Elisha, m. Mrs. C[h]loe **STRONG**, Oct. 12, 1797, by Sol[omo]n Wales, J.P.	TM	10
Elisha, m. Mrs. Chloe **STRONG**, b. of Union, Oct. 12, 1797	1-M	14
Elisha, d. Apr. 16, 1822	1-D	14
Enoch, Gardiner, s. Elisha & Chloe, b. Feb. 1, 1817	1-B	77
Esther Burnett, d. Marsena & Nabby, b. July 23, 1826	1-B	77
Esther Wales, d. Samuel S. & Esther, b. Nov. 11, 1839	1-B	78

	Vol.	Page
NEEDHAM, (cont.)		
Jane Elizabeth, d. Elisha & Chloe, b. May 22, 1820	1-B	77
Jane Elizabeth, d. Samuel S. & Esther, b. Aug. 19, 1837	1-B	78
Laerany, d. Elisha & Chloe, b. Apr. 3, 1811	1-B	14
Marsena, s. Elisha & Chloe, b. July 12, 1800	1-B	14
Marsena, m. Abigail **WALES**, b. of Union, June 19, 1823, by W[illia]m Foster, J.P.	1-M	14
Marsena Wales, s. Marsena & Nabby, b. Jan. 4, 1832, at Stafford	1-B	78
Polly, d. Elisha & Chloe, b. Nov. 26, 1802	1-B	14
Samuel S., m. Esther **WALES**, Dec. 13, 1836, by Rev. Washington Munger	1-M	57
Samuel S., m. Mary **FOSTER**, b. of Union, Apr. 6, 1841, by Rev. Samuel S. Needham	1-M	65
Solomon, s. Elisha & Chloe, b. July 20, 1808	1-B	14
Tryphena, d. Elisha & Chloe, b. Nov. 22, 1813	1-B	14
NELSON, Sylvanus, of South Brimfield, m. Abigail **BEAMAN**, Jan. 30, 1803, by Sol[omo]n Wales, J.P., at his house	TM	16
NEWELL, Abigail Woolcott, d. Timothy & Caroline, b. June 8, 1806	1-B	14
Amey Louisa, d. Nathaniel, Jr. & Amey, b. Oct. 7, 1809	1-B	14
Amy Louisa, of Union, m. Daniel **HURLBUTT**, of Trumbull Co., O., Aug. 14, 1837, by Rev. Alvin Underwood	1-M	26
Caroline, d. Timothy & Caroline, b. Feb. 12, 1808	1-B	14
Caroline Sophia, d. David L. & Caroline C., b. July 21, 1842	1-B	119
David L., m. Caroline **CRAWFORD**, b. of Union, Nov. 29, 1835, by John H. Willis	1-M	14
David Lawson, s. Nathaniel, Jr. & Amey, b. June 6, 1811	1-B	14
David Mellen, s. David L. & Caroline C., b. May 14, 1838	1-B	119
Lucius Blakeley, s. Nathaniel, Jr. & Amey, b. Sept. 16, 1816	1-B	77
Lucius Blakeley, s. Nathaniel & Amy, d. July 23, 1818	1-D	14
Mellen, s. David L. & Caroline C., b. May 14, 1838	1-B	78
Nathaniel, Jr., m. Mrs. Amy **LAWSON**, b. of Union, Dec. 7, 1808	1-M	14
Nathaniel, d. Feb. 11, 1817	1-D	14
Nathaniel Ossian, s. Nathaniel & Amey, b. Sept. 21, 1824	1-B	77
Nathaniel Ossian, s. Nathaniel & Amy, d. Oct. 22, 1824, ae 32 d.	1-D	14
Nathaniel Ossian, s. Nathaniel & Amey, b. Dec. 4, 1825	1-B	77
Roscius Clinton, s. Nathaniel, Jr. & Amey, b. Dec. 11, 1814	1-B	14
Silas Wright, s. David L. & Caroline C., b. Nov. 21, 1844	1-B	119
Timothy Woolcott, s. Nathaniel, Jr. & Amey, b. Dec. 24, 1812	1-B	14
Timothy Wolcott, s. Nathaniel & Amy, d. Mar. 16, 1828, ae 15	1-D	14
Timothy Wolcott, s. David L. & Caroline C., b. July 17, 1836	1-B	78
NICHOLS, Malachi, m. Mrs. Patty **BLODGETT**, May 8, 1792, by Sol[omo]n Wales, J.P.	TM	3
NILES, John, m. Eliza Ann **BLANDING**, July 3, 1842, by Moses C. Sessions, J.P.	1-M	57
OAKS, David, m. Sally Ann **WEEKS**, b. of Ware, Mass., [Nov.] 17, [1836], by Ebenezer Lindsey, J.P.	1-M	15
OLDS, Jesse, of Sturbridge, m. Lula **BULLARD**, of South Brimfield, Sept. 7, 1795, by Sol[omo]n Wales, J.P.	TM	7
ORMSBY, Nathaniel, m. Polly **BURLEY**, Feb. 6, 1822, by Zenas E. Leonard, [of] Sturbridge	1-M	15
Susan Andelucia, d. Nathaniel & Polly, b. Oct. 31, 1822	1-B	15
OSGOOD, Lydia, Mrs., of Stafford, m. Eleazer **ABBE**, of Mansfield, Feb. 16, 1801, by Sol[omo]n Wales, J.P.	TM	14

UNION VITAL RECORDS

	Vol.	Page
PADDOCK, Joanna, Mrs., of Holland, m. Cyrael **CADY**, of Orange, Feb. 29, 1796, by Sol[omo]n Wales, J.P.	TM	7
Oliver, of Holland, m. Mrs. Anna **WOODWARD**, of Roxbury, Feb. 14, 1793, by Sol[omo]n Wales, J.P.	TM	4
PAINE, PANE, Aaron Arnold, [s.] Arnold & Harriet Maria, b. Mar. 11, 1846	1-B	106
Ann Maria, [d.] Arnold & Harriet Mariah, b. Feb. 9, 1844	1-B	106
Arnold, m. Harriet **HATCH**, b. of Union, Apr. 20, 1841, by Rev. Samuel J. Curtiss	1-M	52
Harriet, [d.] Arnold & Harriet Maria, b. Mar. 23, 1845	1-B	106
Lucy, [d.] Arnold & Harriet Mariah, b. Jan. 30, 1843	1-B	106
Mary Jane, [d.] Arnold & Harriet Mariah, b. Mar. 9, 1842	1-B	106
Stephen, of Woodstock, m. Rhoda **LEONARD**, of Union, Dec. 15, 1825, by Luther Crawford, J.P.	1-M	16
PARK, [see under **PARKS**]		
PARKER, Roswell, m. Eunice **PARKHURST**, Mar. 25, 1836, by Ebenezer Lindsey, J.P.	1-M	52
PARKHURST, Abigail T., m. Silas **McLELLAN**, Mar. 25, 1836, by Ebenezer Lingsbury*, J.P. (*Kingsbury?)	1-M	42
Eunice, m. Roswell **PARKER**, Mar. 25, 1836, by Ebenezer Lindsey, J.P.	1-M	52
PARKS, PARK, PARKE, Eleanor Ward, d. Ebenezer & Anner, b. Apr. 3, 1767	2LR	268
Elias, s. Jeremiah & Hannah, b. Oct. 20, 1762	2LR	294
Mary, d. Jeremiah & Hannah, b. Sept. 23, 1767	2LR	268
Shubael, s. Jeremiah & Hannah, b. Jan. 17, 1765	2LR	267
PARVIN, [see under **POWIN**]		
PATCH, Ephraim, s. Ephraim & Penelopy, b. Oct. 26, 1751	2LR	289
PATRIDGE, Charlotte P., of Union, m. Elwell P. **BURLEY**, of Holland, Mass., Apr. 9, 1840, by G. H. Woodward	1-M	61
PAUL, PAULL, Aaline, d. Chauncey & Polly, b. Oct. 23, 1827	1-B	82
[A]lantha, d. Samuel & Margaret, b. Jan. 22, 1805	1-B	16
Alantha, of Union, m. Abial L. **PRATT**, of Southbridge, Mass., May 5, 1831, by Rev. Alvan Underwood, of Woodstock	1-M	51
Amanda, d. Samuel & Margaret, b. Dec. 25, 1801	1-B	16
Amanda, of Union, m. Amasa **HASKELL**, of Woodstock, Aug. 24, 1823, by Ingoldsby W. Crawford, J.P.	1-M	30
Ann, d. Matthew, Jr. & Mary, b. Apr. 6, 1768	2LR	266
Anna, Mrs., m. Alpheas **TWIST**, Feb. 5, 1798, by Sol[omo]n Wales, J.P.	TM	10
Anna, d. Robert, Jr. & Anna, d. Mar. 26, 1802	1-D	16
Anne, d. Matthew & Sarah, d. Mar. 25, 1755	2LR	291
Anson, s. Samuel & Margaret, b. Apr. 11, 1800	1-B	16
Calista Rebeckah Leonard, d. Samuel & Silence Newell, b. Dec. 2, 1843	1-B	128
Chauncey, s. Robert, Jr. & Anna, b. Feb. 10, 1788	1-B	16
Chauncey, m. Polly **ARMOUR**, b. of Union, Sept. 17, 1820, by Ingoldsby W. Crawford, J.P.	1-M	16
Chauncey, Jr., s. Chauncey & Polly, b. Apr. 15, 1837	1-B	104
Elbridge Gerry, s. Chauncey & Polly, b. Dec. 22, 1830	1-B	29
Elizabeth, d. Robert, Jr. & Elizabeth, b. Nov. 18, 1760	2LR	294
Elizabeth, Mrs., m. Jonathan **MUNGER**, b. of Union, Dec. 1, 1791	1-M	13
Elizabeth, d. Robert, Jr. & Anna, b. Aug. 9, 1795	1-B	16

BARBOUR COLLECTION

	Vol.	Page
PAUL, PAULL, (cont.)		
Elizabeth, wid., d. Oct. 24, 1804, in the 82nd y. of her age	1-D	16
Eltham, s. Samuel & Margaret, b. Jan. 23, 1799	1-B	16
Eltham Richmond, s. Eltham & Mary Ann, b. Aug. 6, 1827	1-B	29
Esther, m. Thomas **LAWSON**, Dec. 31, 1754	2LR	295
Eunice, d. Matthew, Jr. & Mary, b. Sept. 24, 1756	2LR	293
Eunice, d. William, Jr. & Mary, d. Sept. 25, 1756	2LR	291
Hannah, d. May 4, 1845, ae 71 y.	1-D	18
Joan (?)*, d. Matthew & Sarah, d. [ ], 1754, in the 25th (?) y. of her age (*Ann?)	2LR	291
John, s. Matthew & Sarah, d. Sept. 5, 1755	2LR	291
John, s. Matthew, Jr. & Mary, b. Mar. 13, 1759	2LR	293
Joseph, s. Robert, Jr. & Elizabeth, b. Mar. 16, 1766	2LR	268
Joseph, s. Robert, Jr. & Elizabeth, d. Apr. 9, 1766	2LR	270
Lantha, see under Alantha		
Laransa, d. Samuel & Margaret, b. Sept. 18, 1807	1-B	82
Luransa, d. June 30, 1835 (Laransa ?)	1-D	17
Liberty, s. Chauncey & Polly, b. Nov. 16, 1824	1-B	82
Luransa, see under Laransa		
Marcia, m. Lyman **SESSIONS**, Jan. 16, 1823, by Rev. Henry Smith	1-M	29
Martha, d. Robert, Jr. & Elizabeth, b. Oct. 20, 1762	2LR	294
Martha, d. Robert, Jr. & Anna, b. Oct. 22, 1799	1-B	16
Marvin Knowlton, s. Chauncey & Polly, b. Aug. 22, 1829	1-B	29
Mary, d. Matthew & Mary, b. May 28, 1766	2LR	268
Mary, m. Eleazer **KINNEY**, b. of Union, Nov. 24, 1791, by Sol[omo]n Wales, J.P.	TM	3
Mary, wid., d. Apr. 2, 1797	1-D	16
Maryan, d. Robert, Jr. & Elizabeth, b. May 21, 1759	2LR	293
Mary Ann, wid., d. Jan. 10, 1772	2LR	270
Matthew, Jr., m. Mary **LAWSON**, Nov. 13, 1755	2LR	295
Matthew, s. Robert, Jr. & Elizabeth, b. Apr. 25, 1767	2LR	268
Matthew, d. Feb. 18, 1793	1-D	16
Mehetable, wid., d. Dec. 18, 1796	1-D	16
Moses White, s. Chauncey & Polly, b. May 30, 1826	1-B	82
Newman, s. Robert & Anna, b. Mar. 1, 1803	1-B	16
Orlando, s. Chauncey & Polly, b. Sept. 23, 1821	1-B	54
Orlando, s. Chauncey & Polly, b. Nov. 19, 1839, ae 18 y.	1-D	17
Phebe, d. Matthew, Jr. & Mary, b. Oct. 9, 1764	2LR	268
Polly, d. Robert, Jr. & Anna, b. Apr. 9, 1794	1-B	16
Polly, m. Dr. Shubael **HAMMOND**, b. of Union, Oct. 4, 1812	1-M	8
Polly, d. Robert, d. Aug. 17, 1863, at Dexter, N.Y.; bd. at Union. She was the wid. of Dr. Shubael **HAMMOND**	1-D	9
Robert, m. Elizabeth **WATSON**, Nov. 23, 1752	2LR	295
Robert, s. Matthew & Mary, b. Nov. 14, 1760	2LR	294
Robert, Jr., m. Mrs. Anna **SESSIONS**, b. of Union, Nov. 14, 1793	1-M	16
Robert, d. Jan. 10, 1804, in the 76th y. of his age	1-D	16
Robert, d. Dec. 21, 1821, ae 61	1-D	16
Robert B., m. Ann E. **KINNEY**, b. of Union, Mar. 16, 1852, by Rev. Samuel J. Curtice	1-M	83
Robert Bruce, s. Chauncey & Polly, b. June 5, 1823	1-B	82
Ruth, d. Robert, Jr. & Elizabeth, b. Mar. 20, 1764	2LR	267
Samuel, s. Matthew, Jr. & Mary, b. June 3, 1762	2LR	294
Samuel, m. Mrs. Margaret **MOORE**, b. of Union, Apr. 24, 1798	1-M	16

UNION VITAL RECORDS 109

	Vol.	Page
PAUL, PAULL, (cont.)		
Samuel, Jr., s. Samuel & Margaret, b. Aug. 2, 1809	1-B	82
Samuel, d. Apr. 2, 1844, ae 82	1-D	18
Sarah had d. Mary **SALMON**, b. Dec. 3, 1758	2LR	293
Sarah Ann, d. Chauncey & Polly, b. Sept. 7, 1834	1-B	103
William, s. Robert, Jr. & Elizabeth, b. Apr. 27, 1758	2LR	293
William, s. Robert & Elizabeth, d. Apr. 19, 175[ ]	2LR	291
PEABLES, Emory, m. Frances A. **BROWN**, Jan. 21, 1849, by Harvey Walker, J.P.	1-M	77
PEAK, PEAKE, PECK, PEACK, Abijah, s. Christopher & Rebeckah, d. [ ]	2LR	291
Anna, m. Ebenezer **WARD**, June 23, 1748	2LR	295
Dorcas, d. Moses & Sibble, b. Mar. 19, 1763	2LR	267
Louis, m. Samuel **MARCY**, Jr., Apr. 10, 1763	2LR	290
Martha, d. Samuel & Abigail, b. Aug. 31, 1765	2LR	267
Moses, m. Sibbel **MARCY**, Feb. 29, 1763	2LR	290
Samuel, m. Abigail **FULLER**, Dec. 6, 1764	2LR	290
Seruah, d. Samuel & Abigail, b. Mar. 30, 1767	2LR	268
Seruah, d. Samuel & Abigail, d. Apr. 13, 1767	2LR	270
Zerviah, m. Jeremiah **BADGER**, Jan. 15, 1767	2LR	290
PECANKER, Gene, m. Robert **NEDSON**, Apr. 4, 1802, by Sol[omo]n Wales, J.P.	TM	11
PECK, [see under **PEAK**]		
PERRIN, Phebe, of Woodstock, m. William **WALKER**, of Union, Oct. 7, 1827, by Neh[emiah] B. Beardsley	1-M	24
PERRY, PERREY, John, m. Mrs. Sally **BELCHER**, of Stafford, Apr. 25, 1802, by Sol[omo]n Wales, J.P.	TM	15
Mary Ann, d. Squire & Olive, b. Dec. 11, 1820	1-B	82
Rhoda, Mrs., of Gera, m. Berah **GAUNDEY**, of South Brimfield, Oct. 31, 1793, by Sol[omo]n Wales, J.P.	TM	6
Ruammey, of Stafford, m. Luke **BURLEY**, of Union, Nov. 22, 1808	1-M	2
PHILLIPS, James, m. Almira **CORBIN**, Mar. 15, 1835, by Luther Crawford, J.P.	1-M	51
Jonathan, m. Pol[l]ey **DENDLESON**, b. of Brimfield, Aug. 1, 1792, by Sol[omo]n Wales, J.P.	TM	4
Lydia C., m. Isaac B. **BOOTH**, b. of Union, Apr. 4, 1833, by Augustus Moore, J.P.	1-M	49
PIERCE, PERCE, PEIRCE, Elizabeth, d. Francis & Elizabeth, b. Feb. 9, 1767	2LR	268
Elizabeth, d. Francis & Elizabeth, d. Feb. 21, 1767	2LR	270
Francis, s. Francis & Elizabeth, b. May 10, 1768	2LR	266
Lidia, m. Robert **CRAWFORD**, June 16, 1757	2LR	295
PLIMPTON, Aland, s. Elisha & Bathsheba, b. July 16, 1803, in Sturbridge	1-B	54
Bethsheba, w. Elisha, d. July 31, 1815	1-D	16
Billings, s. Elisha & Bathsheba, b. Mar. 7, 1799, in Sturbridge	1-B	54
Dwight, s. Elisha & Bathsheba, b. Aug. 24, 1805, in Sturbridge	1-B	54
Elijah, s. Elisha & Bathsheba, b. June 16, 1801, in Sturbridge	1-B	54
Louisa, d. Elisha & Bathsheba, b. Oct. 30, 1812	1-B	54
Mary, d. Elisha & Bathsheba, b. Nov. 10, 1796, in Sturbridge	1-B	54
Matilda, d. Elisha & Bathsheba, b. Nov. 24, 1810	1-B	54
Pearley, s. Elisha & Bathsheba, b. Dec. 6, 1807	1-B	54
PLUMBLEY, PLUMBY, PLUMBEY, Alexander, s. Daniel &		

	Vol.	Page
PLUMBLEY, PLUMBY, PLUMBEY, (cont.)		
Abigail, b. Sept. 26, 1749	2LR	289
Mary, d. Daniel & Abigail, b. Oct. 6, 1765, in Belchartstown	2LR	268
Samuel, s. Daniel & Abigail, b. Sept. 6, 1758	2LR	289
PORTER, Nathan, m. Susannah **TANNER**, June 26, 1785, by Sol[omo]n Wales, J.P.	TM	1
POTTER, Almeda J., of Willington, m. W[illia]m M. **CRAWFORD**, of Union, Oct. 9, 1854, by Rev. Samuel J. Curtis	1-M	73
John, m. Dorothy **FOSTER**, Oct. 25, 1821, by Luther Crawford, J.P.	1-M	16
Marcus N., of Sturbridge, N.Y., m. Persis **HAMMOND**, of Union, Feb. 12, 1851, by Rev. Samuel J. Curtiss	1-M	81
POWIN*, Lovel, m. Mrs. Hulda **GOODHILL**, b. of Holland, July 24, 1793, by Sol[omo]n Wales, J.P. (***PARVIN**?)	TM	5
PRATT, Abial L., of Southbridge, Mass., m. Alantha **PAUL**, of Union, May 5, 1831, by Rev. Alvan Underwood, of Woodstock	1-M	51
Alantha, w. Abial L., d. June 11, 1835*. Recorded Oct. 24, 1832 (*Should be 1832)	1-D	17
Samuel Abial, s. Abial L. & Alantha, b. June 10, 1832	1-B	29
William S., of Vernon, Ct., m. Sarah S. **DIXON**, Oct. 2, 1842, by Rev. Samuel J. Curtis	1-M	52
PRESTON, Hannah had s. Ebenezer **WALKER**, b. Sept. 10, 1801	1-B	58
Medina, s. Stephen & Clarissa, b. Sept. 23, 1793	1-B	16
PULNAM*, Mercy, m. Albert **CRAWFORD**, May 10, 1846, by Rev. Samuel J. Curtiss (***PUTNAM**?)	1-M	67
PUTNAM, Freeman, m. Huldah **MORSE**, b. of Union, Nov. 20, 1853, by Rev. Samuel J. Curtice	1-M	89
PUTNEY, Andrew Nelson, s. Ezra A. & Phila, b. Apr. 24, 1836	1-B	103
Andrew Nelson, d. Sept. 8, 1838	1-D	17
David Wales, s. Ezra A. & Phila, b. June 2, 1844	1-B	128
Eliza, d. Ezra & Elizabeth, b. Apr. 17, 1817	1-B	54
Eliza, of Union, m. Hiram **WALLIS**, of Mass., Jan. 29, [1835], by Rev. Washington Munger, of Holland, Mass. Intention published.	1-M	46
Eliza, d. Ezra A. & Phila, b. Feb. 14, 1842	1-B	104
Elizabeth, d. Oct. 29, 1845	1-D	18
Ezra, m. Mrs. Elizabeth **COYE**, b. of Union, Oct. 6, 1807	1-M	16
Ezra, d. Mar. 21, 1846	1-D	18
Ezra A., m. Phila **WALES**, Apr. 18, 1833, by Rev. Stephen Fairbanks	1-M	51
Ezra Alanson, s. Ezra & Elizabeth, b. Apr. 9, 1812	1-B	16
Joseph, d. Aug. 26, 1838	1-D	17
Joseph, s. Ezra A. & Phila, b. Aug. 24, 1839	1-B	104
Lewis, s. Ezra A. & Phila, b. Jan. 26, 1834	1-B	103
Mary Taylor, d. Ezra & Elizabeth, b. Feb. 13, 1811	1-B	16
Mary Taylor, d. Ezra & Elizabeth, d. Mar. 19, 1811	1-D	16
Mary Taylor, d. Ezra A. & Phila, b. Aug. 21, 1839	1-B	104
Mehetable, Mrs., m. Ethan **SABIN**, b. of Union, Nov. 26, 1801, by Sol[omo]n Wales, J.P.	TM	14
Nelson, s. Ezra & Elizabeth, b. Aug. 22, 1808	1-B	16
Polly, w. Ezra, d. Dec. 5, 1806	1-D	16
Renssalear Osborn, s. Ezra & Elizabeth, b. May 19, 1814	1-B	54
Rufus Coye, s. Ezra & Elizabeth, b. Aug. 17, 1820	1-B	54
Samuel, m. Martha **SHUMWAY**, b. of Sturbridge, Aug. 20, 1837,		

UNION VITAL RECORDS 111

	Vol.	Page
PUTNEY, (cont.)		
by Rev. Abial Williams	1-M	52
RANDALL, Betsey, m. Nathaniel **McINTIRE**, b. of Sturbridge, Sept. 3, 1826, by Neh[emiah] B. Beardsley	1-M	32
RANSOM, Job, of Colrain, m. Martha **ARMOUR**, of Bennington, Aug. [ ], 1784, by Sol[omo]n Wales, J.P.	TM	1
[RAYMOND], [see under **RIMOND**]		
RESBROOK, [see also **ROSEBROOKS**], Walter, of Holland, m. Mrs. Mary **STRONG**, of Union, Feb. 17, 1803, by Sol[omo]n Wales, J.P.	TM	16
RICHARDS, William, of Sturbridge, m. Mary **HISCOCK**, of Union, Jan. 11, 1838, by Rev. Stephen Fairbanks	1-M	18
RICHARDSON, Elicta, d. William Augustus & Dolly, b. May 17, 1825	1-B	87
Ruth, Mrs., of Brookfield, m. Nathaniel **CHICKERING**, of Weston, Feb. 22, 1804, by Sol[omo]n Wales, J.P.	TM	17
William Sanford, s. William Augustus & Dolly, b. Aug. 9, 1827	1-B	87
RIDER, Elizabeth, m. Jason **FERRY**, Apr. 1, 1829, by Augustus Moore, J.P.	1-M	27
Mary A., m. Stephen A. **LAMB**, Sept. 8, 1845, by Rev. Samuel J. Curtiss	1-M	54
Sally, Mrs., of Charlton, m. Alexander **McKINSTREY**, of Sturbridge, Jan. 14, 1802, by Sol[omo]n Wales, J.P.	TM	13
RIMOND, Mary, m. Archilus **HINES**, of Holland, Jan. 2, 1788, by Sol[omo]n Wales, J.P.	TM	2
RINGE, Thomas, m. Mary Ann **SESSIONS**, b. of Union, Sept. 26, 1852, by Rev. Samuel J. Curtice	1-M	84
RIPLEY, Lidia, m. Samuel **WOOD**, Jan. 11, 1749/50	2LR	295
ROBBINS, Frances P., m. Nathan **ARNLEY**, Jan. 9, 1845, by Rev. Samuel J. Curtiss	1-M	75
Sally, Mrs., of Sturbridge, m. Ephraim **MUNGER**, of Union, Feb. 6. 1794	1-M	13
ROBINSON, ROBENSON, Harriet B., of Barre, m. James **BARRY**, of New Salem, Aug. 17, 1833, by Augustus Moore, J.P.	1-M	49
Peter, of Lebanon, m. Mrs. Polly **TAYLOR**, of Union, Feb. 19, 1794, by Sol[omo]n Wales, J.P.	TM	6
ROGERS, Joseph, Jr., of South Brimfield, m. Mrs. Gene **SMALLEDGE**, of Union, Aug. 28, 1803, by Sol[omo]n Wales, J.P.	TM	17
ROOD, ROODE, Joseph Bol[l]es, s. Abigail **BOL[L]ES**, b. Jan. 5, 1820	1-B	76
Rufus, m. Mrs. Rebeckah **HISCOCK**, Nov. 29, 1798, by Sol[omo]n Wales, J.P.	TM	10
ROOP, Lucy, Mrs., of Union, m. Joshua **DUPE**, of Stafford, Sept. 24, 1793, by Sol[omo]n Wales, J.P.	TM	6
ROOT, Charles, of Coventry, m. Mrs. Mary **UTLEY**, of Union, Dec. 27, 1792, by Sol[omo]n Wales, J.P.	TM	4
ROSEBROOKS, [see also **RESBROOK**], Mary, m. John **CRAWFORD**, Dec. 14, 1758	2LR	295
ROSS, Rebeckah, m. Matthew **LAWSON**, b. of Union, Feb. 19, 1795	1-M	12
ROYCE, Alpheas, s. John & Huldah, b. Apr. 5, 1793	1-B	18
Elmathan, d. John & Huldah, b. Mar. 28, 1797 (Son ?)	1-B	18
Huldah*, d. John & Huldah, b. Oct. 27, 1782 (*Followed by the name "Rice")	1-B	18
Irena, d. John & Huldah, b. Aug. 28, 1785	1-B	18
John, s. John & Huldah, b. Mar. 8, 1791	1-B	18

BARBOUR COLLECTION

	Vol.	Page
ROYCE, (cont.)		
Lois, d. John & Huldah, b. Dec. 19, 1783	1-B	18
Phebe, d. John & Huldah, b. Apr. 15, 1789	1-B	18
Rosanna, d. John & Huldah, b. May 2, 1787	1-B	18
Vina, d. John & Huldah, b. Apr. 24, 1795	1-B	18
RUBY, RULY, Acey, d. Thomas & Elizabeth, b. June 6, 1815	1-B	63
Achsah, of Union, m. William **HARVEY,** of Palmer, Mass., May 22, 1834, by Augustus Moore, J.P.	1-M	25
Amanda, d. Thomas & Elizabeth, b. Oct. 24, 1802	1-B	63
Amanda, of Union, m. [ ] **HOWARD,** of Palmer, Apr. 5, 1827, by Neh[emiah] B. Beardsley	1-M	25
Anjaline, d. Thomas & Elizabeth, b. Jan. 9, 1822	1-B	63
Angeline, m. Samuel W. **MOORE,** b. of Union, Nov. 7, 1842, by Rev. Washington Munger	1-M	64
Annis, d. Thomas & Elizabeth, b. Dec. 12, 1805	1-B	63
Annis, of Union, m. Daniel **STEERS,** of Bolton, Nov. 3, 1825, by Neh[emiah] B. Beardsley	1-M	33
Arial Fuller, s. Thomas & Elizabeth, b. May 4, 1813	1-B	63
Betsey, d. Thomas & Elizabeth, b. Jan. 7, 1804	1-B	63
David Thomas, s. Thomas H. & Almeda, b. Jan. 27, 1836	1-B	64
Edmond, s. Thomas & Elizabeth, b. Nov. 18, 1817	1-B	63
Eliza, d. James & Mary, b. Feb. 27, 1805	1-B	18
Esther, d. Thomas & Elizabeth, b. Dec. 9, 1808	1-B	63
Harriet, d. Thomas & Elizabeth, b. Aug. 14, 1825	1-B	64
Harriet, m. Nathaniel **SESSIONS,** b. of Union, Oct. 10, 1842, by Moses C. Sessions, J.P.	1-M	66
James, of Union, m. Mary **LAMB,** of Ashford, Dec. 31, 1801	1-M	18
James, s. Thomas & Elizabeth, b. May 13, 1807	1-B	63
John, s. John & Esther, b. Apr. 9, 1784	1-B	18
Julia Ann, d. Thomas & Elizabeth, b. Nov. 9, 1819	1-B	63
Julia Frances, d. James, 2d, & Nancy W., b. Mar. 31, 1842	1-B	64
Lucinda, d. John & Esther, b. Dec. 7, 1793	1-B	18
Lucinda, of Union, m. Daniel **STEERS,** of Palmer, Mar. 29, 1827, by Neh[emiah] B. Beardsley	1-M	21
Orrel, d. Thomas & Elizabeth, b. Aug. 23, 1801	1-B	18
Orrilla, of Union, m. Paris H. **BOWERS,** of Thompson, Mar. 14, 1824, by William Foster, J.P.	1-M	33
Polly, Mrs., of Union, m. Jason **FERRY,** of Stafford, Feb. 12, 1801, by Sol[omo]n Wales, J.P.	TM	12
Polly, d. James & Mary, b. Feb. 20, 1803	1-B	18
Ruth M., m. Franklin **SEBLY,** b. of Union, Oct. 9, 1854, by Rev. Samuel J. Curtice	1-M	91
Ruth Maria, d. Thomas H. & Almeda, b. Dec. 30, 1837	1-B	64
Thomas, of Union, m. Mrs. Elizabeth **FULLER,** of Stafford, Feb. 11, 1801, by Sol[omo]n Wales, J.P.	TM	12
Thomas, of Union, m. Elizabeth **FULLER,** of Stafford, Feb. 11, 1801	1-M	18
Thomas How, s. Thomas & Elizabeth, b. Aug. 18, 1811	1-B	63
William, s. Thomas & Elizabeth, b. Oct. 23, 1823	1-B	64
RUGGLES, Abigail, of Pomfret, m. Samuel **SESSIONS,** of Union, Oct. 11, 1769	2LR	290
RULY, [see under **RUBY**]		
RUSS, Tryphenia, of Ashford, m. Esek S. **BOWERS,** of Thompson,		

UNION VITAL RECORDS

	Vol.	Page
RUSS, (cont.)		
[June], 4, [1826], by Luther Crawford, J.P.	1-M	34
RUSSELL, Cynthia, m. Benjamin **JAMES**, b. of Ashford, Feb. 8, 1794	1-M	10
Pearly, of Willington, m. Lydia **SNELL**, of Union, June 17, last [1822], by W[illia]m Foster, J.P.	1-M	18
SABIN, Ethan, m. Mrs. Mehetable **PUTNEY**, b. of Union, Nov. 26, 1801, by Sol[omo]n Wales, J.P.	TM	14
Martha, of Thompson, m. Stephen **FAIRBANKS**, of Union, Apr. 10, 1810	1-M	6
SALMON, Mary, d. Sarah **PAULL**, b. Dec. 3, 1758	2LR	293
SANGER, David, s. John & Dorothy, b. Apr. 26, 1751	2LR	288
Dorothy, s. John & Dorothy, b. Apr. 25, 1749	2LR	288
SAVERY, SEVERY, Elias, s. Marshall & Chloe, b. Aug. 4, 1803	1-B	43
Elijah, s. Harmon & Jemima, b. Mar. 17, 1806	1-B	65
Elijah, m. Polly **LILLIE**, b. of Union, Sept. 14, 1828, by Neh[emiah] B. Beardsley	1-M	21
Elijah Sanford, s. Elijah & Polly, b. Aug. 9, 1844	1-B	130
Elisha, s. Elijah & Polly, b. Sept. 15, 1842	1-B	112
Eunice E., m. Ashley D. **STUDLEY**, Mar. 29, 1846, by Rev. Samuel J. Curtiss	1-M	35
Eunice E., m. Ashley D. **STUDLEY**, Mar. 29, 1846, by Rev. Samuel J. Curtiss	1-M	91
Fanny, d. Harmon & Jemima, b. Oct. 13, 1816	1-B	71
Fanny, m. Harvey L. **HOLMES**, b. of Union, Nov. 7, 1852, by Rev. Samuel J. Curtice	1-M	84
Fanny Polly, d. Elijah & Polly, b. Dec. 25, 1831	1-B	112
Fidellia, m. Joseph **MILLER**, of Wales, Mass., May 8, 1847, by Rev. Samuel J. Curtiss	1-M	70
Hammond, of Uxbridge, m. Jemima **WALKER**, of Union, May 11, 1803, by Sol[omo]n Wales, J.P.	TM	16
Harriet, d. Harmon & Jemima, b. Jan. 17, 1810	1-B	65
Harriet, d. Levi & Sophia, b. Feb. 10, 1829	1-B	88
Lucy, d. Hammon & Jemima, b. Mar. 15, 1804	1-B	57
Lucy, d. Harmon & Jemima, b. July 12, 1808	1-B	65
Lucy, d. Elijah & Polly, b. Dec. 29, 1835	1-B	112
Marshall, of Uxbridge, m. Mrs. C[h]loe **WALKER**, of Union, Aug. 30, 1800, by Sol[omo]n Wales, J.P.	TM	13
Marshall, of Uxbridge, m. Chloe **WALKER**, of Union, Aug. 30, 1801	1-M	19
Martha Aristy, d. Elias & Aatteresty(?), b. July 10, 1846	1-B	130
Philelia, d. Elijah & Polly, b. Dec. 4, 1829	1-B	88
Polly, d. Elijah & Polly, b. July 5, 1839	1-B	112
R[e]uben, s. Harmon & Jemima, b. Mar. 5, 1812	1-B	65
Rosanna, m. Ebenezer **WYMAN**, b. of Union, Nov. 29, 1807	1-M	23
Thomas, of Uxbridge, m. Jemima **WALKER**, of Union, May 11, 1803	1-M	19
William Clark, s. Elias & Attesty, b. Mar. 23, 1829	1-B	88
SCARBOROUGH, Elizabeth, m. Lucius **THAYER**, Mar. 7, 1847, by Rev. Samuel J. Curtiss	1-M	71
Huldah, m. Luke **MORSE**, b. of Union, Feb. 1, 1841, by Rev. Samuel J. Curtiss	1-M	64
Huldah, of Ashford, m. Danford **MORSE**, of Union, Jan. 18, 1846, by Augustus Moore, J.P.	1-M	70

BARBOUR COLLECTION

SCARBOROUGH, (cont.)

	Vol.	Page
Mary, m. Harrison **WELDS**, Sept. 8, 1845, by Rev. Samuel J. Curtiss	1-M	72
Pamela, m. Horatio **CASE**, Nov. 8, 1846, by Rev. Samuel J. Curtiss	1-M	73

SEBLY, Franklin, m. Ruth M. **RUBY**, b. of Union, Oct. 9, 1854, by Rev. Samuel J. Curtice — 1-M 91

SELDON, Thomas, of New Stamford, m. Matilda **CHAFFE**, of Union, Feb. 27, 1786, by Sol[omo]n Wales, J.P. — TM 1

SESSIONS, Abigail, d. Apr. [ ] — 2LR 291

	Vol.	Page
Abijah, s. Abijah & Hannah, b. Apr. 12, 1791	1-B	57
Abijah, Jr., of Union, m. Elizabeth **CHILD**, of Woodstock, May 25, 1814	1-M	29
Abijah,, d. May 22, 1834, ae 80 y. 11 m. 20 d. W[illia]m P. Sessions, Exec.	1-D	20
Abner, s. Ebenezer & Huldah, b. Feb. 22, 1770	2LR	266
Alexander Hamilton, s. Abijah, Jr. & Elizabeth, b. Jan. 7, 1816	1-B	71
Amanda M., of Union, m. Jared **CONVERSE**, of Ashford, Mar. 27, 1851, by Ebenezer Lindsey, J.P.	1-M	80
Amanda Melissa, d. Moses C. & Elizabeth, b. June 29, 1830	1-B	55
Amos, s. Ebenezer, Jr. & Sally, b. July 17, 1819	1-B	72
Anna, d. Walter & Anna, b. Jan. 9, 1793	1-B	19
Anna, Mrs., m. Robert **PAUL**, Jr., b. of Union, Nov. 14, 1793	1-M	16
Bethiah, d. Abijah & Elizabeth, b. Feb. 22, 1827	1-B	109
Caroline, d. Ebenezer, Jr. & Sally, b. Feb. 20, 1815	1-B	72
Charlotte, d. Walter & Anna, b. Feb. 21, 1795	1-B	19
Daniel Loomis, s. Walter & Anna, b. Feb. 1, 1800	1-B	43
Darius, s. Nathaniel & Fanny, b. May 8, 1804	1-B	43
Ebenezer, of Union, m. Huldah **HAYWARD**, of Ashford, May 18, 1769	2LR	290
Ebenezer, s. Ebenezer & Huldah, b. May 7, 1782	1-B	19
Ebenezer, 3d, m. Sally **HAWSE**, b. of Union, Nov. 21, 1805	1-M	19
Elijah, s. Ebenezer, 3d, & Sally, b. May 31, 1811	1-B	65
Elizabeth, d. Nathaniel & Phanna, b. Apr. 2, 1806	1-B	57
Elizabeth, w. W[illia]m T. **SESSIONS**, d. July 11, 1840, ae 59 y.	1-D	20
Elizabeth C., m. Rejoice F. **TOWN**, Aug. 22, 1843, by Rev. Waldo Lyon	1-M	71
Elizabeth Chloe, d. Moses C. & Elizabeth, b. Aug. 14, 1824	1-B	88
Ellen Jane, [d. Moses Chandler & Elizabeth], b. Jan. 22, 1841	1-B	133
Fanny, d. Nathaniel & Fanny, b. Aug. 4, 1795	1-B	43
Fanna, m. William **EATON**, b. of Union, Nov. 28, 1822, by William Foster, J.P.	1-M	5
Fanny, wid. [of Nathaniel], d. Mar. 3, 1843, ae 84	1-D	22
Gilbert, s. Ebenezer, 3d, & Sally, b. May 25, 1809	1-B	65
Hannah, d. John & Alles, b. Jan. 11, 1770	2LR	266
Hannah, d. Abijah & Hannah, b. Dec. 11, 1789	1-B	57
Hannah, d. Nathaniel & Fanny, b. Feb. 22, 1797	1-B	43
Hannah, of Brimfield, m. Walter **LOOMIS**, of Union, [ ]	1-M	12
Horace Warren, s. Moses C. & Elizabeth, b. July 24, 1828	1-B	55
Irene, d. Nathaniel & Irene, b. Apr. 12, 1785	1-B	19
Irena, w. Nathaniel, d. Dec. 3, 1793	1-D	19
Jared Dana, s. Abijah & Elizabeth, b. Dec. 27, 1820. Recorded May 2, 1836	1-B	56
Joanna, d. Abijah & Hannah, b. Feb. 11, 1784	1-B	57

UNION VITAL RECORDS

	Vol.	Page
SESSIONS, (cont.)		
Joanna, wid., d. Mar. 20, 1797, in the 67th y. of her age	1-D	19
John, of Union, m. Alles **GOODALE**, of Pomfret, Nov. 5, 1766	2LR	290
John H., s. Abner & Esther, b. June 4, 1797	1-B	43
John Schuyler, s. Walter & Anna, b. Mar. 20, 1897* (*Probably 1797)	1-B	43
Louisa, d. Abijah & Hannah, b. Mar. 10, 1782	1-B	57
Louisa, m. Charles **FOSTER**, b. of Union, June 6, 1809	1-M	6
Louisa Foster, d. Abijah & Elizabeth, b. Nov. 11, 1834	1-B	109
Lydia, d. Nathaniel & Irene, b. Mar. 5, 1787	1-B	19
Lyman, s. Abijah & Hannah, b. Apr. 7, 1793	1-B	57
Lyman, m. Marcia **PAUL**, Jan. 16, 1823, by Rev. Henry Smith	1-M	29
Mariah Louisa, d. Moses C. & Elizabeth, b. Aug. 14, 1826	1-B	55
Mary, d. Abner & Mary, b. Feb. 1, 1753	2LR	292
Mary, wid., d. Apr. 26, 1782	1-D	2
Mary, wid., d. Apr. 26, 1782	1-D	19
Mary Ann, d. Ebenezer, Jr. & Sally, b. July 9, 1817	1-B	72
Mary Ann, d. Abijah & Elizabeth, b. Oct. 11, 1829	1-B	109
Mary Ann, m. Thomas **RINGE**, b. of Union, Sept. 26, 1852, by Rev. Samuel J. Curtice	1-M	84
Meletiah Curtis, d. Abijah & Elizabeth, b. Apr. 16, 1823	1-B	109
Moses C., m. Elizabeth **KINNEY**, b. of Union, Jan. 2, 1821, by William Foster, J.P.	1-M	29
Moses Chandler, s. Nathaniel & Fanny, b. Mar. 5, 1799	1-B	43
Moses Chandler, [s. Moses Chandler & Elizabeth], b. July 30, 1844	1-B	133
Nathaniel, s. Nathaniel & Irene, b. Aug. 20, 1790	1-B	19
Nathaniel, of Union, m. Fanny **CHANDLER**, of Woodstock, Oct. 30, 1794	1-M	19
Nathaniel, s. Moses C. & Elizabeth, b. Feb. 21, 1822	1-B	72
Nathaniel, d. Oct. 5, 1824, ae 74	1-D	22
Nathaniel, m. Harriet **RUBY**, b. of Union, Oct. 10, 1842, by Moses C. Sessions, J.P.	1-M	66
Olive, d. Abijah & Hannah, b. Nov. 24, 1794	1-B	57
Olive, of Union, m. Asa **HAWSE**, Jr., of Woodstock, May 20, 1824, by Neh[emiah] B. Beardsley	1-M	31
Orilla, of Union, m. Leonard M. **STOCKWELL**, of Sutton, Mar. 19, 1828, by Nehemiah B. Beardsley	1-M	21
Orinda had d. Almira **ARMOUR**, b. Dec. 26, 1811	1-B	72
Orinda, m. Amasa **COYE**, b. of Union, June 30, 1825, by Rev. Alvan Underwood, of Woodstock	1-M	37
Orrel, d. Ebenezer, 3rd, & Sally, b. July 6, 1806	1-B	57
Polly, d. Abijah & Hannah, b. Feb. 18, 1786	1-B	57
Polly, d. Nathaniel & Fanny, b. Jan. 19, 1801	1-B	43
Roxa Child, d. Abijah & Elizabeth, b. Sept. 19, 1818. Recorded May 2, 1836	1-B	56
Samuel, of Union, m. Abigail **RUGGLES**, of Pomfret, Oct. 11, 1769	2LR	290
Sarah Lucinda, [d. Moses Chandler & Elizabeth], b. Dec. 21, 1832	1-B	133
Sarah Winchester, d. Abijah & Hannah, b. Sept. 5, 1780	1-B	57
Sarah Winchester, Mrs., m. Hendrick **GREGG**, May 16, 1803, by Sol[omo]n Wales, J.P.	TM	17
Silence, d. Abner & Mary, b. Feb. 1, 1749/50	2LR	288
Silence, m. James **ENOS**, Oct. 18, 1764	2LR	290
Susan Mary, [d. Moses Chandler & Elizabeth], b. May 21, 1835	1-B	133

116 BARBOUR COLLECTION

	Vol.	Page
SESSIONS, (cont.)		
Susannah, Mrs., of Union, m. William **WRIGHT**, of Augusta, N.Y., Feb. 25, 1802, by Sol[omo]n Wales, J.P.	TM	14
Walter, s. John & Allice, b. May 29, 1767	2LR	268
Walter, s. John & Alles, b. July 22, 1768	2LR	266
Walter, m. Anna **LOOMIS**, b. of Union, July 20, 1786	1-M	19
W[illia]m P., m. Laura **MORRIS**, Jan. 19, 1841, by Augustus Moore, J.P.	1-M	65
William Pitt, s. Abijah & Hannah, b. Feb. 9, 1779	1-B	57
SHAW, Abner, m. Harriet **MOORE**, b. of Brimfield, Mass., Aug. 31, 1842, by French Crawford, J.P	1-M	66
SHEDDON, Cheney Plimpton, s. John, Jr. & Polly, b. Apr. 17, 1803	1-B	65
Elijah, s. John, Jr. & Polly, b. Mar. 4, 1811	1-B	65
Harriet, d. John, Jr. & Polly, b. Jan. 4, 1809	1-B	65
Mary Louisa, d. John, Jr. & Polly, b. Feb. 27, 1807	1-B	65
Sophrononia, d. John, Jr. & Polly, b. Oct. 30, 1801	1-B	65
SHEPHARD, Samuel, of Sturbridge, m. Almira **HOLMAN**, of Union, Oct. 16, 1827, by Neh[emiah] B. Beardsley	1-M	21
SHUMWAY, Martha, m. Samuel **PUTNEY**, b. of Sturbridge, Aug. 20, 1837, by Rev. Abial Williams	1-M	52
Sarah, Mrs., m. Levi **WALKER**, Jan. 10, 1799, by Sol[omo]n Wales, J.P.	TM	10
Sarah, m. Levi **WALKER**, b. of Union, Jan. 10, 1799	1-M	23
[SIBLY], [see under **SEBLY**]		
SIMMONS, [see also **SIMONS**], George K., d. Nov. 6, 1847. Was killed with five others on the Revil Road near Boston	1-D	22
Lora Elizabeth, d. George K. & Elizabeth, b. Jan. 14, 1847 ? Recorded Dec. 7, 1847	1-B	130
SIMONS, [see also **SIMMONS**], Mary, of Union, m. Ebenezer **HUMPHREY**, of Ashford, May 5, 1795, by Sol[omo]n Wales, J.P.	TM	7
Richard, s. Paul & Mary, b. Jan. 26, 1759	2LR	293
SMALLEDGE, Gene, Mrs., of Union, m. Joseph **ROGERS**, Jr., of South Brimfield, Aug. 28, 1803, by Sol[omo]n Wales, J.P.	TM	17
John, s. Joseph & Jane, b. May 28, 1751	2LR	292
Polly, Mrs., m. Eli **CLARK**, Mar. 5, 1801, by Sol[omo]n Wales, J.P.	TM	12
Polly, d. Sally Thompson, b. May 13, 1805	1-B	57
SMITH, Andrew, s. Nathaniel M. & Lucy, b. July 3, 1824	1-B	87
Benjamin, of Holland, m. Margaret **MOORE**, of Union, Apr. 9, 1794, by Sol[omo]n Wales, J.P.	TM	6
Benjamin, of Holland, m. Wid. Abigail **MOOR**, of Union, Apr. 9, 1794, by Sol[omo]n Wales, J.P.	TM	8
Charles Hammond, s. Judson & Cynthia, b. Feb. 16, 1839	1-B	112
Ebenezer G., m. Eliza **DORSETT**, b. of Union, June 8, 1825, by Rev. Alvan Underwood, of Woodstock	1-M	35
Edson, m. Sophronia **MARSH**, Feb. 19, 1845, by Rev. Samuel J. Curtis	1-M	68
Emily, d. Judson & Cynthia, b. Sept. 6, 1840	1-B	112
Judson, m. Cynthia **HAMMOND**, b. of Union, Jan. 17, 1838, by Rev. Alvan Underwood	1-M	65
Linus, of Southbridge, Mass., m. Lorett A. **WALES**, of Union, May 1, 1853, by Rev. Samuel J. Curtiss	1-M	35
Orlando Paul, s. Judson & Cynthia, b. Sept. 5, 1841	1-B	112

	Vol.	Page
SMITH, (cont.)		
Persis, Mrs., of Sturbridge, m. Levi **MARBLE**, Oct. 25, 1793, by Sol[omo]n Wales, J.P.	TM	5
Sarah, Mrs., m. John **TERRY**, b. of Conway, Dec. 2, 1797, by Sol[omo]n Wales, J.P.	TM	9
SNA—, Tabitha, m. Samuel **HENDRICKES**, June 19, 1755	2LR	295
SNELL, Abigail Rice, d. Thomas & Hannah, b. May 28, 1813	1-B	71
Asa F., m. Lovisa **EATON**, b. of Union, Dec. 6, 1821, by William Foster, J.P.	1-M	29
Asa Farnham, s. Joseph & Lydia, b. May 2, 1794	1-B	19
Betsey, d. Joseph & Lydia, b. July 19, 1792	1-B	19
Betsey, m. Marcus **BUGBEE**, b. of Union, Mar. 4, 1830, by Nehemiah B. Beardsley	1-M	34
Edmund, s. Thomas & Hannah, b. Jan. 2, 1815	1-B	72
Erastus, s. Joseph & Lydia, b. May 27, 1795	1-B	43
Erastus Gilbert, s. Joseph, Jr. & Hannah, b. Dec. 11, 1814	1-B	71
Hannah Sophronia, d. Joseph, Jr. & Hannah, b. Apr. 19, 1819	1-B	71
Joseph, s. Joseph & Lydia, b. Feb. 24, 1791	1-B	19
Joseph, Jr., of Union, m. Hannah **CHAFFEE**, of Ashford, Nov. 25, 1813	1-M	19
Joseph William, s. Joseph, Jr. & Hannah, b. Mar. 12, 1824	1-B	72
Lydia, of Union, m. Pearly **RUSSELL**, of Willington, June 17, last, [1822], by W[illia]m Foster, J.P.	1-M	18
Mary Ann, d. Joseph, Jr. & Hannah, b. Sept. 24, 1816	1-B	71
Milton, s. Asa F. & Lovisa, b. Apr. 25, 1823	1-B	72
Persis Strong, d. Thomas & Hannah, b. Feb. 25, 1818, at Willington	1-B	72
Thomas, m. Hannah **STRONG**, b. of Union, Feb. 20, 1812	1-M	19
SNOW, Matilda, m. Orrin **LYON**, b. of Union, Sept. 3, 1837, by Rev. Nathan D. Benedict	1-M	48
SPENCER, Schuyler, of Southbridge, m. Rebecca **HISCOCK**, of Union, Jan. 1, 1829, by Ingoldsby W. Crawford, J.P.	1-M	17
SPRAGUE, SPRAGE, Charity, m. Abner **LOOMIS**, July 12, 1754	2LR	295
Olive, d. Thomas & Hannah, b. Aug. 9, 1768	2LR	269
Olive, m. Giles **BADGER**, Jan. 7, 1790, by Sol[omo]n Wales, J.P.	TM	2
Peris, d. Apr. 3, 1758	2LR	291
Peres, s. Calvin & Elizabeth, b. Apr. 13, 1768	2LR	266
Sarah, m. Cyrus **BAILEY**, July 20, 1797, by Sol[omo]n Wales, J.P.	TM	9
SQUIRE, Ephraim W., of Eastford, m. Sarah J. **CLEAVELAND**, of Union, Mar. 26, 1853, by Rev. Samuel J. Curtiss	1-M	68
Hannah, m. George W. **TOWN**, b. of Union, Mar. 20, 1853, by Rev. Samuel J. Curtice	1-M	86
STEBBINS, Hiram, of Wilbraham, Mass., m. Mary A. **HOUGHTON**, of Union, Apr. 9, 1844, by Rev. Samuel J. Curtiss	1-M	68
STEERS, Daniel, of Bolton, m. Annis **RUBY**, of Union, Nov. 3, 1825, by Neh[emiah] B. Beardsley	1-M	33
Daniel, of Palmer, m. Lucinda **RUBY**, of Union, Mar. 29, 1827, by Neh[emiah] B. Beardsley	1-M	21
STOCKWELL, Leonard M., of Sutton, m. Orilla **SESSIONS**, of Union, Mar 19, 1828, by Nehemiah B. Beardsley	1-M	21
STONE, Benjamin, s. Samuel & Mary Ann, b. Apr. 26, 1795	1-B	19
Benjamin, s. Samuel & Mary Ann, d. Dec. 18, 1798, in the 4th y. of his age	1-D	19
Benjamin, of Sturbridge, m. Phebe **LILLEY**, of Union, Apr. 17,		

	Vol.	Page
STONE, (cont.)		
1842, by Rev. Samuel J. Curtiss	1-M	65
Emily, d. Samuel, Jr. & Lucy, b. Nov. 25, 1823	1-B	72
Joseph, s. Samuel & Mary Ann, b. Nov. 27, 1792	1-B	19
Joseph, d. Apr. 22, 1818, in the 89th y. of his age	1-D	19
Lydia, w. Joseph, d. July 1, 1790	1-D	19
Lydia, d. Samuel, Jr. & Lucy, b. Dec. 8, 1821	1-B	71
Mary Ann, w. Samuel, d. Sept. 13, 1842, ae 83 y.	1-D	22
Polly, d. Samuel & Mary Ann, b. June 16, 1790	1-B	43
Samuel, s. Samuel & Mary Ann, b. Feb. 11, 1798	1-B	43
Susanna, d. Samuel & Maryann, d. Dec. 29, 1804, in the 20th y. of her age	1-D	16
STOWELL, Calvin, s. Daniel & Anne, b. Apr. 12, 1767	2LR	268
Marvin, s. Seth & Dinah, b. Mar. 15, 1789	1-B	19
Seth, d. Apr. 3, 1798	1-D	19
STRALTON*, Sally, Mrs., of Brimfield, m. Daniel **FOSTER**, of Andover, Oct. 1, 1790, by Sol[omo]n Wales, J.P. (***STRATTON** ?)	TM	2
STRONG, Abigail, wid. Alexander, d. Mar. 2, 1834, ae 76 y. 9 m. 4 d.	1-D	20
Alexander, s. Alexander & Abigail, b. Apr. 21, 1792	1-B	19
Alexander, Jr., m. Lucinda **GRIGGS**, b. of Union, Nov. 28, 1816	1-M	29
Alexander, d. Feb. 25, 1826, ae 77 y. 3 m. 8 d.	1-D	19
Alexander Stoughton, s. Alexander & Lucinda, b. Mar. 30, 1827	1-B	88
Alvin, s. Alexander, Jr. & Lucinda, b. Jan. 17, 1818	1-B	71
Alvin, see also Elven		
Arvine, s. Alexander, Jr. & Lucinda, b. Aug. 31, 1822	1-B	72
C[h]loe, Mrs., m. Elisha **NEEDHAM**, Oct. 12, 1797, by Sol[omo]n Wales, J.P.	TM	10
Chloe, Mrs., m. Elisha **NEEDHAM**, b. of Union, Oct. 12, 1797	1-M	14
Diantha, d. Alexander, Jr. & Lucinda, b. May 16, 1820	1-B	71
Eben, s. Alexander & Abigail, b. Jan. 9, 1795	1-B	19
Elven, s. Alexander & Abigail, d. Jan. 14, 1803	1-D	19
Elven, see also Alvin		
Eunice Emeline, d. Elias & Atteresty, b. May 24, 1825	1-B	87
Hannah, d. Samuel & Martha, b. Dec. 8, 1750	2LR	292
Hannah, m. Thomas **SNELL**, b. of Union, Feb. 20, 1812	1-M	19
Horatio, s. Alexander & Lucinda, b. Feb. 16, 1833	1-B	56
John, s. Samuel & Martha, d. Mar. 25, 1756	2LR	270
Lucinda, Jr., d. Alexander & Lucinda, b. May 23, 1830	1-B	55
Lucy, m. Solomon **WALES**, Oct. 3, 1754	2LR	295
Martha, Mrs., of Union, m. Nehemiah **MAY**, of Holland, Jan. 16, 1794, by Sol[omo]n Wales, J.P.	TM	8
Martha, wid., d. Mar. 5, 1798	1-D	19
Mary, Mrs., of Union, m. Walter **RESBROOK**, of Holland, Feb. 17, 1803, by Sol[omo]n Wales, J.P.	TM	16
Rebeckah, Mrs., m. Edward **FOSTER**, Nov. 27, 1800, by Sol[omo]n Wales, J.P.	TM	12
Rebeckah, m. Edward **FOSTER**, Jr., b. of Union, Nov. 27, 1800	1-M	6
Return, s. Samuel & Martha, b. [ ] 30, 1755	2LR	292
Salmon, m. Philena **HORTON**, b. of Union, Jan. 9, 1812	1-M	19
Salmon Horton, s. Salmon & Philena, b. Oct. 25, 1812	1-B	65
Samuel, of Union, m. Anna **NEEDHAM**, of South Brimfield, Sept. 19, 1770	2LR	290

UNION VITAL RECORDS

	Vol.	Page
STRONG, (cont.)		
Warren, s. Alexander, Jr. & Lucinda, b. Nov. 19, 1824	1-B	87
STUDLEY, Ashley D., m. Eunice E. **SAVERY**, Mar. 29, 1846, by Rev. Samuel J. Curtiss	1-M	35
Ashley D., m. Eunice E. **SEVERY**, Mar. 29, 1846, by Rev. Samuel J. Curtiss	1-M	91
SUMNER, Ebenezer, of Ashford, m. Dorothy **WYMAN**, of Union, Feb. 7, 1813	1-M	19
Sarah, d. Josiah & Ann, b. Nov. 1, 1748	2LR	288
Sarah, d. Josiah & Ann, d. Jan. 11, 1749/50	2LR	288
William, s. Josiah & Ann, b. July 1, 1750	2LR	288
TANNER, Susannah, m. Nathan **PORTER**, June 26, 1785, by Sol[omo]n Wales, J.P.	TM	1
TAYLOR, Polly, Mrs., of Union, m. Peter **ROBENSON**, of Lebanon, Feb. 19, 1794, by Sol[omo]n Wales, J.P.	TM	6
TERRY, Joanna Merrebeth, see under Joanna Merrebeth **FERRY**		
John, m. Mrs. Sarah **SMITH**, b. of Conway, Dec. 2, 1797, by Sol[omo]n Wales, J.P.	TM	9
THAYER, Lucius, m. Elizabeth **SCARBOROUGH**, Mar. 7, 1847, by Rev. Samuel J. Curtiss	1-M	71
THOMPSON, Abigail, Mrs., of Brimfield, m. Hooker **BALLARD**, of Westmoreland, Sept. 30, 1793, by Sol[omo]n Wales, J.P.	TM	5
Anna, Mrs., of Union, m. David **HISCOX**, Jr., of Ashford, May 10, 1805	1-M	8
Derastus, s. James, Jr. & Rachel, b. Jan. 23, 1791	1-B	20
Dinah, of Union, m. Daniel **FREEMAN**, of Mansfield, Oct. 24, 1842, by Rev. Samuel S. Curtiss	1-M	28
George, Jr., of Union, m. Nancy **HOWLET**, of Woodstock, Mar. 14, 1816	1-M	20
Grosvenor, s. Rufus & Sarah, b. Feb. 21, 1791	1-B	20
Lyman E., of Mansfield, m. Dinah **JOHNSON**, of Union, Oct. 3, 1833, by Augustus Moore, J.P.	1-M	20
Patience, d. James, Jr. & Rachel, b. Feb. 16, 1793	1-B	20
Roxana had d. Salona **BURLEY**, b. June 24, 1807	1-B	51
Sally had d. Polly **SMALLEDGE**, b. May 13, 1805	1-B	57
TOURTELLOT, Adeline, of Union, m. Dwight B. **WHITTEMORE**, of Sturbridge, Mass., Jan. 1, 1837, by Moses C. Sessions, J.P.	1-M	59
Augustus, of Sturbridge, m. Anna **CLEVELAND**, of Union, May 31, 1832, by Augustus Moore, J.P.	1-M	20
Smith, m. Sarah **LELAND**, Apr. 2, 1848, by Rev. Samuel J. Curtiss	1-M	76
TOWN, Abial, s. Joseph & Rhoba, b. Feb. 4, 1828	1-B	124
Elisha, of Sturbridge, m. Mrs. Eleanor **BOND**, of Holland, Aug. 18, 1796, by Sol[omo]n Wales, J.P.	TM	9
Esther, of Union, m. Timothy D. **BUTTERWORTH**, of Holland, Jan. 9, 1851, by Ebenezer Lindsey, J.P.	1-M	79
Est[h]er Wales, d. Joseph & Rhoba, b. Jan. 9, 1832	1-B	124
George W., m. Sally **CASS**, b. of Union, Apr. 12, 1847, by Ingoldsby W. Crawford, J.P.	1-M	72
George W., m. Hannah **SQUIRE**, b. of Union, Mar. 20, 1853, by Rev. Samuel J. Curtice	1-M	86
Herman, d. Joseph & Rhoba, b. Aug. 30, 1810, at Thompson (Son ?)	1-B	123
Hiram, s. Joseph & Rhoba, b. May 5, 1806, at Thompson	1-B	123
Hiram, m. Betsey **WALES**, b. of Union, Dec. 20, 1829, by		

	Vol.	Page
TOWN, (cont.)		
Neh[emiah] B. Beardsley	1-M	20
Hiram Judson, s. Hiram & Betsey, b. Apr. 7, 1834	1-B	20
Jos[eph] Warner, m. Maria S. **EDSON**, b. of Petersham, Mass., May 9, 1848, by Rev. Samuel J. Curtis	1-M	76
Laura, d. Joseph & Rhoba, b. Apr. 2, 1820	1-B	123
Laura, d. Joseph & Rhoba, d. Nov. 27, 1829	1-D	26
Laura, d. Hiram & Betsey, b. Oct. 30, 1830	1-B	20
Lucinda, d. Joseph & Rhoba, b. Mar. 13, 1818, at Thompson	1-B	123
Lucy, d. Joseph & Rhoby, b. Jan. 26, 1825	1-B	124
Lucy, of Union, m. Edwin B. **WEBBER**, of Holland, Mass., Jan. 22, 1843, by Rev. Samuel J. Curtiss	1-M	69
Luther, s. Joseph & Rhoba, b. Dec. 20, 1812, at Thompson	1-B	123
Mary Ann Lyon, d. Joseph & Rhoba, b. Aug. 1, 1822	1-B	123
Nancy, d. Joseph & Rhoba, b. Feb. 7, 1808, at Thompson	1-B	123
Nancy, of Union, m. William G. **YOUNG**, of Southbridge, Oct. 3, 1833, by Augustus Moore, J.P.	1-M	53
Rejoice F., m. Elizabeth C. **SESSIONS**, of Union, Aug. 22, 1843, by Rev. Waldo Lyon	1-M	71
Rhoba, w. Joseph, d. Feb. 17, 1840	1-D	26
Walter, s. Joseph & Rhoba, b. Apr. 3, 1815, at Thompson	1-B	123
Walter, s. Joseph & Rhoba, d. Dec. 29, 1816, at Thompson	1-D	26
Walter, s. Joseph & Rhoby, b. Aug. 15, 1830	1-B	124
Walter, s. Joseph & Rhoba, d. Sept. 19, 1830	1-D	26
TREAT, John, of Granvil, m. Mrs. Elizabeth **FEARSELL**, of Holland, May 14, 1793, by Sol[omo]n Wales, J.P.	TM	5
TRUMBULL, Mary S., of Union, m. William W. **MOORE**, of Holland, Apr. 28, 1834, by John Crawford, J.P.	1-M	42
TWIST, Alpheas, m. Esther **LAWSON**, b. of Union, Feb. 3, 1795	1-M	20
Alpheas, m. Mrs. Anna **PAULL**, Feb. 5, 1798, by Sol[omo]n Wales, J.P.	TM	10
TYLER, Job, Jr., of Ashford, m. Charlotte **UTLEY**, of Union, Mar. 1, 1792, by Sol[omo]n Wales, J.P.	TM	3
Margaret, m. Hezekiah **FULLER**, Feb. 15, 1748	2LR	295
UNDERWOOD, Betsey Jane, d. George, b. Jan. 4, 1845	1-B	22
Cintha, of Holland, m. Festus **MOORE**, of Union, July 8, 1829, by Augustus Moore, J.P.	1-M	41
George Riley, s. George, b. Apr. 4, 1842	1-B	22
Palmer Stanton, s. Sullivan & Fanny, b. Feb. 18, 1836	1-B	21
UPHAM, Edwin W., s. Ichabod T. & Abigail, b. May 31, 1823. Recorded Mar. 26, 1844	1-B	22
Edwin W., m. Nancy D. **CORBIN**, Nov. 12, 1848, by Rev. Samuel J. Curtis	1-M	78
Jonathan C., s. Ichabod T. & Abigail, b. Aug. 16, 1828. Recorded Mar. 26, 1844	1-D	22
Sarah F., d. Ichabod T. & Abigail, b. Oct. 22, 1830. Recorded Mar. 26, 1844	1-B	22
UTLEY, Almira, d. Jonathan, Jr. & Rebeckah, b. Nov. 17, 1791	1-B	21
Charlotte, of Union, m. Job **TYLER**, Jr., of Ashford, Mar. 1, 1792, by Sol[omo]n Wales, J.P.	TM	3
Martha, d. Jonathan, Jr. & Rebeckah, b. Sept. 24, 1793	1-B	21
Mary, Mrs., of Union, m. Charles **ROOT**, of Coventry, Dec. 27, 1792, by Sol[omo]n Wales, J.P.	TM	4

UNION VITAL RECORDS

	Vol.	Page
UTLEY, (cont.)		
Patience, Mrs., m. Shubael **MOOR**, b. of Union, Feb. 20, 1794, by Sol[omo]n Wales, J.P.	TM	8
Simeon, s. Jonathan, Jr. & Rebeckah, b. Nov. 21, 1794	1-B	21
VAN SHAACH, A. H., m. Mary **FAULKNER**, Nov. 25, 1847, by Rev. Samuel J. Curtiss	1-M	22
VINTON, Justus H., Rev., of Willington, m. Calista **HOLMAN**, of Union, [May*] 9, [1834], by Rev. Samuel S. Mallory, Willington (*April ?)	1-M	22
Porter, m. Polly **BUGBEE**, July 27, 1828, by Augustus Moore, J.P.	1-M	22
WAKEFIELD, WEEKFIELD, Chester, s. John & Eless, b. Apr. 30, 1760	2LR	293
Eliza, Mrs., of Stafford, m. Luke **HISCOCK**, of Union, June 15, 1845, by Amos Babcock, Holland, Mass.	1-M	62
Huldah, d. John & Elice, b. Oct. 19, 1763	2LR	267
Levi, s. John & Elles, b. Nov. 5, 1761	2LR	294
WALBRIDGE, Arseneth, Mrs., of Stafford, m. Lemuel **MUNROW**, of Charlton, Aug. 27, 1789, by Sol[omo]n Wales, J.P.	TM	2
WALES, Aaron Allen, s. Gideon & Betsey, b. Nov. 6, 1808	1-B	58
Abigail, w. Gideon, d. Nov. 21, 1798	1-D	23
Abigail, m. Marsena **NEEDHAM**, b. of Union, June 19, 1823, by W[illia]m Foster, J.P.	1-M	14
Abigail Lemira, d. Gideon, Jr. & Polly, b. Nov. 6, 1831	1-B	99
Alvin, s. Linus & Mary, b. May 8, 1817	1-B	81
Andrew Jackson, s. Linus & Mary, b. Aug. 15, 1815	1-B	81
Anne, m. Abijah **LARNED**, Dec. 31, 1753	2LR	295
Arvine Rensal[l]ear, s. Gideon, Jr. & Polly, b. May 29, 1833	1-B	100
Betsey, m. Chester P. **MORRIS**, Mar. 24, 1785, by Sol[omo]n Wales, J.P.	TM	1
Betsey, d. Gideon & Betsey, b. Mar. 28, 1811	1-B	58
Betsey, m. Hiram **TOWN**, b. of Union, Dec. 20, 1829, by Neh[emiah] B. Beardsley	1-M	20
Betsey, of Union, m. Marvin **HOWARD**, of Eastford, Oct. 26, 1851, by Rev. Henry B. Blake, of So. Coventry	1-M	82
Celinda, d. Aaron A. & Maria, b. Apr. 13, 1837	1-B	117
Deidamia, d. Eleazer & Mary, b. June 9, 1803	1-B	44
Delight A., m. Thomas **HORTON**, b. of Union, Apr. 22, 1850, by Rev. Samuel J. Curtiss	1-M	79
Derexa, d. Eleazer & Mary, b. Feb. 16, 1809	1-B	58
Ebenezer, of Union, m. Mary **WHITING**, of Ashford, May 22, 1793	1-M	23
Eben[eze]r, s. Eben[eze[r & Esther, d. Apr. 20, 17[ ]	2LR	291
Eleazer, s. Solomon & Lucy, b. July 30, 1756	2LR	289
Eleazer, m. Deadamia **CHAFFE**, June 11, 1783, by Sol[omo]n Wales, J.P.	TM	18
Eleazer, s. Eleazer & Mary, b. May 16, 1794	1-B	23
Elijah, d. Mar. 28, 1826	1-D	23
Elizabeth, d. Timothy & Sarah, b. Mar. 20, 1764	2LR	267
Elvira Belenda, d. Aaron A. & Maria, b. Oct. 18, 1839	1-B	117
Esther, d. Solomon & Lucy, b. Feb. 13, 1768	2LR	268
Esther, of Union, m. Jacob **BARNET**, of Lime, Nov. 8, 1791, by Sol[omo]n Wales, J.P.	TM	3
Esther, d. Gideon & Betty, b. Jan. 22, 1805	1-B	44
Esther, m. Samuel S. **NEEDHAM**, Dec. 13, 1836, by Rev.		

WALES, (cont.)

	Vol.	Page
Washington Munger	1-M	57
Eunice, d. Solomon & Lucy, b. Jan. 27, 1759	2LR	289
Eunice, d. Eleazer & Mary, b. May 17, 1805	1-B	58
Gideon, s. Solomon & Lucy, b. Mar. 20, 1769	2LR	267
Gideon, of Union, m. Abigail **GALLOP**, of Montville, Jan. 25, 1798	1-M	23
Gideon, [twin with Nabby], s. Gideon & Abigail, b. Oct. 31, 1798	1-B	44
Gideon, of Union, m. Betsey **ALLEN**, of Sturbridge, Oct. 30, 1800, by Sol[omo]n Wales, J.P.	TM	12
Gideon, of Union, m. Bettey **ALLEN**, of Sturbridge, Oct. 30, 1800	1-M	23
Gideon, Jr., m. Polly **BOYDEN**, b. of Union, Jan. 19, 1830, by Neh[emiah] B. Beardsley	1-M	45
Irene, d. Ebenezer & Deborah, b. Aug. 3, 1750	2LR	288
John, s. Eleazer & Mary, b. Jan. 12, 1798	1-B	44
Joseph, s. Elijah & Rachel, b. Aug. 14, 1792	1-B	23
Linus, m. Mary **LOWRING**, b. of Union, Aug. 18, 1811	1-M	23
Lorett A., of Union, m. Linus **SMITH**, of Southbridge, Mass., May 1, 1853, by Rev. Samuel J. Curtiss	1-M	35
Lorett Adelia, d. Aaron A. & Maria, b. Mar. 2, 1834	1-B	116
Lucy, d. Solomon & Lucy, b. June 18, 1761	2LR	294
Lucy, w. Solomon, d. Dec. 29, 1772	2LR	270
Lucy, d. Gideon & Betty, b. Feb. 6, 1803	1-B	44
Lucy, m. Nathan **KINNEY**, b. of Union, Jan. 18, 1830, by Ingoldsby W. Crawford, J.P.	1-M	11
Lucy Jane, d. Aaron A. & Maria, b. Nov. 11, 1844	1-B	117
Lydia, d. Ebenezer & Rebeckah, b. Mar. 9, 1752	2LR	288
Lydia, d. Nov. 24, 1754	2LR	291
Mary Aliza, d. Linus & Mary, b. July 14, 1820	1-B	81
Mary E., of Union, m. James F. **HAMILTON**, of Stafford, Mar. 6, 1844, by Rev. Samuel J. Curtiss	1-M	39
Nabby, [twin with Gideon], d. Gideon & Abigail, b. Oct. 31, 1798	1-B	44
Nancy, d. Linus & Mary, b. Sept. 20, 1825	1-B	81
Palace, d. Elijah & Rachel, b. Sept. 21, 1787	1-B	23
Palace, d. Elijah & Rachel, d. Sept. 17, 1791	1-D	23
Phila, d. Linus & Mary, b. May 25, 1812	1-B	59
Phila, m. Ezra A. **PUTNEY**, Apr. 18, 1833, by Rev. Stephen Fairbanks	1-M	51
Sally, Mrs., m. Samuel **WHITTEMORE**, b. of Mansfield, Jan. 1, 1794, by Sol[omo]n Wales, J.P.	TM	6
Samuel, s. Eleazer & Mary, b. Dec. 17, 1800	1-B	44
Sarah, [twin with Shubael], d. Ebenezer & Deborah, b. Oct. 6, 1754	2LR	292
Shubael, [twin with Sarah], s. Ebenezer & Deborah, b. Oct. 6, 1754	2LR	292
Solomon, m. Lucy **STRONG**, Oct. 3, 1754	2LR	295
Solomon, s. Eleazer & Mary, b. Mar. 1, 1796	1-B	23
Solomon, d. Mar. 20, 1805	1-D	23
Solomon Alexander, s. Gideon, Jr. & Polly, b. Jan. 21, 1836	1-B	100
Timothy, m. Sarah **LOOMIS**, Nov. 11, 1762	2LR	290
Triphena, d. Elijah & Rachel, b. Jan. 5, 1790	1-B	23
Triphena, d. Elijah & Rachel, d. Mar. 27, 1790	1-D	23

WALKER

	Vol.	Page
Abigail P., of Union, m. Charles M. **CURTISS**, of Eastford, Dec. 17, 1854, by Rev. Samuel J. Curtiss	1-M	73
Abigail Persis, d. Ira & Maria, b. Apr. 21, 1836	1-B	99
Andrew Dwight, s. Harvey & Julia A., b. Jan. 29, 1843	1-B	118

UNION VITAL RECORDS

	Vol.	Page
WALKER, (cont.)		
Andrew White, s. Harvey & Juliet A., b. Apr. 17, 1836	1-B	110
Andrew White, s. Harvey & Julia A., d. Oct. 23, 1838	1-D	23
Asa, s. Benjamin & Lydia, b. Jan. 11, 1746/7	2LR	287
Benjamin, s. Benjamin & Abigail, b. June 16, 1755	2LR	292
Benoni, of Union, m. Abigail **KINNEY**, of Woodstock, Nov. 14, 1799	1-M	23
Betsey, d. Ezra & Anna, b. May 1, 1792	1-B	23
C[h]loe, Mrs., of Union, m. Marshall **SEVERY**, of Uxbridge, Aug. 30, 1800, by Sol[omo]n Wales, J.P.	TM	13
Chloe, of Union, m. Marshall **SAVERY**, of Uxbridge, Aug. 30, 1801	1-M	19
Danforth Perry, s. John N. & Nancy, b. Sept. 26, 1827, at Ashford	1-B	116
Daniel, s. John N., b. Oct. 25, 1837, at Ashford	1-B	116
Ebenezer, s. Hannah **PRESTON**, b. Sept. 10, 1801	1-B	58
Elizabeth, d. Stephen & Abigail, b. Apr. 12, 1813	1-B	59
Elizabeth, d. Stephen & Abigail, d. May 9, 1813	1-D	23
Elizabeth, d. Benjamin & Abigail, b. Mar. 1, [ ]	2LR	293
Emeline Jane, d. Joseph & Rebeckah Wilson, b. May 6, 1833	1-B	99
Eward, m. Daniel **BADGER**, Jr., b. of Union, Oct. 5, 1769	2LR	290
Ezra, s. Pearley & Rebeckah, b. July 31, 1794	1-B	23
Frank, s. Joseph & Rebeckah Wilson, b. Dec. 27, 1830	1-B	99
George W., of Hartford, Conn., m. Almira **MOORE**, of Holland, Mass., Oct. 13, 1836, by Moses C. Sessions, J.P.	1-M	59
Henry, s. Ezra & Anna, b. July 1, 1778	1-B	23
Hezekiah, m. Jerusha **AMES**, Nov. 23, 1767	2LR	290
Huldah, d. Pearley & Rebeckah, b. Aug. 2, 1798	1-B	44
Huldah Ainsworth, d. Pearley & Rebeckah, b. Sept. 2, 1798	1-B	44
Ira, s. Benoni & Abigail, b. Feb. 17, 1801, at Woodstock	1-B	58
Ira, m. Maria **MORSE**, b. of Union, Mar. 11, 1830, by Neh[emiah] B. Beardsley	1-M	45
Ira, Jr., s. Ira & Maria, b. June 14, 1833	1-B	100
Ira, Jr., s. Ira & Maria, d. June 15, 1835	1-D	23
Jacob, s. Edward & Mary, b. Feb. 19, 1755	2LR	293
James, s. Nathaniel & Dinah, b. Feb. 9, 1755	2LR	292
James, of Woodstock, m. Mary **HISCOCK**, of Union, Nov. 5, 1838, by Rev. Stephen Fairbanks	1-M	60
Jemima, of Union, m. Hammond **SAVARY**, of Uxbridge, May 11, 1803, by Sol[omo]n Wales, J.P.	TM	16
Jemima, of Union, m. Thomas **SAVERY**, of Uxbridge, May 11, 1803	1-M	19
John Newman, s. Pearley & Rebeckah, b. Mar. 21, 1803	1-B	44
John Quincy, s. John N. & Nancy, b. July 25, 1832, at Ashford	1-B	116
Joseph, of Ashford, m. Rebecca **JAMES**, of Union, June 25, 1829, by Ingoldsby W. Crawford, J.P.	1-M	24
Josephine, d. Harvey & Juliett A., b. Mar. 30, 1841	1-B	110
Josephine, d. Harvey & Julia A., b. Mar. 30, 1841	1-B	118
Laura White, d. Harvey & Juliett A., b. July 14, 1839	1-B	110
Laura White, d. Harvey & Julia A., b. July 14, 1839	1-B	118
Levi, m. Mrs. Sarah **SHUMWAY**, Jan. 10, 1799, by Sol[omo]n Wales, J.P.	TM	10
Levi, m. Sarah **SHUMWAY**, b. of Union, Jan. 10, 1799	1-M	23
Lois, m. Jason **FENTON**, b. of Sturbridge, June 27, 1796, by Sol[omo]n Wales, J.P.	TM	8

WALKER, (cont.)

	Vol.	Page
Lydia, of Brookfield, Mass., m. Amasa **COY**, of Union, July 2, 1848, by Rev. Samuel J. Curtis	1-M	57
Margaret, m. Daniel **BELKNAP**, Feb. 19, 1807	1-M	2
Maria, w. Ira & d. of Jeremiah & Perris Morse, b. Jan. 9, 1807. Recorded Dec. 28, 1832	1-B	90
Mary, of Union, m. Hiram **DODGE**, of Medway, Nov. 8, 1837, by Moses C. Sessions, J.P.	1-M	4
Mehetable, d. Simon & Elizabeth, b. Sept. 23, 1795	1-B	23
Mercy Orrilla, d. Benoni & Abigail, b. Feb. 16, 1814, at Ellington	1-B	59
Minerva, d. Benoni & Abigail, b. Apr. 26, 1820	1-B	81
Nancy, d. James & Polly, b. Jan. 14, 1807, at Sturbridge	1-B	58
Nancy, m. Eli **COYE**, Feb. 19, 1827, by James D. Barnett, Woodstock	1-M	38
Nathan, m. Ruby **LILLIE**, Oct. 6, 1841, by Rev. Samuel J. Curtiss	1-M	69
Nathaniel, s. Setephen & Abigail, b. Dec. 20, 1809	1-B	58
Nathaniel, d. July 1, 1754, in the 54th y. of his age	2LR	291
Obediah, s. Edward & Maray, b. May 18, [ ]	2LR	293
Olive, d. Ezra & Anna, b. Sept. 28, 1787	1-B	23
Orrin, s. Ira & Marian*, b. June 5, 1839 (*Maria ?)	1-B	100
Palmer, s. Pearley & Rebeckah, b. Nov. 4, 1800* (*Perhaps 1801)	1-B	44
Parma, d. John N. & Nancy, b. Feb. 23, 1830, at Ashford	1-B	116
Pearley, s. Ezra & Abigail, b. July 22, 1767	2LR	268
Pearley, s. Pearley & Rebeckah, b. Aug. 28, 1796	1-B	23
Pearley, Jr., of Ashford, m. Sally **HOWARD**, of Union, June 6, 1826, by Ingoldsby W. Crawford, J.P.	1-M	24
Polly had s. John Lyman **KEYES**, b. Nov. 16, 1810. Reputed father John **KEYES**. Recorded Mar. 26, 1830	1-B	40
Rachel, d. Simons & Elizabeth, b. Mar. 20, 1793	1-B	23
Rebeckah, d. John N. & Nancy, b. Jan. 25, 1836, at Ashford	1-B	116
Reward, d. Benjamin & Abigail, b. Aug. 19, 1750	2LR	288
Robert, s. Edward & Mary, b. Mar. 11, 1752	2LR	293
Sally, d. Benoni & Abigail, b. Nov. 4, 1798, at Woodstock	1-B	58
Sally, d. Benoni & Abigail, b. Feb. 21, 1817	1-B	59
Stephen, s. Nathaniel, Jr. & Ruth (?), b. Jan. 1, 1747/8	2LR	287
Susannah, Mrs., of Union, m. Amasa **DOLPH**, of Holland, May 18, 1800, by Sol[omo]n Wales, J.P.	TM	11
Wayram Bugbee, s. Pearley & Rebeckah, b. Sept. 9, 1792	1-B	23
William, s. Benoni & Abigail, b. Feb. 24, 1804	1-B	28
William, m. Irena **COY**, b. of Union, Feb. 2, 1823, by William Foster, J.P.	1-M	23
William, of Union, m. Phebe **PERRIN**, of Woodstock, Oct. 7, 1827, by Neh[emiah] B. Beardsley	1-M	24
Wyllys, s. Ezra & Anna, b. Feb. 21, 1784	1-B	23
Zuriah had d. Roseanna **HALLIDAY**, b. Mar. 3, 1765; d. Apr. 19, 1765	2LR	267

WALLIS,

Hiram, of Mass., m. Eliza **PUTNEY**, of Union, Jan. 29, [1835], by Rev. Washington Munger, of Holland, Mass. Int. Pub.	1-M	46

WARD,

Aaron, s. John & Abigail, b. Oct. 11, 1748	2LR	288
Abigail, w. John, d. Jan. 5, 1746	1-D	2b
Abigail, d. Jesse & Elizabeth, b. Dec. 11, 1757	2LR	289
Abigail, d. Jesse & Elizabeth, b. Dec. 11, 1757	1-D	2b
Amasa, s. Ebenezer & Aanna, b. July 31, 1763	2LR	267

	Vol.	Page
WARD, (cont.)		
Anna, d. Uriah & Elizabeth, b. Apr. 2, 1743	2LR	269
Anna, d. Moses & Eunice, b. Oct. 1, 1760	2LR	294
Anna, [twin with Elijah], d. Ebenezer & Anna, b. May 21, 1761	2LR	294
Benjamin, s. Ebenezer & Anna, b. Feb. 29, 1752	2LR	292
Christopher, s. Ebenezer & Anna, b. Nov. 3, 1757	1-D	2b
Christopher, s. Ebenezer & Anna, b. Nov. 5, 1757	2LR	289
Cloa, d. Uriah & Elizabeth, d. Mar. 19, 1740	1-D	2b
Comfort, s. Uriah & Elizabeth, b. Apr. 4, 1752	2LR	288
David, s. Obadiah & Est[h]er, b. July 31, 1750	1-D	2b
David, s. Obediah & Est[h]er, b. July 31, 1750	2LR	288
Dorcas, d. John & Abigail, d. Dec. 9, 1748	2LR	291
Dorcas, d. Ebenezer & Anna, b. Jan. 31, 1755	2LR	292
Ebenezer, m. Anna **PEAKE**, June 23, 1748	2LR	295
Ebenezer, s. William & Rachel, d. Oct. 25, 1767	2LR	270
Elijah, [twin with Anna], s. Ebenezer & Anna, b. May 21, 1761	2LR	294
Elijah, [twin with Rebeckah], s. Ebenezer & Anne, b. May 21, 1761	1-D	2b
Elizabeth, d. Uriah & Elizabeth, b. Oct. 29, 1738	2LR	269
Elizabeth, m. Daniel **BASCOM**, Oct. 9, 1760	2LR	295
Elizabeth, w. Iriah, d. Aug. 22, 1768	2LR	270
Eunice, d. Moses & Eunice, b. Oct. 1, 1760	1-D	2b
Humphrey, s. Jesse & Elizabeth, b. Nov. 16, 1769	2LR	266
Jesse, m. Elizabeth **ABBE**, May 22, 17[ ]	2LR	295
Joanna, d. John & Abigail, b. Dec. 11, 1749	2LR	288
John, s. John & Abigail, b. Jan. 1, 1746/7	2LR	287
Judeth, wid., d. Jan. 21, 1746	2LR	270
Lois, d. Jesse & Elizabeth, b. May 8, 1768	2LR	266
Lucene, d. Jesse & Elizabeth, b. May 2, 1766	2LR	266
Lucretia, d. Ebenezer & Anna, b. Nov. 10, 1749	2LR	292
Marg[a]ret, d. Moses & [E]unice, b. Dec. 8, 1766	2LR	268
Mary, d. Moses & Eunice, b. May 12, 175[ ]	2LR	288
Mary, d. Moses & Eunice, b. May 12, 1750	1-D	2b
Mindwell, d. Uriah & Elizabeth, b. June 11, 1749	2LR	288
Nathan (?), s. John & Abigail, d. Dec. 9, 1743	2LR	291
Olive, d. Moses & Eunice, b. May 4, 1757	2LR	267
Rachel, m. Samuel **ABBOTT**, b. of Union, Jan. 11, 1770	2LR	290
Rebeckah, [twin with Elijah], d. Ebenezer & Anne, b. May 21, 1761	1-D	2b
Royal, s. Abijah & Anna, b. Feb. 28, 1767	2LR	268
Samuel, s. Moses & Eunes, b. Sept. 17, 1754	2LR	292
Samuel, s. Moses & Eunice, b. Sept. 17, 175[ ]	1-D	2b
Tabitha, d. Uriah & Elizabeth, b. Oct. 14, 1746	2LR	287
Tabitha, d. W[illia]m & Sara[h], b. Apr. 24, 1771	1-D	2b
Tabithy, d. Moses & Eunice, b. Feb. 28, 1763	2LR	267
Uriah, s. William, 2d, & Sarah, b. May 11, 1769	2LR	266
W[illia]m, d. Jan. 8, 1731. "Was the first person who died in Union"	1-D	2b
WATERMAN, William, of Sturbridge, Mass., m. Diantha Christiana **NEDSON**, of Woodstock, Sept. 24, 1853, by Rev. Samuel J. Curtice	1-M	88
WATKINS, Hiram, of Ashford, m. Ruth **HANES***, of Union, Oct. 9, 1834, by Rev. Stephen Fairbanks (***HAWES** ?)	1-M	46
WATSON, Elizabeth, m. Robert **PAULL**, Nov. 23, 1752	2LR	295
Lucretia, m. Josiah R. **JAMES**, Oct. 12, 1845, by Rev. Samuel J. Curtiss	1-M	10

	Vol.	Page
WEBB, Ann, d. Joshua & Hannah, b. Aug. 21, 1761	2LR	294
Luther, s. Joshua & Hannah, b. Oct. 23, 1763	2LR	268
Mary, d. Joshua & Hannah, b. Jan. 27, 1760	2LR	293
WEBBER, Edwin B., of Holland, Mass., m. Lucy **TOWN**, of Union, Jan. 22, 1843, by Rev. Samuel J. Curtiss	1-M	69
Eli, of Holland, Mass., m. Phebe **MOORE**, Jr., of Union, Jan. 23, 1845, by Augustus Moore, J.P.	1-M	69
Lydia, m. Josiah **EATON**, Jr., b. of Union, Sept. 11, 1806	1-M	5
Samuel, of Munson, m. Mrs. Mary **MERIAM**, of Union, Sept. 15, 1803, by Sol[omo]n Wales, J.P.	TM	17
Samuel, Jr., of Union, m. Roxalana **GLEASURE**, of Holland, Feb. 14, 1812	1-M	23
Samuel Shepard, s. Samuel, Jr. & Roxallana, b. Dec. 14, 1812	1-B	58
Zida, of Holland, m. French **CRAWFORD**, of Union, Jan. 1, 1829, by Ingoldsby W. Crawford, J.P.	1-M	43
WEBSTER, Jedediah P., of Wilbraham, m. Diana **HAUGHTON**, of Union, [Oct.] 8, [1837], by Rev. Leonard Gage, of Ashford	1-M	60
WEEKS, Sally Ann, m. David **OAKS**, b. of Ware, Mass., [Nov.] 17, [1836], by Ebenezer Lindsey, J.P.	1-M	15
WELD, WELDS, Bethiah, of Sturbridge, m. William **MOORE**, of Union, May 30, 1796	1-M	13
Harrison, m. Mary **SCARBOROUGH**, Sept. 8, 1845, by Rev. Samuel J. Curtiss	1-M	72
WELLS, Washington, of Great Barrington, m. Mrs. Mary **CARPENTER**, of Sturbridge, Nov. 2, 1798, by Sol[omo]n Wales, J.P.	TM	10
WENTWORTH, Benjamin Mills, of Dorchester, m. Nancy **LILLIE**, of Union, Nov. 29, 1827, by Neh[emiah] B. Beardsley	1-M	24
Sabra Aurilla, d. Benjamin M. & Nancy, b. Aug. 3, 1830	1-B	81
WESTON, Anna, of Willington, m. John **HUNT**, of Union, Sept. 8, 1791	1-M	8
Rhodolphus, Rev., of Carthage, Ill., m. Minerva **HOLMAN**, of Union, Sept. 1, 1840, by Rev. Samuel J. Curtiss	1-M	60
WHITE, Elizabeth, m. Joseph **ENOS**, Mar. 7, 1750	2LR	295
Julia Ann, d. Moses & Betsey, b. Apr. 16, 1816	1-B	21
Julia Ann, d. Moses & Betsey, b. Apr. 16, 1816	1-B	59
Julia Ann, d. Moses & Betsey, b. Apr. 16, 1816	1-B	81
WHITING, Mary, of Ashford, m. Ebenezer **WALES**, of Union, May 22, 1793	1-M	23
WHITON, Amy, of Ashford, m. Samuel **MOOR**, of Union, Jan. 30, 1798	1-M	13
Chauncey, of Ashford, m. Lucinda **MOORE**, of Union, Mar. 26, 1833, by Rev. Elliott Palmer	1-M	45
WHITTEMORE, David G., of Sturbridge, Mass., m. Huldah **JOHNSON**, of Union, Nov. 25, 1849, by Rev. Samuel J. Curtiss	1-M	79
Dwight B., of Sturbridge, Mass., m. Adeline **TOURTELLOT**, of Union, Jan. 1, 1837, by Moses C. Sessions, J.P.	1-M	59
Samuel, m. Mrs. Sally **WALES**, b. of Mansfield, Jan. 1, 1794, by Sol[omo]n Wales, J.P.	TM	6
WILBUR, Elizabeth, of Woodstock, m. Luther **CRAWFORD**, of Union, June 14, 1792	1-M	3
Hannah, m. Elijah **HOLMAN**, b. of Union, Jan. 5, 1834, by Rev. Leonard Gage, of Ashford	1-M	25
WILLIAMS, Abigail, d. Elisha & Abigail, b. May 16, [ ]	2LR	293
Abijah, s. William & Azubah, b. Sept. 24, 1750	2LR	288

UNION VITAL RECORDS

	Vol.	Page
WILLIAMS, (cont.)		
Abijah, s. William & Azubah, d. Nov. 28, 1754	2LR	291
Abijah, s. William & Azubah, b. May 23, 1762	2LR	267
Ann, d. William & Azubah, d. Nov. 22, 1754	2LR	291
Anna, d. William & Azubah, b. Jan. 9, 1747/8	2LR	288
Asahel, s. William & Azubah, b. Jan. 7, [ ]	2LR	293
Betsey, m. Johnathan **LILLEY**, b. of Union, July 2, 1843, by Rev. Samuel J. Curtiss	1-M	48
Daniel, s. Elisha & Abigail, b. May 22, 1758	2LR	293
Elias, s. Elisha & Abigail, b. Feb. 27, 1769	2LR	266
Eliphalet, s. William & Azubah, b. Nov. 6, 1754	2LR	292
Elisha, s. Elisha & Abigail, b. July 21, 1754 (Date conflicts with date of Stephen's birth)	2LR	293
Esther, d. William & Azubah, b. Nov. 15, [ ]	2LR	293
Joseph, s. William & Azubah, b. July 17, 1764	2LR	268
Leonard, m. Melinda **WYMAN**, b. of Union, Aug. 11, 1833, by John Crawford, J.P.	1-M	45
Samuel, s. Elisha & Abigail, b. Apr. 20, 1756	2LR	293
Stephen, s. Elisha & Abigail, b. Jan. 5, 1754 (Date conflicts with date of Elisha's birth)	2LR	293
Sybel, d. William & Azubah, b. Feb. 11, 1748/9	2LR	288
William, m. Azubah **MEDCAFF**, Feb. 17, 1746/7	2LR	295
William, s. William & Azubah, b. Aug. 19, 1752	2LR	288
WILSON, Harvey, of Springfield, Mass., m. Sarah M. **LEWIS**, of Union, Jan. 5, 1851, by Rev. Samuel J. Curtiss	1-M	80
WINCHESTER, Sarah, m. Rev. Caleb **HITCHCOCK**, Nov. 30, 1750	2LR	295
WOOD, Allathear, d. Samuel & Lidia, b. Aug. 1, [ ]	2LR	293
David, s. Samuel & Lydia, b. Nov. 13, 1750	2LR	288
Faith, d. Samuel & Lydia, b. June 7, 1756	2LR	293
Irenay, d. Samuel & Lydia, b. June 7, 1754	2LR	292
Lydia, d. Samuel & Lydia, b. Mar. 26, 1752	2LR	292
Samuel, m. Lidia **RIPLEY**, Jan. 11, 1749/50	2LR	295
Samuel, s. Samuel & Lydia, b. Apr. 12, 1758	2LR	293
WOODWARD, Anna, Mrs., of Roxbury, m. Oliver **PADDOCK**, of Holland, Feb. 14, 1793, by Sol[omo]n Wales, J.P.	TM	4
WRIGHT, John, s. Simeon & Mary, b. Jan. 13, 175[ ]	2LR	293
Joseph Warren, s. Gardner & Jemima, b. May 18, 1798	1-B	44
Mary, d. Simeon & Mary, b. Mar. 1, 1757	2LR	289
Mary, Mrs., of Union, m. Rufus **FISK**, of Brandon, Vt., Jan. 5, 1800, by Sol[omo]n Wales, J.P.	TM	11
Schuyler M., of Woodstock, m. Phebe **CLARK**, of Union, May 21, 1837, by Ebenezer Lindsey, J.P.	1-M	59
William, of Augusta, N.Y., m. Mrs. Susannah **SESSIONS**, of Union, Feb. 25, 1802, by Sol[omo]n Wales, J.P.	TM	14
WYMAN, Alinda, d. Ebenezer & Rosanna, b. Dec. 8, 1815	1-B	59
Deray, s. Ebenezer & Rosannah, b. July 7, 1813	1-B	59
Dorothy, of Union, m. Ebenezer **SUMNER**, of Ashford, Feb. 7, 1813	1-M	19
Ebenezer, m. Rosanna **SAVERY**, b. of Union, Nov. 29, 1807	1-M	23
John, s. Ebenezer & Rosannah, b. Apr. 31, 1807 (sic)	1-B	59
Lucy, d. Ebenezer & Mary, b. Jan. 2, 1743	2LR	293
Lucy, m. Uriah **CARPENTER**, Jr., Dec. 5, 1759	2LR	295
Mary, m. Caleb **LOOMIS**, Jr., Jan. 7, 1758	2LR	295

	Vol.	Page
WYMAN, (cont.)		
Matilda, d. Ebenezer & Rosannah, b. Sept. 22, 1810	1-B	59
Melinda, m. Leonard **WILLIAMS**, b. of Union, Aug. 11, 1833, by		
John Crawford, J.P.	1-M	45
Ruth, d. Ebenezer & Mary, b. Sept. 15, 1745	2LR	293
YOUNG, William G., of Southbridge, m. Nancy **TOWN**, of Union, Oct.		
3, 1833, by Augustus Moore, J.P.	1-M	53

VOLUNTOWN VITAL RECORDS
1708 - 1850

	Vol.	Page
ABBOTT, Mary Ann, of R.I., m. Solomon **MATTESON**, June 7, 1857, by Samuel Gates, J.P.	2	61
ADAMS, Catharine, d. William & Marg[a]ret, b. May 24, 1738	1	45
Hellen, d. Austin, ae 36, resid. of Griswold, b. Oct. 11, 1850	3	25
Helen, d. Sept. 26, 1865, ae 15; b. in Griswold	3	75
James, s. James & Elizabeth, b. July 11, 1755	1	36
John, s. James & Elizabeth, b. Oct. 12, 1750	1	37
Lois, d. James & Elizabeth, b. May 30, 1749	1	37
Lydia, m. Abel W. **MORGAN**, b. of Voluntown, Feb. 20, 1831, by Joseph Wylie, J.P.	2	86
Marg[a]ret, d. James & Elizabeth, b. Nov. 19, 1743	1	37
Martha, m. William **DOUGLASS**, Dec. 13, 1781, by Thomas West, Elder	1	82
Roby, m. Jesse **BRUMBLEY**, Jr., Feb. 15, 1818, by Rev. John Hammon	2	22
Sarah, d. William & Marg[a]ret, b. Apr. 24, 1736	1	45
Sarah, m. William **LO[O]MIS**, Oct. 20, 1815, by Allen Campbell, J.P.	2	45
William, s. James & Elizabeth, b. Feb. 13, 1746	1	37
William, s. William & Mary, b. Oct. 19, 1757	1	45
ALEXANDER, Agniss, d. Joseph & Sarah, b. Feb. 2, 1760	1	76
Agnis, d. John & Lucy, b. Aug. 8, 1775	1	159
Agness, m. Elias **JACKSON**, Sept. 14, 1780, by Rev. Solomon Morgan	1	153
Ame, d. John & Lucy, b. Mar. 29, 1777	1	159
Annah, d. Dec. 18, 1849, ae 63; b. in Griswold	3	61
Anson D., s. Sam[ue]l & Anna, b. Apr. 28, 1829; d. July 20, 1830	2	61-A
Asa, s. John & Lucy, b. Dec. 30, 1795	1	159
Betsey M., m. Charles W. **KENNEDY**, Dec. 9, 1824, by Nathaniel Sheffield, Elder	2	60
Betsey Matilda, d. James & Mary, b. Jan. 23, 1802	1	207
Eliza, d. George & Temperance, b. Mar. 14, 1801	1	228
Elizabeth, d. Joseph & Sarah, b. Sept. 4, 1763	1	76
Elizabeth Stewart, d. James D. & Ruth, b. Feb. 15, 1824	2	55
George, s. Joseph & Sarah, b. Mar. 14, 1773; d. Aug. 7, 1773	1	76
George, s. Joseph & Sarah, b. Nov. 3, 1774	1	76
George, m. Temperance **KINNE**, Nov. 16, 1797, by Allen Campbell, J.P.	1	228
Hannah, d. John & Lucy, b. Nov. 7, 1785	1	159
Harry Augustus, s. James & Mary, b. Mar. 28, 1791	1	207
Harry Gray, s. James & Mary, b. Dec. 16, 1805	1	207
Harvey G., m. Mary **BURDICK**, Apr. 7, 1825, in Hopkinton, by Matthew Stillman, Elder	2	43
Henry Augustus, m. Betsey **GALLUP**, Jan. 23, 1817, by John Wylie, J.P.	2	11
Horace Beardsley, s. James & Mary, b. July 26, 1793; d. June 15,		

BARBOUR COLLECTION

	Vol.	Page
ALEXANDER, (cont.)		
1816, ae 22 y. 11 m.	1	207
Horace Beardsley, s. Thomas D. & Esther, b. Dec. 18, 1819, in Milford, N.Y.	2	42
James, s. Joseph & Sarah, b. July 14, 1761	1	76
James, m. Mary **BABCOCK**, May 8, 1788, by Rev. Micaiah Porter	1	207
James, m. Sarah **TILLINGHAST**, Feb. 1, 1824, by Nathaniel Sheffield, Elder	2	54
James D., m. Ruth S. **GORDON**, Feb. 16, 1823, by James Alexander, J.P.	2	52
James Dorrance, s. James & Mary, b. Mar. 20, 1796	1	207
James Henry, s. Thomas D., & Esther, b. May 7, 1813, in Middlefield, N.Y.	2	42
Jennet, [w. Samuel], d. Apr. 5, 1812	2	61-A
Jerusha, d. John & Lucy, b. July 14, 1798	1	159
John, s. Joseph & Agniss, b. Aug. 24, 1752	1	76
John, m. Lucy **BOWDISH**, Apr. 3, 1774, by John Pembleton, Elder	1	159
John, s. John & Lucy, b. May 25, 1781	1	159
John, s. Joseph, d. Feb. 8, 1813, ae 60 y.	1	159
Joseph, m. Agnis **CAMPBELL**, Dec. 27, 1750, by Rev. Samuel Dorrance	1	76
Joseph, m. Sarah **DORRANCE**, Apr. 5, 1759, by Rev. Samuel Dorrance	1	76
Joseph, s. Joseph & Sarah, b. May 20, 1765	1	76
Joseph C., s. John & Lucy, b. Feb. 5, 1784	1	159
LeRoy L., s. Thomas D. & Esther, b. Sept. 20, 1810, in Aminia, N.Y.	2	42
Luana, d. John & Lucy, b. Apr. 28, 1790	1	159
Lucy, d. John & Lucy, b. Dec. 18, 1787	1	159
Martha Loisa, d. Harry A. & Betsey, b. Oct. 24, 1817, in Paris, N.Y.	2	11
Mary, d. Joseph & Sarah, b. Feb. 3, 1770	1	76
Mary Babcock, d. James D. & Ruth, b. June 14, 1826, in Griswold	2	55
Mary Marilla, d. Thomas D. & Esther, b. Sept. 13, 1815, in Middlefield, N.Y.	2	42
Orin Anson, s. Samuel & Jennet, b. Aug. 18, 1811; d. Mar. 29, 1812	2	61-A
Orin Avery, s. Sam[ue]l & Anna, b. Apr. 5, 1824	2	61-A
Rachel S., d. Harry A. & Betsey, b. Apr. 16, 1820, in Paris, N.Y.	2	11
Roxanna, d. George & Temperance, b. May 17, 1799	1	228
Samuel, s. Joseph & Sarah, b. Apr. 22, 1767	1	76
Samuel, m. Jennet **KENNEDY**, May 14, 1809, by Allen Campbell, J.P.	2	61-A
Samuel, m. Anna **AVERY**, Aug. 22, 1821, by Rev. Horatio Waldo	2	61-A
Samuel, d. Apr. 24, 1851, ae 85	3	62
Sarah, d. John & Lucy, b. June 11, 1779	1	159
Sarah Celinda, d. James & Mary, b. Aug. 6, 1799	1	207
Sarah Celinda, of Voluntown, m. Isaac **GALLUP**, of Plainfield, Feb. 6, 1822, by Rev. Orrin Fowler	2	39
Sarah Clinton, d. Thomas D. & Esther, b. Sept. 14, 1817, in Middlefield, N.Y.	2	42
Sarah D., d. Sam[ue]l & Anna, b. May 1, 1831	2	61-A
Sarah D., ae 19, m. Gershom P. **DOUGLASS**, ae 21, b. of Voluntown, July 21, 1850, by Rev. Henry Robinson	3	3
Thomas D., m. Esther **DORRANCE**, Apr. 16, 1809, by Rev. Israel Day, of Killingly	2	42

VOLUNTOWN VITAL RECORDS 131

	Vol.	Page
ALEXANDER, (cont.)		
Thomas Douglass, s. James & Mary, b. Oct. 13, 1788	1	207
William, s. John & Lucy, b. July 1, 1793	1	159
ALLEN, Agnes, m. John **CAMPBELL**, Nov. 19, 1719	1	4
Deborah, m. John **WYLIE**, 4th, Nov. 4, 1773, by Rev. Solomon Morgan	1	130
Esther, m. Jonathan Ransford **MINOR**, Nov. 20, 1766, by Timothy Whitman, Elder	1	111
George, s. Sylvester & Mary, b. June 14, 1779	1	126
John, s. Sylvester & Mary, b. Oct. 10, 1776	1	126
Sarah, d. Sylvester & Mary, b. Mar. 4, 1774	1	126
Sylvester, s. Sylvester & Mary, b. Feb. 27, 1782	1	126
William, s. Sylvester & Mary, b. Feb. 20, 1772	1	126
ALMY, Abigail, d. Elisha & Mary, b. Mar. 28, 1783	1	181
Elisha, m. Mary **RICE**, wid. of Charles **RICE**, of Scituate, Dec. 24, 1777, by Jeremiah Angell, J.P.	1	181
John, s. Elisha & Mary, b. Dec. 15, 1780	1	181
Mary, d. Elisha & Mary, b. Oct. 7, 1778	1	181
Nancy, d. Elisha & Mary, b. Sept. 13, 1785	1	181
AMES, [see also **EAMES**], William C., m. Marcia **POTTER**, Apr. 12, 1827, by Rev. Zelotes Fuller, Jr.	2	71
ANDREW, ANDREWS, Abigail, d. John & Rebecca, b. Jan. 31, 1806	1	237
Elizabeth, d. James, manufacturer, ae 30, b. Oct. 30, 1850	3	25
Elnathan, s. John & Rebecca, b. Feb. 24, 1790, in Coventry	1	237
Elnathan, m. Phebe **TILLINGHAST**, Feb. 18, 1816, by John Wylie, J.P.	2	5
Hannah, d. John & Rebecca, b. Oct. 6, 1799, in Coventry	1	237
Henrietta, d. John & Rebecca, b. July 4, 1811	1	237
Huldah, d. John & Rebecca, b. June 26, 1803	1	237
James C., of Westerly, m. Elizabeth **STEDMAN**, of Voluntown, July 2, 1843, by Rev. Charles S. Weaver	2	13
Jane, d. John & Rebecca, b. Mar. 10, 1801, in Coventry	1	237
John, b. Apr. 26, 1769, in Coventry	1	237
John, s. John & Rebecca, b. Nov. 3, 1797, in Coventry	1	237
Mary, twin with Thomas, d. John & Rebecca, b. May 13, 1808	1	237
Rebecca, w. John, b. Apr. 8, 1772, in Coventry	1	237
Rebecca, d. John & Rebecca, b. Nov. 4, 1791, in Coventry	1	237
Sarah, d. John & Rebecca, b. Jan. 2, 1796, in Coventry	1	237
Susanna, d. John & Rebecca, b. Nov. 2, 1793	1	237
Thomas, twin with Mary, s. John & Rebecca, b. May 13, 1808	1	237
ANDREWSON, Marg[a]ret, d. John & Marg[a]ret, b. Jan. [ ], 1744	1	65
Robert, s. John & Marg[a]ret, b. Sept. 9, 1731	1	65
Samuel, s. John & Marg[a]ret, b. Apr. 4, 1748	1	65
William, s. John & Marg[a]ret, b. July 2, 1742	1	65
ARMSTRONG, Charles H., of Ston[ington], m. Eunice W. **KINGSLEY**, of Franklin, Mar. 25, 1844, by Rev. Charles S. Weaver	2	18
ARNOLD, Caroline, d. Otis, ae 36, & Caroline, ae 38, b. Jan. 7, 1849	3	22
Caroline, d. Sept. 11, 1849, ae 6 m.	3	61
Sylvester, ae 21, b. Woodstock, resid. of Norwich, m. Mary E. **RIX**, ae 26, b. Griswold, resid. of Voluntown, Nov. 21, 1847, by Rev. Charles S. Weaver	3	1
ARTHUR, Mary, d. Bartholomew & Marcy, b. Apr. 28, 1753	1	75
AUSTIN, Solomon, m. Mary **CAS[E]Y**, Dec. 12, 1819, by James		

132　　　　　BARBOUR COLLECTION

	Vol.	Page
AUSTIN, (cont.)		
Alexander, J.P.	2	32
[**AVERILL**], **AVERIL**, Lucy, m. Samuel **GALLUP**, Dec. 15, 1786, by Rev. Levi Hart	1	204
AVERY, Anna, m. Samuel **ALEXANDER**, Aug. 22, 1821, by Rev. Horatio Waldo	2	61-A
Benjamin, s. Joseph & Rosannah, b. Oct. 8, 1780	1	200
Deborah, d. Joseph & Rosannah, b. Nov. 22, 1766	1	200
Elizabeth, d. Joseph & Rosannah, b. June 18, 1775	1	200
James Gardner, s. Joseph & Rosannah, b. Oct. 7, 1767	1	200
John W., of Groton, m. Louisa **CAMPBELL**, of Voluntown, Nov. 14, 1842, by Rev. Jacob Allen	2	112
Joseph, m. Rosannah **RICE**, Nov. [ ], 1766, by Rev. Samuel Dorrance	1	200
Joseph, s. Joseph & Rosannah, b. June 12, 1773	1	200
Lucy, d. Joseph & Rosannah, b. Mar. 17, 1770	1	200
Mary, d. Joseph & Rosannah, b. Oct. 8, 1777	1	200
Olive, d. Joseph & Rosannah, b. May 4, 1783	1	200
AYER, Ann, d. Nathaniel & Presilla, b. Dec. 13, 1729	1	7
Ann, m. John **KINNE**, May 18, 1749, by Rev. Hezekiah Lord	1	75
Charles B., d. Apr. 27, 1861, ae 9 m. 18 d.	3	71
Jane, d. Peter & Mary, b. July 5, 1756	1	78
Lucrecy, d. Peter & Mary, b. May 14, 1750	1	78
Luke, twin with Thomas, s. Peter & Mary, b. Mar. 5, 1758	1	78
Mary, d. Peter & Mary, b. Aug. 29, 1752	1	78
Nathaniel, s. Peter & Mary, b. July 6, 1754	1	78
Peter, s. Nath[aniel] & Presilla, b. Aug. 7, 1726	1	7
Peter, s. Peter & Mary, b. Sept. 12, 1760	1	78
Pri[s]cilla, d. Peter & Mary, b. Oct. 2, 1762	1	78
Sarah, d. Nath[aniel] & Presil[l]a, b. Apr. 7, 1724; d. Aug. 28, 1726	1	7
Thomas, twin with Luke, s. Peter & Mary, b. Mar. 5, 1758	1	78
AYLESWORTH, Elizabeth, m. Thomas **BA[I]L[E]Y**, Jr., Aug. 18, 1768, by Rev. Samuel Dorrance	1	118
BABCOCK, Albert, ae 21, b. Sterling, resid. of Voluntown, m. Frances **PEIRCE**, ae 17, of Voluntown, July 4, 1849, by Thomas Tillinghast	3	2
Elias, s. Isaiah & Elizabeth, b. Dec. 14, 1757	1	94
Elizabeth, d. Isaiah & Elizabeth, b. Oct. 18, 1768; d. Jan. 14, 1784	1	105
George, m. Sarah **BRIGGS**, June 21, 1798, by Rev. Micaiah Porter	1	229
George A., of Hopkinton, R.I., m. Abby A. **BROWN**, of Voluntown, Mar. 1, 1840, by Rev. Cyrus Miner	2	111
Isaiah, Jr., m. Elizabeth **DOUGLASS**, May 19, 1763, by Robert Dixson, J.P.	1	105
Isaiah, Jr., m. Freelove **BRIGGS**, Aug. 9, 1770, by Robert Dixson, J.P.	1	105
Jonas, s. Isaiah & Elizabeth, b. May 14, 1764	1	94
Levi, s. Isaiah & Freelove, b. June 11, 1771	1	105
Martha, d. Isaiah & Elizabeth, b. Nov. 20, 1764; d. June 23, 1810, in Paris, N.Y.	1	105
Martha, m. Patrick **CAMPBELL**, Dec. 7, 1786, by Rev. Micaiah Porter	1	212
Martha, alias **CAMPBELL**, d. June 23, 1810, ae 46 y.	1	212
Mary, d. Isaiah & Elizabeth, b. Nov. 14, 1766	1	105

VOLUNTOWN VITAL RECORDS

	Vol.	Page
BABCOCK, (cont.)		
Mary, m. James **ALEXANDER**, May 8, 1788, by Rev. Micaiah Porter	1	207
Mary E., d. Sept. [ ], 1854, ae 35; b. in R. Island	3	65
Phebe, m. Amos **LAWRENCE**, Dec. 5, 1784, by Rev. Micaiah Porter	1	176
Prudence, d. Apr. 23, 1864, ae 81; b. in Westerly, R.I.	3	74
Samuel, s. Isaiah & Elizabeth, b. Dec. 2, 1761	1	94
Sarah, d. Hoxsie, wagon maker, ae 38, & Elizabeth, ae 32, b. Nov. 1, 1850	3	25
-----, child of Daniel, farmer, & Mary C., b. Mar. 31, 1850	3	25
BACON, Bradhu[r]st, s. Jacob & Dorothy, b. July 1, 1721	1	1
Dorithy, m. Robert **PARKE**, Oct. 19, 1724	1	8
John F., m. Mary A. **ROB[B]INS**, Oct. 21, 1824, by Sterry Kinne, J.P.	2	60
John F., m. Rebecca **KENNEDY**, b. of Voluntown, Mar. 15, 1840, by Rev. Jacob Allen	2	83
Lucy, m. Joseph **EATON**, Mar. 1, 1750, by Rev. Cogswell	1	52
BAGGS, Roxa A., d. Dec. 29, 1866, ae 29; b. in Hopkinton, R.I.	3	77
[BAILEY], BALEY, BALY, Amy, m. Rufus **VAUGHEN**, Sept. 16, 1780, by John Dixson, Esq.	1	174
Balidel, d. Elisha & Freelove, b. Mar. 14, 1766	1	107
Elisha, m. Freelove **TYLER**, Apr. 11, 1765, by Robert Dixson, J.P.	1	107
Esther, m. Anthony **BROWN**, Nov. 16, 1780, by James Gordon, J.P.	1	162
Frederick, s. Elisha & Freelove, b. Apr. 22, 1772	1	107
Lucretia, d. Elisha & Freelove, b. Sept. 3, 1767	1	107
Merebiah, d. Elisha & Freelove, b. Dec. 3, 1769	1	107
Thomas, Jr., m. Elizabeth **AYLESWORTH**, Aug. 18, 1768, by Rev. Samuel Dorrance	1	118
Thomas, s. Thomas, Jr. & Elizabeth, b. May 24, 1769	1	118
BALDWIN, Daniel A., of Montville, m. Lydia A. **COLEGROVE**, of Voluntown, May 22, 1853, by Elisha Potter, J.P.	2	139
John, m. Anna **ROSE**, Jan. 11, 1825, by Sterry Kinne, J.P.	2	63
William Henry, of N. Stonington, m. Sally **DOUGLASS**, of Voluntown, Mar. 25, 1838, by Rev. Charles s. Weaver	2	66
BALLARD, Esther, m. James **WILKESON**, July 16, 1770, by Samuel St[e]wart, J.P.	1	63
BANNER, Jonathan, d. May 8, 1863, ae 67; b. in England	3	72
BARBER, Aaron, d. Nov. 15, 1862, ae 55; b. in R. Island	3	72
Ann, of Richmond, R.I., m. John **HOXIE**, Jr., of Exeter, R.I., Oct. 20, 1850, by Gershom Palmer, Elder	2	137
Caleb, s. Jabez & Thankfull, b. Nov. 16, 1815, in Cranston, R.I.	2	5
Charles H., s. Caleb & Mary Ann **BARBER**, b. June 1, 1846, at Griswold	2	136
Emily A., d. Caleb & Mary Ann, b. Dec. 18, 1839	2	136
Jaba, s. Henry & Anna, b. Jan. 9, 1795	1	234
Jabez, m. Thankful **LEWIS**, Sept. 18, 1814, by Allen Campbell, J.P.	2	5
John G., d. Feb. 19, 1851, ae 19; b. in W. Greenwich	3	62
Lydia, m. Daniel K. **LARKHAM**, July 12, 1818, by Gershom Palmer, Elder	2	44
Marilla, m. George **BLIVEN**, b. of Griswold, Mar. 15, 1847, by Rev. Charles S. Weaver	2	25
Nabby, m. Roswell **PALMER**, b. of Exeter, R.I., Oct. 29, 1829, by		

	Vol.	Page
BARBER, (cont.)		
Nathaniel Sheffield, Elder	2	82
Nelson, d. May 11, 1867, ae 10; b. in R. Island	3	78
Reynolds, of Exeter, R.I., m. Wid. Sarah **LEWIS**, of Voluntown, Apr. 25, 1831, by Nathaniel Sheffield, Elder	2	88
Sabra, d. Henry & Anna, b. Feb. 3, 1797	1	234
Smith, s. Henry & Anna, b. Mar. 7, 1799	1	234
Thomas J., of Westerly, m. Roxy **LEWIS**, of Voluntown, Feb. 9, 1840, by Rev. Charles S. Weaver	2	24
Tift L., m. Sarah **WINTERBOTTOM**, b. of Voluntown, Nov. 28, 1844, by Rev. Charles S. Weaver	2	118
BARNET[T], Rebecca, m. Samuel **STEWART**, Jr., Sept. 13, 1781, by Rev. Alexander Miller	1	161
BARRETT, Moses, m. Mary **DOW**, Oct. 22, 1747, by Rev. Samuel Dorrance	1	44
Stephen, s. Moses & Mary, b. Oct. 3, 1748	1	44
BARTON, Sarah A., ae 20, m. W[illia]m **BELCHER**, ae 22, b. Exeter, resid. of Providence, Sept. 24, 1849, by Rev. Cha[rle]s S. Weaver	3	3
BASS, Mary, m. Thomas **WEDGE**, Jan. 25, 1760, by Nathaniel Huntington, J.P.	1	98
BASSETT, BASSET, Albert, s. Ralph, farmer & merchant, ae 30, & Sarah, ae 29, b. June 24, 1849	3	22
Albert Anson, s. George & Sarah, b. Apr. 8, 1813	1	218
Alice, d. Apr. 28, 1849, ae 59	3	60
Augusta, d. Dec. 16, 1857, ae 4	3	67
Celie, d. James & Elizabeth, b. Dec. 1, 1793, in Preston	1	211
Clarissa, d. James & Elizabeth, b. Apr. 4, 1795	1	211
Clary, m. Moses **KENNEDY**, b. of Voluntown, Mar. 11, 1827, by Nathaniel Sheffield, Elder	2	71
Elijah, s. James & Elizabeth, b. Nov. 12, 1791	1	211
Emmela Augusta, d. George & Sabra, b. Dec. 3, 1815	1	218
George, s. James & Elizabeth, b. Aug. 21, 1788, in Middleborough, Mass.	1	211
George, m. Sabra **CRARY**, Feb. 2, 1812, by Allen Campbell, J.P.	1	218
George, m. Alice **SMITH**, of Voluntown, Feb. [ ], 1840, by Rev. Charles S. Weaver	2	43
George*, ae 58, mechanic, b. in Griswold, res. of Voluntown, m. Sally **LARKHAM**, ae 50, a farmer's widow, b. in Coventry, R.I., res. of Voluntown, July 15, 1849, by Harvey Campbell. (*His 2d marriage)	3	2
George, Capt., m. Sally **LARKHAM**, b. of Voluntown, July 20, 1849, by Harvey Campbell, J.P.	2	134
Ida C., d. Nov. 19, 1866, ae 6	3	77
James, s. James & Elizabeth, b. May 2, 1790, in Preston	1	211
James, d. Dec. 16, 1857, e 92; b. in Norton, Mass.	3	67
Lydia, d. James & Elisabeth, b. Jan. 29, 1797	1	211
Lydia, m. Charles W. **KENNEDY**, b. of Voluntown, [ ], by Nathaniel Sheffield, Elder	2	61
Mary Ellen, d. Dec. 1, 1866, ae 11	3	77
Massa, s. James & Elizabeth, b. Apr. 18, 1799	1	211
Polly, d. James & Elizabeth, b. Nov. 20, 1786, in Middleborough, Mass.	1	211

	Vol.	Page
BASSETT, BASSET, (cont.)		
Polly, m. Amos **CHAPMAN**, Jr., Sept. 27, 1804, by Amos Crandall, Minister	1	253
Ralph, s. George & Sabra, b. Apr. 3, 1819	1	218
Sally, d. James & Elizabeth, b. Sept. 20, [ ]	1	211
Sarah E., of Voluntown, m. Frances A. **SPAULDING**, of Griswold, Apr. 6, 1830, by Nathaniel Sheffield, Elder	2	83
Susan Maria, d. George & Sabra, b. Mar. 14, 1822	1	218
BATES, BAITES, Abigel, d. Frances & Mary, b. Mar. 16, 1722	1	5
Chester, ae 25, of Providence, m. Sally M. **GALLUP**, Jan. [1850?], by Rev. Peleg Peckham	3	3
Frances, s. Francis & Mary, b. May 1, 1727	1	5
Martha, d. Frances & Mary, b. May 26, 1720; d. Mar. 13, 1726/7, in ye 7th year of her age	1	5
Mary, d. Frances & Mary, b. Apr. 31, 1718	1	5
Mary, had d. Freelove **JACKSON**, reputed d. of Archibald **JACKSON**, b. June 8, 1788	1	206
Susanna, d. Frances & Mary, b. July 28, 1724	1	5
William, s. Francis & Mary, b. May 6, 1716	1	5
BEEBE, Lydia, d. Stephen & Abigail, b. Apr. 22, 1796	1	190
Martin, s. Stephen & Abigail, b. Dec. 14, 1804	1	190
Russel[l], s. Stephen & Abigail, b. Mar. 3, 1802	1	190
Samuel, s. Stephen & Abigail, b. Oct. 7, 1799	1	190
BELCHER, W[illia]m, ae 22, b. in Exeter, resid. of Providence, m. Sarah A. **BARTON**, ae 20, Sept. 24, 1849, by Rev. Cha[rle]s S. Weaver	3	3
BELLEW, Ann, d. Peter & Temperance, b. June 30, 1771	1	124
BENJAMIN, Elam, d. Nov. 19, 1861, ae 76; b. in Preston	3	71
[BENNETT], BENNET, BENET, Agnes, d. Benjamin, Jr. & Marg[a]ret, b. Apr. 3, 1770	1	95
Anne, m. Samuel **EAMES**, Nov. 10, 1774, by Rev. Eliphelet Write	1	140
Ebenezer, s. Benjamin & Thankfull, b. Feb. 2, 1764	1	73
Elizabeth, of Liberty, N.Y., m. James **DOUGLASS**, Aug. 10, 1820, by William Parks, J.P.	1	124
Frances, m. Elias **COREY (CAREY** ?), July 14, 1844, by Rev. Charles S. Weaver	2	20
Han[n]ah, d. Joseph & Jemime, b. Mar. 3, 1720	1	4
Hennery, s. Benjamin & Thankfull, b. Apr. 24, 1756	1	73
John, s. Benjamin & Thankful, b. Sept. 19, 1753	1	73
Lucy, d. Benjamin & Thankfull, b. May 26, 1768	1	73
Luther, s. Lydia, b. Mar. 24, 1785	1	20
Lydia, d. Benjamin & Thankfull, b. Sept. 22, 1760	1	73
Margeret, d. Benjamin & Margeret, b. [ ]	1	95
Nathan, s. Thomas & Jemima, b. Sept. 9, 1723	1	9
Rhoda, d. Dec. 26, 1863, ae 46; b. Mass.	3	73
William, s. Benjamin, Jr. & Marg[a]ret, b. June 29, 1785	1	95
BENTLEY, David, m. Serena **DEWEY**, b. of N. Stonington, Aug. [ ], by Elder Cha[rle]s Randall. Entered Oct. 7, 1840	2	23
Jesse P., s. Gilbert, farmer, ae 23, & Mary, ae 23, b. Apr. 12, 1849	3	23
BILLINGS, Charles, of Griswold, m. Sally **LEWIS**, of Voluntown, Aug. 24, 1823, by James Alexander, J.P.	2	53
Charles, d. Sept. 13, 1855, ae 56; b. Griswold	3	66
Hannah, m. Deac. Joseph **PALMER**, Feb. 8, 1778, by Rev.		

BARBOUR COLLECTION

	Vol.	Page
BILLINGS, (cont.)		
Solomon Morgan	1	118
Horatio M., of Griswold, m. Mary A. **FISH**, of Voluntown, Jan. 30, 1838, by Benj[amin] Gallup, Jr., J.P.	2	101
Mary E., m. Isaac **GLASKO**, b. of Griswold, Feb. 2, 1844, by Rev. Charles S. Weaver	2	11
Phebe E., of Canterbury, m. David **STANTON**, July 4, 1847, by Rev. Charles S. Weaver	2	35
William, of N. Stonington, m. Hannah **WEAVER**, of Voluntown, Aug. 18, 1822, by Amos Treat, J.P.	2	46
BILSON, John H., d. Dec. 14, 1858, ae 5; b. R.I.	3	68
BITGOOD, Albert E., s. Elisha & Betsey, b. July 2, 1836	2	127
Alexander Hamilton, s. Jonathan & Hannah, b. July 4, 1806	2	17
Allen, s. John, 2d, & Lydia, b. Mar. 17, 1803	1	210
Allen, s. John, b. Mar. 17, 1803	2	132
Allen, of Voluntown, m. Betsey **ROUSE**, of Voluntown, Dec. 5, 1822, by Nathaniel Sheffield, Elder	2	50
Andrew J., s. Elisha & Betsey, b. July 12, 1845	2	127
Betsey, d. Sam[ue]l & Elizabeth, b. Aug. 10, 1795, in Westerly	1	260
Betsey, b. Aug. 28, 1805	2	127
Betsey A., d. Elisha & Betsey, b. July 26, 1834	2	127
Carlston Bloomfield, s. Jonathan & Hannah, b. Aug. 26, 1812	2	17
Caroline Matilda, d. Jonathan & Hannah, b. Dec. 6, 1814	2	17
Charles W., m. Tacy A. **WEAVER**, b. of Voluntown, Jan. 16, 1853, by Rev. John H. Baker	2	114
Charles Worden, s. Samuel B. & Susan, b. Mar. 25, 1826	2	23
Charlotte, of Voluntown, m. Joseph **CONGDON**, of Coventry, R.I., Sept. 26, 1847, by Rev. Charles S. Weaver	2	125
Cinthia G., d. John, Jr. & Mary, b. Nov. 25, 1816	2	37
Darius B., ae 33, of Voluntown, m. Mary **FLETCHER**, ae 17, b. Pawtucket, R.I., resid. of Voluntown, Dec. 15, 1850, by Charles S. Weaver	3	4
Dirius Bradford, s. Sam[ue]l B. & Susan, b. July 11, 1818	2	23
Deliverance (**STANTON**), [w. Jonathan], d. July [ ], 1811	2	17
Dolly, d. Sam[ue]l & Elizabeth, b. Aug. 21, 1803	1	260
Elisha, s. John, 2d, & Lydia, b. Nov. 27, 1782	1	210
Elisha, s. John, 2d, & Lydia, b. Aug. 19, 1801	1	210
Elisha, s. John, b. Aug. 19, 1801	2	127
Elisha, d. Feb. 15, 1866, ae 64	3	76
Franklin S., s. Elisha & Betsey, b. Mar. 16, 1843	2	127
Hannah A., d. John & Mary, b. May 30, 1823	2	62
Hannah Smith, d. Sam[ue]l B. & Susan, b. Aug. 12, 1840	2	22
Harriet A., m. John R. **BRIGGS**, b. of Voluntown, Oct. 6, 1850, by Rev. H. Forbush	2	140
Harriet Irena, d. Sam[ue]l B. & Susan, b. Aug. 3, 1837	2	22
Harriet L., d. Allen & Betsey, b. Nov. 2, 1829	2	132
Harriet L., ae 20, of Voluntown, m. John R. **BRIGGS**, ae 19, farmer, b. in Warwick, R.I., res. of Voluntown, Oct. 6, 1850, by Henry Forbush	3	4
Harvey A., s. Allen & Betsey, b. Jan. 15, 1838	2	132
Joel, s. John, 2d, & Lydia, b. Nov. 30, 1799	1	210
Joel K., s. Elisha & Betsey, b. July 16, 1840	2	127
John, s. John, 2d, & Lydia, b. May 20, 1787, in Richmondtown	1	210

VOLUNTOWN VITAL RECORDS

	Vol.	Page
BITGOOD, (cont.)		
John, s. John, 2d, & Lydia, b. Feb. 4, 1796	1	210
John, Jr., m. Mary **SHEFFIELD**, Oct. 15, 1815, by Stafford Green, Elder	2	37
John, h. Mary, d. Mary 14, [1859], ae 66	3	69
John Foster, s. Samuel B. & Susan, b. Apr. 8, 1824	2	23
John H., s. John & Mary, b. Sept. 23, 1829	2	62
John W., s. Elisha & Betsey, b. July 20, 1847	2	127
Jonathan, s. John, 2d, & Lydia, b. Jan. 26, 1780, in Stonington	1	210
Jonathan, m. Hannah **STANTON**, July 4, 1799, by Rev. Micaiah [Porter]	2	17
Jonathan, m. Deliverance **STANTON**, Mar. 27, 1808, by Allen Campbell, J.P.	2	17
Jonathan, m. Hannah **GREEN**, Nov. 17, 1811, by Allen Campbell, J.P.	2	17
Joseph, m. Marcy **GREEN**, July 28, 1799, by Amos Crandall, Elder	1	235
Joseph S., s. John, Jr. & Mary, b. Sept. 7, 1818	2	37
Joseph Stanton, s. Jonathan & Hannah, b. Aug. 13, 1803	2	17
Lucy Ann, d. Samuel & Susannah, b. June 10, 1825	1	260
Lydia, d. Jonathan & Hannah, b. Sept. 31, 1800	2	17
Lydia, m. Henry **SAUNDERS**, Feb. 17, 1822, by Amos Treat, J.P.	2	43
Lydia A., d. Elisha & Betsey, b. June 3, 1831	2	127
Lydia A., d. Clark, farmer, ae 30, & Eliza A., ae 21, b. Oct. 11, 1849	3	25
Marcy, m. Elijah **SCRANTON**, Sept. 26, 1824, by Sterry Kinne, J.P.	2	56
Martin H., s. Sam[ue]l B. & Susan, b. May 31, 1816	2	23
Martin H., d. May 5, 1865, ae 49	3	75
Mary, w. John, d. May 12, [1859], ae 68	3	69
Mary Ann, d. John & Mary, b. Mar. 12, 1826	2	62
Mary Elizabeth, d. Sally, b. Nov. 29, 1819	2	33
Mary Elizabeth, d. Samuel B. & Susan, b. Aug. 16, 1834	2	23
Mary Jane, d. Nov. 1, 1863, ae 10	3	73
Matilda R., m. George A. **LAWTON**, b. of Voluntown, July 30, 1843, by Rev. Charles S. Weaver	2	44
Olive, d. Sam[ue]l & Elizabeth, b. Aug. 12, 1798	1	260
Orilla, d. John & Mary, b. Feb. 23, 1832	2	62
Polly, d. John, 2d, & Lydia, b. June 6, 1792, in Hopkinton	1	210
Polly, d. John, 2d, & Lydia, b. Aug. 26, 1793, in Hopkinton	1	210
Polly, m. Simon **GATES**, Sept. 8, 1808, by Rev. Amos Crandal[l]	1	182
Polly, d. Nov. 15, 1853, ae 53, widow	3	63
Remington, s. John, 2d, & Lydia, b. Dec. 1, 1789, in Hopkinton	1	210
Roxa M., d. John, Jr. & Mary, b. Mar. 11, 1821	2	62
Sally, d. Sam[ue]l & Elizabeth, b. Mar. 7, 1801	1	260
Sally, m. Albert W. **MORGAN**, Mar. 28, 1824, by Amos Treat, J.P.	2	56
Samuel B., m. Susan **CLARK**, Nov. 12, 1815, by John Wylie, J.P.	2	23
Samuel B., d. Feb. 13, 1862, ae 69	3	71
Samuel Babcock, s. Sam[ue]l & Elizabeth, b. July 8, 1793, in Westerly	1	260
Sam[ue]l Clark, s. Sam[ue]l B. & Susan, b. May 28, 1820	2	23
Sarah, d. John, 2d, & Lydia, b. Aug. 28, 1784, in Stonington	1	210
Sarah C., d. John & Mary, b. July 22, 1834	2	62
Sarah J., d. Elisha & Betsey, b. Nov. 11, 1838	2	127
Susan Dianna, d. Sam[ue]l B. & Susan, b. Apr. 11, 1822	2	23
Tacy, d. Dec. 11, 1865, ae 31	3	75

138   BARBOUR COLLECTION

	Vol.	Page
BITGOOD, (cont.)		
Thomas B., d. Mar. [ ], 1853, ae 45	3	64
Varnum, s. John, 2d, & Lydia, b. Mar. 7, 1798	1	210
William H., s. Elisha & Betsey, b. Apr. 30, 1850	2	127
William H., s. Elisha, farmer, & Betsey, b. Apr. 30, 1850	3	25
BLIVEN, Cynthia, of Exeter, m. William A. **DOUGLASS**, of Voluntown, Nov. 1, 1840, by Rev. Charles S. Weaver	2	36
Dolly, ae 68, of N. Stonington, m. Louis **MAIN**, ae 66, b. Griswold, resid. of Voluntown, Mar. 8, 1849, by [ ] Barber	3	1
George, m. Marilla **BARBER**, b. of Griswold, Mar. 15, 1847, by Rev. Charles S. Weaver	2	25
Thomas, of Stonington, m. Louisa S. **SMITH**, of Voluntown, Nov. 19, 1848, by Rev. Jesse B. Denison. Witnesses: Daniel Gorton, Charles H. Kinne	2	123
Thomas, ae 24, m. Louisa **SMITH**, ae 24, b. of Voluntown, Nov. 19, 1848, by Rev. Jesse B. Denison	3	2
BLOSS, David, s. Menassah & Lydia, b. June 27, 1783	1	71
Menassah, m. Lydia **GRIFFITH**, Dec. 19, 1782, by Rev. Micaiah Porter	1	71
BLY, Benjamin, d. Jan. 12, 1853, ae 80, widower; b. Mass.	3	63
Joseph, s. Benjamin & Joanna, b. Apr. 19, 1762	1	102
BOARDMAN, Samuel, m. Nancy **WYLIE**, Aug. 22, 1793, by Rev. Micaiah Porter	1	226
Welcum, s. Sam[ue]l & Nancy, b. Dec. 16, 1793	1	226
BOWDISH, Lucy, m. John **ALEXANDER**, Apr. 3, 1774, by John Pembleton, Elder	1	159
Polly, m. Abraham **ELLIS**, Aug. 22, 1790, by Rev. Micaiah Porter	1	208
BOWEN, Charles, s. Phillip A., ae 32, & Charlotte, ae 26, b. Sept. 13, 1848	3	22
Charles, d. Feb. 24, 1849, ae 5 m.	3	60
Henry H., s. Phillip A., farmer, ae 34, b. Oct. 23, 1850	3	26
Mary, m. Thomas **COLE**, Mar. 11, 1724	1	10
Phebe, m. James **BRIGGS**, Apr. 13, 1789, by Archibald Kosson, J. Common Pleas	1	205
BOYD, Abigail, m. Joseph **SPENCER**, Apr. 19, 1792, by Joshua Dunlap, J.P.	1	173
BRACKETT, [see under **BROCKETT**]		
BRADY, Mary, d. Dec. 24, 1848, ae 35; b. in Ireland	3	60
BRAMAN, Anna, d. James & Elizabeth, b. Aug. 28, 1734	1	28
Benjamin, s. James & Elizabeth, b. June 6, 1738	1	28
Elizabeth, d. James & Elizabeth, b. Mar. 2, 1730	1	28
Esther, d. James & Elizabeth, his widow, b. Feb. 1, 1740	1	28
Harriet, of Voluntown, m. Thomas J. **BROWN**, of Hopkinton, Dec. 27, 1846, by Rev. Charles S. Weaver	2	11
James, s. James & Elizabeth, b. Oct. 13, 1732	1	28
John, s. James & Elizabeth, b. Apr. 12, 1731	1	28
Thomas, s. James & Elizabeth, b. May 25, 1736	1	28
BRANCH, Alice, d. May 20, 1850, ae 71; b. Griswold	3	61
Jonathan, d. Feb. 3, 1852	2	62
Lydia, d. Dec. 12, 1829	2	62
Sarah, m. John **DOUGLASS**, Mar. 24, 1774, by Robert Dixson, J.P.	1	129
BRAYTON, BRATON, Benjamin, of N. Ston[ington], m. Susan **PALMER**, of N. Ston[ington], June 30, 1844, by Rev.		

VOLUNTOWN VITAL RECORDS 139

	Vol.	Page
BRAYTON, BRATON, (cont.)		
Charles S. Weaver	2	19
Sarah A., d. Benjamin, corder, ae 40, & Susan, ae 34, resid. of Griswold, b. June 8, 1850	3	24
BREED, Sally, m. Gershom **RAY**, Dec. 12, 1819, in N. Stonington, by Jonathan Miner, Elder	2	19
Sally, m. Gershom **RAY**, Dec. 12, 1819	2	59
BRIGGS, Alfred, s. Daniel & Cynthia, b. Aug. 7, 1831	2	84
Amy, d. John & Zilpha, b. Feb. 27, 1774, in W. Greenwich	1	160
Archibald, s. James & Phebe, b. Mar. 8, 1790	1	205
Barbary, d. John & Zilpha, b. Sept. 20, 1776	1	160
Benjamin, s. William & Elizabeth. b. May 26, 1792	1	133
Betsey, d. James & Phebe, b. Mar. 30, 1796	1	205
Carnii, s. John & Zilpha, b. Sept. 12, 1787	1	160
Cynthia S., d. Sept. 13, 1849, ae 37; b. Sterling	3	61
Daniel, s. William & Elizabeth, b. Dec. 29, 1777	1	133
Daniel, s. James & Phebe, b. Apr. 13, 1808	1	205
Daniel, of Voluntown, m. Lucretia Parkhurst **TILLINGHAST**, July 4, 1850, by Rev. John Lovejoy, of Norwich	2	135
Daniel, d. Jan. 27, 1857, ae 49	3	67
Edwin, twin with Emma, s. Daniel & Cynthia, b. Oct. 22, 1833	2	84
Elisha, s. James & Phebe, b. Feb. 11, 1798	1	205
Elisha, s. James & Phebe, b. Aug. 26, 1799	1	205
Elizabeth, [w. William], d. Nov. 11, 1795	1	133
Elizabeth, d. James & Phebe, b. Dec. 17, 1803	1	205
Ellen Francis, d. Daniel & Cynthia, b. Sept. 10, 1844	2	84
Ellen Maria, d. Daniel & Cynthia, b. May 6, 1841	2	84
Emily F., d. July 4, 1856, ae 2; b. in R. Island	3	67
Emma, twin with Edwin, d. Daniel & Cynthia, b. Oct. 22, 1833	2	84
Emma, d. June 24, [1860], ae 8 y.; b. Sterling	3	70
Esther, d. John & Zilpha, b. Jan. 17, 1779	1	160
Freelove, m. Isaiah **BABCOCK**, Jr., Aug. 9, 1770, by Robert Dixson, J.P.	1	105
George, d. Aug. 1854, ae 28	3	64
George Henry, s. Samuel & Sally, b. Oct. 31, 1827	2	21
Hannah, d. William & Elizabeth, b. Dec. 6, 1780	1	133
Hannah, w. William, d. Dec. 31, 1817	1	133
Harmy, d. John & Elizabeth, b. Mar. 19, 1817	2	16
Horace A., of Norwich, m. Susan M. **STANTON**, of Voluntown, Nov. 25, 1849, by Rev. H. Forbush	2	140
Ira Elmer, d. July 23, 1864, ae 4 m.	3	74
Isaac, s. Noah & Elizabeth, b. Mar. 29, 1750; d. Nov. 1, 1776	1	85
Isaac, s. William & Elizabeth, b. Dec. 30, 1776	1	133
James, s. Noah & Elizabeth, b. June 1, 1760	1	85
James, m. Phebe **BOWEN**, Apr. 13, 1789, by Archibald Kosson, J. Common Pleas	1	205
James, s. James & Phebe, b. Jan. 19, 1806	1	205
James Harvey, s. Samuel & Sally, b. Mar. 24, 1824	2	21
Jared, s. Daniel & Cynthia, b. Oct. 31, 1835	2	84
John, s. Noah & Elizabeth, b. Sept. 9, 1757	1	85
John, s. John & Zilpha, b. July 2, 1785	1	160
John, s. William & Elizabeth, b. June 16, 1786	1	133
John R., m. Harriet A. **BITGOOD**, b. of Voluntown, Oct. 6, 1850,		

	Vol.	Page
BRIGGS, (cont.)		
by Rev. H. Forbush	2	140
John R., ae 19, farmer, b. in Warwick, R.I., res. of Voluntown, m. Harriet L. **BITGOOD**, ae 20, of Voluntown, Oct. 6, 1850, by Henry Forbush	3	4
Joseph William, s. Samuel & Sally, b. Apr. 15, 1822	2	21
Lillis, d. John & Zelpha, b. Jan. 19, 1781	1	160
Margaret, of Voluntown, m. John **GORDON**, of Sterling, Jan. 23, 1828, by Orin Fowler, V.D.M.	2	72
Mary, d. July 9, 1866, ae 74; b. Groton	3	76
Mary Ann, of Voluntown, m. Albert **FRINK**, of Plainfield, Nov. 8, 1848, by Rev. Jacob Allen	2	90
Mary Wilson, d. Daniel & Cynthia, b. Feb. 14, 1838	2	84
Nancy M., ae 16, b. in R.I., resid. of W. Greenwich, m. Mason C. **TRASH**, ae 17, b. in R.I., resid. of W. Greenwich, Dec. 9, 1849, by Elder Cha[rle]s S. Weaver	3	2
Nathan, s. John & Elizabeth, b. Sept. 2, 1822	2	16
Nathan, of Sterling, m. Elizabeth S. **GORDON**, of Voluntown, Feb. 22, 1847, by Rev. Jacob Allen	2	124
Noah, s. Paris & Elizabeth, b. May 26, 1779	1	133
Noah, s. William & Elizabeth, b. Oct. 4, 1787	1	133
Noah, m. Elizabeth **GALLUP**, Oct. 1, 1812, by John Wyle, J.P.	1	212
Pardon, s. John & Zilpha, b. June 9, 1783	1	160
Paris, m. Elizabeth **SMITH**, Dec. 21, 1775, by Samuel Stewart, J.P.	1	133
Phebe, d. James & Phebe, b. Jan. 27, 1802	1	205
Phebe, d. Jan. 16, 1850, ae 82; b. Coventry, R.I.	3	61
Phebe, d. Sept. 23, 1853, ae 52, single	3	63
Polly, d. James & Phebe, b. Aug. 15, 1791	1	205
Ruth, d. Paris & Elizabeth, b. June 7, 1777	1	133
Samuel, s. William & Elizabeth, b. Feb. 17, 1795	1	133
Samuel, m. Sally **TILLINGHAST**, Mar. 12, 1818, by John Wylie, J.P.	2	21
Samuel, d. Apr. 15, 1850, ae 55	3	61
Samuel S., s. James & Phebe, b. Mar. 18, 1794	1	205
Sarah, d. Noah & Elizabeth, b. Mar. 11, 1752	1	85
Sarah, m. George **BABCOCK**, June 21, 1798, by Rev. Micaiah Porter	1	229
Sarah Jane, d. Feb. 5, 1863, ae 8 m.	3	72
Sarah Melinda, d. Daniel & Synthia, b. Sept. 22, 1829	2	84
Susan[n]a, d. Noah & Elizabeth, b. Sept. 26, 1754	1	85
Susan[n]a, d. Paris & Elizabeth, b. July 13, 1783	1	133
Susanna, m. John **STEWART**, Oct. 5, 1786, by Rev. Mecaiah Porter	1	113
Treat, s. William, farmer, ae 26, & Mary, ae 22, b. Aug. [ ], 1849	3	24
William, m. Elizabeth **GALLUP**, Jan. 11, 1776, by Rev. Solomon Morgan	1	133
William, m. Hannah **STEAVENS**, May 3, 1798	1	133
BROCKETT, Angeline, ae 22, b. Preston, resid. of Voluntown, m. Joseph S. **LARKHAM**, ae 28, b. Voluntown, resid. of Westerly, R.I., Sept. 30, 1849, by Elder Cha[rle]s S. Weaver	3	2
BROMLEY, [see under **BRUMBLEY**]		
BROUGHTON, Hannah, m. Seth **KINNE**, Sept. 30, 1778, by Rev. Solomon Morgan	1	148
John, m. Lucy **PERKINS**, Dec. 17, 1778, by Rev. Solomon Morgan	1	116

	Vol.	Page
BROWN, Abby A., of Voluntown, m. George A. **BABCOCK**, of Hopkinton, R.I., Mar. 1, 1840, by Rev. Cyrus Miner	2	111
Alexander, s. Robert & Jane, b. Nov. 1, 1762	1	53
Ann, d. Robert & Jane, b. Apr. 11, 1770	1	53
Ann E., d. Sept. 3, 1854, ae 2	3	64
Anthony, m. Esther **BA[I]LEY**, Nov. 16, 1780, by James Gordon, J.P.	1	162
Charity, d. Robert & Jane, b. July 22, 1755, in Newport, R.I.	1	53
C[h]loe, m. Amos **WEDGE**, Apr. 10, 1776, by Simeon Brown, Elder	1	135
Daniel, s. Anthony & Esther, b. Nov. 13, 1781, in Fostertown	1	162
Denison, m. Lucy Ann **POTTER**, Mar. 27, 1831, by Minor Rob[b]ins, J.P.	2	86
Eunice, m. Jesse **PALMER**, Oct. 8, 1815, by Elias Hewitt, J.P.	2	4
Francis W., m. Fanny E. **CURTIS**, b. of S. Kingston, R.I., Nov. 25, 1847, by Rev. Charles S. Weaver	2	125
Harriet, d. July 5, 1851, ae 25; b. Hopkinton, R.I.	3	62
James D., d. Oct. 8, 1854, ae 2 m.	3	64
James Russell, s. Thomas & Hepey A., b. Nov. 2, 1840	2	149
John, s. Robert & Jane, b. Sept. 12, 1760	1	53
John, of Griswold, m. Susan **GRIFFIN**, of Voluntown, Dec. 3, 1820, by Nathaniel Sheffield, Elder	2	38
Joseph, d. Sept. 27, 1854, ae 2 m.	3	64
Mary, d. Anthony & Esther, b. Nov. 18, 1784	1	162
Mary A., of N. Stonington, m. Nelson B. **HOLMAN**, Apr. 6, 1828, by Benjamin Gallup, J.P.	2	73
Noah, s. Robert & Jane, b. Aug. 7, 1765	1	53
Rebeckah, d. Anthony & Esther, b. Aug. 3, 1789	1	162
Ruth, d. Robert & Jane, b. Mar. 22, 1772	1	53
Samuel, s. Robert & Jane, b. Nov. 12, 1757	1	53
Samuel, s. Anthony & Esther, b. Apr. 6, 1787	1	162
Sarah A., d. May 9, 1861, ae 25; b. in R. Island	3	70
Stephen H., m. Apr. 17, [1860], ae 2; b. Coventry, R.I.	3	69
Susan, of Hopkinton, R.I., m. Bonaparte **CAMPBELL**, of Voluntown, Nov. 11, 1819, in Hopkinton, by Matthew Stillman, Elder	2	4
Susanna had s. Isaac Brown **TANNER**, reputed s. Isaac **TANNER**, b. Sept. 7, 1770, in Hopkinton, R.I.	1	206
Thomas J., of Hopkinton, m. Harriet **BRAMAN**, of Voluntown, Dec. 27, 1846, by Rev. Charles S. Weaver	2	11
William, s. Anthony & Esther, b. June 13, 1783	1	162
-----, d. Mar. 6, 1849, ae 3 d.	3	60
-----, s. Thomas, ae 25, & Harriet, ae 24, b. Mar. [1849]	3	22
-----, (female), d. [, 1855?], ae 1	3	66
BRUMBLEY, BROMLEY, Alas, m. Huldah **LARKINS**, Oct. 15, 1826, by Sterry Kinne, J.P.	2	66
Amanda M., m. George L. **CHAMPLAIN**, Jan. 11, 1852, by Benjamin Gallup, 2d, J.P.	2	114
C[h]loe, m. Simeon **STEVENS**, Jr., Dec. 22, 1803, by Rev. Amos Crandall	1	251
Desire, m. Seth **MORGAN**, Apr. 13, 1782	1	167
Elisha, of Hopkinton, R.I., m. Cordelia **PALMER**, of Voluntown, Nov. 14, 1844, by John E. Lindley, J.P.	2	118
Elizabeth, of Voluntown, m. Joseph **CLEVELAND**, of Troy, Mass.,		

	Vol.	Page
BRUMBLEY, BROMLEY, (cont.)		
Aug. 29, 1820, by Amos Treat, J.P.	2	38
James W., m. Abby **JA[C]QUES**, b. of Griswold, June 29, 1854, by Samuel Gates, J.P.	2	148
Jesse, Jr., m. Roby **ADAMS**, Feb. 15, 1818, by Rev. John Hammon	2	22
Philura, of N. Stonington, m. Isaac **YORK**, of N. Stonington, Nov. 12, 1848, by Rev. Charles S. Weaver	3	1
Thankful, m. John **DOUGLASS**, Jan. 2, 1820, by James Alexander, J.P.	2	47
William G., d. July 9, 1854, ae 60; b. in Hopkinton, R.I.	3	65
BUMP, Lucy, m. Joshua **FENNER**, Feb. 22, 1829, by Benjamin Gallup, J.P.	2	81
BUNDY, Benajah, s. Benjamin & Hepsibah, b. May 28, 1731	1	15
Benajah, m. Mary **HER[R]INGTON**, the last day of Mar. 1754, by Josiah Bennet[t], Elder, of Scituate	1	46
Simeon, s. Benjamin & Hepsibah, b. Feb. 4, 1734	1	15
Simeon, s. Benajah & Mary, b. Feb. 10, 1755	1	46
BURDICK, Ann, d. June 21, 1863, ae 53	3	72
Benj[amin] F., d. Aug. 29, 1866, ae 5 m.	3	77
Caleb, m. Roxanna **KINNIE**, Mar. 13, 1823, by Sterry Kinne, J.P.	2	52
Charles, s. Maxson & Eunice, b. July 14, 1815	2	8
Dudley, m. Sally **LEWIS**, Nov. 13, 1825, by James Alexander, J.P.	2	62
Ellen, d. Sept. 7, 1866, ae 11; b. in Griswold	3	77
Emily, d. Apr. 5, 1856, ae 28	3	66
Esther, d. Benjamin M., farmer, ae 54, & Ann, ae 40, b. Dec. 23, 1849	3	25
Francis, d. Nov. 17, 1865, ae 12	3	75
Hannah S., m. Paul **RATHBUN**, b. of Voluntown, Apr. 9, 1826, by James Alexander, J.P.	2	68
Joseph, s. Joshua & Katheriah, b. Oct. 7, 1795	1	228
Katy, m. Peter **LEWIS**, Mar. 10, 1805, by Allen Campbell, J.P.	1	162
Lucinda, m. Thomas **REYNOLDS**, b. of Voluntown, Dec. 15, 1822, by James Alexander, J.P.	2	51
Lydia, d. Jan. 26, 1851; resid. Griswold	3	62
Mary, m. Harvey G. **ALEXANDER**, Apr. 7, 1825, in Hopkinton, by Matthew Stillman, Elder	2	43
Maxson, m. Eunice **CRARY**, Jan. 10, 1813, by Allen Campbell, J.P.	2	8
Nelson H., d. Nov. 2, 1866, ae 16; b. in Sterling	3	77
Polly, m. William **POTTER**, Nov. 29, 1818, by Allen Campbell, J.P.	2	48
Rebecca, of Voluntown, m. Ichabod **HALL**, of Groton, Mar. 24, 1844, by Rev. Charles S. Weaver	2	18
Rebecca, d. Dec. 3, 1847, ae 75; b. in Hopkinton, R.I.	3	59
Sarah, m. Luce **WINTERBOTTOM**, b. now res. in Voluntown, June 23, 1833, by Joseph Wylie, J.P.	2	94
Stanton, Jr., m. Emily **CRANDALL**, Sept. 7, 1846, by Rev. Charles S. Weaver	2	65
Stanton, d. June 3, 1849, ae 28; b. in Hopkinton, R.I.	3	60
Susan, m. Stillman K. **LEWIS**, b. of Voluntown, Sept. 11, 1842, by Rev. Charles S. Weaver	2	44
BURDON, Phebe, d. Joseph & Bethaney, b. Mar. 9, 1779	1	101
BURLINGAME, Peter, m. Elizabeth **MOUNTGOMERY**, Apr. 23, 1789, by Rev. Micaiah Porter	1	160
BURNS, Sarah, m. William **CAMPBELL**, Oct. 14, 1752, by Rev. David		

VOLUNTOWN VITAL RECORDS 143

	Vol.	Page
BURNS, (cont.)		
Godard	1	80
BUSHNELL, Alfred, d. Mar. [ ], 1853, ae 42; b. in Griswold; single	3	63
Edgar J., d. Oct. 28, [1859], ae 3 m.	3	69
Edna J., d. Nov. 5, [1859], ae 3 m.	3	69
Emily, d. Mar. 3, 1858, ae 38	3	68
Ruth, m. Ephraim **CAMPBELL**, May 14, 1780, by Andrew Lee, Clerk	1	152
BUTLER, BUTTLER, Abigel, [twin with Ann], d. Sam[ue]ll & An[n], b. June 12 or 27, 1722	1	6
An[n], [twin with Abigel], d. Sam[ue]ll & An[n], b. June 12, 1722	1	6
Han[n]ah, d. Sam[ue]ll & An[n], b. May 4, 1724	1	6
Isaiah, s. John & Jemime, b. Jan. 16, 1743	1	8
Jeremiah, s. John & Ruth, b. July 14, 1724	1	8
John, s. John & Ruth, b. Nov. 28, 1721	1	8
Joseph, s. Sam[ue]ll & An[n], b. Aug. 2, 1714	1	6
Latuenies, s. Sam[ue]ll & Ann, b. May 12, 1714	1	6
Rebeka, d. Sam[ue]ll & An[n], b. May 28, 1717	1	6
Thankful, d. John & Ruth, b. Jan. 17, 1727	1	8
BUTTON, Abby Ann, of Hopkinton, R.I., m. John **NICHOLS**, of Exeter, Nov. 20, 1853, by Samuel Gates, J.P.	2	137
Amee, d. Matthias & Mary, b. Jan. 26, 1747/8	1	31
Ann, d. Matthais & Mary, b. Oct. 20, 1733	1	31
Benjamin, s. Matthias & Mary, b. Oct. 1, 1740	1	31
Charles H., ae 18, farmer, of Voluntown, m. Abby **PALMER**, ae 30, b. in Hopkinton, R.I., res. of Voluntown, Mar. 20, 1851, by Rev. Lathrop P. Weaver	3	3
Charles N., m. Abby Ann **PALMER**, Mar. 20, 1851, by Lathrop B. Weaver	2	139
Eliphel, d. Matthias & Mary, b. Oct. 26, 1736	1	31
Eunice, m. Wait **RANDALL**, Mar. 9, 1800, by Peleg Randall, Elder	1	241
Hannah, d. John & Hannah, b. Feb. 17, 1754	1	60
Harriet, d. Nov. 25, 1854, ae 17	3	65
John, m. Hannah **STANBURY**, May 24, 1753, by Rev. Samuel Dorrance	1	60
John, s. John & Hannah, b. Jan. 31, 1756	1	60
Keziah, m. Nathan L. **YOUNG**, Dec. 1, 1844, by Rev. Charles S. Weaver	2	118
Martha, d. Matthias & Mary, b. Jan. 30, 1738	1	31
Mary, d. John & Hannah, b. Apr. 28, 1761	1	60
Peter, s. Matthias & Mary, b. June 20, 1749	1	31
Thankful, d. Matthias & Mary, b. Sept. 6, 1746	1	31
CADY, CADE, Barnibus, s. William & Sarah, b. Jan. 24, 1727/8	1	7
Elias, s. William & Sarah, b. Jan. 21, 1723/4	1	7
Elias, d. Mar. 13, 1727	1	7
Isaac, s. William & Sarah, b. Apr. 20, 1730	1	7
Jacob, Jr., m. Martha **DOWNER**, Mar. 20, 1763, by Jeremiah Kinne, J.P.	1	114
Jacob, m. Dorothy **MORGAN**, Dec. 27, 1770, by Rev. Levi Hart	1	80
Jacob, d. Apr. 4, 1781	1	114
Joanna, m. John **RHOAD[E]S**, Mar. 16, 1748, by Nathaniel Brown, J.P.	1	46
Lydia, d. Jacob, Jr. & Martha, b. July 9, 1763	1	114

BARBOUR COLLECTION

	Vol.	Page
CADY, CADE, (cont.)		
Lydia, m. William **WILKINSON**, Mar. 11, 1784, by Rev. Micaiah Porter	1	178
Nich[o]lles, s. William & Sarah, b. Nov. 27, 1725 & is the 7th son	1	7
Ridley, s. William & Sarah, b. Mar. 3, 1721	1	7
CAMPBELL, Abby, d. Dr. Harvey & Eliza, b. Nov. 29, 1832	2	26
Agnes, d. John & Agnes, b. Sept. 27, 1726	1	4
Agnis, d. John & Agnis, b. Sept. 27, 1726	1	22
Agnis, m. Joseph **ALEXANDER**, Dec. 27, 1750, by Rev. Samuel Dorrance	1	76
Agness, d. Isaac & Ann, b. Dec. 30, 1756	1	84
Agnes, d. Moses & Sarah, b. Nov. 26, 1758	1	103
Agness, d. James & Dinah, b. Nov. 20, 1766, in Groton	1	52
Agness, m. Joseph **KENNEDY**, Dec. 10, 1778, by Rev. Solomon Morgan	1	256
Albert, s. Dr. Harvey & Eliza, b. Oct. 5, 1836	2	26
Alexander, s. John & Mary, b. Nov. 9, 1756	1	55
Alexander, s. Joseph & Hannah, b. Feb. 18, 1767	1	87
Al[l]en, s. James & Dinah, b. Feb. 24, 1749/50	1	53
Allen, s. Moses & Sarah, b. Feb. 17, 1766	1	103
Allen, m. Sarah **KINNE**, June 18, 1778, by Rev. Levi Hart	1	151
Allen, s. John A., & Molly, b. Jan. 31, 1805	1	252
Allen, s. James & Mary, b. Oct. 19, 1810	1	238
Allen, Dr., d. Mar. 6, 1829	2	82
Allen B., m. Julia **POTTER**, b. of Voluntown, Nov. 13, 1842, by Rev. Charles S. Weaver	2	44
Allen Brown, s. Bonaparte & Susan, b. Feb. 7, 1821	2	4
Alpha Rockwell, s. Allen & Sarah, b. Sept. 30, 1803	1	152
Ann, d. John, Jr. & Mary, b. Nov. 18, 1750	1	55
Ann, d. Mar. 21, 1853, ae 44; b. in Scotland. Married.	3	63
Anna, d. Moses & Sarah, b. May 7, 1774	1	103
Anson, s. Dr. Harvey & Eliza, b. Apr. 30, 1839; d. Apr. 19, 1840	2	26
Archibald, s. Charles & Patience, b. Feb. 16, 1761	1	56
Barbara, d. John A. & Molly, b. Mar. 1, 1806	1	252
Benjamin, s. James & Agness, b. July 15, 1755	1	57
Benjamin, s. James, Jr. & Elizabeth, b. Dec. 14, 1790	1	161
Bounaparte, s. Allen & Sarah, b. Sept. 15, 1801	1	152
Bonaparte, of Voluntown, m. Susan **BROWN**, of Hopkinton, R.I., Nov. 11, 1819, in Hopkinton, by Matthew Stillman, Elder	2	4
Bonaparte, m. Maria **CAMPBELL**, b. of Griswold, Mar. 15, 1847, by Rev. Charles S. Weaver	2	21
Calvin, s. Ezra K. & Maria, b. June 18, 1825	2	10
Calvin, m. Sarah D. **KENNEDY**, b. of Voluntown, Sept. 12, 1847, by Rev. Jacob Allen	2	116
Charles, Jr., m. Patience **KEN[N]EDY**, Mar. 20, 1750, by Rev. Jabez Wight, of Norwich	1	56
Charles, m. Jennet **KENNEDY**, Jan. 29, 1756, by Rev. Samuel Dorrance	1	76
Charles, s. Charles & Patience, b. Aug. 26, 1769	1	56
Charles, of Griswold, m. Polly P. **POTTER**, of Voluntown, Feb. 2, 1844, by Rev. Charles S. Weaver	2	11
Charles, s. Calvin, farmer, ae 26, & Sarah, ae 23, b. Aug. 18, 1850	3	27
Charles Clark, s. Alpha R. & Clarissa, b. May 20, 1823	2	95

VOLUNTOWN VITAL RECORDS 145

	Vol.	Page
CAMPBELL, (cont.)		
Cynthe Ann, d. Joseph & Hannah, b. Sept. 29, 1764	1	87
Cyrus, s. Harvey & Eliza, b. Apr. 9, 1842	2	26
Cyrus, d. July 7, 1856, ae 14	3	66
Daniel, s. Robert & Mary, b. Mar. 12, 1733; d. Sept. 11, 1733	1	11
Daniel, s. Robert & Mary, b. July 29, 1743	1	20
Daniel, s. James & Dinah, b. Apr. 3, 1751 (O.S.)	1	53
Daniel, s. Samuel & Esther, b. June 15, 1764	1	101
Daniel, s. James, d. Sept. 17, 1775, at Groton	1	52
Daniel, s. Moses & Sarah, b. Sept. 23, 1776	1	103
Daniel, s. John, Jr. & Jane, b. May 4, 1783	1	164
Daniel, m. Susanna **KENNEDY**, Dec. 21, 1797, by Allen Campbell, J.P.	1	230
Daniel G., s. Winthrop & Susan, b. Oct. 23, 1816	2	12
Daniel L., m. Keziah **GALLUP**, Oct. 21, 1823, by Sterry Kinne, J.P.	2	54
Daniel Lee, s. Allen & Sarah, b. Apr. 21, 1798	1	151
David, s. James & Hannah, b. Apr. 23, 1727	1	17
David, s. Joseph & Hannah, b. June 9, 1758	1	87
David, s. Samuel & Esther, b. Dec. 13, 1767	1	101
Dinah, d. James & Dinah, b. Jan. 20, 1757	1	53
Dinah, m. John **HUNTER**, Mar. 10, 1778, by Samuel Stewart, J.P.	1	155
Dorothy, d. Joseph & Hannah, b. June 9, 1772	1	87
Dwight Bailey, s. Alpha R. & Clarissa, b. Nov. 25, 1831	2	95
Edwin, s. Harvey & Eliza, b. Jan. 11, 1841	2	26
Eleanor, d. Moses & Sarah, b. Dec. 18, 1768	1	103
Elizabeth, d. Robert & Mary, b. Oct. 1, 1736	1	20
Elizabeth, d. James & Hannah, b. Jan. 22, 1738/9	1	17
Elizabeth, m. William **CRERY**, Nov. 12, 1741, by Rev. Samuel Dorrance	1	60
Elizabeth, d. Charles & Patience, b. Feb. 12, 1757	1	56
Elizabeth, d. James & Dinah, b. Dec. 10, 1761	1	53
Elizabeth, d. Samuel & Esther, b. Feb. 19, 1770	1	101
Elizabeth, d. Moses & Sarah, b. Dec. 18, 1778	1	103
Elizabeth, m. William **HUSTON**, Oct. 4, 1781, by Rev. Solomon Morgan	1	156
Elizabeth, m. Joseph **HUSTON**, Apr. 1, 1784, by Rev. Micaiah Porter	1	170
Elizabeth, d. Patrick & Martha, b. Oct. 27, 1792	1	212
Elizabeth, d. Ezra K. & Maria, b. June 25, 1823	2	10
Emma, d. Dr. Harvey & Elizabeth, b. May 21, 1831	2	27
Ephraim, s. Charles & Patience, b. May 4, 1759	1	56
Ephraim, m. Ruth **BUSHNELL**, May 14, 1780, by Andrew Lee, Clerk	1	152
Esther, d. James & Dinah, b. Jan. 25, 1753 (N.S.)	1	53
Esther, twin with Mary, d. Samuel & Esther, b. Mar. 14, 1772	1	101
Ezra Francis, s. Ezra K. & Maria, b. Nov. 14, 1821	2	10
Ezra K., m. Maria **COOK**, Dec. 7, 1820, by Rev. Horatio Waldo of Griswold	2	10
Ezra K., d. May 3, 1833	2	10
Ezra Kinne, s. Allen & Sarah, b. Nov. 18, 1796	1	151
Frances, d. Dr. Harvey & Eliza, b. Oct. 18, 1834	2	26
Frances Jane, d. Alpha R. & Clarissa, b. Oct. 14, 1829	2	95
Frederick, s. Joseph & Hannah, b. July 14, 1760	1	87

	Vol.	Page
CAMPBELL, (cont.)		
Genet, d. Dr. Harvey & Eliza, b. Feb. 9, 1844	2	26
Genet, see also Jennet		
George, s. John, Jr. & Mary, b. May 8, 1749	1	55
George, s. James & Agness, b. Nov. 8, 1764	1	57
Grace, d. James & Hannah, b. July 1, 1747	1	17
Hannah, d. James & Hannah, b. Jan. 15, 1731	1	17
Hannah, d. Samuel & Esther, b. Jan. 24, 1766	1	101
Hannah, d. Joseph & Hannah, b. Oct. 9, 1778	1	87
Harriet, d. Patrick & Martha, b. Feb. 15, 1799	1	212
Harvey, s. Allen & Sarah, b. Mar. 12, 1779; d. Nov. 26, 1782	1	151
Harvey, s. Allen & Sarah, b. Sept. 30, 1792	1	151
Harvey, Dr., m. Sally **COOK**, Dec. 3, 1818, by Rev. Horatio Waldo, of Griswold	2	27
Harvey, of Voluntown, m. Eliza **COOK**, of Griswold, July 8, 1828, by Rev. Orin Fowler	2	27
Harvey, s. Dr. Harvey & Eliza, b. Oct. 4, 1829	2	27
Horatio N., s. Winthrop & Susan, b. Mar. 13, 1815, in Preston	2	12
Isaac, m. Ann **DIXSON**, Dec. 11, 1755, by Rev. Joseph Fish, of Stonington	1	84
Isaac, s. Charles & Patience, b. Mar. 2, 1763	1	56
Isaac, m. Elizabeth **EDMOND**, Jan. 17, 1793, by Allen Campbell, J.P.	1	219
Isaiah, s. Patrick & Martha, b. Sept. 29, 1794	1	212
James, s. John & Agness, b. July 5, 1724	1	4
James, m. Hannah **TAILLOR**, June 3, 1725	1	17
James, Jr., m. Dinah **MACMAINES**, May 11, 1749, by Rev. Samuel Dorrance	1	53
James, 3d, m. Agnes **WALLING**, Nov. 8, 1750, by Rev. Jabez Wight, of Norwich	1	57
James, s. James & Hannah, b. Feb. 25, 1752	1	16
James, s. James & Dinah, b. Mar. 20, 1759; d. Mar. 20, 1762	1	53
James, s. James & Agness, b. May 12, 1760	1	57
James, s. James & Dinah, b. Apr. 12, 1768	1	53
James, Jr., m. Elizabeth **WYLIE**, Jan. 14, 1790, by Rev. Micaiah Porter	1	161
James, s. John, Jr. & Jane, b. Mar. 3, 1797	1	164
James, Jr., m. Mary **TERRY**, Dec. 14, 1797, by Stephen Reynolds, J.P.	1	238
James, s. James & Mary, b. July 5, 1803	1	238
James, s. John & Agnes, d. Nov. 3, 1810	1	22
James, m. Sally **POTTER**, Jan. 8, 1826, by Sterry Kinne, J.P.	2	63
Jane, d. John & Agness, b. Dec. 7, 1720	1	4
Jean, d. Robert & Mary, b. Jan. 19, 1738/9	1	20
Jean, d. James & Dinah, b. May 29, 1760	1	53
Jean (Jane), m. John **CAMPBELL**, Jr., May 2, 1782, by Samuel Stewart, J.P.	1	164
Jennet, d. John, Jr. & Mary, b. Oct. 18, 1752	1	55
Jennet, d. Charles & Jennet, b. Oct. 16, 1756	1	76
Jennet, see also Genet		
John, m. Agnes **ALLEN**, Nov. 19, 1719	1	4
John, s. John & Agness, b. Sept. 23, 1728	1	4
John, Jr., m. Mary **FORGESON**, June 2, 1748, by Rev. Samuel		

	Vol.	Page
CAMPBELL, (cont.)		
Dorrance	1	55
John, s. James & Dinah, b. Dec. 5, 1754	1	53
John, s. Moses & Sarah, b. Mar. 25, 1770	1	103
John, s. James, d. Oct. 3, 1775	1	52
John, Jr., m. Jean (Jane) **CAMPBELL**, May 2, 1782, by Samuel Stewart, J.P.	1	164
John A., m. Molly **WYLIE**, Nov. 25, 1802, by Allen Campbell, J.P.	1	252
John Allen, s. Allen & Sarah, b. Mar. 31, 1781	1	151
John Dixson, s. Moses, Jr. & Phebe, b. Nov. 28, 1790	1	214
John Ken[n]edy, s. Charles & Patience, b. June 6, 1772	1	56
John Lee, s. Bonaparte & Susan, b. Dec. 4, 1882	2	4
Joseph, m. Hannah **KEN[N]EDY**, June 24, 1756, by Rev. Samuel Dorrance	1	87
Joseph, s. Joseph & Hannah, b. Aug. 28, 1762	1	87
Joseph, Jr., m. Anna **WHIPPLE**, Mar. 30, 1788, by Rev. Micaiah Porter	1	199
Laurinda, d. Moses, Jr. & Phebe, b. Jan. 20, 1794	1	214
Louisa, d. Harvey & Sally, b. Feb. 10, 1823	2	27
Louisa, of Voluntown, m. John W. **AVERY**, of Groton, Nov. 14, 1842, by Rev. Jacob Allen	2	112
Lucynda, d. Allen & Sarah, b. May 19, 1790	1	151
Lucius, s. Ezra K. & Maria, b. May 14, 1827	2	10
Lucretia, d. Harvey & Sally, b. Dec. 25, 1820; d. Jan. 1, 1821	2	27
Lucy, d. James & Agness, b. July 7, 1753	1	57
Luther, s. Isaac & Elizabeth, b. Nov. 12, 1793	1	219
Luther, s. John A. & Molly, b. Jan. 4, 1804; d. Jan. 1, 1811	1	252
Lydia, d. Robert & Mary, b. Aug. 21, 1730	1	11
Lydia, d. John, Jr. & Jane, b. Jan. 6, 1795	1	164
Lydia E., d. James M. & Sally, b. June 21, 1830	2	87
Lydia T., of Voluntown, m. William **PIKE**, of Sterling, Aug. 20, 1822, by Amos Treat, J.P.	2	46
Lydia Terry, d. James & Mary, b. Sept. 23, 1800	1	238
Maria, d. Harvey & Sally, b. Aug. 19, 1819	2	27
Maria, of Voluntown, m. William P. **HARRIS**, of Groton, Mar. 18, 1846, by Rev. Jacob Allen	2	120
Maria, m. Bonaparte **CAMPBELL**, b. of Griswold, Mar. 15, 1847, by Rev. Charles S. Weaver	2	21
Martha, d. John & Agnis, b. Apr. 30, 1732	1	22
Martha, d. James & Hannah, b. June 19, 1744	1	17
Martha, d. William & Sarah, b. Dec. 29, 1753	1	80
Martha, d. Moses & Sarah, b. Apr. 24, 1772	1	103
Martha (**BABCOCK**), [w. Patrick], d. June 23, 1810, ae 46 y.	1	212
Mary, d. Robert & Mary, b. Aug. 19, 1734	1	20
Mary, d. James & Hannah, b. Feb. 27, 1735	1	17
Mary, d. Charles, Jr. & Patience, b. Apr. 5, 1751	1	56
Mary, m. David **KEN[N]EDY**, Jan. 10, 1759	1	104
Mary, d. James & Dinah, b. July 8, 1763	1	53
Mary, m. Joseph **WYLIE**, May 10, 1768, by Robert Dixson, J.P.	1	122
Mary, d. Joseph & Hannah, b. May 7, 1770, in Coventry	1	87
Mary, twin with Esther, d. Samuel & Esther, b. Mar. 14, 1772	1	101
Mary, m. Moses **WYLIE**, May 8, 1777, by Samuel Stewart, J.P.	1	143
Mary, m. Joseph **DOUGLASS**, Aug. 11,1791, by Rev. Micaiah		

148 BARBOUR COLLECTION

CAMPBELL, (cont.)

	Vol.	Page
Porter	1	215
Mary A., d. James M. & Sally, b. Oct. 4, 1827	2	87
Moses, s. John & Agness, b. Sept. 14, 1730; d. Jan. 29, 1736/7	1	4
Moses, s. John & Agnes, b. Apr. 14, 1737	1	22
Moses, m. Sarah **DIXSON**, Dec. 1, 1757, by Rev. Samuel Dorrance	1	103
Moses, s. Moses & Sarah, b. Mar. 12, 1764	1	103
Moses, Jr., m. Phebe **STEWART**, Sept. 10, 1789, by Rev. Micaiah Porter	1	214
Moses Douglass, s. Patrick & Martha, b. Oct. 21, 1790	1	212
Nathan, s. James & Hannah, b. Oct. 24, 1732; d. June 8, 1740	1	17
Nathan, s. James & Hannah, b. Apr. 15, 1750	1	16
Olive, d. John, Jr. & Jane, b. Feb. 27, 1790; d. Nov. 17, 1805	1	164
Orin A., s. James & Mary, b. Jan. 21, 1814; d. Dec. 22, 1815	1	238
Orson, s. Alpha R. & Clarissa, b. Apr. 12, 1827	2	95
Patience, d. Charles & Patience, b. Nov. 2, 1754	1	56
Patience, m. Peter **WYLIE**, b. of Voluntown, Feb. 20, 1777, by Samuel Stewart, Esq.	1	136
Patrick, s. Moses & Sarah, b. Apr. 27, 1760	1	103
Patrick, m. Martha **BABCOCK**, Dec. 7, 1786, by Rev. Micaiah Porter	1	212
Phebe, d. Charles & Patience, b. Jan. 20, 1753	1	56
Polly, d. Moses & Sarah, b. May 11, 1783	1	103
Prudence, m. Andrew **EDMOND**, Sept. 9, 1773, by Rev. Samuel Dorrance	1	79
Rebeckah, d. Robert & Mary, b. Oct. 2, 1728	1	11
Rebecca, m. John **HUNTER**, June 13, 1751, by Rev. Dorrance	1	88
Rebecca, d. William & Sarah, b. Apr. 25, 1756	1	80
Rebecca, d. James & Dinah, b. Sept. 27, 1770; d. Sept. 28, 1775	1	52
Rebecka, d. John, Jr. & Jane, b. Sept. 20, 1784	1	164
Robert, d. Feb. 14, 1725, ae 52 y.	1	9
Robert, m. Mary **MACKMAINS**, Apr. 13, 1727, by Rev. Joseph Coite	1	11
Robert, s. Robert & Mary, b. May 3, 1741	1	20
Robert, s. James & Agnes, b. July 1, 1751	1	57
Roseannah S., m. Allen C. **GORDON**, b. of Voluntown, Sept. 22, 1845, by Rev. Jacob Allen	2	121
Rosena, d. Alpha R. & Clarissa, b. Aug. 23, 1824	2	95
Rowena, d. Allen & Sarah, b. May 19, 1787	1	151
Roxanna, d. John A. & Molly, b. Dec. 23, 1814	1	252
Ruth, d. Charles & Patience, b. July 12, 1767	1	56
Sabra, d. James & Agness, b. Mar. 1, 1762	1	57
Sally, d. James, Jr. & Elizabeth, b. July 5, 1792	1	161
Sally, d. Patrick & Martha, b. Dec. 17, 1796	1	212
Sally, m. Daniel **GORDON**, Apr. 19, 1804, by Allen Campbell, J.P.	1	257
Sally, d. Harvey & Sally, b. June 5, 1827; d. May 6, 1837	2	27
Sally (**COOK**), [w. Harvey], d. Mar. 3, 1828	2	27
Samuel, s. James & Hannah, b. June 3, 1729; d. May 1, 1735	1	17
Samuel, s. James & Hannah, b. Jan. 8, 1736/7	1	17
Samuel, m. Esther **SMITH**, Apr. 10, 1760, by Jacob Perkins, J.P.	1	101
Samuel, s. Samuel & Esther, b. Nov. 4, 1762	1	101
Sarah, d. John & Agness, b. July 31, 1722	1	4
Sarah, d. James & Hannah, b. Sept. 13, 1740	1	17

	Vol.	Page
CAMPBELL, (cont.)		
Sarah, m. John **WYLIE**, Jr., Dec. 9, 1742, by Rev. Samuel Dorrance	1	49
Sarah, d. Robert & Mary, b. Oct. 15, 1745	1	20
Sarah, m. Robert **JACKSON**, Nov. 13, 1746, by Rev. Samuel Dorrance	1	59
Sarah, m. Robert **JACKSON**, Nov. 13, 1746, by Rev. Samuel Dorrance	1	87
Sarah, d. James & Agness, b. July 1, 1757	1	57
Sarah, d. Moses & Sarah, b. June 30, 1762	1	103
Sarah, d. James & Dinah, b. Dec.9, 1764	1	53
Sarah, m. Robert **HUSTON**, Apr. 2, 1778, by Rev. Solomon Morgan	1	148
Sarah, d. Allen & Sarah, b. Aug. 15, 1785	1	151
Sarah, m. Roswell **PALMER**, Apr. 8, 1790, by Rev. Micaiah Porter	1	233
Sarah, w. Dr. Allen, d. Sept. 9, 1832	2	82
Sarah, d. Nov. 24, 1850, ae 23; b. in Griswold	3	62
Sarah Malvina, d. James & Mary, b. May 19, 1818	1	238
Solomon, s. Robert & Mary, b. June 13, 1749	1	20
Susan, d. June 5, 1853, ae 63, married	3	63
Susan[n]a, d. Samuel & Esther, b. Jan. 27, 1761	1	101
Susan[n]a, d. Charles & Patience, b. June 6, 1774	1	56
Welcome, s. John A. & Molly, b. Oct. 1, 1809	1	252
William, s. James & Hannah, b. Mar. 1, 1726	1	17
William, m. Sarah **BURNS**, Oct. 14, 1752, by Rev. David Godard	1	80
William, s. Joseph & Hannah, b. July 7, 1774	1	87
William Henry, s. James & Mary, b. Nov. 2, 1798	1	238
Winthrop, s. John, Jr. & Jane, b. Dec. 16, 1786	1	164
Winthrop, m. Susan D. **GORDON**, Mar. 6, 1814, by Allen Campbell, J.P.	2	12
Winthrop, d. Feb. 25, 1867, ae 80	3	78
CAP[E]WELL, Henry A., d. Jan. 15, 1853, ae 32; b. in R.I.; married.	3	63
CAREY, CARY, [see also **CORY**], Alice A., m. Miner **WILCOX**, b. of Voluntown, Apr. 10, 1844, by Harvey Campbell, J.P.	2	116
Betsey, m. Richard D. **ROB[B]INS**, May 26, 1803, by Joseph Wylie, J.P. (Perhaps "**CORY**")	1	258
CARPENTER, Nabby, m. James **LOOMIS**, Sept. 10, 1826, by Sterry Kinne, J.P.	2	70
CARR, KAR, KERR, David, m. Ann **JAC[K]SON**, Apr. 25, 1741, by Rev. Samuel Dorrance	1	42
Elizabeth, m. Samuel **GORDON**, Nov. 20, 1735, by Rev. Dorrance	1	24
Elizabeth, d. David & Ann, b. Mar. 1, 1746	1	42
Janet, m. John **GORDON**, Mar. 30, 1732, by Rev. Samuel Dorrance	1	14
John, s. David & Ann, b. June 14, 1747	1	42
William, s. David & Ann, b. Aug. 28, 1744	1	42
CAS[E]Y, Mary, m. Solomon **AUSTIN**, Dec. 12, 1819, by James Alexander, J.P.	2	32
CASWELL, Ansel, s. George & Elizabeth, b. July 23, 1779, in Middleborough, Mass.; d. Dec. 31, 1803	1	211
Betsey, d. George & Elizabeth, b. Nov. 18, 1783, in Middleborough, Mass.	1	211
Charity, d. George & Elizabeth, b. May 6, 1781, in Middleborough, Mass.	1	211
CHAMPEON, Lucy, m. Nathaniel **DEAN**, Jr., Mar. 4, 1741, by John Griswold, Esq.	1	30

150 BARBOUR COLLECTION

	Vol.	Page
CHAMPLAIN, Charles H. F., s. Lyman & Sybel, b. Nov. 14, 1836	2	123
Daniel, m. Mary Elizabeth **POTTER**, b. of Voluntown, Dec. 2, 1849, by Rev. H. Forbush	2	140
Daniel, ae 20, spinner, b. in Voluntown, res. of Griswold, m. Mary E. **POTTER**, ae 17, weaver, b. in Voluntown, res. of Griswold, Dec. 2, 1849, by Rev. Henry Forbush	3	2
George L., s. Lyman & Sybel, b. Nov. 1, 1832, at Griswold	2	123
George L., m. Amanda M. **BROMLEY**, Jan. 11, 1852, by Benjamin Gallup, 2d, J.P.	2	114
Hannah, m. George **LAMPHEAR**, Oct. 12, 1828, by Sterry Kinne, J.P.	2	70
Mary F., d. Lyman & Sybel, b. Aug. 13, 1841	2	123
Sarah D., d. Lyman & Sybel, b. June 16, 1830, at Griswold	2	123
CHAPMAN, Abel, m. Prudence **THOMPSON**, Feb. 12, 1818, by Jonathan Miner, Elder	2	30
Abel, d. Apr. 26, 1849, ae 55 y.	2	31
Abel, Deac., d. Apr. 26, 1849, ae 55; b. in N. Stonington	3	60
Adam, m. Amy **GEER**, Dec. 26, 1822, by Sterry Kinne, J.P.	2	52
Amos, Jr., m. Polly **BASSET**, Sept. 27, 1804, by Amos Crandall, Minister	1	253
Amos, d. Jan. 3, 1814	1	237
Amos Smith, s. John & Esther, b. Apr. 17, 1818	1	158
Benjamin Franklin, s. Abel & Prudence, b. Nov. 26, 1830	2	30
Benjamin Kinny, s. Adam & Amy, b. May 12, 1834	2	78
Betsey, d. Amos, Jr. & Polly, b. June 19, 1806	1	253
Caroline, d. Abel & Prudence, b. Feb. 16, 1821	2	30
Caroline, of Voluntown, m. Elijah M. **PELLET**, of Norwich, Jan. 2, 1849, by Rev. Jacob Allen	2	126
Caroline, ae 28, school-teacher, of Voluntown, m. Elijah M. **PELLET**, ae 31, carpenter, res. of Norwich, June 2, 1849, by Rev. Jacob Allen	3	2
Catharine B., of Voluntown, m. Orrin **HINCKLEY**, of Griswold, Feb. 10, 1845, by Rev. Jacob Allen	2	120
Daniel Campbell, s. Amos & Abigail, b. June 25, 1801	1	237
Elizabeth, d. Abel & Prudence, b. Nov. 25, 1832	2	31
Enoch B., d. Aug. 13, 1858, ae 30 y.	2	31
Enoch B., d. Aug. 13, 1858, ae 30	3	68
Enoch Burdick, s. Abel & Prudence, b. July 20, 1828	2	30
Eunice Ann, d. Daniel C. & Philura, b. July 23, 1834	2	73
Frances, d. June 1, 1833	2	78
Francis, d. Adam & Amy, b. Mar. 28, 1825	2	30
Gardner, of N. Stonington, m. Jane E. **KINGSLEY**, of Franklin, Nov. 18, 1845, by Rev. Charles S. Weaver	2	8
Hannah M., of N. Stonington, m. Thomas G. **KINGSLEY**, of Franklin, Mar. 25, 1844, by Rev. Charles S. Weaver	2	18
Harriet Newell, d. Adam & Amy, b. Dec. 26, 1830	2	78
Harriet Newell, d. Sept. 3, 1833	2	78
Henry Lee, s. Daniel C. & Philura, b. Sept. 12, 1828	2	73
Henry Smith, s. Adam & Amey, b. Sept. 28, 1842	2	78
Jacob Allen, s. Adam & Amy, b. Sept. 27, 1840	2	78
James, d. Mar. 23, 1856, ae 1 y. 2 m. 17 d.	3	66
James C., d. May 26, 1844	2	78
James Cushman, s. Adam & Amy, b. Feb. 25, 1823	2	30

VOLUNTOWN VITAL RECORDS 151

	Vol.	Page
CHAPMAN, (cont.)		
Joel Avery, s. Adam & Amy, b. Nov. 1, 1838	2	78
John, m. Esther **SWAN**, Feb. 13, 1814, by Allen Campbell, J.P.	1	158
John Calvin, s. John & Esther, b. Nov. 10, 1814	1	158
John Jackson, s. Adam & Mary, b. Oct. 20, 1829	2	78
Josiah Fuller, s. John & Esther, b. Jan. 20, 1822	1	158
Katharine B., d. Abel & Prudence, b. Nov. 28, 1823	2	30
Lucy, m. John **LAWTON**, Apr. 9, 1809, by Rev. Amos Crandall	1	258
Lucy, d. Adam & Amy, b. Aug. 6, 1844	2	78
Martha Phillips, d. Abel & Prudence, b. Dec. 14, 1836	2	31
Mary Augusta, d. Daniel C. & Philura, b. Mar. 7, 1828	2	73
Nabby, d. Amos & Abigail, b. Mar. 11, 1804; d. Dec. 5, 1805	1	237
Otis L., d. Dec. 25, 1863, ae 29	3	73
Otis Lane, s. Abel & Prudence, b. Jan. 8, 1835	2	31
Phebe Esther, d. John & Esther, b. May 17, 1816	1	158
Prentice, m. Patty **CHURCH**, Jan. 14, 1827, by Sterry Kinne, J.P.	2	70
Rachel, ae 23, tailoress, of Voluntown, m. Ralph **PHILLIPS**, ae 24, farmer, b. in Voluntown, res. of Griswold, July 1, 1844, by Rev. Henry Forbush	3	3
Rachel A., of Voluntown, m. Ralph P. **PHILLIPS**, of Griswold, July 1, 1850, by Rev. H. Forbush	2	140
Rachel Amanda, d. Abel & Prudence, b. Dec. 25, 1826	2	30
Ralph Thompson, s. Abel & Prudence, b. Jan. [ ], 1819; d. June 27, 1824	2	30
Roena, d. Daniel C. & Philura, b. Oct. 13, 1831	2	73
Sally, m. Atwood **PHILLIPS**, Nov. 28, 1816, by John Wylie, J.P.	2	13
Sarah, d. June 5, 1833	2	78
Sarah Matilda, d. Abel & Prudence, b. Sept. 6, 1838	2	31
Susan Thayer, d. Adam & Amy, b. Apr. 21, 1836	2	78
W[illia]m B., of N. Stonington, m. Esther S. **MAIN**, of Voluntown, Nov. 25, 1847, by Rev. James M. Phillips	2	94
-----, d. Adam & Amy, b. July 8, 1827; d. July 11, 1827	2	78
CHAPPELL, Henry N., m. Martha **NICHOLS**, b. of R.I., Sept. 5, 1844, by Rev. Charles S. Weaver	2	21
CHASE, William, s. Benjamin & Elizabeth, b. Dec. 29, 1781	1	100
CHEESEBOROUGH, CHEESBOROUGH, Albert F., s. Erastus F., ae 33, & Susan, ae 28, b. Oct. 28, 1848	3	22
Amille, m. Jonathan **STANTON**, Oct. [ ], 1806, by Peleg Randall, Elder	1	167
Lucy, d. Mar. 1, [1860], ae 72; b. in N. Stonington	3	69
Mary Ann, of Stonington, m. W[illia]m C. **STANTON**, of Voluntown, Nov. 17, 1834, at Stonington, by Elder Jerome S. Anderson, of Stonington	2	110
CHESTER, David Clinton, s. wid. of Thomas **GREEN**, b. Feb. 22, 1830	2	83
CHURCH, Alfred, of Hopkinton, R.I., m. Abby **COON**, of Voluntown, Nov. 21, 1833, by Jonathan Minor, Elder	2	97
Amy, m. Matthew **COY**, Dec. 10, 1752, by Benjamin Randall, J.P.	1	67
Catharine, m. Joel **KINNE**, Aug. 20, 1815, by Alexander Stewart, J.P.	2	64
Catherine A., of Voluntown, m. Elroy **YORK**, of Griswold, Nov. 3, 1844, by Rev. Charles S. Weaver	2	47
Happy K., d. Betsey, b. Apr. 27, 1827	2	127
Happy K., m. John N. **GALLUP**, b. of Voluntown, Apr. 16, 1849, by		

	Vol.	Page
CHURCH, (cont.)		
Rev. Jesse B. Denison. Witnesses: W[illia]m W. Thompson, Lydia A. Bitgood	2	133
Happy K., ae 22, b. in Griswold, now of Voluntown, m. John N. GALLUP, ae 20, farmer, of Voluntown, Apr. 16, 1849, by Rev. Jesse B. Denison	3	2
John J., s. Rufus & Eliza, b. July 25, 1850, at Exeter	2	134
Patty, m. Prentice **CHAPMAN**, Jan. 14, 1827, by Sterry Kinne, J.P.	2	70
Sam[ue]ll, Sr., d. Nov. 27, 1724, ae 90 y.	1	8
CLARK, Abby, of Richmond, d. of Moses **CLARK**, Jr., m. David R. **POTTER**, of Voluntown, Aug. 10, 1834, by Samuel Reynolds, J.P.	2	40
Charles H., d. Oct. 13, 1866, ae 5; b. in Richmond, R.I.	3	77
John, s. William & Mary, b. May 12, 1771	1	124
Judeth, m. David R. **POTTER**, Sept. 9, 1816, by John Wylie, J.P.	2	40
Lois, m. Wells **HOXSIE**, Aug. 27, 1801, by Amos Crandall, Elder	1	243
Mary, d. William & Mary, b. July 9, 1767	1	124
Mary A., of Hopkinton, m. Samuel **GREEN**, of Voluntown, May 10, 1840, by Rev. Charles S. Weaver	2	29
Mary A., m. Benjamin F. **WORDEN**, of R.I., May 26, 1845, by Rev. Charles S. Weaver	2	5
Rebeckah, d. William & Mary, b. May 14, 1769	1	124
Rodman, s. William & Mary, b. Feb. 12, 1764	1	124
Ruth, d. William & Mary, b. Mar. 3, 1776	1	124
Susan, m. Samuel B. **BITGOOD**, Nov. 12, 1815, by John Wylie, J.P.	2	23
Weeden, s. William & Mary, b. Oct. 14, 1778	1	124
Wells, s. William & Mary, b. Jan. 29, 1761	1	124
CLEVELAND, Joseph, of Troy, Mass., m. Elizabeth **BRUMBLEY**, of Voluntown, Aug. 29, 1820, by Amos Treat, J.P.	2	38
Joseph, d. Feb. 1, 1854, ae 65; b. in East Town, Mass.	3	64
Lucy, d. Nov. 3, 1861, ae 45 y.; b. in Griswold	3	71
COALS, [see also **COLE, COWLES & COATS**], Elizabeth, m. Capt. James **KINNE**, May 1, 1793, by Joshua Babcock, J.P.	1	180
COATS, [see also **COALS**], Silas, m. Zerviah **MEECH**, Nov. 28, 1816, by Gustavus F. Davis, Elder	2	24
Silas A., s. Silas & Zerviah, b. Jan. 18, 1818	2	24
COGSWELL, Elizabeth, m. Wheeler **GALLUP**, May 2, 1782, by Rev. Levi Hart	1	184
COLE, [see also **COALS, COWLES & COATS**], Amos, s. Thomas & Mariam, b. Nov. 28, 1759	1	93
Ann, d. Thomas & Mary, b. Sept. 17, 1731	1	10
Ann, d. Thomas, d. May 28, 1751	1	10
Anne, d. Thomas & Lois, b. May 22, 1787	1	180
Azel, s. Noah & Molly, b. July 27, 1778	1	119
Dorithy, d. John & Hannah, b. May 20, 1753	1	41
Ellmon, s. Noah & Molly, b. Mar. 5, 1775	1	119
Easther, d. Thomas & Mary, b. Oct. 24, 1737	1	10
Esther, d. John & Hannah, b. Feb. 18, 1760	1	41
Esther, m. James **FORDICE**, Mar. 5, 1761, by Jeremiah Kinne, Esq.	1	102
Eunice, d. Thomas & Mariam, b. Mar. 12, 1765	1	93
Ezekiel, s. Noah & Molly, b. Jan. 5, 1782	1	119
Ezekiel, s. Noah & Molly, d. Nov. 10, 1792	1	119

VOLUNTOWN VITAL RECORDS 153

	Vol.	Page
COLE, (cont.)		
Ezra, s. John & Hannah, b. Oct. 23, 1757	1	41
Ezra, s. Noah & Molly, b. Feb. 1, 1777	1	119
Ezra, m. Susan COLE, Apr. 6, 1779, by John Dixson, J.P.	1	147
Frederick, s. Noah & Molly, b. June 30, 1787	1	119
Han[n]ah, w. Thomas, d. Dec. 3, 1723, ae 41 y.	1	10
Hannah, d. Thomas & Mary, b. Sept. 22, 1729	1	10
Hannah, d. Thomas [& Mary], d. June 10, 1748	1	10
Hannah, d. John & Hannah, b. July 23, 1749	1	41
Hannah, m. Moses LITTLE, Mar. 8, 1770, by Samuel Stewart, J.P.	1	109
Hezekiah, gdf. of Ruth, d. May 15, 1781	1	82
Jeremiah, s. Thomas & Mariam, b. July 3, 1772	1	93
John, s. Thomas & Mary, b. Oct. 24, 1725	1	10
John, m. Hannah NEWMAN, Nov. 13, 1746, by Rev. Greenwood,. of Rehoboth	1	41
John, s. John & Hannah, b. Jan. 14, 1751	1	41
John, s. Noah & Molly, b. May 31, 1784	1	119
Levi, s. Thomas & Mariam, b. Nov. 20, 1766	1	93
Lydia, d. John & Hannah, b. Aug. 8, 1768	1	41
Lydia, m. Ephraim COLVIN, May 31, 1787, by Joshua Dunlap, Esq.	1	194
Mariam, d. Thomas & Mariam, b. May 9, 1770	1	93
Martha, d. Thomas & Mary, b. Nov. 17, 1739	1	10
Mary, d. Thomas & Mary, b. Sept. 24, 1727	1	10
Mary, m. Stephen STOYELL, Jan. 4, 1753, by Rev. Samuel Dorrance	1	70
Mary, d. John & Hannah, b. Aug. 29, 1755	1	41
Mary, d. Thomas & Mariam, b. May 9, 1763	1	93
Mary, had Elizabeth reputed d. Benadam GALLUP, b. Feb. 21, 1783	1	93
Molly, d. Noah & Molly, b. Aug. 26, 1789	1	119
Moses, s. Noah & Molly, b. Sept. 17, 1771	1	119
Newman, s. Noah & Molly, b. May 3, 1773	1	119
Noah, s. John & Hannah, b. Aug. 9, 1747	1	41
Noah, m. Molly LITTLE, Nov. 29, 1770, by Eliphalet Wright	1	119
Patience, d. Thomas & Mary, b. Aug. 2, 1733	1	10
Patience, d. Thomas [& Mary], d. Jan. 21, 1755	1	10
Ruth, d. Hezekiah & Patience, b. Sept. 4, 1777	1	82
Ruth, w. of Hezekiah, d. July 12, 1793	1	82
Samuel, s. Thomas & Mariam, b. July 23, 1775	1	93
Sarah, d. Ezra & Susan, b. June 10, 1781	1	147
Silas, s. Thomas & Mariam, b. Sept. 10, 1758	1	93
Spencer, s. Thomas & Mariam, b. Sept. 14, 1761	1	93
Spencer, m. Eunice PARKE, Jan. 13, 1785, by Rev. Jonathan Fuller	1	177
Susan, m. Ezra COLE, Apr. 6, 1779, by John Dixson, J.P.	1	147
Thomas, m. Mary BOWEN, Mar. 11, 1724	1	10
Thomas, s. Thomas & Mary, b. Aug. 24, 1735	1	10
Thomas, Jr., m. Mariam KINNE, Dec. 7, 1757, by Robert Dixson, J.P.	1	93
Thomas, s. John & Hannah, b. May 27, 1762	1	41
Thomas, s. Thomas & Mariam, b. Oct. 10, 1768	1	93
Thomas, Jr., m. Lois FRINK, Nov. 3, 1785, by Rev. Joel Benedict	1	180
Zeruah, m. Azariah WINSLOW, Jan. 26, 1786, by Rev. Israel Day	1	182
COLEGROVE, Benjamin, Jr., m. Sarah LARKHAM, Mar. 1, 1789, by Rev. Micaiah Porter	1	216

154   BARBOUR COLLECTION

	Vol.	Page
COLEGROVE, (cont.)		
Benjamin, s. Benjamin, Jr. & Sarah, b. Jan. 25, 1790	1	216
Christopher, of Lisbon, m. Lydia **ROUSE**, of Voluntown, May 10, 1840, by Rev. Charles S. Weaver	2	32
Eleazer, m. Judy **GREEN**, Dec. 31, 1796, by Allen Campbell, J.P.	1	232
Eliphalet, s. Benjamin, Jr. & Sarah, b. July 22, 1794	1	216
Ely, s. Eleazer & Judy, b. Oct. 28, 1801	1	232
Fanny, d. Eleazer & Judy, b. Aug. 22, 1799	1	232
Hannah Maria, d. Eleazer & Judy, b. Sept. 14, 1803	1	232
James, s. Jeremiah & Hannah, b. Oct. 4, 1777	1	145
Lot, s. Benjamin, Jr. & Sarah, b. Mar. 5, 1792	1	216
Lucinda, d. Eleazer & Judy, b. Dec. 24, 1797	1	232
Lydia A., of Voluntown, m. Daniel A. **BALDWIN**, of Montville, May 22, 1853, by Elisha Potter, J.P.	2	139
Nancy, d. Jeremiah & Hannah, b. Feb. 23, 1779	1	145
Patience, d. Benj[amin], Jr. & Sarah, b. June 3, 1800	1	216
Prudence, d. Benjamin, Jr. & Sarah, b. Mar. 2, 1798	1	216
Rowena, d. Eleazer & Judy, b. Aug. 28, 1805	1	232
Sally, d. Benjamin, Jr. & Sarah, b. June 11, 1796	1	216
Sally, d. Eleazer & Judy, b. Jan. 28, 1798	1	232
Stephen, m. Elizabeth **PARTELO[W]**, June 12, 1794, by Rev. Micaiah Porter	1	221
Stephen, d. Apr. [ ], 1854	3	65
Thankfull, d. Stephen & Elizabeth, b. Jan. 14, 1795	1	221
COLLINS, Willard M., ae 21, m. Harriet **KENYON**, ae 18, b. of Hopkinton, R.I., Jan. 14, 1849, by John Sheffield	3	1
Willard W., of Hopkinton, R.I., m. Harriet E. **KENYON**, of Voluntown, Jan. 14, 1849, by Rev. John Sheffield	2	137
Zerviah, d. James & Ruth **HAMBLEN**, b. Jan. 8, 1762	1	68
COLVIN, Ephraim, m. Lydia **COLE**, May 31, 1787, by Joshua Dunlap, Esq.	1	194
Freeman, s. Ephraim & Lydia, b. Feb. 18, 1789	1	194
Newman, s. Ephraim & Lydia, b. Feb. 14, 1788; d. Feb. 26, 1788	1	194
CONGDON, Charlotte J., d. Charlotte, ae 34, b. Sept. 26, 1849. Father decd.	3	25
Clark, d. Dec. 4, 1863, ae 68; b. in R. Island	3	73
George W., s. George, colored, blacksmith, ae 25, b. Sept. 25, 1850	3	25
Hannah, m. William **KINNEY**, b. of Voluntown, June, 19, 1853, by John E. Lindley, J.P.	2	143
Jonathan, d. Oct. 4, 1854, ae 29	3	64
Joseph, of Coventry, R.I., m. Charlotte **BITGOOD**, of Voluntown, Sept. 26, 1847, by Rev. Charles S. Weaver	2	125
Joseph, d. [June 15, 1849 (?)], ae 35; b. in R.I.	3	60
Mary E., d. Oliver H., ae 36, dresser-tender, b. Sept. 15, 1849	3	24
Mary E., d. Sept. 28, 1849; ae 2 w.	3	61
COOK, Eliza, of Griswold, m. Harvey **CAMPBELL**, of Voluntown, July 8, 1828, by Rev. Orin Fowler	2	27
Margery, m. Garshom **DORRANCE**, May 4, 1749, by Rev. Samuel Dorrance	1	49
Maria, m. Ezra K. **CAMPBELL**, Dec. 7, 1820, by Rev. Horatio Waldo, of Griswold	2	10
Ruth, m. Samuel **FISH**, Dec. 11, 1748, by Joseph Palmer, Esq.	1	92
Sally, m. Dr. Harvey **CAMPBELL**, Dec. 3, 1818, by Rev. Horatio		

	Vol.	Page
COOK, (cont.)		
Waldo, of Griswold	2	27
Zeruviah, m. Samuel **ROB[B]ENS**, Mar. 6, 1777, by Rev. Levi Hart	1	156
COON, Abby, of Voluntown, m. Alfred **CHURCH**, of Hopkinton, R.I., Nov. 21, 1833, by Jonathan Minor, Elder	2	97
Asa S., m. Katura **EG[G]LESTON**, Feb. 9, 1823, by Sterry Kinne, J.P.	2	52
COOPER, COPER, Abigail, d. Ebenezer & Mary, b. Aug. 26, 1719	1	2
Anne, m. Ebenezer **SMITH**, May 1, 1763, by John Rice, J.P.	1	102
Sarah, d. Ebenezer & Mary, b. July 7, 1716	1	2
Thomas C., m. Elizabeth **POTTER**, Oct. 13, 1839, by Rev. Charles S. Weaver	2	25
CORNING, Elizabeth, d. Charles & Hannah, b. Dec. 19, 1804	1	246
Hannah, d. Charles & Hannah, b. Nov. 26, 1802	1	246
John R., s. Charles & Hannah, b. Jan. 13, 1807	1	246
Joseph, d. Feb. 1, 1866, ae 76	3	76
CORY, COREY, [see also **CAREY, CARY**], Caroline, d. Aug. [ ], 1855, ae 6 m.	3	66
Elias, m. Frances **BENNET[T]**, July 14, 1844, by Rev. Charles S. Weaver	2	20
Eliza Ann, m. Stephen **RICHMOND**, of R.I., Dec. 2, 1849, by Gershom Palmer, Elder	2	137
Eliza Ann, ae 15, m. Stephen **RICHMOND**, ae 23, farmer, of R.I., Dec. 2, 1849, by Elder Gershom Palmer	3	3
Henry E., m. Julia Ann **SULLIVAN**, b. of Voluntown, Sept. 6, 1851, by Elder William R. Slocum	2	140
John R., m. Hannah **DOUGLASS**, b. of Voluntown, Mar. 12, 1820, by James Alexander, J.P.	2	19
Joseph, m. Sarah E. **WATSON**, b. of Voluntown, Dec. 8, 1849, by Amos Witter, J.P.	2	135
Joseph, d. Oct. [ ], 1855, ae 4 y.	3	66
Mary M., of Voluntown, m. Nathaniel S. Richmond, of Voluntown, Sept. 5, 1841, by Rev. Charles S. Weaver	2	43
Sheffield, Jr., m. Rhoby **RATHBUN**, Dec. 8, 1817, by Allen Campbell, J.P.	2	25
Susan, of Griswold, m. John T. **YOUNG**, of Voluntown, Dec. 25, 1836, by Harvey Campbell, J.P.	2	97
Susan, of Griswold, m. John I. **YOUNG**, of Voluntown, Dec. 25, 1836, by Harvey Campbell, J.P.	2	100
-----, male, d. Jan. 6, 1864, ae 6 d.	3	73
COWLES, [see also **COLE** and **COALS**], Charles H., s. Martin L., farmer, ae 29, b. Aug. 13, 1850	3	26
Martin L., m. Olive M. **GALLUP**, b. of Voluntown, Oct. 27, 1845, by Rev. Warren Emmerson	2	122
COY, COYE, David, s. Matthew & Amy, b. Apr. 20, 1761	1	67
[E]unice, d. Matthew & Amy, b. Dec. 4, 1759	1	67
Joseph, s. Matthew & Amy, b. Feb. 4, 1765	1	67
Matthew, m. Amy **CHURCH**, Dec. 10, 1752, by Benjamin Randall, J.P.	1	67
Nathan, s. Matthew & Amy, b. Feb. 5, 1755	1	67
Phebe, d. Benjamin & Mary, b. Nov. 5, 1760	1	101
Phebe, d. Matthew & Amy, b. Jan. 14, 1767	1	67
Sarah, d. Matthew & Amy, b. May 3, 1769	1	67

BARBOUR COLLECTION

	Vol.	Page
CRANDALL, CRANDAL, Adah, d. Eld. Amos & Esther, b. July 23, 1807	1	239
Amos, Elder, m. Esther **KINNE**, Feb. 22, 1798, by Allen Campbell, J.P.	1	239
Anna, m. Daniel **KEIGWIN**, b. of Voluntown, Sept. 24, 1801, by Allen Campbell, J.P.	2	103
Charity, d. Joseph & Olive, b. Mar. 4, 1770	1	85
Clarissa, d. Elder Amos & Esther, b. July 5, 1802	1	239
Dolly, m. John **RHOADES**, Jr., Apr. 27, 1788, by Amos Crandall, Jr., Elder	1	197
Emily, d. Ira K. & Zilpha, b. June 15, 1828	2	90
Emily, m. Stanton **BURDICK**, Jr., Sept. 7, 1846, by Rev. Charles S. Weaver	2	65
Esther, d. Elder Amos & Esther, b. Apr. 16, 1799	1	239
Esther, m. Joseph **SWEET**, Mar. 5, 1818, by John Wylie, J.P.	2	48
Hannah, d. Elder Amos & Esther, b. [ ]	1	239
Henry, s. Ira K. & Zilpha, b. Nov. 30, 1829	2	90
Ira Kinne, s. Eld. Amos & Esther, b. Dec. 2, 1805	1	239
John A., of Bristol, N.Y., m. Phebe **GEER**, of Voluntown, Mar. 27, 1831, by Daniel Keigwin, J.P.	2	86
Martin, s. Elder Amos & Esther, b. July 1, 1801	1	239
Sarah, m. Thomas **LARKHAM**, Nov. 25, 1790, by Henry Joslin, Elder	1	211
Sophia, d. Benjamin, of Hopkinton, R.I., m. Henry W. **DOUGLASS**, s. Joseph, of Voluntown, Sept. 1, 1825, by Matthew Stillman, Elder	2	104
William, s. Ira K. & Zilpha, b. June 21, 1831	2	90
CRARY, CRERY, Archibald, s. William & Elizabeth, b. Nov. 24, 1748	1	60
Charles Samuel, s. George & Betsey, b. Aug. 10, 1817	2	22
Christopher, m. Elizabeth **ROB[B]INS**, Mar. 7, 1737, by John Cook, Esq.	1	79
Desire, d. Ezra & Dorithy, b. Apr. 29, 1760	1	78
Elias, s. Ezra & Dorithy, b. Feb. 13, 1764	1	78
Elisha, s. Robert & Sarah, b. Mar. 7, 1752	1	63
Elizabeth, m. Elisha **POTTER**, b. of Voluntown, Jan. 18, 1846, by Rev. Jacob Allen, of Sterling	2	57
Esther, d. William & Elizabeth, b. Sept. 20, 1742	1	60
Esther, m. John **WYLIE**, Jr., Mar. 25, 1773, by Rev. Solomon Morgan	1	126
Eunice, d. Robert & Sarah, b. Feb. 18, 1747	1	63
Eunice, m. Maxson **BURDICK**, Jan. 10, 1813, by Allen Campbell, J.P.	2	8
Ezra, s. Christopher & Elizabeth, b. July 30, 1737	1	79
Ezra, m. Dorithy **RANDALL**, Dec. 29, 1756, by Jeremiah Kinne, Esq.	1	78
George, m. Betsey **SKINNER**, Jan. 4, 1815, by John Wylie, J.P.	2	22
George K., s. George & Betsey, b. Sept. 15, 1816	2	22
Huldah, d. Robert & Sarah, b. May 6, 1743	1	63
James, s. William & Elizabeth, b. Oct. 30, 1751	1	60
James, of Plainfield, m Elizabeth **WYLIE**, of Voluntown, Jan. 22, 1829, by Rev. Otis Lane	2	74
James, d. Oct. 26, 1844, ae 45	2	74
Joanna, reputed d. George **CRARY** & Betsey **SKINNER**, b. Oct.10,		

VOLUNTOWN VITAL RECORDS 157

	Vol.	Page
CRARY, CRERY, (cont.)		
1813	2	22
John, s. Robert & Sarah, b. Mar. 25, 1745	1	63
Lois, d. Robert & Sarah, b. Apr. 10, 1750	1	63
Lucy, d. James & Elizabeth, b. Jan. 13, 1832, at Plainfield	2	74
Nathan, d. Ezra & Dorithy, b. Mar. 9, 1762	1	78
Nathaniel, s. Ezra & Dorithy, b. Nov. 13, 1766	1	78
Prudence, d. William & Elizabeth, b. Sept. 6, 1746	1	60
Robert, Jr., m. Sarah **TRACY**, June 3, 1742, by Rev. Wight, of Norwich	1	63
Sabra, m. George **BASSET[T]**, Feb. 2, 1812, by Allen Campbell, J.P.	1	218
Samuel, of Plainfield, m. Olive C. **KENNEDY**, of Voluntown, Sept. 9, 1835, by Peleg Peckham, Elder	2	99
Sarah, d. William & Elizabeth, b. Mar. 1, 1744	1	60
Sarah Harmony, d. James & Elizabeth, b. June 19, 1830, at Plainfield	2	74
William, m. Elizabeth **CAMPBELL**, Nov. 12, 1741, by Rev. Samuel Dorrance	1	60
William, s. William & Elizabeth, b. July 11, 1756	1	60
CROSS, George W., m. Amy **GARDNER**, b. of R.I., July 6, 1846, by Rev. Charles S. Weaver	2	9
CROSWELL, Daniel, twin with Jonathan, s. Mingale & Sarah, b. Aug. 30, 1756	1	30
[E]unis, d. Mingale & Sarah, b. May 31, 1750	1	30
John, s. Mingale & Sarah, b. May 17, 1752	1	30
Jonathan, twin with Daniel, s. Mingale & Sarah, b. Aug. 30, 1756	1	30
Mark, s. Mingale & Sarah, b. Sept. 16, 1760	1	30
CURTIS, Fanny E., m. Francis W. **BROWN**, b. of S. Kingston, R.I., Nov. 25, 1847, by Rev. Charles S. Weaver	2	125
CUTLER, Job N., of Plainfield, m. Mary Elizabeth **WYLIE**, of Voluntown, May 24, 1836, by Rev. Samuel Rockwell, of Plainfield	2	25
CYRUS, Jeff, s. Sarah, b. Sept. 9, 1768, in Charlestown, R.I.	1	179
Jeffrey, m. Sarah **STANTON**, July 2, 1789, by Rev. Micaiah Porter	1	198
Sarah, d. Jeffrey & Bettsa, b. Sept. 25, 1792	1	198
DARLING, Elizabeth, d. Michail & Hannah, b. July 11, 1774	1	138
James, s. Michail & Hannah, b. Aug. 27, 1768	1	138
John, s. Michail & Hannah, b. Apr. 20, 1771	1	138
Mary, d. Michail & Hannah, b. Oct. 24, 1766	1	138
Mich[a]il, m. Hannah **DIXSON**, May 1, 1766, by Robert Dixson, J.P.	1	138
Sarah, d. Michail & Hannah, b. Oct. 30, 1777	1	138
DAVEY, Mary, d. Mar. [ ], 1851, ae 4; b. in N. Stonington, resid. N. Stonington	3	62
DAVIS, Lucy M., ae 23, of Griswold, m. Atwood W. Phillips, ae 27, b. Voluntown, resid. of Griswold, Mar. 20, 1850, by C. S. Weaver, Elder	3	2
Martin, of Griswold, m. Eunice E. **PALMER**, of Voluntown, Feb. 17, 1840, by Rev. Charles S. Weaver	2	32
Richard, of Griswold, m. Freelove **KINNE**, of Voluntown, Dec. 15, 1839, by Rev. Charles S. Weaver	2	24
William H., of R.I., m. Mary C. **KENYON**, of Voluntown, Apr. 4, 1841, by Rev. Charles S. Weaver	2	37
DAWLEY, George, of Norwich, m. Roxa S. **GALLUP**, of Voluntown,		

158   BARBOUR COLLECTION

	Vol.	Page
DAWLEY, (cont.)		
Apr. 8, 1849, by Rev. Jesse B. Denison. Witnesses: John S. Gallup, Samuel A. Edmond	2	133
DEAN, Champeon, s. Nathaniel & Lucy, b. Dec. 28, 1741; d. Mar. 14, 1742	1	30
Joanna, d. Nathaniel & Joanna, b. June 18, 1727	1	7
Jonathan, s. Nathaniel & Joannah, b. May 24, 1725	1	7
Jonathan, s. Nath[aniel] & Joan[n]a, b. May 24, 1725	1	9
Mary, m. Isaac **GALLUP**, Jr., Apr. 24, 1788, by Rev. Micaiah Porter	1	210
Nathan, s. Nathaniel & Lucy, b. Jan. 13, 1745/6	1	30
Nathaniel, Jr., m. Lucy **CHAMPEON**, Mar. 4, 1741, by John Griswold, Esq.	1	30
R[e]ubin, s. Nathaniel & Lucy, b. May 25, 1743	1	30
Sam[ue]ll, s. Nath[aniel] & Johan[n]a, b. May 4, 1723	1	7
DENISON, Amos, s. Amos & Sarah, b. Dec. 28, 1777	1	23
Stephen A., of Westerly, R.I., m. Philura D. **ROUSE**, of Griswold, Oct. 22, 1854, by Rev. Benedict Johnson, Jr.	2	148
DENNIS, George H., of Norwich, m. Sarah **TIFT**, of Voluntown, Nov. 2, 1845, by Rev. Alfred Burnham	2	94
James, m. Polly **NORTH[R]UP**, May 4, 1823, by Sterry Kinne, J.P.	2	53
DEWEY, Serena, m. David **BENTLEY**, b. of N. Stonington, Aug. [ ], by Elder Cha[rle]s Randall. Entered Oct. 7, 1840	2	23
-----, s. William, laborer, & [ ], b. Apr. 21, 1850	3	23
DIXSON, DIXON, Agness, d. James & Jenet, b. Sept. 26, 1722; d. Mar. 30, 1787* (*handwritten correction on original manuscript)	1	26
Agnis, d. John, Jr. & Mary, b. May 20, 1738	1	23
Agness, m. William **JAC[K]SON**, Dec. 25, 1744, by Rev. Samuel Dorrance	1	77
Agness, m. John **DORRANCE**, Jan. 18, 1759, by Rev. Samuel Dorrance	1	99
Agnes, d. John & Jean, b. Feb. 27, 1768	1	185
Ann, m. Isaac **CAMPBELL**, Dec. 11, 1755, by Rev. Joseph Fish, of Stonington	1	84
Archibald, s. John & Jane, b. Apr. 4, 1772	1	185
Barbary, d. John & Jane, b. Mar. 19, 1770	1	185
Barnet[t], s. Thomas, 3d, & Jane, b. Mar. 19, 1782	1	146
Benjamin, s. John & Jane, b. May 14, 1776	1	185
Charles, s. Thomas & Lydia, b. Nov. 2, 1770	1	163
David, s. John & Jane, b. May 14, 1780	1	185
Edward N., d. June 3, [1860], ae 14 m.	3	70
Ele[a]ner, m. Samuel **KESSON**, Jan. 23, 1744/5, by Rev. Samuel Dorrance	1	52
Elizabeth, d. Robert & Sarasana, b. May 24, 1762	1	98
Elizabeth, d. John & Jane, b. Mar. 18, 1763	1	96
Elizabeth, d. John & Jane, b. Oct. 21, 1782	1	185
Eunice, d. Thomas & Lydia, b. Apr. 22, 1764	1	163
Fanny, d. Robert & Sarasana, b. June 10, 1772	1	98
George, s. Robert & Sarasana, b. July 15, 1781	1	98
Hannah, m. Mich[a]il **DARLING**, May 1, 1766, by Robert Dixson, J.P.	1	138
Harriet, d. Robert & Sarasana, b. Jan. 7, 1784	1	98
Isabell, d. James & Jennet, b. Sept. 2, 1742	1	26
James, s. James & Jenet, b. Mar. 16, 1738	1	26

	Vol.	Page
DIXSON, DIXON, (cont.)		
James, s. John & Jenet, b. Apr. 12, 1746	1	34
James, s. Thomas & Lydia, b. June 11, 1760, in Plainfield	1	163
*James, h. of Jenett; d. Mar. 30, 1787 (*handwritten addition to manuscript)	1	26
John, s. James & Jenet, b. June 25, 1726	1	26
John, s. Robert & Elizabeth, b. Nov. 16, 1733	1	29
John, Jr., m. Mary KEN[N]EDY, Oct. 8, 1735, by Thomas Thomson, Minister	1	23
John, s. John, Jr. & Mary, b. May 10, 1740	1	23
John, m. Jenet KEN[N]EDY, Aug. 7, 1741, by Rev. Samuel Dorrance	1	34
John, Jr., m. Jane GORDON, Jan. 5, 1758, by Rev. Samuel Dorrance	1	96
John, s. Thomas & Lydia, b. Aug. 30, 1761	1	163
John, m. Jane GORDON, May 3, 1764, by Rev. Samuel Dorrance	1	185
John, s. John & Jane, b. Mar. 17, 1765	1	185
Lydia, d. Thomas & Lydia, b. Sept. 19, 1771	1	163
Marg[a]ret, d. James & Jenet, b. Sept. 25, 1734	1	26
Marian, d. John, Jr. & Mary, b. Aug. 30, 1742	1	23
Maryan, d. Robert & Sarasana, b. May 7, 1767	1	98
Marian, d. John & Jane, b. Sept. 23, 1784	1	185
Mary, d. James & Jenet, b. May 13, 1740	1	26
Mary, d. John & Jenet, b. July 1, 1744; d. May [ ], 1751	1	34
Mary, d. John & Jenet, b. Mar. 21, 1752	1	34
Mary, m. Jacob **PATRICK**, Dec. 23, 1756, by Rev. Samuel Dorrance	1	86
Mary, d. Robert & Sarasana, b. Aug. 2, 1759	1	98
Mary, d. Thomas & Lydia, b. Dec. 25, 1762	1	163
Mary, d. John & Jane, b. Apr. 25, 1774	1	185
Mary Ann, m. John **GORDON**, Jr., June 9, 1763, by Rev. Samuel Dorrance	1	108
Nancy, d. Thomas & Lydia, b. Jan. 22, 1766	1	163
Nancy, d. Robert & Sarasana, b. Aug. 12, 1774	1	98
Olive, d. Thomas, 3d, & Jane, b. Apr. 6, 1778	1	146
Rebecca, d. John & Jane, b. Apr. 13, 1765	1	96
Robert, m. Elizabeth **HASTON**, Jan. 29, 1729/30, by Rev. Samuel Dorrance	1	29
Robert, s. John, Jr. & Mary, b. July 22, 1736	1	23
Robert, s. John, m. Sarasana **DORRANCE**, Jan. 26, 1758, by Rev. Samuel Dorrance	1	98
Robert, s. Robert & Sarasana, b. Apr. 3, 1770	1	98
Robert H., ae 22, b. Sterling, resid. of Voluntown, m. Hannah **KENNEDY**, ae 18, of Voluntown, Oct. 16, 1849, by Rev. Peleg Peckham	3	3
Samuel, s. Robert & Sarasana, b. Aug. 10, 1764	1	98
Samuel, s. John & Jane, b. Apr. 30, 1778	1	185
Sarah, d. James & Jenet, b. June 14, 1729	1	26
Sarah, m. John **MOUN[T]GOMERY**, Jr., Feb. 12, 1756, by Rev. Dorrance	1	86
Sarah, m. Moses **CAMPBELL**, Dec. 1, 1757, by Rev. Samuel Dorrance	1	103
Thomas, s. James & Jenet, b. Mar. 14, 1732	1	26
Thomas, s. John, Jr. & Mary, b. Jan. 8, 1746/7	1	23

160   BARBOUR COLLECTION

	Vol.	Page
DIXSON, DIXON, (cont.)		
Thomas, s. Robert & Sarasana, b. June 3, 1777	1	98
Thomas Parker, s. Thomas, 3d, & Jane, b. Apr. 1, 1780	1	146
Varnum, s. Thomas & Lydia, b. May 12, 1774	1	163
William, s. John & Jenet, b. Nov. 16, 1742; d. Mar. [ ], 1746	1	34
William, s. John & Jenet, b. Apr. 5, 1748	1	34
William, s. Thomas & Lydia, b. Sept. 4, 1767	1	163
DOLEFOR, Dorithy, of E. Greenwich, m. Benjamin **WILLIAMS**, of Voluntown, Feb. 26, 1722/3, by John Nicholes, J.P.	1	7
DONLEY, Mary, d. Thomas, common laborer, ae 28, b. Oct. 20, 1850	3	26
DORRANCE, Barton, s. Garshom & Margery, b. Nov. 10, 1749	1	49
Charlotte, d. Lemuel & Mary, b. Mar. 24, 1773	1	135
Daniel, s. Garshom & Margery, b. Feb. 26, 1752; d. Nov. 1, 1753	1	49
David, m. [Anna] **HURLBUTT**, Feb. 2, 1786, by Rev. James Cogswell	1	189
Elisha, s. David & Anna, b. Sept. 23, 1787	1	189
Elizabeth, d. James & Elizabeth, b. Oct. 16, 1734	1	67
Elizabeth, d. Sept. 10, 1750	1	11
Elizabeth, d. Garshom & Margery, b. Oct. 18, 1754	1	49
Elizabeth, m. Benadam **GALLUP**, Mar. 31, 1785, by Rev. Micaiah Porter	1	213
Elizabeth, d. James & Esther, b. [ ]	1	172
Esther, d. James, Jr. & Esther, b. Dec. 22, 1793	1	172
Esther, m. Thomas D. **ALEXANDER**, Apr. 16, 1809, by Rev. Israel Day, of Killingly	2	42
Esther, w. (?) of James, s. James & Elizabeth, d. Mar. 9, 1814	1	68
Esther, w. James, d. Mar. 9, 1814	1	172
George, s. Samuel & Elizabeth, b. Mar. 7, 1735/6	1	11
George, s. James & Elizabeth, b. June 25, 1736	1	67
Gershom, s. Rev. Samuel & Elizabeth, b. May 24, 1727	1	11
Garshom, m. Margery **COOK**, May 4, 1749, by Rev. Samuel Dorrance	1	49
Henry, s. James, Jr. & Esther, b. May 6, 1782	1	172
James, s. James & Elizabeth, b. Apr. 1, 1742	1	67
James, s. Samuel & Elizabeth, b. July 30, 1743	1	11
James, Jr., m. Esther **HALL**, Apr. 19, 1781, by James Bradford, Esq.	1	172
James, s. James [& Elizabeth], d. Mar. 17, 1814	1	68
James, d. Mar. 17, 1814	1	172
John, s. Samuel & Elizabeth, b. July 12, 1733	1	11
John, s. James & Elizabeth, b. Feb. 18, 1738	1	67
John, m. Agness **DIXSON**, Jan. 18, 1759, by Rev. Samuel Dorrance	1	99
Lemuel, s. Samuel & Elizabeth, b. Nov. 28, 1746	1	11
Lemuel, m. Mary **GORDON**, May 14, 1772, by Rev. Samuel Dorrance	1	135
Lemuel, s. Lemuel & Mary, b. Dec. 5, 1774	1	135
Marg[a]ret, d. James & Elizabeth, b. Apr. 1, 1749	1	68
Mary, m. John **KELSON**, Oct. 14, 1731, by Rev. Samuel Dorrance	1	16
Mary, d. James & Elizabeth, b. Sept. 15, 1744	1	67
Mary, d. John & Agness, b. Dec. 12, 1759	1	99
Mary, m. John **SMITH**, Aug. 5, 1781, by John Dixson, J.P.	1	166
Mary, d. James, Jr. & Esther, b. Sept. 2, 1786	1	172
Samuel, Rev., m. Elizabeth **SMITH**, Aug. 1, 1726, by Rev. Joseph Coite	1	11

VOLUNTOWN VITAL RECORDS

	Vol.	Page
DORRANCE, (cont.)		
Samuel, s. James & Elizabeth, b. Apr. 28, 1740	1	67
Samuel, s. Samuel & Elizabeth, b. Oct. 10, 1740	1	11
Samuel, Rev., m. Madame Mary **OWEN**, July 1, 1755, by Rev. David Jewett, of New London	1	72
Samuel, [s. James & Elizabeth], d. June 7, 1799	1	68
Sarah, d. James & Elizabeth, b. Aug. 28, 1733; d. Sept. 14, 1830	1	67
Sarah, m. Joseph **ALEXANDER**, Apr. 5, 1759, by Rev. Samuel Dorrance	1	76
Sarasana (?), d. Samuel & Elizabeth, b. Apr. 30, 1738	1	11
Sarasana, m. Robert **DIXSON**, s. John, Jan. 26, 1758, by Rev. Samuel Dorrance	1	98
DOUGLASS, Allen Campbell, s. Joseph & Mary, b. Mar. 5, 1797	1	215
Alvin, s. James, Jr. & Lucy, b. Dec. 16, 1816	1	188
Andrew, s. Samuel & Agness, b. Oct. 16, 1767	1	81
Andrew M., s. W[illia]m, Jr. & Mary, b. Apr. 19, 1828	1	149
Anna, d. James, Jr. & Lucy, b. Nov. 10, 1814	1	188
Anne, d. John & Sarah, b. July 20, 1776	1	129
Benjamin C., s. Henry W. & Sophia, b. Oct. 25, 1826	2	104
Betsey Alvira, d. John & Thankfull, b. Mar. 11, 1823	2	47
Betsey Alvira, d. [Joseph, Jr. & Elizabeth (?)], [ ]	2	49
Catharine, d. Samuel & Agness, b. June 16, 1759	1	81
Charles P., s. W[illia]m & Betsey, b. June 1, 1824	2	112
Daniel, s. Samuel & Agness, b. Nov. 27, 1769	1	81
Daniel McMain, s. Joseph & Mary, b. June 15, 1798	1	215
David, s. William & Ruth, b. Mar. 31, 1809	1	191
David G., d. July 9, 1862, ae 53	3	71
David G., [s. William & Ruth], d. July 10, 1862. (The name "David" is used in recording the birth in 1809)	1	191
Desire, d. William & Mary, b. Mar. 21, 1769	1	81
Dinah, twin with Mary, d. Joseph & Mary, b. Dec. 20, 1792	1	215
Dinah, m. Earl **DOUGLASS**, b. of Voluntown, Mar. 12, 1823, by Nathaniel Sheffield, Elder	2	53
Dinah Mary, d. Aug. 3, 1856, ae 26	3	66
Earl, s. James & Sarah, b. Oct. 26, 1799, in Sterling	1	192
Earl, m. Dinah **DOUGLASS**, b. of Voluntown, Mar. 12, 1823, by Nathaniel Sheffield, Elder	2	53
Edwin A., s. William A., farmer, ae 35, & Cynthia, ae 30, b. Nov. 11, 1848	3	22
Elizabeth, d. James & Jennit, b. May 11, 1732	1	29
Elizabeth, d. Thomas & Martha, b. Apr. 4, 1745	1	74
Elizabeth, d. William & Mary, b. Feb. 8, 1761	1	81
Elizabeth, m. Isaiah **BABCOCK**, Jr., May 19, 1763, by Robert Dixson, J.P.	1	105
Elizabeth, m. Ephraim **GATES**, Apr. 25, 1793, by Allen Campbell, J.P.	1	222
Emily A., d. W[illia]m & Betsey, b. June 27, 1830	2	112
Emma A., d. Oct. 7, 1862, ae 1 y. 2 m.	3	71
Easther, d. Joseph & Mary, b. Mar. 7, 1800	1	215
Fanny H., d. W[illia]m & Betsey, b. Jan. 20, 1822	2	112
Gershom P., ae 21, m. Sarah D. **ALEXANDER**, ae 19, b. of Voluntown, July 21, 1850, by Rev. Henry Robinson	3	3
Hannah, d. Thomas & Martha, b. Jan. 12, 1756	1	74

DOUGLASS, (cont.)

	Vol.	Page
Hannah, d. William & Mary, b. Apr. 20, 1773	1	81
Hannah, m. John **GALLUP**, Jr., May 5, 1774, by Robert Dixson, Esq.	1	129
Hannah, d. James & Sarah, b. May 12, 1791, in Kingsbury	1	192
Hannah, m. John R. **COREY**, b. of Voluntown, Mar. 12, 1820, by James Alexander, J.P.	2	19
Harry William, s. Joseph & Mary, b. May 24, 1803	1	215
Hendrick, s. James, Jr. & Lucy, b. June 1, 1824	1	188
Henry W., s. Joseph, of Voluntown, m. Sophia **CRANDALL**, d. Benjamin, of Hopkinton, R.I., Sept. 1, 1825, by Matthew Stillman, Elder	2	104
James, s. James & Jenet, b. July 28, 1736	1	29
James, s. Samuel & Agness, b. Mar. 12, 1761	1	81
James, s. William & Mary, b. May 1, 1762	1	81
James, f. James, d. Jan. 23, 1770	1	29
James, s. John & Sarah, b. Feb. 20, 1775	1	129
James, m. Sarah **ROUSE**, Mar. 16, 1788, by Rev. Micaiah Porter	1	192
James, Jr., m. Lucy **PETTIS**, June 25, 1812, by Allen Campbell, J.P.	1	188
James, m. Elizabeth **BENNET[T]**, of Liberty, N.Y., Aug. 10, 1820, by William Parks, J.P.	1	124
James, d. Jan. 27, 1850, ae 88	3	61
Jenet, d. James & Jenet, b. June 11, 1743	1	29
Jenet, d. Samuel & Agness, b. Feb. 4, 1758	1	81
Jennet, m. John **HUSTON**, Feb. 14, 1788, by Rev. Micaiah Porter	1	195
Joel W., s. Henry W. & Sophia, b. Mar. 14, 1833	2	104
John, s. James & Jenet, b. June 9, 1741	1	29
John, s. Thomas & Martha, b. July 28, 1747	1	74
John, m. Isabel **GORDON**, Feb. 1, 1770, by Robert Dixson, J.P.	1	119
John, m. Sarah **BRANCH**, Mar. 24, 1774, by Robert Dixson, J.P.	1	129
John, twin with Zephaniah, s. John & Sarah, b. Dec. 27, 1779	1	129
John, m. Thankful **BROMLEY**, Jan. 2, 1820, by James Alexander, J.P.	2	47
Joseph, s. William & Mary, b. Sept. 2, 1766	1	81
Joseph, m. Mary **CAMPBELL**, Aug. 11, 1791, by Rev. Micaiah Porter	1	215
Joseph, s. Joseph & Mary, b. June 4, 1794	1	215
Joseph, Jr., m. Elizabeth **LITHBRIDGE**, Nov. 30, 1818, by Gershom Palmer, Elder	2	49
Joseph, Sr., d. Aug. 8, 1847	1	215
Joseph, d. Aug. 8, 1847, ae 81	3	59
Joseph, d. June 21, 1865, ae 72	3	75
Joseph H., s. Henry W. & Sophia, b. Nov. 24, 1828	2	104
Joseph H., of Voluntown, m. Sarah **PRATT**, of W. Greenwich, Aug. 25, 1850, by Charles S. Weaver	3	4
Laura, d. James, Jr. & Lucy, b. Apr. 7, 1813	1	188
Leland, s. James, Jr. & Lucy, b. Mar. 13, 1819	1	188
Lucinda, d. William, Jr. & Ruth, b. Oct. 27, 1794; d. [ ]	1	191
Lucinda, of Voluntown, m. Nathan **LILLIBRIDGE**, of Griswold, Sept. 14, 1840, by Rev. Charles S. Weaver	2	33
Lydia, d. William & Ruth, b. [ ]	1	191
Lydia S., m. John L. **SMITH**, b. of Voluntown, Mar. 31, 1831, by Nathaniel Sheffield, Elder	2	86

	Vol.	Page
DOUGLASS, (cont.)		
Marg[a]ret, d. James & Jenet, b. Nov. 9, 1738	1	29
Marg[a]ret, m. Robert **JACKSON**, Apr. 16, 1772, by Samuel Stewart, J.P.	1	87
Marianna, d. July 1, 1855, ae 45; b. in Exeter, R.I.	3	66
Martha, d. Thomas & Martha, b. Apr. 29, 1750	1	74
Martha, d. William, Jr. & Ruth, b. May 18, 1798	1	191
Martha M., d. Henry W. & Sophia, b. Feb. 18, 1835	2	104
Mary, d. Thomas & Martha, b. May 22, 1753	1	74
Mary, d. Samuel & Agness, b. Jan. 25, 1764	1	81
Mary, d. William & Mary, b. Mar. 23, 1765	1	81
Mary, w. William, d. Dec. 29, 1779	1	81
Mary, d. William, Jr. & Ruth, b. June 15, 1788	1	191
Mary, twin with Dinah, d. Joseph & Mary, b. Dec. 20, 1792; d. Jan. 18, 1793	1	215
Mary, d. Joseph & Mary, b. Aug. 8, 1795	1	215
Mary, [w. Joseph], d. May 3, 1837, ae 74 y.	1	215
Mary, w. William, 2d, d. Jan. 22, 1846	1	149
Mary Ann, d. Joseph, Jr. & Elizabeth, b. Oct. [ ], 1821, in West Greenwich	2	49
Nancy, d. Samuel & Agness, b. Jan. 7, 1757	1	81
Nelson Perry, s. William, Jr. & Mary, b. Nov. 29, 1816	1	148
Olive, d. John & Isabel, b. Dec. 4, 1775	1	119
Polly, m. John **HUNTER**, b. of Voluntown, June 7, 1826, by Nathaniel Sheffield, Elder	2	69
Quocko (?), m. Lucy **SNELLEN**, June 22, 1788, by Rev. Micaiah Porter	1	198
Rachel, d. Samuel & Angess, b. Dec. 23, 1775	1	81
Rhoda, d. James, Jr. & Lucy, b. Sept. 6, 1821	1	188
Robert, s. Samuel & Agness, b. Oct. 24, 1772	1	81
Rosa, d. Aug. 12, 1866, ae 13	3	76
Ruth, d. William & Mary, b. June 10, 1771	1	81
Ruth, d. William, Jr. & Ruth, b. Sept. 1, 1791	1	191
Ruth, w. William, d. Dec. 5, 1817	1	191
Ruth, m. Elisha **MORGAN**, Sept. 26, 1827, by Sterry Kinne, J.P.	2	72
Ruth Lucinda, d. William, Jr. & Mary, b. Feb. 8, 1818	1	148
Sally, d. William, Jr. & Mary, b. May 24, 1819	1	148
Sally, of Voluntown, m. William Henry **BALDWIN**, of N. Stonington, Mar. 25, 1838, by Rev. Charles S. Weaver	2	66
Samuel, s. James & Jennet, b. Dec. 22, 1729	1	29
Samuel, m. Agness **EDMOND**, Jan. 8, 1756, by Rev. Samuel Dorrance	1	81
Samuel, s. Samuel & Agness, b. Oct. 28, 1765	1	81
Samuel, s. John & Sarah, b. July 3, 1784	1	129
Sanford, s. John & Thankfull, b. May 10, 1820	2	47
Sarah, d. William, Jr. & Ruth, b. Jan. 23, 1802	1	191
Sarah, w. James, d. Oct. 24, 1818	1	124
Sarah, m. Nicholas **SAUNDERS**, Feb. 20, 1825, by Amos Treat, J.P.	2	60
Sarah, d. Mar. 31, 1866, ae 46; b. in R.I.	3	77
Stephen, s. William & Mary, b. July 9, 1747	1	81
Stephen, m. Susanna **POTTER**, Apr. 12, 1798, by Allen Campbell, J.P.	1	233
Susan E., d. W[illia]m & Betsey, b. Aug. 13, 1827	2	112

	Vol.	Page
DOUGLASS, (cont.)		
Susan[n]a, d. John & Isabel, b. Nov. 23, 1777	1	119
Theodata, d. John & Thankfull, b. July 5, 1821	2	47
Thomas, m. Martha **GALLUP**, Jan. 4, 1737, by Timothy Peirce, Asst.	1	74
Thomas, s. John & Isabel, b. Nov. 27, 1780	1	155
Thomas A., s. Joseph, Jr. & Elizabeth, b. Nov. 14, 1819	2	49
Thomas W., s. Henry W. & Sophia, b. Feb. 18, 1831	2	104
Thomas Winslow, s. Joseph & Mary, b. Jan. 10, 1801	1	215
William, s. James & Jenit, b. Feb. 15, 1728	1	29
William, m. Mary **PETTIS**, May 1, 1760, by Edward Perry, J.P.	1	81
William, s. William & Mary, b. Aug. 23, 1763	1	81
William, m. Martha **ADAMS**, Dec. 13, 1781, by Thomas West, Elder	1	82
William, Jr., m. Ruth **WILKINSON**, Mar. 13, 1788, by Rev. Micaiah Porter	1	191
William, s. James & Sarah, b. Feb. 13, 1789	1	192
William, [s. James & Jenit], d. July 7, 1806	1	29
William, Jr., m. Mary **RATHBUN**, Apr. 8, 1813, in Exeter, R.I., by Ellet Locke, Elder	1	148
William, m. Betsey **JONES**, Apr. 15, 1821, by Or[r]in Fowler, V.D.M.	1	191
William, d. Apr. 30, 1848, ae 85	3	59
William A., of Voluntown, m. Cynthia **BLIVEN**, of Exeter, Nov. 1, 1840, by Rev. Charles S. Weaver	2	36
William Avery, s. William, Jr. & Mary, b. Mar. 5, 1814	1	148
William C., d. Sept. 23, 1857, ae 2; b. in Richmond, R.I.	3	68
Zephaniah, twin with John, s. John & Sarah, b. Dec. 27, 1779	1	129
-----, male, d. June 11, [1860], ae 1 d.	3	70
DOW, Aaron, s. Ebenezer & Martha, b. Mar. 12, 1733	1	14
Aaron, s. Ebenezer & Susannah, b. June 19, 1772	1	71
Asa, s. Benjamin & Mary, b. Feb. 11, 1759	1	96
Asa, [s. Benjamin & Mary], d. Aug. 9, 1778	1	96
Asa, s. Ebenezer & Susannah, b. Nov. 22, 1780	1	107
Benjamin, s. Ebenezer & Martha, b. Nov. 6, 1735	1	14
Benjamin, m. Mary **HUTCHINSON**, May 17, 1758, by Rev. Hezekiah Lord	1	96
Benjamin, m. Marcy **KILLAM**, Sept. 27, 1768, by William Witter, J.P.	1	96
Benjamin, s. Benjamin & Marcy, b. Feb. 11, 1775	1	96
Clarry, d. Nathan & Agness, b. May 27, 1789	1	190
Daniel, s. Ebenezer & Martha, b. May 13, 1723	1	1
Daniel, s. Ebenezer & Martha, b. May 13, 1723	1	14
Daniel, s. Benjamin & Marcy, b. Apr. 22, 1771	1	96
Ebenezer, m. Martha **HARES**, Dec. 29, 1720	1	1
Ebenezer, m. Martha **HARRES**, Dec. 29, 1720, by Rev. Joseph Coit	1	14
Ebenezer, s. Ebenezer & Martha, b. Mar. 17, 1731	1	14
Ebenezer, Jr., m. Susannah **HUTCHINSON**, July 31, 1761, by Samuel Coit, J.P.	1	71
Ebenezer, s. Ebenezer & Susannah, b. Apr. 13, 1770	1	71
Ebenezer, d. Oct. 2, 1775	1	14
Elisha, s. Ebenezer, Jr. & Susannah, b. Apr. 26, 1762; d. June 17, 1762	1	71

VOLUNTOWN VITAL RECORDS 165

	Vol.	Page
DOW, (cont.)		
Elisha, s. Benjamin & Mary, b. May 27, 1765	1	96
Elisha, s. Benjamin & Mary, d. Aug. 11, 1789	1	150
Han[n]ah, d. Ebenezer & Martha, b. Oct. 23, 1721	1	1
Hannah, d. Ebenezer & Martha, b. Oct. 23, 1721; d. Apr. 9, 1741, ae 20 y.	1	14
Hannah, d. Ebenezer, Jr. & Susannah, b. Apr. 1, 1768	1	71
Hannah, m. Jesse **MATTESON**, Mar. 26, 1789, by Rev. Micaiah Porter	1	86
John, s. Benjamin & Marcy, b. Aug. 13, 1769	1	96
John, 3d, of Plainfield, m. Harty **ELLIS**, of W. Greenwich, Mar. 1, 1818, by John Wylie, J.P.	2	19
Lucy, d. Benjamin & Marcy, b. Apr. 1, 1773	1	96
Martha, d. Ebenezer, Jr. & Susannah, b. Apr. 18, 1766	1	71
Martha, w. Deac. Ebenezer, d. Jan. 4, 1791, ae 95 y.	1	14
Mary, d. Ebenezer & Martha, b. Dec. 8, 1726	1	1
Mary, d. Ebenezer & Martha, b. Dec. 8, 1726	1	14
Mary, m. Moses **BARRETT**, Oct. 22, 1747, by Rev. Samuel Dorrance	1	44
Mary, d. Ebenezer, Jr. & Susannah, b. Apr. 18, 1764; d. May 21, 1785	1	71
Mary, [w. Benjamin], d. May 20, 1766	1	96
Moses, s. Benjamin & Marcy, b. May 26, 1777; d. Dec. 22, 1778	1	96
Nancy, d. Nathan & Agness, b. Jan. 12, 1794	1	190
Nathan, s. Ebenezer & Martha, b. Feb. 9, 1724/5; d. Aug. 26, 1726	1	1
Nathan, s. Ebenezer & Martha, b. Mar. 1, 1738	1	14
Nathan, s. Benjamin & Mary, b. Mar. 20, 1761	1	96
Nathan, m. Agness **GORDON**, Sept. 16, 1787, by Rev. Micaiah Porter	1	190
Rebeckah, d. Ebenezer & Martha, b. Feb. 3, 1729	1	1
Rebeckah, d. Ebenezer & Martha, b. Feb. 3, 1729	1	14
Rebecca, d. Benjamin & Mary, b. June 22, 1763	1	96
Ruth, d. Ebenezer & Susannah, b. Oct. 6, 1778; d. Oct. 1778	1	107
Sarah, d. Benjamin & Mary, b. June 26, 1779	1	150
Stephen, s. Ebenezer, Jr. & Susannah, b. July 20, 1774	1	107
Susannah, d. Ebenezer & Susannah, b. Oct. 6, 1776	1	107
DOWNER, Martha, m. Jacob **CADY**, Jr., Mar. 20, 1763, by Jeremiah Kinne, J.P.	1	114
DOWNING, Sarah, m. Richard **KEIGWIN**, Aug. 5, 1735, by Rev. Samuel Dorrance	1	21
DRAPER, Rowland, of Voluntown, m. Hannah M. **PALMER**, of Exeter, May 31, 1840, by Rev. Charles S. Weaver	2	32
DUNLAP, Frederick, s. Ladely & Cynthy, b. Feb. 26, 1785	1	30
EAGLESTON, [see under **EGGLESTON** and **ECCLESTON**]		
EAMES, [see also **AMES**], Abner, m. Rachel **MANSFIELD**, Oct. 14, 1756	1	90
Abner, s. Mark & Anne, b. Oct. 8, 1765	1	95
Amos, s. David & Rachel, b. May 21, 1761	1	120
Anne, d. Mark & Anne, b. Nov. 4, 1760	1	95
Anthony, s. Mark & Anne, b. July 3, 1753	1	95
David, s. Mark & Anne, b. Apr. 11, 1762	1	95
Desire, d. Anthony & [ ], b. Oct. 15, 1745	1	89
Eadey, d. Mark & Anne, b. Mar. 26, 1775	1	95

166   BARBOUR COLLECTION

	Vol.	Page
EAMES, (cont.)		
Eliphelet, s. Samuel & Anne, b. May 28, 1775	1	140
Elizabeth, d. Mark & Anne, b. Mar. 8, 1759	1	95
Elizabeth, d. Samuel & Anne, b. Oct. 23, 1778	1	140
Esther, d. David & Rachel, b. May 21, 1757	1	120
Hannah, d. David & Rachel, b. Oct. 5, 1754	1	120
Isaac, s. David & Rachel, b. Oct. 30, 1752	1	120
Isaac, s. Samuel & Anne, b. Aug. 11, 1780	1	140
Jeddediah, s. John & Mary, b. May 12, 1772	1	142
Jesse, s. John & Mary, b. June 10, 1764	1	142
John, m. Mary **MILLER**, Nov. 25, 1756	1	142
John, s. John & Mary, May 17, 1762	1	142
John, m. Mary **RUDE**, Apr. 2, 1778, by Rev. Eliphalet Write	1	142
Joshua, s. David & Rachel, b. Aug. 11, 1763	1	120
Lemuel, s. David & Rachel, b. Nov. 23, 1769	1	120
Lydia, d. John & Mary, b. Aug. 23, 1758	1	142
Marcy, m. John **MANSFIELD**, Nov. 26, 1759	1	128
Marg[a]ret, d. John & Mary, b. May 18, 1760	1	142
Mark, m. Anne **GRICE**, May 24, 1750, by Rev. Nehemiah Barker	1	95
Mark, s. Mark & Anne, b. Mar. 11, 1755	1	95
Martha, d. Mark & Anne, b. Apr. 26, 1757	1	95
Martha, twin with Mary, d. John & Mary, b. July 18, 1767	1	142
Mary, twin with Martha, d. John & Mary, b. July 18, 1767	1	142
Mary, w. John, d. Sept. 30, 1773	1	142
Mary, d. Samuel & Anne, b. Mar. 28, 1777	1	140
Miller, s. John & Mary, b. Aug. 3, 1769	1	142
Neomi, d. Anthony & [ ], b. Sept. 17, 1751	1	89
Priscilla, d. Anthony & [ ], b. Aug. 9, 1747	1	89
Rachel, d. Mark & Anne, b. Apr. 30, 1770	1	95
Robert, s. Mark & Anne, b. July 22, 1768	1	95
Samuel, s. Mark & Anne, b. Nov. 16, 1751	1	95
Samuel, m. Anne **BENNET[T]**, Nov. 10, 1774, by Rev. Eliphelet Write	1	140
Tabitha, d. David & Rachel, b. Mar. 3, 1751	1	120
Zephaniah, s. Anthony & [ ], b. Nov. 12, 1749	1	89
EATON, Ebenezer, s. Joseph & Lucy, b. Dec. 20, 1750	1	52
Easther, d. Joseph & Easther, b. Sept. 6, 1746	1	40
Hannah, d. Joseph & Lucy, b. July 3, 1758	1	52
Joseph, m. Lucy **BACON**, Mar. 1, 1750, by Rev. Cogswell	1	52
Lucy, d. Joseph & Lucy, b. Jan. 31, 1753	1	52
ECCLESTON, ECCLESTONE, [see also **EGGLESTON**], Charles C., s. Samuel & Margaret, b. June 6, 1833	2	102
Content, m. John **REYNOLDS**, b. of Voluntown, Dec. 29, 1833, by William C. Stanton, J.P.	2	55
Dorcas, d. Apr. 24, 1848, ae 30; b. in N. Stonington	3	59
Eliza C., d. Samuel & Margaret, b. Dec. 26, 1828	2	102
Ellen J., d. Feb. 8, 1864, ae 18; b. in Stonington	3	73
Gardiner W., ae 22, b. in Richmond, R.I., resid. of Voluntown, m. Hannah **PALMER**, ae 18, of Voluntown, Feb. 23, 1850, by Rev. J. B. Denison	3	2
John, d. Feb. 12, [1859], ae 88	3	69
John S., s. Samuel & Margaret, b. Apr. 5, 1831	2	102
John W., m. Joanna **TERRY**, Mar. 5, 1829, by Minor Rob[b]ins, J.P.	2	81

	Vol.	Page
ECCLESTON, ECCLESTONE, (cont.)		
Louisa, d. Dec. 5, 1857, ae 16	3	67
Polly C., d. Samuel & Margaret, b. Dec. 28, 1822	2	102
Samuel H. C., s. Samuel & Margaret, b. Nov. 29, 1826	2	102
William W., of Voluntown, m. Dorcas **MAIN**, of N. Stonington, Dec. 31, 1837, by Benj[ami]n Gallup, Jr., J.P.	2	106
W[illia]m W., m. Sally **MAINE**, Feb. 23, 1851, by Lathrop B. Weaver	2	139
William W., ae 36, farmer, of Voluntown, m. Sally **MAIN**, ae 40, b. in N. Stonington, res. of Voluntown, Feb. 23, 1851, by Rev. Lathrop P. Weaver. (His 2d marriage)	3	3
-----, s. Gardner W., manufacturer, ae 22, & Hannah, ae 18, b. July 28, 1850	3	23
EDMOND, Agness, m. Samuel **DOUGLASS**, Jan. 8, 1756, by Rev. Samuel Dorrance	1	81
Allen, s. Andrew & Esther, b. July 24, 1790	1	79
Andrew, s. Andrew & Catharine, b. Oct. 4, 1740	1	62
Andrew, s. James & Ann, b. July 7, 1760	1	100
Andrew, m. Prudence **CAMPBELL**, Sept. 9, 1773, by Rev. Samuel Dorrance	1	79
Andrew, s. Andrew & Prudence, b. Sept. 22, 1781	1	79
Ann, d. James & Ann, b. May 4, 1766	1	100
Calvin, s. James & Ann, b. July 27, 1768	1	100
Dinah, d. Andrew & Esther, b. Apr. 23, 1786	1	79
Dinah, m. Nathaniel C. **GALLUP**, Mar. 3, 1808, by Rev. Levi Hart	1	175
Elizabeth, d. Robert & Elizabeth, b. Apr. 17, 1759	1	72
Elizabeth, m. Isaac **CAMPBELL**, Jan. 17, 1793, by Allen Campbell, J.P.	1	219
James, m. Ann **KEN[N]EDY**, July 27, 1759, by Rev. Samuel Dorrance	1	100
James, s. Andrew & Esther, b. July 14, 1784	1	79
Jennet, d. Andrew & Catharine, b. Aug. 31, 1746	1	62
Jennet, d. James & Ann, b. May 11, 1762	1	100
Jennet, m. Jonathan **MILLET**, Sept. 1, 1763	1	117
John, s. Andrew & Catharine, b. Dec. 14, 1737	1	62
Jonathan, s. Robert & Elizabeth, b. May 14, 1761 (sic)	1	72
Ken[n]edy, s. William & Rachel, b. Apr. 3, 1764	1	118
Mary, d. Andrew & Catharine, b. Apr. 4, 1744	1	62
Molly, twin with Peggy, d. Andrew & Prudence, b. June 27, 1778	1	79
Peggy, twin with Molly, d. Andrew & Prudence, b. June 27, 1778	1	79
Rachel, d. William & Rachel, b. June 6, 1766	1	118
Robert, m. Elizabeth **MORY**, Dec. 29, 1757, by Rev. Samuel Dorrance	1	72
Samuel, s. Robert & Elizabeth, b. Apr. 4, 1761 (sic)	1	72
Samuel, s. William & Rachel, b. Aug. 6, 1768	1	118
Samuel Stewart, s. Andrew & Esther, b. Feb. 2, 1788	1	79
Susanna, d. Andrew & Prudence, b. Aug. 12, 1775	1	79
William, s. Andrew & Catharine, b. Mar. 31, 1742	1	62
William, m. Rachel **KEN[N]EDY**, June 23, 1763, by Jeremiah Kinne, J.P.	1	118
Zip[p]orah, d. James & Ann, b. May 16, 1764	1	100
EDWARDS, Eunice, d. Isaac C., farmer, & Lucy A., b. Oct. 10, 1848	3	23
George, ae 42, farmer, m. Phebe **PALMER**, ae 54, b. of Hopkinton,		

168   BARBOUR COLLECTION

	Vol.	Page
EDWARDS, (cont.)		
R.I., Dec. 24, 1848, by Benjamin Gallup	3	1
George W., m. Phebe **PALMER**, Dec. 24, 1848, by Benjamin Gallup, 2d, J.P.	2	131
Patience, m. Joseph **WELLS**, Sept. 5, 1768, by Thomas Wells, J.P.	1	110
-----, d. Nathan, farmer, & Matilda, b. Mar. 17, 1849	3	23
-----, s. Isaac C., farmer, & Lucy A., b. Nov. 16, 1850	3	27
EGGLESTON, EGLETON, EGELETON, EAGLESTON, EGLESTON, [see also **ECCLESTON**], Clark, s. John & Content, b. Feb. 14, 1807	2	9
Daniel, s. John & Content, b. Jan. 15, 1796	2	9
Isaac, Jr., m. Mary **PART[E]LOW**, Jan. 15, 1755, by Wait Palmer, Elder	1	57
John W., s. John & Content, b. Sept. 15, 1794	2	9
Joseph, twin with Samuel, s. John & Content, b. Mar. 14, 1802	2	9
Katura, m. Asa S. **COON**, Feb. 9, 1823, by Sterry Kinne, J.P.	2	52
Robert, m. Phebe **WILSON**, Jan. 13, 1823, by Sterry Kinne, J.P.	2	52
Robert S., s. John & Content, b. May 1, 1804	2	9
Samuel, twin with Joseph, s. John & Content, b. Mar. 14, 1802	2	9
William W., s. John & Content, b. Sept. 3, 1814	2	9
ELDREDGE, Abram, of Dartmouth, Mass., m. Susan C. **GATES**, of Voluntown, Mar. 2, 1845, by Rev. Richard B. Eldredge	2	120
William, s. Desire, b. Nov. 28, 1813	2	33
[ELLIOTT], ELIOT, Andrew, m. Hannah **PALMER**, Aug. 18, 1745, by Joseph Palmer, Esq.	1	65
Andrew, s. Andrew & Hannah, b. Nov. 27, 1751	1	65
Andrew, m. Brigget **HARRIS**, Mar. 25, 1767, by Jeremiah Kinne, J.P.	1	65
Asenath, d. Andrew & Hannah, b. Mar. 9, 1748	1	65
George, s. Andrew & Hannah, b. Mar. 1, 1757	1	65
Gedian, twin with John, s. Andrew & Hannah, b. Sept. 26, 1763	1	65
Hannah, w. Andrew, d. May 21, 1766	1	65
Hannah, d. Andrew & Bridget, b. Feb. 27, 1768	1	65
Jacob, s. Andrew & Hannah, b. Feb. 14, 1759	1	65
John, twin with Gedian, s. Andrew & Hannah, b. Sept. 26, 1763	1	65
Jonathan Palmer, s. Andrew & Hannah, b. May 4, 1766	1	65
Joseph, s. Andrew & Hannah, b. July 13, 1761	1	65
Molly, d. Andrew & Hannah, b. July 18, 1746	1	65
Sarah, d. Andrew & Hannah, b. Aug. 6, 1750; d. Dec. 15, 1750	1	65
Sarah, d. Andrew & Hannah, b. Aug. 16, 1754	1	65
ELLIS, Abraham, m. Polly **BOWDISH**, Aug. 22, 1790, by Rev. Micaiah Porter	1	208
Harty, of W. Greenwich, m. John **DOW**, 3d, of Plainfield, Mar. 1, 1818, by John Wylie, J.P.	2	19
EUSTISTON, Lydia, m. John **REYNOLDS**, Dec. 28, 1823, by Amos Treat, J.P.	2	54
FAIRMAN, Abigail, of Killingly, m. William **WILLIAMS**, of Voluntown, Feb. 3, 1742/3, by Joseph Leavens, J.P.	1	38
Jonathan, s. Jonathan & Mary, b. July 10, 1744	1	39
FARE, Grace, d. John & Hannah, b. May 31, 1751	1	19
FELLOWS, Mary, m. Jonas **MARSH**, Sept. 4, 1732	1	19
FENNER, [see also **TANNER**], Arthur, of Hopkinton, R.I., m. Content **JACKSON**, now residing in Hopkinton, June 13, 1830, by		

	Vol.	Page
FENNER, (cont.)		
Nathaniel Sheffield, Elder	2	85
John, d. Dec. 29, 1853, ae 3	3	64
John L., s. Luther, farmer, ae 33, & Lucy, ae 25, b. May 30, 1850	3	25
Joseph, of Sterling, m. Lucinda **REYNOLDS**, Feb. 13, 1834, by Nathaniel Sheffield, Elder	2	97
Joshua, m. Lucy **BUMP**, Feb. 22, 1829, by Benjamin Gallup, J.P.	2	81
Mary Alice, d. June 10, [1860], ae 5	3	70
FERGUSON, [see under **FORGESON**]		
FISH, Asa, s. Moses, Jr. & Jerusha, b. July 27, 1792	1	145
Asa, s. Moses, Jr. & Jerusha, b. July 27, 1792	1	223
Asa, m. Betsey **LESTER**, May 10, 1812, by Peleg Randall, Elder	2	7
Betsey, d. Moses, Jr. & Jerusha, b. Feb. 1, 1799	1	145
Betsey, d. Moses, Jr. & Jerusha, b. Feb. 1, 1799	1	223
Betsey, d. June 25, 1864, ae 65	3	74
Byron D., d. Nov. 9, 1863, ae 10 m.	3	73
Charles H., s. Moses, Jr. & Susanna, b. Oct. 12, 1821	2	6
Daniel, s. Moses & Elizabeth, b. Dec. 10, 1758	1	73
Daniel, s. Samuel & Ruth, b. Nov. 19, 1763	1	92
Elias, s. Samuel & Ruth, b. Nov. 19, 1753	1	92
Elias, m. [E]unice **FISH**, Dec. 11, 1777, by Rev. Solomon Morgan	1	147
Elisha, s. Moses, Jr. & Jerusha, b. Oct. 13, 1783	1	145
Elisha, s. Moses, Jr. & Jerusha, b. Oct. 13, 1785	1	223
Elisha Eldredge N., s. Moses, Jr. & Susanna, b. Jan. 4, 1828	2	6
Elisha P., s. Levi & Rebecca, b. Oct. 21, 1826	2	100
Elisha P., d. Oct. [ ], 1856, ae 30	3	67
Elizabeth, d. Moses & Elizabeth, b. Oct. 7, 1746	1	73
Elizabeth, d. Samuel & Ruth, b. Dec. 11, 1761	1	92
Emmeline, d. Asa & Betsey, b. Oct. 29, 1813	2	7
Enos, s. Elias & Eunice, b. Dec. 11, 1799	1	147
Eunice, d. Moses & Elizabeth, b. Mar. 16, 1752	1	73
[E]unice, m. Elias **FISH**, Dec. 11, 1777, by Rev. Solomon Morgan	1	147
Eunice Caroline, d. Levi & Rebecca, b. Jan. 6, 1814	1	242
Frances L., s. Moses, Jr. & Susanna, b. Mar. 17, 1820	2	6
George F., s. Moses, Jr. & Susanna, b. Feb. 5, 1834	2	6
Henry Palmer, b. Sept. 14, 1830	1	147
James L., s. Moses, Jr. & Susanna, b. Apr. 5, 1837	2	6
Joanna M., of Voluntown, m. James M. **PHILLIPS**, of Russel, Mass., Dec. [ ], 1846, by Rev. Charles S. Weaver	2	8
Joanna Melvena, d. Levi & Rebecca, b. Feb. 14, 1819	1	243
John, s. Elias & Eunice, b. Sept. 30, 1798	1	147
John, m. Nancy **WHEELER**, of Voluntown, Sept. 25, 1825, by Benjamin Gallup, J.P.	2	61
John Phelps, b. Jan. 24, 1829	1	147
Jonas, s. Elias & Eunice, b. Nov. 16, 1786	1	147
Jonas, d. Jan. 2, 1851, ae 64	3	62
Jonathan Clinton P., s. Moses, Jr. & Susanna, b. Nov. 5, 1839	2	6
Levi, s. Moses, Jr. & Jerusha, b. Apr. 10, 1786	1	145
Levi, s. Moses, Jr. & Jerusha, b. Apr. 10, 1786	1	223
Levi, m. Rebecca **FISH**, Dec. 13, 1807, by Peleg Randall, Elder	1	242
Levi H., m. Amy **SAUNDERS**, b. of Voluntown, Jan. 12, 1834, by Jonathan Miner, Elder	2	57
Levi Hart, s. Levi & Rebecca, b. June 13, 1809	1	242

	Vol.	Page
FISH, (cont.)		
Lucy, d. Samuel & Ruth, b. Dec. 4, 1758	1	92
Lucy, d. Moses, Jr. & Jerusha, b. Apr. 9, 1796	1	145
Lucy, d. Moses, Jr. & Jerusha, b. Apr. 9, 1796	1	223
Lucy, m. Spencer **SAUNDERS**, Dec. 22, 1822, by Amos Treat, J.P.	2	51
Lucy Ann, d. Levi & Rebecca, b. July 2, 1821	1	243
Mahala, d. Moses, Jr. & Jerusha, b. Aug. 29, 1779	1	145
Mahala, d. Moses, Jr. & Jerusha, b. Aug. 29, 1780	1	223
Mary A., of Voluntown, m. Horatio M. **BILLINGS**, of Griswold, Jan. 30, 1838, by Benj[amin] Gallup, Jr., J.P.	2	101
Mary Ann, d. Moses, Jr. & Susanna, b. Apr. 9, 1818	2	6
Mary Ann, b. May 24, 1826	1	147
Mary N., s. Moses, Jr. & Susanna, b. Feb. 27, 1824	2	6
Moses, m. Elizabeth **MORGAN**, Nov. 7, 1745, by Rev. Crosswell	1	73
Moses, s. Moses & Elizabeth, b. Mar. 20, 1749	1	73
Moses, Jr., m. Jerusha **PHILLIPS**, Feb. 12, 1778, by Rev. Levi Hart	1	145
Moses, s. Ellias & Eunice, b. Apr. 21, 1788	1	147
Moses, s. Moses, Jr. & Jerusha, b. Oct. 3, 1789	1	145
Moses, s. Moses, Jr. & Jerusha, b. Oct. 3, 1789	1	223
Moses, Jr., m. Susanna **REYNOLDS**, Oct. 8, 1815, by Jonathan Miner, Elder	2	6
Moses, d. Aug. 8, 1836	1	145
Rachel, d. Moses, Jr. & Jerusha, b. Dec. 14, 1781	1	145
Rachel, d. Moses, Jr. & Jerusha, b. Dec. 14, 1782	1	223
Rachel, d. Sept. 29, 1864, ae 86	3	74
Rebeckah, d. Elias & Eunice, b. Sept. 30, 1783	1	147
Rebecca, m. Levi **FISH**, Dec. 13, 1807, by Peleg Randall, Elder	1	242
Rebecca M., m. Philetus T. **PARTELOW**, Feb. 14, 1830, by Levi Kneeland	2	83
Rebecca Merilla, d. Levi & Rebecca, b. Jan. 5, 1808	1	242
Ruth, d. Samuel & Ruth, b. June 12, 1755	1	92
Sally Irena, d. Moses, Jr. & Susanna, b. Sept. 5, 1831	2	6
Samuel, m. Ruth **COOK**, Dec. 11, 1748, by Joseph Palmer, Esq.	1	92
Samuel, s. Elias & Eunice, b. Apr. 15, 1781	1	147
Sarah, d. Samuel & Ruth, b. Apr. 21, 1757	1	92
Spicer Stanton, b. June 30, 1833	1	147
Susan J., d. Moses, Jr. & Susanna, b. Oct. 4, 1826	2	6
Thomas, s. Elias & Eunice, b. Apr. 2, 1791	1	147
Thomas Leland, s. Levi & Rebecca, b. July 6, 1811	1	242
William Pendleton, s. Moses, Jr. & Susanna, b. June 15, 1816	2	6
FISK, Martha, d. Apr. 24, 1849, ae 14; b. in Voluntown, resid. Griswold	3	60
FLETCHER, Mary, ae 17, b. Pawtucket, R.I., resid. of Voluntown, m. Darius B. **BITGOOD**, ae 33, of Voluntown, Dec. 15, 1850, by Charles S. Weaver	3	4
FORDICE, James, m. Esther **COLE**, Mar. 5, 1761, by Jeremiah Kinne, Esq., d. July 8, 1761	1	102
Lucy, d. James & Esther, b. Dec. 26, 1761	1	102
FORGESON, FARGISSON, Jennit, m. John **KEN[N]EDY**, Aug. 14, 1735, by Rev. [ ], of Charlestown	1	21
Mary, m. John **CAMPBELL**, Jr., June 2, 1748, by Rev. Samuel Dorrance	1	55
FOSTER, Sillas, s. Thomas & Masy, b. Mar. 7, 1721; d. Dec. 8, 1721, ae 10 m. 1 d.	1	3

VOLUNTOWN VITAL RECORDS 171

	Vol.	Page
FRENCH, Abigel, d. Nath[aniel] & Abigel, b. June 14, 1721	1	3
Hannah, relict of Jonathan, m. Thomas **GALLUP**, Jan. 4, 1721/22, by Capt. Thomas Williams, J.P.	1	3
Jonathan, d. Feb. 17, 1720/21, in ye 32nd year of his age	1	3
FRINK, Abigail, [w. Zacchariah], d. June 13, 1805	1	71
Albert, of Plainfield, m. Mary Ann **BRIGGS**, of Voluntown, Nov. 8, 1848, by Rev. Jacob Allen	2	90
Amos, s. Zac[c]hariah & Elizabeth, b. July 22, 1740	1	18
Anna, d. Uzziel, Jr. & Eunice, b. Oct. 16, 1810	1	249
Daniel, s. Zac[c]hariah & Abigale, b. May 7, 1754	1	71
Daniel, m. Lydia **MULKIN**, Dec. 20, 1770, by Samuel Coit, J.P.	1	26
Daniel, s. Zachariah, Jr. & Mercy, b. Dec. 14, 1802	1	231
Elias, s. Joshua & Ann, b. Sept. 12, 1766	1	109
Elias, s. Zachariah, Jr. & Marcy, b. Sept. 24, 1796	1	231
Elizabeth, d. Uzziel & Huldah, b. Mar. 31, 1762	1	92
Eunice, m. Uzziel **FRINK**, Jr., May 26, 1802, by Elder Avery, of Stonington	1	249
Eunice, d. Uzziel, Jr. & Eunice, b. Aug. 29, 1803	1	249
Eunice, of Norwich, m. Daniel Ayres **KEIGWIN**, of Voluntown, Feb. 12, 1838, by Daniel Keigwin, J.P.	2	62
Ezra, s. Zachariah, Jr. & Marcy, b. Feb. 10, 1801	1	231
Hannah, m. John **GALLUP**, Apr. 9, 1747, by Rev. Joseph Fish	1	50
Israel, s. Zac[c]hariah & Elizabeth, b. Aug. 25, 1752	1	18
Israel, m. Esther **PHILIPS**, Nov. 2, 1775, by Rev. John Fuller	1	134
Joshua, s. Zachariah & Elizabeth, b. Mar. 21, 1738	1	18
Joshua, m. Ann **GALLUP**, Mar. 31, 1763, by Rev. Samuel Dorrance	1	109
Lois, d. Zachariah & Elizabeth, b. Feb. 3, 1748	1	18
Lois, d. Joshua & Ann, b. Jan. 30, 1769	1	109
Lois, m. Thomas **COLE**, Jr., Nov. 3, 1785, by Rev. Joel Benedict	1	180
Lucy, d. Israel & Esther, b. Sept. 27, 1776	1	134
Lucy G., d. Uzziel, Jr. & Eunice, b. Mar. 16, 1808	1	249
Lydia, m. Ezekiel **SMITH**, Jan. 8, 1798, by Silas Westcot[t], J.P.	1	230
Marcy, m. Zachariah **FRINK**, Jr., Oct. 22, 1795, by Rev. Micaiah Porter	1	231
Marg[a]ret, d. Uzziel & Marg[a]ret, b. July 30, 1783	1	92
Margaret, m. Russel[l] **STEVENS**, Nov. 17, 1796, by Rev. Micaiah Porter	1	218
Margaret, d. Uzziel, Jr. & Eunice, b. Feb. 28, 1806	1	249
Margaret, d. Mar. 1, 1826, ae 89 y.	1	249
Mary, d. Joshua & Ann, b. Apr. 9, 1774	1	109
Mattathias, s. Zachariah & Elizabeth, b. Feb. 11, 1743	1	18
Mercy, d. Joshua & Ann, b. Sept. 14, 1771	1	109
Moses, s. Zachariah, Jr. & Marcy, b. Mar. 10, 1799	1	231
Prudence, d. Zachariah & Elizabeth, b. Mar. 16, 1750	1	18
Rachel, d. Zachariah & Elizabeth, b. June 21, 1745	1	18
Rachel, m. Abel **KINNE**, Oct. 3, 1771, by Jeremiah Kinne, J.P.	1	123
Rachel, d. Daniel & Lydia, b. Dec. 20, 1772	1	26
Sabra, d. Daniel & Lydia, b. Dec. 19, 1782	1	26
Sabra, m. Ethel **PHILLIPS**, Mar. 10, 1803, by Joseph Wylie, J.P.	1	254
Samuel, s. Joshua & Ann, b. Oct. 16, 1764	1	109
Samuel, m. Marg[a]ret **G[A]LLUP**, Mar. 16, 1786, by Rev. Joel Benedict	1	186
Susan G., d. Uzziel & Eunice, b. July 21, 1813	1	249

BARBOUR COLLECTION

	Vol.	Page
FRINK, (cont.)		
Uzziel, s. Zachariah & Elizabeth, b. Jan. 26, 1735/6	1	18
Uzziel, m. Huldah **KINNE**, Mar. 3, 1757, by Jeremiah Kinne, J.P.	1	92
Uzziel, m. Marg[a]ret **PALMER**, Mar. 28, 1776, by James Bradford, J.P.	1	92
Uzziel, s. Uzziel & Marg[a]ret, b. June 3, 1778	1	92
Uzziel, Jr., m. Eunice **FRINK**, May 26, 1802, by Elder Avery, of Stonington	1	249
Uzziel, s. Uzziel & Eunice, b. Oct. 5, 1815	1	249
Uzziel, d. May 15, 1826, ae 48 y.	1	249
Zachariah, m. Elizabeth **GALLUP**, Mar. 4, 1730, by Rev. Coit; d. Dec. 28, 1777	1	18
Zachariah, s. Zachariah & Elizabeth, b. Jan. 10, 1731	1	18
Zachariah, Jr., m. Abigale **KINNE**, Feb. 21, 1753, by Jeremiah Kinne, J.P.	1	71
Zachariah, s. Daniel & Lydia, b. Apr. 11, 1775	1	26
Zachariah, Jr., m. Marcy **FRINK**, Oct. 22, 1795, by Rev. Micaiah Porter	1	231
Zachariah, Jr., d. May 11, 1804	1	231
Zachariah, d. Dec. 8, 1804	1	71
Zephaniah, s. Zachariah & Elizabeth, b. May 29, 1733	1	18
FRYERS, Rebecca, m. James **GORDON**, July 28, 1768, by Rev. Ezra Styles	1	149
GALLUP, Albin, of West Greenwich, R.I., m. Susanna **WALDO**, of Hampton, [Conn.] Aug. 29, 1822, by Benjamin Gallup, Jr., J.P.	2	50
Amy, d. Benjamin & Amy, b. June 27, 1770	1	140
Amy, m. William **GALLUP**, Jr., Sept. 2, 1790, by Rev. Micaiah Porter	1	223
Amey, d. Benjamin, Jr. & Huldah, b. June 13, 1808	2	3
Amy, of Voluntown, m. Benjamin **GALLUP**, 2d, Dec. 1, 1825, by Benjamin Gallup, J.P.	2	63
Amey S., d. Nov. 3, 1848, ae 26	3	60
Andrew E., s. Nathaniel C. & Dinah, b. Sept. 18, 1810	1	175
Ann, m. Joshua **FRINK**, Mar. 31, 1763, by Rev. Samuel Dorrance	1	109
Asal, s. John & Elizabeth, b. Feb. 24, 1712	1	2
Benadam, s. Isaac & Marg[a]ret, b. Nov. 17, 1761	1	47
Benadam, m. Elizabeth **DORRANCE**, Mar. 31, 1785, by Rev. Micaiah Porter	1	213
Benadam, d. Mar. 30, 1850, ae 90; b. in Voluntown, resid. Sterling	3	61
Benjamin, m. Theody **PARKE**, May 22, 1735, by Rev. Samuel Dorrance	1	16
Benjamin, m. Amy **KINNE**, Jan. 20, 1763, by Rev. Levi Hart	1	140
Benjamin, s. Benjamin & Amy, b. May 25, 1774	1	140
Benjamin, s. Nath[aniel] & Keziah, b. Dec. 27, 1801	1	243
Benjamin, Jr., m. Huldah **KINNE**, Jan. 3, 1806, by Peleg Randall, Elder	2	3
Benjamin, s. Benjamin, Jr. & Huldah, b. July 10, 1811	2	3
Benjamin, 2d, m. Amy **GALLUP**, of Voluntown, Dec. 1, 1825, by Benjamin Gallup, J.P.	2	63
Benjamin, Jr., m. Caroline L. **KENNEY**, of Voluntown, Oct. 30, 1831, by Joseph Wylie, J.P.	2	91
Benjamin, 2d, m. Amey **STANTON**, b. of Voluntown, Mar. [ ], 1846, by Charles S. Weaver, Pastor	2	8

	Vol.	Page
GALLUP, (cont.)		
Benj[amin], d. Aug. 23, 1854, ae 80	3	64
Benjamin V., m. Juliette **KENNEDY**, b. of Voluntown, Oct. 8, 1848, by Rev. Alfred Burnham	2	128
Betsey, m. Henry Augustus **ALEXANDER**, Jan. 23, 1817, by John Wylie, J.P.	2	11
Betsey, d. Apr. 14, 1853, ae 48; b. in R.I. Married	3	63
Betsey Therisa, d. David & Lucy, b. Jan. 7, 1816, in Stonington	2	96
Charles E., s. Isaac & Olive, b. Mar. 26, 1833	2	141
Clarissa Ann, d. Isaac & Olive, b. Apr. 17, 1827	2	141
Cynthia, d. Benjamin & Amy, b. Dec. 22, 1784	1	141
Daniel, s. John & Hannah, b. Mar. 7, 1755	1	50
Daniel, s. John & Lydia, b. Feb. 9, 1778	1	132
Daniel A., of Sterling, m. Barbara L. **GORDON**, of Voluntown, Oct. 1, 1843, by Rev. Jacob Allen	2	24
Daniel B., s. Benj[amin], 2d, ae 46, & Amey E., ae 26, b. May 17, 1848	3	21
Daniel B., d. June 23,1849, ae 1	3	59
David, of Plainfield, m. Lucy **HANCOCK**, of Stonington, Mar. 30, 1815, by Jonathan Minor, Elder; d. Jan. 9, 1848	2	96
David, d. Jan. 8, 1848, ae 58; b. in Plainfield	3	59
David Nelson, s. David & Lucy, b. Jan. 8, 1821	2	96
Dolly, d. Wheeler & Elizabeth, b. Apr. 1, 1783	1	184
Dolly, d. John & Lydia, b. May 14, 1786	1	132
Dor[o]thy, d. John & Elizabeth, b. Mar. 22, 1721	1	2
Dorithy, d. John & Hannah, b. June 11, 1765	1	50
Elizabeth, d. John & Elizabeth, b. Apr. 9, 1714	1	2
Elizabeth, m. Zachariah **FRINK**, Mar. 4, 1730, by Rev. Coit	1	18
Elizabeth, d. John & Hannah, b. June 2, 1753	1	50
Elizabeth, d. Isaac & Marg[a]ret, b. Jan. 22, 1755	1	47
Elizabeth, m. William **BRIGGS**, Jan. 11, 1776, by Rev. Solomon Morgin	1	133
Elizabeth, m. Micaiah **PORTER**, Nov. 22, 1781, by Rev. Solomon Morgan	1	157
Elizabeth, reputed, d. Benadam **GALLUP** & Mary **COLE**, b. Feb. 21, 1783	1	93
Elizabeth, d. Wheeler & Elizabeth, b. Mar. 6, 1785	1	184
Elizabeth, d. Benadam & Elizabeth, b. Nov. 24, 1791	1	213
Elizabeth, m. Noah **BRIGGS**, Oct. 1, 1812, by John Wyle, J.P.	1	212
Emily, d. Sept. 14, 1865, ae 45	3	75
Esther, d. Benjamin & Amy, b. Apr. 17, 1780	1	140
Eunice, d. Benjamin & Amy, b. Mar. 8, 1787	1	141
Francis E., s. John, farmer, ae 22, & Happy, ae 23, b. Apr. 4, 1850	3	24
Francis E., d. Nov. 14, 1850, ae 9 m.; b. in Voluntown, resid. of Griswold	3	62
Freelove, m. Abel **KINNE**, Apr. 9, 1789, by Elder Whitman	1	124
George, s. Benedam & Elizabeth, b. Dec. 21, 1785	1	213
Han[n]ah, d. John & Elizabeth, b. Jan. 29, 1719	1	2
Hannah, d. John & Hannah, b. Feb. 15, 1748	1	50
Hannah, d. John & Lydia, b. Nov. 1, 1782	1	132
Hannah, d. Nath[aniel] & Keziah, b. Dec. 29, 1788	1	243
Hannah, d. John, Jr. & Hannah, b. Nov. 23, 1789	1	129
Hannah, m. Avery **KINNE**, Feb. 27, 1814, by Allen Campbell, J.P.	1	235

174 BARBOUR COLLECTION

	Vol.	Page
GALLUP, (con.t.)		
Harvey, s. Nathaniel & Rachel, b. May 23, 1791	1	169
Huldah, d. Wheeler & Elizabeth, b. Mar. 7, 1789	1	184
Isaac, m. Marg[a]ret **GALLUP**, Mar. 29, 1749, by Rev. Eben[eze]r Rosseter	1	47
Isaac, s. Isaac & Marg[a]ret, b. June 14, 1751; d. Oct. 20, 1766, ae 16 y.	1	47
Isaac, s. Isaac & Marg[a]ret, b. Oct. 8, 1766	1	47
Isaac, s. Capt. Isaac [& Marg[a]ret], d. Oct. 20, 1766	1	47
Isaac, s. John, Jr. & Hannah, b. Feb. 19, 1781	1	129
Isaac, Jr., m. Mary **DEAN**, Apr. 24, 1788, by Rev. Micaiah Porter	1	210
Isaac, m. Olive **PARK[E]**, Nov. 14, 1819, by Rev. Asa Meech; d. Dec. 4, 1850	2	141
Isaac, of Plainfield, m. Sarah Celinda **ALEXANDER**, of Voluntown, Feb. 6, 1822, by Rev. Orrin Fowler	2	39
Isaac, b. Feb. 19, 1781; d. Dec. 4, 1850	2	141
Jabez, s. Nathaniel C. & Dinah, b. Mar. 19, 1809	1	175
Jabish, s. John & Hannah, b. May 12, 1759	1	50
James, s. Benadam & Elizabeth, b. Feb. 22, 1788	1	213
James, ae 20, of Sterling, m. Patience **STONE**, of Sterling, Oct. [ ], 1849, by Rev. Jacob Allen	3	3
James H., s. Isaac & Olive, b. Aug. 9, 1825	2	141
Jared A., s. Isaac & Olive, b. Mar. 10, 1837	2	141
John, s. John & Elizabeth, b. June 9, 1724	1	2
John, m. Hannah **FRINK**, Apr. 9, 1747, by Rev. Joseph Fish	1	50
John, s. Isaac & Marg[a]ret, b. Dec. 29, 1749	1	47
John, s. John & Hannah, b. July 23, 1751	1	50
John, Capt., d. Dec. 29, 1755, ae 81 y.	1	69
John, 3d, m. Lydia **RANDALL**, Oct. 24, 1773, by Rev. Solomon Morgan	1	132
John, Jr., m. Hannah **DOUGLASS**, May 5, 1774, by Robert Dixson, Esq.	1	129
John, s. John & Hannah, b. Feb. 19, 1775	1	129
John, s. Nathan & Zeruiah, b. Feb. 26, 1787	1	188
John, d. Jan. 7, 1789	1	132
John D., s. Isaac & Olive, b. Oct. 1, 1820	2	141
John Henry, s. David & Lucy, b. Dec. 15, 1826	2	96
John N., m. Happy K. **CHURCH**, b. of Voluntown, Apr. 16, 1849, by Rev. Jesse B. Denison. Witnesses: W[illia]m W. Thompson, Lydia A. Bitgood	2	133
John N., ae 20, farmer, of Voluntown, m. Happy K. **CHURCH**, ae 22, b. in Griswold, now of Voluntown, Apr. 16, 1849, by Rev. Jesse B. Denison	3	2
Joseph, s. Isaac & Marg[a]ret, b. Mar. 24, 1772	1	47
Josephine, d. Apr. 19, 1849, ae 18	3	60
Keturah, d. Benjamin & Amy, b. Feb. 22, 1790	1	141
Keziah, d. Nath[aniel] & Keziah, b. July 1, 1799	1	243
Keziah, m. Daniel L. **CAMPBELL**, Oct. 21, 1823, by Sterry Kinne, J.P.	2	54
Keziah, [w. Nathaniel], d. Sept. 23, 1824	1	243
Kinne, s. Nath[aniel] & Keziah, b. Sept. 27, 1794	1	243
Lee, ae 20, m. Elizabeth [ ], b. of Sterling, Jan. [1850?], by Rev. Peleg Peckham	3	3

VOLUNTOWN VITAL RECORDS

	Vol.	Page
GALLUP, (cont.)		
Lucy, d. Benjamin & Amy, b. May 17, 1776	1	140
Lucy, m. Thomas **GALLUP**, Apr. 3, 1794, by Peleg Randall, Elder	1	204
Lucy, m. John **KINNE**, Jan. 1, 1800, by Allen Campbell, J.P.	1	235
Lucy Celinda, d. David & Lucy, b. July 30, 1824	2	96
Lydia, d. Thomas & Lucy, b. Nov. 28, 1804	1	204
Lydia, d. Dec. 13, 1863, ae 30; b. in W. Greenwich	3	73
Lyman, s. Nath[aniel] & Keziah, b. Feb. 4, 1791	1	243
Marg[a]ret, m. Isaac **GALLUP**, Mar. 29, 1749, by Rev. Eben[eze]r Rosseter	1	47
Marg[a]ret, d. Isaac & Marg[a]ret, b. Aug. 26, 1768	1	47
Margaret, d. Benjamin & Amy, b. Nov. 18, 1782	1	141
Marg[a]ret, m. Samuel **FRINK**, Mar. 16, 1786, by Rev. Joel Benedict	1	186
Marg[a]ret, d. Benadam & Elizabeth, b. Jan. 11, 1790	1	213
Martha, d. John & Elizabeth, b. Sept. 3, 1716	1	2
Martha, m. Thomas **DOUGLASS**, Jan. 4, 1737, by Timothy Peirce, Asst.	1	74
Martha, d. Isaac & Marg[a]ret, b. Feb. 17, 1757	1	47
Martha, d. Benjamin & Amy, b. Apr. 16, 1778	1	140
Martha, d. John, Jr. & Hannah, b. Apr. 20, 1784	1	129
Martha M., d. Isaac & Olive, b. Mar. 10, 1822	2	141
Mary Jane, d. David & Lucy, b. Mar. 4, 1831	2	96
Mercy, d. Benjamin & Amy, b. Apr. 17, 1772	1	140
Molly, m. Wheeler **GALLUP**, July 2, 1815, by Joseph Wylie, J.P.	1	175
Nathan, s. John & Hannah, b. Feb. 11, 1763	1	50
Nathan, m. Zeruiah **GALLUP**, Jan. 19, 1786, by Rev. Micaiah Porter	1	188
Nathaniel, s. Isaac & Marg[a]ret, b. Dec. 24, 1758	1	47
Nathaniel, s. Benjamin & Amy, b. Jan. 14, 1765	1	140
Nathaniel, m. Rachel **SMITH**, Jan. 30, 1783, by Rev. Micaiah Porter	1	169
Nathaniel, m. Keziah **KINNE**, Sept. 7, 1786, by Rev. Micaiah Porter	1	243
Nathaniel, s. Nath[aniel] & Keziah, b. Mar. 10, 1806; d. Sept. 26, 1824	1	243
Nath[aniel], d. Oct. 26, 1815	1	243
Nathaniel C., m. Dinah **EDMOND**, Mar. 3, 1808, by Rev. Levi Hart	1	175
Nathaniel C., s. Nathaniel C. & Dinah, b. Mar. 14, 1814	1	175
Nathaniel Cogswell, s. Wheeler & Elizabeth, b. Mar. 15, 1787	1	184
Noyes B., s. Isaac & Olive, b. Jan. 12, 1831	2	141
Olive D., d. Isaac & Olive, b. Jan. 21, 1835	2	141
Olive M., m. Martin L. **COWLES**, b. of Voluntown, Oct. 27, 1845, by Rev. Warren Emmerson	2	122
Origen S., s. Benjamin, Jr., farmer, & Caroline L., b. Dec. 31, 1850	3	24
Orrin W., s. Nathaniel C. & Dinah, b. July 17, 1812	1	175
Peleg Hancock, s. David & Lucy, b. May 3, 1817	2	96
Phebe, d. Thomas & Lucy, b. Oct. 7, 1798	1	204
Prudence, d. Nathaniel & Rachel, b. July 24, 1785	1	169
Rachel, d. Nathaniel & Rachel, b. June 12, 1788; d. May 30, 1789	1	169
Ralph P., s. Isaac & Olive, b. Feb. 28, 1829	2	141
Rebecca, d. John, Jr. & Hannah, b. Dec. 3, 1786	1	129
Roxa S., of Voluntown, m. George **DAWLEY**, of Norwich, Apr. 8, 1849, by Rev. Jesse B. Denison. Witnesses: John S. Gallup, Samuel A. Edmond	2	133

176   BARBOUR COLLECTION

	Vol.	Page
GALLUP, (cont.)		
Roxelina, [w. Simon], d. Aug. 18, 1828	2	54
Sabara, d. John & Lydia, b. Feb. 7, 1774	1	132
Sally, d. Wheeler & Elizabeth, b. Mar. 17, 1791	1	184
Sally M., m. Chester **BATES**, ae 25, of Providence, Jan. [ ], [1850?], by Rev. Peleg Peckham	3	3
Samuel, s. John & Hannah, b. Apr. 7, 1761	1	50
Samuel, m. Lucy **AVERIL[L]**, Dec. 15, 1786, by Rev. Levi Hart	1	204
Sarah B., d. Isaac & Olive, b. Mar. 16, 1844	2	141
Silas, s. Thomas & Esther, b. Mar. 15, 1800, in Coventry	1	236
Simon, m. Roxelina **ROB[B]INS**, Feb. 12, 1824, by Sterry Kinne, J.P.	2	54
Tempe, d. Nath[aniel] & Keziah, b. Oct. 6, 1792	1	243
Thomas, m. Hannah, relict of Jonathan **FRENCH**, Jan. 4, 1721/22, by Capt. Thomas Williams, J.P.	1	3
Thomas, s. Benjamin & Amy, b. Nov. 20, 1768; d. Feb. 3, 1770	1	140
Thomas, s. John & Lydia, b. Apr. 17, 1775	1	132
Thomas, s. John, Jr. & Hannah, b. June 4, 1777	1	129
Thomas, s. Nath[aniel] & Keziah, b. Nov. 21, 1786	1	243
Thomas, m. Lucy **GALLUP**, Apr. 3, 1794, by Peleg Randall, Elder	1	204
Thomas, Jr., m. Easther **WESTCOT[T]**, Feb. 7, 1799, by Benjamin Greene, J.P.	1	236
Uzziel, s. Benjamin & Theody, b. July 30, 1737	1	16
Wheeler, s. John & Hannah, b. Jan. 20, 1757	1	50
Wheeler, m. Elizabeth **COGSWELL**, May 2, 1782, by Rev. Levi Hart	1	184
Wheeler, s. Wheeler & Elizabeth, b. Sept. 30, 1793; d. Dec. 23, 1796	1	184
Wheeler, m. Molly **GALLUP**, July 2, 1815, by Joseph Wylie, J.P.	1	175
William, s. John & Elizabeth, b. Sept. 2, 1710	1	2
William, reputed s. of William, decd., & Est[h]er **SMITH**, b. Aug. 18, 1735	1	18
William, s. John & Hannah, b. Oct. 8, 1749	1	50
William, s. Isaac & Marg[a]ret, b. Apr. 12, 1764	1	47
William, m. Mary **WHIP[P]LE**, Apr. 17, 1769, by Robert Dixson, J.P.	1	88
William, Jr., m. Amy **GALLUP**, Sept. 2, 1790, by Rev. Micaiah Porter	1	223
William, s. Thomas & Lucy, b. Mar. 18, 1796	1	204
William W., s. Isaac & Olive, b. Oct. 19, 1823	2	141
Zeruiah, d. Benjamin & Amy, b. Jan. 20, 1767	1	140
Zeruiah, m. Nathan **GALLUP**, Jan. 19, 1786, by Rev. Micaiah Porter	1	188
Zeruiah, d. William & Amy, b. May 21, 1791	1	223
GARDEN, Mary, m. Lemuel **DORRANCE**, May 14, 1772, by Rev. Samuel Dorrance	1	135
GARDNER, Amy, m. George W. **CROSS**, b. of R.I., July 6, 1846, by Rev. Charles S. Weaver	2	9
Bra[y[ton, s. William & Zerviah, b. Oct. 9, 1779	1	101
Rowland, m. Rachel **LAWTON**, b. of Griswold, Sept. 15, 1850, by Charles S. Weaver	3	4
Thankfull, m. Amos **KEIGWIN**, Nov. 30, 1780, by John Maxson, J.P.	1	154
Willard, ae 24, b. in Exeter, R.I., resid. of Voluntown, m. Susan		

	Vol.	Page
GARDNER, (cont.)		
PHILLIPS, ae 24, of Voluntown, Feb. 11, 1849, by Gershom Palmer	3	2
GARY, Ezekiel, m. Thankfull **HALL**, [ ]	1	105
Thankfull, d. Ezekiel & Thankfull, b. Dec. 1, 1764	1	105
GASTON, Alexander, m. Mary **WILLSON**, Sept. 29, 1743, by Rev. Samuel Dorrance	1	82
Alexander, s. Alexander & Mary, b. Oct. 28, 1754	1	82
Alexander, s. John & Ruth, b. Aug. 5, 1772	1	173
David, s. Alexander & Mary, b. Feb. 13, 1757	1	82
Janet, d. Alexander & Mary, b. Jan. 5, 1753	1	82
John, s. Alexander & Mary, b. Mar. 3, 1746	1	82
John, Jr., m. Ruth **MILLER**, Oct. 24, 1771, by Rev. Alexander Miller, of Plainfield	1	173
Marg[a]ret, d. John & Ruth, b. Dec. 13, 1781	1	173
Mary, d. Alexander & Mary, b. Dec. 27, 1750	1	82
Robert, d. Alexander & Mary, b. Dec. 8, 1747	1	82
William, s. Alexander & Mary, b. Aug. 9, 1749	1	82
GATES, Abigail P., d. Caleb & Marcy, b. Aug. 3, 1800	2	18
Allen Moses, s. Ephraim & Elizabeth, b. Apr. 8, 1807	1	222
Charles, of Voluntown, m. Lucy Ann **PALMER**, of N. Stonington, July 5, 1840, by Rev. Charles S. Weaver	2	32
Dorcas, d. Caleb & Marcy, b. Mar. 7, 1795, in W. Greenwich	2	18
Elijah, s. Elijah & Anna, b. Aug. 14, 1794	1	197
Ephraim, m. Elizabeth **DOUGLASS**, Apr. 25, 1793, by Allen Campbell, J.P.	1	222
Ezra Plum[m]er, s. Ephraim & Elizabeth, b. Jan. 31, 1800	1	222
Grosvenor B., s. Simon & Mary, b. June 18, 1809	2	82
Jennet Douglass, d. Ephraim & Elizabeth, b. June 22, 1796	1	222
Jerusha, m. Thomas **KEIGWIN**, Dec. 26, 1765, by Samuel Coit, J.P.	1	111
Joseph Ephraim, s. Ephraim & Elizabeth, b. Nov. 13, 1804	1	222
Mary, d. Ephraim & Elizabeth, b. Mar. 3, 1794	1	222
Peggy, d. Elijah & Anna, b. Mar. 25, 1797	1	197
Phebe, d. Caleb & Marcy, b. Dec. 13, 1786, in W. Greenwich	2	18
Phebe, m. Samuel **GREEN**, Jr., Feb. 6, 1806, by Amos Crandel[l], Elder	1	189
Polly, d. Elijah & Anna, b. July 7, 1792	1	197
Prudence, d. Caleb & Marcy, b. Mar. 15, 1790, in W. Greenwich	2	18
Samuel, s. Caleb & Marcy, b. Feb. 25, 1797, in W. Greenwich	2	18
Samuel, Col., of Pensacola, Florida, m. Kezia **ROB[B]INS**, of Voluntown, July 11, 1830, by Rev. Levi Kneeland	2	85
Simeon, s. Caleb & Marcy, b. June 14, 1784, in W. Greenwich	2	18
Simon, m. Polly **BITGOOD**, Sept. 8, 1808, by Rev. Amos Crandal[l]	1	182
Susan C., of Voluntown, m. Abram **ELDREDGE**, of Dartmouth, Mass., Mar. 2, 1845, by Rev. Richard B. Eldredge	2	120
Thomas S., s. Simon & Polly, b. Sept. 24, 1820	1	182
William, s. Caleb & Marcy, b. Feb. 13, 1788, in W. Greenwich	2	18
William Douglass, s. Ephraim & Elizabeth, b. Aug. 31, 1802	1	222
GEER, GEERS, Amy, m. Adam **CHAPMAN**, Dec. 26, 1822, by Sterry Kinne, J.P.	2	52
Ezra P., m. Fanny M. **REYNOLDS**, Feb. 20, 1831, by Minor Rob[b]ins, J.P.	2	86

	Vol.	Page
GEER, GEERS, (cont.)		
Kezia, m. Manassah **MINOR**, Nov. 9, 1726	1	13
Laury, d. George, of N. Stonington, m. Lothrop **ROUSE**, s. Reuben, of Voluntown, Apr. 22, 1827, at Hopkinton, by Matthew Stillman, Elder	2	73
Nancy, m. Joseph H. **SMITH**, b. of Voluntown, Dec. 21, 1834, by Daniel Keigwin, J.P.	2	89
Phebe, of Voluntown, m. John A. **CRANDALL**, of Bristol, N.Y., Mar. 27, 1831, by Daniel Keigwin, J.P.	2	86
GIBSON, Elizabeth, d. John & Sarah, b. May 4, 1728	1	10
James, s. John & Sarah, b. Apr. 1, 1726	1	10
Jennet, d. John & Mary, b. May 22, 1732	1	55
Jennet, m. George **GORDON**, Dec. 20, 1748, by Rev. Samuel Dorrance	1	51
John, s. John & Mary, b. Feb. 12, 1736	1	55
Mary, d. John & Mary, b. Oct. 5, 1734	1	55
Susan[n]a, d. John & Mary, b. Apr. 25, 1738	1	55
GILMORE, GILLMORE, Ann, d. George & Ann, b. Apr. 20, 1771	1	139
George, s. George & Ann, b. Nov. 13, 1774	1	139
Peter A., d. June 25, 1856, ae 62; b. in England	3	66
Sarah, d. George & Ann, b. Sept. 30, 1772	1	139
GLASKO, Isaac, m. Mary E. **BILLINGS**, b. of Griswold, Feb. 2, 1844, by Rev. Charles S. Weaver	2	11
GOODELL, Miriam, m. Ira **KINNE**, Nov. 12, 1765, by James Cogswell, Clerk	1	117
GORDON, [see also **GORTON, JORDAN** and **JURDON**], Abby, of Voluntown, m. John **WILLCOX**, of W. Greenwich, R.I., Jan. 9, 1851, by Rev. Henry Forbush, of Plainfield	2	139
Agnes, d. Samuel & Elizabeth, b. Jan. 20, 1743	1	24
Agness, d. John & Jennet, b. Nov. 15, 1745	1	14
Agness, d. John & Jennet, b. Nov. 15, 1745	1	90
Agness, d. John & Mary Ann, b. Mar. 6, 1766	1	108
Agness, m. Nathan **DOW**, Sept. 16, 1787, by Rev. Micaiah Porter	1	190
Albert, s. Daniel & Sally, b. Jan. 1, 1810	1	257
Alexander, s. John & Janet, b. Feb. 6, 1732/3; d. Jan. 9, 1754	1	14
Alexander, s. Samuel & Elizabeth, b. Feb. 19, 1749	1	24
Allen C., s. Daniel & Sally, b. Sept. 17, 1817	1	257
Allen C., m. Roseannah S. **CAMPBELL**, b. of Voluntown, Sept. 22, 1845, by Rev. Jacob Allen	2	121
Ann Mercy, d. Gideon W. & Sophronia, b. May 1, 1831	2	76
Barbara L., of Voluntown, m. Daniel A. **GALLUP**, of Sterling, Oct. 1, 1843, by Rev. Jacob Allen	2	24
Barbara P., d. Daniel & Sally, b. June 6, 1825	1	257
Betsey, d. James & Rebecca, b. May 13, 1773	1	149
Betty, d. John & Janet, b. Oct. 15, 1736	1	14
Betty, d. John & Jennet, d. Mar. 31, 1774	1	90
Caroline, d. William S. & Eunice, b. Feb. 21, 1826	2	79
Charles Middleton, s. Gideon W. & Sophronia, b. Mar. 17, 1845	2	76
Daniel, s. John & Janet, b. Oct. 6, 1734	1	14
Daniel, s. John & Rosanna, b. Aug. 14, 1782	1	168
Daniel, m. Sally **CAMPBELL**, Apr. 19, 1804, by Allen Campbell, J.P.	1	257
Daniel, d. June 2, 1856, ae 75	3	66

VOLUNTOWN VITAL RECORDS 179

	Vol.	Page
GORDON, (cont.)		
Elizabeth, d. Samuel & Elizabeth, b. Mar. 6, 1747	1	24
Elizabeth, [w. Thomas], d. Nov. 7, 1822, ae 51 y.	2	26
Elizabeth S., of Voluntown, m. Nathan **BRIGGS**, of Sterling, Feb. 22, 1847, by Rev. Jacob Allen	2	124
Emily, d. William S. & Eunice, b. Mar. 30, 1828	2	79
Esther, d. Robert & Jane, b. Dec. 23, 1757	1	75
Eunice Elizabeth, d. William S. & Eunice, b. Aug. 10, 1821	2	79
Francis Henry, s. Gideon W. & Sophronia, b. May 16, 1837	2	76
George, s. Robert & Mary, b. Aug. 23, 1726	1	22
George, m. Jennet **GIBSON**, Dec. 20, 1748, by Rev. Samuel Dorrance	1	51
George, s. George & Jennet, b. May 10, 1755	1	51
George Wright, s. James & Rebecca, b. Sept. 11, 1776	1	149
Gideon W., d. Aug. 18, [1860], ae 67; b. in Sterling	3	70
Henry, s. George & Jenet, b. Apr. 12, 1765	1	51
Huldah M., d. Thomas & Elizabeth, b. Jan. 9, 1807	2	26
Isaac, s. George & Jennet, b. Nov. 2, 1772; d. May 16, 1774	1	51
Isabell, d. John & Jennet, b. Oct. 27, 1747	1	90
Isabel, m. John **DOUGLASS**, Feb. 1, 1770, by Robert Dixson, J.P.	1	119
James, s. John & Janet, b. Jan. 14, 1740/41	1	14
James, m. Rebecca **FRYERS**, July 28, 1768, by Rev. Ezra Styles	1	149
James, s. George & Jennet, b. Apr. 19, 1770	1	51
James, s. James & Rebecca, b. Oct. 4, 1774	1	149
Jain, d. Robert & Mary, b. Dec. 13, 1728	1	22
Jane, m. John **DIXSON**, Jr., Jan. 5, 1758, by Rev. Samuel Dorrance	1	96
Jane, m. John **DIXSON**, May 3, 1764, by Rev. Samuel Dorrance	1	185
Jain, d. George & Jennet, b. Apr. 1, 1767	1	51
Janet, w. John, d. Dec. 28, 1784	1	14
Jean, d. John & Janet, b. Sept. 11, 1738	1	14
Jean, d. Samuel & Elizabeth, b. Jan. 31, 1745	1	24
John, m. Janet **KERR**, Mar. 30, 1732, by Rev. Samuel Dorrance	1	14
John, s. Samuel & Elizabeth, b. Sept. 7, 1736	1	24
John, s. John & Jennet, b. Jan. 18, 1749/50	1	14
John, s. John & Jennet, b. Jan. 18, 1749/50	1	90
John, s. George & Jennet, b. Sept. 2, 1762	1	51
John, Jr., m. Mary Ann **DIXSON**, June 9, 1763, by Rev. Samuel Dorrance	1	108
John, Jr., m. Rosanna **PARKE**, Oct. 25, 1781, by Rev. Solomon Morgan	1	168
John, s. Robert & Nancy, b. Sept. 5, 1792	1	234
John, s. Daniel & Sally, b. June 9, 1805	1	257
John, of Sterling, m. Margaret **BRIGGS**, of Voluntown, Jan. 23, 1828, by Orin Fowler, V.D.M.	2	72
John Fryers, s. James & Rebecca, b. Aug. 5, 1771	1	149
Joseph, s. George & Jennet, b. Aug. 4, 1750	1	51
Mary, d. Robert & Mary, b. Oct. 6, 1733	1	22
Mary, d. John & Jennet, b. Feb. 4, 1752	1	14
Mary, d. John & Jennet, b. Feb. 4, 1752	1	90
Mary, d. Samuel & Elizabeth, b. Aug. 15, 1753	1	24
Mary, d. George & Jennet, b. Nov. 24, 1757	1	51
Mary, d. John & Mary Ann, b. July 14, 1774	1	108
Mary, d. Daniel & Sally, b. Sept. 14, 1812	1	257

180   BARBOUR COLLECTION

	Vol.	Page
GORDON, (cont.)		
Nancy, d. James & Rebecca, b. Apr. 26, 1778	1	149
Phebe M., d. Thomas & Elizabeth, b. Feb. 20, 1796	2	26
Phebe Mary, m. John **TILLINGHAST**, Sept. 11, 1817, by John Wylie, J.P.	2	23
Ralph, s. Daniel & Sally, b. June 26, 1807	1	257
Rebeckah, d. John & Jennet, b. Aug. 3, 1743	1	14
Rebeckah, d. John & Jennet, b. Aug. 3, 1743	1	90
Robert, s. Robert & Mary, b. Mar. 14, 1731	1	22
Robert, s. George & Jennet, b. Jan. 20, 1753; d. Jan. 7, 1755	1	51
Robert, m. Jane **KESSON**, Apr. 21, 1757, by Rev. Samuel Dorrance	1	75
Robert, s. John & Mary Ann, b. July 2, 1768	1	108
Rosannah, d. William S. & Eunice, b. Dec. 28, 1823	2	79
Ruth S., d. Thomas & Elizabeth, b. Oct. 1, 1793	2	26
Ruth S., m. James D. **ALEXANDER**, Feb. 16, 1823, by James Alexander, J.P.	2	52
Samuel, m. Elizabeth **KAR[R]**, Nov. 20, 1735, by Rev. Dorrance	1	24
Samuel, s. Samuel & Elizabeth, b. Oct. 19, 1740	1	24
Samuel, s. John & Mary Ann, b. Apr. 8, 1764	1	108
Samuel Stewart, s. John & Rosanna, b. Dec. 13, 1783	1	168
Sarah, d. John & Jennet, b. July 14, 1754	1	14
Sarah, d. John & Jennet, b. July 14, 1754; d. Aug. 16, 1769	1	90
Sarah, d. Apr. 8, 1863, ae 78	3	72
Sarah R., d. Daniel & Sally, b. July 18, 1820	1	257
Sarah R., of Voluntown, m. Carlton H. **WEBSTER**, of Norwich, Feb. 16, 1840, by Rev. Jacob Allen	2	105
Susan, d. Daniel & Sally, b. Aug. 28, 1815	1	257
Susan D., m. Winthrop **CAMPBELL**, Mar. 6, 1814, by Allen Campbell, J.P.	2	12
Susan Dorrance, d. John & Rosanna, b. June 3, 1789	1	168
Susanna, d. George & Jennet, b. Apr. 4, 1760	1	51
Thad[d]eus Cook, s. William S. & Eunice, b. Apr. 25, 1816	2	79
Thomas, s. Samuel & Elizabeth, b. Feb. 19, 1751	1	24
Thomas, s. John & Mary Ann, b. Dec. 9, 1771	1	108
Thomas, m. Elizabeth **STEWART**, Dec. 23, 1792, by Rev. Micaiah Porter	2	26
William, s. George & Jennet, b. Feb. 23, 1776	1	51
William S., s. John & Rosanna, b. June 24, 1792	1	168
William Stewart, s. William S. & Eunice, b. Nov. 4, 1818	2	79
-----, male, d. Oct. 1, [1860], ae 3 m.	3	70
-----, male, d. Mar. 7, 1862, ae 13 d.	3	71
GORE, Desire, w. Samuel, d. Sept. 11, 1772	1	24
Dorothy, m. Comfort **TITUS**, June 27, 1765, by Rev. Samuel Dorrance	1	93
Ebenezer, s. Samuel & Desire, b. Feb. 3, 1762	1	24
Elijah, m. Sarah **LITTLE**, Dec. 11, 1767	1	137
Elijah, s. Elijah & Sarah, b. Sept. 5, 1768, in Killingly	1	137
Elizabeth, d. Samuel & Desier, b. Dec. 15, 1738	1	25
Ezekiel, s. Elijah & Sarah, b. Nov. 20, 1770	1	137
Hannah, d. Samuel & Desier, b. June 26, 1741	1	25
John, s. Samuel & Desier, d. Aug. 15, 1773	1	25
Marg[a]ret, d. Elijah & Sarah, b. Feb. 10, 1773	1	137
Samuel, s. Elijah & Sarah, b. Apr. 10, 1775	1	137

VOLUNTOWN VITAL RECORDS 181

	Vol.	Page
GORTON, [see also GORDON], Anthony, s. James & Charity, b. Aug. 7, 1810, in Coventry, R.I.	2	28
Archibald, s. James & Charity, b. July 22, 1802	2	28
Benjamin, s. James & Charity, b. Sept. 2, 1797	2	28
Charity, d. James & Charity, b. Sept. 18, 1813, in Coventry, R.I.	2	28
Dolly L., d. James, Jr. & Dolly, b. Feb. 10, 1827	2	144
Edwin Gilbert, s. James, Jr. & Dolly, b. Mar. 30, 1833	2	144
Elizabeth, d. William & Wealthian, b. Mar. 1, 1785	1	141
Emily, d. Aug. 6, 1857, ae 18	3	67
Emily M., d. James, Jr. & Dolly, b. Nov. 12, 1836	2	144
Ira, s. James & Charity, b. Sept. 24, 1805	2	28
James, s. William & Welthian, b. July 26, 1771, in W. Greenwich, R.I.	1	141
James, m. Charity RATHBUN, Apr. 28, 1791, by Phinehas Kenyon, J.P.	2	28
James, s. James & Charity, b. Nov. 30, 1794	2	28
James M., s. James, Jr. & Cynthia, b. Apr. 24, 1817	2	144
Olive, m. Lot LARKHAM, Jr., Nov. 28, 1816, by Stafford Greene, Elder	2	14
Patience A., of Voluntown, m. Joseph S. PHILLIPS, of W. Greenwich, R.I., Feb. 20, 1848, by Rev. Charles S. Weaver	2	125
Phebe, d. William & Wealthian, b. Oct. 18, 1776	1	141
Sarah, d. William & Wealthian, b. Apr. 24, 1774	1	141
Sarah, m. Joseph TILLINGHAST, Sept. 14, 1788, by Rev. Micaiah Porter	1	221
Simeon R., s. James & Charity, b. Dec. 12, 1799	2	28
Tillinghast, s. William & Wealthian, b. Sept. 23, 1787	1	141
Wate, m. Benjamin WATERMAN, b. of Voluntown, Sept. 9, 1827, by Daniel Keigwin, J.P.	2	81
Welthen, d. James & Charity, b. May 3, 1792, in W. Greenwich	2	28
William, s. William & Wealthian, b. Dec. 21, 1782	1	141
William, s. James & Charity, b. Feb. 29, 1808	2	28
William, m. Waty UNDERWOOD, May 6, 1821, by Amos Treat, J.P.	2	39
GRANT, Rebecca, m. Elisha KINNEY, Feb. 11, 1816, by Nathan Pendleton, J.P.	2	31
GRAY, James, s. Robert & Ann, b. May 13, 1754	1	41
Jane, d. Robert & Ann, b. Oct. 3, 1751	1	41
John, s. Robert & Ann, b. Nov. 26, 1759 [sic]	1	41
Robert, s. Robert & Ann, b. Jan. 8, 1745	1	41
Thomas, s. Robert & Ann, b. Jan. 23, 1749	1	41
William, s. Robert & Ann, b. June 24, 1759 [sic]	1	41
GREEN, GREENE, Amelia M., d. Oct. 5, [1860], ae 1-1/2 m.	3	70
Benjamin, s. William & Elizabeth, b. Mar. 15, 1735	1	15
Caswell, m. Content REYNOLDS, Feb. 12, 1812, by Alexander Stewart, J.P.	1	247
Caswell, see also Cogswell		
Charles A., s. Charles B., farmer, ae 30, & Ruth M., ae 30, b. Aug. 23, 1849	3	24
Charles A., d. Dec. 1, 1863, ae 14	3	73
Charles Bradford, s. Cogswell & Tenty, b. Aug. 22, 1821	2	84
Cogswell, m. Tenty REYNOLDS, Jan. 12, 1810, at Preston, by Alexander Stewart, J.P.	2	84

GREEN, GREENE, (cont.)

	Vol.	Page
Cogswell, d. Oct. 13, 1864, ae 77	3	74
Cogswell, see also Caswell		
Daniel, d. Sept. 19, 1840	2	22
Diana, d. Samuel, Jr. & Phebe, b. Oct. 15, 1806	1	189
Elisha, d. May 8, [1859], ae 88; b. Griswold	3	69
Frederick, m. Dolly **ROUSE**, Dec. 9, 1828, by Sterry Kinne, J.P.	2	74
Freelove, d. Nov. 2, 1849, ae 80 y.; b. in Westerly, R.I.	3	61
Hannah, d. Samuel, b. Sept. 24, 1788	1	247
Hannah, m. Jonathan **BITGOOD**, Nov. 17, 1811, by Allen Campbell, J.P.	2	17
Harriet, d. Cogswell & Tenty, b. Apr. 29, 1818	2	84
John, m. Mehitable **TUCKERMAN**, Mar. 18, 1784, by Rev. Micaiah Porter	1	213
Jonathan, s. John & Mehitable, b. Nov. 4, 1786	1	213
Joseph, s. William & Elizabeth, b. July 16, 1729, in Preston	1	15
Judy, m. Eleazer **COLEGROVE**, Dec. 31, 1796, by Allen Campbell, J.P.	1	232
Julia, of Canterbury, m. Chauncey **LAMPHERE**, of N. Stonington, Nov. 29, 1837, by Benjamin Gallup, Jr., J.P.	2	101
Louis (Lois ?), m. Gideon **POPPLESTONE**, b. of Voluntown, Dec. 9, 1789, by Allen Campbell, J.P.	1	135
Lucy, d. Elisha Cheesebrough & Mahala, b. Dec. 4, 1803	1	247
Marcy, m. Joseph **BITGOOD**, July 28, 1799, by Amos Crandall, Elder	1	235
Marg[a]ret, m. William **VAUGHAN**, b. of Voluntown, Dec. 5, 1776, by Samuel Stewart, J.P.	1	137
Martha, m. Resolved **WILLCOX**, b. of Voluntown, Sept. 3, 1827, by Nathaniel Sheffield, Elder	2	72
Martin Malbrough, s. Cosgwell, b. Dec. 8, 1824	2	84
Mary, d. John & Mehetable, b. Aug. 10, 1789	1	213
Mary, m. Harvey **PHILLIPS**, b. of Plainfield, Apr. 8, 1838, by Daniel Keigwin, J.P.	2	107
Otis, m. Celinda **RATHBUN**, b. of Voluntown, Mar. [ ], 1846, by Rev. Charles S. Weaver	2	8
Prudence, d. Aug. 6, 1857, ae 65; b. in Westerly	3	67
Robert, s. John & Mehetable, b. Dec. 17, 1784	1	213
Ruth, d. Samuel, b. Apr. 5, 1791	1	247
Sally, m. Caleb **POTTER**, Nov. 16, 1797, by Allen Campbell, J.P.	1	219
Samuel, Jr., m. Phebe **GATES**, Feb. 6, 1806, by Amos Crandel[l], Elder	1	189
Samuel, of Voluntown, m. Mary A. **CLARK**, of Hopkinton, May 10, 1840, by Rev. Charles S. Weaver	2	29
Silence, m. Simeon **HOXSIE**, Sept. 3, 1807, by Allen Campbell, J.P.	1	230
Stephen, s. Samuel, b. June 18, 1785	1	247
Tenty, [w. Cogswell], d. June 18, 1828	?	84
Thomas A., s. Cogswell & Tenty, b. Jan. 27, 1813	2	84
William, s. William & Elizabeth, b. Sept. 23, 1732	1	15
William, s. Cogswell & Tenty, b. Jan. 25, 1816	2	84
W[illia]m H.C., d. Apr. 14, 1856, ae 25	3	66
GREENEL, David, d. Sept. 23, 1867, ae 66; b. in W. Canada	3	78
GRICE, Anne, m. Mark **EAMES**, May 24, 1750, by Rev. Nehemiah Barker	1	95

	Vol.	Page
GRIFFIN, Joseph, s. David & Marg[a]ret, b. Feb. 4, 1784	1	103
Susan, of Voluntown, m. John **BROWN**, of Griswold, Dec. 3, 1820, by Nathaniel Sheffield, Elder	2	38
GRIFFITH, Lydia, m. Menassah **BLOSS**, Dec. 19, 1782, by Rev. Micaiah Porter	1	71
Mary, m. Joseph **SWEET**, Jan. 27, 1774, by Robert Dixson, J.P.	1	141
GROSS, Salome, d. Feb. 16, 1866, ae 8; b. in R. Island	3	76
GROW, Julia, m. Orrin T. **KINNEY**, b. of Voluntown, Dec. 30, 1832, by Joseph Wylie, J.P.	2	94
HALEY, Leley, m. Thomas **RICHA[RD]SON**, Dec. 30, 1754, by Robert Dixson, J.P.	1	51
HALL, David, d. Oct. [1854?], ae 48	3	64
Esther, m. James **DORRANCE**, Jr., Apr. 19, 1781, by James Bradford, Esq.	1	172
Eunice, m. Thomas **WEAVER**, Jr., Dec. 11, 1793	1	223
Ichabod, of Groton, m. Rebecca **BURDICK**, of Voluntown, Mar. 24, 1844, by Rev. Charles S. Weaver	2	18
Leonard, d. Feb. 26, 1866, ae 66; b. in Plainfield	3	76
Mary, d. Feb. 18, 1860, ae 2 m.	3	69
Phebe, m. Benjamin **MARS**, Sept. 2, 1790, by Rev. Micaiah Porter	1	177
Thankfull, m. Ezekiel Gary [ ]	1	105
HAMBLEN, Lucy, d. Keziah, b. Mar. 16, 1763	1	68
Ruth, had s. Zerviah **COLLINS**, by James **COLLINS**, b. Jan. 8, 1762	1	68
Ruth, d. May 9, 1764	1	68
HAMILTON, Henry B., of Voluntown, m. Mary M. **POTTER**, of Griswold, June 28, 1847, by Rev. Charles S. Weaver	2	35
HANCOCK, Lucy, of Stonington, m. David **GALLUP**, of Plainfield, Mar. 30, 1815, by Jonathan Minor, Elder	2	96
Lydia C., m. Reuben **RANDALL**, Jr., Nov. 16, 1816, by Allen Campbell, J.P.	2	20
Sybel, m. Nathan **WILLCOX**, Feb. 25, 1821, by Sterry Kinney, J.P.	2	29
HANDY, John, m. Lucy **LAMPHIRE**, b. of Exeter, R.I., Nov. 14, 1849, by Gershom Palmer, Elder	2	137
John, ae 35, farmer, of R.I., m. Lucy **LAMPHERE**, ae 14, Dec. 15, 1849, by Elder Gershom Palmer	3	3
HANSEY, William Robinson, s. Andrew & Sarah, b. June 30, 1790	1	68
HARRINGTON, [see also **HERRINGTON**], Charity, d. Apr. 10, [1859], ae 38	3	69
Dianthia E., d. Mar. 15, 1865, ae 31	3	74
James C., ae 21, b. W. Greenwich, resid. of Plainfield, m. Charity **PHILLIPS**, ae 28, b. in Voluntown, resid. of Plainfield, May 7, 1849, by Rev. C. S. Weaver	3	2
-----, female, d. Mar. 15, 1865, ae 1 hour	3	75
HARRIS, HARES, HARRES, Brigget, m. Andrew **EL[L]IOT[T]**, Mar. 25, 1767, by Jeremiah Kinne, J.P.	1	65
Harvey, d. Mar. 14, 1865, ae 32; b. in Sterling; soldier	3	74
Martha, m. Ebenezer **DOW**, Dec. 29, 1720	1	1
Martha, m. Ebenezer **DOW**, Dec. 29, 1720, by Rev. Joseph Coit	1	14
Mary, [of Voluntown], m. Job **RATHBON**, of N. Kingstown, R.I., Sept. 1, 1737, by Rev. Samuel Dorrance	1	19
Reuben, d. May 8, 1867, ae 68; b. in Stonington	3	78
William P., of Groton, m. Maria **CAMPBELL**, of Voluntown, Mar.		

	Vol.	Page
HARRIS, HARES, HARRES, (cont.)		
18, 1846, by Rev. Jacob Allen	2	120
HART, Alice, m. Nathan B. **HOXSIE**, Nov. 2, 1840, by Rev. Edmund A. Standish. Witness: Nelson Gallup	2	112
HARWOOD, Polly, ae 45, b. Sterling, Ct., resid. of Voluntown, m. Alfred **WHIPPLE**, ae 50, b. Scituate, R.I., resid. of Voluntown, ae 50, b. Scituate, R.I., resid. of Voluntown, Sept. 2, 1849, by Rev. Cha[rle]s S. Weaver	3	2
HASTON, [see also **HUSTON**], Agness, d. William & Agness, b. Apr. 3, 1752	1	97
Elizabeth, m. Robert **DIXSON**, Jan. 29, 1729/30, by Rev. Samuel Dorrance	1	29
Elizabeth, d. William & Agnes, b. May 24, 1754	1	97
John, s. William & Agness, b. July 10, 1746	1	97
Joseph, s. William & Agness, b. May 1, 1759	1	97
Marg[a]ret, d. William & Agness, b. May 31, 1761	1	97
Robert, s. William & Agness, b. Feb. 4, 1750	1	97
Samuel, s. William & Agness, b. Sept. 28, 1763	1	97
Thomas, s. William & Agness, b. Mar. 12, 1767	1	97
William, m. Agnes **HINDMAN**, May 28, 1745, by Rev. Samuel Dorrance	1	97
William, s. William & Agness, b. Dec. 28, 1756	1	97
HATCH, Abby, d. Sept. 24, 1854, ae 2; b. in R. Island	3	64
George, m. Mary L. **HOWE**, b. of Canterbury, Oct. 10, 1842, by Rev. Jacob Allen	2	108
Penelope, d. Sept. 1, 1854, ae 3; b. in R. Island	3	65
-----, male, d. July 30, 1864, stillborn	3	74
HAVENS, Martha, d. Robert & Rebecca, b. Jan. 10, 1724/5	1	5
Robert, s. Robert & Rebecca, b. May 20, 1721	1	5
Ruth, d. Robert & Rebecca, b. June 29, 1717	1	5
Thomas, s. Robert & Rebecca, b. May 4, 1723	1	5
HAWKINS, John, d. May 11, 1848, ae 1; b. in Hopkinton, R.I.	3	59
Lewis N., of Voluntown, m. Eliza A. **SWEET**, of Griswold, Feb. 29, 1864, by Thomas L. Shipman, of Jewett City	2	106
Sarah, d. William, ae 33, & Sally, ae 34, b. Feb. 1, 1849	3	22
William, m. Sally **WATSON**, May 30, 1837, by Kinne Gallup, J.P.	2	83
HAYWARD, Louisa, d. Sept. 15, 1857, ae 58	3	68
HAZARD, Thomas C., d. Apr. 14, 1850, ae 81 y.; b. in Kingston	3	61
HENRY, Elizabeth, m. James **MACGONEGALL**, Jr., Oct. 27, 1742, by Rev. Cotton, of Providence	1	39
HERD, [see under **HURD**]		
HERRICK, Freelove, m. Jonathan **PALMER**, May 5, 1749, by Joseph Palmer, J.P.	1	71
Sally B., d. June 14, 1854, ae 36; b. in Griswold	3	65
HERRINGTON, HERINGTON, [see also **HARRINGTON**], Isa[a]c, s. Isa[a]c & Jemimy, b. May 8, 1722	1	6
Jemime, d. Isa[a]c & Jemimy, b. Dec. 29, 1715	1	6
Mary, m. Benajah **BUNDY**, the last day of Mar. 1754, by Josiah Bennet[t], Elder, of Scituate	1	46
Samuel, s. Isa[a]c & Jemimy, b. Sept. 4, 1720	1	6
Sarah, d. Isa[a]c & Jemimy, b. June 10, 1719	1	6
Timothy, s. Isa[a]c & Jemimy, b. Dec. 27, 1717	1	6
HEWIT[T], Arthur, s. Henery & Sarah, b. Jan. 2, 1752	1	90

	Vol.	Page
HEWIT[T], (cont.)		
Hannah, m. James **KINNE**, Jr., Jan. 15, 1761, by Rev. Joseph Fish	1	106
Henry, m. Sarah **KINNE**, Jan. 23, 1751	1	90
Sabra, d. Henery & Sarah, b. Mar. 10, 1754	1	90
Sabra, m. Joseph **RANDALL**, Jr., Apr. 20, 1775	1	138
Serrey, s. Henery & Sarah, b. Apr. 7, 1756	1	90
HILL, Betsey, d. Crommel[l] & Jenne, b. Sept. 12, 1788	1	170
Elizabeth, m. Ruebin **RANDALL**, July 6, 1789, by Joshua Babcock, J.P.	1	220
Hannah, m. Lewis Peck **JAMES**, b. of Voluntown, May 30, 1802, by Amos Crandall, Elder	1	245
James, s. Crommel[l] & Jenne, b. July 14, 1790	1	170
John, s. John & Olive, b. Apr. 21, 1790	1	218
Joseph, s. Parker & Elizabeth, b. Dec. 11, 1781	1	158
Phebe, d. Jonathan & Phebe, b. Jan. 31, 1779	1	158
Polly, d. Daniel & Sarah, b. Aug. 21, 1782	1	148
Roba, d. Jonathan & Phebe, b. July 27, 1777	1	158
Robert, s. Crommell & Jenne, b. Apr. 9, 1792	1	170
Smith, s. John & Olive, b. Dec. 29, 1792	1	218
HILLIARD, Jonathan, m. Sarah **STEWART**, Apr. 19, 1819, by James Alexander, J.P.	2	29
Sarah (**STEWART**), [w. Jonathan], d. Jan. 10, 1820, ae 32 y.	2	29
Temperance, w. Jonathan, Sr., d. Sept. 30, 1822, ae 87 y.	2	29
HINCKLEY, Orrin, of Griswold, m. Catharine B. **CHAPMAN**, of Voluntown, Feb. 10, 1845, by Rev. Jacob Allen	2	120
HINDMAN, Agnes, m. William **HASTON**, May 28, 1745, by Rev. Samuel Dorrance	1	97
Margaret, m. James **MON[T]GUM[E]RY**, Mar. 4, 1756, by Robert Dixson, Esq.	1	59
HODGE, Elijah, s. Elijah & Sarah, b. May 4, 1774	1	64
Sarah, m. John **LOWDEN**, Aug. 15, 1776, by Rev. George Gilmore	1	110
HOLLAND, Daniel, d. June 28, 1849, ae 37; b. in R.I.	3	60
HOLLY, Mary, m. James **WYLIE**, 3d, Jan. 29, 1778, by Rev. Levi Hart	1	132
HOLMAN, Nelson B., m. Mary A. **BROWN**, of N. Stonington, Apr. 6, 1828, by Benjamin Gallup, J.P.	2	73
HOLMES, George, m. Sarah **PALMER**, b. of Griswold, Nov. 24, 1848, by Rev. Charles S. Weaver	3	1
HOPKINS, Elisha, m. Welthian **TILLINGHAST**, Mar. 30, 1820, by James Alexander, J.P.	2	29
Jennet, d. Robert & Agness, b. June 26, 1743; d. Apr. 1, 1746	1	88
Jennet, d. Robert & Agness, b. Apr. 9, 1746	1	88
Judith, d. Robert & Agness, b. Sept. 7, 1749	1	88
Martha, d. Robert & Agness, b. July 8, 1755	1	88
Mary, d. Robert & Agness, b. May 21, 1738	1	88
Nathaniel, of Charlestown, R.I., m. Joanna **NEWKEY**, of Voluntown, Apr. 13, 1851, by Elisha Potter, J.P.	2	124
Nathaniel, ae 30, farmer, b. in Charlestown, R.I., res. of Voluntown, m. Joanna **NEWKEY**, ae 24, of Voluntown, people of color, Apr. 13, 1851, by Elisha Potter, Esq.	3	3
Robert, s. Robert & Agness, b. May 23, 1752	1	88
Samuel, s. Robert & Agness, b. Aug. 26, 1740	1	88
HOUGHTON, John, m. Philena **MAIN**, May 31, 1827, by Sterry Kinne, J.P.	2	71

	Vol.	Page
HOWARD, Joseph H., d. July 12, 1863, ae 36; b. in Mass.	3	72
Nancy, d. Sept. 5, 1866, ae 55; b. in Mansfield, Mass.	3	76
HOWE, Mary L., m. George **HATCH**, b. of Canterbury, Oct. 10, 1842, by Rev. Jacob Allen	2	108
Sarah Ann, of Voluntown, m. William **PHILLIPS**, of Plainfield, July 13, 1845, by Rev. Charles E. Weaver	2	5
HOXSIE, HOXIE, Arnold Clark, s. Wells & Lois, b. Mar. 6, 1802	1	243
Artemas, s. Christopher & Huldah, b. Aug. 6, 1805	1	236
Charloty, d. Christopher & Huldah, b. Mar. 9, 1817	1	236
Cyrena, d. Christopher & Huldah, b. Feb. 2, 1808	1	236
Huldah, d. Christopher & Huldah, b. May 22, 1811	1	236
John, Jr., of Exeter, R.I., m. Ann **BARBER**, of Richmond, R.I., Oct. 20, 1850, by Gershom Palmer, Elder	2	137
Joseph, s. Christopher & Huldah, b. Nov. 30, 1809	1	236
Lydia A., d. Sept. 18, 1855, ae 2-1/2; b. in Griswold	3	66
Mary, d. Christopher & Huldah, b. July 2, 1815	1	236
Nathan B., m. Alice **HART**, Nov. 2, 1840, by Rev. Edmund A. Standish. Witness: Nelson Gallup	2	112
Olive, d. Christopher & Huldah, b. Jan. 15, 1804	1	236
Phebe J. Tillinghast, d. Christopher & Huldah, b. July 2, 1813	1	236
Simeon, m. Silence **GREEN**, Sept. 3, 1807, by Allen Campbell, J.P.	1	230
Wells, m. Lois **CLARK**, Aug. 27, 1801, by Amos Crandall, Elder	1	243
-----, child of Joseph, farmer, & Mary, b. Apr. 31, 1850	3	25
HUGHES, Sarah, d. Mar. 2, 1860, ae 2 y.; b. in Sterling	3	69
HULL, Thomas H., m. Freelove E. **PALMER**, b. of N. Stonington, Feb. 24, 1840, by Rev. Cyrus Miner	2	111
HUNTER, Agness, d. Robert & Jane, b. Feb. 4, 1746	1	53
Andrew, s. Robert & Jane, b. Mar. 13, 1748	1	53
Andrew, m. Agness **WYLIE**, Oct. 7, 1773	1	128
Esther, d. Robert & Jane, b. June 16, 1759	1	53
George, s. John & Rebeckah, b. Dec. 3, 1753	1	88
Hannah, d. William & Mary, b. Oct. 5, 1753	1	77
Jeane (Jane), d. John & Dinah, b. June 5, 1779; d. June 16, 1806	1	155
John, m. Rebecca **CAMPBELL**, June 13, 1751, by Rev. Dorrance	1	88
John, s. John & Rebeckah, b. Sept. 25, 1755	1	88
John, s. Robert & Jane, b. Sept. 27, 1756	1	53
John, m. Dinah **CAMPBELL**, Mar. 10, 1778, by Samuel Stewart, J.P.	1	155
John, m. Polly **DOUGLASS**, b. of Voluntown, June 7, 1826, by Nathaniel Sheffield, Elder; d. Nov. 2, 1826	2	69
Larkin, s. William & Mary, b. Nov. 22, 1755	1	77
Lucretia, d. William & Mary, b. Dec. 15, 1757	1	77
Marg[a]ret, d. Robert & Jane, b. Mar. 28, 1752	1	53
Mary, m. Gawen* **MILLER**, Jan. 8, 1741, by Rev. Samuel Dorrance (*Garven?)	1	64
Mary, d. William & Mary, b. Mar. 6, 1751	1	77
Mary, d. John & Rebeckah, b. July 1, 1752	1	88
Robert, m. Jane **WYLIE**, Dec. 9, 1742, by Rev. Dorrance	1	53
Robert, s. Robert & Jane, b. Nov. 23, 1754	1	53
Samuel, s. Robert & Jane, b. Feb. 11, 1750	1	53
Sarah, d. Andrew & Agness, b. Oct. 9, 1774	1	128
Thankfull, d. William & Mary, b. Apr. 21, 1760	1	77
HURD, HEARD, HERD, Dorcus, m. Incom **POTTER**, Jan. 8, 1824, by		

	Vol.	Page
HURD, HEARD, HERD, (cont.)		
James Alexander, J.P.	2	54
Hannah, d. Josiah & Phebe, b. Jan. 16, 1763	1	108
Jacob, s. Jacob & Amey, b. Oct. 18, 1757	1	35
Joseph, s. Josiah & Phebe, b. May 6, 1768	1	108
Josiah, s. Jacob & Amy, b. Aug. 19, 1754	1	35
Martha, d. Josiah & Phebe, b. Feb. 13, 1771	1	108
Nancy, m. Gardiner **SUL[L]IVAN**, Aug. 25, 1821, by Amos Treat, J.P.	2	39
Olive, m. Albert L. **LEWIS**, Apr. 1, 1827, by Sterry Kinne, J.P.	2	71
Phebe, d. Josiah & Phebe, b. Sept. 4, 1761	1	108
Rachel, d. Josiah & Phebe, b. Dec. 6, 1769	1	108
Rhoda, d. Josiah & Phebe, b. Feb. 20, 1766	1	108
Robert, s. Jacob & Amy, b. Apr. 2, 1756	1	35
Sarah, d. Jacob & Amy, b. Apr. 30, 1753	1	35
William, s. Josiah & Phebe, b. Mar. 12, 1759	1	108
HURLBUTT, [Anna], m. David **DORRANCE**, Feb. 2, 1786, by Rev. James Cogswell	1	189
HUSTON, [see also **HASTON**], Alice, d. Joseph & Elizabeth, b. Oct. 3, 1786	1	170
Elizabeth, m. Joseph **WYLIE**, July 30, 1801, by Allen Campbell, J.P.	1	123
John, m. Jennet **DOUGLASS**, Feb. 14, 1788, by Rev. Micaiah Porter	1	195
Joseph, m. Elizabeth **CAMPBELL**, Apr. 1, 1784, by Rev. Micaiah Porter	1	170
Joseph, d. Apr. 4, 1788	1	170
Robert, m. Sarah **KINNE**, Feb. 23, 1775, by Rev. Levi Hart	1	148
Robert, s. Robert & Sarah, b. Nov. 23, 1775, in Preston	1	148
Robert, m. Sarah **CAMPBELL**, Apr. 2, 1778, by Rev. Solomon Morgan	1	148
Sarah, w. Robert, d. Mar. 15, 1776	1	148
William, m. Elizabeth **CAMPBELL**, Oct. 4, 1781, by Rev. Solomon Morgan	1	156
William, s. Joseph & Elizabeth, b. Jan. 10, 1785; d. Dec. 21, 1785	1	170
HUTCHINS, HUCHENS, Amy, m. Samuel **KINNE**, May 8, 1776, by Jeremiah Kinne, Esq.	1	136
Noah, s. Benjamin & Judith, b. Mar. 27, 1758	1	82
HUTCHINSON, Burton, s. Elisha & Mary, b. May 9, 1786	1	144
Elisha, s. Elisha & Mercy, b. July 6, 1779	1	144
John, s. Elisha & Mercy, b. June 12, 1781	1	144
Lydia, m. John **KEIGWIN**, Jr., Oct. 27, 1768, by Robert Dixson, J.P.	1	113
Mary, m. Benjamin **DOW**, May 17, 1758, by Rev. Hezekiah Lord	1	96
Nathan Dow, s. Elisha & Mercy, b. Aug. 15, 1784	1	144
Sally, m. William **WEAVER**, Sept. 26, 1822, by Sterry Kinne, J.P.	2	51
Susannah, m. Ebenezer **DOW**, Jr., July 31, 1761, by Samuel Coit, J.P.	1	71
Susanna, d. Elisha & Mercy, b. Oct. 10, 1777	1	144
JACKSON, JACSON, Agness, d. William & Agness, b. June 20, 1751	1	77
Alexander, s. Elias & Nancy, b. Feb. 6, 1785, in New Concord	1	244
An[n], d. Robert & Mary, b. May 15, 1715	1	11
Ann, m. David **CARR**, Apr. 25, 1741, by Rev. Samuel Dorrance	1	42
Anna, d. Theophilus & Else, b. Nov. 21, 1750	1	43

188   BARBOUR COLLECTION

	Vol.	Page
JACKSON, JACSON, (cont.)		
Archibald, s. Robert & Sarah, b. Apr. 24, 1758	1	59
Archibald, s. Elias & Nancy, b. Oct. 24, 1795	1	244
Asher, s. Elias & Nancy, b. Mar. 28, 1800	1	244
Betsey, d. Elias & Nancy, b. Mar. 27, 1783, in New Concord	1	244
Content, now residing in Hopkinton, m. Arthur **FENNER**, of Hopkinton, R.I., June 13, 1830, by Nathaniel Sheffield, Elder	2	85
Elies, s. Robert & Sarah, b. Dec. 31, 1753	1	87
Elias, m. Agness **ALEXANDER**, Sept. 14, 1780, by Rev. Solomon Morgan	1	153
Elias, s. Elias & Nancy, b. Jan. 26, 1802	1	244
Elizabeth, d. Robert & Sarah, b. Dec. 30, 1751	1	59
Eunice, d. Robert & Sarah, b. Sept. 22, 1748	1	59
Freelove, reputed d. Archibald **JACKSON** & Mary **BATES**, b. June 8, 1788	1	206
Freelove, of Voluntown, m. Gideon **TANNER**, of Hopkinton, Apr. 1, 1804, by Joseph **WYLIE**, J.P.	2	45
Hillence, s. William & Agness, b. May 2, 1749	1	77
Hope, d. Robert & Sarah, b. Dec. 24, 1760	1	59
Jacob, s. Theophilus & Else, b. Apr. 6, 1755	1	43
James, s. William & Agness, b. Apr. 1, 1758	1	77
Lorinda, d. Elias & Nancy, b. Aug. 24, 1797	1	244
Martha, twin with Sarah, d. William & Agness, b. Nov. 20, 1753	1	77
Mary, d. William & Agness, b. Apr. 22, 1747	1	77
Mary, d. Robert & Sarah, b. Aug. 1, 1756	1	87
Milton, s. Elias & Nancy, b. Oct. 31, 1788	1	244
Nancy, d. Elias & Nancy, b. Jan. 31, 1793	1	244
Olive, d. Theophilus & Else, b. Feb. 13, 1749	1	43
Olive, d. Elias & Nancy, b. Mar. 6, 1787	1	244
Polly, d. Elias & Nancy, b. Oct. 14, 1790	1	244
Robert, s. Robert & Mary, b. Jan. 20, 1723/4	1	11
Robert, m. Sarah **CAMPBELL**, Nov. 13, 1746, by Rev. Samuel Dorrance	1	59
Robert, m. Sarah **CAMPBELL**, Nov. 13, 1746, by Rev. Samuel Dorrance	1	87
Robert, s. William & Agness, b. Apr. 5, 1760	1	77
Robert, s. Robert & Sarah, b. Aug. 22, 1762	1	59
Robert, m. Marg[a]ret **DOUGLASS**, Apr. 16, 1772, by Samuel Stewart, J.P.	1	87
Sally, d. Elias & Nancy, b. Oct. 28, 1781, in New Concord	1	244
Samuel, s. Robert & Mary, b. May 17, 1719	1	11
Sarah, twin with Martha, d. William & Agness, b. Nov. 20, 1753	1	77
Theophilus, s. Robert & Mary, b. June 17, 1722	1	11
Theophilus, m. Else **STRANEHAN**, Oct. 9, 1746, by Rev. Samuel Dorrance	1	43
Theophilus, s. Theophilus & Else, b. May 2, 1753	1	43
William, s. Robert & Mary, b. Sept. 17, 1720	1	11
William, m. Agness **DIXSON**, Dec. 25, 1744, by Rev. Samuel Dorrance	1	77
William, s. William & Agness, b. Dec. 1, 1755	1	77
JACQUAYS, JAQUES, JAQUAYS, Abby, m. James W. **BROMLEY**, b. of Griswold, June 29, 1854, by Samuel Gates, J.P.	2	148
Betsey Samantha, d. Hazzard & Betsey, b. Mar. 4, 1826	2	67

VOLUNTOWN VITAL RECORDS

	Vol.	Page
JACQUAYS, JAQUES, JAQUAYS, (cont.)		
Hazzard, m. Betsey **TANNER**, Oct. 21, 1824, by Amos Treat, J.P.	2	56
Sary Ann, d. Hazzard & Betsey, b. Mar. 3, 1831	2	67
JAMES, Amanzer P., s. Joseph S. & Esther, b. July 2, 1825; d. Jan. 30, 1833, ae 7 y. 5 m. 28 d.	2	126
Bridget Julia, d. Charles T. & Bridget, b. Oct. 21, 1849	2	130
Charles D., s. Charles T. & Bridget, b. June 19, 1851	2	130
Charles T., s. Joseph S. & Esther, b. Apr. 16, 1822	2	126
Clark B., d. Dec. 5, 1854, ae 20	3	65
Elizabeth, m. Benjamin **WILLIAMS**, Feb. 25, 1779, by John Dixson, J.P.	1	138
Emma A., d. Clark, ae 41, & Mary Jane, ae 39, b. Aug. 2, 1848	3	21
Frances, d. Nov. 14, 1854, ae 4	3	65
Frances L., d. Sept. 7, 1849, ae 4 y.	3	61
Frances L., d. Clarke, farmer, ae 42, & Mary, ae 40, b. July 29, 1850	3	24
Hannah, ae 21, b. W. Greenwich, resid. of Voluntown, m. George W. **SWAN**, ae 20, b. N. Stonington, resid. of Voluntown, June 4, 1849, by Charles S. Weaver	3	1
Joseph D., s. Joseph S. & Esther, b. July 20, 1834	2	126
Joseph S., s. Silas & Sabra, b. Jan. 27, 1804	1	245
Joseph S., s. Joseph S. & Esther, b. Dec. 29, 1827; d. Jan. 25, 1833, ae 5 y. 24 d.	2	126
Julia A., d. Joseph S. & Esther, b. Sept. 28, 1823	2	126
Lewis Peck, m. Hannah **HILL**, b. of Voluntown, May 30, 1802, by Amos Crandall, Elder	1	245
Mary E., d. Nov. 26, 1854, ae 2	3	65
Mary Esther, d. Silas A. & Esther Ann, b. Oct. 21, 1851	2	146
Silas A., s. Joseph S. & Esther, b. Oct. 9, 1831	2	126
Silas A., ae 17, m. Esther Ann **PALMER**, ae 15, b. of Voluntown, Jan. 9, 1848, by Gershom Palmer	3	1
Silas A., d. Sept. 23, 1865, ae 34	3	75
JAMESON, JEMMASON, Agness, d. Robert & Nancy, b. Apr. 25, 1766	1	66
Alexander, s. Robert & Nancy, b. Sept. 10, 1764	1	66
Ann, d. Robert & Nancy, b. Apr. 26, 1752	1	66
Benjamin, s. Robert & Nancy, b. Aug. 15, 1768	1	66
Elizabeth, d. Robert & Nancy, b. Aug. 5, 1757	1	66
Hannah, d. Robert & Nancy, b. Dec. 29, 1761	1	66
Hester, d. John & Roseanah, b. May 29, 1726	1	10
John, s. Robert & Nancy, b. June 17, 1749	1	66
Joseph, s. Robert & Nancy, b. May 23, 1763	1	66
Mary, d. Robert & Nancy, b. Mar. 12, 1751	1	66
Robert, s. Robert & Nancy, b. June 10, 1755	1	66
Rosannah, d. Robert & Nancy, b. Dec. 24, 1758	1	66
Samuel, s. Robert & Nancy, b. Mar. 13, 1760	1	66
Sarah, m. Joseph **PARKE**, May 27, 1735, by Rev. Samuel Dorrance	1	70
William, s. Robert & Nancy, b. Dec. 19, 1753	1	66
JAQUES, [see under **JACQUAYS**]		
JEFFORDS, Ann, [d. Joshua & Ann], b. Jan. 20, 1715	1	2
Hannah, [d. Joshua & Ann], b. Mar. 10, 1725	1	2
Margary, [d. Joshua & Ann], b. July 10, 1708	1	2
Mary, d. Joshua & Ann, b. May 18, 1718	1	2
Mehitable, d. Joshua & Ann, b. July 10, 1720	1	2
Pashance, [d. Joshua & Ann], b. Oct. 23, 1713	1	2

BARBOUR COLLECTION

	Vol.	Page
JEFFORDS, (cont.)		
Penellope, [d. Joshua & Ann], b. Sept. 28, 1722	1	2
Sarah, [d. Joshua & Ann], b. June 10, 1727	1	2
William, [s. Joshua & Ann], b. Dec. 7, 1711	1	2
JENCKES, Sarah, d. Dec. 15, 1866, ae 33; b. in Killingly	3	76
Winfield S., d. Oct. 12, 1866, ae 5 m.	3	76
JONES, Aaron, s. Moses & Dorithy, b. Nov. 14, 1757	1	94
Betsey, m. William **DOUGLASS**, Apr. 15, 1821, by Or[r]in Fowler, V.D.M.	1	191
Lydia, m. Obadiah **RHOADES**, Dec. 30, 1773, by Rev. Witt	1	127
JORDAN, JURDON, [see also **GORDON**], Mary, d. Oct. 22, 1864, ae 50; b. in R. Island	3	74
Rebecca, m. John **NEY**, May [ ], 1802, by Allen Campbell, J.P.	1	186
KALSON, KELSON, Allice, m. Deliverance **SPAULDING**, Apr. 15, 1756, by Rev. Samuel Dorrance	1	16
Elizabeth, d. John & Mary, b. Feb. 8, 1735	1	16
Jean, d. John & Mary, b. Jan. 27, 1737	1	16
John, m. Mary **DORRANCE**, Oct. 14, 1731, by Rev. Samuel Dorrance	1	16
John, s. John & Mary, b. June 23, 1739	1	16
Mary, d. John & Mary, b. Mar. 17, 1747	1	16
Samuel, s. John & Mary, b. June 14, 1733; d. [ ]	1	16
Samuel, s. John & Mary, b. Jan. 26, 1745	1	16
Sarah, d. John & Mary, b. Apr. 24, 1749	1	16
William, s. John & Mary, b. Sept. 23, 1741	1	16
KARR, [see under **CARR**]		
KASSON, [see also **KESSON**], Adam, s. Thomas & Elce, b. Nov. 30, 1743	1	48
Elce, d. Thomas & Elce, b. May 22, 1747	1	48
Elizabeth, d. Thomas & Elce, b. Jan. 29, 1749/50	1	48
Sarah, d. Thomas, d. May 10, 1744	1	48
Thomas, d. Mar. 1750	1	48
KEE, Jerusha, m. Alexander **WILLIAMS**, Feb. 18, 1783, by Rev. Eliphalet Write	1	171
KEIGWIN, Amos, s. John & Deborah, b. June 10, 1749	1	13
Amos, s. John, Jr. & Lydia, b. Apr. 12, 1774	1	113
Amos, m. Thankfull **GARDNER**, Nov. 30, 1780, by John Maxson, J.P.	1	154
Amos T., of Griswold, m. Alice K. **LARKHAM**, of Voluntown, Dec. 14, 1828, by Nathaniel Sheffield, Elder	2	74
Amos Treat, s. Ephraim & Eunice, b. Mar. 22, 1807	1	195
Ann, d. Richard & Sarah, b. Apr. 10, 1740	1	21
Anna, d. Jan. 7, 1821	2	103
Anne, d. Nicholas & Huldah, b. Oct. 27, 1765	1	100
Barton C., s. Daniel & Celinda, b. Apr. 22, 1823	2	103
Betsey, s. James & Sarah, b. Apr. 30, 1775	1	102
Betsey, d. Ephraim & Eunice, b. July 28, 1794, in Preston	1	195
Damon D., d. May 8, [1860], ae 4 d.	3	69
Daniel, s. Nicholas & Huldah, b. Jan. 29, 1774	1	100
Daniel, m. Anna **CRANDALL**, b. of Voluntown, Sept. 24, 1801, by Allen Campbell, J.P.	2	103
Daniel A., s. Daniel & Anna, b. July 19, 1811	2	103
Daniel Ayres, of Voluntown, m. Eunice **FRINK**, of Norwich, Feb.		

	Vol.	Page
KEIGWIN, (cont.)		
12, 1838, by Daniel Keigwin, J.P.	2	62
Daniel Kennedy, s. Ephraim & Eunice, b. June 12, 1790	1	195
Deborah, d. John & Deborah, b. Apr. 4, 1729	1	13
Deborah, d. Thomas & Jerusha, b. Mar. 8, 1775	1	111
Deborah, w. Lieut. John, d. July 20, 1791, ae 83 y.	1	12
Elias, s. Thomas & Jerusha, b. Feb. 22, 1773	1	111
Elisha, s. John & Lydia, b. Aug. 17, 1776	1	113
Elizabeth, d. John & Deborah, b. Aug. 19, 1746	1	13
Elisabeth, d. Thomas & Jerusha, b. Oct. 7, 1766	1	111
Elizabeth, m. Elisha **TUCKER**, Oct. 29, 1786, by Rev. Micaiah Porter	1	149
Ephraim, s. James & Sarah, b. Sept. 26, 1766	1	102
Ephraim, m. Eunice **KENNEDY**, Jan. 1, 1789, by Rev. Micaiah Porter	1	195
Ephraim, s. Ephraim & Eunice, b. June 21, 1800, in Preston	1	195
Erastus C., s. Daniel & Anna, b. Mar. 17, 1814	2	103
Eunice, d. Ephraim & Eunice, b. Nov. 1, 1802, in Preston	1	195
Ezra, s. James & Sarah, b. Aug. 7, 1769	1	102
Ezra Whip[p]le, s. Ephraim & Eunice, b. Nov. 14, 1810	1	195
Hannah, d. Richard & Sarah, b. May 25, 1742	1	21
Hannah R., d. Daniel & Anna, b. Feb. 21, 1817; d. Aug. 17, 1820	2	103
Harriet, d. Ephraim & Eunice, b. Mar. 27, 1805	1	195
James, s. John & Deborah, b. Apr. 15, 1736	1	13
James, m. Sarah **MULKIN**, May 1, 1763, by Samuel Coit, J.P.	1	102
James, s. Ephraim & Eunice, b. May 17, 1796, in Preston	1	195
Jerusha, d. Thomas & Jerusha, b. Apr. 19, 1779	1	111
John, m. Deborah **PARKE**, Aug. 15, 1728; d. July 8, 1775	1	13
John, s. John & Deborah, b. Apr. 26, 1731	1	13
John, s. John & Deborah, d. July 26, 1740	1	13
John, s. John & Deborah, b. July 28, 1742	1	13
John, s. Thomas & Jerusha, b. Oct. 17, 1768	1	111
John, Jr., m. Lydia **HUTCHINSON**, Oct. 27, 1768, by Robert Dixson, J.P.	1	113
John, Lieut., d. July 8, 1775	1	12
John, s. James & Sarah, b. May 24, 1778	1	103
Joseph, s. Nicholas & Huldah, b. Nov. 14, 1763	1	100
Lucy A., d. Daniel & Anna, b. Sept. 19, 1819; d. Oct. [ ], 1821	2	103
Marg[a]ret, d. Richard & Sarah, b. June 21, 1747	1	21
Mary, d. Richard & Sarah, b. Apr. 13, 1744	1	21
Mehetabell, d. Thomas & Jerusha, b. Mar. 9. 1777	1	111
Molly, d. John & Lydia, b. Aug. 14, 1778	1	113
Nathan, s. John & Deborah, b. June 4, 1740	1	13
Nicholas, s. Richard & Sarah, b. Sept. 18, 1736	1	21
Nicholas, m. Huldah **STARKWEATHER**, Nov. 15, 1759, by Jeremiah Kinne, J.P.	1	100
Olive, d. Nicholas & Huldah, b. Mar. 16, 1769	1	100
Phebe, d. John, Jr. & Lydia, b. Jan. 6, 1772	1	113
Richard, m. Sarah **DOWNING**, Aug. 5, 1735, by Rev. Samuel Dorrance	1	21
Sally L., d. Daniel & Anna, b. July 9, 1806	2	103
Sarah, d. Nicholas & Huldah, b. Sept. 7, 1761	1	100
Sarah, d. Ephraim & Eunice, b. June 8, 1792, in Preston	1	195

	Vol.	Page
KEIGWIN, (cont.)		
Stephen S., s. Daniel & Anna, b. Mar. 1, 1809	2	103
Sterry S., s. Daniel & Anna, b. Oct. 11, 1803	2	103
Thomas, s. John & Deborah, b. Sept. 5, 1733; d. July 25, 1740	1	13
Thomas, s. John & Deborah, b. Aug. 15, 1744	1	13
Thomas, m. Jerusha **GATES**, Dec. 26, 1765, by Samuel Coit, J.P.	1	111
Thomas, s. John, Jr. & Lydia, b. Nov. 6, 1769	1	113
William, s. John & Deborah, b. Apr. 19, 1738	1	13
William, s. Thomas & Jerusha, b. Dec. 7, 1770	1	111
-----, s. Daniel & Celinda, b. Feb. 14, 1827; d. Mar. 8, 1827	2	103
KENNEDY, KENEDY, Abigail, twin with Rachel, d. Hugh & Rachel, b. Jan. 21, 1741	1	61
Alexander, s. Hugh & Rachel, b. July 20, 1745	1	61
Ann, d. John & Jennit, b. July 23, 1736	1	21
Ann, m. James **EDMOND**, July 27, 1759, by Rev. Samuel Dorrance	1	100
Ann, d. Daniel & Lucretia, b. Nov. 17, 1769	1	112
Anne, m. Oliver **PERKINS**, Jr., Dec. 27, 1792, by Rev. Micaiah Porter	1	222
Charles W., m. Betsey M. **ALEXANDER**, Dec. 9, 1824, by Nathaniel Sheffield, Elder	2	60
Charles W., d. June 24, 1849, ae 49	3	60
Charles W., m. Lydia **BASSETT**, b. of Voluntown, [ ], by Nathaniel Sheffield, Elder	2	61
Charles Whipple, s. Joseph & Agness, b. Jan. 16, 1800	1	256
Clarissa, d. May 24, 1849, ae 53	3	60
Daniel, s. John & Jennet, b. Aug. 10, 1743	1	21
Daniel, m. Lucretia **WHIPPLE**, Dec. 5, 1764, by Rev. Jo[h]nson, of Groton	1	112
Daniel, s. Joseph & Agness, b. Aug. 2, 1786	1	256
Daniel, s. John & Polly, b. May 14, 1811	1	240
David, s. Hugh & Rachal, b. July 6, 1730	1	61
David, m. Mary **CAMPBELL**, Jan. 10, 1759	1	104
Dixson, s. Joseph & Agness, b. May 31, 1802	1	256
Eliza, d. John & Polly, b. June 29, 1806	1	240
Elizabeth, d. Hugh & Rachal, b. Mar. 28, 1731	1	61
Elizabeth, d. John & Jennet, b. July 31, 1751	1	21
Elizabeth, m. Lot **LARKHAM**, Jr., Apr. 28, 1796, by Rev. Micaiah Porter	1	227
Ellis, d. Daniel & Lucretia, b. May 31, 1775 (Alice ?)	1	112
[E]unice, d. Daniel & Lucretia, b. Oct. 24, 1767	1	112
Hannah, d. Hugh & Rachel, b. Oct. 28, 1737	1	61
Hannah, m. Joseph **CAMPBELL**, June 24, 1756, by Rev. Samuel Dorrance	1	87
Hannah, ae 18, of Voluntown, m. Robert H. **DIXSON**, ae 22, b. Sterling, resid. of Voluntown, Oct. 16, 1849, by Rev. Peleg Peckham	3	3
Hugh, s. Hugh & Rachel, b. Jan. 6, 1739	1	61
Hugh, s. David & Mary, b. Sept. 30, 1762	1	104
James Harvey, s. John & Mary, b. Apr. 6, 1803	1	240
Jenet, m. John **DIXSON**, Aug. 7, 1741, by Rev. Samuel Dorrance	1	34
Jennet, m. Charles **CAMPBELL**, Jan. 29, 1756, by Rev. Samuel Dorrance	1	76
Jennet, d. Joseph & Agness, b. July 31, 1780	1	256

	Vol.	Page

KENNEDY, KENEDY, (cont.)

	Vol.	Page
Jennet, m. Samuel **ALEXANDER**, May 14, 1809, by Allen Campbell, J.P.	2	61-A
John, m. Jennit **FARGISSON**, Aug. 14, 1735, by Rev. [ ], of Charlestown	1	21
John, s. John & Jennet, b. Sept. 5, 1741	1	21
John, s. David & Mary, b. Feb. 1, 1767	1	104
John, s. Joseph & Agness, b. Nov. 15, 1797	1	256
John, m. Polly **WITHEY**, Oct. 4, 1798, by Rev. Levi Hart	1	240
John A., s. John & Polly, b. Feb. 12, 1814; d. Apr. 12, 1817	1	240
Joseph, s. John & Jennet, b. Aug. 3, 1749	1	21
Joseph, m. Agness **CAMPBELL**, Dec. 10, 1778, by Rev. Solomon Morgan	1	256
Joseph, s. Joseph & Agness, b. Sept. 17, 1789	1	256
Joseph, Jr., m. Sarah **LO[O]MIS**, Jan. 29, 1826, by James Alexander, J.P.	2	65
Joseph, d. Oct. 7, [1859], ae 71	3	69
Joseph Whipple, s. John & Polly, b. Jan. 30, 1800	1	240
Julian, of Voluntown, m. George **SPAULDING**, of Canterbury, Aug. 21, 1843, by Rev. Jacob Allen	2	55
Juliette, m. Benjamin V. **GALLUP**, b. of Voluntown, Oct. 8, 1848, by Rev. Alfred Burnham	2	128
Lucretia, d. Daniel & Lucretia, b. Apr. 28, 1773	1	112
Marian, d. Hugh & Rachel, b. May 3, 1733	1	61
Mary, d. Hugh & Rachel, b. Nov. 28, 1726	1	61
Mary, m. John **DIXSON**, Jr., Oct. 8, 1735, by Thomas Thomson, Minister	1	23
Mary, d. John & Jennet, b. Oct. 13, 1738	1	21
Mary, d. David & Mary, b. Dec. 21, 1764	1	104
Mary, d. Daniel & Lucretia, b. Sept. 10, 1765	1	112
Mary Lucretia, d. John & Polly, b. July 12, 1819	1	240
Moses, m. Clary **BASSETT**, b. of Voluntown, Mar. 11, 1827, by Nathaniel Sheffield, Elder	2	71
Moses, d. Oct. 2, 1864, ae 71	3	74
Moses Campbell, s. Joseph & Agness, b. May 29, 1793	1	256
Olive C., of Voluntown, m. Samuel **CRARY**, of Plainfield, Sept. 9, 1835, by Peleg Peckham, Elder	2	99
Olive Campbell, d. John & Polly, b. Sept. 25, 1808	1	240
Patience, m. Charles **CAMPBELL**, Jr., Mar. 20, 1750, by Rev. Jabez Wight, of Norwich	1	56
Phebe, d. Joseph & Agness, b. Aug. 18, 1795	1	256
Rachel, twin with Abigail, d. Hugh & Rachel, b. Jan. 21, 1741	1	61
Rachel, m. William **EDMOND**, June 23, 1763, by Jeremiah Kinne, J.P.	1	118
Rachel, d. David & Mary, b. Mar. 3, 1772	1	104
Rebec[c]a, d. David & Mary, b. June 5, 1769	1	104
Rebecca, m. John F. **BACON**, b. of Voluntown, Mar. 15, 1840, by Rev. Jacob Allen	2	83
Robert, s. David & Mary, b. Jan. 20, 1761	1	104
Sally, d. Joseph & Agness, b. Sept. 1, 1784	1	256
Sarah D., m. Calvin **CAMPBELL**, b. of Voluntown, Sept. 12, 1847, by Rev. Jacob Allen	2	116
Susanna, m. Daniel **CAMPBELL**, Dec. 21, 1797, by Allen		

	Vol.	Page
KENNEDY, KENEDY, (cont.)		
Campbell, J.P.	1	230
Temperance, d. Hugh & Rachel, b. Nov. 28, 1735	1	61
Thomas, d. Aug. 27, 1866, ae 16; b. in Foster, R.I.	3	77
William, s. Hugh & Rachal, b. Sept. 30, 1728	1	61
KENYON, [see also **KINYON**], Eliza A., of Voluntown, m. W[illia]m C. **LAMPHIRE**, of N. Stonington, Oct. 17, 1847, by Rev. James M. Phillips	2	124
Harriet, ae 18, m. Willard M. **COLLINS**, ae 21, b. of Hopkinton, R.I., Jan. 14, 1849, by John Sheffield	3	1
Harriet E., of Voluntown, m. Willard W. **COLLINS**, of Hopkinton, R.I., Jan. 14, 1849, by Rev. John Sheffield	2	137
Margaret, d. Feb. 18, 1857, ae 11 m.; b. in Coventry	3	67
Martha A., ae 14, of Griswold, m. Edwin **PEIRCE**, ae 19, b. Killingly, resid. of Griswold, Nov. 25, 1850, by Samuel Cogswell	3	4
Mary, of Exeter, R.I., m. William B. **WILLCOX**, of Griswold, Ct., Nov. 8, 1830, by Nathaniel Sheffield, Elder	2	86
Mary C., of Voluntown, m. William H. **DAVIS**, of R.I., Apr. 4, 1841, by Rev. Charles S. Weaver	2	37
Phillip, of Plainfield, m. Sarah **KENNEY**, of Voluntown, Feb. 3, 1833, by Peleg Peckham, Elder	2	34
Sally, d. Aug. 16, 1866, ae 82	3	76
William, of Plainfield, m. Hannah **KINNE**, of Voluntown, Mar. 16, 1829, by Levi Kneeland, Evangelist	2	81
KESSON, [see also **KASSON**], Jane, m. Robert **GORDON**, Apr. 21, 1757, by Rev. Samuel Dorrance	1	75
Jane, d. Samuel & Ele[a]nor, b. June 18, 1765	1	52
Joseph, s. Samuel & Ele[a]ner, b. Oct. 16, 1747	1	52
Marg[a]ret, d. Samuel & Ele[a]ner, b. Jan. 23, 1749/50	1	52
Olive, d. Samuel & Ele[a]nor, b. Aug. 20, 1758	1	52
Phebe, d. Samuel & Ele[a]nor, b. Sept. 16, 1752	1	52
Samuel, m. Ele[a]ner **DIXSON**, Jan. 22, 1744/5, by Rev. Samuel Dorrance	1	52
Samuel, s. Samuel & Ele[a]nor, b. Aug. 29, 1761	1	52
Sarah, d. Samuel & Ele[a]nor, b. Mar. 1, 1746	1	52
Thomas, s. Samuel & Ele[a]nor, b. Apr. 6, 1756	1	52
KILE, Ann, d. William & Elizabeth, b. Oct. 7, 1727	1	15
Elizabeth, d. William & Elizabeth, b. Sept. 5, 1730	1	15
Ephraim, s. William & Elizabeth, b. May 12, 1737	1	15
Jane, d. William & Elizabeth, b. Apr. 6, 1735	1	15
John, s. William & Elizabeth, b. Mar. 2, 1733	1	15
Miriam, d. William & Elizabeth, b. July 8, 1739	1	15
Sarah, d. William & Elizabeth, b. Mar. 14, 1742	1	15
KILLAM, Marcy, m. Benjamin **DOW**, Sept. 27, 1768, by William Witter, J.P.	1	96
KILTON, KELTON, Caleb H., s. Isaac J. & Phebe, b. Oct. 21, 1838; d. Sept. 20, 1839	2	98
Hannah F., d. Isaac J. & Phebe A., b. May 25, 1840	2	98
Isaac J., Jr., s. Isaac J. & Phebe A., b. Sept. 23, 1850	2	98
Isaac J., s. Isaac J., weaver, ae 39, b. Sept. 23, 1850	3	26
KIMBALL, Sarah Jane, d. Nov. 10, 1866, ae 21	3	77
Virginia, d. Nov. 6, 1862, ae 22	3	71

	Vol.	Page
KING, Ellen, d. June 27, 1850, ae 21; b. in Ireland	3	62
KINGSLEY, Eunice W., of Franklin, m. Charles H. **ARMSTRONG**, of Ston[ington], Mar. 25, 1844, by Rev. Charles S. Weaver	2	18
Jane E., of Franklin, m. Gardner **CHAPMAN**, of N. Stonington, Nov. 18, 1845, by Rev. Charles S. Weaver	2	8
Thomas G., of Franklin, m. Hannah M. **CHAPMAN**, of N. Stonington, Mar. 25, 1844, by Rev. Charles S. Weaver	2	18
KINNEY, KINNE, KINNY, KENNEY, A[a]ron J., s. John & Lucy, b. Sept. 9, 1819	1	234
Abby, d. Mar. 24, 1866, ae 57; b. in R. Island	3	76
Abel, s. Moses & Abigail, b. June 22, 1748	1	40
Abel, m. Rachel **FRINK**, Oct. 3, 1771, by Jeremiah Kinne, J.P.	1	123
Abel, s. Abel & Rachel, b. Feb. 2, 1779	1	123
Abel, m. Freelove **GALLUP**, Apr. 9, 1789, by Elder Whitman	1	124
Abel, h. Rachel, d. Mar. 2, 1834	1	123
Abel, d. Nov. 26, 1853, ae 42, single	3	63
Abel Nelson, s. John & Lucy, b. Feb. 15, 1810	1	235
Abigale, m. Zachariah **FRINK**, Jr., Feb. 21, 1753, by Jeremiah Kinne, J.P.	1	71
Abigail, d. Ira & Miriam, b. Aug. 14, 1771	1	117
Abigail, wid. of Deac. Moses, d. Jan. 18, 1804	1	40
Alfred Avery, s. John & Lucy, b. Mar. 6, 1808	1	235
Alice, d. Ira & Miriam, b. May 16, 1774	1	117
Allen, s. Abell & Freelove, b. Aug. 1, 1791	1	124
Amy, m. Benjamin **GALLUP**, Jan. 20, 1763, by Rev. Levi Hart	1	140
Amy Angeline, d. Joel & Catharine, b. Aug. 25, 1826	2	64
Angeline, m. Lathrop P. **WEAVER**, b. of Voluntown, Mar. 31, 1844, by Rev. Charles Randall	2	118
Anna M., d. Apr. 3, 1867, ae 6	3	78
Anne, d. John & Ann, b. June 12, 1758	1	75
Archelus, s. James, d. Sept. 25, 1756	1	79
Archibald, s. Sterry & Sally, b. Apr. 16, 1815	2	34
Asher, s. James & Hannah, b. Aug. 18, 1767	1	106
Avery, s. Abel & Freelove, b. Feb. 12, 1790	1	124
Avery, m. Hannah **GALLUP**, Feb. 27, 1814, by Allen Campbell, J.P.	1	235
Avery, d. Dec. 6, 1861, ae 71 y. 9 m. 24 d.	3	71
Backus, s. Ira & Meriam, b. Aug. 11, 1791	1	202
Betsey, d. Samuel & Amy, b. Sept. 15, 1790	1	136
Caroline, d. Sterry & Sally, b. May 31, 1813	2	34
Caroline L., of Voluntown, m. Benjamin **GALLUP**, Jr., Oct. 30, 1831, by Joseph Wylie, J.P.	2	91
Catharine, d. Feb. 7, 1867, ae 73; b. in R. Island	3	78
Catharine (**CHURCH**), w. Joel, b. Jan. [ ], 1795	2	64
Catharine Ellen, d. Charles H. & Lucy, b. Sept. 12, 1846	2	107
Charles, s. James & Hannah, b. Nov. 21, 1783	1	106
Charles Edwin, s. Martin & Sarah, b. Oct. 1, 1845	2	115
Charles H., m. Lucy **RICHMOND**, Apr. 12, 1837, by Rev. Charles S. Weaver	2	107
Charles Hutchins, s. Joel & Catharine, b. May 24, 1816	2	64
Chester, s. Ira & Miriam, b. Dec. 13, 1772	1	117
Cyrus, m. Comfort **PALMER**, Apr. 10, 1770, by Jeremiah Kinne, Esq.	1	123

196   BARBOUR COLLECTION

	Vol.	Page
KINNEY, KINNE, KINNY, KENNEY, (cont.)		
Daniel, s. Jeremiah & Mary, b. May 10, 1747	1	74
Daniel James, s. John & Mary, b. May 15, 1824	2	41
Darius, s. Ira & Miriam, b. May 25, 1767	1	117
Ebenezer, s. James & Sarah, b. June 30, 1728	1	79
Elbert M., d. Aug. 22, 1866, ae 2	3	77
Elijah, s. James & Sarah, b. Aug. 7, 1743	1	79
Elisha, s. John & Ann, b. Oct. 21, 1753	1	75
Elisha, s. Samuel & Amy, b. May 23, 1782	1	136
Elisha, m. Rebecca **GRANT**, Feb. 11, 1816, by Nathan Pendleton, J.P.	2	31
Elizabeth, d. Jeremiah & Mary, b. Mar. 23, 1749	1	74
Elizabeth, d. Abel & Rachel, b. Aug. 4, 1783	1	123
Elizabeth, d. Oct. 22, 1863, ae 13	3	73
Elizabeth A., d. Martin, farmer, & Sally, b. Apr. 22, 1850	3	24
Elsey A., d. Charles H., farmer, & Lucy, b. Feb. 18, 1849	3	23
Elsey Angeline, d. Charles H. & Lucy, b. Feb. 18, 1849	2	107
Elvina, d. Feb. 24, 1866, ae 1	3	77
Emanuel, s. John & Mary, b. Jan. 16, 1827	2	41
Emma Jane, d. Sam[ue]l P. & Lydia C., b. June 26, 1857	2	100
Emma Katharine, d. Martin & Sarah, b. Mar. 1, 1847	2	115
Emmary Mary, d. Nov. 20, 1866, ae 7 y. 6 m.	3	77
Esther, d. Ira & Miriam, b. Jan. 4, 1770	1	117
Esther, m. Elder Amos **CRANDALL**, Feb. 22, 1798, by Allen Campbell, J.P.	1	239
Ethel Phillips, s. John & Mary, b. Sept. 18, 1829	2	41
Ezra, s. Cyrus & Comfort, b. Jan. 14, 1771	1	123
Francis W[illia]m, s. Elisha & Rebecca, b. Jan. 3, 1819	2	31
Franklin S., d. Oct. 5, 1854, ae 2	3	65
Freelove, of Voluntown, m. Richard **DAVIS**, of Griswold, Dec. 15, 1839, by Rev. Charles S. Weaver	2	24
Freelove, d. July 16, 1849, ae 98; b. in Groton	3	59
Freelove, d. John & Lucy, b. Mar. [ ]	1	235
George Gallup, s. John & Lucy, b. Apr. 24, 1806	1	235
George Washington, s. Joel & Katharine, b. Aug. [ ], 1838	2	64
Hannah E., d. Martin, farmer, & Sally, b. Sept. 16, 1848	3	22
Hannah, d. James & Hannah, b. July 24, 1769* (*July 4th ?)	1	106
Hannah, d. Abell & Freelove, b. Nov. 13, 1795	1	124
Hannah, d. John & Lucy, b. May 8, 1802	1	235
Hannah, of Voluntown, m. William **KENYON**, of Plainfield, Mar. 16, 1829, by Levi Kneeland, Evangelist	2	81
Hannah, d. Peleg A. & Amy J., b. Apr. 10, 1847	2	79
Hannah E., d. Mar. 3, 1849, ae 6 m.	3	59
Hannah E., d. Martin & Sally, b. Sept. 16, 1849	3	21
Happy, d. Joel & Katharine, b. Oct. 29, 1833	2	64
Happy Ann, s. Charles H. & Lucy, b. May 21, 1841	2	107
Harriet, d. Sterry & Sally, b. July 17, 1817	2	34
Huldah, m. Uzziel **FRINK**, Mar. 3, 1757, by Jeremiah Kinne, J.P.	1	92
Huldah, d. Abel & Rachel, b. Oct. 2, 1774	1	123
Huldah, m. Benjamin **GALLUP**, Jr., Jan, 3, 1806, by Peleg Randall, Elder	2	3
Ira, m. Miriam **GOODELL**, Nov. 12, 1765, by James Cogswell, Clerk	1	117

VOLUNTOWN VITAL RECORDS

	Vol.	Page
KINNEY, KINNE, KINNY, KENNEY, (cont.)		
Ira, s. Ira & Miriam, b. Jan. 31, 1778	1	117
Ira Allison, s. Joel & Katharine, b. Jan. 11, 1836	2	64
James, s. James & Sarah, b. Aug. 21, 1734	1	79
James, m. Mary **ROB[B]ENS**, Sept. 28, 1750, by Rev. Hezekiah Lord	1	79
James, Jr., m. Hannah **HEWIT[T]**, Jan. 15, 1761, by Rev. Joseph Fish	1	106
James, s. James & Hannah, b. Nov. 9, 1772	1	106
James, Capt., m. Elizabeth **COALS**, May 1, 1793, by Joshua Babcock, J.P.	1	180
James, d. Oct. 31, 1807	1	180
James, s. Sterry & Sally, b. June 2, 1809	2	34
James M., d. Dec. 14, 1866, ae 31	3	77
James Maddeson, s. John & Esther, b. Sept. 3, 1835	1	234
Jerome, s. Jeremiah & Mary, b. Mar. 27, 1743	1	74
Jesse, s. Moses & Abigail, b. Feb. 6, 1749/50	1	40
Joel, s. Samuel & Amy, b. Jan. 31, 1793	1	136
Joel, m. Catharine **CHURCH**, Aug. 20, 1815, by Alexander Stewart, J.P.	2	64
Joel D., d. Oct. 4, 1854, ae 4	3	65
Joel S., m. Elcey A. **WAIT**, b. of Voluntown, Oct. 1, 1843, by Rev. H. Farbush	2	69
Joel Starkweather, s. Joel & Catharine, b. June 20, 1823	2	64
John, m. Ann **AYER**, May 18, 1749, by Rev. Hezekiah Lord	1	75
John, s. Abel & Rachel, b. Jan. 27, 1777	1	123
John, m. Lucy **GALLUP**, Jan. 1, 1800, by Allen Campbell, J.P.	1	235
John, 2d, d. July 12, 1849, ae 56; b. in Plainfield	3	59
John, d. Apr. [ ], 1856, ae 79	3	67
John J., s. Joel & Katharine, b. July 18, 1829	2	64
John Packer, s. John & Lucy, b. May 1, 1804	1	235
Joseph, s. Samuel & Amy, b. May 30, 1777; d. July 18, 1777	1	136
Joseph, s. Ira & Miriam, b. Feb. 4, 1780	1	117
Joseph Cutler, s. Joel & Catharine, b. July 1, 1818	2	64
Jude, d. John & Ann, b. Apr. 11, 1751	1	75
Julia, ae 18 m. John **PALMER**, ae 19, farmer, b. of Voluntown, Mar. 11, 1849, by Gershom Palmer	3	1
Julia Ann, d. Joel & Katharine, b. Mar. 16, 1832	2	64
Julia Ann, d. Joel, dec., of Voluntown, m. John Hunter **PALMER**, of Voluntown, s. Gershom, Mar. 11, 1849, by Gershom Palmer, Elder	2	131
Kezia, d. James, Jr. & Hannah, b. Sept. 25, 1765	1	106
Keziah, m. Nathaniel **GALLUP**, Sept. 7, 1786, by Rev. Micaiah Porter	1	243
Keziah, d. July 18, 1850, ae 33	3	61
Keziah Maria, d. John & Mary, b. Jan. 12, 1815, in Plainfield	2	41
Levi, s. John & Mary, b. Jan. 23, 1817	2	41
Levi, d. Aug. 5, 1845	2	59
Lois, d. James & Sarah, b. July 10, 1738	1	79
Lois, m. Simeon **STEAVENS**, Oct. 10, 1770, by Jeremiah Kinne, Esq.	1	131
Lucy, d. Nathan & Elizabeth, b. Oct. 10, 1752	1	80
Lucy, d. Samuel & Amy, b. Aug. 28, 1779	1	136

KINNEY, KINNE, KINNY, KENNEY, (cont.)

	Vol.	Page
Lucy Ann, d. Anson J. & Sarah C., b. July 24, 1854	2	146
Lucy F., w. John, d. Nov. 20, 1833	1	235
Lucy (RICHMOND), w. Charles H., b. Nov. 20, 1819, at Exeter	2	107
Lydia, d. John & Ann, b. Aug. 3, 1755	1	75
Lydia Marcy, d. John & Mary, b. May 25, 1821	2	41
Lyman, s. Samuel & Amy, b. Nov. 2, 1784; d. Oct. 24, 1788	1	136
Manuel, s. Jeremiah & Mary, b. Nov. 10, 1740	1	74
Mariam, m. Thomas COLE, Jr., Dec. 7, 1757, by Robert Dixson, J.P.	1	93
Martin, m. Sarah THOMPSON, b. of Voluntown, Jan. 1, 1844, by Rev. H. Farbush	2	115
Martin Van Beurin, s. Charles H. & Lucy, b. Apr. 17, 1839	2	107
Mary, d. Jeremiah & Mary, b. Apr. 30, 1745	1	74
Mary, w. Jeremiah, d. Jan. 29, 1785	1	74
Mary A., m. Henry LILLIBRIDGE, b. of Griswold, Mar. [ ], 1846, by Rev. Charles S. Weaver	2	9
Mary Adelaide, d. Charles H. & Lucy, b. Sept. 1, 1844	2	107
Matilda, d. John & Lucy, b. Aug. 9, 1800	1	235
Miriam, d. Ira & Miriam, b. May 23, 1782	1	117
Moses, s. Ira & Miriam, b. June 7, 1768	1	117
Moses, Deac., d. July 18, 1788, ae 79 y.	1	40
Nathan, m. Elizabeth TUBBS, Feb. 27, 1749, by Wait Palmer, Elder, in Stonington	1	80
Orrin, s. Sterry & Sally, b. June 25, 1807	2	34
Orrin T., m. Julia GROW, b. of Voluntown, Dec. 30, 1832, by Joseph Wylie, J.P.	2	94
Peleg A., s. John & Lucy, b. Sept. 14, 1814	1	234
Peleg G., s. Peleg A. & Amy, b. Feb. 12, 1849	2	79
Peleg G., s. Peleg A. & Amey J., b. Feb. 12, 1849	3	21
Peleg G., s. Peleg A., farmer, & Mary J., b. Feb. 12, 1849	3	22
Polly, d. Samuel & Amy, b. Apr. 30, 1795	1	136
Prentis, s. Cyrus & Comfort, b. Oct. 16, 1773	1	123
Priscilla, d. John & Ann, b. July 18, 1749	1	75
Prudence, d. Abel & Rachel, b. Dec. 19, 1785	1	123
Rachel, d. Abel & Rachel, b. May 15, 1781	1	123
Rachel, w. Abel, d. May 22, 1788	1	123
Rachel, d. Peleg A. & Amy, b. Mar. 16, 1851	2	79
Roxanna, d. Samuel & Ama, b. July 11, 1798	1	136
Roxanna, m. Caleb BURDICK, Mar. 13, 1823, by Sterry Kinne, J.P.	2	52
Ruth, d. Nathan & Elizabeth, b. Apr. 19, 1757	1	80
Sabra, d. James & Hannah, b. Apr. 10, 1786	1	106
Sally, d. Samuel & Amy, b. May 11, 1787; d. July 22, 1797	1	136
Samuel, s. Jeremiah & Mary, b. Apr. 13, 1753	1	74
Samuel, m. Amy HUTCHINS, May 8, 1776, by Jeremiah Kinne, Esq.	1	136
Samuel, s. Sterry & Sally, b. July 31, 1811	2	34
Samuel L., d. Jan. 27, 1853, ae 11; b. in Griswold. Single	3	63
Samuel P., m. Lydia C. PHILLIPS, Sept. 10, 1848, by Lathrop P. Weaver, of Norwich	2	100
Samuel Palmer, s. Joel & Catharine, b. May 27, 1820	2	64
Sarah, d. James & Sarah, b. Aug. 23, 1732	1	79

	Vol.	Page
KINNEY, KINNE, KINNY, KENNEY, (cont.)		
Sarah, m. Henry **HEWIT[T]**, Jan. 23, 1751	1	90
Sarah, m. Robert **HUSTON**, Feb. 23, 1775, by Rev. Levi Hart	1	148
Sarah, m. Allen **CAMPBELL**, June 18, 1778, by Rev. Levi Hart	1	151
Sarah, of Voluntown, m. Phillip **KENYON**, of Plainfield, Feb. 3, 1833, by Peleg Peckham, Elder	2	34
Sarah R., d. Mar. 19, 1853, ae 42, married	3	63
Seth, s. Moses & Abigail, b. May 18, 1752	1	40
Seth, m. Hannah **BROUGHTON**, Sept. 30, 1778, by Rev. Solomon Morgan	1	148
Solomon, s. James & Hannah, b. Jan. 20, 1777	1	106
Stary, s. James & Hannah, b. Dec. 27, 1780	1	106
Sterry, m. Sally **ROBBINS**, Jan. 16, 1806, by Rev. Amos Crandall	2	34
Sterry, m. Abba **ROB[B]INS**, Apr. 1, 1824, by James Alexander, J.P.	2	56
Susanna, d. Jeremiah & Mary, b. Sept. 5, 1751	1	74
Temperance, d. James & Hannah, b. Oct. 3, 1774	1	106
Temperance, m. George **ALEXANDER**, Nov. 16, 1797, by Allen Campbell, J.P.	1	228
Thomas, s. Nathan & Elizabeth, b. Oct. 12, 1754	1	80
Thomas, s. Ira & Miriam, b. Mar. 23, 1776	1	117
Vina, d. Ira & Miriam, b. May 13, 1784	1	117
Waterman, s. John & Mary, b. Feb. 13, 1819	2	41
William, m. Hannah **CONGDON**, b. of Voluntown, June 19, 1853, by John E. Lindley, J.P.	2	143
Zachariah, s. Cyrus & Comfort, b. Feb. 24, 1772	1	123
-----, female, d. Feb. 26, 1861, ae 19 d.	3	70
KINYON, [see also **KENYON**], Mumford, m. Hannah **WAGE**, Jan. 12, 1796, by Rev. Micaiah Porter	1	203
KITTLE, Charles, s. Elias & Mary, b. Oct. 9, 1766	1	109
William, s. Elias & Mary, b. May 26, 1765	1	109
KNIGHT, Aaron, d. Apr. 17, 1850, ae 70, resid. of Voluntown & Sterling	3	61
Celia, d. Feb. 11, 1863, ae 48; b. in R. Island	3	72
Earl, d. Nov. 19, 1862, ae 80; b. in Cranston, R.I.	3	72
Horace W., d. June 1, 1860, ae 1-1/2	3	70
KNOX, Brittana Maria, d. Robert & Jane, b. May 20, 1762	1	30
LAMPHEAR, LAMPHERE, LAMPHIRE, Chauncey, of N. Stonington, m. Julia **GREEN**, of Canterbury, Nov. 29, 1837, by Benjamin Gallup, Jr., J.P.	2	101
George, m. Hannah **CHAMPLAIN**, Oct. 12, 1828, by Sterry Kinne, J.P.	2	70
Lucy, m. John **HANDY**, b. of Exeter, R.I., Nov. 14, 1849, by Gershom Palmer, Elder	2	137
Lucy, ae 14, m. John **HANDY**, ae 35, farmer, of R.I., Dec. 15, 1849, by Elder Gershom Palmer	3	3
W[illia]m C., of N. Stonington, m. Eliza A. **KENYON**, of Voluntown, Oct. 17, 1847, by Rev. James M. Phillips	2	124
LARKER, Isebel, m. Peter **MILLER**, Dec. 2, 1731	1	91
LARKHAM, Albert, m. Julia **REED**, b. of Griswold, Sept. 17, 1843, by Rev. H. Farbush	2	67
Alice K., of Voluntown, m. Amos T. Keigwin, of Griswold, Dec. 14, 1828, by Nathaniel Sheffield, Elder	2	74
Allice Kennedy, d. Lot & Elizabeth, b. Apr. 19, 1803	1	227

LARKHAM, (cont.)

	Vol.	Page
Daniel K., m. Lydia **BARBER**, July 12, 1818, by Gershom Palmer, Elder	2	44
Daniel Kennedy, s. Lot, Jr. & Elizabeth, b. Mar. 8, 1797	1	227
Daniel Miner, s. Daniel K. & Lydia, b. Mar. 21, 1822	2	44
Erastus R., m. Nancy **LARKIN**, Feb. 11, 1823, at Hopkinton, R.I., by Matthew Stillman, Elder	2	19
Erastus Renssalear, s. Lot & Elizabeth, b. July 5, 1801	1	227
George E., s. William H., farmer, ae 30, & Hannah, ae 25, b. Nov. 12, 1849	3	24
John, m. Desire **MORGAN**, Feb. 6, 1785, by Rev. Micaiah Porter	1	216
John, s. John & Desire, b. Oct. 14, 1786	1	216
Joseph S., ae 28, b. Voluntown, resid. of Westerly, R.I., m. Angeline **BROCKETT**, ae 22, b. Preston, resid. of Voluntown, Sept. 30, 1849, by Elder Cha[rle]s S. Weaver	3	2
Joseph Sheffield, s. Daniel K. & Lydia, b. Jan. 1, 1821, in Hopkinton, R.I.	2	44
Julia M., d. William H., ae 28, & Hannah E., ae 23, b. Dec. 26, 1847	3	21
Lance L., of Griswold, m. Diadama **ROUSE**, of Voluntown, Sept. 4, 1840, by Rev. Charles S. Weaver	2	33
Lanselot, s. Lot & Elizabeth, b. Feb. 15, 1810	1	227
Lot, Jr., m. Elizabeth **KENNEDY**, Apr. 28, 1796, by Rev. Micaiah Porter	1	227
Lot, Jr., m. Olive **GORTON**, Nov. 28, 1816, by Stafford Greene, Elder	2	14
Patience, d. Lot & Prudence, b. Nov. 17, 1779	1	199
Sally, ae 50, a farmer's widow, b. in Coventry, R.I., res. of Voluntown, m. George **BASSETT**, ae 58, mechanic, b. in Griswold, res. of Voluntown, July 15, 1849, by Harvey Campbell	3	2
Sally, m. Capt. George **BASSETT**, b. of Voluntown, July 20, 1849, by Harvey Campbell, J.P.	2	134
Sarah, m. Benjamin **COLEGROVE**, Jr., Mar. 1, 1789, by Rev. Micaiah Porter	1	216
Thomas, m. Sarah **CRANDAL[L]**, Nov. 25, 1790, by Henry Joslin, Elder	1	211

LARKINS, LARKIN

	Vol.	Page
Betsey, m. Gardner **TABOR**, May 29, 1825, by Sterry Kinne, J.P.	2	63
George H., d. Aug. 22, 1865, ae 2 y. 2 m.; b. in Griswold	3	75
Huldah, m. Alas **BRUMBLEY**, Oct. 15, 1826, by Sterry Kinne, J.P.	2	66
Nancy, m. Erastus R. **LARKHAM**, Feb. 11, 1823, at Hopkinton, R.I., by Matthew Stillman, Elder	2	19
Thompson, m. Mary Weaver, July 13, 1823, by Sterry Kinne, J.P.	2	70
-----, female, d. Sept. 1, 1865, ae 45 min.	3	75

LARYBE

	Vol.	Page
Dorithy, m. John **SAFFORD**, Aug. 18, 1711. Entered Mar. 22, 1722	1	4

LASSLY

	Vol.	Page
James, s. John & Catherine, b. Apr. 15, 1742	1	43
John, s. John & Catherine, b. July 28, 1743	1	43

LAWRENCE, LORRANCE

	Vol.	Page
Allen, s. David & Sarah, b. Mar. 3, 1787	1	227
Amos, m. Phebe **BABCOCK**, Dec. 5, 1784, by Rev. Micaiah Porter	1	176
Amy, d. Amos & Phebe, b. Jan. 31, 1785	1	176
Betsey, d. Amos & Phebe, b. July 10, 1786	1	176
Esther, d. David & Marvil, b. Sept. 26, 1798	1	227

	Vol.	Page
LAWRENCE, LORRANCE, (cont.)		
Levi, s. David & Marvel, b. Apr. 30, 1795	1	227
Warren, s. Amos & Phebe, b. Apr. 22, 1788, in Providence	1	176
LAWTON, Betsey Maria, d. John & Lucy, b. May 14, 1815, in Sterling	1	258
George A., m. Matilda R. **BITGOOD**, b. of Voluntown, July 30, 1843, by Rev. Charles S. Weaver	2	44
John, m. Lucy **CHAPMAN**, Apr. 9, 1809, by Rev. Amos Crandall	1	258
John B., of Voluntown, m. Esther **LEWIS**, of Exeter, R.I., Sept. 3, 1837, by Weeden Barber, Elder, of Hopkinton	2	108
John Babcock, s. John & Lucy, b. July 10, 1818	1	258
Lucy H., d. John & Lucy, b. Mar. 19, 1811	1	258
Phebe Eliza, d. John & Lucy, b. Feb. 13, 1820	1	258
Rachel, m. Rowland **GARDNER**, b. of Griswold, Sept. 15, 1850, by Charles S. Weaver	3	4
LEE, Abby Jane, d. Sept. 5, 1866, ae 9	3	77
Calvin H., s. Henry J., farmer, ae 33, b. Aug. 21, 1850	3	26
Henry J., d. Dec. 19, 1858, ae 40; b. in Westerly	3	68
Henry M., d. Jan. 6, 1853, ae 64; b. in Ledyard. Married.	3	63
LESTER, Betsey, m. Asa **FISH**, May 10, 1812, by Peleg Randall, Elder	2	7
Lydia, d. Aug. 26, 1849, ae 33; b. in N. Stonington	3	61
LEWIS, Albert L., m. Olive **HURD**, Apr. 1, 1827, by Sterry Kinne, J.P.	2	71
Allen C., s. Peter & Katy, b. Oct. 10, 1815	1	162
Ame, d. Silvester & Sarah, b. July 2, 1750, in Exeter	1	142
Amy, twin with Peter, d. Eleazer & Thankful, b. Mar. 13, 1781	1	153
Betsey, m. Isaac **RANDALL**, Jr., Dec. 3, 1815, by Gershom Palmer, Elder	2	10
Caleb, s. Silvester & Sarah, b. Apr. 22, 1757	1	142
Caroline, d. Aug. 26, 1867, ae 24; b. in Exeter	3	78
Charles Albert, s. Albert L. & Olive, b. Mar. 6, 1829	2	87
Charles H., d. Mar. 6, 1864, ae 30; b. in Plainfield	3	74
Clark, s. Samuel & Sarah, b. Feb. 20, 1778, in Hopkintown	1	166
Cinthia, m. Rufus **RANDALL**, Mar. 22, 1818, by Allen Campbell, J.P.	2	20
Deborah, d. Silvester & Sarah, b. Apr. 2, 1763	1	142
Dille G., d. Caleb & Sarah, b. Sept. 17, 1807	1	248
Emma, d. Dec. 26, 1863, ae 11	3	73
Esther, of Exeter, R.I., m. John B. **LAWTON**, of Voluntown, Sept. 3, 1837, by Weeden Barber, Elder, of Hopkinton	2	108
George, s. Peter & Katy, b. Mar. 1, 1807	1	162
Griffin, s. Silvester & Sarah, b. Oct. 17, 1767	1	142
Hannah, d. Samuel & Sarah, b. July 14, 1783	1	166
Hannah, d. James B. & Susan, b. Apr. 29, 1836	2	109
Jacob, of Exeter, R.I., m. Roxana **WRIGHT**, of Hopkinton, R.I., Oct. 21, 1850, by Rev. H. Forbush	2	140
James, s. Silvester & Sarah, b. Oct. 22, 1765	1	142
James B., d. Oct. 24, 1850, ae 44; b. in R. Island	3	62
James H., s. James B. & Susan, b. Feb. 7, 1830	2	109
James M., s. Peter & Katey, b. July 28, 1822	1	162
James M., m. Hannah **WAIT**, b. of Voluntown, Nov. 26, 1843, by Rev. Charles S. Weaver	2	44
Jason, d. Feb. [ ], 1864, ae 39, b. in Voluntown, resid. of Groton	3	73
Job, s. James B. & Susan, b. Sept. 2, 1838	2	109
John, s. Silvester & Sarah, b. Nov. 9, 1760	1	142

BARBOUR COLLECTION

LEWIS, (cont.)

	Vol.	Page
John, s. Caleb & Sarah, b. Dec. 27, 1791, in Exeter	1	248
John, d. Mar. 23, 1861, ae 35, Colored	3	71
[John ?], d. [　　　　　], ae 1; b. in Hopkinton, R.I.	3	59
John Button, s. Eleazer & Thankful, b. May 31, 1789	1	153
John R., s. James B., ae 49, & Susan, ae 46, b. Feb. 1, 1849, resid. of Griswold	3	22
Joseph S., s. James B. & Susan, b. Oct. 29, 1834	2	109
Julia F., of Hopkinton, R.I., m. Joseph T. **PALMER**, of Voluntown, Jan. 6, 1861, by Elisha Potter, J.P.	2	135
Lucy, d. Samuel & Sarah, b. Nov. 3, 1781, in Hopkinton	1	166
Lucy, d. Caleb & Sarah, b. Nov. 26, 1797	1	248
Lydia, d. Peter & Katy, b. Nov. 25, 1808	1	162
Lydia A., d. James B. & Susan, b. Oct. 25, 1831	2	109
Martha, m. Peter **MORGAN**, Apr. 5, 1781, by Elder Pembleton	1	214
Martha, d. Samuel & Sarah, b. Sept. 30, 1785	1	166
Martha, d. Caleb & Sarah, b. July 1, 1802	1	248
Martha, of Voluntown, m. Richard **WATSON**, of Exeter, R.I., Nov. 28, 1822, by Nathaniel Sheffield, Elder	2	51
Mary, d. Eleazer & Thankfull, b. May 3, 1784	1	153
Obadiah, d. Feb. 7, 1850, ae 84; b. in Exeter, R.I.	3	61
Oliver, d. June 6, 1857, ae 30 y.; b. in W. Greenwich	3	67
Peleg, s. Silvester & Sarah, b. July 15, 1754, in W. Greenwich	1	142
Peleg, s. Caleb & Sarah, b. May 20, 1804	1	248
Peter, twin with Amy, s. Eleazer & Thankful, b. Mar. 13, 1781	1	153
Peter, m. Katy **BURDICK**, Mar. 10, 1805, by Allen Campbell, J.P.	1	162
Peter, d. Sept. 11, 1843	2	111
Phebe D., d. James B. & Susan, b. Mar. 22, 1833	2	109
Reynolds, s. Caleb & Sarah, b. Dec. 14, 1789	1	248
Rosey A., d. Peter & Katey, b. Jan. 4, 1818	1	162
Roxy, of Voluntown, m. Thomas J. **BARBER**, of Westerly, Feb. 9, 1840, by Rev. Charles S. Weaver	2	24
Ruth, d. Silvester & Sarah, b. Oct. 29, 1769	1	142
Sally, of Voluntown, m. Charles **BILLINGS**, of Griswold, Aug. 24, 1823, by James Alexander, J.P.	2	53
Sally, m. Dudley **BURDICK**, Nov. 13, 1825, by James Alexander, J.P.	2	62
Samuel, s. Silvester & Sarah, b. June 28, 1752, in Coventry, R.I.	1	142
Samuel, s. Samuel & Sarah, b. Feb. 9, 1775, in Hopkintown	1	166
Sarah, d. Silvester & Sarah, b. Aug. 29, 1748, in W. Greenwich	1	142
Sarah, d. Samuel & Sarah, b. June 20, 1776, in Hopkintown	1	166
Sarah, d. Caleb & Sarah, b. May 11, 1800	1	248
Sarah, wid., of Voluntown, m. Reynolds **BARBER**, of Exeter, R.I., Apr. 25, 1831, by Nathaniel Sheffield, Elder	2	88
Stillman K., m. Susan **BURDICK**, b. of Voluntown, Sept. 11, 1842, by Rev. Charles S. Weaver	2	44
Stillman P., s. Peter & Katey, b. Feb. 22, 1820	1	162
Thankful, d. Caleb & Sarah, b. July 5, 1795, in W. Greenwich	1	248
Thankful, m. Jabez **BARBER**, Sept. 18, 1814, by Allen Campbell, J.P.	2	5
Thankfull, wid., m. Roger **SHELDON**, b. of Exeter, R.I., Oct. 27, 1830, by Nathaniel Sheffield, Elder	2	85
William P., s. Peter & Katey, b. July 21, 1824	1	162

	Vol.	Page
LILLIBRIDGE, LITHIBRIDGE, Elizabeth, m. Joseph **DOUGLASS**, Jr., Nov. 30, 1818, by Gershom Palmer, Elder	2	49
Henry, m. Mary A. **KINNEY**, b. of Griswold, Mar. [ ], 1846, by Rev. Charles S. Weaver	2	9
Nathan, of Griswold, m. Lucinda **DOUGLASS**, of Voluntown, Sept. 14, 1840, by Rev. Charles S. Weaver	2	33
LINDSEY, LINDLEY, John E., m. Laura **ROB[B]INS**, Nov. 27, 1828, by Sterry Kinne, J.P.	2	70
Laura M., d. Mar. 28, 1858, ae 56	3	68
LITTLE, Molly, m. Noah **COLE**, Nov. 29, 1770, by Eliphalet Wright	1	119
Moses, m. Hannah **COLE**, Mar. 8, 1770, by Samuel Stewart, J.P.	1	109
Sarah, m. Elijah **GORE**, Dec. 11, 1767	1	137
LITTLEFIELD, Lewis, m. Mary Ann **SABINS**, Apr. 13, 1851, by Benjamin Gallup, 2d, J.P.	2	139
Lewis, ae 51, farmer, b. in Newport, R.I., res. of Voluntown, m. Mary **SABINS**, ae 50, b. in Griswold, res. of Voluntown, Apr. 13, 1851, by Benj[amin] Gallup, 2d. (His 2d marriage)	3	3
Lucinda, d. May 28, 1850, ae 18; b. in Exeter, R.I.	3	61
LOGAN, Hugh, s. John & Marg[a]ret, b. Sept. 14, 1736	1	23
James, s. John & Marg[a]ret, b. June 30, 1731 (twin with John)	1	23
John, twin with James, s. John & Marg[a]ret, b. June 30, 1731	1	23
Martha, d. John & Marg[a]ret, b. Sept. 14, 1726	1	23
Mary, d. John & Marg[a]ret, b. Oct. 19, 1724	1	23
Mary, [d. John & Marg[a]ret], d. Mar. 27, 1739	1	23
LOOMIS, LOMIS, Eliza, of Voluntown, m. James M. **MATTESON**, of W. Greenwich, R.I., Sept. 20, 1846, by Rev. Jacob Allen	2	111
James, s. William & Sarah, b. May 26, 1797	1	229
James, s. William & Lydia, b. May 26, 1797	2	45
James, m. Nabby **CARPENTER**, Sept. 10, 1826, by Sterry Kinne, J.P.	2	70
Nelson, s. James & Nabby, b. June 12, 1828	2	93
Ralph, s. James & Nabby, b. July 2, 1840	2	93
Sarah, m. Joseph **KENNEDY**, Jr., Jan. 29, 1826, by James Alexander, J.P.	2	65
Sarah, d. Aug. 11, 1864, ae 90; b. in Richmond, R.I.	3	74
William, m. Sarah **ADAMS**, Oct. 20, 1815, by Allen Campbell, J.P.	2	45
LOVE, Mary, d. Thomas & Jenet, b. Oct. 25, 1730	1	24
LOWDEN, LOUDEN, Deborah, [w. John], d. Apr. 15, 1776	1	110
Deborah, d. John & Sarah, b. July 9, 1779	1	110
Guile, s. John & Sarah, b. Aug. 9, 1777	1	110
Hannah, d. John & Deborah, b. Oct. 26, 1768	1	110
Jane, d. John & Deborah, b. Jan. 27, 1767	1	110
John, m. Deborah **WEDGE**, Jan. 22, 1766, by Robert Dixson, J.P.	1	110
John, s. John & Deborah, b. Aug. 1, 1774	1	110
John, m. Sarah **HODGE**, Aug. 15, 1776, by Rev. George Gilmore	1	110
Mary, m. Allen **STEVENSON**, Jan. 12, 1775	1	139
Priscilla, d. John & Deborah, b. July 6, 1770	1	110
Thomas, s. John & Deborah, b. May 12, 1772	1	110
MAC--- [see also **Mc---**]		
MACGONEGALL, MEGONIGALL, MEGONIGILL, Ann, d. James & Elizabeth, b. Apr. 23, 1752	1	39
Elizabeth, d. James & Elizabeth, b. July 3, 1746	1	39
Hannah, d. James & Elizabeth, b. Apr. 15, 1755	1	39

BARBOUR COLLECTION

	Vol.	Page
MACGONEGALL, MEGONIGALL, MEGONIGILL, (cont.)		
Henry, s. James & Elizabeth, b. Sept. 26, 1743	1	39
James, Jr., m. Elizabeth **HENRY**, Oct. 27, 1742, by Rev. Cotton, of Providence	1	39
Jane, d. John & Jane, b. Aug. 2, 1752; d. Oct. 4, 1754	1	27
John, s. John & Jane, b. July 27, 1747; d. Oct. 3, 1754	1	27
John, s. John & Jane, b. Nov. 29, 1755	1	27
Marg[a]ret, d. John & Jane, b. June 11, 1742	1	27
Mary, d. John & Jane, b. Oct. 15, 1736	1	27
Mary, d. James & Elizabeth, b. Oct. 27, 1745	1	39
Mary, w. James, d. Oct. 19, 1754	1	38
Robert, s. John & Jane, b. Mar. 22, 1745	1	27
Rowland, s. John & Jane, b. Mar. 27, 1750; d. Oct. 12, 1754	1	27
Thomas, s. John & Jane, b. Apr. 10, 1759	1	27
William, s. John & Jane, b. July 15, 1739	1	27
William, s. James & Elizabeth, b. Apr. 28, 1750; d. Oct. 13, 1754	1	39
MACMAINES, MACKMAINS, Dinah, m. James Campbell, Jr. May 11, 1749, by Rev. Samuel Dorrance	1	53
Mary, m. Robert **CAMPBELL**, Apr. 13, 1727, by Rev. Joseph Coite	1	11
Sarah, m. James **WYLIE**, Aug. 14, 1746, by Rev. Hezekiah Lord	1	83
MACWETHY, Elizabeth, d. David & Abigail, b. Feb. 5, 1734	1	32
Esther, d. David & Abigail, b. June 20, 1741	1	32
Hannah, d. David & Abigail, b. Oct. 11, 1743	1	32
Isaac, s. David & Abigail, b. Oct. 26, 1745	1	32
Rachel, d. David & Abigail, b. Aug. 12, 1748	1	32
R[e]ubeen, s. David & Abigail, b. Aug. 31, 1731	1	32
Ruth, d. David & Abigail, b. Oct. 16, 1736	1	32
Simeon, s. David & Abigail, b. Mar. 7, 1739	1	32
MADISON, Eliza, d. Jan. 1, 1849, ae 29; b. in Hopkinton	3	60
MAINE, MAIN, David, of N. Stonington, m. Sarah M. **PALMER,** of Voluntown, Jan. 2, 1848, by Rev. Charles S. Weaver	2	125
David, ae 25, machinist, b. in N. Stonington, res. of Westerly, m. Sarah **PALMER,** ae 26, weaver, b. in Voluntown, res. of Westerly, Jan. 2, 1848, by Rev. Charles S. Weaver	3	1
Dorcas, of N. Stonington, m. William W. **ECCLESTONE,** of Voluntown, Dec. 31, 1837, by Benj[ami[n Gallup, Jr., J.P.	2	106
Dorcas, m. William **MAINE,** b. of N. Stonington, Jan. 2, 1848, by Rev. Charles S. Weaver	2	125
Dorcas, ae 20, weaver, b. in N. Stonington, res. of Westerly, m. William **MAIN,** ae 23, machinist, b. in N. Stonington, res. of Westerly, Jan. 2, 1848, by Rev. Charles S. Weaver	3	1
Esther S., of Voluntown, m. W[illia]m B. **CHAPMAN,** of N. Stonington, Nov. 25, 1847, by Rev. James M. Phillips	2	94
George W., m. Julia A. **SLOCUM,** b. of N. Stonington, Dec. 9, 1838, by Benjamin Gallup, Jr., J.P.	2	108
Louis, ae 66, b. Griswold, resid. of Voluntown, m. Dolly **BLIVEN,** ae 68, of N. Stonington, Mar. 8, 1849, by [ ] Barber	3	1
Mary Ann, of N. Stonington, m. Benjamin T. **NEWTON,** of Voluntown, Dec. 31, 1837, by Benjamin Gallup, Jr., J.P.	2	105
Parmelia, d. Feb. 28, 1858, ae 32; b. in N. Stonington	3	68
Philena, m. John **HOUGHTON,** May 31, 1827, by Sterry Kinne, J.P.	2	71
Sally, m. W[illia]m W. **ECCLESTONE,** Feb. 23, 1851, by Lathrop		

	Vol.	Page
MAINE, MAIN, (cont.)		
B. Weaver	2	139
Sally, ae 40, b. in N. Stonington, res. of Voluntown, m. William W. **ECCLESTON**, ae 36, farmer, of Voluntown, Feb. 23, 1851, by Rev. Lathrop P. Weaver. (Her 3d marriage)	3	3
William, m. Dorcas **MAINE**, b. of N. Stonington, Jan. 2, 1848, by Rev. Charles S. Weaver	2	125
William, ae 23, machinist, b. in N. Stonington, res. of Westerly, m. Dorcas **MAIN**, ae 20, weaver, b. in N. Stonington, res. of Westerly, Jan. 2, 1848, by Rev. Charles S. Weaver	3	1
——, s. David P., machinist, ae 26, & Sarah, ae 27, b. Nov. 24, 1848	3	22
MANSFIELD, Calven, s. John & Marcy, b. July 6, 1762	1	128
John, m. Marcy **EAMES**, Nov. 26, 1759	1	128
John, s. John & Marcy, b. July 1, 1767	1	128
Maryann, d. John & Mary, b. May 10, 1783	1	128
Rachel, m. Abner **EAMES**, Oct. 14, 1756	1	90
Sarah, m. Christopher **PARKE**, Nov. 5, 1754, by Robert Dixson, Esq.	1	85
Thomas, s. John & Marcy, b. Feb. 14, 1769	1	128
MARS, (*See also **MORSE**) (*handwritten on original manuscript), Benjamin, m. Phebe **HALL**, Sept. 2, 1790, by Rev. Micaiah Porter	1	177
Daniel, s. Benjamin & Phebe, b. Mar. 16, 1793	1	177
Henry, s. Benjamin & Phebe, b. June 16, 1791	1	177
MARSH, William, s. Jonas & Mary, b. June 6, 1733	1	19
MARTIN, Mary, m. Isaac **PARK[E]**, Mar. 9, 1775, by John Green, Esq.	1	134
MASON, Allen, s. Jenckes & Sibbel, b. Sept. 12, 1792	1	202
Daniel, s. Jenckes & Sibbel, b. Apr. 25, 1790	1	202
Jenckes, m. Sibbel **WOOD**, Mar. 22, 1784, by Charles Thompson, Elder	1	202
Lydia, d. Jenckes & Sibbel, b. Mar. 7, 1788	1	202
Massy, d. Jenckes & Sibbel, b. Mar. 14, 1785	1	202
MATTESON, MATESON, MATTISON, Abraham, s. Daniel & Elizabeth, b. Nov. 26, 1796, in Pownal, Bennngton County, Vt.	1	245
Archabald, s. Thomas & Thankfull, b. Feb. 16, 1783	1	175
Hendrick Dow, s. Jesse & Hannah, b. May 19, 1791	1	86
James, d. Oct. 18, [1859], ae 20; b. in Cranston, R.I.	3	69
James M., of W. Greenwich, R.I., m. Eliza **LOOMIS**, of Voluntown, Sept. 20, 1846, by Rev. Jacob Allen	2	111
Jesse, m. Hannah **DOW**, Mar. 26, 1789, by Rev. Micaiah Porter	1	86
Jude, d. Thomas & Thankfull, b. July 25, 1785	1	175
Mary, d. Thomas & Thankfull, b. Aug. 11, 1788	1	175
Solomon, s. Caleb & Lucy, b. Sept. 27, 1789	1	206
Solomon, m. Mary Ann **ABBOTT**, of R.I., June 7, 1857, by Samuel Gates, J.P.	2	61
Stephen Allen, s. Jesse & Hannah, b. Jan. 15, 1790, in W. Greenwich	1	86
Susanna, w. Abraham, b. Nov. 2, 1793, in Coventry, R.I.	1	245
Susanna, d. Abraham & Susanna, b. Mar. 26, 1816, in Coventry, R.I.	1	245
Thomas, m. Thankfull **SWEET**, June 7, 1782, by Elder Elisha Green	1	175
Urin, d. Oct. 1, [1860], ae 10 m. 10 d.	3	70
MAXON, George, ae 22, laborer, b. in Hopkinton, R.I., res. of Hopkinton, m. Lucy **RANDALL**, ae 24, weaver, b. in Voluntown, res. of Voluntown, May 8, 1848, by Rev. Charles S. Weaver	3	1

206   BARBOUR COLLECTION

	Vol.	Page
MAXON, (cont.)		
George J., of Hopkinton, R.I., m. Lucy E. **RANDALL**, of Voluntown, May 8, 1848, by Rev. Charles S. Weaver	2	130
Mc——, [see also **MAC——**]		
McCRACKEN, -----, 2 males, s. William, stonemason, ae 43, of Griswold, b. [1849 or 1850]	3	24
-----, male twins, d. Nov. [ ], 1849, ae 2 m.; b. in Griswold, resid. of Griswold	3	61
McKAY, Hugh, d. Nov. 29, 1862, ae 52	3	71
Hugh, d. Nov. 29, 1863, ae 52; b. in Ireland	3	73
McNALLY, Andrew, d. Sept. 24, 1858, ae 64; b. in Ireland	3	68
MEECH, Zerviah, m. Silas **COATS**, Nov. 28, 1816, by Gustavus F. Davis, Elder	2	24
MERRIS, Amanda, of Exeter, R.I., m. Henry B. Reynolds, of Voluntown, Mar. 27, 1825, by Nathaniel Sheffield, Elder	2	60
MILLER, Alexander, s. Peter & Isabell, b. June 27, 1735	1	91
Alexander, s. Alexander & Esther, b. June 12, 1752	1	89
Alexander, s. Robert & Jane, [ ]	1	91
Anne, d. Gawen (?) & Mary, b. Nov. 26, 1742	1	64
Catharine, d. Gawen (?) & Mary, b. July 13, 1753	1	64
Daniel, s. Peter & Isabell, b. Apr. 20, 1737	1	91
Daniel, d. Dec. 10, 1737	1	91
Daniel, s. Robert & Jane [ ]	1	91
Dorcas, d. Alexander & Esther, b. Feb. 16, 1742/3	1	89
Elizabeth, d. Gawen (?) & Mary, b. Apr. 13, 1755	1	64
Esther, d. Alexander & Esther, b. June 23, 1754	1	89
Gawen (Garven ?), m. Mary **HUNTER**, Jan. 8, 1741, by Rev. Samuel Dorrance	1	64
James, s. Alexander & Esther, b. Oct. 14, 1746	1	89
Jane, w. Robert, d. June 20, 1723	1	91
Jane, w. Rob[e]rd, d. July 4, 1723, in ye 44th year of her age	1	7
Jane, d. Peter & Barbere, b. Sept. 1, 1746	1	91
Jane, d. Peter, d. Oct. 17, 1748	1	91
John, s. Alexander & Esther, b. July 22, 1750	1	89
Lydia, d. Peter & Barbere, b. Dec. 21, 1749	1	91
Lydia, d. Peter, d. June 10, 1750	1	91
Marg[a]ret, d. Peter & Barberi, b. Jan. 29, 1739	1	91
Marg[a]ret, d. Gawen (?) & Mary, b. July 19, 1744	1	64
Marg[a]ret, d. Peter, d. May 2, 1756	1	91
Marg[a]ret, d. Alexander & Esther, b. May 23, 1756	1	89
Martha, d. Peter & Barberi, b. Mar. 25, 1744	1	91
Mary, d. Alexander & Esther, b. Apr. 25, 1737	1	89
Mary, d. Gawen (?) & Mary, b. Apr. 1, 1751	1	64
Mary, m. John **EAMES**, Nov. 25, 1756	1	142
Peter, m. Isebel **LARKER**, Dec. 2, 1731	1	91
Peter, s. Peter & Barberi, b. June 20, 1742	1	91
Peter, s. Peter, d. June 3, 1743	1	91
Peter, s. Robert & Jane [ ]	1	91
Robert, d. Aug. 2, 1727	1	91
Robert, s. Peter & Isabell, b. Mar. 17, 1733	1	91
Robert, s. Alexander & Esther, b. Dec. 7, 1744	1	89
Robert, s. Peter, d. May 7, 1749	1	91
Ruth, d. Alexander & Esther, b. Oct. 26, 1748	1	89

VOLUNTOWN VITAL RECORDS

	Vol.	Page
MILLER, (cont.)		
Ruth, m. John **GASTON**, Jr., Oct. 24, 1771, by Rev. Alexander Miller, of Plainfield	1	173
MILLET, Andrew, s. Jonathan & Jenet, b. Nov. 29, 1767	1	117
Barberry, d. Jonathan & Jenet, b. Feb. 22, 1766	1	117
Daniel, s. Jonathan & Jennet, b. Feb. 2, 1774	1	117
Hannah, d. Jonathan & Jennet, b. Nov. 18, 1769	1	117
John, s. Jonathan & Jenet, b. Sept. 29, 1765	1	117
Jonathan, m. Jennet **EDMOND**, Sept. 1, 1763	1	117
Samuel, s. Jonathan & Jennet, b. Feb. 2, 1772	1	117
MINOR, MINER, Allen, s. Jonathan Ransford & Esther, b. Nov. 10, 1771	1	111
Ephraim, s. Jonathan & Ann, b. Aug. 10, 1754	1	48
Hannah, d. Jonathan Ransford & Esther, b. Sept. 29, 1767	1	111
Jonathan Ransford, m. Esther **ALLEN**, Nov. 20, 1766, by Timothy Whitman, Elder	1	111
Kezia, d. Manassah & Kezia, b. Nov. 6, 1727	1	13
Lucrecey, d. Manassah & Kezia, b. Feb. 16, 1733	1	13
Lucrecey, m. Amos **YORK**, Nov. 8, 1750, by Jeremiah Kinne, J.P.	1	64
Ledia, d. Jonathan & Ann, b. Jan. 15, 1749/50; d. Mar. 27, 1753	1	48
Lydia, d. Jonathan Ransford & Esther, b. Apr. 17, 1776	1	111
Manassah, m. Kezia **GEERS**, Nov. 9, 1726	1	13
Ransford Avery, s. Jonathan Ransford & Esther, b. Mar. 10, 1774	1	111
Samuel, s. Jonathan & Ann, b. June 27, 1752	1	48
Samuel, s. Jonathan Ransford & Esther, b. Aug. 9, 1769	1	111
Stephen, s. Jonathan Ransford & Esther, b. Oct. 27, 1778; d. June 8, 1781	1	111
-----, stillborn s. William F., farmer, ae 35, & Abby, ae 30, by May 8, 1850	3	24
MOFFITT, Lydia L., d. July 9, 1866, ae 29; b. in Vermont	3	76
MONTGOMERY, MONGUMRY, MOUNTGUMRY, MOUNGOMERY, Abigail, d. Asa & Martha, b. Dec. 3, 1776	1	201
Agness, d. John, Jr. & Sarah, b. July 18, 1757	1	86
Asa, s. John & Mary, b. May 2, 1747	1	72
Asa, s. Asa & Martha, b. Jan. 25, 1781	1	201
Charles, s. John & Mary, b. May 30, 1742	1	72
Charles, s. John & Sarah, b. June 15, 1763	1	86
Ebenezer, s. Robert & Hannah, b. June 23, 1768	1	187
Elias, s. John & Sarah, b. July 31, 1765	1	86
Elizabeth, d. Robert & Hannah, b. Mar. 4, 1770	1	187
Elizabeth, d. Asa & Martha, b. Apr. 4, 1778	1	201
Elizabeth, m. Peter **BURLINGAME**, Apr. 23, 1789, by Rev. Micaiah Porter	1	160
Esther, d. Asa & Martha, b. Oct. 30, 1769	1	201
Ezekiel, s. John & Mary, b. Dec. 4, 1744	1	72
Hannah, d. Robert & Hannah, b. May 21, 1772	1	187
Huldah, d. Asa & Martha, b. Feb. 18, 1773	1	201
James, m. Margaret **HINDMAN**, Mar. 4, 1756, by Robert Dixson, Esq.	1	59
James, s. John & Sarah, b. Mar. 4, 1768	1	86
Jean, d. Robert & Hannah, b. June 16, 1782	1	187
Jenitt, d. John & Sarah, b. May 14, 1759	1	86
Jenney, d. James & Marg[a]ret, b. Dec. 19, 1756	1	59

BARBOUR COLLECTION

	Vol.	Page
MONTGOMERY, MONGUMRY, MOUNTGUMRY, MOUNGOMERY, (cont.)		
John, Jr., m. Sarah **DIXSON**, Feb. 12, 1756, by Rev. Dorrance	1	86
John, s. Robert & Hannah, b. Feb. 12, 1766	1	187
Josiah, s. John & Mary, b. Mar. 5, 1737/8	1	72
Josiah, s. Robert & Hannah, b. Oct. 1, 1764	1	187
Lydia, d. John & Sarah, b. Sept. 2, 1770	1	86
Martha, d. Asa & Martha, b. May 29, 1774	1	201
Mary, w. John, d. Aug. 22, 1750, ae 46 y.	1	72
Mary, d. John & Sarah, b. Mar. 20, 1761	1	86
Mary, d. Asa & Martha, b. July 16, 1768	1	201
Mary, d. Robert & Hannah, b. Aug. 3, 1786	1	187
Robert, s. John & Mary, b. Jan. 8, 1740	1	72
Robert, s. Robert & Hannah, b. Aug. 4, 1778	1	187
Sally, d. John & Sarah, b. Mar. 5, 1773	1	86
Sarah, d. Robert & Hannah, b. May 15, 1776	1	187
William, s. John & Mary, b. Feb. 10, 1735/6	1	72
William, s. Asa & Martha, b. Apr. 25, 1771	1	201
MORGAN, Abel W., m. Lydia **ADAMS**, b. of Voluntown, Feb. 20, 1831, by Joseph Wylie, J.P.	2	86
Abel W., d. July 3, [1860], ae 56	3	70
Abel Wilkinson, s. Wheeler & Polly, b. Sept. 18, 1804	1	224
Abigale, d. Nathaniel & Ele[a]nor, b. May 13, 1767	1	115
Albert W., m. Sally **BITGOOD**, Mar. 28, 1824, by Amos Treat, J.P.	2	56
Anne, d. Seth & Desire, b. May 20, 1788	1	167
Charlotte, d. June 2, 1860, ae 72; b. in Windham	3	70
Desier, d. Ebenezer & Desire, b. July 4, 1765	1	94
Desire, w. Ebenezer, d. Feb. 21, 1784	1	94
Desire, m. John **LARKHAM**, Feb. 6, 1785, by Rev. Micaiah Porter	1	216
Desire, d. Wheeler & Polly, b. Mar. 8, 1792	1	224
Dinah, d. Wheeler & Polly, b. Jan. 7, 1795	1	224
Dorothy, m. Jacob **CADY**, Dec. 27, 1770, by Rev. Levi Hart	1	80
Ele[a]ner, d. Nathaniel & Ele[a]nor, b. Apr. 6, 1770	1	115
Elisha, s. Wheeler & Polly, b. Dec. 18, 1798	1	224
Elisha, m. Ruth **DOUGLASS**, Sept. 26, 1827, by Sterry Kinne, J.P.	2	72
Elizabeth, m. Moses **FISH**, Nov. 7, 1745, by Rev. Crosswell	1	73
Hannah, d. Nathaniel & Ele[a]ner, b. July 11, 1774	1	115
Hannah had d. Hope Almira **WILCOX**, reputed d. of Henry **WILCOX**, b. Feb. 5, 1804	1	115
Hannah, d. Feb. 5, 1849, ae 95 (perhaps 75)	3	59
Harvey, s. Seth & Desire, b. Apr. 29, 1783	1	167
Lucynda, d. Peter & Martha, b. May 23, 1788	1	214
Lucy, d. Solomon & Eunice, b. Dec. 6, 1778	1	154
Lydia, d. Wheeler & Polly, b. Jan. 24, 1784	1	224
Marcy, d. Wheeler & Polly, b. Aug. 11, 1788	1	224
Mary, d. Peter & Martha, b. June 12, 1783	1	214
Mary, d. Wheeler & Polly, b. Apr. 8, 1791	1	224
Nathan Lewis, s. Peter & Martha, b. Dec. 25, 1790	1	214
Nathaniel, m. Eleanor **RANDALL**, Oct. 16, 1766, by Jeremiah Kinne, J.P.	1	115
Nathaniel, s. Nathaniel & Ele[a]ner, b. July 4, 1772	1	115
Nathaniel, Lieut., d. Sept. 27, 1776, at Westchester	1	115
Nathaniel, s. Peter & Martha, b. Jan. 23, 1786	1	214

	Vol.	Page
MORGAN, (cont.)		
Olive, d. Nathaniel & Ele[a]ner, b. Sept. 26, 1776	1	115
Olive, d. Wheeler & Polly, b. July 6, 1802	1	224
Park[e], s. Solomon & Eunice, b. Aug. 13, 1774	1	154
Peter, s. Ebenezer & Desier, b. Jan. 15, 1758	1	94
Peter, m. Martha **LEWIS**, Apr. 5, 1781, by Elder Pembleton	1	214
Sally, m. William **PEIRCE**, Jan. 7, 1786	1	194
Seth, m. Desire **BRUMBLEY**, Apr. 13, 1782	1	167
Temperance, m. Gideon **PALMER**, June 19, 1776, by Rev. Solomon Morgan	1	143
Wheeler, s. Ebenezer & Desier, b. Jan. 31, 1761	1	94
Wheeler, m. Polly **WILKINSON**, Dec. 24, 1780, by Rev. Solomon Morgan	1	224
Wheeler, s. Wheeler & Polly, b. Jan. 11, 1797	1	224
William, s. Solomon & Eunice, b. Jan. 15, 1777	1	154
William Allen, s. Wheeler & Polly, b. Feb. 5, 1790	1	224
MORSE, Anna, d. Benjamin & Phebe, b. Sept. 24, 1795	1	218
[See also **MARS** (handwritten on original manuscript)]		
MORY, MORRAY, MOWRY, Agnes, d. Gilbert & Elizabeth, b. Feb. 3, 1742	1	36
Elizabeth, d. Gilbert & Elizabeth, b. May 3, 1747	1	36
Elizabeth, m. Robert **EDMOND**, Dec. 29, 1757, by Rev. Samuel Dorrance	1	72
Esther, d. Gilbert & Elizabeth, b. July 2, 1745	1	36
Gilbert, s. Gilbert & Elizabeth, b. Apr. 20, 1751	1	36
James, s. Gilbert & Elizabeth, b. Nov. 1, 1743	1	36
Jane, d. Gilbert & Elizabeth, b. Mar. 25, 1749	1	36
John, of Exeter, R.I., m. Eunice **PALMER**, of Voluntown, Apr. 27, 1828, by Benjamin Gallup, J.P.	2	73
Lathrop, s. Joseph & Mary, b. Aug. [ ], 1753	1	63
Ruhamer, d. Joseph & Mary, b. July [ ], 1755	1	63
Samuel, s. Joseph & Mary, b. Aug. 15, 1750	1	63
MOTT, Hannah, d. Samuel & Hannah, b. July 13, 1758	1	92
Samuel, m. Hannah **STORY**, Apr. 14, 1757, by Jeremiah Kinne, Esq.	1	92
MOWRY, [see under **MORY**]		
MULKINS, MULKIN, Lydia, m. Daniel **FRINK**, Dec. 20, 1770, by Samuel Coit, J.P.	1	26
Mary, alias Mary **NEWKEY**, of Voluntown, m. Moses **SABINS**, of Griswold, Sept. 12, 1845, by John E. Lindley, J.P.	2	118
Sarah, m. James **KEIGWIN**, May 1, 1763, by Samuel Coit, J.P.	1	102
MURPHY, Ira Gallup, s. Archibald & Sabra, b. Oct. 11, 1802, in Bridgewater, Oneida County, N.Y.	1	132
NEWKEY, Joanna, of Voluntown, m. Nathaniel **HOPKINS**, of Charlestown, R.I., Apr. 13, 1851, by Elisha Potter, J.P.	2	124
Joanna, ae 24, of Voluntown, m. Nathaniel **HOPKINS**, ae 30, farmer, b. in Charlestown, R.I., res. of Voluntown, people of color, Apr. 13, 1851, by Elisha Potter, Esq.	3	3
Mary, alias Mary **MULKINS**, of Voluntown, m. Moses **SABINS**, of Griswold, Sept. 12, 1845, by John E. Lindley, J.P.	2	118
NEWMAN, Hannah, m. John **COLE**, Nov. 13, 1746, by Rev. Greenwood, of Rehoboth	1	41
NEWTON, NUTON, Abram, s. Nathan, b. May 5, 1801	2	58

	Vol.	Page
NEWTON, NUTON, (cont.)		
Amos, s. Matthew & Elizabeth, b. Mar. 27, 1767	1	104
Anna, d. Aug. 31, 1849, ae 81; b. in Stonington	3	61
Benjamin F., s. Nathan, b. June 14, 1816	2	58
Benjamin T., of Voluntown, m. Mary Ann **MAINE**, of N. Stonington, Dec. 31, 1837, by Benjamin Gallup, Jr., J.P.	2	105
Charlotte, d. Nathan, b. July 26, 1808	2	58
Charlotte, of Voluntown, m. Stephen **REYNOLDS**, of Griswold, Nov. 22, 1846, by Rev. Ebenezer Blake	2	75
Clarissa, d. Stephen & Huldah, b. Feb. 5, 1797	1	183
Content, d. Matthew & Elizabeth, b. Nov. 2, 1753	1	104
Content, d. Amos & Anna, b. Apr. 13, 1797	1	188
Content, of Voluntown, m. Archibald **WEAVER**, of Coventry, R.I., Apr. 18, 1822, by Amos Treat, J.P.	2	46
Daniel, s. Matthew & Elizabeth, b. Nov. 20, 1761	1	104
Elijah, s. Nathan, b. July 6, 1798	2	58
Elizabeth, d. Matthew & Elizabeth, b. Feb. 13, 1765	1	104
Elizabeth, d. Nathan, b. Apr. 13, 1800	2	58
George, s. Nathan P., farmer, ae 38, & Mercy, ae 33, b. Aug. 1, 1850	3	23
George B., s. Nathan, b. May 23, 1810	2	58
Hannah E., d. Nathaniel P., ae 36, & Mercy, ae 30, b. Feb. 11, 1848	3	21
Henry, s. Matthew & Elizabeth, b. Apr. 30, 1755	1	104
Isaac, s. Nathan, b. July 1, 1802	2	58
Israel, s. Matthew & Tacy, b. Dec. 9, 1788	1	104
Jabez, s. Matthew & Elizabeth, b. Mar. 6, 1769	1	104
Jabez, [s. Matthew & Elizabeth], d. Apr. 28, 1837	1	104
Jacob, s. Nathan, b. Oct. 6, 1803	2	58
Mary, d. Matthew & Elizabeth, b. Mar. 10, 1757	1	104
Mary, d. Nathan, b. Sept. 5, 1806	2	58
Mary, of Voluntown, m. James **WEAVER**, of Coventry, Sept. 29, 1822, by Amos Treat, J.P.	2	50
Nathan, s. Matthew & Elizabeth, b. June 9, 1771	1	104
Nathan G., s. Nathan, b. May 27, 1814	2	58
Sarah, d. Sept. [ ], 1854, ae 4	3	65
Sarah C., d. Henry, farmer, & Sally, b. Dec. 9, 1849	3	24
Sheffield, s. Nathan, b. Feb. 23, 1805	2	58
Stephen, m. Huldah **STEVENS**, Dec. 4, 1794, by Allen Campbell, J.P.	1	183
Tacy, m. Elisha **POTTER**, Nov. 28, 1822, by Sterry Kinne, J.P.	2	51
William, s. Matthew & Elizabeth, b. May 28, 1759	1	104
William Albert, d. Aug. 21, 1862, ae 22	3	71
-----, female, d. Nov. [ ], 1865; b. in R. Island	3	75
NEY, Hannah, d. John & Rebecca, b. Sept. 5, 1805	1	186
John, m. Rebecca **JURDON**, May [ ], 1802, by Allen Campbell, J.P.	1	186
Nathan, s. John & Rebecca, b. Feb. 14, 1803	1	186
NICHOLS, NICHOS, John, of Exeter, m. Abby Ann **BUTTON**, of Hopkinton, R.I., Nov. 20, 1853, by Samuel Gates, J.P.	2	137
Martha, m. Henry N. **CHAPPELL**, b. of R. Island, Sept. 5, 1844, by Rev. Charles S. Weaver	2	21
Stephen, of Exeter, m. Betsey **RATHBUN**, of Voluntown, May 15, 1842, by Rev. Charles S. Weaver	2	43
NORTH[R]UP, Polly, m. James **DENNIS**, May 4, 1823, by Sterry		

	Vol.	Page
NORTH[R]UP, (cont.)		
Kinne, J.P.	2	53
[O'BRIEN], O'BRIENE, O'BRIENT, John, d. Mar. 27, 1866, ae 11, m.;		
b. in W. Greenwich	3	77
Nell[i]e, d. Thomas & Mary, b. Oct. 7, 1754	1	84
OWEN, Mary, Madame, m. Rev. Samuel **DORRANCE**, July 1, 1755, by		
Rev. David Jewett, of New London	1	72
PALMER, Abby, ae 30, b. in Hopkinton, R.I., res. of Voluntown, m.		
Charles H. **BUTTON**, ae 18, farmer, of Voluntown, Mar. 20,		
1851, by Rev. Lathrop P. Weaver	3	3
Abby Ann, m. Charles N. **BUTTON**, Mar. 20, 1851, by Lathrop B.		
Weaver	2	139
Alfred, s. Allen C. & Polly, b. Feb. 6, 1825	2	80
Allen Campbell, s. Russell* & Sarah, b. July 12, 1791. (*Should be		
"**ROSWELL**")	1	233
Amos Randall, s. Benjamin & Hannah, b. Mar. 15, 1815; d. Jan. [ ],		
1825	2	99
Asenath, d. Roswell & Sarah, b. Nov. 1, 1793	1	233
Benjamin, s. Elijah & Lucretia, b. Mar. 23, 1793	1	225
Benjamin, d. Apr. 2, 1849, ae 92	3	59
Benjamin W., s. Benjamin & Hannah, b. Jan. 25, 1813	2	99
Carrie Frances, d. June 19, 1864, ae 2 y. 7 m.; b. in Hopkinton, R.I.	3	74
Celinda, m. George **RATHBUN**, b. of Voluntown, July 12, 1840, by		
Rev. Charles S. Weaver	2	33
Charles H., of R.I., m. Frances **WILLCOX**, Apr. 8, 1845, by Rev.		
Charles S. Weaver	2	5
Comfort, m. Cyrus **KINNE**, Apr. 10, 1770, by Jeremiah Kinne, Esq.	1	123
Content, m. Joseph **RANDALL**, Dec. 25, 1754, by Weight Palmer,		
Elder	1	114
Cordelia, of Voluntown, m. Elisha **BRUMBLEY**, of Hopkinton,		
R.I., Nov. 14, 1844, by John E. Lindley, J.P.	2	118
Courtland Edwin, s. Benjamin & Hannah, b. Mar. 3, 1828	2	99
Daniel, s. Samuel & Lucretia, b. Apr. 22, 1763	1	106
Daniel, d. Aug. 17, 1772, ae 69 y.	1	106
David W., s. Joseph & Nabby, b. June 5, 1807	1	202
Dinah, d. Roswell & Sarah, b. Oct. 10, 1802	1	233
Dinah Mary, d. Gershom & Mary, b. Dec. 23, 1829	2	145
Dinah Mary, d. Gershom, m. Jabez Thurston **PHILLIPS**, s. Daniel,		
all of Voluntown, Jan.14, 1844, by Gershom Palmer, Elder	2	113
Dolly, d. Elijah & Lucretia, b. Dec. 23, 1776	1	225
Elijah, twin with Elisha, s. Joseph & Catharine, b. Sept. 23, 1750	1	122
Elijah, m. Lucretia **PALMER**, Mar. 28, 1773	1	225
Elisha, twin with Elijah, s. Joseph & Catharine, b. Sept. 23, 1750	1	122
Elisha, m. Huldah **PALMER**, Nov. 30, 1769, by Jeremiah Kinne,		
J.P.	1	122
Elisha, s. Elijah & Lucretia, b. Aug. 31, 1786	1	225
Elizabeth, d. Samuel & Lucretia, b. Sept. 18, 1759	1	106
Elizabeth, twin with Joseph, d. David & Grace, b. Dec. 7, 1767	1	146
Elizabeth, d. Roswell & Sarah, b. Nov. 5, 1797	1	233
Esther, m. Jonathan **PALMER**, Nov. 23, 1774, by Eleazer Brown,		
Elder	1	130
Esther Ann, d. Gershom & Mary, b. July 20, 1833	2	145
Esther Ann, ae 15, m. Silas A. **JAMES**, ae 17, b. of Voluntown,		

BARBOUR COLLECTION

	Vol.	Page
PALMER, (cont.)		
Jan. 9, 1848, by Gershom Palmer	3	1
Eugene Hunter, s. John H. & Julia Ann **PALMER**, b. Nov. 22, 1851	2	131
[E]unice, d. David & Grace, b. Jan. 25, 1772	1	146
Eunice, of Voluntown, m. John **MOWRY**, of Exeter, R.I., Apr. 27, 1828, by Benjamin Gallup, J.P.	2	73
Eunice, m. David **SMITH**, b. of N. Stonington, Mar. 20, 1841, by Benjamin Gallup, Jr., J.P.	2	108
Eunice Ann, d. Benjamin & Hannah, b. May 15, 1819	2	99
Eunice E., of Voluntown, m. Martin **DAVIS**, of Griswold, Feb. 17, 1840, by Rev. Charles S. Weaver	2	32
Eunice E., d. Ethel, ae 42, & Elizabeth, ae 30, b. June 18, 1848	3	21
Freelove E., m. Thomas H. **HULL**, b. of N. Stonington, Feb. 24, 1840, by Rev. Cyrus Miner	2	111
Freelove Emma, d. Benjamin & Hannah, b. Aug. 3, 1821	2	99
Gershom, s. Elijah & Lucretia, b. Nov. 22, 1774	1	225
Gideon, m. Temperance **MORGAN**, June 19, 1776, by Rev. Solomon Morgan	1	143
Grace, d. David & Grace, b. Mar. 31, 1766	1	146
Hannah, m. Andrew **EL[L]IOT**, Aug. 18, 1745, by Joseph Palmer, Esq.	1	65
Hannah, m. Peleg **RANDAL[L]**, Mar. 12, 1772, by Jeremiah Kinne, Esq.	1	131
Hannah, m. Peleg **RANDALL**, Mar. 12, 1772, by Jeremiah Kinne, J.P.	1	174
Hannah, m. Gershom **RAY**, Jan. 26, 1783, by Eleazer Brown, Elder	1	248
Hannah, ae 18, of Voluntown, m. Gardiner W. **ECCLESTONE**, ae 22, b. Richmond, R.I., resid. of Voluntown, Feb. 23, 1850, by Rev. J. B. Denison	3	2
Hannah E., d. Benjamin & Hannah, b. Apr. 4, 1817	2	99
Hannah E., m. Zebulon F. **STANTON**, b. of Voluntown, Feb. 23, 1834, by Elisha Potter, J.P.	2	98
Hannah M., of Exeter, m. Rowland **DRAPER**, of Voluntown, May 31, 1840, by Rev. Charles S. Weaver	2	32
Huldah, m. Elisha **PALMER**, Nov. 30, 1769, by Jeremiah Kinne, J.P.	1	122
Huldah, d. Elijah & Lucretia, b. Dec. 28, 1797	1	225
Jabez, d. May 11, 1848, ae 66; b. in Hopkinton, R.I.	3	59
James, s. David & Grace, b. Mar. 6, 1764	1	146
James, s. Roswell & Sarah, b. Aug. 6, 1792	1	233
Jarus, d. Nov. [ ], 1856, ae 78	3	67
Jesse, s. Elijah & Lucretia, b. July 23, 1795	1	225
Jesse, m. Eunice **BROWN**, Oct. 8, 1815, by Elias Hewitt, J.P.	2	4
John, ae 19, farmer, m. Julia **KENNEY**, ae 18, b. of Voluntown, Mar. 11, 1849, by Gershom Palmer	3	1
John H., d. Nov. 5, 1854, ae 3	3	65
John H., d. July 30, 1857, ae 25	3	67
John Hunter, s. Roswell & Sarah, b. Oct. 31, 1800	1	233
John Hunter, s. Gershom & Mary, b. Apr. 12, 1832	2	145
John Hunter, of Voluntown, s. Gershom, m. Julia Ann **KINNE**, d. of Joel, decd., of Voluntown, Mar. 11, 1849, by Gershom Palmer, Elder	2	131
John M., of Exeter, m. Amy E. **POTTER**, of R.I., Sept. 2, 1844, by		

	Vol.	Page
PALMER, (cont.)		
Rev. Charles S. Weaver	2	19
Jonathan, m. Freelove **HERRICK**, May 5, 1749, by Joseph Palmer J.P.	1	71
Jonathan, s. Joseph & Catharine, b. Feb. 10, 1753	1	130
Jonathan, m. Esther **PALMER**, Nov. 23, 1774, by Eleazer Brown, Elder	1	130
Joseph, s. Joseph & Susannah, b. Nov. 18, 1778; m. Nabby **WHEELER**, May 12, 1805, by Peleg Randall, Elder	1	202
Joseph, m. Lidea **PALMER**, Dec. 2, 1762, by Jeremiah Kinne, J.P.	1	112
Joseph, twin with Elizabeth, s. David & Grace, b. Dec. 7, 1767	1	146
Joseph, 3d, m. Content **WHEELER**, Apr. 27, 1768, by Joseph Denison, J.P.	1	116
Joseph, Deac., m. Hannah **BILLINGS**, Feb. 8, 1778, by Rev. Solomon Morgan	1	118
Joseph, s. Elijah & Lucretia, b. Mar. 23, 1784	1	225
Joseph, m. Nabby **WHEELER**, May 12, 1805, by Peleg Randall, Elder	1	202
Joseph T., of Voluntown, m. Julia F. **LEWIS**, of Hopkinton, R.I., Jan. 6, 1861, by Elisha Potter, J.P.	2	135
Julia, ae 20, b. Exeter, R.I., resid. of Griswold, m. Nathaniel **WILCOX**, ae 25, b. in W. Greenwich, resid. of Griswold, Sept. 2, 1849, by Elder Cha[rle]s S. Weaver	3	2
Katurah, d. Dec. 7, 1865, ae 65; b. in Exeter, R.I.	3	75
Leland, s. Allen C. & Polly, b. Mar. 21, 1823	2	80
Louis, wid., d. Aug. 10, 1853, ae 78	3	63
Lucretia, d. Samuel & Lucretia, b. Sept. 13, 1757	1	106
Lucretia, m. Elijah **PALMER**, Mar. 28, 1773	1	225
Lucy Ann, of N. Stonington, m. Charles **GATES**, of Voluntown, July 5, 1840, by Rev. Charles S. Weaver	2	32
Luther Allen, s. Allen C. & Polly, b. Apr. 20, 1827	2	80
Lidea, m. Joseph **PALMER**, Dec. 2, 1762, by Jeremiah Kinne, J.P.	1	112
Lydia, d. Elijah & Lucretia, b. Apr. 5, 1789	1	225
Lydia E., d. Apr. [ ], 1856, ae 6	3	67
Lyea E., d. Ethel, farmer, ae 43, & Elizabeth, ae 39, b. Mar. 3, 1850	3	23
Marg[a]ret, d. Samuel & Lucretia, b. June 4, 1761	1	106
Marg[a]ret, m. Uzziel **FRINK**, Mar. 28, 1776, by James Bradford, J.P.	1	92
Margaret, m. Thomas **PALMER**, July 13, 1780, by Rev. Solomon Morgan	1	153
Mary, w. Deac. Joseph, d. June 13, 1777, ae 88 y.	1	118
Mary, d. Nov. 26, 1854, ae 60	3	65
Nabby, d. Joseph & Nabby, b. Sept. 7, 1809	1	202
Nancy, d. David & Grace, b. Apr. 20, 1777	1	146
Nathaniel, s. Gideon & Temperance, b. Nov. 9, 1777	1	143
N[ ], d. Roswell & Sarah, b. [ ]	1	233
Phebe, m. Amos **RANDALL**, Apr. 25, 1765, by Jeremiah Kinne, J.P.	1	115
Phebe, d. Elijah & Lucretia, b. Apr. 16, 1781	1	225
Phebe, of Voluntown, m. Henry **RAY**, of Norwich, Dec. [ ], 1846, by Rev. Charles S. Weaver	2	11
Phebe, m. George W. **EDWARDS**, Dec. 24, 1848, by Benjamin Gallup, 2d, J.P.	2	131

	Vol.	Page
PALMER, (cont.)		
Phebe, ae 54, m. George **EDWARDS**, ae 42, farmer, b. of Hopkinton, R.I., Dec. 24, 1848, by Benjamin Gallup	3	1
Phebe Maria, d. Benjamin & Hannah, b. July 5, 1825	2	99
Prudence, d. Dec. 8, 1848, ae 64; b. N. Stonington	3	60
Rebeckah, d. Samuel & Lucretia, b. May 25, 1756	1	106
Rebecca, d. Elijah & Lucretia, b. Dec. 27, 1778	1	225
Roswell, m. Sarah **CAMPBELL**, Apr. 8, 1790, by Rev. Micaiah Porter	1	233
Roswell, s. Roswell & Sarah, b. June 10, 1804	1	233
Roswell, m. Nabby **BARBER**, b. of Exeter, R.I., Oct. 29, 1829, by Nathaniel Sheffield, Elder	2	82
Sarah, d. David & Grace, b. Feb. 1, 1770	1	146
Sarah, d. Roswell & Sarah, b. Nov. 23, 1795	1	233
Sarah, m. George **HOLMES**, b. of Griswold, Nov. 24, 1848, by Rev. Charles S. Weaver	3	1
Sarah, ae 26, weaver, b. in Voluntown, res. of Westerly, m. David **MAIN**, ae 25, machinist, b. in N. Stonington, res. of Westerly, Jan. 2, 1848, by Rev. Charles S. Weaver	3	1
Sarah M., of Voluntown, m. David **MAINE**, of N. Stonington, Jan. 2, 1848, by Rev. Charles S. Weaver	2	125
Susan, of N. Ston[ington], m. Benjamin **BRATON**, of N. Ston[ington], June 30, 1844, by Rev. Charles S. Weaver	2	19
Thomas, m. Margaret **PALMER**, July 13, 1780, by Rev. Solomon Morgan	1	153
Tully, d. Nov. 22, 1867, ae 72; b. in S. Kingston	3	78
Walter, of [ ], m. Fanny **STEWART**, of Springfield, Mar. 25, 1844, by Rev. Charles S. Weaver	2	19
Zebulon, s. Gideon & Temperance, b. Oct. 8, 1779	1	143
Ziporah, d. David & Grace, b. May 17, 1762	1	146
Ziporah, m. Isaac **RANDALL**, May 25, 1790, by Joshua Babcock, J.P.	1	209
-----, d. Benjamin W., ae 36, & Betsey A., ae 30, b. May 10, 1849	3	22
-----, female, d. Nov. 23, 1855, ae 1 y. 3 m.	3	66
PARKE, PARK, Abigail, d. Nehemiah & Mary, b. Feb. 26, 1757	1	47
Bethuel, s. Isaac & Mary, b. Mar. 12, 1777; d. Mar. 15, 1780	1	134
Christopher, m. Sarah **MANSFIELD**, Nov. 5, 1754, by Robert Dixson, Esq.	1	85
Christopher, s. Christopher & Sarah, b. Sept. 22, 1761	1	85
Deborah, m. John **KEIGWIN**, Aug. 15, 1728	1	13
Deborah, d. Isaac & Mary, b. Aug. 24, 1775	1	134
Desire, d. Robert & Dorithy, b. Oct. 22, 1733	1	36
Dorithy, d. Robert & Dorithy, b. Aug. 4, 1729	1	8
Elizabeth, d. Robert & Dorithy, b. Sept. 28, 1742	1	36
Elizabeth, d. John & Sarah, b. Aug. 3, 1744	1	34
Elizabeth, m. Thomas **SHAW**, Oct. 15, 1767, by William Witter, J.P.	1	97
Elizabeth, d. Robert & Elizabeth, b. July 20, 1770	1	121
Elizabeth, d. Nehemiah, Jr. & Marg[a]ret, b. Mar. 25, 1772	1	125
Esther, d. John & Sarah, b. Dec. 14, 1742	1	34
Eunice, twin with Lois, d. Joseph & Sarah, b. Feb. 14, 1745	1	70
Eunice, d. Robert & Elizabeth, b. Oct. 10, 1767	1	121
Eunice, m. Spencer **COLE**, Jan. 13, 1785, by Rev. Jonathan Fuller	1	177
Ezekiel, s. Robert & Dorithy, b. Jan. 22, 1726/7; d. Apr. 9, 1727	1	8

VOLUNTOWN VITAL RECORDS 215

	Vol.	Page
PARKE, PARK, (cont.)		
Ezekiel, s. Robert & Dorithy, b. Mar. 12, 1728	1	8
Hannah, d. Nehemiah, Jr. & Marg[a]ret, b. June 27, 1776	1	125
Isaac, m. Mary **MARTIN**, Mar. 9, 1775, by John Green, Esq.	1	134
Isaac, s. Isaac & Mary, b. Mar. 7, 1783	1	134
Jared, s. Isaac & Mary, b. July 16, 1787	1	134
Jemima, d. Benjamin & Mary, b. Apr. 17, 1748	1	84
John, m. Sarah **SPAULDING**, Dec. 7, 1741	1	34
John, s. John & Sarah, b. Feb. 16, 1745/6	1	34
John, s. Nehemiah & Mary, b. Apr. 27, 1759	1	47
John, m. Rosannah **STEWART**, June 20, 1776, by Rev. Solomon Morgan	1	40
John, s. John & Rosannah, b. Apr. 12, 1777	1	40
Joseph, m. Sarah **JAMESON**, May 27, 1735, by Rev. Samuel Dorrance	1	70
Joseph, s. Joseph & Sarah, b. Aug. 13, 1748	1	70
Joseph, s. Robert & Elizabeth, b. Sept. 5, 1773	1	121
Joshua, s. Nehemiah & Mary, b. Oct. 11, 1764	1	47
Lois, twin with Eunice, d. Joseph & Sarah, b. Feb. 14, 1745	1	70
Lucy, d. Robert & Elizabeth, b. Sept. 15, 1760	1	121
Lydia, d. Benjamin & Mary, b. Sept. 18, 1749	1	84
Martha, d. Robert & Tamson, d. Sept. 19, 1724, ae 21 y.	1	9
Martha, d. Robert & Dorithy, b. July 21, 1725	1	8
Marten, s. Isaac & Mary, b. Feb. 1, 1780	1	134
Mary, d. Benjamin & Mary, b. Oct. 3, 1731	1	84
Mary, d. Nehemiah & Mary, b. May 21, 1768	1	47
Matthais, s. Nehemiah & Mary, b. Apr. 13, 1761	1	47
Nathan, s. Robert & Dorithy, b. Apr. 30, 1731	1	8
Nathan, s. Nehemiah, Jr. & Marg[a]ret, b. May 20, 1774	1	125
Nehemiah, Jr., m. Marg[a]ret **STEWART**, Dec. 27, 1771, by Samuel Stewart, J.P.	1	125
Nehemiah, s. Nehemiah, Jr. & Marg[a]ret, b. July 29, 1778	1	125
Olive, d. Christopher & Sarah, b. May 11, 1755	1	85
Olive, b. Nov. 13, 1795; m. Isaac **GALLUP**, Nov. 14, 1819, by Rev. Asa Meech	2	141
Phebe, d. Robert & Dorithy, b. June 25, 1736	1	36
Robert, m. Dorithy **BACON**, Oct. 19, 1724	1	8
Robert, Lieut., d. May 12, 1752, ae 76 y.	1	69
Robert, s. Robert & Elizabeth, b. Feb. 12, 1776	1	121
Rosanna, m. John **GORDON**, Jr., Oct. 25, 1781, by Rev. Solomon Morgan	1	168
Ruth, d. Christopher & Sarah, b. Aug. 20, 1756	1	85
Samuel, s. Robert & Elizabeth, b. Jan. 29, 1762	1	121
Sarah, d. Joseph & Sarah, b. Jan. 1, 1742/3	1	70
Sarah, d. John & Sarah, b. Sept. 21, 1747	1	34
Sarah, d. Robert & Elizabeth, b. Feb. 10, 1765	1	121
Theody, m. Benjamin **GALLUP**, May 22, 1735, by Rev. Samuel Dorrance	1	16
Ward, s. Christopher & Sarah, b. Jan. 5, 1759	1	85
William, d. Nov. 29, 1724, ae 27 y.	1	9
-----, s. William & Mary, b. Nov. 24, 1724; d. the same day	1	9
PARKER, Jedidiah, s. Elisha & Mol[l]ey, b. Mar. 5, 1772	1	45
PARTELOW, PARTELO, PARTLOW, Asahel, m. Mary **KENNEDY**,		

216 BARBOUR COLLECTION

	Vol.	Page
PARTELOW, PARTELO, PARTLOW, (cont.)		
Mar. 15, 1787, by Rev. Micaiah Porter	1	226
Deborah, d. Asahel & Mary, b. Apr. 25, 1793, in Plainfield	1	226
Elizabeth, m. Stephen **COLEGROVE**, June 12, 1794, by Rev. Micaiah Porter	1	221
Ezra, m. Nancy **SAUNDERS**, Nov. 16, 1828, by Sterry Kinne, J.P.	2	70
Lydia, d. Thomas & Martha, b. Oct. 28, 1787	2	14
Lydia had d. Hannah, b. Apr. 14, 1811	2	14
Lydia had d. Almira, b. Apr. 17, 1817	2	14
Mary, m. Isaac **EAGLESTON**, Jr., Jan. 15, 1755, by Wait Palmer, Elder	1	57
Philetus T., m. Rebecca M. **FISH**, Feb. 14, 1830, by Levi Kneeland	2	83
Rosanna, d. Asahel & Mary, b. Dec. 22, 1788; d. Mar. 7, 1790	1	226
We[a]lthy, d. Asahel & Mary, b. Feb. 10, 1791, in Plainfield	1	226
Welcom[e] Jonas, s. Asahel & Mary, b. July 6, 1795	1	226
-----, m. Joseph **WOODMANCY**, of N. Stonington, [ ], 1850, by Charles S. Weaver	3	4
PATRICK, PATTRICK, PATRIACH, Benajah, s. Jacob & Zeruah, b. June 1, 1770	1	119
Ebenezer, s. Matthew & Elizabeth, b. Oct. 3, 1752	1	12
Jacob, s. Matthew & Elizabeth, b. May 24, 1733	1	12
Jacob, m. Mary **DIXSON**, Dec. 23, 1756, by Rev. Samuel Dorrance	1	86
Jacob, s. Jacob & Zeruah, b. Feb. 13, 1764	1	119
James, s. Jacob & Mary, b. Mar. 3, 1758	1	86
Joshua, s. Jacob & Zeruah, b. Feb. 24, 1762	1	119
Lydia, d. Matthew & Elizabeth, b. June 28, 1731	1	12
Mary, d. Jacob & Zeruah, b. Dec. 25, 1765	1	119
Mather*, m. Elizabeth **ROGERS**, Nov. 23, 1726, by Rev. Samuel Dorrance. (*Matthew)	1	12
Matthew, s. Jacob & Zeruah, b. Feb. 27, 1768	1	119
Robert, s. Matthew & Elizabeth, b. Apr. 29, 1740	1	12
Spencer Phypps, s. Jacob & Zeruah, b. Jan. 6, 1773	1	119
William, s. Matthew & Elizabeth, b. Apr. 15, 1738	1	12
PAUL, Jesse E., m. Eliza S. **TREAT**, Mar. 14, 1824, by Amos Treat, J.P.	2	56
PECKHAM, James H., of N. Stonington, m. Harriet **RANDALL**, of Voluntown, Nov. 30, 1845, by Rev. Charles S. Weaver	2	8
PELLET, Elijah M., of Norwich, m. Caroline **CHAPMAN**, of Voluntown, Jan. 2, 1849, by Rev. Jacob Allen	2	126
Elijah M*., ae 31, carpenter, res. of Norwich, m. Caroline **CHAPMAN**, ae 28, school-teacher, of Voluntown, June 2, 1849, by Rev. Jacob Allen. (*His 2d marriage)	3	2
PENDOCK, Levina, m. Ebenezer **WILLIAMS**, May 17, 1789, by Rev. Israel Day, of Killingly	1	217
PERKINS, Amos, s. Oliver & Ruth, b. July 7, 1758, in Norwich	1	193
Caleb, s. Oliver & Ruth, b. Apr. 1, 1777	1	193
Charity, m. Ethel **PHILLIPS**, June 17, 1819, by James Alexander, J.P.	1	254
Ebenezer, s. Ebenezer & Han[n]ah, b. July 1, 1721	1	5
Eliphaz, s. Eliphaz & Lydia, b. Mar. 6, 1788	1	196
Elisha, s. Oliver & Ruth, b. July 28, 1760, in Westerly	1	193
Han[n]ah, d. Ebenezer & Han[n]ah, b. Aug. 8, 1722	1	5
John, s. Christopher & Rebecca, b. July 6, 1777	1	94

VOLUNTOWN VITAL RECORDS 217

	Vol.	Page
PERKINS, (cont.)		
John, d. Apr. 4, 1849, ae 50; b. in Sterling, resid. of Griswold	3	60
John Milton, s. Oliver, Jr. & Anne, b. Oct. 25, 1793	1	222
Lemmuwell, s. Ebenezer & Han[n]ah, b. Apr. 2, 1720 (sic)	1	5
Lucy, m. John **BROUGHTON**, Dec. 17, 1778, by Rev. Solomon Morgan	1	116
Mary, d. Oliver & Ruth, b. Nov. 4, 1765, in Scituate	1	193
Mary C., of Exeter, m. Israel **PRATT**, of Voluntown, Jan. 9, 1820, in Sterling, by Nathaniel Sheffield, Elder	2	66
Newman, s. Oliver & Ruth, b. Aug. 22, 1762, in Westerly	1	193
Oliver, s. Oliver & Ruth, b. Oct. 22, 1770, in Scituate	1	193
Oliver, Jr., m. Anne **KENNEDY**, Dec. 27, 1792, by Rev. Micaiah Porter	1	222
Ransom, s. Oliver & Ruth, b. Apr. 8, 1768, in Scituate	1	193
Rufus, of Exeter, R.I., m. Jemima **PHILLIPS**, of Voluntown, Oct. 6, 1822, by James Alexander, J.P.	2	50
Ruth, d. Oliver & Ruth, b. Aug. 15, 1773	1	193
Sally, m. Elias **RATHBUN**, Jr., Jan. 24, 1819, by Gershom Palmer, Elder	2	35
Susannah, d. Oliver & Ruth, b. Mar. 23, 1780	1	193
Vallintine, s. Ebenezer & Han[n]ah, b. Dec. 26, 1719 (sic)	1	5
PETTIS, Amy, d. Stephen & Amy, b. Dec. 23, 1788	1	183
Lucy, m. James **DOUGLASS**, Jr., June 25, 1812, by Allen Campbell, J.P.	1	188
Mary, m. William **DOUGLASS**, May 1, 1760, by Edward Perry, J.P.	1	81
Nathan, s. Stephen & Anna (Ama ?), b. June 12, 1786	1	183
PHILLIPS, Almyra Roseannah Dulcena Hannah, d. Jabez T. & Dinah Mary, b. Sept. 30, 1852	2	113
Alzada W., d. Daniel & Sally, b. Apr. 23, 1829	2	119
Amos, s. Joseph, ae 35, & Marian, ae 28, b. Dec. 22, 1849	3	22
Amos Chapman, s. Atwood & Sally, b. Aug. 13, 1822; d. July 2, 1823	2	13
Amos J., s. Joseph & Merriam, b. Dec. 22, 1847	2	29
Annah, d. July 8, 1861, ae 1 y. 8 m.	3	71
Attwood, s. Nathaniel & We[a]lthy, b. Apr. 14, 1792	1	176
Atwood, m. Sally **CHAPMAN**, Nov. 28, 1816, by John Wylie, J.P.	2	13
Atwood W., ae 27, b. in Voluntown, resid. of Griswold, m. Lucy M. **DAVIS**, ae 23, b. in Griswold, resid. of Griswold, Mar. 20, 1850, by C. S. Weaver, Elder	3	2
Atwood Williams, s. Atwood & Sally, b. Sept. 29, 1817	2	13
Bishop, s. Ethel & Sabra, b. Oct. 30, 1804	1	254
Charity, ae 28, b. in Voluntown, resid. of Plainfield, m. James C. **HARRINGTON**, ae 21, b. in W. Greenwich, resid. of Plainfield, May 7, 1849, by Rev. C. S. Weaver	3	2
Charles, m. Sally **WORDEN**, b. of Hopkinton, R.I., Jan. 2, 1847, by Rev. Ebenezer Blake	2	116
Clarissa, d. Nathaniel & We[a]lthy, b. Nov. 10, 1804	1	176
Content, m. Nicholas **RANDALL**, Nov. 28, 1777, by Rev. Levi Hart	1	165
Daniel H., d. May 16, 1865, ae 80	3	75
Elisha Perkins, m. Mary **REMINGTON**, Feb. 6, 1806, by Silas Westcot[t], J.P.	1	178
Eliza Ann, d. Elisha P. & Mary, b. Sept. 18, 1810	1	178
Esther, m. Israel **FRINK**, Nov. 2, 1775, by Rev. John Fuller	1	134

218 BARBOUR COLLECTION

	Vol.	Page
PHILLIPS, (cont.)		
Esther, d. Jabez T. & Dinah Mary, b. Jan. 12, 1849	2	113
Esther, d. Thurston, ae 35, & Dinah M., ae 19, b. Jan. 12, 1849, (farmer)	3	23
Esther, d. Oct. 12, 1856, ae 6	3	66
Ethel, m. Sabra **FRINK**, Mar. 10, 1803, by Joseph Wylie, J.P.	1	254
Ethel, m. Charity **PERKINS**, June 17, 1819, by James Alexander, J.P.	1	254
Ethel, d. Apr. 25, 1827	2	69
Eunice, d. Ethel & Sabra, b. Feb. 25, 1811	1	254
Godfr[e]y, s. Nathaniel & We[a]lthy, b. Dec. 19, 1796	1	176
Harriet Newell, d. Pearley & Anna, b. Sept. 17, 1817	2	75
Harry G., d. Sept. 7, [1860], ae ?	3	70
Harvey, m. Mary **GREEN**, b. of Plainfield, Apr. 8, 1838, by Daniel Keigwin, J.P.	2	107
Henry C., of Plainfield, m. Harriet E. **ROUSE**, of Voluntown, May 23, 1852, by Benjamin Gallup, 2d, J.P.	2	142
Irena, d. Elisha P. & Mary, b. Aug. 24, 1807	1	178
Israel D., s. Daniel & Sally, b. Aug. 4, 1809	2	119
Jabez T., s. Daniel & Sally, b. Jan. 2, 1814	2	119
Jabez Thurston, s. Daniel, m. Dinah Mary **PALMER**, d. Gershom, all of Voluntown, Jan. 14, 1844, by Gershom Palmer, Elder	2	113
James M., of Russel, Mass., m. Joanna M. **FISH**, of Voluntown, Dec. [ ], 1846, by Rev. Charles S. Weaver	2	8
Jemima, d. Ethel & Sabra, b. June 21, 1806	1	254
Jemima, of Voluntown, m. Rufus **PERKINS**, of Exeter, R.I., Oct. 6, 1822, by James Alexander, J.P.	2	50
Jerusha, m. Moses **FISH**, Jr., Feb. 12, 1778, by Rev. Levi Hart	1	145
John H., s. Daniel & Sally, b. Mar. 16, 1808	2	119
Joseph, m. Merriam **PHILLIPS**, b. of Voluntown, Mar. 10, 1840, by Rev. Charles S. Weaver	2	29
Joseph S., of W. Greenwich, R.I., m. Patience A. **GORTON**, of Voluntown, Feb. 20, 1848, by Rev. Charles S. Weaver	2	125
Joshua P., s. Oliver, farmer, ae 22, & Clarinda, ae 24, b. May 17, 1849	3	23
Lucy, d. Nathaniel & We[a]lthy, b. Nov. 14, 1789	1	176
Lucy, of Canterbury, Ct., m. Gardner **WORDEN**, of Charlestown, R.I., Jan. 3, 1830, by Nathaniel Sheffield, Elder	2	82
Lydia C., d. Daniel & Sally, b. June 6, 1827	2	119
Lydia C., m. Samuel P. **KINNE**, Sept. 10, 1848, by Lathrop P. Weaver, of Norwich	2	100
Maata (Martha ?), d. Nathaniel & We[a]lthy, b. June 19, 1799	1	176
Martha Celinda, d. Pearly & Anna, b. Apr. 3, 1814	2	75
Mary Ann Prudence, d. Atwood & Sally, b. Mar. 19, 1824	2	13
Mary Jane, d. Jabez T. & Dinah Mary, b. Mar. 28, 1845	2	113
Mercy, d. Feb. 11, 1866, ae 21	3	76
Merriam, m. Joseph **PHILLIPS**, b. of Voluntown, Mar. 10, 1840, by Rev. Charles S. Weaver	2	29
Merriannah, d. Daniel & Sally, b. Aug. 7, 1820	2	119
Nabby Elizabeth, d. Atwood & Sally, b. Nov. 27, 1820	2	13
Nathaniel, s. Nathaniel & We[a]lthy, b. July 25, 1787	1	176
Orry Elizabeth, d. Pearley & Anna, b. Aug. 5, 1822	2	75
Palmer, s. Jabez T. & Dinah Mary, b. Oct. 15, 1846	2	113

	Vol.	Page
PHILLIPS, (cont.)		
Parley, s. Nathaniel & We[a]lthy, b. June 4, 1785	1	176
Batty, of Plainfield, m. Russell **TANNER**, Nov. 10, 1851, by Rev. Henry Robinson, of Plainfield	2	68
Pearly, m. Anna **TUCKER**, Sept. 13, 1812	2	75
Phebe E., d. Daniel & Sally, b. Feb. 2, 1816	2	119
Ralph, ae 24, farmer, b. in Voluntown, res. of Griswold, m. Rachel **CHAPMAN**, ae 23, tailoress, of Voluntown, July 1, 1844, by Rev. Henry Forbush	3	3
Ralph P., of Griswold, m. Rachel A. **CHAPMAN**, of Voluntown, July 1, 1850, by Rev. H. Forbush	2	140
Rebecca Matilda, d. Atwood & Sally, b. Feb. 19, 1819	2	13
Sabra B., d. Daniel & Sally, b. May 17, 1818	2	119
Sally, d. July 9, 1864, ae 79; b. in Exeter, R.I.	3	74
Sally Fear, d. Elisha P. & Mary, b. Sept. 14, 1812	1	178
Susan, ae 24, of Voluntown, m. Willard **GARDNER**, ae 24, b. in Exeter, R.I., resid. of Voluntown, Feb. 11, 1849, by Gershom Palmer	3	2
Susan C., d. Daniel & Sally, b. Jan. 12, 1825	2	119
Uzziel, s. Ethel & Sabra, b. Oct. 24, 1808	1	254
William, of Plainfield, m. Sarah Ann **HOWE**, of Voluntown, July 13, 1845, by Rev. Charles E. Weaver	2	5
PIERCE, PEIRCE, Betsey, d. W[illia]m & Sally, b. Oct. 11, 1787	1	194
Ebenezer, s. W[illia]m & Sally, b. Apr. 12, 1795	1	194
Edwin, ae 19, b. in Killingly, resid. of Griswold, m. Martha A. **KENYON**, ae 14, of Griswold, Nov. 25, 1850, by Samuel Cogswell	3	4
Frances, ae 17, of Voluntown, m. Albert **BABCOCK**, ae 21, b. in Sterling, resid. of Voluntown, July 4, 1849, by Thomas Tillinghast	3	2
Frederick, s. W[illia]m & Sally, b. Feb. 13, 1800	1	194
John Morgan, s. W[illia]m & Sally, b. Oct. 2, 1804	1	194
Lucy, d. Ebenezer & Margaret, b. May 23, 1726	1	8
Marg[a]ret, d. Benjamin & Elizabeth, b. Jan. 24, 1744/5	1	35
Peter, s. W[illia]m & Sally, b. Apr. 9, 1793	1	194
Phebe, m. John **SMITH**, Nov. 24, 1736, by Timothy Peirce, Esq.	1	25
Solomon, s. W[illia]m & Sally, b. Apr. 15, 1807	1	194
Susanna, d. W[illia]m & Sally, b. June 16, 1802	1	194
William, m. Sally **MORGAN**, Jan. 7, 1786	1	194
William, s. W[illia]m & Sally, b. Sept. 10, 1790	1	194
PIKE, William, of Sterling, m. Lydia T. **CAMPBELL**, of Voluntown, Aug. 20, 1822, by Amos Treat, J.P.	2	46
POLLOCK, Marvel, d. Apr. 8, 1867, ae 97; b. in R. Island	3	78
POPE, Hannah, d. Angel & Anne, b. Apr. 7, 1780	1	152
POPPLESTONE, Gideon, m. Louis **GREEN**, b. of Voluntown, Dec. 9, 1789, by Allen Campbell, J.P.	1	135
PORTER, Benjamin, s. Micaiah & Elizabeth, b. May 7, 1788	1	157
Isaac, s. Micaiah & Elizabeth, b. Oct. 11, 1783	1	157
Jabez, s. Rev. Micaiah & Elizabeth, b. Dec. 22, 1796	1	157
John, s. Rev. Micaiah & Elizabeth, b. Jan. 25, 1795	1	157
Martha, d. Rev. Micaiah & Elizabeth, b. Feb. 11, 1799	1	157
Micaiah, m. Elizabeth **GALLUP**, Nov. 22, 1781, by Rev. Solomon Morgan	1	157

	Vol.	Page
PORTER, (cont.)		
Phebe, d. Micaiah & Elizabeth, b. Mar. 11, 1790	1	157
William, s. Micaiah & Elizabeth, b. Feb. 10, 1786	1	157
POTTER, Alice L., m. Erastus **WILLIAMS**, b. of Voluntown, Apr. 26, 1835, by Elisha Potter, J.P.	2	101
Alice Lucinda, d. David R. & Judeth, b. Nov. 14, 1814	2	40
Amy E., of R.I., m. John M. **PALMER**, of Exeter, Sept. 2, 1844, by Rev. Charles S. Weaver	2	19
Arnold, d. Apr. 3, 1854, ae 78; b. in Richmond, R.I.	3	64
Barber, d. Jan. 2, 1848, ae 67; b. in Richmond, R.I.	3	59
Betsey, of Voluntown, m. Charles W. **THOMPSON**, of N. Stonington, Jan. 25, 1821, by Amos Treat, J.P.	2	39
Caleb, m. Sally **GREEN**, Nov. 16, 1797, by Allen Campbell, J.P.	1	219
Caleb, d. Aug. 4, 1848	1	219
Caleb, d. Aug. 4, 1848, ae 75; b. in Richmond, R.I.	3	59
Caleb P., s. Elisha & Tacy, b. Jan. 14, 1824	2	57
Caleb P., m. Eliza A. **STANTON**, b. of Voluntown, May 7, 1848, by Rev. Charles S. Weaver	2	129
Caleb P., ae 24, school-teacher, m. Eliza A. **STANTON**, ae 21, seamstress, b. of Voluntown, May 7, 1848, by Elder Charles S. Weaver	3	1
Candace, d. William & Reuby, b. May 18, 1840	2	48
David R., m. Judeth **CLARK**, Sept. 9, 1816, by John Wylie, J.P.	2	40
David R., s. David R. & Judeth, b. Mar. 1, 1822	2	40
David R., of Voluntown, m. Abby **CLARK**, of Richmond, d. of Moses **CLARK**, Jr., Aug. 10, 1834, by Samuel Reynolds, J.P.	2	40
David R., m. Content **REYNOLDS**, b. of Voluntown, May 12, 1844, by Harvey Campbell, J.P.	2	117
David R., d. June 16, [1859], ae 77; b. in Richmond, R.I.	3	69
David R., d. June 16, 1859, ae 67 y.	2	40
David R., d. June 16, 1859	2	117
Dwight Clark, s. David R. & Judeth, b. May 26, 1825	2	40
Dwight R., d. Sept. 19, 1848, ae 23	3	60
Dwight R., Jr., d. Jan. 5, 1849, ae 26	3	60
Elisha, s. Caleb & Sarah, b. Feb. 23, 1801	1	219
Elisha, m. Tacy **NEWTON**, Nov. 28, 1822, by Sterry Kinne, J.P.	2	51
Elisha, m. Elizabeth **CRARY**, b. of Voluntown, Jan. 18, 1846, by Rev. Jacob Allen, of Sterling	2	57
Elizabeth, d. Bennett & Elizabeth, b. May 10, 1774	1	101
Elizabeth, d. Caleb & Sarah, b. Oct. 17, 1798	1	219
Elizabeth, w. Income, d. May 13, 1822	2	111
Elizabeth, m. Thomas C. **COOPER**, Oct. 13, 1839, by Rev. Charles S. Weaver	2	25
Elizabeth, d. July 29, 1864, ae 59	3	74
Fanny Abba, d. David R. & Judeth, b. May 28, 1817	2	40
Hellen, d. William & Reuby, b. Jan. 7, 1839	2	48
Incom[e], m. Dorcus **HURD**, Jan. 8, 1824, by James Alexander, J.P.	?	54
Income, d. Feb. 28, 1844, ae 99 y.	2	111
Judeth, w. David R., d. Dec. 4, 1833	2	40
Julia, m. Allen B. **CAMPBELL**, b. of Voluntown, Nov. 13, 1842, by Rev. Charles S. Weaver	2	44
Lucy Ann, m. Denison **BROWN**, Mar. 27, 1831, by Minor Rob[b]ins, J.P.	2	86

	Vol.	Page
POTTER, (cont.)		
Marcia, m. William C. **AMES**, Apr. 12, 1827, by Rev. Zelotes Fuller, Jr.	2	71
Mary E., ae 17, weaver, b. in Voluntown, res. of Griswold, m. Daniel **CHAMPLAIN**, ae 20, spinner, b. in Voluntown, res. of Griswold, Dec. 2, 1849, by Rev. Henry Forbush	3	2
Mary Elizabeth, m. Daniel **CHAMPLAIN**, b. of Voluntown, Dec. 2, 1849, by Rev. H. Forbush	2	140
Mary M., of Griswold, m. Henry B. **HAMILTON**, of Voluntown, June 28, 1847, by Rev. Charles S. Weaver	2	35
Nathan, m. Nabby **RATHBUN**, Dec. 7, 1817, by Allen Campbell, J.P.	2	36
Nathan P., s. Nathan & Nabby, b. Mar. 18, 1819	2	36
Polly Matilda, d. Nathan & Nabby, b. June 18, 1823	2	36
Polly P., of Voluntown, m. Charles **CAMPBELL**, of Griswold, Feb. 2, 1844, by Rev. Charles S. Weaver	2	11
Sally, m. James **CAMPBELL**, Jan. 8, 1826, by Sterry Kinne, J.P.	2	63
Sally, wid. of Caleb, d. Apr. 21, 1854	1	219
Sally, d. Apr. 21, 1854, ae 76; b. in Westerly, R.I.	3	65
Sally Arnold, d. David R. & Judeth, b. Nov. 9, 1818	2	40
Susan Lucinda, d. William & Polly, b. Dec. 25, 1823	2	48
Susanna, m. Stephen **DOUGLASS**, Apr. 12, 1798, by Allen Campbell, J.P.	1	233
William, m. Polly **BURDICK**, Nov. 29, 1818, by Allen Campbell, J.P.	2	48
William, d. Feb. 10, 1849	2	48
William, d. Feb. 10, 1849	2	111
William Henry, s. William & Reuby, b. Mar. 20, 1843	2	48
-----. Stillborn, s. Caleb P., school-teacher, ae 27, resid. of Griswold, b. Oct. 11, 1850	3	26
PRATT, Israel, of Voluntown, m. Mary C. **PERKINS**, of Exeter, Jan. 9, 1820, in Sterling, by Nathaniel Sheffield, Elder	2	66
John F., Sir, d. Oct. 1, 1865, ae 4	3	76
Nancy A., d. Sept. 24, 1865, ae 2 y. 4 m.	3	75
Sarah, of W. Greenwich, m. Joseph H. **DOUGLASS**, of Voluntown, Aug. 25, 1850, by Charles S. Weaver	3	4
William C., d. Dec. 11, 1857, ae 10 m.	3	67
PRENTICE, Hezekiah, d. Apr. 12, 1865, ae 70 y.; b. in Griswold	3	75
RAFFERTY, Mary, d. Mar. 4, 1851, ae 67; b. in Ireland	3	62
Patrick A., s. James, common laborer, resid. of New Haven, b. Oct. [ ], 1850	3	26
Sarah, d. James, ae 33, & Catharine, ae 24, b. Mar. 3, 1849	3	22
RANDALL, Amos, m. Phebe **PALMER**, Apr. 25, 1765, by Jeremiah Kinne, J.P.	1	115
Amos, s. Amos & Phebe, b. Mar. 22, 1768	1	115
Asa, s. Peleg & Hannah, b. Sept. 3, 1779	1	174
Asa, s. Isaac & Elizabeth, b. June 2, 1793	1	209
Asa Lewis, s. Rufus & Cintha, b. May 16, 1818	2	20
Benjamin, s. Amos & Phebe, b. Mar. 4, 1781	1	115
Christopher, s. Joseph & Content, b. Nov. 17, 1758	1	114
Content, d. Joseph & Content, b. Mar. 10, 1766	1	114
Cate, d. Amos & Phebe, b. Nov. 23, 1776	1	115
Dolly, d. Rial & Mary, b. Mar. 4, 1791	1	220

RANDALL, (cont.)

	Vol.	Page
Dorithy, m. Ezra **CRERY**, Dec. 29, 1756, by Jeremiah Kinne, Esq.	1	78
Eleanor, m. Nathaniel **MORGAN**, Oct. 16, 1766, by Jeremiah Kinne, J.P.	1	115
Elisha, s. Amos & Phebe, b. Mar. 8, 1790	1	116
Ephraim, s. Isaac & Elizabeth, b. July 14, 1796	1	209
Esther, d. Amos & Phebe, b. Mar. 14, 1775	1	115
Esther, d. Peleg & Hannah, b. Feb. 16, 1796	1	174
Eunice, d. Wait & Eunice, b. Dec. 21, 1800	1	241
Frederic A., d. Aug. 26, 1864, ae 9; b. in R. Island	3	74
Freelove, d. Peleg & Hannah, b. Aug. 29, 1784	1	174
Hannah, d. Peleg & Hannah, b. Dec. 18, 1781	1	174
Harriet, of Voluntown, m. James H. **PECKHAM**, of N. Stonington, Nov. 30, 1845, by Rev. Charles S. Weaver	2	8
Huldah, d. Greenfield & Anna, b. Oct. 17, 1751	1	46
Huldah, d. Peleg & Hannah, b. May 8, 1790	1	174
Ichabod, s. Joseph & Content, b. Oct. 2, 1761	1	114
Isaac, s. Joseph & Content, b. Dec. 23, 1763	1	114
Isaac, m. Ziporah **PALMER**, May 25, 1790, by Joshua Babcock, J.P.	1	209
Isaac, s. Isaac & Zip[p]orah, b. May 16, 1791	1	209
Isaac, m. Elizabeth **REYNOLDS**, Aug. 12, 1792, by Joshua Babcock, J.P.	1	209
Isaac, Jr., m. Betsey **LEWIS**, Dec. 3, 1815, by Gershom Palmer, Elder	2	10
Jonas, s. Nathan & Ele[a]nor, b. Sept. 8, 1756	1	43
Joseph, m. Content **PALMER**, Dec. 25, 1754, by Weight Palmer, Elder	1	114
Joseph, s. Joseph & Content, b. Jan. 12, 1756	1	114
Joseph, Jr., m. Sabra **HEWIT[T]**, Apr. 20, 1775	1	138
Joseph, s. Peleg & Hannah, b. Mar. 14, 1793	1	174
Joseph A., s. Reuben, Jr. & Lydia, b. Aug. 19, 1817	2	20
Joseph A., d. Feb. 9, [1859], ae 42	3	69
Kate, see Cate		
Keturah, s. Amos & Phebe, b. Apr. 18, 1784	1	115
Lucretia, d. Rial & Mary, b. May 20, 1792	1	220
Lucy, ae 24, weaver, b in Voluntown, res. of Voluntown, m. George **MAXON**, ae 22, laborer, b. in Hopkinton, R.I., res. of Hopkinton, May 8, 1848, by Rev. Charles S. Weaver	3	1
Lucy E., of Voluntown, m. George J. **MAXON**, of Hopkinton, R.I., May 8, 1848, by Rev. Charles S. Weaver	2	130
Lydia, m. John **GALLUP**, 3d, Oct. 24, 1773, by Rev. Solomon Morgan	1	132
Lydia, d. Peleg & Hannah, b. Apr. 18, 1787	1	174
Mary, d. Nicholas & Content, b. June 17, 1782	1	165
Mary, m. Rial **RANDALL**, June 18, 1786, by Joshua Babcock, J.P.	1	220
Nicholass, s. Nathan & Ele[a]nor, b. May 21, 1753	1	43
Nicholas, m. Content **PHILLIPS**, Nov. 28, 1777, by Rev. Levi Hart	1	165
Nicholas, s. Nicholas & Content, b. July 25, 1779	1	165
Palmer, s. Amos & Phebe, b. Aug. 29, 1772	1	115
Paul Palmer, s. Peleg & Hannah, b. Dec. 24, 1798	1	174
Peleg, m. Hannah **PALMER**, Mar. 12, 1772, by Jeremiah Kinne, Esq.	1	131

	Vol.	Page
RANDALL, (cont.)		
Peleg, m.Hannah **PALMER**, Mar. 12, 1772, by Jeremiah Kinne, J.P.	1	174
Peleg, s. Peleg & Hannah, b. May 9, 1775	1	131
Peleg, s. Peleg & Hannah, b. May 9, 1775	1	174
Phebe, d. Amos & Phebe, b. Feb. 7, 1770	1	115
Polly, d. Rial & Mary, b. Oct. 27, 1787	1	220
Rebecca, d. Nicholas & Content, b. Nov. 2, 1780	1	165
Reuben, s. Joseph & Content, b. Apr. 1, 1757	1	114
Ruebin, m. Elizabeth **HILL**, July 6, 1789, by Joshua Babcock, J.P.	1	220
Reubin, s. Reubin & Elizabeth, b. May 3, 1793	1	220
Reuben, Jr., m. Lydia C. **HANCOCK**, Nov. 16, 1816, by Allen Campbell, J.P.	2	20
Reuben, Sr., d. Apr. 19, 1839	1	220
Reuben, d. Dec. 5, 1867, ae 75	3	78
Riel, s. Amos & Phebe, b. June 25, 1766	1	115
Rial, m. Mary **RANDALL**, June 18, 1786, by Joshua Babock, J.P.	1	220
Roswell, s. Peleg & Hannah, b. May 17, 1777	1	174
Rufus, s. Reuben & Elizabeth, b. July 24, 1796	1	220
Rufus, m. Cinthia **LEWIS**, Mar. 22, 1818, by Allen Campbell, J.P.	2	20
Ruth, d. Apr. 28, 1867, ae 92	3	78
Sarah, d. Greenfield & Anna, b. Apr. 5, 1749	1	46
Sarah, m. Samuel **WELLS**, Jr., Jan. 9, 1758, by Maj. Samuel Coit, J.P.	1	93
Stephen, s. Amos & Phebe, b. Apr. 2, 1788	1	116
Wait, m. Eunice **BUTTON**, Mar. 9, 1800, by Peleg Randall, Elder	1	241
William, s. Amos & Phebe, b. Mar. 7, 1779	1	115
Zip[p]orah, w. Isaac, d. May 31, 1791	1	209
RATHBUN, RATHBON, Amanda Alvina, d. Elias, Jr. & Sally, b. Dec. 15, 1821	2	35
Betsey, of Voluntown, m. Stephen **NICHOS**, of Exeter, May 15, 1842, by Rev. Charles S. Weaver	2	43
Charity, m. James **GORTON**, Apr. 28, 1791, by Phinehas Kenyon, J.P.	2	28
Celinda, m. Otis **GREEN**, b. of Voluntown, Mar. [ ], 1846, by Rev. Charles S. Weaver	2	8
Elias, Jr., m. Sally **PERKINS**, Jan. 24, 1819, by Gershom Palmer, Elder	2	35
Elias, s. Elias, Jr. & Sally, b. May 17, 1824, in Exeter	2	35
Elias, d. Feb. 19, 1843	2	112
Elijah L., s. Elias, Jr., & Sally, b. Jan. 22, 1820	2	35
George, m. Celinda **PALMER**, b. of Voluntown, July 12, 1840, by Rev. Charles S. Weaver	2	33
Job, of N. Kingstown, R.I., m. Mary **HARRIS**, [of Voluntown], Sept. 1, 1737, by Rev. Samuel Dorrance	1	19
John, of Hopkinton, m. Fanny **SEARS**, of Griswold, Feb. 10, 1841, by Rev. Charles S. Weaver	2	35
Mary, m. William **DOUGLASS**, Jr., Apr. 8, 1813, in Exeter, R.I., by Ellet Locke, Elder	1	148
Nabby, m. Nathan **POTTER**, Dec. 7, 1817, by Allen Campbell, J.P.	2	36
Paul, m. Hannah S. **BURDICK**, b. of Voluntown, Apr. 9, 1826, by James Alexander, J.P.	2	68
Phebe, d. Apr. 30, 1866, ae 24	3	76
Rhoby, m. Sheffield **COREY**, Jr., Dec. 8, 1817, by Allen		

	Vol.	Page
RATHBUN, RATHBON, (cont.)		
Campbell, J.P.	2	25
RAY, Daniel, s. Daniel & Elizabeth, b. Jan. 14, 1753	1	30
Gershom, m. Hannah **PALMER**, Jan. 26, 1783, by Eleazer Brown, Elder	1	248
Gershom, s. Gershom & Hannah, b. June 29, 1786	1	248
Gershom, m. Sally **BREED**, Dec. 12, 1819, in N. Stonington, by Jonathan Miner, Elder	2	19
Gershom, m. Sally **BREED**, Dec. 12, 1819	2	59
Gideon, s. Gershom & Hannah, b. Sept. 4, 1790	1	248
Hannah, d. Gershom & Hannah, b. Jan. 29, 1784	1	248
Henry, of Norwich, m. Phebe **PALMER**, of Voluntown, Dec. [ ], 1846, by Rev. Charles S. Weaver	2	11
Jabez B., ae 26, of Voluntown, m. Mary A. **WILBUR**, ae 21, of Griswold, Mar. 11, 1849, by Charles S. Weaver	3	1
Jabez Breed, s. Gershom & Sally, b. Apr. 24, 1823	2	59
Lucy, d. Gershom & Hannah, b. Dec. 13, 1799	1	248
Palmer, s. Gershom & Hannah, b. Mar. 10, 1797	1	248
Sally, d. Dec. 15, 1865, ae 83; b. in N. Stonington	3	76
Sinda, d. Gershom & Hannah, b. July 5, 1788	1	248
William B., s. Jabez B., farmer, ae 28, & Mary, ae 22, b. Feb. 5, 1850	3	23
READ*, Diantha, d. July 6, 1865, ae 43; b. in N. Stonington (*Perhaps **ROOD**?)	3	75
Julia, m. Albert **LARKHAM**, b. of Griswold, Sept. 17, 1843, by Rev. H. Farbush	2	67
REMINGTON, Mary, m. Elisha Perkins **PHILLIPS**, Feb. 6, 1806, by Silas Westcot[t], J.P.	1	178
REYNOLDS, Content, m. Caswell **GREEN**, Feb. 12, 1812, by Alexander Stewart, J.P.	1	247
Content, m. David R. **POTTER**, b. of Voluntown, May 12, 1844, by Harvey Campbell, J.P.	2	117
Elizabeth, m. Isaac **RANDALL**, Aug. 12, 1792, by Joshua Babcock, J.P.	1	209
Fanny M., m. Ezra P. **GEER**, Feb. 20, 1831, by Minor Rob[b]ins, J.P.	2	86
Henry B., of Voluntown, m. Amanda **MERRIS**, of Exeter, R.I., Mar. 27, 1825, by Nathaniel Sheffield, Elder	2	60
John, m. Lydia **EUSTISTON**, Dec. 28, 1823, by Amos Treat, J.P.	2	54
John, m. Content **ECCLESTONE**, b. of Voluntown, Dec. 29, 1833, by William C. Stanton, J.P.	2	55
Lucinda, m. Joseph **FENNER**, of Sterling, Feb. 13, 1834, by Nathaniel Sheffield, Elder	2	97
Samuel T., m. Eunice **WILLCOX**, b. of Voluntown, Feb. 11, 1828, by Nathaniel Sheffield, Elder	2	72
Sarah, d. John & Sarah, b. Nov. 21, 1760	1	92
Stephen, of Griswold, m. Charlotte **NEWTON**, of Voluntown, Nov. 22, 1846, by Rev. Ebenezer Blake	2	75
Susanna, m. Moses **FISH**, Jr., Oct. 8, 1815, by Jonathan Miner, Elder	2	6
Tenty, m. Cogswell **GREEN**, Jan. 12, 1810, at Preston, by Alexander Stewart, J.P.	2	84
Thomas, m. Lucinda **BURDICK**, b. of Voluntown, Dec. 15, 1822,		

	Vol.	Page
REYNOLDS, (cont.)		
by James Alexander, J.P.	2	51
RHOADES, RHOADS, RHODES, Abigel, d. Obed & Abigel, b. Dec. 31, 1719	1	6
Benjamin, s. Obadiah, Jr. & Mary, b. Jan. 3, 1754	1	45
Clarissa, d. John & Rebeckah, b. Mar. 16, 1775	1	144
Elezier, s. Eleizer & Marg[a]ret, b. Nov. 30, 1768	1	116
Elisha, s. Obadiah, Jr. & Lydia, b. Aug. 30, 1779	1	127
Jane, d. Obadiah, Jr. & Mary, b. Feb. 15, 1752	1	45
Jane, m. Oliver **STEWART**, Jr., Feb. 13, 1772, by Sam[ue]ll Stewart, J.P.	1	127
John, s. Obediah & Abiga[i]l, b. Apr. 15, 1727	1	6
John, m. Joanna **CADY**, Mar. 16, 1748, by Nathaniel Brown, J.P.	1	46
John, s. Obadiah, Jr. & Mary, b. Dec. 15, 1749	1	45
John, Jr., m. Rebeckah **STEWART**, Nov. 14, 1771, by Samuel Stewart, J.P.	1	144
John, s. John & Rebeckah, b. Sept. 29, 1773	1	144
John, Jr., m. Dolly **CRANDALL**, Apr. 27, 1788, by Amos Crandall, Jr., Elder	1	197
Martha, d. Obediah & Abiga[i]l, b. May 29, 1725; d. Oct. 7, 1727, in ye second year of her age	1	6
Mary, d. Eleizer & Marg[a]ret, b. Aug. 21, 1766	1	116
Obediah, s. Obediah & Abigel, b. July 20, 1722	1	6
Obadiah, Jr., m. Mary **STANDBERRY**, June 4, 1747, by Rev. Samuel Dorrance	1	45
Obadiah, s. Obadiah, Jr. & Mary, b. June 5, 1748	1	45
Obadiah, m. Susanna **TORRY**, Nov. 27, 1761, by Rev. Sylvanus White of Southampton	1	61
Obadiah, m. Lydia **JONES**, Dec. 30, 1773, by Rev. Witt	1	127
Obadiah, s. Obadiah & Lydia, b. Sept. 16, 1774	1	127
Obadiah, d. Oct. 18, 1781	1	61
Polly, d. Obadiah & Lydia, b. July 4, 1776	1	127
Rebeckah, d. John & Rebeckah, b. May 24, 1772	1	144
Samuel, s. John & Rebeckah, b. May 18, 1777	1	144
Samuel, s. Obadiah & Lydia, b. July 6, 1783	1	127
Susanna, d. John & Joanna, b. Jan. 25, 1764	1	94
Susan[n]a, d. Obadiah & Lydia, b. Sept. 6, 1781	1	127
Susanna, w. Obadiah, d. Oct. 17, 1781	1	61
RICE, Elizabeth, d. Oct. 6, [1859], ae 54; b. in Coventry, R.I.	3	69
Mary, wid. of Charles **RICE**, of Scituate, m. Elisha **ALMY**, Dec. 24, 1777, by Jeremiah Angell, J.P.	1	181
Rosannah, m. Joseph **AVERY**, Nov. [ ], 1766, by Rev. Samuel Dorrance	1	200
RICHARDSON, RICHASON, Henry S., ae 22, b. in Plainfield, resid. of Providence, m. Susan C. **TANNER**, ae 26, of Voluntown, Sept. 24, 1849, by Rev. C. S. Weaver	3	3
Mary Ann, m. Charles P. **SHELDON**, b. of Voluntown, Mar. 5, 1843, by W[illia]m C. Stanton, J.P.	2	101
Phebe, d. Thomas & Leley, b. Oct. 5, 1755	1	51
Thomas, m. Leley **HALEY**, Dec. 30, 1754, by Robert Dixson, J.P.	1	51
RICHMOND, Adoline A., d. Asa, farmer, ae 34, & Nancy, ae 29, b. July 16, 1850	3	24
Benjamin, d. Nov. [ ], 1854, ae 2	3	64

226 BARBOUR COLLECTION

	Vol.	Page
RICHMOND, (cont.)		
Charles Alexander, s. Benj[amin], 2d, & Sabra, b. Sept. 10, 1853	2	147
James T., d. July 23, 1863, ae 18	3	72
James Treat, s. Benj[amin], 2d, & Sabra, b. Dec. 13, 1845	2	147
Lucy, b. Nov. 20, 1819, at Exeter; m. Charles H. **KINNEY**, Apr. 12, 1837, by Rev. Charles S. Weaver	2	107
Lydia Margaret, d. Benj[amin], 2d, & Sabra, b. July 4, 1847	2	147
Nathaniel S., of Voluntown, m. Mary M. **CORY**, of Voluntown, Sept. 5, 1841, by Rev. Charles S. Weaver	2	43
Patience, d. Nov. 1, 1854, ae 53, b. in W. Greenwich	3	65
Sabra, d. Feb. 8, 1854, ae 30	3	65
Stephen, of R.I., m. Eliza Ann **CORY**, Dec. 2, 1849, by Gershom Palmer, Elder	2	137
Stephen, ae 23, farmer, of R.I., m. Eliza Ann **COREY**, ae 15, Dec. 2, 1849, by Elder Gershom Palmer	3	3
RIPLEY, Sally, d. Oct. 25, 1858, ae 57	3	68
RIX, Ephraim, d. June 3, 1848, ae 89; b. in Griswold	3	59
Mary E., ae 26, b. in Griswold, resid. of Voluntown, m. Sylvester **ARNOLD**, ae 21, b. Woodstock, resid. of Norwich, Nov. 21, 1847, by Rev. Charles S. Weaver	3	1
ROB[E]RDS, Elizabeth, d. Jonathan & Bridget, b. July 17, 1723	1	1
Mary, d. Jonathan & Bridget, b. Mar. 15, 1718	1	1
Rebecca, d. Jonathan & Bridget, b. Mar. 17, 1721	1	1
ROBBINS, ROBENS, ROBINS, Abba, m. Sterry **KINNE**, Apr. 1, 1824, by James Alexander, J.P.	2	56
Abby, d. July 3, 1854, ae 53	3	64
Archibald, s. Brintnell & Mary, b. June 15, 1778	1	151
Archibald, m. Rebecca S. **WEAVER**, b. of Voluntown, Sept. 17, 1843, by Rev. Charles S. Weaver	2	14
Archibald, d. Aug. 1, 1848, ae 25; b. in Industryville	3	59
Brintnell, s. Moses & Kezia, b. Mar. 22, 1756	1	62
Elizabeth, m. Christopher **CRERY**, Mar. 7, 1737, by John Cook, Esq.	1	79
Esther Jane, d. Richard D. & Abby, b. Apr. 27, 1837	2	76
Frederick Minor, s. Moses & Abigail, b. Aug. 21, 1799	1	242
George W., m. Julia **TANNER**, Nov. 25, 1827, by Sterry Kinne, J.P.	2	66
Henrietta, d. Archibald, ae 25, & Rebecca, ae 22, b. Dec. 11, 1847, in Industryville	3	21
Henrietta, d. Nov. 6, 1848, ae 43	3	60
Kezia, d. Brintnell & Mary, b. May 12, 1780	1	151
Kezia, of Voluntown, m. Col. Samuel **GATES**, of Pensacola, Florida, July 11, 1830, by Rev. Levi Kneeland	2	85
Laura, m. John E. **LINDLEY**, Nov. 27, 1828, by Sterry Kinne, J.P.	2	70
Mary, m. James **KINNE**, Sept. 28, 1750, by Rev. Hezekiah Lord	1	79
Mary A., m. John F. **BACON**, Oct. 21, 1824, by Sterry Kinne, J.P.	2	60
Merinda, d. Moses & Abigail, b. Aug. 31, 1794	1	242
Minor, s. Moses & Kezia, b. Nov. 25, 1747	1	62
Minor, s. Samuel & Zeruviah, b. July 22, 1781	1	156
Moses Brintnell, s. Moses & Abigail, b. Jan. 26, 1797	1	242
Nancy, d. Richard D. & Betsey, b. Mar. 29, 1804	1	258
Orrin C., s. Richard D. & Betsey, b. Apr. 24, 1817	1	259
Phebe E., m. Russel[l] D. **STEWART**, b. of Voluntown, Nov. 26, 1829, by Nathaniel Sheffield, Elder	2	82

	Vol.	Page
ROBBINS, ROBENS, ROBINS, (cont.)		
Richard Chester, s. Richard D. & Betsey, b. Mar. 22, 1815	1	258
Richard D., d. Nov. 15, 1864, ae 81	3	74
Richard D., m. Betsey **CARY (CORY** ?), May 26, 1803, by Joseph Wylie, J.P.	1	258
Roxelina, m. Simon **GALLUP,** Feb. 12, 1824, by Sterry Kinne, J.P.	2	54
Sally, m. Sterry **KINNEY,** Jan. 16, 1806, by Rev. Amos Crandall	2	34
Samuel, s. Moses & Kezia, b. Oct. 9, 1749	1	62
Samuel, m. Zeruviah **COOK,** Mar. 6, 1777, by Rev. Levi Hart	1	156
Samuel S., m. Hannah L. **THAYER,** of Bozrah, Aug. 29, 1822, by Amos Treat, J.P.	2	46
Sarah, d. Moses & Kezia, b. July 17, 1752	1	62
Sarah, d. Samuel & Zeruviah, b. Feb. 22, 1778	1	156
Thad[d]eus Cook, s. Moses & Abigail, b. Dec. 23, 1787	1	242
Thomas, d. Oct. 29, 1850, ae 87; b. in Exeter, R.I.	3	62
Thomas Jefferson, s. Moses & Abigail, b. Nov. 25, 1801	1	242
Tyler, ae 28, b. in Voluntown, resid. of Richmond, R.I., m. Sarah **TUCKER,** b. in Voluntown, resid. of Richmond, R.I., May 12, 1849, by Charles S. Weaver	3	1
Welcome Arnold, s. Moses & Abigail, b. Feb. 3, 1791	1	242
William Nelson, s. Richard D. & Betsey, b. Mar. 22, 1819	1	259
William Nelson, s. Richard D. & Betsey, b. Mar. 22, 1819	2	76
Zeruviah, d. Samuel & Zeruviah, b. Apr. 19, 1779	1	156
ROBINSON, Frank, d. Jan. 3, 1864, ae 20	3	73
RODMAN, Thomas C., s. Thomas, Manufacturer, b. June 23, 1849	3	23
ROGERS, Ann, m. Thomas **STUART,** Jan. 27, 1735/6, by Rev. Samuel Dorrance	1	58
Elizabeth, m. Mather **PATRIACH,** (Matthew **PATRICK),** Nov. 23, 1726, by Rev. Samuel Dorrance	1	12
William, d. Feb. 15, 1863, ae 50; b. in Griswold. Colored	3	72
RONAN, Agness, d. Aug. 14, 1863, ae 6 d.	3	72
Thomas, d. Jan. 5, 1865, ae 13 y. 4 m.; b. in Norwich	3	74
ROSE, Anna, m. John **BALDWIN,** Jan. 11, 1825, by Sterry Kinne, J.P.	2	63
Clarrisa, d. Dec. 26, 1864, ae 75; b. in Weston	3	74
ROUSE, Betsey, d. Reuben, b. June 19, 1798; m. Allen Bitgood	2	132
Betsey, m. Allen **BITGOOD,** b. of Voluntown, Dec. 5, 1822, by Nathaniel Sheffield, Elder	2	50
Diadama, of Voluntown, m. Lance L. **LARKHAM,** of Griswold, Sept. 4, 1840, by Rev. Charles S. Weaver	2	33
Dolly, m. Frederick **GREEN,** Dec. 9, 1828, by Sterry Kinne, J.P.	2	74
Emily E., d. Lothrop & Philura, b. Dec. 27, 1835	2	15
Harriet E., of Voluntown, m. Henry C. **PHILLIPS,** of Plainfield, May 23, 1852, by Benjamin Gallup, 2d, J.P.	2	142
Herrick, s. Reuben & Nancy, b. June 8, 1814	2	83
Julia A., d. Lathrop, common laborer, ae 38, & Philura, resid. of Griswold, b. Apr. 7, 1850	3	24
Lathrop, d. Feb. 7, 1867, ae 68	3	78
Lothrop, s. Reuben, of Voluntown, m. Laury **GEER,** d. George, of N. Stonington, Apr. 22, 1827, at Hopkinton, by Matthew Stillman, Elder	2	73
Lydia, of Voluntown, m. Christopher **COLEGROVE,** of Lisbon, May 10, 1840, by Rev. Charles S. Weaver	2	32
Mary, d. Apr. 6, 1849, ae 28; b. in N. Stonington	3	60

228   BARBOUR COLLECTION

	Vol.	Page
ROUSE, (cont.)		
Mary, d. Aug. 27, 1863, ae 18	3	72
Philura D., d. Lothrop & Philura, b. Nov. 2, 1827	2	15
Philura D., of Griswold, m. Stephen A. **DENISON**, of Westerly, R.I., Oct. 22, 1854, by Rev. Benedict Johnson, Jr.	2	148
Reuben E., s. Lothrop & Philura, b. Oct. 3, 1837	2	15
Robert, s. Elias & Hannah, b. Mar. 27, 1774	1	124
Sarah, m. James **DOUGLASS**, Mar. 16, 1788, by Rev. Micaiah Porter	1	192
Zilpha, of Plainfield, m. Daniel W. **SNELL**, b. Warwick, resid. of Plainfield, Oct. 13, 1850, by Charles S. Weaver	3	4
RUDE, Mary, m. John **EAMES**, Apr. 2, 1778, by Rev. Eliphalet Write	1	142
Welcum, s. Stephen & Eliabeth, b. Apr. 3, 1789	1	208
SABIN, SABINS, Mary, ae 50, b. in Griswold, res. of Voluntown, m. Lewis **LITTLEFIELD**, ae 51, farmer, b. in Newport, R.I., res. of Voluntown, Apr. 13, 1851, by Benj[amin] Gallup, 2d	3	3
Mary Ann, m. Lewis **LITTLEFIELD**, Apr. 13, 1851, by Benjamin Gallup, 2d, J.P.	2	139
Moses, of Griswold, m. Mary **NEWKEY**, alias Mary **MULKINS**, of Voluntown, Sept. 12, 1845, by John E. Lindley, J.P.	2	118
Moses, d. May 25, 1849, ae 28; b. in Hopkinton, R.I.	3	60
SAFFORD, Desier, d. John & Dorithy, b. Oct. 18, 1717	1	4
Dorithy, d. John & Dorithy, b. Aug. 18, 1712	1	4
Elizabeth, d. John & Dorithy, b. Sept. 4, 1724	1	4
Est[h]er, d. John & Dorithy, b. Apr. 15, 1720	1	4
Han[n]ah, d. John & Dorithy, b. Nov. 24, 1714	1	4
John, m. Dorithy **LARYBE**, Aug. 18, 1711. Entered Mar. 22,1722	1	4
John, d. Dec. 12, 1724, ae 37 y.	1	4
Sarah, d. John & Dorithy, b. Sept. 4, 1721	1	4
SAMPSON, Elijah, s. W[illia]m & Olive, b. Apr. 25, 1801	1	246
John, s. W[illia]m & Olive, b. Mar. 20, 1803	1	246
Olive, d. W[illia]m & Olive, b. Jan. 19, 1797	1	246
Sophy, d. W[illia]m & Olive, b. Feb. 9, 1793	1	246
SAUNDERS, Abbie A., d. Pardon & Rebecca, b. Sept. 19, 1842	2	92
Amy, m. Levi H. **FISH**, b. of Voluntown, Jan. 12, 1834, by Jonathan Miner, Elder	2	57
Benjamin T., s. Pardon & Rebecca, b. Apr. 2, 1847; d. Nov. 26, 1847	2	92
Charles Henry, s. Pardon & Rebecca, b. July 17, 1837	2	92
Emma L., d. Pardon & Rebecca, b. Sept. 19, 1842; d. Oct. 12, 1847	2	92
Emma L., d. Oct. 12, 1848, ae 3	3	59
Frank E., d. Sept. 22, 1866, ae 2	3	77
Henry, m. Lydia **BITGOOD**, Feb. 17, 1822, by Amos Treat, J.P.	2	43
Horace, d. Nov. 26, 1848, ae 1	3	59
John Leland, s. William & Sarah, b. Feb. 11, 1831	2	88
John W., s. Pardon & Rebecca, b. Jan. 16, 1833	2	92
Joseph Allen, s. Pardon & Rebecca, b. Nov. 28, 1834; d. Sept. 5, 1849, in Preston	2	92
Junia Etta, d. Sept. 11, 1866, ae 7	3	77
Lydia Lucinda, d. William & Sarah, b. Apr. 12, 1834	2	88
Nancy, m. Ezra **PARTILO[W]**, Nov. 16, 1828, by Sterry Kinne, J.P.	2	70
Nicholas, s. William & Nancy, b. Apr. 7, 1805, in Hopkinton, R.I.	2	88
Nicholas, m. Sarah **DOUGLASS**, Feb. 20, 1825, by Amos Treat, J.P.	2	60
Nicholas Denison, s. William & Sarah, b. June 8, 1828	2	88

VOLUNTOWN VITAL RECORDS 229

	Vol.	Page
SAUNDERS, (cont.)		
Pardon, m. Rebecca **TENNANT**, b. of Voluntown, Nov. 20, 1831, by Joseph Wylie, J.P.	2	92
Pardon B., s. Pardon & Rebecca, b. Dec. 12, 1839	2	92
Sarah Laura, d. William & Sarah, b. Feb. 1, 1826	2	88
Spencer, m. Lucy **FISH**, Dec. 22, 1822, by Amos Treat, J.P.	2	51
William, d. Feb. 13, 1862, ae 89; b. in R. Island	3	71
SCRANTON, Elijah, m. Marcy **BITGOOD**, Sept. 26, 1824, by Sterry Kinne, J.P.	2	56
Samuel, d. Nov. 29, 1849, ae 70 y.	3	61
Stafford, a pensioner, d. Oct. 27, 1826	2	71
Thomas, d. Mar. 26, 1857, ae 72	3	68
SEARS, Fanny, of Griswold, m. John **RATHBUN**, of Hopkinton, Feb. 10, 1841, by Rev. Charles S. Weaver	2	35
James, m. Hannah **WELLS**, Apr. 28, 1766, by Simeon Brown, Elder	1	110
SHAW, Elizabeth, d. Thomas & Prudence, b. May 25, 1763	1	99
Lavina, d. Thomas & Elizabeth, b. June 26, 1769	1	97
Peleg, s. Thomas & Prudence, b. July 21, 1760	1	99
Thomas, m. Elizabeth **PARKE**, Oct. 15, 1767, by William Witter, J.P.	1	97
SHEFFIELD, Mary, m. John **BITGOOD**, Jr., Oct. 15, 1815, by Stafford Green, Elder	2	37
Nancy, of Westerly, m. James H. Stedman, of Voluntown, July 2, 1843, by Rev. Charles S. Weaver	2	13
SHELDON, Charles, d. Apr. 24, 1848, ae 70	3	59
Charles P., m. Mary Ann **RICHARDSON**, b. of Voluntown, Mar. 5, 1843, by W[illia]m C. Stanton, J.P.	2	101
George T., d. Nov. 20, 1857, ae 55; b. Hopkinton, R.I	3	67
John K., d. Aug. 27, 1862, ae 30	3	71
Mary, m. John **WELLS**, Mar. 27, 1766, by Rev. Levey Hart	1	107
Roger, m. Wid. Thankfull **LEWIS**, b. of Exeter, R.I., Oct. 27, 1830, by Nathaniel Sheffield, Elder	2	85
Sally, d. Sept. 8, 1855, ae 19 y.	3	66
-----, s. George, farmer, ae 42, b. Feb. 8, 1850	3	24
SHIPPEL, Hannah E., d. May 18, 1866, ae 9; b. in Coventry, R.I.	3	76
-----, female, d. May 6, 1866, ae 11 m.; b. in R. Island	3	76
SIMMONS, Abraham, s. Prince & Sarah, b. Aug. 19, 1783	1	179
Amy, d. Prince & Sarah, b. July 26, 1773	1	179
Hannah, d. Prince & Sarah, b. Dec. 1, 1781	1	179
Isaac, s. Prince & Sarah, b. Mar. 9, 1771	1	179
Jonathan, s. Prince & Sarah, b. June 15, 1776	1	179
Mark, s. Prince & Sarah, b. May 24, 1785	1	179
Molly, d. Prince & Sarah, b. Oct. 26, 1779	1	179
SISCO, Hannah, d. Jacob & Elizabeth, b. July 8, 1739	1	28
SKILLION, Mary, m. John **WILLIAMS**, Dec. 27, 1770, by Alexander Miller, Elder	1	120
SKINNER, Betsey, had d. Joanna **CRARY**, reputed d. George **CRARY**, b. Oct. 10, 1813	2	22
Betsey, m. George **CRARY**, Jan. 4, 1815, by John Wylie, J.P.	2	22
SLOCUM, Ira A., d. May 21, 1860, ae 3 y.; b. in N. Stonington	3	70
Joseph J., s. Latham H., ae 34, & Lucy, ae 28, b. Sept. [ ], 1847	3	21
Josephine, d. Aug. 31, [1860], ae 12; b. in N. Stonington	3	70
Julia A., m. George W. **MAINE**, b. of N. Stonington, Dec. 9, 1838,		

230   BARBOUR COLLECTION

	Vol.	Page
SLOCUM, (cont.)		
by Benjamin Gallup, Jr., J.P.	2	108
Sophia, d. Stephen, ae 36, & Eliza, ae 31, b. Nov. [ ], 1847	3	21
SMITH, Abbie Maria, d. Alexander C. & Maria, b. Oct. 31, 1836; d. Dec. 11, 1837	2	16
Abbie Maria, d. Alexander C. & Mariah, b. Feb. 17, 1841	2	16
Abel, s. John & Phebe, b. Aug. 31, 1748	1	25
Alexander Campbell, s. John C. & Alice, b. June 1, 1813	2	77
Alice, of Voluntown, m. George **BASSETT**, Feb. [ ], 1840, by Rev. Charles S. Weaver	2	43
Alice Elizabeth, d. Alexander C. & Maria, b. Sept. 27, 1838	2	16
Almira, d. Ezekiel & Lydia, b. Dec. 26, 1810, in Preston	1	230
Amanda F., d. Ezekiel & Lydia, b. [ ], 1819	1	230
Ann, d. Ebenezer & Anne, b. Aug. 17, 1769	1	102
Anne, d. Daniel & Marcy, b. May 2, 1752	1	91
Benjamin, s. Lemuel & Martha, b. Aug. 30, 1738	1	33
Benjamin, d. Oct. 1, 1757	1	33
Calvin, s. Francis, Jr. & Elizabeth, b. Mar. 18, 1782	1	150
Charles, s. Ezekiel & Lydia, b. Aug. 25, 1801	1	230
Charles H., s. David, farmer, ae 31 & Eunice, ae 42, resid. of N. Stonington, b. Sept. 5, 1849	3	23
Clarissa, d. Ezekiel & Lydia, b. Sept. 16, 1808, in Preston	1	230
Daniel, s. Daniel & Marcy, b. Sept. 21, 1755	1	91
David, m. Eunice **PALMER**, b. of N. Stonington, Mar. 20, 1841, by Benjamin Gallup, Jr., J.P.	2	108
Diantha Marilla, d. John C., b. Mar. 6, 1823; d. Dec. 12, 1823	2	77
Dyer, formerly of Richmond, R.I., now residing in Sterling, Ct., m. Asenath **YOUNG**, of Voluntown, June 29, 1823, by Nathaniel Sheffield, Elder	2	53
Ebenezer, s. Francis & Rachel, b. May 22, 1754	1	44
Ebenezer, m. Anne **COOPER**, May 1, 1763, by John Rice, J.P.	1	102
Ebenezer, s. Ebenezer & Anne, b. June 6, 1767	1	102
Elizabeth, m. Rev. Samuel **DORRANCE**, Aug. 1, 1726, by Rev. Joseph Coite	1	11
Elizabeth, m. Paris **BRIGGS**, Dec. 21, 1775, by Samuel Stewart, J.P.	1	133
Elizabeth, d. Francis, Jr. & Elizabeth, b. Mar. 12, 1780	1	150
Elizabeth, d. May 29, 1858, ae 78; b. in R. Island	3	68
Erastus, s. John C. & Alice, b. June 4, 1816	2	77
Est[h]er, had s. William **GALLUP**, b. Aug. 18, 1735, reputed s. of William **GALLUP**, decd.	1	18
Esther, m. Samuel **CAMPBELL**, Apr. 10, 1760, by Jacob Perkins, J.P.	1	101
Est[h]er, mother of William **GALLUP**	1	18
Ezekiel, s. Ezekiel **SMITH** & Elizabeth **THAYER**, b. May 27, 1774	1	20
Ezekiel, m. Lydia **FRINK**, Jan. 8, 1798, by Silas Westcot[t], J.P.	1	230
Frances, s. Lemuel & Martha, b. Jan. 9, 1737	1	33
Francis, m. Rachel **SPAULDING**, Feb. 3, 1742, by John Crery, J.P.	1	44
Francis, s. Francis & Rachel, b. Mar. 23, 1749	1	44
Hannah, d. John & Phebe, b. Mar. 25, 1742	1	25
Hannah, d. Francis, Jr. & Elizabeth, b. Mar. 5, 1778	1	150
Hannah, d. June 25, 1849, ae 95; b. in R. Island	3	60
Isaac, s. Lemuel & Martha, b. Nov. 2, 1744	1	33
Israel, s. Ezekiel & Lydia, b. Jan. 19, 1804	1	230

VOLUNTOWN VITAL RECORDS 231

	Vol.	Page
SMITH, (cont.)		
J. Henry, d. Aug. 19, 1863, ae 22	3	72
James, of Plainfield, m. Jennet **STEWART**, of Voluntown, Oct. 31, 1791, by Rev. Micaiah Porter	1	217
James L., d. Feb. 8, 1862, ae 19	3	72
Jedediah, s. John & Phebe, b. Sept. 30, 1750; d. Sept. 25, 1752	1	25
John, m. Phebe **PEIRCE**, Nov. 24,1736, by Timothy Peirce, Esq.	1	25
John, s. John & Phebe, b. Sept. 4, 1737	1	25
John, s. Lemuel & Martha, b. Mar. 7, 1749	1	33
John, s. Ebenezer & Anne, b. May 25, 1764	1	102
John, s. Ebenezer & Anne, b. June 26, 1772	1	102
John, m. Mary **DORRANCE**, Aug. 5, 1781, byJohn Dixson, J.P.	1	166
John, s. John & Mary, b. Mar. 6, 1782	1	166
John Congdon, s. Alexander C. & Mariah, b. Apr. 4, 1843	2	16
John L., m. Lydia S. **DOUGLASS**, b. of Voluntown, Mar. 31, 1831, by Nathaniel Sheffield, Elder	2	86
John Q. A., d. May 23, 1849, ae 24	3	60
John Quincy, s. John C. & Alice, b. Apr. 8, 1825	2	77
Jonathan, s. Ebenezer & Anne, b. Feb. 28, 1778	1	102
Joseph, s. Lemuel & Martha, b. Sept. 5, 1742	1	33
Joseph H., m. Nancy **GEER**, b. of Voluntown, Dec. 21, 1834, by Daniel Keigwin, J.P.	2	89
Joseph H., d. June 8, 1863, ae 53	3	72
Joseph Huston, s. John C. & Alice, b. Apr. 26, 1809	2	77
Lemuel, s. Lemuel & Martha, b. Sept. 7, 1740	1	33
Lemuel, d. Sept. 21, 1759	1	33
Lemuel Alexander, s. Joseph H. & Nancy, b. Feb. 23, 1838	2	89
Lemuel Wylie, s. John C. & Alice, b. Feb. 6, 1811	2	77
Louisa, ae 24, m. Thomas **BLIVEN**, ae 24, b. of Voluntown, Nov. 19, 1848, by Rev. Jesse B. Denison	3	2
Louisa S., of Voluntown, m. Thomas **BLIVEN**, of Stonington, Nov. 19, 1848, by Rev. Jesse B. Denison. Witnesses: Daniel Gorton, Charles H. Kinne	2	123
Luther, s. Lemuel & Martha, b. Oct. 1, 1755	1	33
Luther, s. Francis, Jr. & Elizabeth, b. Sept. 20, 1784	1	150
Lydia, d. Ezekiel & Lydia, b. Feb. 21, 1800	1	230
Lydia, d. Sept. 20, 1861, ae 1 y. 6 m.	3	71
Margaret, d. Ezekiel & Lydia, b. May 16, 1812	1	230
Mariah, d. July 26, 1848, ae 33; b. in W. Greenwich, R.I.	3	59
Martha, d. Lemuel & Martha, b. Apr. 23, 1751	1	33
Mary, d. Lemuel & Martha, b. Apr. 26, 1753	1	33
Mary, d. Ezekiel & Lydia, b. Mar. 24, 1816 (Full name Mary Laura)	1	230
Orlando Hallam, s. John C. & Alice, b. Jan. 31, 1821	2	77
Phebe, d. John & Phebe, b. Apr. 25, 1752	1	25
Rachel, d. Francis & Rachel, b. Sept. 19, 1760	1	44
Rachel, m. Nathaniel **GALLUP**, Jan. 30, 1783, by Rev. Micaiah Porter	1	169
Rachel, d. Francis & Elizabeth, b. Sept. 14, 1787	1	150
Ruth, d. John & Phebe, b. Mar. 19, 1744	1	25
Ruth, m. John **STEWART**, Mar. 20, 1766, by Rev. Samuel Dorrance	1	113
Sarah, d. Ebenezer & Anne, b. Feb. 23, 1775	1	102
Susannah, d. John & Phebe, b. Mar. 28, 1739; d. Apr. 9, 1739	1	25

	Vol.	Page
SMITH, (cont.)		
Susan[n]a, d. John & Phebe, b. June 25, 1746	1	25
Thomas, s. Cornelius & Hannah, b. Apr. 6, 1760	1	28
Timothy, s. John & Phebe, b. Apr. 28, 1740	1	25
Willerd, s. Lemuel & Martha, b. Dec. 23, 1746	1	33
William Henry, s. John C. & Alice, b. Dec. 15, 1818	2	77
Zachariah F., s. Ezekiel & Lydia, b. Feb. 14, 1806, in Preston	1	230
SNELL, Daniel W., b. Warwick, resid. of Plainfield, m. Zilpha **ROUSE,** of Plainfield, Oct. 13, 1850, by Charles S. Weaver	3	4
SNELLEN, Lucy, m. Quocko (?) **DOUGLASS,** June 22, 1788, by Rev. Micaiah Porter	1	198
SPAULDING, Deliverance, m. Allice **KALSON,** Apr. 15, 1756, by Rev. Samuel Dorrance	1	16
Frances A., of Griswold, m. Sarah E. **BASSETT,** of Voluntown, Apr. 6, 1830, by Nathaniel Sheffield, Elder	2	83
George, of Canterbury, m. Julian **KENNEDY,** of Voluntown, Aug. 21, 1843, by Rev. Jacob Allen	2	55
Rachel, m. Francis **SMITH,** Feb. 3, 1742, by John Crery, J.P.	1	44
Sarah, m. John **PARKE,** Dec. 7, 1741	1	34
-----, s. George, farmer, & Julia Ann, b. Feb. [ ], 1849	3	23
SPENCER, Abraham, s. Joseph & Abigail, b. Jan. 28, 1793	1	173
Elizabeth, d. May 7, 1857, ae 22; b. in N. Scituate	3	68
Joseph, m. Abigail **BOYD,** Apr. 19, 1792, by Joshua Dunlap, J.P.	1	173
STANBURY, STANDBERRY, Hannah, m. John **BUTTON,** May 24, 1753, by Rev. Samuel Dorrance	1	60
Mary, m. Obadiah **RHOAD[E]S,** Jr., June 4, 1747, by Rev. Samuel Dorrance	1	45
STANTON, Alexas J., d. Oct. 27, 1865, ae 17	3	75
Alexis Jewet, s. William C., ae 41, & Mary A., ae 37, b. May 13, 1848	3	21
Amey, m. Benjamin **GALLUP,** 2d, b. of Voluntown, Mar. [ ], 1846, by Rev. Charles S. Weaver	2	8
Amy, d. Dec. 29, 1848, ae 43; b. in Griswold	3	60
Benjamin, s. Joseph & Mary, b. May 21, 1789; d. Nov. [ ], 1809	1	255
David, m. Phebe E. **BILLINGS,** of Canterbury, July 4, 1847, by Rev. Charles S. Weaver	2	35
Deliverance, d. Joseph & Mary, b. Nov. 2, 1787; d. July [ ], 1811	1	255
Deliverance, m. Jonathan **BITGOOD,** Mar. 27, 1808, by Allen Campbell, J.P.	2	17
Eliza A., m. Caleb P. **POTTER,** b. of Voluntown, May 7, 1848, by Rev. Charles S. Weaver	2	129
Eliza A., ae 21, seamstress, m. Caleb P. **POTTER,** ae 24, schoolteacher, b. of Voluntown, May 7, 1848, by Elder Charles S. Weaver	3	1
Eliza Ann, d. Jonathan & Amilla, b. Mar. 17, 1827	1	167
George Washington, s. Jonathan & Amilla, b. Nov. 16, 1822; d. Aug. 7, 1833	1	167
Hannah, d. Joseph & Mary, b. July 21, 1779, in Exeter; d. Oct. 19, 1806, in Voluntown	1	255
Hannah, m. Jonathan **BITGOOD,** July 4, 1799, by Rev. Micaiah [Porter]	2	17
Henry Allen, s. Jonathan & Amilla, b. Feb. 9, 1825	1	167
James M., s. Jonathan & Ammilla, b. July 28, 1818	1	167

VOLUNTOWN VITAL RECORDS

	Vol.	Page
STANTON, (cont.)		
James M., m. Rhoda Ann **SYMMS**, b. of Voluntown, Feb. 19, 1843, by Rev. H. Forbush	2	114
John, s. Joseph & Mary, b. Mar. 13, 1791	1	255
Jonathan, m. Amille **CHEESEBOROUGH**, Oct. [ ], 1806, by Peleg Randall, Elder	1	167
Jonathan, d. Oct. 24, 1848, ae 66; b. in Stonington	3	60
Joseph, b. Mar. 25, 1753; d. Apr. 18, 1806	1	255
Joseph, s. Joseph & Mary, b. Sept. 21, 1785; d. Mar. [ ], 1808	1	255
Lydia Ann, d. W[illia]m C. & Mary Ann, b. Mar. 17, 1836	2	110
Lydia D., twin with Zebulon F., d. Jonathan & Amilla, b. July 13, 1811; d. Aug. 1, 1833	1	167
Marcy G., d. Jonathan & Amilla, b. May 5, 1809; d. Mar. 13, 1833	1	167
Mary, w. Joseph, b. Sept. 1, 1753; d. Sept. [ ], 1809	1	255
Mary, d. Joseph & Mary, b. Feb. 18, 1784; d. May 1, 1810	1	255
Mercy Amelia, d. W[illia]m C. & Mary Ann, b. July 17, 1837	2	110
Phebe, d. Joseph & Mary, b. Aug. 16, 1793; d. Jan. [ ], 1810	1	255
Prudence Eliza, d. W[illia]m C. & Mary Ann, b. May 17, 1842; d. Oct. 25, 1842, ae 5 m. 7 d.	2	110
Sabra, d. Joseph & Mary, b. June 10, 1782; d. July 2, 1805	1	255
Sarah, m. Jeffrey **CYRUS**, July 2, 1789, by Rev. Micaiah Porter	1	198
Sarah Eleanor, d. W[illia]m C. & Mary Ann, b. Aug. 9, 1845	2	110
Serena J., d. W[illia]m C., farmer, ae 43, & Mary A., ae 39, b. Feb. 22, 1850	3	24
Susan M., of Voluntown, m. Horace A. **BRIGGS**, of Norwich, Nov. 25, 1849, by Rev. H. Forbush	2	140
Susanna, d. Joseph & Mary, b. Oct. 1, 1780, in Exeter; d. Nov. [ ], 1820	1	255
Susannah W., d. Mar. 14, 1854, ae 28	3	64
William C., s. Jonathan & Amilla, b. July 28, 1807	1	167
W[illia]m C., of Voluntown, m. Mary Ann **CHEES[E]BROUGH**, of Stonington, Nov. 17, 1834, at Stonington, by Elder Jerome S. Anderson, of Stonington	2	110
William Henry, s. W[illia]m C. & Mary Ann, b. Aug. 11, 1839	2	110
Zebulon F., twin with Lydia D., s. Jonathan & Amilla, b. July 13, 1811	1	167
Zebulon F., m. Hannah E. **PALMER**, b. of Voluntown, Feb. 23, 1834, by Elisha Potter, J.P.	2	98
STAPLES, Freelove, m. Samson **WILLIAMS**, June 5, 1777, by Rev. John Fuller	1	54
STARKWEATHER, Huldah, m. Nicholas **KEIGWIN**, Nov. 15, 1759, by Jeremiah Kinne, J.P.	1	100
STEARNES, Cynthia, m. Robert **WILSON**, Jr., May 14, 1772	1	196
STEDMAN, Elizabeth, of Voluntown, m. James C. **ANDREW**, of Westerly, July 2, 1843, by Rev. Charles S. Weaver	2	13
Hannah A., of Voluntown, m. Henry F. **STILLMAN**, of Westerly, Apr. 4, 1841, by Rev. Charles S. Weaver	2	37
James H., of Voluntown, m. Nancy **SHEFFIELD**, of Westerly, July 2, 1843, by Rev. Charles S. Weaver	2	13
John B., d. Dec. 22, 1863, ae 78; b. in R. Island	3	73
STEPHENS, [see also **STEVENS**], Hannah, of Voluntown, m. John **WHITMAN**, of Griswold, Sept. 23, 1844, by Rev. Charles S. Weaver	2	22

234 BARBOUR COLLECTION

	Vol.	Page
STEVENS, STEAVENS, [see also **STEPHENS**], Elizabeth, d. Jarad & Lucy, b. Sept. 16, 1772	1	44
Elizabeth, d. Simeon & C[h]loe, b. May 12, 1817	1	251
Hannah, m. William **BRIGGS**, May 3, 1798	1	133
Huldah, d. Simeon & Lois, b. Apr. 29, 1772	1	131
Huldah, m. Stephen **NEWTON**, Dec. 4, 1794, by Allen Campbell, J.P.	1	183
Jesse Brumbley, s. Simeon, Jr. & C[h]loe, b. June 11, 1806	1	251
Lois Anna, d. Simeon & C[h]loe, b. Jan. 17, 1815	1	251
Russell, s. Simeon & Lois, b. Feb. 15, 1776	1	131
Russel[l], m. Margaret **FRINK**, Nov. 17, 1796, by Rev. Micaiah Porter	1	218
Simeon, m. Lois **KINNE**, Oct. 10, 1770, by Jeremiah Kinne, Esq.	1	131
Simeon, Jr., m. C[h]loe **BRUMBLEY**, Dec. 22, 1803, by Rev. Amos Crandall	1	251
Squire, s. Simeon, Jr. & C[h]loe, b. Oct. 6, 1804	1	251
Thomas A., s. Simeon & C[h]loe, b. Aug. 30, 1808	1	251
Uzziel, s. Simeon & Lois, b. Sept. 25, 1773	1	131
STEVENSON, Allen, m. Mary **LOUDEN**, Jan. 12, 1775	1	139
Allen, s. Allen & Mary, b. Oct. 9, 1776	1	139
John, s. Allen & Mary, b. Apr. 19, 1775	1	139
Mary, d. Allen & Mary, b. Jan. 26, 1778	1	139
STEWART, STEWARTT, STUART, Abigale, d. Oliver, Jr. & Jane, b. Jan. 7, 1773	1	127
Alexander, s. Thomas & Ann, b. Nov. 1, 1736	1	58
Alexander, s. Samuel & Elizabeth, b. Sept. 6, 1744	1	37
Alexander, s. John & Susannah, b. Nov. 22, 1798	1	113
Allen, s. Oliver, Jr. & Jane, b. Sept. 13, 1775	1	127
Ann, d. Samuel & Elizabeth, b. June 22, 1755	1	37
Anne, d. Thomas & Ann, b. Jan. [ ], 1756	1	58
Anne, d. John & Ruth, b. Feb. 6, 1774	1	113
Celend, d. Samuel & Elizabeth, b. May 20, 1759	1	37
Charity, d. Thomas & Ann, b. Oct. 10, 1748	1	58
Charles, s. John & Susanna, b. July 17, 1792	1	113
Clarissa, d. John & Susanna, b. May 15, 1789	1	113
Dinah, d. Thomas & Ann, b. Sept. 19, 1744	1	58
Elias, s. Thomas & Ann, b. Mar. 24, 1742	1	58
Elizabeth, d. Thomas & Ann, b. May 29, 1746	1	58
Elizabeth, d. Samuel & Elizabeth, b. Apr. 19, 1747	1	37
Elizabeth, d. John & Ruth, b. June 28, 1771	1	113
Elizabeth, m. Thomas **GORDON**, Dec. 23, 1792, by Rev. Micaiah Porter	2	26
Fanny, of Springfield, m. Walter **PALMER**, of [ ], Mar. 25, 1844, by Rev. Charles S. Weaver	2	19
George Dorrance, s. Samuel & Rebecca, b. June 12, 1782	1	161
Hannah, d. Thomas & Ann, b. May 26, 1750	1	58
Jennet, d. Samuel & Elizabeth, b. July 2, 1749	1	37
Jennet, of Voluntown, m. James **SMITH**, of Plainfield, Oct. 31, 1791, by Rev. Micaiah Porter	1	217
John, s. Thomas & Ann, b. May 27, 1738	1	58
John, s. Samuel & Elizabeth, b. Sept. 6, 1742	1	37
John, m. Ruth **SMITH**, Mar. 20, 1766, by Rev. Samuel Dorrance	1	113
John, m. Susanna **BRIGGS**, Oct. 5, 1786, by Rev. Mecaiah Porter	1	113

STEWART, STEWARTT, STUART, (cont.)

	Vol.	Page
John, s. John & Susanna, b. Oct. 28, 1790	1	113
John, d. Jan. 21, 1802	1	113
Joshua, s. Thomas & Ann, b. Sept. 5, 1739	1	58
Marg[a]ret, d. Thomas & Ann, b. Jan. 8, 1752	1	58
Marg[a]ret, m. Nehemiah **PARKE**, Jr., Dec. 27, 1771, by Samuel Stewart, J.P.	1	125
Mary, d. Samuel & Elizabeth, b. Apr. 24, 1757	1	37
Nathaniel, s. Nathaniel & Experience, b. Dec. 30, 1745	1	38
Oliver, Jr., m. Jane **RHOADES**, Feb. 13, 1772, by Sam[ue]ll Stewart, J.P.	1	127
Phebe, d. John & Ruth, b. Apr. 5, 1769	1	113
Phebe, m. Moses **CAMPBELL**, Jr., Sept. 10, 1789, by Rev. Micaiah Porter	1	214
Rebeckah, m. John **RHOAD[E]S**, Jr., Nov. 14, 1771, by Samuel Stewart, J.P.	1	144
Rosan[n]a, d. Samuel & Elizabeth, b. Sept. 19, 1753	1	37
Rosannah, m. John **PARKE**, June 20, 1776, by Rev. Solomon Morgan	1	40
Russel[l] D., m. Phebe E. **ROB[B]INS**, b. of Voluntown, Nov. 26, 1829, by Nathaniel Sheffield, Elder	2	82
Ruth, d. John & Ruth, b. June 25, 1776	1	113
Ruth, w. John, d. Nov. 14, 1776	1	113
Sabara, d. Samuel & Elizabeth, b. July 20, 1763	1	37
Sabra,d. Samuel & Rebecca, b. Sept. 28, 1784	1	161
Sally, d. Samuel & Rebecca, b. May 17, 1790	1	161
Samuel, s. Thomas & Ann, b. July 15, 1741	1	58
Samuel, s. Samuel & Elizabeth, b. Mar. 10, 1761	1	37
Samuel, s. John & Ruth, b. Feb. [ ], 1767	1	113
Samuel, Jr., m. Rebecca **BARNET[T]**, Sept. 13, 1781, by Rev. Alexander Miller	1	161
Sarah, d. John & Susanna, b. Sept. 15, 1787	1	113
Sarah, m. Jonathan **HILLIARD**, Apr. 19, 1819, by James Alexander, J.P.; d. Jan. 10, 1820, ae 32 y.	2	29
Susan[n]a, d. Samuel & Elizabeth, b. Sept. 15, 1751	1	37
Susannah, d. John & Susannah, b. June 26, 1795	1	113
Susannah, w. John, d. July 30, 1818	1	113
Thomas, m. Ann **ROGERS**, Jan. 27, 1735/6, by Rev. Samuel Dorrance	1	58
Thomas, s. Samuel & Elizabeth, b. May 26, 1767	1	37
William, s. Thomas & Ann, b. Aug. 8, 1754	1	58
William, s. Samuel & Elizabeth, b. June 9, 1772	1	37

STILLMAN, Henry F., of Westerly, m. Hannah A. **STEDMAN**, of Voluntown, Apr. 4, 1841, by Rev. Charles S. Weaver — 2, 37

STONE, Patience, of Sterling, m. James **GALLUP**, ae 20, of Sterling, Oct. [ ], 1849, by Rev. Jacob Allen — 3, 3

Susan[n]a, m. Roger **WILLIAMS**, Apr. 25, 1744, by Rev. Samuel Dorrance — 1, 35

STORY, Hannah, m. Samuel **MOTT**, Apr. 14, 1757, by Jeremiah Kinne, Esq. — 1, 92

STOWELL, [see under **STOYELL**]

STOYELL, Aaron, s. Stephen & Mary, b. July 10, 1765 — 1, 70

Amos, twin with Martha, s. Stephen & Mary, b. Dec. 28, 1767 — 1, 70

236 BARBOUR COLLECTION

	Vol.	Page
STOYELL, (cont.)		
Ann, d. Stephen & Mary, b. Oct. 1, 1753	1	70
Hannah, d. Stephen & Mary, b. Jan. 6, 1755	1	70
Isaac, s. Stephen & Mary, b. Mar. 16, 1772	1	70
James, s. Stephen & Mary, b. Feb. 17, 1763	1	70
John, twin with Thomas, s. Stephen & Mary, b. Nov. 18, 1760	1	70
Martha, twin with Amos, d. Stephen & Mary, b. Dec. 28, 1767	1	70
Mary, twin with Stephen, d. Stephen & Mary, b. Jan. 12, 1759	1	70
Sarah, d. Stephen & Mary, b. Dec. 3, 1756	1	70
Stephen, m. Mary **COLE**, Jan. 4, 1753, by Rev. Samuel Dorrance	1	70
Stephen, twin with Mary, s. Stephen & Mary, b. Jan. 12, 1759	1	70
Thomas, twin with John, s. Stephen & Mary, b. Nov. 18, 1760	1	70
STRANEHAN, Else, m. Theophilus **JACKSON**, Oct. 9, 1746, by Rev. Samuel Dorrance	1	43
STRANGE, Hannah, d. Dec. 14, 1862, ae 40; b. in R. Island	3	72
Hannah, d. Nov. [ ], 1863, ae 40; b. in R. Island	3	73
Herbert, d. Sept. 3, 1865, ae 1 y. 7 m. 8 d.	3	75
Louisa, d. Apr. 15, 1863, ae 10	3	72
-----, s. William, spinner, ae 26, & Mary, ae 18, resid. of Griswold, b. [1848 or 1849]	3	22
STUART, [see under **STEWART**]		
STUBBS, Samuel, d. Nov. 15, 1866, ae 2 y. 4 m.	3	77
SULLIVAN, SULIVAN, Gardiner, m. Nancy **HURD**, Aug. 15, 1821, by Amos Treat, J.P.	2	39
Julia Ann, m. Henry E. **CORY**, b. of Voluntown, Sept. 6, 1851, by Elder William R. Slocum	2	140
SWAN, Amos Stiles, s. Amos & Esther, b. Oct. 1, 1811, in N. Stonington. Entered at the request of John Chapman, who married the said Esther	1	158
Esther, m. John **CHAPMAN**, Feb. 13, 1814, by Allen Campbell, J.P.	1	158
George W., ae 20, b. in N. Stonington, resid. of Voluntown, m. Hannah **JAMES**, ae 21, b. in W. Greenwich, resid. of Voluntown, June 4, 1849, by Rev. Charles S. Weaver	3	1
Joseph S., of Stonington, m. Abby **WHIPPLE**, of Voluntown, Feb. 18, 1828, by Rev. Jabez S. Swan	2	72
SWEET, Amos C., s. Joseph & Esther, b. May 28, 1819	2	48
Caroline, d. Joseph & Esther, b. Feb. 10, 1827	2	48
Clarissa, d. Joseph & Esther, b. Oct. 21, 1824	2	48
Daniel E., d. Dec. 16, 1863, ae 80; b. in R. Island	3	73
Denison, d. Nov. 12, 1852, ae 22, single	3	63
Eliza A., of Griswold, m. Lewis N. **HAWKINS**, of Voluntown, Feb. 29, 1864, by Thomas L. Shipman, of Jewett City	2	106
Harriet J., d. Mar. 23, 1863, ae 26	3	72
Isaac, s. Joseph & Mary, b. Jan. 7, 1775	1	141
James, s. Griffin & Else, b. Oct. 25, 1760, in Coventry	1	69
Joseph, m. Mary **GRIFFETH**, Jan. 27, 1774, by Robert Dixson, J.P.	1	141
Joseph, m. Esther **CRANDALL**, Mar. 5, 1818, by John Wylie, J.P.	2	48
Marg[a]ret, d. Griffen & Else, b. May 2, 1762	1	69
Samuel, s. Griffen & Else, b. June 1, 1764	1	69
Thankful, m. Thomas **MATTESON**, June 7, 1782, by Elder Elisha Green	1	175
Varnum, m. Mary **WILLCOX**, b. of Voluntown, July 5, 1827, by Daniel Keigwin, J.P.	2	81

VOLUNTOWN VITAL RECORDS 237

	Vol.	Page
SYMMS, Rhoda Ann, m. James M. **STANTON**, b. of Voluntown, Feb. 19, 1843, by Rev. H. Forbush	2	114
TABOR, TABER, Gardner, m. Betsey **LARKINS**, May 29, 1825, by Sterry Kinne, J.P.	2	63
Joseph, d. Oct. 5, 1865, ae 15 y. 6 m..; b. in Exeter, R.I.	3	75
TALBOT, TALBUT, Ebenezer, s. Job & Elizabeth, b. Mar. 7, 1777	1	121
Elizabeth, d. Job & Elizabeth, b. May 9, 1774	1	121
John, s. Job & Elizabeth, b. Jan. 26, 1772	1	121
Sarah, d. Job & Elizabeth, b. July 7, 1769	1	121
TANNER, [see also **FENNER**], Alfred K., s. Joseph & Amy, b. Apr. 7, 1852	2	144
Allen, d. Mar. 12, 1855, ae 64; b. in R. Island	3	66
Amy H., d. Oct. 25, 1865, ae 51; b. in R. Island	3	75
Betsey, m. Hazzard **JAQUAYS**, Oct. 21, 1824, by Amos Treat, J.P.	2	56
Betsey Ann, d. Gideon & Freelove, b. Aug. 26, 1815	2	45
Charles A., s. Josiah & Polly, b. Jan. 18, 1826	2	93
Daniel, s. Gideon & Freelove, b. May 15, 1819	2	45
Dolly Celinda, d. Josiah & Polly, b. June 12, 1823	2	93
Elisha Brown, s. Isaac B. & Anna, b. Jan. 18, 1795	1	206
Freelove, [w. Gideon], d. Jan. 26, 1824	2	45
Georgeanna A., d. Noah, ae 26, & Sally, ae 20, b. Apr. 23, 1848	3	21
Gideon, of Hopkinton, m. Freelove **JACKSON**, of Voluntown, Apr. 1, 1804, by Joseph Wylie, J.P.	2	45
Giles Browning, s. Isaac B., & Anna, b. May 19, 1790, in S. Kingston, R.I.	1	206
Henry Hubbard, s. Isaac B. & Anna, b. Feb. 11, 1799	1	206
Isaac Brown, reputed s. of Isaac **TANNER** & Susanna **BROWN**, b. Sept. 7, 1770, in Hopkinton, R.I.	1	206
Isaac W., s. Josiah & Polly, b. Dec. 24, 1814	2	93
Isaiah, s. Isaac B. & Anna, b. Nov. 20, 1792	1	206
James D., s. Gideon & Freelove, b. Aug. 22, 1811	2	45
John, s. Gideon & Freelove, b. July 29, 1822	2	45
John Phillips, s. Isaac B. & Anna, b. Mar. 5, 1801	1	206
Julia, m. George W. **ROB[B]INS**, Nov. 25, 1827, by Sterry Kinne, J.P.	2	66
Mary Bates, d. Gideon & Freelove, b. Aug. 12, 1808	2	45
Mary E., d. Josiah & Polly, b. Jan. 12, 1828	2	93
Nancy, d. Isaac B. & Anna, b. Jan. 24, 1797	1	206
Nathan P., d. Sept. 9, 1858, ae 6	3	68
Nathaniel, d. Feb. 6, 1863, ae 72 y.; b. in R. Island	3	72
Orra Augustus, d. Josiah & Polly, b. July 13, 1817	2	93
Parmelia Electa, d. Josiah & Polly, b. Feb. 7, 1820	2	93
Russel[l], s. Giles B. & Sally (**LEWIS**), b. Aug. 12, 1823	2	76
Russell, m. Patty **PHILLIPS**, of Plainfield, Nov. 10, 1851, by Rev. Henry Robinson, of Plainfield	2	68
Sally Marilla, d. Giles B. & Sally (**LEWIS**), b. June 12, 1814	2	76
Susan C., ae 26, of Voluntown, m. Henry S. **RICHARDSON**, ae 22, b. Plainfield, resid. of Providence, Sept. 24, 1849, by Rev. C. S. Weaver	3	3
Susan M., d. June 12, 1856, ae 19; b. in R. Island	3	67
Warren L., 3d, s. Joseph & Amy R., b. June 25, 1850	2	144
Warren L., s. Joseph, farmer, ae 47, & Ann H., ae 36, b. June 25, 1850	3	25

	Vol.	Page
TANNER, (cont.)		
William C., s. Josiah & Polly, b. Mar. 8, 1834	2	93
[**TAYLOR**], **TAILLOR**, Hannah, m. James **CAMPBELL**, June 3, 1725	1	17
TENNANT, Rebecca, m. Pardon **SAUNDERS**, b. of Voluntown, Nov. 20, 1831, by Joseph Wylie, J.P.	2	92
TERRY, David K., ae 21, farmer, of Griswold, m. Susan A. **THOMPSON**, ae 22, weaver, of Voluntown, Nov. 2, 1848, by Rev. J. B. Denison	3	1
David K., of Griswold, m. Susan A. **THOMPSON**, of Voluntown, Nov. 12, 1848, by Rev. Jesse B. Denison. Witness: Clark Reynolds	2	131
Joanna, m. John W. **ECCLESTON**, Mar. 5, 1829, by Minor Rob[b]ins, J.P.	2	81
Mary, d. William & Mary, b. Apr. 6, 1775, in Exeter, m. James **CAMPBELL**, Jr., Dec. 14, 1797, by Stephen Reynolds, J.P.	1	238
Mary, m. James **CAMPBELL**, Jr., Dec. 14, 1797, by Stephen Reynolds, J.P.	1	238
THAYER, Elizabeth, had s. Ezekiel **SMITH**, b. May 27, 1774, & the father was Ezekiel **SMITH**	1	20
Hannah L., of Bozrah, m. Samuel S. **ROB[B]INS**, Aug. 29, 1822, by Amos Treat, J.P.	2	46
THOMAS, Aaron, s. William & Patience, b. Apr. 16, 1729	1	1
Amos, s. William & Patience, b. Mar. 16, 1716	1	1
Daniel, twin with Temp[e]rance, s. William & Patience, b. Oct. 30, 1718	1	1
Elizabeth, d. William & Patience, b. Nov. 25, 1723	1	1
Hann[ah], twin with Nathan, d. William & Patience, b. Mar. 20, 1721	1	1
Nathan, twin with Hann[ah], s. William & Patience, b. Mar. 20, 1721	1	1
Patience, d. William & Patience, b. May 12, 1726	1	1
Survia, d. William & Patience, b. Apr. 27, 1712	1	1
Temp[e]rance, twin with Daniel, d. William & Patience, b. Oct. 30, 1718	1	1
THOMPSON, THOMSON, Asa, 2d, m. Elizabeth **VAUGHAN**, b. residing in Jewett City, Ct., June 3, 1831, by Nathaniel Sheffield, Elder	2	89
Charles W., of N. Stonington, m. Betsey **POTTER**, of Voluntown, Jan. 25, 1821, by Amos Treat, J.P.	2	39
Elisha Chester, s. Charles W. & Betsey, b. June 11, 1831; d. Apr. 18, 1838	2	80
John, s. Thomas & Jane, b. Oct. 25, 1746	1	67
Julia, d. Charles W. & Betsey, b. May 10, 1835	2	80
Martha, d. Thomas & Jane, b. Apr. 13, 1741	1	67
Moses, d. Sept. 27, 1852	2	23
Phebe Esther, d. Charles W. & Betsey, b. Sept. 30, 1827	2	80
Polly Elizabeth, d. Charles W. & Betsey, b. Oct. 26, 1824	2	80
Prudence, m. Abel **CHAPMAN**, Feb. 12, 1818, by Jonathan Miner, Elder	2	30
Sally, d. Charles W. & Betsey, b. Feb. 19, 1823	2	80
Sarah, m. Martin **KINNEY**, b. of Voluntown, Jan. 1, 1844, by Rev. H. Farbush	2	115
Susan A., ae 22, weaver, of Voluntown, m. David K. **TERRY**, ae 21, farmer, of Griswold, Nov. 2, 1848, by Rev. J. B. Denison	3	1

	Vol.	Page
THOMPSON, THOMSON, (cont.)		
Susan A., of Voluntown, m. David K. **TERRY**, of Griswold, Nov. 12, 1848, by Rev. Jesse B. Denison. Witness: Clark Reynolds	2	131
Susan Amelia, d. Charles W. & Betsey, b. Jan. 9, 1826	2	80
Susan[n]a, d. Thomas & Jane, b. May 31, 1743	1	67
Thomas, s. Thomas & Jane, b. Feb. 6, 1748	1	67
William, s. Thomas & Jane, b. Feb. 10, 1750	1	67
THROOP, Susanna, m. William **WILLIAMS**, July 31, 1753, by Rev. Solomon Williams, of Lebanon	1	38
THURSTON, Ezra, s. Obed & Phebe, b. Nov. 11, 1783	1	209
Susannah, d. Obed & Phebe, b. Dec. 12, 1779	1	209
TIFT, Mary, of R.I., m. Nicholas **VINCENT**, of R.I., July 6, 1846, by Rev. Charles S. Weaver	2	9
Sarah, of Voluntown, m. George H. **DENNIS**, of Norwich, Nov. 2, 1845, by Rev. Alfred Burnham	2	94
TILLINGHAST, Almira, d. Feb. 14, 1850, ae 45; b. in R. Island	3	61
Betsey Amanda, d. James & Nabby, b. Jan. 30, 1813	2	15
Charles A., s. Joseph & Sarah, b. May 16, 1808	1	229
Charlotte, d. James & Nabby, b. July 14, 1822, in Sterling	2	15
Harvey, s. Joseph & Sarah, b. Aug. 23, 1810	1	229
James, s. Joseph & Sarah, b. Sept. 15, 1789	1	221
John, m. Phebe Mary **GORDON**, Sept. 11, 1817, by John Wylie, J.P.	2	23
Joseph, m. Sarah **GORTON**, Sept. 14, 1788, by Rev. Micaiah Porter	1	221
Joseph, d. Mar. 3, 1815	1	229
Joseph Allen, s. James & Nabby, b. June 19, 1815	2	15
Joseph Gorton, s. Joseph & Sarah, b. Mar. 20, 1802	1	229
Louisa, d. Mar. 10, 1850, ae 24; b. in R. Island	3	61
Lucretia Parkhurst, m. Daniel **BRIGGS**, of Voluntown, July 4, 1850, by Rev. John Lovejoy, of Norwich	2	135
Lydia, d. Joseph & Sarah, b. Mar. 29, 1792, in W. Greenwich; d. Sept. [ ], 1794	1	221
Marcy, d. Joseph & Sarah, b. June 20, 1796, in Stephentown, N.Y.	1	221
Phebe, d. Joseph & Sarah, b. Apr. 26, 1794	1	221
Phebe, m. Elnathan **ANDREW**, Feb. 18, 1816, by John Wylie, J.P.	2	5
Sally, m. Samuel **BRIGGS**, Mar. 12, 1818, by John Wylie, J.P.	2	21
Sarah, d. Joseph & Sarah, b. May 5, 1799	1	221
Sarah, m. James **ALEXANDER**, Feb. 1, 1824, by Nathaniel Sheffield, Elder	2	54
Sylvester, d. Jan. 5, 1858, ae 65; b. in W. Greenwich, R.I.	3	68
Welthan, d. Joseph & Sarah, b. Mar. 30, 1805	1	229
Welthian, m. Elisha **HOPKINS**, Mar. 30, 1820, by James Alexander, J.P.	2	29
William Toilson, s. Joseph & Eliza, b. Oct. 8, 1824	2	59
----, d. Benjamin, school-teacher, ae 32, & Mary A., ae 27, b. June 12, 1849	3	23
TITUS, Comfort, m. Dorothy **GORE**, June 27, 1765, by Rev. Samuel Dorrance	1	93
Desire, d. Comfort & Dorothy, b. Feb. 13, 1769	1	93
Nathaniel, s. Comfort & Dorothy, b. Mar. 31, 1766	1	93
Sylvanus, s. Comfort & Dorithy, b. Feb. 5, 1772	1	93
TORRY, Susanna, m. Obadiah **RHO[A]DES**, Nov. 27, 1761, by Rev. Sylvanus White, of Southampton	1	61

	Vol.	Page
TRACY, Sarah, m. Robert **CRERY**, Jr., June 3, 1742, by Rev. Wiht, of Norwich	1	63
TRASH, Mason C., ae 17, b. in R. Island, resid. of W. Greenwich, m. Nancy M. **BRIGGS**, ae 16, b. in R. Island, resid. of W. Greenwich, Dec. 9, 1849, by Elder Cha[rle]s S. Weaver	3	2
TREAT, Amos, d. Feb. 24, [1859], ae 89; b. in Preston, Ct.	3	69
Diantha R., m. Joseph **WYLIE**, Apr. 10, 1825, by Amos Treat, J.P.	2	60
Eliza S., m. Jesse E. **PAUL**, Mar. 14, 1824, by Amos Treat, J.P.	2	56
Rebecca, d. Nov. 25, 1848, ae 76; b. in Coventry, Ct.	3	60
TUBBS, Elizabeth, m. Nathan **KINNE**, Feb. 27, 1749, by Wait Palmer, Elder, in Stonington	1	80
TUCKER, Amos T., d. May 7, 1860, ae 4 m. 4 d.	3	70
Ann, d. Samuel & Ann, b. Nov. 16, 1753	1	42
Anna, m. Edward **TYLER**, of Preston, Nov. 25, 1773, by Samuel Stewart, J.P.	1	19
Anna, m. Pearly **PHILLIPS**, Sept. 13, 1812	2	75
Anne, d. Elisha & Elizabeth, b. Jan. 1, 1788	1	149
Elisha, s. Samuel & Ann, b. Oct. 15, 1765	1	42
Elisha, m. Elizabeth **KEIGWIN**, Oct. 29, 1786, by Rev. Micaiah Porter	1	149
Elizabeth, d. Samuel & Ann, b. Oct. 8, 1763	1	42
Elizabeth, d. Samuel & Ann, b. June 14, 1769	1	42
Ephraim, s. Samuel & Ann, b. July 3, 1761	1	42
Eunice, d. Samuel & Ann, b. Aug. 3, 1751	1	42
Happy C., d. July 15, [1860], ae 36; b. in Griswold	3	70
John, s. Samuel & Ann, b. June 14, 1769	1	42
Kezia, d. Samuel & Ann, b. Jan. 3, 1757	1	42
Olive, d. Elisha & Elizabeth, b. May 16, 1789	1	149
Samuel, s. Samuel & Ann, b. Apr. 22, 1749	1	42
Sarah, b. in Voluntown, resid. of Richmond, R.I., m. Tyler **ROB[B]INS**, ae 28, b. in Voluntown, resid. of Richmond, R.I., May 12, 1849, by Charles S. Weaver	3	1
Susannah, [ ]	1	149
Zoath, s. Samuel & Ann, b. Jan. 12, 1759	1	42
TUCKERMAN, Mehitable, m. John **GREENE**, Mar. 18, 1784, by Rev. Micaiah Porter	1	213
TYLER, Amy, m. John **WYLIE**, May 1, 1794, by Rev. Levi Hart, of Preston	1	250
Archibald, d. Dec. 16, 1866, ae 78; b. in Foster, R.I.	3	76
Edward, of Preston, m. Anna **TUCKER**, Nov. 25, 1773, by Samuel Stewart, J.P.	1	19
Elizabeth, m. Samuel **WELLS**, Sept. 18, 1755, by Samuel Coit, J.P.	1	31
Elizabeth, d. John & Mary [sic], b. Apr. 25, 1826 [sic]. (Mother's name should be "Sarah" and date "1726")	1	6
Freelove, m. Elisha **BA[I]L[E]Y**, Apr. 11, 1765, by Robert Dixson, J.P.	1	107
John, s. John & Sarah, b. Aug. 16, 1728	1	6
Sarah, d. John & Mary [sic], b. Apr. 11, 1721 (Mother's name should be "Sarah")	1	6
Sarah, d. John & Sarah, b. Dec. 3, 1723	1	6
William, s. John & Sary, b. Apr. 4, 1718	1	6
UNDERWOOD, Waty, m. William **GORTON**, May 6, 1821, by Amos Treat, J.P.	2	39

	Vol.	Page
VAUGHAN, VAUGHEN, Abel, s. William & Marg[a]ret, b. Feb. 26, 1780	1	137
Amey, d. William & Marg[a]ret, b. June 9, 1788	1	137
Asaph, s. William & Marg[a]ret, b. Oct. 26, 1777	1	137
Barbary, d. Jesse & Phebe, b. Apr. 22, 1785	1	203
Charles, s. Jesse & Phebe, b. Sept. 26, 1770, in Coventry	1	203
Cornel, s. Jesse & Phebe, b. Mar. 18, 1772, in East Greenwich	1	203
Daniel, s. Jesse & Phebe, b. June 10, 1777	1	203
Deborah, d. Jesse & Phebe, b. Aug. 29, 1779	1	203
Elisha, s. Jesse & Phebe, b. Oct. 5, 1776	1	203
Elizabeth, d. William & Marg[a]ret, b. May 22, 1782	1	137
Elizabeth, m. Asa **THOMPSON**, 2d, b. residing in Jewett City, Ct., June 3, 1831, by Nathaniel Sheffield, Elder	2	89
James, s. Rufus & Amy, b. Oct. 10, 1784	1	174
Jesse, s. Jesse & Phebe, b. July 26, 1781	1	203
John, s. William & Marg[a]ret, b. Aug. 19, 1785	1	137
Johnson, s. Jesse & Phebe, b. Aug. 26, 1783	1	203
Mercy, d. Rufus & Amy, b. Sept. 9, 1781	1	174
Phebe, d. Jesse & Phebe, b. Feb. 22, 1787	1	203
Rufus, m. Amy **BA[I]LEY**, Sept. 16, 1780, by John Dixson, Esq.	1	174
Russel[l], s. Jesse & Phebe, b. Sept. 26, 1774, in Coventry, R.I.	1	203
William, m. Marg[a]ret **GREEN**, b. of Voluntown, Dec. 5, 1776, by Samuel Stewart, J.P.	1	137
Zazerus, s. Rufus & Amy, b. Jan. 30, 1783	1	174
VINCENT, Nicholas, of R.I., m. Mary **TIFT**, of R.I., July 6, 1846, by Rev. Charles S. Weaver	2	9
WAGE, Hannah, m. Mumford **KINYON**, Jan. 12, 1796, by Rev. Micaiah Porter	1	203
WAIT, Elcey A., m. Joel S. **KINNEY**, b. of Voluntown, Oct. 1, 1843, by Rev. H. Farbush	2	69
Hannah, m. James M. **LEWIS**, b. of Voluntown, Nov. 26, 1843, by Rev. Charles S. Weaver	2	44
WALDO, Susanna, of Hampton, [Conn.] m. Albin **GALLUP**, of West Greenwich, R.I., Aug. 29, 1822, by Benjamin Gallup, Jr., J.P.	2	50
WALKER, Cyress W., d. Sept. 14, 1856, ae 25	3	67
Peter, s. Peter & Hannah, b. Mar. 23, 1755	1	30
WALLING, Agnes, m. James **CAMPBELL**, 3d, Nov. 8, 1750, by Rev. Jabez Wight, of Norwich	1	57
WATERMAN, Benjamin, m. Wate **GORTON**, b. of Voluntown, Sept. 9, 1827, by Daniel Keigwin, J.P.	2	81
Waitey, d. Apr. 8, 1853, ae 90, widow; b. in R. Island	3	63
WATSON, Jeffrey, d. Jan. 6, 1864, ae 77; b. in R. Island	3	73
Richard, of Exeter, R.I., m. Martha **LEWIS**, of Voluntown, Nov. 28, 1822, by Nathaniel Sheffield, Elder	2	51
Sally, m. William **HAWKINS**, May 30, 1837, by Kinne Gallup, J.P.	2	83
Sarah E., m. Joseph **CORY**, b. of Voluntown, Dec. 8, 1849, by Amos Witter, J.P.	2	135
WEAVER, Archibald, of Coventry, R.I., m. Content **NEWTON**, of Voluntown, Apr. 18, 1822, by Amos Treat, J.P.	2	46
Content, d. Aug. 16, 1853, ae 56, widow	3	63
Frances Ellen, d. Lathrop P. & Amey A., b. May 20, 1847	2	117
Hannah, of Voluntown, m. William **BILLINGS**, of N. Stonington, Aug. 18, 1822, by Amos Treat, J.P.	2	46

WEAVER, (cont.)

	Vol.	Page
James, of Coventry, m. Mary **NEWTON**, of Voluntown, Sept. 29, 1822, by Amos Treat, J.P.	2	50
Lathrop P., m. Angeline **KINNEY**, b. of Voluntown, Mar. 31, 1844, by Rev. Charles Randall	2	118
Laurette M., d. James B., ae 48, & Almira, ae 43, b. July 22, 1848, in Industryville	3	21
Lydia, d. Alston, ae 38, & Louisa, ae 34, b. Nov. 13, 1847, in Industryville	3	21
Mary, m. Thompson **LARKINS**, July 13, 1828, by Sterry Kinne, J.P.	2	70
Mary, d. Oct. [ ], 1853, ae 20	3	64
Rebecca S., m. Archibald **ROB[B]INS**, b. of Voluntown, Sept. 17, 1843, by Rev. Charles S. Weaver	2	14
Sarah, d. July [ ], 1853, ae 60; b. in Preston	3	64
Tacy A., m. Charles W. **BITGOOD**, b. of Voluntown, Jan. 16, 1853, by Rev. John H. Baker	2	114
Thomas, Jr., m. Eunice **HALL**, Dec. 11, 1793	1	223
William, m. Sally **HUTCHINSON**, Sept. 26, 1822, by Sterry Kinne, J.P.	2	51
William, d. June 8, 1856, ae 78; b. in R. Island	3	66
-----, stillborn d. Charles S., minister, ae 47, & Diana, b. July 1, 1850	3	24

WEBSTER, Carlton H., of Norwich, m. Sarah R. **GORDON**, of Voluntown, Feb. 16, 1840, by Rev. Jacob Allen

	Vol.	Page
	2	105

WEDGE, Abigail, d. William & Mary, b. Aug. 23, 1741, in Plainfield

	Vol.	Page
	1	69
Amos, s. Isaac & Priscilla, b. Apr. 12, 1755	1	32
Amos, m. C[h]loe **BROWN**, Apr. 10, 1776, by Simeon Brown, Elder	1	135
Amos, s. Amos & C[h]loe, b. July 17, 1788	1	135
Asahel, s. John & Zerviah, b. Feb. 28, 1746	1	27
C[h]loe, d. Amos & C[h]loe, b. Oct. 6, 1781	1	135
Daniel, s. William & Mary, b. Apr. 10, 1743, in Plainfield	1	69
Deborah, d. Isaac & Priscilla, b. Mar. 28, 1748	1	32
Deborah, m. John **LOWDEN**, Jan. 22, 1766, by Robert Dixson, J.P.	1	110
Deborah, d. Amos & C[h]loe, b. Sept. 14, 1778	1	135
[E]unice, d. John & Zerviah, b. May 27, 1739	1	27
Hannah, d. Isaac & Priscilla, b. July 1, 1750	1	32
Hannah, d. William & Mary, b. Feb. 14, 1751	1	69
Hannah, d. Amos & C[h]loe, b. Apr. 2, 1777	1	135
Isaac, m. Priscilla **WELLS**, Feb. 22, 1742/3, by Rev. Samuel Dorrance	1	32
Isaac, s. Isaac & Priscilla, b. Dec. 14, 1752	1	32
Jemima, d. William & Mary, b. June 27, 1755	1	69
Jemima, d. Thomas & Mary, b. Sept. 25, 1761	1	98
John, s. John & Zerviah, b. Aug. 14, 1743	1	27
Lois, d. John & Zerviah, b. Feb. 8, 1741	1	27
Mary, d. William & Mary, b. June 27, 1748; d. Jan. 28, 1762	1	69
Nathaniel, s. William & Mary, b. May 14, 1752	1	69
Phebe, d. Amos & C[h]loe, b. Mar. 13, 1780	1	135
Priscilla, d. Isaac, Jr. & Priscilla, b. Feb. 4, 1744	1	32
Thomas, s. William & Mary, b. June 8, 1739, in Plainfield	1	69
Thomas, m. Mary **BASS**, Jan. 25, 1760, by Nathaniel Huntington, J.P.	1	98
William, s. William & Mary, b. May 10, 1746	1	69

VOLUNTOWN VITAL RECORDS 243

	Vol.	Page
WEEKS, Celinda, d. June 22, 1861, ae 48; b. in Hopkinton, R.I.	3	71
WELCH, WELLCH, Amy, d. Samuel & Amy, b. July 25, 1735	1	20
Ann, d. Tho[mas] & An[n], b. June 23, 1716	1	5
Daniel, s. Tho[ma]s & An[n], b. Aug. 26, 1718	1	5
Han[n]ah, d. Tho[mas] & An[n], b. Sept. 17, 1721	1	5
Mary, d. Samuel & Amy, b. [ ] 21, 1726	1	12
Mary, d. Samuel & Amy, b. June 2, 1747	1	12
Samuel, s. Samuel & Amy, b. Apr. 16, 1730	1	20
Thomas, s. Tho[mas] & An[n], b. Mar. 31, 1714	1	5
WELLS, Hannah, m. James **SEARS**, Apr. 28, 1766, by Simeon Brown, Elder	1	110
John, s. Samuel & Hannah, b. July 26, 1741	1	31
John, m. Mary **SHELDON**, Mar. 27, 1766, by Rev. Levey Hart	1	107
Joseph, s. Samuel & Hannah, b. Oct. 16, 1746	1	31
Joseph, m. Patience **EDWARDS**, Sept. 5, 1768, by Thomas Wells, J.P.	1	110
Joseph, s. Joseph & Patience, b. Dec. 11, 1777	1	110
Mara, d. Samuel & Hannah, b. Nov. 23, 1750	1	31
Patience, d. Joseph & Patience, b. June 1, 1775	1	110
Prescilla, m. Isaac **WEDGE**, Feb. 22, 1742/3, by Rev. Samuel Dorrance	1	32
R[e]ubin, s. Samuel & Elizabeth, b. July 25, 1759	1	31
Samuel, m. Elizabeth **TYLER**, Sept. 18, 1755, by Samuel Coit, J.P.	1	31
Samuel, Jr., m. Sarah **RANDALL**, Jan. 9, 1758, by Maj. Samuel Coit, J.P.	1	93
Thankfull, d. Samuel & Hannah, b. Dec. 19, 1743	1	31
WESTCOT, WESTCOAT, Benjamin, d. Apr. 27, 1861, ae 21 y.	3	70
Easther, m. Thomas **GALLUP**, Jr., Feb. 7, 1799, by Benjamin Greene, J.P.	1	236
WHALLEY, WHALEY, Ann, d. Sam[ue]l & Pashance, b. Jan. 24, 1716	1	3
James, S. Sam[ue]ll & Pashance, b. Nov. 16, 1721	1	3
John, s. Sam[ue]ll & Pashance, b. May 28, 1724	1	3
Pashance, d. Sam[ue]l & Pashance, b. Dec. 24, 1713	1	3
Theophiles, s. Sam[ue]ll & Pashance, b. Aug. 10, 1718	1	3
Timothy, s. Samuel & Pashance, b. Mar. 14, 1727	1	3
WHEELER, Annie, d. Nov. 12, 1861, ae 17; b. in Bloomfield	3	71
Content, m. Joseph **PALMER**, 3d, Apr. 27, 1768, by Joseph Denison, J.P.	1	116
Nabby, m. Joseph **PALMER**, May 12, 1805, by Peleg Randall, Elder	1	202
Nancy, of Voluntown, m. John **FISH**, Sept. 25, 1825, by Benjamin Gallup, J.P.	2	61
WHIPPLE, Abby, of Voluntown, m. Joseph S. **SWAN**, of Stonington, Feb. 18, 1828, by Rev. Jabez S. Swan	2	72
Alfred, ae 50, b. Scituate, R.I., resid. of Voluntown, m. Polly **HARWOOD**, ae 45, b. Sterling, Ct., resid. of Voluntown, Sept. 2, 1849, by Rev. Chas. S. Weaver	3	2
Anna, m. Joseph **CAMPBELL**, Jr., Mar. 30, 1788, by Rev. Micaiah Porter	1	199
George H., s. Robert, farmer, ae 33, b. Dec. 13, 1850	3	26
Lucretia, m. Daniel **KEN[N]EDY**, Dec. 5, 1764, by Rev. Jo[h]nson, of Groton	1	112
Mary, m. William **GALLUP**, Apr. 17, 1769, by Robert Dixson, J.P.	1	88

244   BARBOUR COLLECTION

	Vol.	Page
WHITING, Amos, s. Enock & Thankfull, b. July 7, 1744	1	20
Hannah, d. Enock & Thankfull, b. Aug. 11, 1735	1	20
John, s. Enock & Thankfull, b. May 2, 1737	1	20
WHITMAN, John, of Griswold, m. Hannah **STEPHENS**, of Voluntown, Sept. 23, 1844, by Rev. Charles s. Weaver	2	22
WILBUR, Mary A., ae 21, of Griswold, m. Jabez B. **RAY**, ae 26, of Voluntown, Mar. 11, 1849, by Charles S. Weaver	3	1
WILCOX, WILLCOX, Celinda M., d. Miner & Alice Ann, b. Sept. 17, 1847	2	138
Erasmus D., d. Dec. 19, 1849, ae 1	3	61
Erasmus S., d. John, ae 38, & Mary, ae 36, b. May 15, 1848	3	22
Eunice, m. Samuel T. **REYNOLDS**, b. of Voluntown, Feb. 11, 1828, by Nathaniel Sheffield, Elder	2	72
Frances, m. Charles H. **PALMER**, of R. Island, Apr. 8, 1845, by Rev. Charles S. Weaver	2	5
Hamilton M., s. Miner & Alice Ann, b. Apr. 9, 1845	2	138
Hope Almira, reputed d. Henry **WILCOX** & Hannah **MORGAN**, b. Feb. 5, 1804	1	115
John, of W. Greenwich, R.I., m. Abby **GORDON**, of Voluntown, Jan. 9, 1851, by Rev. Henry Forbush, of Plainfield	2	139
Mary, m. Varnum **SWEET**, b. of Voluntown, July 5, 1827, by Daniel Keigwin, J.P.	2	81
Miner, m. Alice A. **CAREY**, b. of Voluntown, Apr. 10, 1844, by Harvey Campbell, J.P.	2	116
Nathan, m. Sybel **HANCOCK**, Feb. 25, 1821, by Sterry Kinney, J.P.	2	29
Nathan, d. June 15, 1849, ae 50; b. in N. Stonington	3	60
Nathaniel, ae 25, b. in W. Greenwich, resid. of Griswold, m. Julia **PALMER**, ae 20, b. in Exeter, R.I., resid. of Griswold, Sept. 2, 1849, by Elder Cha[rle]s S. Weaver	3	2
Resolved, m. Martha **GREENE**, b. of Voluntown, Sept. 3, 1827, by Nathaniel Sheffield, Elder	2	72
Samuel, d. June 20, 1866, ae 84; b. in R. Island	3	76
Sarah Ann, d. Apr. 14, [1860], ae 10; b. in Mass.	3	69
Sarah M., d. Amos, ae 38, & Eliza, ae 37, b. June 19, 1848	3	21
Thomas Records, s. Benjamin & Elizabeth, b. Apr. 4, 1802	1	245
William B., of Griswold, Ct., m. Mary **KENYON**, of Exeter, R.I., Nov. 8, 1830, by Nathaniel Sheffield, Elder	2	86
WILKINSON, WILKESON, Abel, d. Mar. 20, 1838	2	107
Jacob Cady, s. William & Lydia, b. Dec. 27, 1784	1	178
James, m. Esther **BALLARD**, July 16, 1770, by Samuel St[e]wart, J.P.	1	63
John Mumford, s. William & Lydia, b. June 5, 1786	1	178
Lydia, d. Jan. 27, 1850, ae 18; b. in Coventry, R.I.	3	61
Marvel, d. James & Esther, b. May 11, 1771	1	63
Polly, m. Wheeler **MORGAN**, Dec. 24, 1780, by Rev. Solomon Morgan	1	224
Ruth, m. William **DOUGLASS**, Jr., Mar. 13, 1788, by Rev. Micaiah Porter	1	191
Thankfull, d. John & Deborah, b. Sept. 22, 1769	1	84
William, m. Lydia **CADY**, Mar. 11, 1784, by Rev. Micaiah Porter	1	178
WILLIAMS Abigail, d. William & Abigail, b. Sept. 15, 1747	1	38
Alexander, s. Roger & Susan[n]a, b. June 2, 1753	1	35
Alexander, m. Jerusha **KEE**, Feb. 18, 1783, by Rev. Eliphalet Write	1	171

VOLUNTOWN VITAL RECORDS 245

	Vol.	Page
WILLIAMS, (cont.)		
Anna, d. Ebenezer & Levina, b. Jan. 14, 1791	1	217
Benjamin, of Voluntown, m. Dorithy **DOLEFOR**, of E. Greenwich, Feb. 26, 1722/3, by John Nicholes, J.P.	1	7
Benjamin, s. William & Susanna, b. May 26, 1759	1	38
Benjamin, m. Elizabeth **JAMES**, Feb. 25, 1779, by John Dixson, J.P.	1	138
Betsey, d. Benjamin & Elizabeth, b. Aug. 12, 1779	1	138
Daniel, s. Richard & Abigail, b. May 17, 1721; d. Nov. 18, 1721, ae 6 m. 1 d.	1	1
Daniel Kee, s. Alexander & Jerusha, b. Mar. 25, 1785	1	171
Ebenezer, s. Roger & Susan[n]a, b. Oct. 19, 1750	1	35
Ebenezer, s. William & Susan[n]a, b. Feb. 19, 1765	1	38
Ebenezer, m. Levina **PENDOCK**, May 17, 1789, by Rev. Israel Day, of Killingly	1	217
Ebenezer, d. Feb. 15, 1793	1	217
Elizabeth, d. William & Abigail, b. May 20, 1750	1	38
Erastus, m. Alice L. **POTTER**, b. of Voluntown, Apr. 26, 1835, by Elisha Potter, J.P.	2	101
Hannah, d. Robert & Martha, b. Jan. 9, 1734	1	12
Hannah, d. William & Abigail, b. Oct. 24, 1743	1	38
Huldah, d. Benjamin & Elizabeth, b. Apr. 7, 1783	1	138
Huston, s. Alexander & Jerusha, b. Nov. 18, 1783	1	171
Ichabod, s. Richard & Abigail, b. Oct. 27, 1722	1	1
Jane, d. Roger & Susan[n]a, b. Jan. 28, 1745	1	35
John, twin with William, s. William & Abigail, b. Mar. 21, 1745	1	38
John, m. Mary **SKILLION**, Dec. 27, 1770, by Alexander Miller, Elder	1	120
Joseph, s. William & Susanna, b. Nov. 2, 1753	1	38
Lucy, d. Alexander & Jerusha, b. Mar. 31, 1789	1	171
Mary, d. Robert & Martha, b. May 6, 1738	1	12
Nancy, d. Benjamin & Elizabeth, b. Feb. 24, 1781	1	138
Nehemiah, s. Robert & Martha, b. Jan. 19, 1739	1	12
Roger, s. Robert & Han[n]ah, b. Apr. 16, 1717	1	2
Roger, m. Susan[n]a **STONE**, Apr. 25, 1744, by Rev. Samuel Dorrance	1	35
Roger, d. July 15, 1777	1	35
Samson, s. Roger & Susan[n]a, b. Mar. 4, 1747	1	35
Samson, m. Freelove **STAPLES**, June 5, 1777, by Rev. John Fuller	1	54
Sarah, d. William & Susanna, b. Dec. 9, 1756	1	38
Susan[n]a, d. Roger & Susan[n]a, b. Nov. 11, 1755; d. June 18, 1757	1	35
Susan[n]a, d. Benjamin & Elizabeth, b. July 14, 1785	1	138
William, s. Robert & Han[n]ah, b. Mar. 23, 1719	1	2
William, of Voluntown, m. Abigail **FAIRMAN**, of Killingly, Feb. 3, 1742/3, by Joseph Leavens, J.P.	1	38
William, twin with John, s. William & Abigail, b. Mar. 21, 1745	1	38
William, m. Susanna **THROOP**, July 31, 1753, by Rev. Solomon Williams, of Lebanon	1	38
Zeruiah, d. William & Susanna, b. Oct. 10, 1761	1	38
WILSON, Archibald, s. Robert, Jr. & Cynthia, b. Jan. 24, 1773	1	196
Jared, s. Robert, Jr. & Cynthia, b. May 13, 1788	1	196
Mary, m. Alexander **GASTON**, Sept. 29, 1743, by Rev. Samuel Dorrance	1	82
Mary, d. Robert, Jr. & Cynthia, b. Jan. 11, 1775	1	196

	Vol.	Page
WILSON, (cont.)		
Olive, d. Robert, Jr. & Cynthia, b. Apr. 26, 1778	1	196
Phebe, m. Robert **EG[G]LESTON**, Jan. 13, 1823, by Sterry Kinne, J.P.	2	52
Robert, Jr., m. Cynthia **STEARNES**, May 14, 1772	1	196
WINSLOW, Azariah, m. Zeruah **COLE**, Jan. 26, 1786, by Rev. Israel Day	1	182
Eddy, s. Azariah & Zeruah, b. Feb. 24, 1786	1	182
Nancy, d. Azariah & Zeruah, b. Apr. 18, 1790	1	182
WINTERBOTTOM, Luce, m. Sarah **BURDICK**, b. now resid. in Voluntown, June 23, 1833, by Joseph Wylie, J.P.	2	94
Sarah, m. Tift L. **BARBER**, b. of Voluntown, Nov. 28, 1844, by Rev. Charles S. Weaver	2	118
WITHEY, Polly, m. John **KENNEDY**, Oct. 4, 1798, by Rev. Levi Hart	1	240
WOOD, Sibbel, m. Jenckes **MASON**, Mar. 22, 1784, by Charles Thompson, Elder	1	202
WOODMANCY, Joseph, of N. Stonington, m. [ ] **PARTELOW**, [ ], 1850, by Charles S. Weaver	3	4
WORDEN, Benjamin F., of R.I., m. Mary A. **CLARK**, May 26, 1845, by Rev. Charles S. Weaver	2	5
Gardner, of Charlestown, R.I., m. Lucy **PHINNEY**, of Canterbury, Ct., Jan. 3, 1830, by Nathaniel Sheffield, Elder	2	82
Sally, m. Charles **PHILLIPS**, b. of Hopkinton, R.I., Jan. 2, 1847, by Rev. Ebenezer Blake	2	116
WRIGHT, Orrin, d. Oct. 16, 1855, ae 1 y. 4 m.	3	66
Roxana, of Hopkinton, R.I., m. Jacob **LEWIS**, of Exeter, R.I., Oct. 21, 1850, by Rev. H. Forbush	2	140
WYLIE, Agness, d. John & Sarah, b. July 26, 1754	1	49
Agness, d. Hugh & Elizabeth, b. Feb. 18, 1755; d. Apr. 28, 1757	1	54
Agness, m. Andrew **HUNTER**, Oct. 7, 1773	1	128
Agness, d. Joseph & Mary, b. May 1, 1775	1	122
Allen, s. Joseph & Mary, b. Mar. 4, 1769	1	122
Allen, s. Allen & Sarah, b. Jan. 18, 1796, in Preston	1	232
Allen, Dr., d. Aug. 5, 1796	1	232
Alva, s. John & Betsey, b. Feb. 16, 1809	1	250
Amy, w. John, d. Aug. 2, 1804	1	250
Barbara, d. Joseph & Mary, b. Sept. 27, 1779	1	122
Betsey, m. John **WYLIE**, Oct. 18, 1804, by John Wylie, J.P.	1	250
Betsey, w. John, d. Aug. 26, 1811	1	250
Betsey Amy, d. John & Betsey, b. May 29, 1811	1	250
Celynda, d. Joseph & Mary, b. Dec. 22, 1781; d. June 27, 1782	1	122
Celynda, d. Joseph & Mary, b. Mar. 23, 1787	1	122
Charles, s. Joseph & Mary, b. Dec. 14, 1772	1	122
Charles Bishop, s. John & Amy, b. [ ]	1	250
Daniel, s. James & Sarah, b. May 31, 1747	1	83
Daniel, s. James, 3d, & Mary, b. Jan. 12, 1779	1	132
Diantha R., d. Aug. 15, 1854, ae 52	3	64
Elizabeth, m. Hugh **WYLIE**, Mar. 25, 1742, by Rev. Hezekiah Lord, Clerk	1	54
Elizabeth, d. Hugh & Elizabeth, b. Jan. 30, 1751	1	54
Elizabeth, d. John & Sarah, b. July 1, 1767	1	49
Elizabeth, Jr., m. John **WYLIE**, 3d, Jan. 14, 1773, by Robert Dixson, J.P.	1	125

VOLUNTOWN VITAL RECORDS

	Vol.	Page
WYLIE, (cont.)		
Elizabeth, d. John & Elizabeth, b. Feb. 26, 1778	1	125
Elizabeth, m. James **CAMPBELL**, Jr., Jan. 14, 1790, by Rev. Micaiah Porter	1	161
Elizabeth, d. Joseph & Elizabeth, b. June 6, 1805	1	123
Elizabeth, of Voluntown, m. James **CRARY**, of Plainfield, Jan. 22, 1829, by Rev. Otis Lane	2	74
Henry, s. John & Betsey, b. Apr. 10, 1806	1	250
Hugh, m. Elizabeth **WYLIE**, Mar. 25, 1742, by Rev. Hezekiah Lord, Clerk	1	54
James, m. Sarah **MacMAINS**, Aug. 14, 1746, by Rev. Hezekiah Lord	1	83
James, s. James & Sarah, b. Apr. 1, 1753	1	53
James, 3d, m. Mary **HOLLY**, Jan. 29, 1778, by Rev. Levi Hart	1	132
James, s. Daniel & Elizabeth, b. Jan. 26, 1784	1	99
Jane, m. Robert **HUNTER**, Dec. 9, 1742, by Rev. Dorrance	1	53
Jean, d. John & Sarah, b. Jan. 24, 1759	1	49
John, Jr., m. Sarah **CAMPBELL**, Dec. 9, 1742, by Rev. Samuel Dorrance	1	49
John, s. John & Sarah, b. Dec. 22, 1746	1	49
John, s. James & Sarah, b. Mar. 6, 1749; d. Aug. 2, 1750	1	83
John, s. James & Sarah, b. Jan. 16, 1751	1	83
John, s. Joseph & Mary, b. Dec. 16, 1770	1	122
John, 3d, m. Elizabeth **WYLIE**, Jr., Jan. 14, 1773, by Robert Dixson, J.P.	1	125
John, Jr., m. Esther **CRERY**, Mar. 25, 1773, by Rev. Solomon Morgan	1	126
John, 4th, m. Deborah **ALLEN**, Nov. 4, 1773, by Rev. Solomon Morgan	1	130
John, s. Moses & Mary, b. July 26, 1782	1	143
John, m. Amy **TYLER**, May 1, 1794, by Rev. Levi Hart, of Preston	1	250
John, m. Betsey **WYLIE**, Oct. 18, 1804, by John Wylie, J.P.	1	250
John Tyler, s. John & Amy, b. Apr. 8, 1802	1	250
Joseph, s. John & Sarah, b. June 26, 1744	1	49
Joseph, m. Mary **CAMPBELL**, May 10, 1768, by Robert Dixson, J.P.	1	122
Joseph, m. Elizabeth **HUSTON**, July 30, 1801, by Allen Campbell, J.P.	1	123
Joseph, s. Joseph & Elizabeth, b. Aug. 27, 1802	1	123
Joseph, d. July 29, 1812, ae 68 y.	1	123
Joseph, m. Diantha R. **TREAT**, Apr. 10, 1825, by Amos Treat, J.P.; d. Dec. 9, 1833	2	60
Lucy, d. John & Amy, b. July 15, 1797	1	250
Marg[a]ret, d. John, Jr. & Elizabeth, b. July 13, 1774	1	125
Mary, d. John & Sarah, b. Apr. 20, 1762	1	49
Mary, w. Joseph, d. May 30, 1801	1	122
Mary Elizabeth, of Voluntown, m. Job N. **CUTLER**, of Plainfield, May 24, 1836, by Rev. Samuel Rockwell, of Plainfield	2	25
Matilda, d. Joseph & Mary, b. May 19, 1791	1	122
Molly, d. Joseph & Mary, b. Nov. 12, 1783	1	122
Molly, m. John A. **CAMPBELL**, Nov. 25, 1802, by Allen Campbell, J.P.	1	252
Moses, s. John & Sarah, b. Nov. 9, 1751	1	49

248   BARBOUR COLLECTION

	Vol.	Page
WYLIE, (cont.)		
Moses, s. John, Jr. & Elizabeth, b. Feb. 24, 1776	1	125
Moses, m. Mary **CAMPBELL**, May 8, 1777, by Samuel Stewart, J.P.	1	143
Moses, s. Moses & Mary, b. Jan. 6, 1793	1	143
Nancy, d. John & Elizabeth, b. June 6, 1785	1	125
Nancy, m. Samuel **BOARDMAN**, Aug. 22, 1793, by Rev. Micaiah Porter	1	226
Patty, d. Moses & Mary, b. Oct. 4, 1789	1	143
Peggy, d. Moses & Mary, b. Sept. 17, 1780	1	143
Peter, s. John & Sarah, b. Feb. 22, 1748/9	1	49
Peter, s. James & Sarah, b. Oct. 31, 1755	1	53
Peter, m. Patience **CAMPBELL**, b. of Voluntown, Feb. 20, 1777, by Samuel Stewart, Esq.	1	136
Peter, s. Moses & Mary, b. June 29, 1778	1	143
Polly, d. Moses & Mary, b. Jan. 28, 1786	1	143
Polly, d. John & Elizabeth, b. Oct. 2, 1792	1	125
Rachel Brown, d. John & Amy, b. Aug. 25, 1799	1	250
Robert, s. Hugh & Elizabeth, b. Apr. 23, 1748	1	19
Robert, s. Hugh & Elizabeth, b. Apr. 23, 1748	1	54
Sally, d. John & Elizabeth, b. Oct. 21, 1783; d. June 4, 1784	1	125
Sally, d. John & Amy, b. July 5, 1795	1	250
Sarah, d. John & Sarah, b. July 22, 1756	1	49
Sarah, d. John & Deborah, b. Jan. 22, 1776	1	130
Sarah, d. Joseph & Mary, b. June 4, 1777	1	122
Simeon, s. John & Deborah, b. Nov. 21, 1774	1	130
Susan[n]a, d. Peter & Patience, b. Apr. 2, 1778	1	136
Thomas, s. Moses & Mary, b. June 12, 1784	1	143
YORK, Amos, m. Lucrecey **MINOR**, Nov. 8, 1750, by Jeremiah Kinne, J.P.	1	64
Elroy, of Griswold, m. Catherine A. **CHURCH**, of Voluntown, Nov. 3, 1844, by Rev. Charles S. Weaver	2	47
Esther, d. Amos & Lucrecey, b. Nov. 13, 1754	1	64
Isaac, of N. Stonington, m. Philura **BROMLEY**, of N. Stonington, Nov. 12, 1848, by Rev. Charles S. Weaver	3	1
Lucretia, d. Amos & Lucretia, b. Apr. 21, 1757	1	64
Naomi, d. Sept. 20, 1865, ae 85; b. in Griswold	3	75
Wealthian, d. Amos & Lucrecey, b. Nov. 3, 1752	1	64
YOUNG, Aseneth, of Voluntown, m. Dyer **SMITH**, formerly of Richmond, R.I., now residing in Sterling, Ct., June 29, 1823, by Nathaniel Sheffield, Elder	2	53
Charles E., s. Benjamin, ae 30, & Eliza R., ae 28, b. July 30, 1848	3	22
Henry, d. Feb. 3, [1859], ae 79; b. in Exeter, R.I.	3	69
Jesse, s. Jesse, ae 37, & Fanny, ae 32, b. Dec. 1, 1847	3	21
John I., of Voluntown, m. Susan **COREY**, of Griswold, Dec. 25, 1836, by Harvey Campbell, J.P.	2	100
John T., of Voluntown, m. Susan **COREY**, of Griswold, Dec. 25, 1836, by Harvey Campbell, J.P.	2	97
Maria, d. Nov. 20, 1862, ae 3; b. in England	3	71
Nathan L., m. Keziah **BUTTON**, Dec. 1, 1844, by Rev. Charles S. Weaver	2	118
Waitey, d. Mar. 4, 1853, ae 94, widow; b. in R. Island	3	63

NO SURNAME

	Vol.	Page
Almira, d. Lydia, who was d. Thomas & Martha **PARTELOW**, b. Apr. 17, 1817	2	14
Elizabeth, m. Lee **GALLUP**, ae 20, b. of Sterling, Jan. [1850 ?], by Peleg Peckham	3	3
Hannah, d. Lydia, who was d. Thomas & Martha **PARTELOW**, b. Apr. 14, 1811	2	14

www.ingramcontent.com/pod-product-compliance
Lightning Source LLC
Chambersburg PA
CBHW050848230426
43667CB00012B/2193